PRINCIPLES of INFORMATION SECURITY

Dr. Michael E. Whitman, CISSP
Herbert J. Mattord, CISSP

Kennesaw State University

THOMSON
COURSE TECHNOLOGY

Australia • Canada • Mexico • Singapore • Spain • United Kingdom • United States

THOMSON

— ★ —™

COURSE TECHNOLOGY

Principles of Information Security

by Michael E. Whitman, Ph.D., CISSP and Herbert J. Mattord, M.B.A., CISSP

Senior Vice President, Publisher:
Kristen Duerr

Executive Editor:
Jennifer Locke

Product Manager:
Barrie Tysko

Developmental Editor:
Betsey Henkels

Associate Production Manager:
Christine Spillett

Associate Product Manager:
Janet Aras

Editorial Assistant:
Christy Urban

Marketing Manager:
Jason Sakos

Text Designer:
Books By Design

Cover Designer:
Janet Lavine

Manufacturing Coordinator:
Denise Powers

Compositor:
GEX Publishing Services

To Rhonda, Rachel, and Alex, thank you for your loving support

—MEW

For Carola, Becky and Lisa; Mom and Max: you kept up the encouragement.

—HJM

Table of Contents

Section II–Security Investigation Phase
Chapter 2

Section III–Security Analysis
Chapter 4
Risk Management: Identifying and Assessing Risk 117

Chapter 5
Risk Management: Assessing and Controlling Risk 153

Section IV–Logical Design
Chapter 6
Blueprint For Security 191

Chapter 7
Planning for Continuity 235

Section V–Physical Design
Chapter 8
Security Technology 273

Chapter 11
Security and Personnel 417

Preface

AS GLOBAL NETWORKS EXPAND the interconnection of the world, the smooth operation of communication and computing systems becomes vital. However, recurring events such as virus and worm attacks and the success of criminal attackers illustrate the weaknesses in current information technologies and the need for heightened security of these systems.

The immediate need for organizations to protect critical information assets continues to increase. In an attempt to secure current systems and networks, organizations must draw on the pool of current information security practitioners. These same organizations will count on the next generation of professionals to have the correct mix of skills and experiences to develop more secure computing environments in the future. Improved texts with supporting materials along with the efforts of college and university faculty are needed to prepare students of technology to recognize the threats and vulnerabilities present in existing systems and to learn to design and develop the secure systems needed in the near future.

The purpose of this textbook is to fill the need for a quality academic textbook in the discipline of Information Security. While there are dozens of quality publications on information security and assurance oriented to the practitioner, there is a dramatic lack of textbooks that provide the student with a balance between security management and the technical components of security. By creating a book specifically oriented toward Information Systems students, we hope to close this gap. Specifically, there is a clear need for Information Systems, Criminal Justice, Political Science, Accounting Information Systems, and other disciplines to gain a clear understanding of the foundations of Information Security, the principles on which managerial strategy can be formulated and from which technical solutions can be selected. The fundamental tenet of this textbook is that Information Security in the modern organization is a problem for management to solve and not a problem of that technology alone can answer—a problem that has important economic consequences and for which management will be held accountable.

Approach

The book provides a broad review of the entire field of information security, background on many related elements, and enough detail to facilitate understanding of the field. It covers the terminology of the field, the history of the field, and an overview of how to manage an information security program. In short, it is "an inch deep and a mile wide".

Certified Information Systems Security Professionals Common Body of Knowledge —Because the authors are Certified Information Systems Security Professionals (CISSP), the CISSP knowledge domains have had an influence in the design of the text. Although care was taken to avoid producing another CISSP study guide, the author's backgrounds have resulted in a treatment that ensures that much of the CISSP Common Body of Knowledge (CBK) has been integrated into the text to some degree.

Chapter-Opening Scenarios — Each chapter opens with a short story that follows the same fictional company as it encounters some of the issues of information security. The discussion questions that accompany each scenario give the student and the instructor the opportunity to discuss the issues that underlay the content.

Offline and Technical Details Boxes — These sections highlight interesting topics and detailed technical issues, giving the student the option of delving into topics more deeply. Chapters include the Offline and Technical Details boxes as needed.

Hands-On Learning — At the end of each chapter, students find a Chapter Summary and Review Questions as well as Exercises and Case Exercises, which give them the opportunity to examine the information security arena outside the classroom. Using the Exercises, the student can research, analyze and write to reinforce learning objectives and deepen their understanding of the text. With the Case Exercises, students use professional judgment, powers of observation, and elementary research, to create solutions for simple information security scenarios.

Author Team

Michael Whitman and Herbert Mattord have jointly developed this text to merge knowledge from the world of academic study with practical experience from the business world.

Michael Whitman, Ph.D., CISSP is an Associate Professor of Information Systems in the Computer Science and Information Systems Department at Kennesaw State University, Kennesaw, Georgia, where he is also the Director of the Masters of Science in Information Systems and the Director of the KSU Center for Information Security Education and Awareness (*infosec.kennesaw.edu*). Dr. Whitman is also the coordinator for the department's Certificate in Information Security and Assurance. Dr. Whitman is an active researcher in Information Security, Fair and Responsible Use Policies, Ethical Computing and Information Systems Research Methods. He currently teaches graduate and undergraduate courses in Information Security, Local Area Networking, and Data Communications. He has published articles in the top journals in his field, including *Information Systems Research*, the *Communications of the ACM*, *Information and Management*, the *Journal of International Business Studies*, and the *Journal of Computer Information Systems*. He is an active member of the Georgia Electronic Commerce Association's Information Security Working Group, the Association for Computing Machinery and the Association for Information Systems. Dr. Whitman is also currently co-authoring a Lab Manual, "The Hands-On Information Security Lab Manual," to be published by Thomson Learning Custom Publishing.

Herbert Mattord, M.B.A. CISSP recently completed 24 years of IT industry experience as an application developer, database administrator, project manager, and information security practitioner to join the faculty as Kennesaw State University. During his career as an IT practitioner, he has been an adjunct professor at Kennesaw State University, Southern Polytechnic State University in Marietta, Georgia, Austin Community College in Austin, Texas, and Southwest Texas State University in San Marcos, Texas. He currently teaches undergraduate courses in Information Security, Data

Communications, Local Area Networks, Database Technology, Project Management, and Systems Analysis & Design. He was formerly the Manager of Corporate Information Technology Security at Georgia-Pacific Corporation, where much of the practical knowledge found in this textbook was acquired.

Structure

Principles of Information Security is structured to follow a model called the Security Systems Development Life Cycle (or SecSDLC). This structured methodology can be used to implement information security in an organization that has little or no formal information security measures in place and can also serve as a method to improve established information security programs. The SecSDLC provides a solid framework very similar to that used in application development, software engineering, traditional systems analysis and design, and networking. The use of a structured methodology provides a supportive but not overriding theme that will guide instructors and students through an examination of the various components of the information domains of information security. To serve this end, this textbook is organized into seven sections, twelve chapters and an Appendix.

Section I—Introduction

Chapter 1—Introduction to Information Security

This opening chapter establishes the foundation for understanding the broader field of Information Security. This is accomplished by defining key terms, explaining essential concepts, and providing a review the origins of the field and its impact on the understanding of Information Security.

Section II—Security Investigation Phase

Chapter 2—The Need for Security

Chapter 2 examines the business drivers behind the security analysis design process. It examines current organization and technology needs of security, emphasizing and building on the concepts presented in Chapter 1. One principle concept is that information security is primarily an issue of management, not technology. Best practices apply technology only after considering the business needs.

The chapter also examines the various threats facing organizations and presents the process of ranking these threats to provide relative priority as the organization begins the security planning process. The chapter continues with a detailed examination of the types of attacks that could occur from these threats, and how they could impact the organization's information and systems. The chapter concludes with a further discussion of the key principles of information security, some of which were introduced in Chapter 1: confidentiality, integrity, availability, authentication and identification, authorization, accountability, and privacy.

Chapter 3—Legal, Ethical and Professional Issues in Information Security

As a fundamental part of the SecSDLC investigation process, a careful examination of current legislation, regulation, and common ethical expectations of both national and international entities provides key insights into the regulatory constraints that govern business. This chapter examines several key laws that shape the field of Information Security, and presents a detailed examination of computer ethics necessary to better educate those implementing security. Although ignorance of the law is no excuse, it's considered better than negligence (knowing and doing nothing). This chapter also presents several legal and ethical issues that are commonly found in today's organizations, as well as formal and professional organizations that promote ethics and legal responsibility.

Section III—Security Analysis

Chapter 4—Risk Management: Identifying and Assessing Risk

Before the design of a new security solution can begin, the security analysts must first understand the current state of the organization and its relationship to security. Does the organization have any formal security mechanisms in place? How effective are they? What policies and procedures have been published to the security managers and end users? This chapter examines the processes necessary to conduct a fundamental security assessment by describing the procedures for identifying and prioritizing threats and assets, and identifying what controls are in place to protect these assets from threats. The chapter also provides a discussion of the various types of control mechanisms available and identifies the steps involved in preparing for the initial risk assessment.

Chapter 5—Risk Management: Assessing and Controlling Risk

As a conclusion to the analysis phase, Chapter 5 presents a thorough examination of the process of risk management. Risk management is the process of identifying, assessing, and reducing risk to an acceptable level and implementing effective control measures to maintain that level of risk. The chapter begins with a discussion of risk analysis and continues through various types of feasibility analyses. Finally the chapter examines quantitative and qualitative assessment measures and evaluation of security controls.

Section IV—Logical Design

Chapter 6—Blueprint for Security

As the first chapter in the logical design phase, Chapter 6 presents a number of widely accepted security models and frameworks. It examines best business practices and standards of due care and due diligence, and offers an overview of the development of security policy. This chapter details the major components, scope, and target audience for each of the levels of security policy. This chapter also explains data classification schemes, both military and private, as well as the security education training and awareness (SETA) program. The chapter concludes with an overview of logical technologies that aid in the design of an effective security blueprint.

Chapter 7—Planning for Continuity

Chapter 7 continues with the logical design scheme in two important areas. First, the chapter examines the planning process that supports business continuity, disaster recovery, and incident response. The chapter describes the organization's role and when the organization should involve outside law enforcement agencies. Second, the chapter examines the integration of security into the traditional systems development life cycle, to ensure that systems developed in-house comply with the desired security profile.

SECTION V—Physical Design

Chapter 8—Security Technology
Supporting the transition from logical to physical design, Chapter 8 outlines the specific security technologies that an organization can select to support security efforts. Topics include firewalls, intrusion detection systems, honey pots, security protocols, virtual private networks (VPNs), and cryptography.

Appendix to Chapter 8—Cryptography
The appendix to Chapter 8 provides additional detail on the history, composition, and function of modern cryptosystems. The appendix focuses on how these algorithms work and how they are used. It also presents a number of protocols used in modern data communications that rely on cryptographic algorithms.

Chapter 9—Physical Security
As a vital part of any information security process, physical security is concerned with the management of the physical facilities, the implementation of physical access control, and the oversight of environmental controls. From designing a secure data center to the relative value of guards and watchdogs to the technical issues of fire suppression and power conditioning, Chapter 9 examines as special considerations for physical security threats.

Section VI—Implementation

Chapter 10—Implementing Security
Chapter 10 examines the elements critical to implementing the design created in the previous stages. Key areas in this chapter include the bull's-eye model for implementing information security and a discussion of whether an organization should outsource each component of security. Change management, program improvement, and additional planning for the business continuity efforts are also discussed.

Chapter 11—Personnel Security
The next area in the implementation stage addresses people issues. Chapter 11 examines both sides of the personnel coin: security personnel and security of personnel. It examines staffing issues, professional security credentials, and the implementation of employment policies and practices. The chapter also discusses how security policy affects, and is affected by, consultants, temporary workers, and outside business partners.

Section VII—Maintenance and Change

Chapter 12—Information Security Maintenance
Last and most important is the discussion on maintenance and change. Chapter 12 presents the ongoing technical and administrative evaluation of the security program. This chapter explores ongoing risk analysis, risk evaluation, and measurement, all of which are part of risk management. The special considerations needed for the varieties of vulnerability analysis needed in the modern organization are explored from Internet penetration testing to wireless network risk assessment.

Instructor Resources

A variety of teaching tools have been prepared to support this textbook and offer many options to enhance the classroom learning experience:

Electronic Instructor's Manual — The Instructor's Manual includes suggestions and strategies for using this text, such as suggestions for lecture topics. The Instructors Manual also includes answers to the review questions and suggested solutions to the exercises at the end of each chapter.

Figure Files — Figure Files allow instructors to create their own presentations using figures taken from the text.

PowerPoint Presentations — This book comes with Microsoft PowerPoint slides for each chapter. These are included as a teaching aid for classroom presentation, to make available to students on the network for chapter review, or to be printed for classroom distribution. Instructors can add their own slides for additional topics they introduce to the class.

Lab Manual — Thompson Learning Custom Publishing is producing a lab manual to accompany this book, which is written by one of the authors: *The Hands-On Information Security Lab Manual* (ISBN 0-759-31283-4). The lab manual provides hands-on security exercises on footprinting, enumeration, and firewall configuration, as well as a number of detailed exercises and cases that supplement the book as a laboratory component or as in-class projects. Contact your Course Technology sales representative for more information.

ExamView — ExamView®, the ultimate tool for objective-based testing needs. ExamView® is a powerful objective-based test generator that enables instructors to create paper, LAN or Web-based tests from testbanks designed specifically for their Course Technology text. Instructors can utilize the ultra-efficient QuickTest Wizard to create tests in less than five minutes by taking advantage of Course Technology's question banks, or customize their own exams from scratch.

Acknowledgments

The authors would like to thank their families for their support and understanding for the many hours dedicated to this project, hours taken in many cases from family activities. Special thanks to Carola Mattord, graduate student of English at Georgia State University. Her reviews of early drafts and suggestions for keeping the writing focused on the students resulted in a more readable manuscript.

Contributors

Several Kennesaw State University students also assisted in the preparation of the textbook, and we thank them for their contributions:

- Anthony J. Nichols — Author of the first draft of the Appendix on cryptography
- Ramona Binder — Research assistant for endnotes

Reviewers

We are indebted to the following individuals for their respective contributions of percep-tive feedback on the initial proposal, the project outline, and the chapter-by-chapter reviews of the text:

- Snehamay Banerjee, Rutgers University
- Michael L. Casper, Central Piedmont Community College
- Lawrence R. Knupp, DeVry University
- Robert Lipton, Pennsylvania State University
- Patrick Massaro, Long Island University
- David Ozag, Gettysburg College
- Denise Padavano, Peirce College
- Sara Robben, DeVry University
- JoAnna Burley Shore, Frostburg State University
- Robert Statica, New Jersey Institute of Technology
- Eileen M. Vidrine, Northern Virginia Community College

Special Thanks

The authors wish to thank the Editorial and Production teams at Course Technology. Their diligent and professional efforts greatly enhanced the final product:

- Barrie Tysko, Product Manager
- Betsey Henkels, Developmental Editor
- Jennifer Locke, Executive Editor
- Christine Spillett, Associate Production Manager
- Janet Aras, Associate Product Manager
- Abby Reip, Photo Researcher

In addition, several professional and commercial organizations and individuals have aided the development of the textbook by providing information and inspiration, and the authors wish to acknowledge their contribution:

- The Human Firewall Council
- PentaSafe Security Technologies, Inc.
- Steven Kahan, Vice President of Marketing, PentaSafe Security Technologies, Inc.
- Charles Cresson Wood
- Georgia-Pacific Corporation
- Carlos Mena, Senior Manager of Corporate IT Privacy and Security, Georgia-Pacific Corporation
- Robert D. Hayes, Director of Corporate Security, Georgia-Pacific Corporation
- Our colleagues in the Department of Computer Science and Information Systems, Kennesaw State University
- Professor Merle King, Chair of the Department of Computer Science and Information Systems, Kennesaw State University

Our Commitment

The authors are committed to serving the needs of the adopters and readers. We would be pleased and honored to receive feedback on the textbook and its supporting materials. You can contact us, through Course Technology, via e-mail at mis@course.com.

Introduction to Information Security

1

> Do not figure on opponents not attacking;
> worry about your own lack of preparation.
>
> **BOOK OF THE FIVE RINGS**

IT STARTED OUT LIKE ANY OTHER DAY for Amy at the Sequential Label and Supply Company. She liked her technical support job at the help desk at good old SLS. It was true that she was working for a stodgy, old manufacturing company and not at some cutting-edge, high-tech startup, but she liked the work. Taking calls and helping the office workers with PC problems was not glamorous, but it was challenging and paid pretty well. She had friends she knew from school who had jobs all over the city and the area. Some worked at bigger companies, some at higher-tech companies, but everyone kept up with each other, and they all agreed that technology jobs were a good way to pay the bills.

The phone rang. That was not a big deal for Amy; after all, that was her job. Using her wireless headset she answered the phone about 35 times an hour, 315 times a day, nine days every two weeks. This time the call started out the same as usual, with a worried user hoping Amy could help him out of a jam. The call display on her screen gave her all the facts: the user's name, his phone number, the department in which he worked, where his office was on the company campus, and a list of all the calls he'd made in the past.

"Hi, Bob," she said. "Did you get that document formatting problem squared away after our last call? "

"Sure did, Amy. Hope we can figure out what's going on today."

"We'll try, Bob, tell me about it."

"Well, my PC is acting weird," Bob said. "When I go to the screen that has my e-mail program running, it doesn't respond to the mouse or the keyboard."

1

Amy didn't think long about her reply, "Did you try a reboot yet, Bob?"

"Sure did. But the window wouldn't close, and I had to turn it off. Once it finished the reboot, and I opened the e-mail program, it's just like it was before—no response at all. The other stuff is working OK, but really, really slowly. Even my Internet browser is sluggish."

"OK Bob. We've tried the usual stuff we can do over the phone. Let me open a case and I'll dispatch a tech over as fast as possible." Amy looked up at the LED tally board on the wall at the end of the room. She saw that there were only two cases dispatched to deskside support at the moment, and since it was the day shift there were four technicians available. "Shouldn't be long at all Bob. Sit tight, and they should be right over." She glanced at the inbound call counter and saw that there were not even enough incoming calls to keep her and the other two first-level technicians busy.

She clicked off the line from Bob and typed her notes into ISIS, their Information Status and Issues System. She assigned the newly generated case to the deskside dispatch queue, knowing the roving deskside team would be paged with the details and attend to Bob in just a few minutes.

Amy looked up to see Charles Moody walking briskly down the hall. Charlie, as he liked to be called, was the senior manager of the server administration team. He was being trailed by three of his senior technicians as he made a beeline from his office to the door of the server room where all the company servers were kept in a controlled environment. They all looked worried.

Amy's screen beeped to alert her of a new e-mail. She glanced down. It beeped again—and again. It started beeping constantly. She clicked on the envelope icon on her screen. After a short delay, the mail window opened. She had 47 new e-mails in her inbox. She double-clicked on one from Davey Martinez, an acquaintance of hers from the Accounting Department. The subject line said, "Wait till you see this." The message body contained, "Look what this has to say about our manager's salaries…" There was an icon for a file attachment that Amy did not recognize. But, she knew Davey, he often sent her interesting and funny e-mails. She double clicked on the icon.

Her PC showed the hourglass pointer icon for a second and then resumed its normal pointer. Nothing happened. She clicked on the icon for the next e-mail message. Nothing happened. Her phone rang again. She clicked on the ISIS icon on her computer desktop to activate the call management software, and activated her headset. "Hello, Sequential Label and Supply, Company Tech Support, how can I assist you today?" She couldn't greet the caller by name because ISIS had not yet opened the screen on her PC.

"Hello, this is Erin Williams in Receiving."

Amy glanced down at the screen. Still no ISIS. She glanced up to the tally board and was surprised to see the inbound call counter tallying up waiting calls like digits on a stopwatch. Amy had never seen so many calls come in at one time

"Hi, Erin," Amy answered pushing her concern about the incoming calls aside. "What's up?"

"Nothing," Erin answered "That's just it." Amy could tell Erin was frustrated about the situation. The rest of the call was as an exact replay of Bob's earlier call, except Amy couldn't type the notes into ISIS and had to jot them down on a legal pad. She also couldn't dispatch to the deskside support team either. She looked at the tally board. It had gone dark. No numbers at all.

Then she saw Charlie running down the hall from the server room. He didn't look worried anymore. He looked scared.

Amy reached for the button to make an outbound call on her phone. She wanted to check with her supervisor about what to do now. There was no dial tone…

DISCUSSION QUESTIONS:

1. What happened to Sequential's network?
2. Did an insider or outsider attack the system?
3. What type of security breach occurred: physical, personal, operational, communications, or network?
4. Was this salami theft, spam, e-mail spoofing, a virus, or a worm?

LEARNING OBJECTIVES:

Upon completion of this material, you should be able to:

- Understand what information security is and how it came to mean what it does today.
- Comprehend the history of computer security and how it evolved into information security.
- Understand the key terms and critical concepts of information security as presented in the chapter.
- Outline the phases of the security systems development life cycle.
- Understand the role of professionals involved in information security in an organizational structure.

Introduction

James Anderson, Vice President of Information Security, Inovant, the world's largest commercial processor of financial payment transactions, believes information security in today's enterprise is a "well-informed sense of assurance that the information risks and controls are in balance."

In the opening scenario of this chapter, it seems clear that the information risks and controls are not in balance. Though Amy has a technical support job and her duties are to solve technical problems, you sense that she does not consider a virus or worm to be the culprit of the company's current ills. Management also shows signs of confusion and seems to be at a loss to contain this kind of situation. If you were in Amy's place and were faced with a similar situation, what would you do? How would you react? Would it occur to you that something far more insidious than a simple technical malfunction was happening to your company? As you study the following chapters and learn more about information security, you will find the answers to these questions. But, before you can begin analyzing the details of information security, it is necessary to review the origins of this field and its impact on your understanding of information security.

The History of Information Security

The history of information security begins with the history of **computer security**. The need for computer security, in other words, the need to secure the physical location of hardware from outside threats, began almost immediately after the first mainframes were developed and put to use. The multiple levels of security to protect these mainframes became the focus for the safety of data integrity. Groups developing code-breaking computations during World War II created the first modern computers[1]. During this time access to sensitive military locations was controlled through the use of badges, keys, and the facial recognition of authorized personnel. The growing needs for maintaining national security, however, including background investigations and ongoing counterintelligence programs, eventually expanded the procedures of computer security to embrace more complex and more technologically sophisticated safeguards. See Figure 1-1 for a brief discussion of decrypting transmissions from the German code machine Enigma.

Earlier versions of the German code machine Enigma were first broken by the Poles in the 1930s. The British and Americans managed to break later, more complex versions during World War II. The increasingly complex versions of the Enigma, especially the submarine or *Unterseeboot* version of the Enigma, caused considerable anguish to allied forces before finally being cracked. The information gained from decrypted transmissions was used to anticipate the actions of German armed forces. "Some ask why, if we were reading the Enigma, we did not win the war earlier. One might ask, instead, when, if ever, we would have won the war if we hadn't read it."

Courtesy of National Security Agency

FIGURE 1-1 The Enigma[2]

In contrast to computer security, information security during those early years was rudimentary and mainly composed of simple document classification schemes. There were no application classification projects for computers or operating systems at that time, because the primary threats to security were physical theft of equipment, espionage against the products of the systems, and sabotage.

The 1960s

One of the first documented security problems that was not physical in nature occurred years later in the early 1960s when a systems administrator was working on an MOTD (message of the day) file, and another administrator was editing the password file. A software glitch mixed the two files, and the entire password file was printed on every output file.[3] During the Cold War of the 1960s, many more mainframes were brought online to accomplish more complex and sophisticated work. At this time, it became necessary to find a way to enable the mainframes to communicate with each other using a less cumbersome process than mailing magnetic tapes between computer centers. In response to this need, the Department of Defense's Advanced Research Project Agency (ARPA) began examining the feasibility of a redundant, networked communications system designed to support the military's need to exchange information. Larry Roberts, known as the Founder of the Internet, developed the project from its inception. The project was named ARPANET, and it is the origin of today's Internet (see Figure 1-2 for an excerpt from the ARPANET Program Plan).

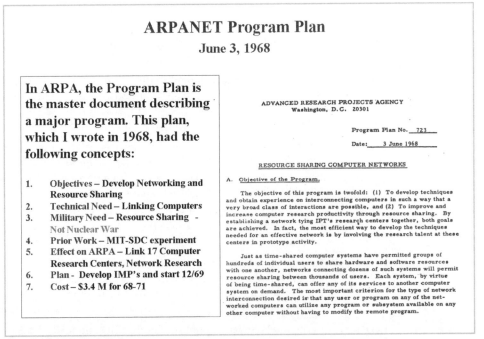

ARPANET Program Plan
June 3, 1968

In ARPA, the Program Plan is the master document describing a major program. This plan, which I wrote in 1968, had the following concepts:

1. **Objectives – Develop Networking and Resource Sharing**
2. **Technical Need – Linking Computers**
3. **Military Need – Resource Sharing - Not Nuclear War**
4. **Prior Work – MIT-SDC experiment**
5. **Effect on ARPA – Link 17 Computer Research Centers, Network Research**
6. **Plan - Develop IMP's and start 12/69**
7. **Cost – $3.4 M for 68-71**

ADVANCED RESEARCH PROJECTS AGENCY
Washington, D.C. 20301

Program Plan No. 723

Date: 3 June 1968

RESOURCE SHARING COMPUTER NETWORKS

A. Objective of the Program.

The objective of this program is twofold: (1) To develop techniques and obtain experience on interconnecting computers in such a way that a very broad class of interactions are possible, and (2) To improve and increase computer research productivity through resource sharing. By establishing a network tying IPT's research centers together, both goals are achieved. In fact, the most efficient way to develop the techniques needed for an effective network is by involving the research talent at these centers in prototype activity.

Just as time-shared computer systems have permitted groups of hundreds of individual users to share hardware and software resources with one another, networks connecting dozens of such systems will permit resource sharing between thousands of users. Each system, by virtue of being time-shared, can offer any of its services to another computer system on demand. The most important criterion for the type of network interconnection desired is that any user or program on any of the networked computers can utilize any program or subsystem available on any other computer without having to modify the remote program.

Courtesy of Dr. Lawrence Roberts

FIGURE 1-2 ARPANET Program Plan[4]

The 1970s and 80s

During the next decade, the ARPANET grew in popularity and use, and so did the potential for its misuse. In December of 1973, Robert M. "Bob" Metcalfe, who is credited with the development of the Ethernet, one of the most popular protocols for networking, indicated that there were fundamental problems with ARPANET security. Individual remote users' sites did not have sufficient controls and safeguards to protect data against unauthorized remote users. Other problems abounded, including the vulnerability of password structure and formats. There were no safety procedures for dial-up connections to the ARPANET. User identification and authorization to the system were nonexistent. Phone numbers were widely distributed and openly publicized on the walls of phone booths, giving hackers easy access to ARPANET. Given the range and frequency of computer security violations and the explosion in numbers of hosts and users on the ARPANET, network security was referred to as network insecurity.[5] In 1978, a famous study was published entitled, "Protection Analysis: Final Report." It focused on a project undertaken by ARPA to discover the vulnerabilities of operating system security. For an outline of this and other seminal studies of computer security, see Table 1-1.

TABLE 1-1 Key Dates for Seminal Works In Early Computer Security

Date	Documents
1968	Maurice Wilkes discusses password security in *Time-Sharing Computer Systems*.
1973	Schell, Downey, and Popek examine the need for additional security in military systems in "Preliminary Notes on the Design of Secure Military Computer Systems."[6]
1975	The Federal Information Processing Standards (FIPS) examines DES (Digital Encryption Standard) in the *Federal Register*.
1978	Bisbey and Hollingworth publish their study "Protection Analysis: Final Report" discussing the Protection Analysis project created by ARPA to better understand the vulnerabilities of operating system security and examine the possibility of automated vulnerability detection techniques in existing system software.[7]
1979	Morris and Thompson author "Password Security: A Case History" published in the *Communications of the Association for Computing Machinery* (ACM). The paper examines the history of a design for a password security scheme on a remotely accessed, time-sharing system.
1979	Dennis Ritchie publishes "On the Security of UNIX" and "Protection of Data File Contents" discussing secure user IDs and secure group IDs, and the problems inherent in the systems.
1984	Grampp and Morris write "UNIX Operating System Security." In this report the authors examine four "important handles to computer security:" physical control of premises and computer facilities, management commitment to security objectives, education of employees, and administrative procedures aimed at increased security.[8]
1984	Reeds and Weinberger publish "File Security and the UNIX System Crypt Command." Their premise was: "No technique can be secure against wiretapping or its equivalent on the computer. Therefore no technique can be secure against the system administrator or other privileged users... the naive user has no chance."[9]

Security that went beyond the protection of the physical location was now needed to protect data integrity. It began with a single paper sponsored by the Department of Defense, the Rand Report R-609, which attempted to define the multiple controls and mechanisms necessary for the protection of a multilevel computer system. The document was classified for almost ten years, and is now referred to as "the paper that started the study of computer security." The following are a few paragraphs from that paper:

"The question of security control in resource-sharing systems was brought into focus for the Department of Defense by a series of events in the spring and summer of 1967. Such systems were being procured in increasing numbers for government installations; the problems of security for them were becoming of pressing concern both to defense contractors and to military operations; the Research Security Administrators had forwarded a position paper through the Defense Supply Agency to the Director for Security Policy in the Office of Assistant Secretary of Defense (Administration) soliciting action. Since the matter involved technical issues, the paper was referred to the Office of the Director of Defense Research and Engineering for consideration.

"In June 1967, the Deputy Director (Administration, Evaluation and Management) requested the Director of the Advanced Research Projects Agency (ARPA) to form a Task Force to study and recommend hardware and software safeguards that would satisfactorily protect classified information in multi-access, resource-sharing computer systems. Within ARPA, the responsibility for this task was forwarded to Mr. Robert W. Taylor, Director of the Office of Information Processing Techniques.

"A series of discussions was held during the summer and fall months of 1967 with people from the university and industrial communities, culminating in the formation by October 1967 of a Task Force consisting of a Steering Group and two Panels. The organizational meeting was held the following month, and thereafter the Panels and the Steering Group met on a regular basis to formulate the recommendations that constitute the body of this Report. The Task Force has operated formally under the authority of the Defense Science Board."[10]

It is important to note this report, because it was the first to identify the role of management and policy issues in computer security. Rand Report R-609 states:

"The wide use of computers in military and defense installations has long necessitated the application of security rules and regulations. A basic principle underlying the security of computer systems has traditionally been that of isolation-simply removing the entire system to a physical environment in which penetrability is acceptably minimized. The increasing use of systems in which some equipment components, such as user access terminals, are widely spread geographically has introduced new complexities and issues. These problems are not amenable to solution through the elementary safeguard of physical isolation."[11]

This paper signaled a pivotal moment in computer security history—when the scope of computer security expanded significantly. The scope grew from the safety of physical locations and hardware to include:

- Safety of the data
- Limiting random and unauthorized access to that data
- Involvement of personnel from multiple levels of the organization

At this stage, the original concept of computer security was beginning to evolve into the more complex and sophisticated system that today we call information security.

MULTICS

Much of the focus for research on computer security centered on a system called MULTICS (Multiplexed Information and Computing Service). Even though this operating system is now obsolete, MULTICS is noteworthy, because it was the first and *only* operating system created with security as its primary goal. It was a mainframe, time-sharing operating system developed in the mid-1960s by a consortium from General Electric (GE), Bell Labs, and the Massachusetts Institute of Technology (MIT).

In mid-1969, not long after the restructuring of the MULTICS project, several of its key players, Ken Thompson, Dennis Ritchie, Rudd Canaday, and Doug McIlroy, created a new operating system called UNIX. While the MULTICS system had planned security with multiple security levels and passwords, the UNIX system did not. Its primary developmental purpose, text processing, did not require the same level of security as its predecessor. In fact, it was not until the early 1970s that even the simplest component of security, the password function, was implemented as a component of the operating system.

In the late 1970s, the microprocessor brought in a new age of computing capabilities. The personal computer, built with this microprocessor technology, became the workhorse of modern computing, thereby decentralizing the exclusive domain of the data center. With decentralization of data, the need for resource sharing increased during the 1980s, driving owners of personal computers to interconnect them. These networking abilities worked for both mainframe and microcomputers, and gave owners the opportunity to make all their computing resources work together.

The 1990s

At the close of the twentieth century, as networks of computers became more common, so too did the need to connect the networks to each other. This gave rise to the Internet, the first manifestation of a global network of networks. This networking resource was made more available to the general public in the 1990s, having previously been the domain of government, academia, and dedicated industry professionals. The Internet brought connectivity to virtually all computers that could reach a phone line or a Local Area Network (LAN) that was itself connected to the Internet. After the Internet was commercialized, the technology became pervasive, reaching almost every corner of the globe with an expanding universe of uses.

There has been a price for this phenomenal growth, however. Since its inception as a tool for sharing defense information, the Internet has grown steadily with the interconnection of millions of networks. At first, these connections were based on *de facto* **standards**, because industry standards for interconnection of networks did not exist at that time. These *de facto* standards did not consider the security of information to be a critical factor, but as these precursor technologies were more widely adopted and they developed into industry standards, some degree of security was brought into the process. However, when security was considered at all, early Internet deployment treated it as a low priority. For example, many of the problems that plague e-mail on the Internet today come from this early lack of security as a major design requirement. Early computing approaches relied on security that was built into the physical environment of the data center that housed the computers. As the requirement for networked computers became the dominant style of computing, however, the ability to physically secure that physical computer was lost, and the stored information became more exposed to security threats.

The Present

Today, the Internet has brought millions of unsecured computer networks into communication with each other. Our ability to secure each computer's stored information is now influenced by the security on every other computer to which it is connected.

As you may have realized through this review of the history of information security, the concept of *computer* security is no longer the main objective for securing computer systems. Computer security has evolved into a component of a complex, multifaceted environment now defined as information security.

What Is Security?

As mentioned in the previous section, computers have evolved into highly sophisticated and complex systems of operation, and the networking environments in which they operate are also incredibly complex. That complexity of relationship between the computer system and the network is proving to be the area of greatest vulnerability. Therefore, an organization's security must no longer be viewed as a low priority.

In general, **security** is "the quality or state of being secure—to be free from danger."[12] It means to be protected from adversaries—from those who would do harm, intentionally or otherwise. National security, for example, is a multilayered system that protects the sovereignty of a state, its assets, resources, and its people. In the same manner, achieving the appropriate level of security for an organization also depends on a multifaceted system.

A successful organization should have the following multiple layers of security in place to protect its operations:

- **Physical security** addresses the issues necessary to protect the physical items, objects, or areas of an organization from unauthorized access and misuse.
- **Personal security** addresses the protection of the individual or group of individuals who are authorized to access the organization and its operations.
- **Operations security** focuses on the protection of the details of a particular operation or series of activities.
- **Communications security** encompasses the protection of an organization's communications media, technology, and content.
- **Network security** is the protection of networking components, connections, and contents.
- **Information security** is discussed in more detail in the following section.

What Is Information Security?

The definition of information security used here is adopted from the concept developed by the National Security Telecommunications and Information Systems Security Committee (NSTISSC).[13] **Information security** is the protection of information and the systems and hardware that use, store, and transmit that information. But, to protect the information and its related systems from danger, such tools as policy, awareness, training and education, and technology are necessary. The NSTISSC model of information security evolved from a concept developed by the computer security industry known as the C.I.A. triangle. The **C.I.A. triangle** has been considered the industry standard for computer security since the development of the mainframe. It is solely based on three characteristics that describe the utility of information, confidentiality, integrity, and availability. The security for these three characteristics of information are as important today as they were at their conception, but are limited in scope, because they no longer encompass the constantly changing environment of the computer industry. The threats to these characteristics of information have evolved into a vast collection of events, including accidental or intentional damage, destruction, theft, unintended or unauthorized modification, or other misuses from human or nonhuman threats. This new environment of many constantly evolving threats has necessitated the development of a more robust intellectual model of the characteristics of information. The updated model addresses the complexities of the current information security environment. The C.I.A. triangle, therefore, has expanded into a list of critical characteristics of information as described in the next section. C.I.A. terminology will be used in this chapter, however, because of the breadth of material that is based on it.

Critical Characteristics of Information

The value of information comes from the characteristics it possesses. Should any one of these characteristics of information change, the value changes, occasionally increasing, but usually decreasing. Some characteristics increase the value of information to users more than other characteristics. For example, the timeliness of information is a critical factor to users, because information often loses all value when it is delivered too late. Though information security professionals and end users share the same understanding of the characteristics of information, each group may give these characteristics different weights. Tensions arise when the need to secure the integrity of information from threats conflicts with the end users' unhindered access to the same information. For example, end users may perceive a tenth of a second delay in computation of data to be an unnecessary annoyance. Information security professionals, however, may perceive that tenth of a second a minor delay for the accomplishment of an important task, like the encryption of data. Each critical characteristic of information is defined in the sections below.

Availability

Availability enables users who need to access information to do so without interference or obstruction, and to receive it in the required format. A user in this case, means not only a person, but also another computer system. However, availability as defined here, does not imply that the information is *accessible* to any user. The availability of information requires the verification of the user as one with authorized access to the information. The information, then, is said to be available to an authorized user when and where needed and in the correct format. To understand this concept more fully, consider the contents of a library, in particular, research libraries that require identification before entrance. Librarians protect the contents of the library, so that it is available only to authorized patrons. This means that the librarian must see and accept a patron's proof of identification before that patron has free and easy access to the contents available in the bookroom. Once authorized patrons have access to the contents of the bookroom, they expect to find the information needed in the required language and in a useable format. For example, this could mean the information is bound in a book and written in English.

Accuracy

Information is **accurate** when it is free from mistakes or errors and it has the value that the end user expects. If information contains a value different from the user's expectations due to the intentional or unintentional modification of its content, it is no longer accurate. Consider the checking account as an example. You assume that the information contained in your checking account is an accurate portrayal of your finances, a portrayal you intend to use for specific purposes. Inaccuracy of the information in your checking account can be caused by external or internal means. If a bank teller, for instance, mistakenly adds or subtracts too much from your account, the value of the information has changed. In turn, as the user of your bank account, you can also accidentally enter an incorrect amount into your account register. This also changes the value of the information. Either way, the changed value of accuracy of your bank account could lead you into making poor or even detrimental decisions.

Authenticity

Authenticity of information is the quality or state of being genuine or original, rather than a reproduction or fabrication. Information is authentic when it is the information that was originally created, placed, stored, or transferred. Consider for a moment some of the assumptions made about e-mail. When you receive e-mail, you assume that a specific individual or group of individuals created and transmitted the e-mail—you assume you know the origin of the e-mail. This is not always the case. **E-mail spoofing**, the process of sending an e-mail message with a modified field, is a problem for many individuals today, because many times the field modified is the address of the originator. Spoofing the address of origin can fool the e-mail recipient into thinking that the message is legitimate traffic. In this way, the spoofer can induce the e-mail readers into opening e-mail they otherwise might not have opened. The attack known as spoofing can also be applied to the transmission of data across a network, as in the case of user data protocol (UDP) packet spoofing, which can enable unauthorized access to data stored on computing systems.

Confidentiality

The **confidentiality** of information is the quality or state of preventing disclosure or exposure to unauthorized individuals or systems. Confidentiality of information is ensuring that only those with the rights and privileges to access a particular set of information are able to do so, and that those who are not authorized are prevented from obtaining access. When unauthorized individuals or systems can view information, confidentiality is breached. To protect the confidentiality of information, you can use a number of measures:

- Information classification
- Secure document storage
- Application of general security policies
- Education of information custodians and end users

Though confidentiality, like most of the characteristics of information, is interdependent with other characteristics, it is closely related to the characteristic known as privacy. The relationship of these two characteristics is covered in more detail in Chapter 3, "Legal and Ethical Issues in Security."

In an organization, the characteristic value of confidentiality of information is especially high when it involves personal information about employees, customers, or patients. Individuals who deal with an organization expect that their personal information will remain confidential, whether the organization is a federal agency, such as the Internal Revenue Service, or a business. Problems arise when companies disclose sensitive information that has been deemed confidential. Sometimes this disclosure occurs on purpose, but there are times when disclosure of confidential information happens by mistake, for example, when confidential information is mistakenly e-mailed to someone *outside* the organization rather than to someone *inside* the organization. The famous case of privacy violation by Eli Lilly and Co. from July, 2001 is outlined in Offline: Unintentional Disclosure.

OFFLINE

Unintentional Disclosure

"ACLU Knocks Eli Lilly for Divulging E-Mail Addresses"[14]
By Julekha Dash, Computerworld, July 9, 2001

"Pharmaceutical firm Eli Lilly and Co. inadvertently divulged the e-mail addresses of 600 patients to one another due to a computer programming error revealed last week. The incident sparked an outcry from the American Civil Liberties Union for the breach of privacy, and analysts noted it's the kind of event that will violate pending health care rules.

"Eli Lilly says a programming error led to mishap.

Patients had signed up for e-mail reminders to take a prescription drug or for other health matters. About 600 patient addresses were identified in a mass e-mail.

"The ACLU has asked the FTC to investigate the error for possible consumer privacy violations.

"The incident occurred when the drug maker sent an electronic message to its registered Web site users to notify them that the site's 'reminder' feature, which alerts them to take their medication, would be discontinued due to a redesign. Instead of each message being sent individually, the system sent one e-mail, whose 'to' field revealed the complete e-mail addresses of about 600 patients, according to Eli Lilly spokeswoman Anne Griffin. Indianapolis-based Eli Lilly makes the antidepressant drug Prozac and other drugs.

The affected patients were those who had signed up for the e-mail reminder service. Griffin described the mistake as an 'isolated event' and the result of a programming error."

©Copyright 2001. Computerworld, Inc. Reprinted with the permission of Computerworld Magazine.

Another example of a breach of security is an employee throwing away a document containing critical information without shredding it. A second example is a hacker who successfully breaks into an internal database of a Web-based organization and steals sensitive information about the clients, such as names, addresses and credit card numbers.

As a consumer, you give up pieces of your confidential information in exchange for convenience or value almost daily. By using a "members only card" at a grocery store, you disclose a bit of your spending habits. When you fill out an online survey, you are exchanging pieces of your personal history for access to online privileges. The bits and pieces of your information that you disclose are copied, sold, replicated, distributed and eventually are coalesced into profiles and even complete dossiers of yourself and your life. A similar aggregation of information used with criminal intent is called **salami theft**. A deli worker knows he or she cannot steal the entire salami, but a few slices here or there can be taken home without notice. Eventually the deli worker has stolen the whole salami. In security, salami theft occurs when an employee steals a few pieces of information at a time, knowing that taking more at one time would be noticeable—but eventually they get the whole thing.

Integrity

The quality or state of being whole, complete, and uncorrupted is the **integrity** of information. The integrity of information is threatened when the information is exposed to corruption, damage, destruction, or other disruption of its authentic state. The threat of corruption can occur while information is being stored or transmitted. Many computer viruses and worms have been created with the specific purpose of corrupting data. For this reason, the key method for detecting a virus or worm is to look for changes in file integrity as shown by the size of the file. Another key methodology for assuring information integrity is through file hashing. With **file hashing**, a file is read by a special algorithm that uses the value of the bits in the file to compute a single large number called a **hash value**. The hash value for any combination of bits is different for each combination. If the computer system performs the same hashing algorithm before trusting the contents of the file and returns a different number than the posted hash value for that file, you know the file has been compromised and the integrity of the information is lost. Therefore, information integrity is the cornerstone of information systems, because information is of no value or use if users cannot verify its integrity.

The corruption of a file does not always come from external forces, such as hackers. Noise in the transmission media, for instance, can cause data to lose its integrity. A low-power signal carrying information can cause the receiving system to record the data with inaccurate values. You attempt to compensate for internal and external threats to the integrity of information by including redundancy bits and check bits. During each transmission, algorithms, hash values, and the error-correcting codes ensure the integrity of the information. Data, which has not been verified in this manner, is retransmitted.

Utility

The **utility** of information is the quality or state of having value for some purpose or end. Information has value when it serves a particular purpose. This means that if information is available, but not in a format meaningful to the end user, it is not useful. For example, if you have ever reviewed the results of the U.S. Census report, you may see that the information can quickly become overwhelming and difficult to interpret. In addition, for a private citizen the census results would probably be of little use. However, if you are a politician, the results of the U.S. Census can inform you about the voters in your district, to what political party they belong, and their race, gender, age, and so on. This information can help you plan your next campaign strategy. The value of the information depends on its utility.

Possession

The **possession** of information is the quality or state of having ownership or control of some object or item. Information is said to be in possession if one obtains it, independent of format or other characteristic. While a breach of confidentiality always results in a breach of possession, a breach of possession does not always result in a breach of confidentiality. Regarding the latter, assume a company stores its critical customer data using an encrypted file system. An employee, who has quit, decides to take a copy of the tape backups to sell the customer records to the competition. The removal of the tapes from their secure environment is a breach of possession. But, because the data is encrypted, neither the employee nor anyone else can read it without the proper decryption methods, therefore there is no breach of confidentiality. Today, individuals caught selling company secrets are facing increasingly stiff fines with the possibility of jail time. Companies are also growing more and more reluctant to hire individuals who have been untrustworthy to previous employers.

NSTISSC Security Model

You can recall the definition for information security presented earlier which is based in part on the National Security Telecommunications and Information Systems Security Committee document called the National Training Standard for Information Security Professionals NSTISSI No. 4011 (see *www.nstissc.gov/html/library.html*). This document presents a comprehensive model for information security and is becoming the evaluation standard for the security of information systems. The security model, as represented in Figure 1-3, shows the three dimensions. If you extrapolate the three dimensions of each axis, you end up with a $3 \times 3 \times 3$ cube with 27 cells representing areas that must be addressed to secure the information systems of today. Your primary responsibility is to make sure that each of the 27 cells is properly addressed during the security process. For example, if you look at the intersection between the technology, integrity, and storage areas, you would expect to see a control or safeguard that indicates that you have addressed the need to use *technology* to protect the *integrity* of information while in *storage*. One technology you could use would be a system to detect host intrusion, that is designed to protect the integrity of information by alerting the security administrators of the potential modification of a critical file. Your job is to examine all cells, and make sure each is addressed to your satisfaction. What is commonly left out of such a model is the need for guidelines and policies that provide direction for the practices and implementations of technologies. The necessity of policy is discussed in later chapters.

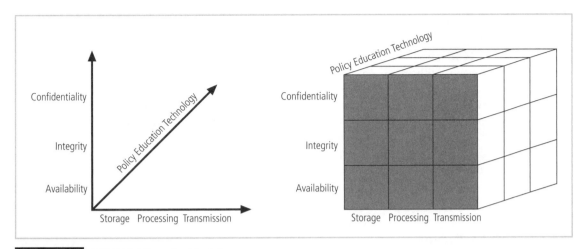

FIGURE 1-3   NSTISSC Security Model

Components of an Information System

As explained previously, information security is protecting information and the systems that store, process, and transmit it. As shown in Figure 1-4, an **Information System (IS)** is much more than computer hardware; it is the entire set of software, hardware, data, people, and procedures necessary to use information as a resource in the organization. These are the five critical components that enable information to be input, processed, output, and stored. Each of these five components of the IS has its own strengths and weaknesses—its own characteristics and uses. More important to remember, each component of the information system has its own security requirements.

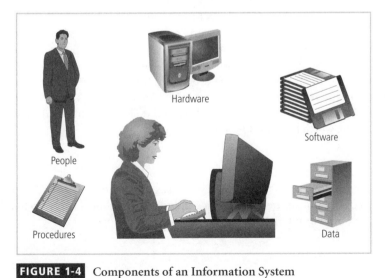

FIGURE 1-4   Components of an Information System

Software

The first major component of an IS is software. The software component of the IS comprises applications, operating systems, and assorted command utilities. Software is perhaps the most difficult IS component to secure. Exploiting errors in software programming results in a substantial portion of the attacks on information. The news is filled with reports warning of holes, bugs, weaknesses, or other fundamental problems in software. Software programs are the vessels that carry the lifeblood of information through an organization. Unfortunately, software programs are often created under the demanding constraints of project management—time, cost, and manpower. Concern for security is applied as an afterthought, rather than developed as an integral component from the beginning. In this way, the information software programming process becomes an easy target of accidental or intentional attacks.

Hardware

The next major component of an IS is hardware. It is the physical technology that houses and executes the software, stores and carries the data, and provides interfaces for the entry and removal of information from the system. Physical security policies deal with hardware as a physical asset and with the protection of these physical assets from harm or theft. We can apply the traditional tools of physical security, such as locks and keys, to restrict access to and interaction with the hardware components of an information system. Securing the physical location of computers and the computers themselves is important, because a breach of physical security can result in a loss of information. Unfortunately, most information systems are built on hardware platforms that cannot guarantee any level of information security if unrestricted access to the hardware is possible.

Reports of laptop thefts in airports are common. A two-person team works to steal a computer as the victim passes it through the conveyor scanning devices. The first perpetrator enters the security area ahead of an unsuspecting target and quickly goes through. Then, the second perpetrator follows the intended victim, but delays walking through the metal detector, until the target places his/her computer on the baggage scanner. As the computer is whisked through, the second agent enters the metal detector, with a substantial collection of keys, coins and the like, slowing the detection process, and allowing the first agent to grab the computer and disappear in a crowded walkway.

While the tragic events of September 11, 2001 have changed the security measures at airports, hardware can still be stolen in these kinds of public places. Although laptops or notebook computers are worth a few thousand dollars, the information contained in them can be worth millions to an organization.

Data

Earlier we discussed the concept of data versus information. It is evident that data stored, processed, and transmitted through a computer system must be protected. Data is usually the main object of intentional attacks.

People

People are often a threat to information security. Legend has it that around 200 B.C., a great army threatened the security and stability of the Chinese empire. So ferocious were the invaders that the Chinese emperor commanded the construction of a great wall that would defend against the Hun invaders. Around 1275 A.D. Kublai Khan finally achieved what the Huns had been trying for thousands of years. Initially, the Khan's army tried to climb over, dig under, and break through the wall. In the end, Khan bribed the gatekeeper to open the gates—and the rest is history. Whether this event actually occurred or not, the moral of the story is that people can be your weakest link. They may not intend to be, but, unless policy, education and training, awareness, and technology are properly employed to prevent them from accidentally or intentionally allowing damage or loss of information, they are the weakest link. Social engineering can be used to prey on the tendency to cut corners and the commonplace nature of human error. It can be used to manipulate the actions of people to obtain access information about a system. This topic is discussed in more detail in Chapter 2, "The Need for Security."

Procedures

Another frequently overlooked component of IS is procedures. Procedures are written instructions for accomplishing a specific task. If an unauthorized user obtains an organization's procedures, a threat to the integrity of the information is posed. For example, a consultant of a bank learned how to wire funds by using the computer center's procedures that were readily available. By taking advantage of a security weakness (lack of authentication), this bank consultant ordered millions of dollars to be transferred by wire to an unauthorized account. Lax security of the information system caused the loss of over ten million dollars before the situation was corrected. Most organizations focus on distributing procedures to their legitimate employees, so that they can access the information system. However, proper education on the protection of those procedures is often lacking. Educating employees about safeguarding the procedures is as important as securing the information system. After all, procedures are information in their own right. Therefore, knowledge of procedures, as with all critical information, should be disseminated among members of the organization only on a need-to-know basis.

Securing the Components

As you can see from the previous sections, security of information and its systems entails securing all components and protecting them from potential misuse and abuse by unauthorized users. When considering the security of information systems components, it is important to understand the concept of the computer as the subject of an attack as opposed to the computer as the object of an attack. When a computer is the **subject of an attack**, it is used as an active tool to conduct the attack. When a computer is the **object of an attack**, it is the entity being attacked. Figure 1-5 illustrates computers as subject and object. There are also two types of attacks: **direct attacks** and **indirect attacks**. An attack is considered direct when a hacker uses his personal computer to break into a system. An attack is considered indirect when a system is compromised and used in a distributed denial of service attack. Direct attacks originate from the threat itself. Indirect attacks originate from a system or resource that itself has been attacked, and is malfunctioning or working under the control of a threat. A computer can be considered to be in both categories at once. Should an attacker compromise a computer system, and then use that compromised system to attack other systems, that computer is both the subject and object of attack.

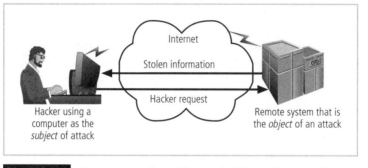

FIGURE 1-5   Computer as the Subject and Object of an Attack

Balancing Security and Access

Take another look at the quotation in the introduction of this chapter. Notice that Jim Anderson does not consider information security as a means to eradicate all threats to a system. When determining information security, it is important to realize that it is impossible to obtain perfect security. Security is not an absolute; it is a process, not a goal. Security should be considered a *balance* between protection and availability. It is possible to have unrestricted access to a system, so that the system is available to anyone, anywhere, anytime, through any means. However, this kind of random access poses a danger to the integrity of the information. On the other hand, complete security of an information system would not allow anyone access. For instance, to achieve the desired security certification, TCSEC C-2, for its Windows operating system, Microsoft had to remove all networking components and operate the computer solely in a secured room.[15]

To achieve balance—to operate an information system to the satisfaction of the user and the security professional—the level of security must allow reasonable access, yet protect against threats. Figure 1-6 shows some of the competing voices that must be reconciled in the security versus access balancing act.

FIGURE 1-6 Balancing Security and Access

Because of today's security concerns and issues, an information system or Data-Processing Department can get too entrenched in its responsibility to manage and protect systems. An imbalance can occur when the needs of the end user are undermined by too heavy a focus on protecting and administering the information systems. Both the information security technologists and end users must exercise patience and cooperation when interacting with each other, as both groups share the same overall goals of the organization—to ensure the data is available when, where, and how it is needed, with minimal delays or obstacles. In an ideal world, this level of availability is met even after concerns about loss, damage, interception, or destruction have been addressed.

Top-Down Approach to Security Implementation

The implementation of information security in an organization must begin somewhere. After all, the security of all systems does not magically appear overnight. It is an incremental process that requires coordination, time, and patience. Security can begin as a grassroots effort in which systems administrators attempt to improve the security of their systems. This is often referred to as a **bottom-up approach**. The key advantage of the bottom-up approach is the technical expertise of the individual administrators. Working with information systems on a day-to-day basis, these administrators possess in-depth knowledge that can greatly enhance the development of an information security system. They know and understand the threats to their systems and the mechanisms needed to successfully protect them. Unfortunately, this approach seldom works, as it lacks a number of critical features, such as participant support and organizational staying power. The levels of organization hierarchy involved with bottom-up and top-down approaches are shown in Figure 1-7.

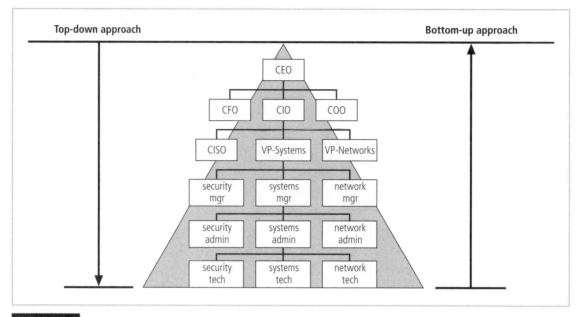

Top-down approach   **Bottom-up approach**

FIGURE 1-7   Approaches to Security Implementation

For any organization-wide effort to succeed, however, management must buy into and totally support an information security system. Such a system must have a **champion**—an executive who moves the project forward, ensures that it is properly managed, and pushes for acceptance throughout the organization. Typically, the champion is the chief information officer (CIO), or other senior executive such as the vice president of information technology (VP-IT). Without this high-level support, many of the midlevel administrators fail to make time for the project or dismiss it as a low priority. Also critical to the success of this type of project is the involvement and support of the end users. These individuals are most directly impacted by the process and outcome of the project and must be included in the information security process. Key end users should be assigned to a developmental team, known as the joint application development team, or JAD. To succeed, the JAD must have staying power. It must be able to survive employee turnover and should not be vulnerable to changes in the personnel who are developing the information security system. This means the processes and procedures must be documented and integrated into the organizational culture. They must be adopted *and promoted* by the organization's management.

An alternative approach, which has a higher probability of success, is called the **top-down approach**. The difference between this approach and the bottom-up approach is significant. With this approach, the project is initiated by upper management who issue policy, procedures and processes, dictate the goals and expected outcomes of the project, and determine who is accountable for each of the required actions. The top-down approach has strong upper-management support, a dedicated champion, usually dedicated funding, a clear planning and implementation process, and the opportunity to influence organizational culture. The most successful top-down approach also involves a formal development strategy referred to as a systems development life cycle.

The Systems Development Life Cycle

Information security must be managed in a manner similar to any other major system implemented in the organization. The best approach for implementing an information security system in an organization with little or no formal security in place is to use a variation of the systems development life cycle (SDLC): the security systems development life cycle (SecSDLC).

Methodology

The **SDLC** is a methodology for the design and implementation of an information system in an organization. A **methodology** is a formal approach to solving a problem based on a structured sequence of procedures. Using a methodology ensures a rigorous process and avoids missing those steps that can lead to compromising the end goal. The goal in this case is creating a comprehensive security posture. A methodology also increases the probability of success. Once a methodology has been adopted, the key milestones are established and a team of individuals is selected and made accountable to accomplish the project goals.

Phases

To understand a formal security development life cycle, it is important to review the basics of the SDLC upon which it is based. The traditional SDLC consists of six general phases. If you have taken a system analysis and design course, you may have been exposed to a model consisting of a different number of phases. The different variations of SDLC range from three to 12 stages, all of which have been mapped into the six presented here. Each of these stages comes from the **waterfall model** pictured in Figure 1-8, in which each phase begins with the results and information gained from the previous phase.

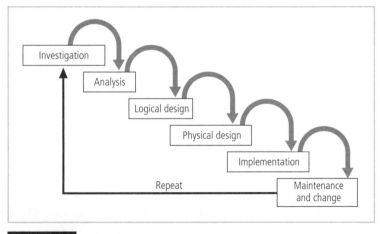

FIGURE 1-8 SDLC Waterfall Methodology

The entire process may be initiated in response to specific conditions or combinations of conditions. The impetus to begin the SecSDLC may be event-driven, that is, started in response to some occurrence in the business community, inside the organization, or within the ranks of employees, customers, or other stakeholders. It may be plan-driven, or a result of a carefully developed implementation strategy. Either way, once the need for information security is recognized, the methodology ensures that development proceeds in an orderly, comprehensive fashion. At the end of each phase comes a structured review or reality check during which the team determines if the project should be continued, discontinued, outsourced, or postponed, depending on the need for additional expertise, organizational knowledge, or resources.

The process begins with an investigation of the problem facing the organization, continues with an analysis of current organizational practices considered in the context of the investigation, and then proceeds into the logical and physical design phases. During the design phases, potential solutions are identified and are associated with evaluation criteria. While in the implementation phase, solutions are evaluated, selected, and acquired through a make-or-buy process. These solutions, whether made or bought, are tested, installed, and tested again. Users of systems are trained and documentation developed. Finally, the system becomes mature and is maintained and modified over the remainder of its operational life. Like any information systems implementation, the SecSDLC may have multiple iterations, as over time, the cycle is repeated. Only through constant examination and renewal can any system, especially an information security program, perform up to expectations in the constantly changing environment in which it is placed. The following sections detail activities of each phase of the traditional SDLC.[16]

Investigation

The first phase, investigation, is the most important. What is the problem the system is being developed to solve? The investigation phase begins with an examination of the event or plan that initiates the process. During the investigation phase, the objectives, constraints, and scope of the project are specified. A preliminary cost benefit analysis is developed to evaluate the perceived benefits and the appropriate levels of cost for those benefits. At the conclusion of this stage, and at every stage following, a feasibility analysis is performed, which assesses the economic, technical, and behavioral feasibilities of the process and ensures that implementation is worth the organization's time and effort.

Analysis

The analysis phase begins with the information gained during the investigation phase. This phase consists primarily of assessments of the organization, the status of current systems, and the capability to support the proposed systems. Analysts begin to determine what the new system is expected to do, and how it will interact with existing systems. This phase ends with the documentation of the findings and an update of the feasibility analysis.

Logical Design

In the logical design phase, the information gained from the analysis phase is used to begin creating a solution system for a business problem. In any systems solution, it is imperative that the first and driving factor is the business need. Then, based on the business need, applications are selected that are capable of providing needed services. Based on the applications needed, data support and structures capable of providing the needed inputs are then chosen. Finally, based on all of the above, specific technologies to implement the physical solution are delineated. The logical design is, therefore, the blueprint for the desired solution. This is discussed in greater detail in Chapter 6. The logical design is implementation independent, meaning that it contains no reference to specific technologies, vendors, or products. It addresses instead how the proposed system will solve the problem at hand. In this stage, analysts generate a number of alternative solutions, each with corresponding strengths and weaknesses, and costs and benefits, allowing for a general comparison of available options. In the end, another feasibility analysis is performed.

Physical Design

During the physical design phase, specific technologies are selected to support the alternatives identified and evaluated in the logical design. The selected components are evaluated based on a make-or-buy decision (develop the components in-house or purchase them from a vendor). Final designs integrate various components and technologies. After yet another feasibility analysis, the entire solution is presented to the organizational management for approval.

Implementation

In the implementation phase, any needed software is created. Components are ordered, received, and tested. Afterwards, users are trained and supporting documentation created. Once all components are tested individually, they are installed and tested as systems. Again a feasibility analysis is prepared, and the sponsors are then presented with the system for a performance review and acceptance test.

Maintenance and Change

The maintenance and change phase is the longest and most expensive phase of the process. This phase consists of the tasks necessary to support and modify the system for the remainder of its useful life cycle. Even though formal development may conclude during this phase, the life cycle of the project continues until it is determined that the process should begin again from the investigation phase. At periodic points, the system is tested for compliance, and the feasibility of continuance versus discontinuance is evaluated. Upgrades, updates, and patches are managed. As the needs of the organization change, the systems that support the organization must also change. It is imperative that those who manage the systems, as well as those who support it, continually monitor the effectiveness of the systems in relation to the organization's environment. When the current system can no longer support the evolving mission of the organization, the project is terminated and a new project is implemented.

The Security Systems Development Life Cycle

The same phases used in the traditional SDLC can be adapted to support the specialized implementation of a security project. While the process may differ in intent and specific activities, the overall methodology is the same. The fundamental process is the identification of specific threats and the creation of specific controls to counter those threats. The SecSDLC unifies the process and makes it a coherent program rather than a series of random, seemingly unconnected actions.

Investigation

The investigation of the SecSDLC begins with a directive from upper management, dictating the process, outcomes, and goals of the project, as well as its budget and other constraints. Frequently, this phase begins with a statement of **program security policy** that outlines the implementation of a security program within the organization. Teams of responsible managers, employees, and contractors are organized, problems analyzed, and scope defined, including specific goals and objectives, and any additional constraints not covered in the program policy. Finally, an organizational feasibility analysis is performed to determine whether the organization has the resources and commitment necessary to conduct a successful security analysis and design.

Analysis

In the analysis phase, the documents from the investigation phase are studied. The development team created during the investigation phase conducts a preliminary analysis of existing security policies or programs, along with documented current threats and associated controls. This phase also includes an analysis of relevant legal issues that could impact the design of the security solution. Increasingly, privacy laws have become a major consideration when making decisions about information systems that manage personal information. Recently, many states have implemented legislation making certain computer-related activities illegal. A detailed understanding of these issues is vital. The risk management task also begins in this stage. **Risk management** is the process of identifying, assessing, and evaluating the levels of risk facing the organization, specifically the threats to the organization's security and to the information stored and processed by the organization.

Logical Design

The logical design phase creates and develops the blueprints for security, and examines and implements key policies that influence later decisions. Also at this stage, critical planning is developed for incident response actions to be taken in the event of partial or catastrophic loss. The planning answers the following questions:

- **Continuity planning:** How will business continue in the event of a loss?
- **Incident response:** What do you do when an attack occurs?
- **Disaster recovery:** What must you do to recover information and vital systems immediately after a disastrous event?

These questions are examined and solutions documented. Next, a feasibility analysis determines whether or not the project should continue or should be outsourced.

Physical Design

In the physical design phase, the security technology needed to support the blueprint outlined in the logical design is evaluated, alternative solutions generated, and a final design agreed upon. The security blueprint may be revisited to keep it in line with the changes needed when the physical design is completed. Criteria needed to determine the definition of successful solutions are also prepared during this phase. Included at this time are the designs for physical security measures to support the proposed technological solutions. At the end of this phase, a feasibility study should determine the readiness of the organization for the proposed project, and then the champion and sponsors are presented with the design. At this time, all parties involved have a chance to approve the project before implementation begins.

Implementation

The implementation phase is similar to the traditional SDLC. The security solutions are acquired (made or bought), tested, and implemented, and tested again. Personnel issues are evaluated and specific training and education programs conducted. Finally, the entire tested package is presented to upper management for final approval.

Maintenance and Change

The maintenance and change phase, though last, is perhaps most important, given the high level of ingenuity in today's threats. Today's information security systems need constant monitoring, testing, modification, updating, and repairing. Traditional applications systems are developed within the framework of the SDLC are not designed to anticipate a vicious attack that would require some degree of application reconstruction. In security, the battle for stable, reliable systems is a defensive one. Often repairing damage and restoring information is a constant effort against an unseen adversary. As new threats emerge and old threats evolve, the information security profile of an organization requires constant adaptation to prevent threats from successfully penetrating sensitive data. For Star Trek fans, this can be likened to the Borg's defensive shield, in which constant changes in methods of attack are met with equally nimble changes in the capabilities of defense. For those of us who are not Star Trek fans, this constant vigilance and security is much like a fortress where threats from outside as well as from within must be constantly monitored and checked with continuously new and more innovative technologies.

Table 1-2 summarizes the steps performed in both the systems development life cycle and the security systems development life cycle. Since the security systems development life cycle is based on the systems development life cycle, the steps in the cycles are similar and those common to both cycles are outlined in column 2. Column 3 shows the security issues unique to the security systems development life cycle that are performed in each phase.

TABLE 1-2 SDLC and SecSDLC Phase Summary

Phases	Steps common to both the systems development life cycle and the security systems development life cycle	Steps unique to the security systems development life cycle
Phase 1: Investigation	■ Outline project scope and goals ■ Estimate costs ■ Evaluate existing resources ■ Analyze feasibility	■ Management defines project processes and goals and documents these in the program security policy
Phase 2: Analysis	■ Assess current system against plan developed in Phase 1 ■ Develop preliminary system requirements ■ Study integration of new system with existing system ■ Document findings and update feasibility analysis	■ Analyze existing security policies and programs ■ Analyze current threats and controls ■ Examine legal issues ■ Perform risk analysis
Phase 3: Logical Design	■ Assess current business needs against plan developed in Phase 2 ■ Select applications, data support, and structures ■ Generate multiple solutions for consideration ■ Document findings and update feasibility analysis	■ Develop security blueprint ■ Plan incident response actions ■ Plan business response to disaster ■ Determine feasibility of continuing and/or outsourcing the project
Phase 4: Physical Design	■ Select technologies to support solutions developed in Phase 3 ■ Select the best solution ■ Decide to make or buy components ■ Document findings and update feasibility analysis	■ Select technologies needed to support security blueprint ■ Develop definition of successful solution ■ Design physical security measures to support technological solutions ■ Review and approve project
Phase 5: Implementation	■ Develop or buy software ■ Order components ■ Document the system ■ Train users ■ Update feasibility analysis ■ Present system to users ■ Test system and review performance	■ Buy or develop security solutions ■ At end of phase, present tested package to management for approval
Phase 6: Maintenance	■ Support and modify system during its useful life ■ Test periodically for compliance with business needs ■ Upgrade and patch as necessary	■ Constantly monitor, test, modify, update, and repair to meet changing threats

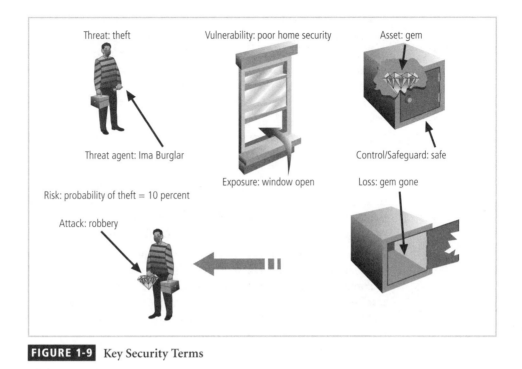

FIGURE 1-9 Key Security Terms

Key Terms

Throughout this chapter and the rest of the textbook, a number of key terms are presented that require careful attention. Some of these terms are illustrated in Figure 1-9.

- **Access:** A subject or object's ability to use, manipulate, modify, or affect another subject or object is referred to as **access**. Authorized users have legal access to a system, whereas hackers have illegal access to a system.

- **Asset:** An **asset** is the organizational resource that is being protected. An asset could be logical, such as a web site, information, or data; or an asset can be physical, such as a person, computer system, or other tangible object. Assets, and particularly information assets, are the focus of our security efforts and are what we are attempting to protect.

- **Attack:** An **attack** is an act that is an intentional or unintentional attempt to cause damage to or otherwise compromise the information and/or the systems that support it. If someone casually reads sensitive information not intended for his or her use, this is considered a passive attack. If a hacker attempts to break into an information system, the attack is considered active. If a lightening strike causes a fire in a building, it would be an unintentional attack.

- **Control**, **safeguard**, or **countermeasure:** These terms represent security mechanisms, policies, or procedures that can successfully counter attacks, reduce risk, resolve vulnerabilities, and otherwise improve the security within an organization. The various levels and types of **controls** are discussed more fully in the following chapters.

- **Exploit:** There are two common uses of this term in security. First, hackers may attempt to **exploit** a system or information by using it illegally for their personal gains. Second, an exploit can be a targeted solution to misuse a specific hole or vulnerability, usually in software, that a hacker creates to formulate an attack. In this regard an exploit is either the attempt to take advantage of a known vulnerability or weakness, or it is a method for taking advantage of a known vulnerability or weakness. In security, the latter is the more common usage.

- **Exposure:** The **exposure** of an information system is a single instance when the system is open to damage. Vulnerabilities can cause an exposure to potential damage or attack from a threat. Total exposure is the degree to which an organization's assets are at risk of attack from a threat. Total exposure is sometimes quantified in dollars by applying a formula based on the value of the asset, the likelihood of the loss (the risk), and the number of exposures. This term is sometimes used as a summation measure of risk across various areas of security in an organization.

- **Hacking:** **Hacking** can be defined positively and negatively: "1: to write computer programs for enjoyment, 2: to gain access to a computer illegally."[17] In the early days of computing, computer enthusiasts were called hacks, or hackers, because they could tear apart the computer instruction code, or even the computer itself, to manipulate its output. The term "hacker" expressed respect for another's ability to make computing technology work as desired in the face of adversity. In recent years, the association with the performance of an illegal activity has negatively tinged the term.

- **Object:** An **object** is a passive entity in the information system that receives or contains information. Objects are assigned specific controls that restrict or prevent access by unauthorized subjects. Examples include printers, servers, databases, or any other shared resource.

- **Risk:** **Risk** is the probability that something can happen. In information security, it could be the probability of a threat to a system, the probability of a vulnerability being discovered, or the probability of equipment or software malfunctioning. Risk can be measured in quantitative terms, as in "a 25% chance of attack," or in qualitative terms, as in "a low probability of malfunctioning."

- **Security blueprint:** The **security blueprint** is the plan for the implementation of new security measures in the organization. Sometimes called a framework, the blueprint presents an organized approach to the security planning process. The security blueprint is the most significant work produced during the design phases of the SecSDLC. See Chapter 6, "Blueprint For Security" for further information on the security blueprint.

- **Security model:** A **security model** is a collection of specific security rules that represents the implementation of a security policy. Some recognized security models are examined in later chapters.

- **Security posture** or **security profile:** The **security posture** or **profile** refers to the implementation of security in an organization. It is a general label for the combination of all policy, procedures, technology, and programs that make up the total security effort currently in place and is sometimes called the information security program.

- **Subject:** A **subject** is an *active* entity that interacts with an information system and causes information to move through the system for a specific purpose. A subject can be an individual, technical component, or computer process. Users, servers, and threads are examples of subjects.

- **Threats:** A **threat** is a category of objects, persons, or other entities that represents a potential danger to an asset. Threats are always present. Some threats manifest themselves in accidental occurrences and others are purposeful. For example, all hackers represent a potential danger or threat to an unprotected information system. Severe storm are always a threat to buildings and their contents.

- **Threat agent:** A **threat agent** is the specific instance or component of a threat. For example, you can think of all hackers in the world as a collective threat, and Kevin Mitnick, who was convicted for hacking into phone systems, as a specific threat agent. Likewise, a specific lightning strike, hailstorm, or tornado is a threat agent that is part of the threat of severe storms.

- **Vulnerability:** Weaknesses or faults in a system or protection mechanism that expose information to attack or damage are known as **vulnerabilities**. They can range from a flaw in a software package, to an unprotected system port, or an unlocked door. Vulnerabilities that have been examined, documented, and published are referred to as **well-known vulnerabilities**.

Security Professionals and the Organization

It takes a wide range of professionals to support a diverse information security program. As noted earlier in this chapter, security must be initiated from the top down. Senior management is the key component and vital force for a successful implementation of an information security program. To develop and execute specific security policies and procedures, additional administrative support is required. Finally, technical expertise is necessary to implement the details of the security operation. The following are descriptions of professionals involved in information security in a typical organization.

Senior Management

Chief information officer: The senior technology officer is typically the chief information officer or CIO, although other titles such as vice president of Information, VP of Information Technology, and VP of Systems may be used. The CIO is primarily responsible for advising the chief executive officer, president, or company owner on the strategic planning that affects the management of information in the organization. The CIO translates the strategic plans of the organization as a whole into strategic information plans for the Information Systems or Data Processing Division of the organization. Once this is accomplished, CIOs work with subordinate managers to develop tactical and operational plans for the division, enabling planning and management of the systems that support the organization.

Chief information security officer (CISO): The chief information security officer is the individual primarily responsible for the assessment, management, and implementation of securing the information in the organization. The CISO may also be referred to as the manager for Security, the security administrator, or a similar title. The CISO usually reports directly to the CIO, although in larger organizations it is not uncommon for one or more layers of management to exist between the two. Care should be exercised however, that the recommendations of the CISO to the CIO are not subordinated to less important issues. The CISO recommendations are important, if not more important, than other technology and information-related decisions. Placement in the organization chart of the CISO and supporting security staff is the subject of current debate. The Offline on where the CIO belongs addresses this issue.

OFFLINE

"Where The Chief Security Officer Belongs"[18]

By Mary Hayes, InformationWeek, February 25, 2002

"Chief security officers usually report to top IT executives, even if their jobs include information and physical security. But should companies consider pulling the CISO out of IT altogether?

"Meta Group analyst Christian Byrnes thinks so. Among the several hundred of the consulting firm's clients that have CISOs, only 3% have them report to executives outside of IT, such as the chief corporate counsel, chief auditor, or chief operating officer. But that 3% are ahead of the pack in recognizing a potential conflict of interest. 'It's a basic audit principle that the people who do and the people who watch shouldn't report to a common manager,' Byrnes says. If IT staffers unwittingly cause a security leak by reconfiguring the network so they can make system changes from their desktops at home, for instance, will that get reported as high in the organization as it should? 'Typically, those breaches don't get reported as security incidents and are kept within IT,' Byrnes says.

"Marc Lewis, who heads the IT practice at Cleveland executive-recruitment firm Christian & Timbers, says a company should have its CISO report to the CEO or chief operating officer if the job includes information and physical security. Because security has grown into an organization wide concern, encompassing everything from the safety of workers to the threat of cyberterrorism, it may not make sense to keep it within IT, Lewis says.

"Yet some CISOs say security management should stay put. 'You want your information security department to be the solution provider and facilitator of risk management for IT,' says David Bauer, chief information security and privacy officer at Merrill Lynch & Co. in New York. 'Otherwise, [security] will be just another audit department, and the IT guys will buy whatever security solutions they want.' Bauer meets with the executive IT team on a regular basis to present his plans, which are directly communicated to the top executive management team; he reports to the head of global technology services.

continued

Some observers point out that a chief IT executive plays an important role in championing information security initiatives and translating them into business terms for the executive team; taking the CISO out from under the top tech person's wing could undermine security strategy.

"At the Port Authority of New York and New Jersey, the director of information security works on strategy with the chief technology officer, who communicates those plans to the executive team. Greg Burnham, CTO at the transportation organization, says that reporting structure makes the most sense. 'General management struggles with understanding the role of the IT infrastructure in the first place,' Burnham says. 'And in most cases, that's where the security problems are.'"

Security Project Team

Information security is a field with a vast array of technical and nontechnical requirements. The **project team** should consist of a number of individuals who are experienced in one or multiple requirements of both the technical and nontechnical areas. Many of the same skills needed to manage and implement security are needed to design it. Members of the security project team fill the following roles:

- The **champion:** As indicated earlier, a senior executive who promotes the project and ensures its support, both financially and administratively, at the highest levels of the organization

- The **team leader:** A project manager, who may be a departmental line manager or staff unit manager, who understands project management, personnel management, and information security technical requirements

- **Security policy developers:** Individuals who understand the organizational culture, existing policies, and requirements for developing and implementing successful policies

- **Risk assessment specialists:** Individuals who understand financial risk assessment techniques, the value of organizational assets, and the security methods to be used

- **Security professionals:** Dedicated, trained, and well-educated specialists in all aspects of information security from both technical and nontechnical standpoint

- **Systems administrators:** Individuals with the primary responsibility for administering the systems that house the information used by the organization

- **End users:** Those whom the new system will most directly impact. Ideally, a selection of users from various departments, levels, and degrees of technical knowledge assist the team in focusing on the application of realistic controls applied in ways that do not disrupt the essential business activities they seek to safeguard

Now that you understand the responsibilities of both senior management and the security project team, we can define the roles of those who own and safeguard the data.

Data Ownership

Three types of data ownership and their respective responsibilities are outlined below:

- **Data owners:** Those responsible for the security and use of a particular set of information. They are usually members of senior management and could be CIOs. The **data owners** usually determine the level of data classification (discussed later) associated with the data, as well as changes to that classification required by organization change. The data owners work with subordinate managers to oversee the day-to-day administration of the data.

- **Data custodians:** Working directly with data owners, **data custodians** are responsible for the storage, maintenance, and protection of the information. Depending on the size of the organization, this may be a dedicated position, such as the CISO, or it may be an additional responsibility of a systems administrator, or other technology manager. The duties of a data custodian often include overseeing data storage and backups, implementing the specific procedures and policies laid out in the security policies and plans, and reporting to the data owner.

- **Data users:** End systems users who work with the information to perform their daily jobs supporting the mission of the organization. Everyone in the organization is responsible for the security of data, so **data users** are included here as individuals with an information security role.

Communities of Interest

Each organization develops and maintains its own unique culture and values. Within that organizational **culture**, there are **communities of interest**. For our purpose, a community of interest is generally thought of as a group of individuals united by shared interests or values within an organization and who share a common goal of making the organization function to meet its objectives. Within the context of this discussion, there are three communities of interest that have roles and responsibilities in information security. In theory each role must complement the other; in practice, this is often not the case.

Information Security Management and Professionals

As described above in individual roles, some organization members are aligned with the goals and mission of the information security community of interest. These job functions and organizational roles focus on protecting the organization's information systems and stored information from attacks.

Information Technology Management and Professionals

Others in the organization are oriented to deliver value to the organization by designing, building, or operating information systems. This community of interest is made up of IT managers and various groups of skilled professionals in systems design, programming, networks, and other related disciplines usually categorized as IT, or information technology. This community has many of the same objectives as the information security community. They focus, however, more on costs of system creation and operation, ease of use for system users, timeliness of system creation, as well as transaction response time. The goals of the IT community and the information security community do not always completely align, and depending on the organizational structure, this may cause conflict.

Organizational Management and Professionals

The organization's general management team and the rest of the resources in the organization make up the other major community of interest. This large group is almost always made up of other subsets of interest as well, including executive management, production management, human resources, accounting, and legal, just to name a few. The IT community often categorizes these groups as users of information technology systems, while the information security community categorizes them as security subjects. The reality is that they are much more than this categorization implies. It is important for us to focus on the fact that all IT systems and information security objectives are created to implement the objectives of the broader organizational community and safeguard their effective use and operation. The most efficient IT systems operated in the most secure fashion ever devised are of no value if they do not bring value to the broad objectives of the organization as a whole.

Information Security: Is It an Art or a Science?

With the level of complexity in today's information systems, the implementation of information security has often been described as a combination of art and science. It is not difficult to see how this perspective has evolved along with the concept of the information security community of interest. The concept of the *security artesan*[19] is based on the way individuals have perceived systems technologists since computers became commonplace. Those with the gift for managing and operating computers and computer-based systems have long been suspected of using more than a little black magic to keep the systems running and functioning as expected. Everyone who has studied computer systems can appreciate the anxiety most people feel when faced with complex technology. Consider the inner workings of the computer: with the mind-boggling functions of the transistors in a CPU, the interaction of various capacitors, and the memory storage units on the circuit boards, it's a miracle these things work at all.

Security as Art

With this in mind, it is easy to see the security administrators and technicians as individuals who implement security, the way a painter applies oils to the canvas. A touch of color here, a brush stroke there, just enough to represent the image the artist wants to convey without overwhelming the viewer, or in security terms, without over restricting the user. There are no hard and fast rules regulating the installation of various security mechanisms. Nor are there many universally accepted complete solutions. While there are many manuals to support individual systems, once these systems are interconnected, there is no magic user's manual for the security of the entire system. This is especially true with the complex levels of interaction between users, policy, and technology controls.

Security as Science

The other view of security is as a science. After all, we are dealing with technology developed by computer scientists and engineers—technology designed to perform at rigorous levels of performance. Even with the complexity of the technology, most scientists would agree that specific scientific conditions cause virtually all actions that occur in computer systems. Almost every fault, security hole, and systems malfunction is a result of the interaction of specific hardware and software. If the developers had sufficient time, they could resolve and eliminate these faults.

The faults that remain are usually the result of malfunctioning technology caused by any one of a thousand possible reasons. There are many sources of recognized and approved security methods and techniques that provide sound technical security advise. Best practices, standards of due care, and other tried-and-true methods can minimize the level of guesswork necessary to secure an organization's information and systems.

Security as a Social Science

There is a third view to incorporate when examining security. It integrates some of the components of art and science, and adds another dimension to the discussion. That is security as a *social science*. Social science examines the behavior of individuals as they interact with systems, whether societal systems or, in our case, information systems. Security begins and ends with the people inside the organization and the people that interact with the system, planned or otherwise. End users who need the very information the security personnel are trying to protect may be the weakest link in the security chain. By understanding some of the behavioral aspects of organizational science and change management, security administrators can greatly reduce the levels of risk caused by end users, and create more acceptable and supportable security profiles. These measures, coupled with appropriate policy and training issues, can substantially improve the performance of end users and result in a more secure system.

Chapter Summary

- Information security evolved from the early field of computer security. The defining moment for information security may well have been when the protection of data integrity gained importance equal to the protection of computing equipment.

- What is Security? Security is the protection from danger, from adversaries, from those who would harm, intentionally or otherwise, the item, object, or area being protected. There are a number of types of security: physical security, personal security, operations security, communications security, national security, and network security, to name a few.

- In this textbook, we are concerned with information security: the protection from danger of information and the systems that use, store, or transmit that information, through the application of policy, education, and technology.

- The critical characteristics of information (confidentiality, integrity, and availability, also known as the C.I.A triangle) must be protected at all times (storage, processing, and transmission). The protection must be implemented by multiple measures (policies, education training and awareness, and technology).

- A typical information system comprises five major components: hardware, software, data, people, and procedures.

- The history of computer security dates back to the mid-1960s.

- Upper management drives the top-down approach to security implementation. This is contrasted with the bottom-up approach or grassroots effort, where each individual chooses security implementation strategies. Involving end users in the project (known as joint application development) can help in the acceptance of the end product.

- The traditional systems development life cycle is an approach to implementing a system in an organization and has been adapted to provide the outline of a security systems development life cycle (SecSDLC). The SecSDLC is based on the traditional systems development life cycle and has many of the same stages. Each stage is focused on the analysis and design of a security posture rather than the development of a specific computer system. The security development life cycle requires a project team consisting of a variety of managerial, technical, and security skills and abilities.

- Threats can turn vulnerabilities into exploits that can be crafted into the supporting elements of an attack. The organization's information assets are at risk to these attacks and can suffer damage. You limit risk by applying a control (or countermeasure or safeguard). Organizations with security programs in place have a security profile or posture, which can be improved by developing a blueprint. An effective security blueprint is based on a well-accepted security model.

- Is information security an art or a science? It has been described as both.

Review Questions

1. What is the difference between a threat agent and a threat?
2. What is the difference between vulnerability and exposure?
3. How has the definition of "hack" evolved over the last 30 years?
4. What type of security was dominant in the early years of computing?
5. What are the three components of the C.I.A. triangle? What are they used for?
6. If the C.I.A. triangle is incomplete, why is it so commonly used in security?
7. Describe the critical characteristics of information. How are they used in the study of computer security?
8. Identify the five components of an information system. Which are most directly impacted by the study of computer security? Which are most commonly associated with its study?
9. In the history of the study of computer security, what system is the father of almost all modern multiuser systems?
10. What paper is the foundation of all subsequent studies of computer security?
11. How is the top-down approach to information security superior to the bottom-up approach?
12. Why is a methodology important in the implementation of information security? How does a methodology improve the process?
13. Who is involved in the security development life cycle? Who leads the process?

14. How does the practice of information security qualify as both an art and a science? How does security as a social science influence its practice?

15. Who is ultimately responsible for the security of information in the organization?

16. What is the relationship between the MULTICS project and early development of computer security?

17. How has computer security evolved into modern information security?

18. What was important about Rand Report R-609?

19. What does it mean to discover an exploit? How does an exploit differ from vulnerability?

20. Who would lead a security team? Should the approach to security be more managerial or technical?

Exercises

1. Look up "the paper that started the study of computer security." Prepare a summary of the key points. What in this paper specifically addresses security in areas previously unexamined?

2. Assume that a security model is needed for the protection of information in your class. Using the NSTISSC model, examine each of the cells and write a brief statement on how you would address the three components represented in that cell.

3. Consider the information stored on your personal computer. For each of the terms listed, find an example and document it: threat, threat agent, vulnerability, exposure, risk, attack, and exploit.

4. Using the Web, identify the chief information officer, chief information security officer, and system administrator for your school. Which of these individuals represents the data owner? Data custodian?

5. Using the Web, find out who Kevin Mitnick was. What did he do? Who caught him? Write a short summary of his activities and why he is infamous.

Case Exercises

I. Security Staff Shortage

Adapted from "Staffing Costs Spur Outsourcing"[20]

By D. Verton, Computerworld, March, 2001.

Many professional organizations are outsourcing information security functions, as they are unable to find sufficient professionals to hire. Even if they can find security experts, they may be too expensive.

"We don't have the people necessary to do the required security tasks around the clock," says the manager of Internet services of one such company.[19]

The solution? Outsourcing. There is an increase in companies that focus on providing security services, particularly monitoring. One in particular, Veritect, located in Reston, Virginia, has a 4000 square foot facility and team of over 150 professionals that can provide round-the-clock security monitoring of information systems. They provide everything from monitored firewalls, intrusion detection systems, networking devices, to physical security for the information systems themselves.

"There's not enough smart security people on the planet for all companies to have their own network defense centers," said Veritect CEO, Don Walker.

Companies should consider the advantages and disadvantages of outsourcing information security before selecting outsourcing as a viable option. The advantages are dedicated professionals focusing on the protection of your systems. The disadvantages are the cost and the fact that the outsourcing company has little more than a commercial interest in protecting your systems. The systems, after all, are not theirs. Placing proprietary information in the hands of strangers is a risk in itself.

The Yankee Group in Boston estimates that there is a potential market for managed security services that could be quite lucrative, estimated at over $2.5 billion by 2005. However the disadvantages listed above have so far limited demand. Most companies would prefer to hire their own trusted employees and hope for the best, while implementing incomplete security solutions, focusing on security perimeters with their own firewalls, and implementing their own intrusion detection systems.

Some companies have cited losing control of their own destiny and losing an appreciation for how security works as reasons against outsourcing, according to a recent survey by Giga Information Group Inc. in Cambridge, Massachusetts.

1. What can outsourcing companies do to gain the confidence of companies?

2. Why would management prefer substandard internal security to professional outsourcing?

II. Spending on Security

Adapted from "Businesses Keep Spending on Security"[21]
By G. Huime, InformationWeek, January, 2002

With the increased attention on all aspects of security, companies are expected to spend more and more on information security, even as overall IT expenditures are leveling or declining.

The recent outbreaks of computer viruses help feed the funding fury. Damages attributed to Code Red and Nimda alone are estimated to be over $3 billion worldwide.

Some spending statistics:

In December 2001, InformationWeek Research interviewed 300 technology executives and reported their spending forecasts as follows:

- Over half will increase spending

- 46 percent are making security their number one focus

- 43 percent will maintain the current level

- Less than two percent will reduce spending

The bulk of this expenditure will be directed at protecting networks. Experts warn that some of this should be spent on ensuring servers are patched and protected.

1. Other than protecting the networks, on what other areas of security should these organizations focus spending?

2. What could cause an organization to fail to increase its security budget in times when security problems are on everyone's mind?

Endnotes

1. For further reading on this subject, consult Andrew Hodges, *Alan Turing: the Enigma* (New York: Walker and Company, 2000).
2. NSA. "The Enigma" [Cited 5 March, 2002]. Available from the World Wide Web. *<http://www.nsa.gov/museum/enigma.html>*.
3. Peter Salus. "Net Insecurity: Then and Now (1969-1998)." *Sane '98 Online.* 19 November 1998. [Cited 1 February 2002]. Available from the World Wide Web <http://www.nluug.nl/events/sane98/aftermath/salus.html>.

4. Roberts, Larry. "Program Plan for the ARPANet" [Cited 5 March 2002] Available from the World Wide Web. <*http://www.ziplink.net/%7Elroberts/ SIGCOMM99_files/frame.htm*>

5. *Ibid.*

6. *Preliminary Notes on the Design of Secure Military Computer Systems*, (Jan. 1973), by Roger R. Schell, Peter J. Downey, and Gerald J. Popek, file, MCI-73-1, ESD/AFSC, Hanscom AFB, Bedford, MA 01731.

7. *Protection Analysis: Final Report*, (May 1978), by Richard Bisbey II and Dennis Hollingworth, final report, ISI/SR-78-13, USC/Information Sciences Institute, Marina Del Rey, CA 90291.

8. F. T. Grampp and R. H. Morris, "UNIX Operating System Security," *AT& Bell Laboratories Technical Journal* 63, no. 8 (1984): 1649-1672.

9. *Net Insecurity: Then and Now (1969-1998).*

10. Willis Ware. "Security Controls for Computer Systems: Report of Defense Science Board Task Force on Computer Security." *Rand Online.* 10 October 1979. [Cited 1 February 2002]. Available from the World Wide Web <http://www.rand.org/publications/R/R609.1/ R609.1.html>.

11. *Ibid.*

12. Merriam-Webster. "security." *Merriam-Webster Online.* [Cited 1 February 2002]. Available from the World Wide Web <http://www.m-w.com/cgi-bin/dictionary>.

13. National Security Telecommunications and Information Systems Security, *National Training Standard for Information Systems Security (Infosec) Professionals*, 20 June 1994, file, 4011, [Cited 1 Feb 2002]. Available from the World Wide Web <http://www.nstissc.gov/Assets/ pdf/4011.pdf>.

14. Julekha Dash, "ACLU Knocks Eli Lilly for Divulging E-Mail Addresses," *Computerworld* 35, no. 28 (9 July 2001): 6.

15. Microsoft. "C2 Evaluation and Certification for Windows NT (Q93662)." *Microsoft Online.* 26 November 2001. [Cited 1 February 2002]. Available from the World Wide Web <http://www.microsoft.com/default.aspx?scid=kb;EN-US;q93362>.

16. adapted from Sandra D. Dewitz, *Systems Analysis and Design and the Transition to Objects* (New York: McGraw Hill Publishers, 1996), 94.

17. Merriam-Webster. "hack." *Merriam-Webster Online.* [Cited 1 February 2002]. Available from the World Wide Web <http://www.m-w.com/cgi-bin/dictionary>.

18. Mary Hayes, "Where The Chief Security Officer Belongs," *InformationWeek*, no. 877 (Feb 25, 2002): 38.

19. D. B. Parker, *Fighting Computer Crime* (New York: Wiley Publishing, 1998), 189.

20. D. Verton, "Staffing Costs Spur Security Outsourcing," *Computerworld* 35, no. 11 (March 2001): 20.

21. G. Hulme, "Businesses Keep Spending on Security," *InformationWeek*, no. 873 (January 2002): 96.

The Need for Security

2

Our bad neighbor makes us early stirrers,
Which is both healthful and good husbandry.
WILLIAM SHAKESPEARE (1564–1616), KING HENRY, IN HENRY V, ACT 4, SC. 1, L. 6-7.

FRED CHIN, CEO, LEANED BACK in his leather chair. He propped his feet up on the long mahogany table in the conference room where the Sequential Label and Supply Board of Directors had just adjourned their quarterly meeting.

"Gladys, what do you think about our computer security problem?" he said to Gladys Williams, the company's CFO. The problem he referred to was last month's outbreak of a malicious virus program on the company's computer network.

Gladys nodded slowly and said, "I think we have a real problem this time, and we need to put together a real solution, not just a quick Band-Aid like the last time." She was referring to the time about 18 months before when someone brought a floppy disk in from home with a virus. The solution then was to take all the floppy drives out of the company computers.

Fred wasn't convinced. "Isn't that just a bunch of technical mumbo-jumbo? Let's just give Charlie another thousand bucks in the next budget to fix it up."

Gladys shook her head. "Fred, you may not understand how things have changed. Our business runs on computers now. I've done some reading on this subject and have some ideas. I've asked Charlie Moody to meet us today to talk about it. He's waiting for us outside now. I'll get him."

She got up, opened the door, and waved Charlie, senior manager for Infrastructure Services, into the conference room.

Fred began, "Hello Charlie, as you know the Board of Directors met today. They received a report on the expenses and lost production from the virus outbreak last month. They have

39

directed us to improve the security of our information systems. Gladys tells me you can help me understand what we need to do about it."

"To start with," Charlie began, "we need to set up an information security program, not just put on another set of Band-Aids. We need a thorough review of our policies and standards, and we need to establish an ongoing risk management program. There are some other things that are part of the process as well, but these would be a good start."

"Sounds expensive," said Fred.

Charlie looked at Gladys, then answered "Well, there may be some extra expenses for specific controls and software tools, and we may slow down our development projects a bit, but this is more of a change in our attitude about security than any gigantic spending spree. I don't have accurate estimates yet, but you can be sure we will put cost benefit worksheets in front of you before we spend any money."

Fred thought about that for a few seconds. "OK. What do we need to do next?"

Gladys answered, "To start with, we need to get going on a project plan to develop our security program. We will use our usual systems development and project management approach, just like developing any other system. There are a few differences, but we can adapt our current models easily. We will need to appoint or hire a person to be responsible for information security."

"Information security? What about computer security?" asked Fred.

Charlie looked at him and said, "Information security includes all the things we use to do business: computers, software, procedures, data, and our people."

"I see," Fred said. "Let's get started. Bring me the project plan and a draft budget next week. We need to get started now. The Audit Committee of the Board meets in four weeks and we need to report our progress."

DISCUSSION QUESTIONS:

1. Do Fred, Gladys, and Charlie agree about this effort?
2. How will Fred measure success when he evaluates Gladys' and Charlie's performance for this project?

LEARNING OBJECTIVES:

Upon completion of this material, you should be able to:

- Understand the business need for information security.
- Understand a successful information security program is the responsibility of an organization's general management and IT management.
- Understand the threats posed to information security and the more common attacks associated with those threats.
- Differentiate *threats* to information systems from *attacks* against information systems.

Introduction

Information security is unlike any other aspect of information technology. It is an arena in which the primary mission is to ensure things remain the same. Organizations spend hundreds of thousands of dollars and employ thousands of man-hours to maintain their current information status. If there were no threats to information and systems, that energy could be channeled directly towards improving the systems that support the information, resulting in vast improvements in ease of use and effectiveness. But, there are those with little better to do than to attempt to access the systems and information for which they have no authorization. Others try to deny access to the same systems by legitimate users. These are but a few of the reasons organizations spend effort and resources on information security.

From Chapter 1 you should have gained an appreciation for the various aspects of information security as well as an understanding of the Security Systems Development Life Cycle (SecSDLC). The first phase of the SecSDLC, investigation, provides an overview of the environment in which security must operate and the problems that security must address. This chapter examines the security environment and identifies the threats to information that create the need for security.

Business Needs First, Technology Needs Last

Information security performs four important functions for an organization:

1. Protects the organization's ability to function
2. Enables the safe operation of applications implemented on the organization's IT systems
3. Protects the data the organization collects and uses
4. Safeguards the technology assets in use at the organization

Protecting the Ability of the Organization to Function

Both general management and IT management are responsible for implementing information security that protects the ability of the organization to function. Decision makers in organizations must set policy and operate their organizations in compliance with the complex, shifting political legislation on the use of technology. Although many business and government managers shy away from addressing information security because of its perceived technical complexity, it is important to understand that information security has more to do with management than with technology. Just as payroll has more to do with management than with the mathematics of computing wages, information security has more to do with policy and enforcement than with the technology of its implementation. As the noted information security author Charles Cresson Wood has said,

> "In fact, a lot of [Information Security] is good management for information technology. Many people think that a solution to a technology problem is more technology. Well, not necessarily. ... So a lot of my work, out of necessity, has been trying to get my clients to pay more attention to information security as a management issue in addition to a technical issue, information security as a people issue in addition to the technical issue."[1]

To assist management in addressing the needs for information security, each of the communities of interest within an organization must effectively communicate in terms of business impact and the cost of business interruption and avoid arguments expressed only in technical terms.

Enabling the Safe Operation of Applications

Today's organizations are under immense pressure to create and operate integrated, efficient, and capable applications. Under this pressure, management is responsible for informed policy choices and the enforcement of decisions that affect applications and the IT infrastructures that support them. The modern organization needs to create an environment that safeguards applications using the organization's IT systems, particularly those elements of the environment that make up the infrastructure of the organization. These elements include operating system platforms, electronic mail (e-mail) and Instant Messenger (IM) applications. Organizations enable these elements either by subscription from an Internet Service provider (ISP) or by building their own. Once the infrastructure is in place, management must understand it has not abdicated to the IT department its responsibility to make choices and enforce decisions, but must continue to oversee the infrastructure.

Protecting Data that Organizations Collect and Use

Many organizations realize that one of their most valuable assets is their data, because without data, an organization loses its record of transactions and/or its ability to deliver value to its customers. Any business, educational institution, or government agency that functions within the modern social context of connected and responsive service relies on information systems to support these services. Even if the transaction is not online, information systems and the data they process enable the creation and movement of goods and services. Therefore, protecting *data in motion* and *data at rest* are both critical aspects of information security. The significant value of data motivates attackers to steal, sabotage, or corrupt it. An effective information security program implemented by management is essential to the protection of the integrity and value of the organization's data.

Safeguarding Technology Assets in Organizations

To perform effectively, organizations must add secure infrastructure services based on the size and scope of the enterprise. For instance, a small business may get by with using an e-mail service provided by an ISP, augmented with a personal encryption tool. But, when an organization grows and more capabilities are needed, additional security services may have to be provided locally. For example, organizational growth could lead to the need for Public Key Infrastructure (PKI), which supports encryption for the organization.

Note that the Cryptography Appendix describes PKI in more detail, but for now you need to know that PKI involves the use of digital certificates to ensure the confidentiality of Internet communications and transactions. Certificate authorities embed an individual's or an organization's public key along with other identifying information into each digital certificate and then cryptographically sign the certificate with a tamper-proof seal, verifying the integrity of the data within it and validating its use.

The PKI offers advanced features such as efficient key management across and between organizations and key recovery when keys are lost. Likewise, as the organization's network grows to accommodate changing needs, more robust technology solutions may be needed to replace security programs the organization has outgrown. An example of a robust solution is a firewall, a device that keeps certain kinds of network traffic out of a private network. Another example is caching network appliances, which are devices that store local copies of Internet content, such as Web pages that are frequently referred to by employees. The appliance displays the pages when the employee looks for that page.

Threats

To make sound decisions about information security, create policies, and enforce them, management must be informed of the various kinds of threats facing the organization, its people applications, data, and information systems. As defined in Chapter 1, a **threat** is an object, person, or other entity that represents a constant danger to an asset. To understand the wide range of threats that pervade the interconnected world, researchers have interviewed practicing information security personnel and examined information security literature on threats. While the categorization of threats may vary, threats are relatively well researched and consequently fairly well understood.

The 2002 Computer Security Institute/Federal Bureau of Investigation (CSI/FBI) Computer Crime and Security Survey is a representative study. The CSI/FBI study found that 90 percent of organizations responding (primarily large corporations and government agencies) detected computer security breaches within the last 12 months. The study also found that 80 percent of these organizations lost money to computer breaches, totaling over $455,848,000, up from $377,828,700 in 2001. The number of attacks that came across the Internet rose from 70 percent in 2001 to 74 percent in 2002.[2]

To better understand the numerous threats facing the organization, a categorization scheme has been developed to group threats by their respective activities.[3] This model consists of twelve general categories organized into five groups that represent a real and present danger to an organization's people, information and systems. The management of an organization must focus resources and efforts toward protecting its information and systems. By examining each threat category in turn, management can most effectively protect its information through policy, education and training, and technology controls. These five groups of real and present danger are:

1. Inadvertent acts
2. Deliberate acts
3. Acts of God
4. Technical failures
5. Management failures

Each organization must prioritize the real and present dangers listed above based on its particular security situation, strategy, and the exposure levels of its assets. Chapters 4 and 5 cover these topics in more detail. For now, remember that when you review the real and present dangers, each act or failure can be represented in more than one threat category. For example, the sabotage of a hacker falls within the deliberate acts category listed above and also could fall within the following categories of the threats listed in Table 2-1: 2, 3, 5, and 7. These threats are summarized in Table 2-1 and then covered in detail in the following sections.

TABLE 2-1 Threats to Information Security[4]	
Categories of threat	Examples
1. Acts of human error or failure	Accidents, employee mistakes
2. Compromises to intellectual property	Piracy, copyright infringement
3. Deliberate acts of espionage or trespass	Unauthorized access and/or data collection
4. Deliberate acts of information extortion	Blackmail of information disclosure
5. Deliberate acts of sabotage or vandalism	Destruction of systems or information
6. Deliberate acts of theft	Illegal confiscation of equipment or information
7. Deliberate software attacks	Viruses, worms, macros, denial-of-service
8. Forces of nature	Fire, flood, earthquake, lightning
9. Deviations in quality of service from service providers	Power and WAN service issues
10. Technical hardware failures or errors	Equipment failure
11. Technical software failures or errors	Bugs, code problems, unknown loopholes
12. Technological obsolescence	Antiquated or outdated technologies

Threat Group 1: Inadvertent Acts

Malicious intent is absent or cannot be proven in the category of threats called **inadvertent acts**. Inadvertent acts discussed in the sections below include: acts of human error or failure, deviations in quality of service-by-service providers, and power irregularities.

Acts of Human Error or Failure

This category includes acts performed without intent or malicious purpose by an individual who is an authorized user with an organization. When people use information systems, sometimes mistakes happen. Inexperience, improper training, the making of incorrect assumptions, and other circumstances can cause these misadventures. But, harmless mistakes can produce extensive damage with catastrophic results. For example, a simple keyboarding error has caused worldwide Internet outages.

> "In April 1997 the core of the Internet suffered a disaster. Internet service providers lost connectivity with other ISPs due to an error in a routine Internet router-table update process. The resulting outage effectively shut down a major portion of the Internet for at least twenty minutes. It has been estimated that about 45 percent of Internet users were affected. In July 1997, the Internet went through yet another more critical global shutdown for millions of users. An accidental upload of a corrupt database to the Internet's root domain servers occurred. Since this provides the ability to address hosts on the net by name (i.e., eds.com), it was impossible to send e-mail or access Web sites within the .com and .net domains for several hours. The .com domain comprises a majority of the commercial enterprise users of the Internet."[5]

Many threats can be prevented with controls, ranging from simple procedures, such as requiring the user to type a critical command twice, to more complex procedures, such as the verification of commands by a second party. An example of the latter is the performance of key recovery actions in PKI systems. Many military applications have robust, dual-approval controls built in. Some systems that have a high potential for data loss or system outages use expert systems to monitor human actions and request confirmation for critical inputs.

Indeed, employees constitute one of the greatest threats to information security. Employees are the individuals closest to the organizational data. They use it in everyday activities to conduct the organization's business. Employee mistakes such as those shown in Figure 2-1 represent a serious threat to the confidentiality, integrity, and availability of data. This is because employee mistakes can easily lead to the following: revelation of classified data, entry of erroneous data, accidental deletion or modification of data, storage of data in unprotected areas, and failure to protect information. Leaving classified information in unprotected areas, such as a desktop, Web site, or even in the trash can, is as much a threat to the protection of information as is the individual who would exploit the information. It creates a vulnerability opportunity that some may not be able to pass up. However, if an individual damages or destroys data on purpose, the act belongs to a different threat category.

FIGURE 2-1 Acts of Human Error or Failure

Deviations in Quality of Service by Service Providers

This category covers situations in which a product or service is not delivered to the organization as expected. Utility companies, service providers, and other value-added organizations form a vast web of interconnected services. The organization's information system depends on the successful operation of many inter-dependent support systems, including power grids, telecom networks, parts suppliers, service vendors, and even the janitorial staff and garbage haulers. Any one of these support systems can experience outages from storms, employee illnesses, or other unforeseen events. Threats in this category manifest in an attacks such as a backhoe taking out a fiber-optic link for an ISP. The backup provider may be online and in service, but may be able to supply only a fraction of the bandwidth the organization needs for full service. This degradation of service is a form of **availability disruption**. Internet service, communications, and power irregularities are three sets of service issues that can dramatically affect the availability of information and systems that are discussed in detail below.

Internet Service Issues.   For organizations that rely heavily on the Internet and the World Wide Web to support continued operations, the threat of the potential loss of Internet service, due to service provider failures, can lead to considerable loss in the availability of information. Many organizations have sales staff and telecommuters working at remote locations. When these offsite employees cannot contact the host systems, manual procedures must be used to continue operations.

When an organization places its Web servers in the care of a Web hosting provider, that provider assumes responsibility for all Internet services as well as for the hardware and operating system software used to operate the Web site. These Web hosting services are usually arranged with an agreement providing minimum service levels known as **Service Level Agreements (SLAs)**. When a service provider fails to meet the SLA, fines may accrue to cover losses incurred by the client, but these mitigating payments seldom cover the losses generated by the outage.

Communications and other Service Provider Issues.   Other utility services can impact organizations as well. Among these are telephone, water, wastewater, trash pickup, cable television, natural or propane gas, and custodial services. The threat of loss of these services can lead to the inability of an organization to function properly. For instance, most facilities require water service to operate an air-conditioning system. Even in Minnesota in February, air-conditioning systems are needed to keep a modern facility operating. Other service interruptions may have less obvious results. If the wastewater system fails, an organization could be prevented from allowing employees into the building. This would stop normal business operations.

Power Irregularities.   The threat of irregularities from power utilities is common and can lead to fluctuations such as power excesses, power shortages, and power losses. This can pose problems for organizations that provide inadequately conditioned power for their information systems equipment. In the U.S., we are "fed" 120-volt, 60-cycle power usually through 15 and 20 amp circuits. When the voltage levels **spike** (a momentary increase), or **surge** (a prolonged increase), this voltage can severely damage or destroy equipment. Equally disruptive are power shortages from a lack of available power. A momentary low voltage or **sag**, or a more prolonged drop in voltage, known as a **brownout**, can cause systems to shut down, reset, or otherwise disrupt availability. Complete loss of power for a moment is known as a **fault**, as opposed to a more lengthy loss, known as a **blackout**. Since sensitive electronic equipment, especially networking equipment, computers, and computer-based systems are susceptible to fluctuations, controls can be applied to manage power quality. With small computers and network systems, quality power-conditioning options such as surge suppressors can smooth out spikes. The more expensive uninterruptible power supply (UPS) can protect against spikes and surges as well as against sags and even blackouts of limited duration.

Threat Group 2: Deliberate Acts

This is a group of threats in which people or organizations engage in purposeful acts designed to harm the people, the organization, or the culture. The harm caused can range from the trivial, such as the sending of unsolicited commercial e-mail, to the catastrophic, such as destroying buildings or whole complexes.

Deliberate Acts of Espionage or Trespass

The threat of deliberate acts of espionage or trespass represents a well-known and broad category of electronic and human activities that can breach the confidentiality of information. When an unauthorized individual gains access to the information an organization is trying to protect, that act is categorized as a deliberate act of espionage or trespass. Attackers can use many different methods to access the information stored in an information system. Some information gathering techniques that are quite legal are forms of research. These techniques are called, collectively, **competitive intelligence**. When information gatherers employ techniques that cross the threshold of what is legal or ethical, they enter the world of **industrial espionage**. Many countries considered allies of the United States engage in industrial espionage against American organizations. When foreign governments are involved, these activities are considered espionage that threatens national security. Some forms of espionage are relatively low-tech. One example, called **shoulder surfing**, is pictured in Figure 2-2. This technique is used in public or semipublic settings when individuals observe information without authorization by looking over another individual's shoulder or spotting information from a distance. Instances of shoulder surfing occur at computer terminals, desks, ATM machines, public phones, or other places where a person is accessing confidential information. There is unwritten etiquette among professionals who address information security in the workplace. When someone can see another person entering personal or private information into a system, the first person should look away politely as the information is entered. Failure to do so constitutes not only a breach of etiquette, but is considered an affront to privacy as well as a threat to the security of the confidential information.

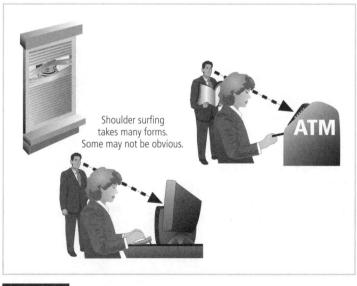

Shoulder surfing
takes many forms.
Some may not be obvious.

FIGURE 2-2 Shoulder Surfing

The threat of **trespass** can lead to unauthorized, real or virtual actions that enable information gatherers to enter premises or systems they have not been authorized to enter. Controls are sometimes implemented to mark the boundaries of an organization's virtual territory. These boundaries give notice to trespassers that they are encroaching on the organization's cyberspace. When an organization needs to protect valuable information and systems, sound principles of authentication and authorization lead employees to valid control methods and technologies. These safeguards employ multiple layers or factors and protect the data they are employed to control.

The classic perpetrator of *deliberate acts of espionage* or *trespass* is the hacker. **Hackers** are "people who use and create computer software for enjoyment "or "to gain access to information illegally."[6] The persona of the hacker is frequently glamorized in fictional accounts as someone who stealthily manipulates through a maze of computer networks, systems, and data to find the information that resolves the dilemma posed in the plot and saves the day. Television and motion pictures are inundated with images of hackers as heroes or heroines. However, the true life of the hacker is far more mundane (see Hacker Profiles, Figure 2-3). In the gritty world of reality, a hacker uses skill, guile, or fraud to attempt to bypass the controls placed around information that is the property of someone else. The hacker frequently spends long hours examining the types and structures of the targeted systems.

There are generally two skill levels among hackers. The first is the **expert hacker**, who develops software scripts and codes exploits used by those in the second category, the novice, or **unskilled hacker**. The expert hacker is usually a master of several programming languages, networking protocols, and operating systems, and also exhibits a mastery of the technical environment of the chosen targeted system. As indicated in the Hack PCWeek Offline, expert hackers are extremely talented individuals who usually have lots of time and energy to devote to attempts to break into other people's information systems.

The threat posed by expert hackers successfully entering a system is high once they have chosen a target. Fortunately for the many poorly protected organizations in the world, there are substantially fewer expert hackers than novice hackers.

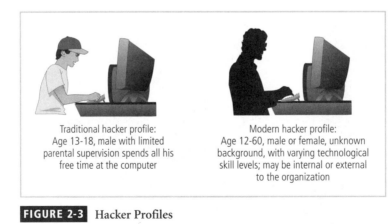

Traditional hacker profile:
Age 13-18, male with limited
parental supervision spends all his
free time at the computer

Modern hacker profile:
Age 12-60, male or female, unknown
background, with varying technological
skill levels; may be internal or external
to the organization

FIGURE 2-3   Hacker Profiles

However, expert hackers have now become bored with directly attacking systems, and have turned to writing software. The programs they are writing are automated exploits that allow novice hackers to become **script kiddies**. These are hackers of limited skill who use expertly written software to exploit a system, but do not fully understand or appreciate the systems they hack. The good news is that if an expert hacker can post a script tool where a script kiddie can find it, systems and security administrators can find it, too. The developers of protection software and hardware and the service providers that keep defensive systems up to date are also informed of the latest in exploit scripts. As a result of preparation and continued vigilance, attacks conducted by scripts are usually predictable, and can be adequately defended against.

OFFLINE

Hack PCWeek

On September 20th, 1999, PC Week did the unthinkable, it set up two computers, one Linux, one Windows NT, and challenged the hacking community to be the first to crack either system, deface the posted Web page, and claim a $1000 reward. Four days later it was hacked. Figure 2-4 shows the configuration of the *www.hackpcweek.com*. The article below provides the technical details of how the hack was accomplished, not by a compromise of the root operating system, but by the exploitation of an add-on CGI script with improper security checks.

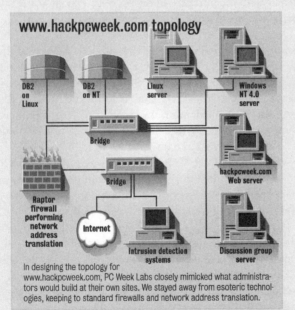

In designing the topology for www.hackpcweek.com, PC Week Labs closely mimicked what administrators would build at their own sites. We stayed away from esoteric technologies, keeping to standard firewalls and network address translation.

FIGURE 2-4 Hack PC Week Configuration

continued

"The Gibraltar Hack: Anatomy of a Break-in"[7]
By Pankaj Chowdhry, PC Week Labs, eWEEK, October 11, 1999.

"The hacker who first broke into the www.hackpcweek.com Web site hails, ironically, from Gibraltar—a location known as the Rock for its impregnability.

"The hack of our site's Linux server, via CGI, was cleverly crafted and methodical. The culprit, Luis Mora, known publicly as Jfs, is certainly a cut above the average hacker, 95 percent of whom can be stopped by a good firewall. It's the 5 percent like Jfs that organizations need to worry about.

"Jfs detailed the lengths to which he went to get into the system, a process that took him a relatively short 20 hours. Our analysis of the steps he took shows that administrators have a lot to be afraid of.

"Jfs first did a standard vulnerability analysis, using a port scanner. Our servers were pretty well locked down, and Jfs didn't find anything except for HTTP port 80. He next looked for Web server fingerprints to find out what software we were running. Our circuit-level firewall was worth its weight in gold here.

"After looking for the obvious stuff, Jfs began to map out our site, beginning with the directory structure. Using the HTML pages, he got a pretty good idea of what he was dealing with.

"He identified the commercial application that was running on our system as PhotoAds, whose source code is available with the purchase of the product. Having come to dead ends at all the networking vulnerabilities, he decided to pay more attention to our commercial scripts.

"With the PhotoAds source code in hand, Jfs tried the standard viewing of the configuration. But because of the server setup he could not get to it. He was able to see our environment configuration script, but this provided him with little useful information.

"Undeterred, Jfs began trying to exploit server-side includes and mod_PERL embedded commands. He tried this in every field and found that a PERL regexp filtered out most input before it got into the HTML. He did, however, find one user-assigned variable that wasn't checked for malicious data. That was all he needed.

"Jfs found that the ENV variable in the HTTP REFERER was left open. He tried to use a server-side include or mod_PERL embedded command to compromise the system. Unfortunately for him, neither of these services was configured on the machine.

"He persisted, this time looking for holes in the PhotoAds CGI scripts. With an obviously extensive knowledge of PERL, he began looking at open() and system() calls.

"He examined all of the variables and found only one to be of substance—the variable for the upload graphics-file name. If he could edit this name, he could write to any file on the system, including index.html—the home page.

"The variable consisted of two elements, a directory variable and a file name variable. The directory variable was hard-coded in the config file, so that was useless.

"The file name variable was filtered by a regexp, so Jfs couldn't upload just anything. In fact, files needed to end in .gif or .jpg to get through. Using www.phrack.com as a resource, Jfs figured out a string that would refer him to the home index.html page.

continued

"He couldn't use a post command to send the string because it strips out all percentage signs, a necessary component of the hack string. This left him with just a get command. Because we configured the upload image size to 0, Jfs was left with only the gif section of the code.

"By examining the code for the script, Jfs found that the graphics width must be less than 350 pixels with a height less than 250 pixels. He got around this by manually setting the sixth through ninth bytes to ascii null.

"He moved on, only to find that any uploaded files are automatically placed in another directory and renamed.

"Jfs attempted to get around the rename function. After examining the script, he saw that there was no error checking on the rename function. This presented the opportunity he was looking for. Using his knowledge of Linux, he figured out that the way to get the script to process past the rename function was to give the script a bad file name that would be skipped, leaving the file with its original name.

"Jfs knew that Linux has a standard maximum file name size of 1,024 bytes. However, he also had to create a number that matched the long file name, which was easy because of the faulty input checking.

"The result was a hack that let Jfs overwrite any file in the file system that was owned by the same user as the CGI process. Unfortunately for him, the CGI process was owned by 'nobody,' and all of the HTML documents were owned by root. He had hit another dead end.

"Using pretty sophisticated knowledge of C, Jfs tried to get an ELF executable into the server, but he had to manually manipulate the binaries because of length restrictions with the get command. This limited Jfs to 8,190 bytes. Because he already had a 1,024-character number, he was left with about 7,000 bytes to code the entire executable.

"Jfs stripped out everything he could and managed to get it under the size requirements.

"This didn't get him the files he needed, so he went after root access—the hacker's Holy Grail. Using the Bugtraq service, he found a cron exploit for which patches hadn't been applied. He modified the hack to get a suidroot. This got him root access—and the ability to change the home page to the chilling: "This site has been hacked. Jfs was here.

"Game over."

The most notorious hacker in recent history is Kevin Mitnick, highlighted in the following Offline. More recently, a juvenile hacker named Mafiaboy, responsible for a series of widely publicized denial-of-service attacks on prominent Web sites, pled guilty to 55 counts of computer mischief, and was sentenced to eight months in juvenile detention.[8] His downfall came from his inability to cover his tracks by deleting the systems logs that tracked his activity, and his need to brag about his exploits in chat rooms.

There are other terms for system rule breakers that may be less familiar. The terms, hacker and **cracker** denote criminal intent. The term cracker is now commonly associated with an individual who "cracks" or removes an application's software protection that is designed to prevent unauthorized duplication. With the removal of the copyright protection, the software can be easily distributed and installed.

A **phreaker** hacks the public telephone network to make free calls, disrupt services, and generally wreak havoc. Phreakers grew in fame in the 1970s, when devices called blue boxes made free telephone calls popular. Later, red boxes were developed to simulate the tones of coins falling in a pay phone, and finally black boxes emulated the line voltage. With the advent of digital communications, these boxes became practically obsolete. Even with the loss of the colored box technologies, phreakers continue to cause problems for the public telephone systems.

OFFLINE

Kevin Mitnick

The most famous hacker to date is Kevin Mitnick. The son of divorced parents, Kevin Mitnick grew up in a lackluster middle-class environment. Kevin got his start as a phreaker, with a local group of juvenile enthusiasts. Eventually the group Kevin hung out with expanded their malicious activities into computer companies. After attacking and physically breaking into the Pacific Bell Computer Center for Mainframe Operations, the group was tracked down, when a former girlfriend of one of the group members turned them in. A 17-year-old, Mitnick was convicted of the destruction of data and theft of equipment, and sentenced to three months in juvenile detention and a year's probation.

Mitnick spent the next few years sharpening his hacking and phreaking skills, and surviving run-ins with the police. He was arrested again in 1983 at the University of Southern California where he was caught breaking into Pentagon computers over the ARPANet. He received six months in another juvenile prison. He disappeared a few years later, after he was issued an arrest warrant for breaking into a credit agency computer database. He was eventually convicted of using illegal telephone cards in 1987 and sentenced to 36 months probation. His next hacking battle pitched him against the FBI. His knowledge of the telephone system frustrated their efforts to apprehend him, until his best friend turned him in. His unusual plea of computer addiction managed to prevent a serious sentence, resulting in one year in prison and six months counseling. By 1992, he had reverted to a relatively normal life until someone was caught illegally using a database and the crime was traced back to Mitnick. After an FBI search of his residence, he was eventually charged with illegally accessing a phone company's computer and associating with a former criminal associate. But, then Kevin Mitnick disappeared.[9]

In 1995, he was finally tracked down and arrested. Because of the severe risk of flight, he was held without bail for nearly five years; eight months of it in solitary confinement. Afraid he would never get to trial, he eventually pleaded guilty to wire fraud, computer fraud and intercepting communications. He is now free on probation and required to get permission to travel or use any technology until January 2003. His newest job is touring the lecture circuit, speaking out in support of information security and against hacking.[10]

Deliberate Acts of Information Extortion

The threat of information extortion is the possibility of an attacker or formerly trusted insider stealing information from a computer system and demanding compensation for its return or for an agreement to not disclose the information. Extortion is common in credit card number theft. For example, Web-based retailer CD Universe was the victim of a theft of data files containing customer credit card information. The culprit was a Russian hacker named Maxus who hacked the online vendor, and stole several hundred thousand credit card numbers. When the company refused to pay the $100,000 blackmail, he posted the card numbers to a Web site, offering them to the criminal community. His Web site became so popular he had to restrict access.[11]

Another example of extortion occurred in June of 2000, when a student was charged with online blackmail. The student discovered how to freely download books from an online digital book company. He threatened to release this information unless he was provided with "a sum equal to the retail value of the content on the company's Web site, a 2001 Volvo wagon, two digital audio players, and unlimited free downloads of the company's content."[12] Since a single conviction for using the Internet to send blackmail threats could result in two years in prison and fines up to $100,000, this student faced a maximum total of 36 years and fines up to $800,000 if convicted on all counts.

Deliberate Acts of Sabotage or Vandalism

Equally popular today is the assault on the electronic face of an organization—its Web site. This category of threat originates with an individual or group of individuals who want to deliberately sabotage the operation of a computer system or business, or perform acts of vandalism to either destroy an asset or damage the image of the organization. These threats can range from petty vandalism by employees to organized sabotage against an organization.

Although not necessarily financially devastating, attacks on the image of an organization are serious. Organizations frequently rely on image to support the generation of revenue. So if an organization's Web site is defaced, a reduction in consumer confidence is probable, reducing the organization's sales and net worth. For example, in the early hours of July 13, 2001, a group known as Fluffi Bunni left their mark on the front page of the SANS Institute. This event was particularly embarrassing to SANS Institute management, since the Institute provides information security instruction and certification. The defacement read, "Would you really trust these guys to teach you security?"[13]

There are innumerable reports of hackers accessing systems, and damaging or destroying critical data. Hacked Web sites once made front-page news immediately, as the perpetrators intended. The impact of these acts has lessened as the volume has increased. The Web site that acts as the clearinghouse for many hacking reports, Attrition.org, has stopped cataloging all web site defacements, because the sheer volume of the acts has outstripped the ability of the volunteers to keep the site up to date.[14]

Compared to Web site defacement, vandalism within a network is more malicious in intent and less public. Today, security experts are noticing a rise in another form of online vandalism in what are described as **hacktivist** or **cyberactivist** operations. In these cases, technology becomes a tool for high-tech civil disobedience and hacking to protest the operations, policies, or actions of an organization or government agency. The following examples illustrate this concept:

"In 1998, the Electronic Disturbance Theater (EDT) took the concept of electronic civil disobedience a step further. They organized a series of Web sit-ins, first against Mexican President Zedillo's Web site and later against President Clinton's White House Web site, the Pentagon, the School of the Americas, the Frankfurt Stock Exchange, and the Mexican Stock Exchange. The purpose was to demonstrate solidarity with the Mexican Zapatistas."[15]

Figure 2-5 shows another hacktivist example. In this case, Greenpeace, a well-known environmental activist organization uses its Web presence to recruit cyberactivists.

FIGURE 2-5   Cyber Activists Wanted

Related to the concept of cyberactivists is the much more sinister **cyberterrorist**. The threat of cyberterrorism can lead to the use of hacking as a method for conducting terrorist activities through network or Internet pathways. In the current war on terrorism, the United States and other governments are developing security measures intended to protect the critical computing and communications networks as well as the physical and power infrastructures. Here is a description of the coining and use of the term cyberterrorism:

> "In the 1980s, Barry Collin, a senior research fellow at the Institute for Security and Intelligence in California, coined the term 'cyberterrorism' to refer to the convergence of cyberspace and terrorism. Mark Pollitt, special agent for the FBI, offers a working definition: 'Cyberterrorism is the premeditated, politically motivated attack against information, computer systems, computer programs, and data which result in violence against noncombatant targets by subnational groups or clandestine agents.'"[16]

Examples of cyberterrorism are currently limited to acts such as the defacement of NATO Web pages during the war in Kosovo. In fact some industry observers have taken the position that cyberterrorism is not a real threat, and instead is merely hype that distracts from the more concrete and pressing information security issues that do need attention.[17] Occasionally, hackers and hacking do become capital issues. In some cases, the hacking lifestyle crosses paths with the darker alleys of the criminal underworld as indicated in the following:

> "But when Boris Floriciz was found hanging from a tree in a Berlin park on Oct. 22, his belt around his neck and his feet dragging the ground, it drew attention even outside the tight-knit world of hackers.
>
> "His friends wonder whether he was caught up in the murkier side of the trade — one of spies, espionage, and black-market criminals. Was it suicide, as police suspect? Or homicide?
>
> "At 26, Floriciz seemed headed for a great future. He'd just finished his computer science degree. International firms sought him as a consultant. He was happy, say his friends, who cannot believe he would take his own life.
>
> "Floriciz's friends wonder if he had become a threat to someone on the wrong side of the business, leading to his death."[18]

When hackers push the envelope and make hacking-related crimes serious public policy issues, the issue moves from the realm of the individual security professional to the realm of government policy-makers and the general public.

Deliberate Acts of Theft

The threat of theft within an organization is a constant problem. **Theft** is the illegal taking of another's property. Within an organization, that property can be physical, electronic, or intellectual. The value of information suffers when it is copied and taken away without the owner's knowledge. Instead of stealing entire computer systems, criminals often steal computer circuit boards and valuable memory chips, which are sold to unscrupulous buyers who disregard their origins.[19]

Physical theft can be controlled quite easily. A wide variety of measures can be used from something as simple as locked doors to trained security personnel and the installation of alarm systems. Electronic theft, however, is a more complex problem to manage and control. When someone steals a physical item, it is easily detected; after all, it has been removed and is no longer present. With the theft of electronic information, the evidence of a crime is not readily apparent. If thieves are clever and cover their tracks carefully, no one may ever know of the crime until it is far too late.

Deliberate Software Attacks

Perhaps the most familiar form of threat is the potential for software attack. Deliberate software attacks occur when an individual or group designs software to attack an unsuspecting system. Most of this software is referred to as **malicious code** or **malicious software**, or sometimes **malware**. These software components or programs are designed to damage, destroy, or deny service to the target systems. Some of the more common instances of malicious code are viruses and worms, Trojan horses, logic-bombs, and back doors.

Equally prominent among the recent incidences of malicious code, are the denial-of-services attacks conducted by Mafiaboy (as mentioned earlier) on Amazon.com, CNN.com, E*TRADE.com, ebay.com, Yahoo.com, Excite.com, and Dell.com. These software-based attacks lasted approximately four hours, and are reported to have caused millions of dollars in lost revenue.[20] The British Internet service provider Cloudnine is suspected of being the first business "hacked out of existence" in a denial-of-service attack in January 2002. This attack was similar to denial-of-service attacks launched by Mafiaboy in February 2000.[21] The following are explanations of common malware threats.

Virus. Computer viruses are segments of code that perform malicious actions. This code behaves very much like a virus pathogen attacking animals and plants, using the cell's own replication machinery to propagate and attack. The code attaches itself to the existing program and takes control of that program's access to the targeted computer. The virus-controlled target program then carries out the virus's plan, by replicating itself into additional targeted systems. Many times the virus code gets into a system with the assistance of the user of the targeted computer. Opening an infected e-mail or some other seemingly trivial action can cause anything from random undesired messages popping up on a user's screen to the complete destruction of entire hard drives of data. Just as their namesake implies, viruses are passed from machine to machine via physical media, e-mail, or other forms of computer data transmission. When these viruses infect a machine, they may immediately scan the local machine for e-mail applications, or even send themselves to every user in the e-mail address book.

One of the most common methods of virus transmission at the opening of the twenty-first century is through e-mail attachment files. Most organizations block e-mail attachments of certain types and also filter all e-mail for known virus strains. In earlier times, viruses were slow moving creatures that transferred viral payloads through the cumbersome movement of diskettes from system to system. Now, computers are networked, and e-mail programs prove fertile ground for computer viruses unless they are suitably controlled. The current software marketplace has several established vendors that provide applications to assist in the control of computer viruses such as Symantec Norton Anti-Virus and McAfee VirusScan.

There are several types of viruses. One is the **macro virus**, which is embedded in automatically executing macro code, common in office productivity software such as word processors, spread sheets, and database applications. Another type, the **boot virus**, infects the key operating systems files located in a computer's boot sector.

Worms. Named for the Tapeworm in John Brunner's novel *The Shockwave Rider*, worms are malicious programs that replicate themselves constantly without requiring another program to provide a safe environment for replication. Worms can continue replicating themselves until they completely fill available resources, such as memory, hard drive space, and network bandwidth. Read the Offline on Robert Morris and the worm he created for a taste of the extent of damage an actual worm can cause. Code Red, Sircam, Nimda (admin spelled backwards), and Klez are recent and dangerous examples of a new class of worm attacks. See Figure 2-6 for screenshots of the Nimda and Sircam viruses. The difference between these newer worm variants and earlier worms is that the newer worms contain multiple exploits that can use any of the many predefined distribution vectors to programmatically distribute the virus (see the section on polymorphism later in this chapter). The Klez virus, pictured in Figure 2-7, delivers a two-barrel payload: it has an attachment that contains the worm, and if the e-mail is viewed on an HTML-enabled browser, it attempts to deliver a macro virus.

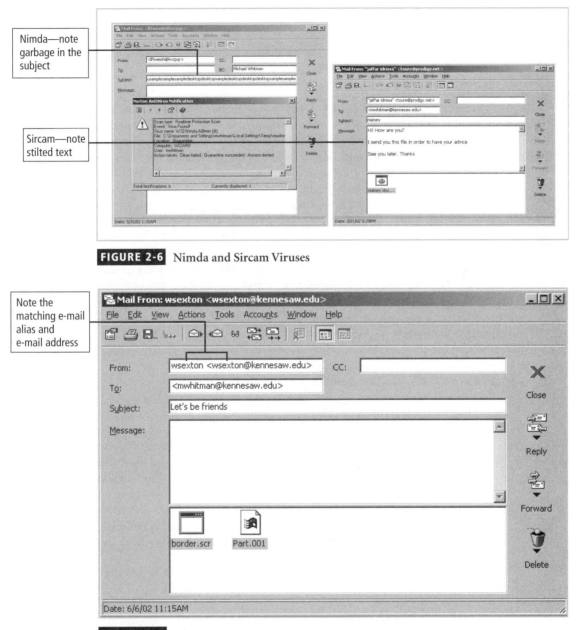

Nimda—note garbage in the subject

Sircam—note stilted text

FIGURE 2-6 Nimda and Sircam Viruses

Note the matching e-mail alias and e-mail address

FIGURE 2-7 Klez Virus

These complex behaviors can be invoked with or without the user downloading or executing the file. Once the worm has infected a computer, it can redistribute itself to all e-mail addresses found on the infected system. Further, a worm can deposit copies of itself onto all Web servers that the infected system can reach, so that users who subsequently visit those sites become infected themselves. Worms also take advantage of open shares found on the network in which an infected system is located, placing working copies of the worm code onto the server so that users of those shares are likely to become infected.

OFFLINE

Robert Morris And The Internet Worm

"Zen and the Art of the Internet"[22]
By Brendan P. Kehoe, January 1992.

"On November 2, 1988, Robert Morris, Jr., a graduate student in Computer Science at Cornell, wrote an experimental, self-replicating, self-propagating program called a worm and injected it into the Internet. He chose to release it from MIT, to disguise the fact that the worm came from Cornell. Morris soon discovered that the program was replicating and reinfecting machines at a much faster rate than he had anticipated—there was a bug. Ultimately, many machines at locations around the country either crashed or became 'catatonic.' When Morris realized what was happening, he contacted a friend at Harvard to discuss a solution. Eventually, they sent an anonymous message from Harvard over the network, instructing programmers how to kill the worm and prevent reinfection. However, because the network route was clogged, this message did not get through until it was too late. Computers were affected at many sites, including universities, military sites, and medical research facilities. The estimated cost of dealing with the worm at each installation ranged from $200 to more than $53,000.

"The program took advantage of a hole in the debug mode of the UNIX *sendmail* program, which runs on a system and waits for other systems to connect to it and give it e-mail, and a hole in the finger daemon *fingerd*, which serves finger requests (a UNIX feature that provides information about users on the system). People at the University of California at Berkeley and MIT had copies of the program and were actively disassembling it (returning the program back into its source form) to try to figure out how it worked.

"Teams of programmers worked nonstop to come up with at least a temporary fix, to prevent the continued spread of the worm. After about twelve hours, the team at Berkeley came up with steps that would help retard the spread of the payload. Another method was also discovered at Purdue and widely published. The information didn't get out as quickly as it could have, however, since so many sites had completely disconnected themselves from the network.

"After a few days, things slowly began to return to normalcy and everyone wanted to know who had done it all. Morris was later named in The New York Times as the author (though this hadn't yet been officially proven, there was a substantial body of evidence pointing to Morris).

"Robert T. Morris was convicted of violating the Computer Fraud and Abuse Act (Title 18), and sentenced to three years of probation, 400 hours of community service, a fine of $10,050, and the costs of his supervision. His appeal, filed in December 1990, was rejected the following March."

Reprinted with permission from Brendan Kehoe of the Zen Internet Group

Trojan horses. **Trojan horses** are software programs that hide their true nature, and reveal their designed behavior only when activated. Trojan horses are frequently disguised as helpful, interesting, or necessary pieces of software, such as readme.exe files often included with shareware or freeware packages. Unfortunately, like their famed namesake in Greek legend, once brought into a position of trust, they are activated and can wreak havoc on the unsuspecting user. Figure 2-8 outlines a typical Trojan horse attack. Around January 20, 1999, Internet e-mail users began receiving e-mail with an attachment of a Trojan horse program named Happy99.exe. When the e-mail was opened, a brief multimedia program displayed fireworks and the message "Happy 1999." While the fireworks display was running, the Trojan horse program was happily installing itself into the user's system. The program continued to propagate itself by following up every e-mail the user sent with a second e-mail to the same user containing the Happy99 Trojan horse program.

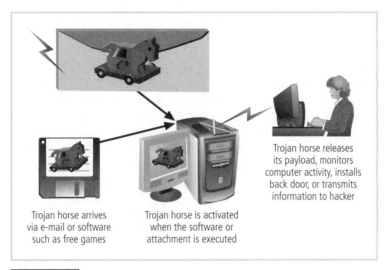

Trojan horse releases its payload, monitors computer activity, installs back door, or transmits information to hacker

Trojan horse arrives via e-mail or software such as free games

Trojan horse is activated when the software or attachment is executed

FIGURE 2-8 Trojan Horse Attack

Back door or **Trap door.** A virus or worm can have a payload that installs a **back door** or **trap door** component in a system. This allows the attacker to access the system at will with special privileges. Examples of these kinds of payloads include Subseven and Back Orifice.

Polymorphism. One of the biggest problems in fighting viruses and worms is the recent development of polymorphic threats. A **polymorphic threat** is one that changes its apparent shape over time, representing a new threat not detectable by techniques that are looking for a preconfigured signature. These threats actually evolve variations in size and appearance to elude detection by antivirus software programs. This means that an e-mail generated by the virus may not match previous examples, making detection more of a challenge.

Virus and Worm Hoaxes. As frustrating as viruses and worms are, perhaps more time and money is spent on resolving **virus hoaxes**. Well-meaning people can disrupt the harmony and flow of an organization when they send random e-mails warning of the latest and most dangerous viruses that are fictitious. When this happens and individuals fail to follow procedures, the network becomes overloaded, and much time and energy is wasted as everyone forwards the message to everyone they know, posts the message on bulletin boards, and begins updating antivirus protection software. There are a number of resources on the Internet, however, that allow individuals to research viruses to determine if they are fact or fiction. For the latest information on real threatening viruses and hoaxes, along with other relevant and current security information, visit the CERT Coordination Center or visit the Urban Legend Reference Pages at *www.snopes.com/inboxer/hoaxes/hoaxes.htm*, or the Hoax Busters Web page at *http://hoaxbusters.ciac.org/*.

Compromises to Intellectual Property

As will be discussed in detail in Chapter 3, many organizations create or support the development of intellectual property as part of their business operations. Intellectual property is defined as "the ownership of ideas and control over the tangible or virtual representation of those ideas. Use of another person's intellectual property may or may not involve royalty payments or permission, but should always include proper credit to the source."[23] Intellectual property for an organization includes trade secrets, copyrights, trademarks, and patents. Once intellectual property (IP) has been defined, and properly identified, breaches to IP constitute a threat to the security of this information. Employees may be privileged to the various types of IP, and may use the property to conduct day-to-day business.

Frequently an organization purchases or leases the IP of other organizations, and must abide by the purchase or licensing agreement for the fair and responsible use of the property. Most common in the category of IP breaches is the unlawful use or duplication of software-based intellectual property, more commonly known as **software piracy**. It may be surprising to learn that many individuals and organizations seldom purchase their software. Since most software is licensed to a particular purchaser, its use is restricted to a single user. If the user copies the program to another computer without securing another license, he or she has violated the copyright. For an example, see the Offline on violating software licenses. Software licenses are strictly enforced through a number of regulatory and private organizations, and software publishers use several control mechanisms to prevent copyright infringement. In addition to the laws surrounding software piracy, two watchdog organizations investigate allegations of software abuse: Software & Information Industry Association (SIIA) at *www.siia.org,* formerly known as the Software Publishers Association, and the Business Software Alliance (BSA) at *www.bsa.org*. Additional details on these organizations and how they operate to preserve IP rights are discussed in Chapter 3, "Legal, Ethical, and Professional Issues in Information Security".

Enforcement of copyright violations, piracy, and the like has been attempted through a number of technical security mechanisms, including digital watermarks, embedded code, required copyright codes, and even intentional bad sectors on software media. The most common reminder of the obligation of the individual to fair and responsible use is the license agreement window that usually pops up during the installation of new software. This screen serves as the legal proof that the user has read and agrees to the license agreement. Unfortunately, simply displaying this screen is not sufficient to prove that legal agreement was reached. For a time, these license agreements were referred to as blow-by screens, as the users found that if they hit the Enter key frequently during installation, these bothersome installation screens quickly vanished, allowing faster installation of the software. Now, it is more common to see a different type of acceptance screen, requiring the selection of a response via mouse click, or a key other than the Enter key.

Another effort to combat piracy is the online registration process. Individuals who install software are often asked or even required to register their software, to obtain technical support, or full use. This process has led to allegations that the process introduces risks to personal privacy, since the individual never really knows exactly what information is obtained from their computer and sent to the software manufacturer.

OFFLINE

Violating Software Licenses

Adapted from "Bootlegged Software Could Cost Community College"[24]
By Natalie Patton, Las Vegas Review Journal, September 18, 1997.

Ever heard of the software police? Not the urban legend they are cast to be, the Washington-based Software Publishers Association (SPA) copyright watchdogs were tipped off that a community college in Las Vegas, Nevada, was using copyrighted software in violation of the software licenses. The SPA spent months investigating the report. Academic Affairs Vice President Robert Silverman said the college was preparing to pay some license violation fines, but was unable to estimate the total amount of the fines. The college cut back on new faculty hires, and set aside over 1.3 million dollars in anticipation of the total cost.

The audit is intensive, examining every computer on campus, including faculty machines, lab machines, even the president's computer. Peter Beruk, the software association's director of domestic antipiracy cases, said the decision to audit a reported violation is only made when there is overwhelming evidence to win a law suit, as the SPA has no legal power other than the threat of legal action. Most of the investigated organizations settle out of court, agreeing to pay the fines, instead of costly court battles.

The process begins with an anonymous tip, usually from an individual inside the organization. Of the hundreds of tips the SPA receives each week, only a handful are selected for on-site visits. If the audited organizations have license violations they are required to destroy illegal copies, repurchase software they wish to keep (at double the face value), and pay the cost of the illegal use.

The community college president suggested the blame for the community college's violations belonged to faculty and students, downloading illegal copies of software from the Internet, or installing software on campus computers without permission, sometimes from home. Some of the faculty suspected that the problem lay in the qualifications and credibility of the campus technology staff. The president promises to put additional staff and rules in place to prevent reoccurrence.

So be good for goodness sake, the software police are watching you.

Threat Group 3: Acts of God

In the last section we discussed threats to hardware and data that involved deliberate intent. However, not all threats occur from deliberate intent. The acts of God category is used for threats that result from forces of nature that cannot be prevented or controlled.

Forces of Nature

Forces of nature, *force majeure*, or acts of God pose some of the most dangerous threats imaginable, because they are unexpected and can occur with very little warning. These threats can disrupt not only the lives of individuals, but also the storage, transmission, and use of information. Many natural forces still affect human affairs. These include fire, flood, earthquake, and lightning as well as volcanic eruption and insect infestation. Some of the more common threats in this group are presented in the list below.

- **Fire:** Usually meant in this context as a structural fire that damages the building housing the computing equipment that comprises all or part of the information system.

Also encompasses smoke damage from the fire and/or water damage from sprinkler systems or firefighters. Can usually be mitigated with fire casualty insurance and/or business interruption insurance.

- **Flood:** An overflowing of water onto land that is normally dry, causing direct damage to all or part of the information system or, to the building that houses all or part of the information system. May also disrupt operations through interruptions in access to the buildings that house all or part of the information system. Can sometimes be mitigated with flood insurance and/or business interruption insurance.

- **Earthquake:** A sudden movement of the earth's crust caused by the release of stress accumulated along geologic faults or by volcanic activity. Earthquakes can cause direct damage to all or part of the information system or, more often, to the building that houses them. May also disrupt operations through interruptions in access to the buildings that house all or part of the information system. Can sometimes be mitigated with specific casualty insurance and/or business interruption insurance, but is usually a specific and separate policy.

- **Lightning:** An abrupt, discontinuous natural electric discharge in the atmosphere. Lightning usually directly damages all or part of the information system an/or its power distribution components. It can also cause fires or other damage to the building that houses all or part of the information system. May also disrupt operations through interruptions in access to the buildings that house all or part of the information system. Can usually be mitigated with multi-purpose casualty insurance and/or business interruption insurance.

- **Landslide or mudslide:** The downward sliding of a mass of earth and rock directly damaging all or part of the information system or, more likely, the building that houses them. May also disrupt operations through interruptions in access to the buildings that house all or part of the information system. Can sometimes be mitigated with casualty insurance and/or business interruption insurance.

- **Tornado or severe windstorm:** A rotating column of air ranging in width from a few yards to more than a mile and whirling at destructively high speeds, usually accompanied by a funnel-shaped downward extension of a cumulonimbus cloud. Storms can directly damage all or part of the information system or, more likely, the building that houses them. May also disrupt operations through interruptions in access to the buildings that house all or part of the information system. Can sometimes be mitigated with casualty insurance and/or business interruption insurance.

- **Hurricane or typhoon:** A severe tropical cyclone originating in the equatorial regions of the Atlantic Ocean or Caribbean Sea or eastern regions of the Pacific Ocean (typhoon), traveling north, northwest, or northeast from its point of origin, and usually involving heavy rains. These storms can directly damage all or part of the information system or, more likely, the building that houses them. Organizations located in coastal or low-lying areas may experience flooding (see above). May also disrupt operations through interruptions in access to the buildings that house all or part of the information system. Can sometimes be mitigated with casualty insurance and/or business interruption insurance.

- **Tsunami:** A very large ocean wave caused by an underwater earthquake or volcanic eruption. These events can directly damage all or part of the information system or, more likely, the building that houses them. Organizations located in coastal areas may experience tsunamis. Tsunamis may also cause disruption to operations through interruptions in access or electrical power to the buildings that house all or part of the information system. Can sometimes be mitigated with casualty insurance and/or business interruption insurance.

▪ **Electro-static discharge (ESD):** Usually, static electricity and ESD are little more than a nuisance. Unfortunately, the mild static shock we receive when walking across a carpet can be costly or dangerous when it ignites flammable mixtures and damages costly electronic components. Static electricity can draw dust into clean-room environments or cause products to stick together. The cost of ESD-damaged electronic devices and interruptions to service can range from only a few cents to several millions of dollars for critical systems. Loss of production time in information processing due to ESD impact is significant. While not usually viewed as a threat, ESD can disrupt information systems and is not usually an insurable loss unless covered by business interruption insurance.

▪ **Dust contamination:** Some environments are not friendly to the hardware components of information systems. Because dust contamination can shorten the life of information systems or cause unplanned downtime, this threat can disrupt normal operations.

Since it is not possible to avoid these threats, management must implement controls to limit damage, and they must also prepare contingency plans for continued operations, such as disaster recovery plans, business continuity plans, and incident response plans to limit losses in the face of these threats.

Threat Group 4: Technical Failures

Sometimes machines break without a discernable cause or in unexpected ways. Such disruptions can have severe negative consequences for unprepared organizations.

Technical Hardware Failures or Errors

Technical hardware failures or errors occur when a manufacturer distributes to users equipment containing a known or unknown flaw. These defects can cause the system to perform outside of expected parameters, resulting in unreliable service or lack of availability. Some errors are terminal, in that they result in the unrecoverable loss of the equipment. Some errors are intermittent, in that they only periodically manifest themselves, resulting in faults that are not easily repeated. For example, equipment can sometimes stop working, or work in unexpected ways. Murphy's Law (and yes, there really was a Murphy) says that if something can possibly go wrong, it will.[25] In other words, it's not *if* something will fail, but when.

One of the best-known hardware failures is the Intel Pentium II chip. The microchip had a defect that caused it to calculate erroneously in certain circumstances. Soon after it was reported, Intel expressed little concern for the defect, stating that it would take an inordinate amount of time to identify a calculation that would interfere with the reliability of the results. Yet within days popular computing journals were publishing a simple calculation to determine if an individual's machine contained the defective chip. Incidentally, the floating-point operation bug was easily detected by comparing the calculation of 4195835 divided by 3145727 between a spreadsheet and a calculator. The Pentium floating-point division bug (FDIV) led to a public relations disaster for Intel that resulted in its first-ever chip recall and a loss of over $475 million. A few months later, disclosure of another bug known as the Dan-0411 flag erratum further impacted the chip manufacturer's public image.[26] In 1998, when Intel released its Xeon chip, it had hardware errors. Intel said, "All new chips have bugs and the process of debugging and improving performance inevitably continues even after a product is in the market."[27]

Technical Software Failures or Errors

This category of threats comes from purchasing software with unknown, hidden faults. Large quantities of computer code are written, debugged, published, and sold only to determine that not all bugs were resolved. Sometimes, unique combinations of certain software and hardware reveal new bugs. These failures range from bugs to untested failure conditions. Sometimes, these items are not errors, but are purposeful shortcuts left by programmers for honest or dishonest reasons. Collectively, shortcut access routes into programs that bypass security checks are called trap doors and can cause severe security breaches.

Software bugs in general are so prolific that entire web sites are dedicated to documenting them. Bugtraq, found at *lists.insecure.com*, provides up-to-the-minute information on the latest security vulnerabilities, including software and hardware bugs.

Threat Group 5: Management Failures

A final category of threats to an organization's information security comes from management's potential lack of sufficient planning and foresight to anticipate the technology needed for evolving business requirements.

Technological Obsolescence

Antiquated or outdated infrastructure leads to unreliable and untrustworthy systems. Management must recognize that when technology becomes outdated, there is a risk of loss of data integrity from attacks. Management's strategic planning should always include an analysis of the technology current in the organization. Ideally, proper planning by management should prevent the risks from technology obsolesce, but when obsolescence is identified, management must take immediate action. IT professionals are instrumental in assisting management in the identification of probable obsolescence.

For example, Symantec recently retired support for a legacy version of its popular antivirus software. Organizations relying on that version must now execute immediate upgrades to a different antivirus control. If IT personnel kept their management informed of the coming retirement, these replacements were made earlier and at lower cost.

Attacks

An **attack** is the deliberate act that exploits vulnerability. It is accomplished by a **threat agent** that damages or steals an organization's information or physical asset. What does this mean? An **exploit** is a technique to compromise a system. **Vulnerability** is an identified weakness of a controlled system with controls that are not present or are no longer effective. An attack is the use of an exploit to achieve the compromise of a controlled system. The following sections discuss each of the major types of attack used against controlled systems.

Malicious Code

This kind of attack includes the execution of viruses, worms, Trojan horses, and active Web scripts with the intent to destroy or steal information. The state of the art in attacking systems in 2002 is the multivector (or polymorphic) worm. These attack programs use up to six known attack vectors to exploit a variety of vulnerabilities in commonly found information system devices. Perhaps the best illustration of **malicious code** was the outbreak of Nimda in September 2001 that used five of the six vectors to spread with startling speed. TruSecure Corporation, an industry source for information security statistics and solutions, reports that Nimda spread to span the Internet address space of 14 countries in less than 25 minutes.[28] Table 2-2 outlines the six categories of known attack vectors.

TABLE 2-2   Attack Replication Vectors

Vector	Description
IP scan and attack	Infected system scans random or local range of IP addresses and targets any of several vulnerabilities known to hackers or left over from previous exploits such as Code Red, Back Orifice, or PoizonBox
Web browsing	If the infected system has write access to any Web pages, it makes all Web content files (.html, .asp, .cgi, and others) infectious, so that users who browse to those pages become infected
Virus	Each infected machine infects certain common executable or script files on all computers to which it can write with virus code that can cause infection
Shares	Using vulnerabilities in file systems and the way many organizations configure them, it copies the viral component to all locations it can reach
Mass mail	By sending e-mail infections to addresses found in the infected system's address book, copies of the infection are sent to many users whose mail-reading programs automatically run the program and infect other systems
Simple Network Management Protocol (SNMP)	In early 2002, the SNMP vulnerabilities known to many in the IT industry were brought to the attention of the multivector attack community. SNMP buffer overflow and weak community string attacks are expected by the end of 2002

Hoaxes

A more devious approach to attacking computer systems is the transmission of a virus hoax, *with a real virus attached*. By masking the attack in a seemingly legitimate message, unsuspecting users more readily distribute it, as they try to do the right thing to avoid infection. They send the attack on to their coworkers and friends, infecting many users along the way.

Back Doors

Using a known or previously unknown and newly discovered access mechanism, an attacker can gain access to a system or network resource through a back door. Sometimes these are features left behind by system designers or maintenance staff (as in trap doors).[29] This kind of attack is hard to detect, because very often the programmer who puts it in place also makes the access exempt from the usual audit logging features of the system.

Password Crack

Attempting to reverse calculate a password is often called **cracking**. A cracking attack is a component of many dictionary attacks. It is used when a copy of the Security Account Manager (SAM) data file can be obtained. The SAM file contains the hashed representation of the user's password. A password can be hashed using the same algorithm and compared to the hashed results. If they are the same, the password has been guessed.

Brute Force

The application of computing and network resources to try every possible combination of options of a password is called a **brute force attack**. Since this is often an attempt to repeatedly guess passwords to commonly used accounts, it is sometimes called a **password attack**. If attackers can narrow the field of accounts to be attacked, they can devote more time and resources to attacking fewer accounts. That is one reason a recommended practice is to change account names for common accounts from the manufacturer's default.

While often effective against low-security systems, password attacks are often not useful against systems that have adopted the usual security practices recommended by manufacturers. Controls that limit the number of attempts allowed per unit of elapsed time are very effective at limiting brute force attacks. Defense against brute force attacks are usually adopted early on in any security effort and are thoroughly covered in the SANS/FBI Top Twenty most critical Internet security vulnerabilities.[30]

Dictionary

This is another form of the brute force attack noted above for guessing passwords. The **dictionary attack** narrows the field by selecting specific accounts to attack and uses a list of commonly used passwords (the dictionary) with which to guess, instead of random combinations. Organizations that use similar dictionaries to disallow passwords during the reset process, guard against easy-to-guess passwords. In addition, rules requiring additional numbers and/or special characters make the dictionary attack less effective.

Denial-of-Service (DoS) and Distributed Denial-of-Service (DDoS)

In a **denial-of-service (DoS)** attack, the attacker sends a large number of connection or information requests to a target (see Figure 2-9). So many requests are made that the target system cannot handle them successfully along with other, legitimate requests for service. This may result in a system crash, or merely an inability to perform ordinary functions. A **distributed denial-of-service (DDoS)** is an attack in which a coordinated stream of requests is launched against a target from many locations at the same time. Most DDoS attacks are preceded by a preparation phase in which many systems, perhaps thousands, are compromised. The compromised machines are turned into **zombies**, directed towards the target, and executed remotely (usually by a transmitted command) by the attacker. DDoS attacks are the most difficult to defend against, and there are presently no controls that any single organization can apply. There are some cooperative efforts to enable DDoS defenses among groups of service providers; among them is Consensus Roadmap for Defeating Distributed Denial of Service Attacks.[31] To use a popular metaphor, DDoS is considered a weapon of mass destruction on the Internet.[32] The reason for the Code Red worm's replication action was the prospect of a distributed denial-of-service (DDoS) attack against the United States White House Web site (*www.WhiteHouse.gov*).[33]

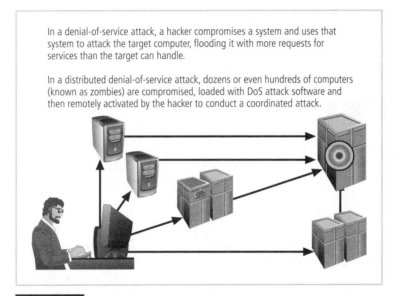

In a denial-of-service attack, a hacker compromises a system and uses that system to attack the target computer, flooding it with more requests for services than the target can handle.

In a distributed denial-of-service attack, dozens or even hundreds of computers (known as zombies) are compromised, loaded with DoS attack software and then remotely activated by the hacker to conduct a coordinated attack.

 **FIGURE 2-9** Denial-of-Service Attacks

Any system connected to the Internet and providing TCP-based network services (such as a Web server, FTP server, or mail server) is potentially subject to this attack. Note that in addition to attacks launched at specific hosts, these attacks could also be launched against routers or other network server systems, if these hosts enable (or turn on) other TCP services (e.g., echo). The consequences of the attack may vary depending on the system; however, the attack itself is fundamental to the TCP protocol used by all systems.[34]

Spoofing

Spoofing is a technique used to gain unauthorized access to computers, whereby the intruder sends messages to a computer with an IP address indicating that the message is coming from a trusted host. To engage in IP spoofing, a hacker must first use a variety of techniques to find an IP address of a trusted host and then modify the packet headers (see Figure 2-10) so that it appears that the packets are coming from that host.[35] Newer routers and firewall arrangements can offer protection against IP spoofing.

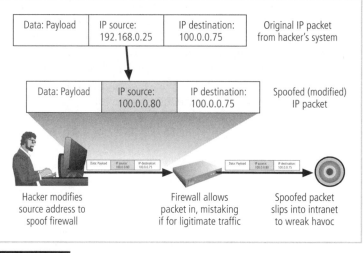

FIGURE 2-10 IP Spoofing

Man-in-the-Middle

In the well-know **man-in-the-middle** or **TCP hijacking** attack, an attacker sniffs packets from the network, modifies them, and inserts them back into the network. It uses IP spoofing (as explained above) to enable an attacker to impersonate another entity on the network. It allows the attacker to eavesdrop as well as to change, delete, reroute, add, forge, or divert data.[36] In a variant on the TCP hijacking session, spoofing involves the interception of an encryption key exchange, where the man-in-the-middle hacker acts as an invisible middleman allowing him to eavesdrop on encrypted communications. Figure 2-11 illustrates this example by showing how a hacker uses public and private encryption keys to intercept messages. For more information on encrypted keys, see the Appendix on Cryptography.

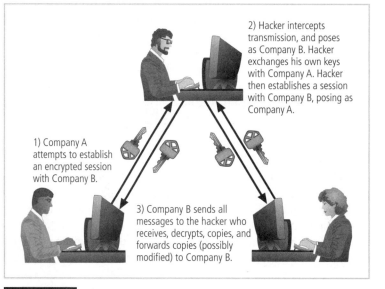

FIGURE 2-11 Man-in-the-Middle Attack

Spam

Spam is unsolicited commercial e-mail. While many consider spam a nuisance rather than an attack, it is emerging as a vector for some attacks. In March 2002, reports emerged of malicious code embedded in MP3 files that were included as attachments to spam.[37]

Mail bombing

Another form of e-mail attack that is also a DoS is called a **mail bomb,** in which an attacker routes large quantities of e-mail to the target. This can be accomplished through social engineering or by exploiting various technical flaws in the Simple Mail Transport Protocol. This results in the target receiving large volumes of unsolicited e-mail, which they are unable to manage. By sending large e-mails with forged header information, poorly configured e-mail systems on the Internet can be tricked into sending many e-mails to an address chosen by the attacker. If many such systems are tricked into the event, the target e-mail address is buried under thousands or even millions of unwanted e-mails.

Sniffers

A **sniffer** is a program or device that can monitor data traveling over a network. Sniffers can be used both for legitimate network management functions and for stealing information from a network. Unauthorized sniffers can be extremely dangerous to a network's security, because they are virtually impossible to detect and can be inserted almost anywhere. This makes them a favorite weapon in the hacker's arsenal. They often work on TCP/IP networks, where they're sometimes called **packet sniffers**.[38] Sniffers add risk to the network, since many systems and users send information on local networks in clear text. A sniffer program shows all the data going by, including passwords and the data inside of files, such as word-processing documents and screens full of sensitive data from applications.

Social Engineering

Within the context of information security, **social engineering** is the process of using social skills to convince people to reveal access credentials or other valuable information to the attacker. This can be done in several ways, usually involving the perpetrator posing as a person higher in the organizational hierarchy than the victim. The false representation may have been preceded by preparatory social engineering against others in the organization to collect seemingly unrelated information. This information used in context of a later attack, makes the false representation more credible. For instance, anyone can call the main switchboard of a company for the name of the CIO. Additional calls to others could use the CIO's name as a way to assume inappropriate authority to request information. Social engineering attacks may include individuals posing as new employees or pathetically requesting assistance to prevent getting fired. Sometimes attackers threaten, cajole, or beg to sway the target. Other variations are possible, as noted here in the excerpt from The Computer Emergency Response Team/Coordination Center (CERT/CC):

> "CERT/CC has received several incident reports concerning users receiving requests to take an action that results in the capturing of their password. The request could come in the form of an e-mail message, a broadcast, or a telephone call. The latest ploy instructs the user to run a "test" program, previously installed by the intruder, which will prompt the user for his or her password. When the user executes the program, the user's name and password are e-mailed to a remote site. These messages can appear to be from a site administrator or root. In reality, they may have been sent by an individual at a remote site, who is trying to gain access or additional access to the local machine via the user's account."[39]

While this advisory may seem very trivial to some experienced users, the fact remains that *many* users have fallen for these tricks (refer to CERT Advisory CA-91.03). A similar social engineering attack involves the infamous Nigerian National Petroleum Company. Over the past year, the authors have received no fewer than four e-mail, fax, and mail solicitations (see Figure 2-12 for a sample letter) asking for assistance in this social engineering effort. This is an old scam making a comeback. The so-called Nigeria National Petroleum Corporation scam is notorious for stealing funds from gullible individuals by requesting additional funding fees and is even suspected of involvement with kidnapping and extortion. On May 23, 2002, six men were arrested in South Africa on suspicion of being involved in this scam. The Secret Service believes this scam has bilked over $100 million from Americans by luring unsuspecting individuals into disclosing personal banking information. For more information, go to *www.secretservice.gov/alert419.shtml*.

The infamous super-hacker Kevin Mitnick (see previous description) once stated,

> "People are the weakest link. You can have the best technology; firewalls, intrusion-detection systems, biometric devices...and somebody can call an unsuspecting employee. That's all she wrote, baby. They got everything."[40]

Buffer Overflow

This is an application error that occurs when more data is sent to a buffer than it can handle. The use of buffers occurs when there is a mismatch in the processing rates between two entities involved in a communication process. When the **buffer overflows**, the attacker can make the target system execute instructions, or the attacker can take advantage of some other unintended consequence of the failure. Sometimes this is limited to a denial-of-service, when the attacked system shuts down for a time until restarted and is therefore unavailable to users. Or the buffer overflow could allow control of the system by the attacker. Either way, data on the attacked system loses integrity.[41] In 1998 Microsoft encountered a buffer overflow problem that is described below:

> "Microsoft acknowledged that if you type a res:// URL (a Microsoft-devised type of URL) which is longer than 256 characters in Internet Explorer 4.0, the browser will crash. No big deal, except that anything after the 256th character can be executed on the computer. This maneuver, known as a buffer overrun, is just about the oldest hacker trick in the book. Tack some malicious code (say, an executable version of the Pentium-crashing FooF code) onto the end of the URL, and you have the makings of a disaster."[42]

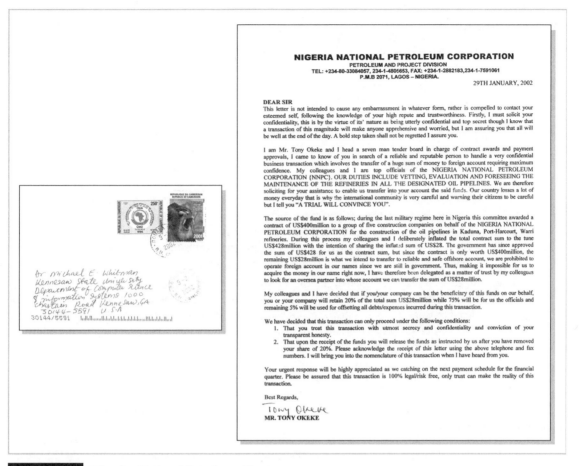

FIGURE 2-12   Nigerian National Petroleum Company

Timing Attack

Relatively new, the **timing attack** works by exploring the contents of a Web browser's cache. These attacks allow a Web designer to create a malicious form of cookie to store on the client's system. This could allow the designer to collect information on access to password-protected sites.[43] Another attack by the same name involves attempting to intercept cryptographic elements to determine keys and encryption algorithms.[44]

Chapter Summary

- An organization's senior management is accountable for information security. The IT Department may have responsibilities as well. An organization needs information security for four important reasons: to protect the ability of the organization to function by implementing information security; to enable the safe operation of applications using the organization's IT systems, particularly the infrastructure of the organization; to protect the data an organization collects and uses both in motion and at rest; and to safeguard the technology assets in an organization by adding secure infrastructure services based on the size and scope of the enterprise.

- A threat is an object, person, or other entity that endangers an asset. A categorization scheme is presented that consists of twelve general categories of real and present danger to an organization's information and systems: acts of human error or failure; deviations in quality of service by service providers; deliberate acts of espionage or trespass; deliberate acts of information extortion; deliberate acts of sabotage or vandalism; deliberate acts of theft; deliberate software attacks; compromises to intellectual property; forces of nature; technical hardware failures or errors; technical software failures or errors; and technological obsolescence.

- An attack is the exploitation of vulnerability by a threat agent to damage or steal an organization's information or physical asset. An exploit is a technique to compromise a system. A vulnerability is an identified weakness of a system that has controls that are not present or are no longer effective. Examples of attacks include: malicious code, hoaxes, back doors, password cracks, brute force attacks, dictionary attacks, denial-of-service (DoS) and distributed denial-of-service (DDoS), spoofing, man-in-the-middle, TCP hijacking, spam, mail bombing, sniffers or packet-sniffers, social engineering, buffer overflows, and timing attacks.

Review Questions

1. Why is information security a management problem? What can management do that technology cannot?

2. Why is data the most important asset an organization possesses? What other assets in the organization require protection?

3. It is important to protect data in motion (transmission) and data at rest (storage). What other state of data is important to protect? Which of the three is most difficult to protect?

4. How does a threat to information security differ from an attack? How can the two overlap?

5. How does protection from intentional (malicious) threats differ from unintentional (accidental) attacks?

6. How can dual controls, such as two-person confirmation, reduce the threats from acts of human error and failure? What other controls can reduce this threat?

7. Why do employees constitute one of the greatest threats to information security?

8. How can a Service Level Agreement provide a safeguard for Internet service provisioning issues?

9. How can an individual protect against shoulder surfing in the organization?

10. How has the perception of the hacker changed over recent years? What is the profile of a hacker today?

11. What is the difference between a skilled hacker and an unskilled hacker (other than the lack of skill)? How does the protection against each differ?

12. What is the difference between a cyberterrorist and a cyberactivist?

13. What are the various types of malware? How do worms differ from viruses? Do Trojan horses carry viruses or worms?

14. Why does polymorphism cause greater concern than traditional malware? How does it affect detection?

15. What is the most common form of violation of intellectual property? How does an organization protect against it? What agencies fight it?

16. What are the various types of *force majeure*? Which type is of greatest concern to an organization in Las Vegas? Oklahoma City? Miami? Los Angeles?

17. How does Murphy's law impact the protection of information?

18. How does technological obsolescence constitute a threat to information security? How can an organization protect against it?

19. What is the difference between an exploit and vulnerability?

20. What are the types of password attacks? What can a systems administrator do to protect against them?

21. What is the difference between a denial-of-service attack and a distributed denial-of-service attack? Which is potentially more dangerous and devastating? Why?

22. What is so dangerous in a spoofing attack? How can e-mail be used or compromised in a spoofing attack?

23. For a sniffer attack to succeed, what must the attacker do? How can an attacker gain access to a network to use the sniffer system?

24. What are some ways a social engineering hacker can attempt to gain information about a user's login and password? How would this type of attack differ if it were targeted towards an administrator's assistant versus a data-entry clerk?

25. What is a buffer overflow and how can it be caused over the Web?

Exercises

1. Consider the statement: an individual threat agent, like a hacker, can be represented in more than one threat category. If a hacker hacks into a network, copies a few files, defaces the Web page, and steals credit card numbers, how many different threat categories does this attack cover?

2. Using the Web, determine what was the extent of Mafiaboy's exploits. How many sites did he compromise and how? How was he caught?

3. Using the Web, look for the "The Official Phreaker's Manual." What information contained in this manual can help a security administrator to protect a communications system.

4. Two studies here mention threats to information security. Using the Web, find other sources of information on threats. Begin with *www.securitystats.com*.

5. Using the categories of threats mentioned here, as well as the various attacks described, review several newspapers and locate examples of each.

Case Exercises

I.   New MyLife Worm Emerges

Adapted from "MyLife.B Worm Deletes Infected PC's Files"[45]
By Dennis Fisher, eWeek Online, March 22, 2002.

MyLife as a Worm. There is a new worm coursing through the Internet's veins. It's known as MyLife.B and is a variant of the original MyLife virus, which has been around for a while.

As with many worms, MyLife.B arrives as an e-mail attachment, which in this case is "Cari.scr." The e-mail carries the subject "bill caricature" and has the text:

"Hiiiii
how are youuuuuuuu?
look to bill caricature it's vvvery ffffunny :-) :-)
i promise you will love it? Ok
buy"[46]

As with many worms of this type, when activated the worm displays a harmless screen shot, in this case a cartoon of Bill Clinton, and then proceeds to run amok in the computer's registry, as well as sending itself to everyone in the Microsoft Outlook address book. It causes the registry to reactivate the worm every time the computer is booted. Unique to this variant is the following time-related effect:

"If the machine boots between 8 a.m. and 9 a.m., the worm deletes files from the PC's C, D, E and F drives as well as in the system directory, according to Craig Schmugar, a virus researcher with Network Associates Inc.'s AVERT team."[47]

The worm is easily detectable, and most antivirus software catch it. The worm was initially identified in late March 2002 and has been labeled as a medium risk by McAfee.

1. If users without virus-detection software received an e-mail with the indicated message, where could they go to determine if it was a legitimate e-mail or potentially contained a virus?

2. What could an organization do to prevent this particular malware from impacting the productivity of its employees?

II.   Worm Disguised as Virus Update

Adapted from "Social Engineering: Low-Tech Tools for Virus Writers"[48]
By Andrew Conry-Murray, Network Magazine, July 2001.

Here's a new spin on an old trick—an e-mail virus, posing as an antivirus update. In May 2001, users began receiving unsolicited updates from Symantec, an antivirus software manufacturer. The e-mail contained a link, purportedly to route the recipient to an antivirus Web site to download a patch for the utility, or even an updated virus signature. In fact the link activated a worm. This type of virus hoax involves social engineering, which is preferred for two reasons:

"First, it's easier than writing exploits that launch without user participation," says Roger Thompson, technical director of malicious code research at TruSecure (*www.trusecure.com*). Second, "People will just click on anything," Thompson adds. Virus writers exploit that, and their targets unwittingly spread the virus, says Vincent Weafer, director of Symantec's AntiVirus Research Center (*www.symantec.com*)."[49]

With the widespread sharing of computer art, games, and a host of other e-mail attachments, we have developed a culture of e-mail users who are overly trusting, clicking on any attachment almost without thinking. This reaction is a security nightmare. Some think that users can be educated not to open unsolicited e-mail. However Thompson disagrees, "Even if you convince users not to click attachments with the common virus extensions, such as a file names clickme.exe, Windows may get in the way by hiding known file extensions."[50]

Technology may help, but isn't the ultimate answer. If the system administrator denies any e-mail, the problem goes away, right? But who can work under these restrictions? Filtering content may also help, but with the ever-changing viruses and worms, it is increasingly difficult to isolate an attachment extension (for example .scr, .exe, .com) that may or may not be used for these sinister deceptions.

1. What non-technical controls or safeguards can combat social engineering? Is end user education truly hopeless?

2. The case presents the solution of prohibiting attachments to solve the problem of users clicking on attachments. How can this solution conflict with the business mission of an organization? What is the fundamental flaw of using this technical solution to a business problem?

Endnotes

1. Daniel S. Levine, "One on One with Charles Cresson Wood of InfoSecurity Infrastructure," *Techbiz Online* (12 October 2001) [Cited 1 February 2002]; available from the World Wide Web http://www.sanfrancisco.bizjournals.com/sanfrancisco/stories/2001/10/15/newscolumn7.html.

2. Computer Security Institute, CSI/FBI "Computer Crime and Security Survey," *Computer Security Institute Online*, (April 7, 2002) [Cited 13 August 2002]; available from the World Wide Web http://www.gocsi.com/press/20020407.htm.

3. Michael Whitman, "Enemy at the Gates: Threats to Information Security," (*Communications of the ACM*, accepted 26 March 2002, forthcoming).

4. *Ibid.*

5. James T. Kennedy, "Internet Intricacies: Don't Get Caught in the Net," *Info War Online* (24 March 2000) [Cited 1 February 2002]; available from the World Wide Web http://www.inforwar.com/articles/00/article_032400a_j.shtml.

6. Merriam-Webster, "hackers," *Merriam-Webster Online* [Cited 1 February 2002]; available from the World Wide Web http://www.m-w.com/cgi-bin/dictionary.

7. Pankaj Chowdhry, "The Gibraltar Hack: Anatomy of a Break-in," *PCWeek* 16, no. 41 (1999): 1,22.

8. Linda Rosencrance, "Teen hacker 'Mafiaboy' sentenced," *ComputerWorld Online* (13 September 2001); available from the World Wide Web http://www.computerworld.com/securitytopics/security/story/0,10801,63823,00.html.

9. Excerpt from *Takedown*, "Kevin Mitnick," *Takedown Online* [Cited 1 February 2002]; available from the World Wide Web http://www.takedown.com/bio/mitnick1.html.

10. Reuters, "Hacker Legend Meets Former Target." *ZDNet Online* (21 February 2002); available from the World Wide Web http://www.zdnet.com.com/2100-1105-842318.html.

11. Brian McWilliams, "Failed Blackmail Attempt Leads to Credit Card Theft," *Internetnews.com Online* (9 January 2000) [Cited 1 February 2002]; available from the World Wide Web http://www.internetnews.com/ec-news/article.php/4_278091.

12. USA Today, "Student Charged with Online Blackmail," *USA Today Online* (7 June 2000) [Cited 1 February 2002]; available from the World Wide Web http://www.usatoday.com/life/cyber/tech/cth969.htm.

13. Lawrence M. Walsh and Anne Saita, "Hacked Off: Black Hat and DefCon Served their Purpose, but Failed to Live up to Expectations," *Information Security Magazine Online* (August 2001) [Cited 1 February 2002]; available from the World Wide Web http://www.infosecuritymag.com/articles/august01/departments_news.shtml.

14. Sam Costello, "Attrition.org stops mirroring Web site defacements," *ComputerWorld Online* (22 May 2001); available from the World Wide Web. http://www.computerworld.com/securitytopics/security/story/0,10801,60769,00.html.

15. Dorothy E. Denning, "Activism, Hacktivism, and Cyberterrorism: The Internet as a Tool for Influencing Foreign Policy," *Info War Online* (4 February 2000) [Cited 1 February 2002]; available from the World Wide Web http://www.infowar.com/class_2/00/class2_020400b_j.shtml.

16. *Ibid.*

17. April Brousseau, "Cybersecurity Threat Evaluated," *2001 MEDiA Student Group Online* [Cited 1 February 2002]; available from the World Wide Web http://media.sa.utoronto.ca/jup460/april.pdf.

18. Infowar.com, "Hacker's Death: Murder or Suicide?" *Info War Online* (2 December 1998) [Cited 1 February 2002]; available from the World Wide Web http://www.infowar.com/hacker/hack_120298d_j.shtml.

19. John Gehl and Suzanne Douglas, "Low-Risk, High Payoff Crime," *Edupage Newsletter Online* (5 October 1997) [Cited 1 February 2002]; available from the World Wide Web http://www.ee.surrey.ac.uk/Contrib/Edupage/1997/10/05-10-1997.html#7.

20. D. Ian Hopper, "'Mafiaboy' Faces up to 3 Years in Prison," *CNN.com Online* (19 April 2000) [Cited 1 February 2002]; available from the World Wide Web http://www.cnn.com/2000/TECH/computing/04/19/dos.charges/index.html.

21. Bernhard Warner, "Internet Firm Hacked Out of Business," *Tech Update Online* [Cited 1 February 2002]; available from the World Wide Web http://www.techupdate.zdnet.com/techupdate/stories/main/0,14179,2844881,00.html.

22. Brendan P. Kehoe, *Zen and the Art of the Internet,* 1st Edition (January 1992) [Cited 1 February 2002]; available from the World Wide Web. http://www.cs.indiana.edu/docproject/zen/zen-1.0_10.html#SEC91.

23. FOLDOC, "Intellectual Property," *FOLDOC Online* (27 March 1997) [Cited 1 February 2002]; available from the World Wide Web http://wombat.doc.ic.ac.uk/foldoc.doc.ic.ac.uk/foldoc/foldoc.cgi?query=Intellectual+property&action=Search.

24. Natalie Patton, "Bootlegged Software Could Cost Community College," *Las Vegas Review Journal Online* (18 September 1997) [Cited 1 February 2002]; available from the World Wide Web http://www.lvrj.com/lvrj_home/1997/Sep-18-Thu-1997/news/6072867.html.

25. Excerpt from *The Desert Wings*, "Murphy's Law was Born Here," [Cited 1 February 2002]; available from the World Wide Web http://www.edwards.af.mil/history/docs_html/tidbits/murphy's_law.html.

26. Alexander Wolfe, "Intel Preps Plan to Bust Bugs in Pentium MPUs," *Electronic Engineering Times* no. 960 (June 1997): 1.

27. Roger Taylor, "Intel to Launch New Chip Despite Bug Reports," *Financial Times* (London), 25 June 1998, 52.

28. Trusecure, "Trusecure Successfully Defends Customers Against Goner Virus," *Trusecure Online* (18 December 2001) [Cited 1 February 2002]; available from the World Wide Web http://www.trusecure.com/html/news/press/2001/prgoner121801.shtml.

29. SANS Institute, "Back Door,? "NSA Glossary of Terms Used in Security and Intrusion Detection," *SANS Institute Online* [Cited 1 February 2002]; available from the World Wide Web http://www.sans.org/newlook/resources/glossary.html>.

30. SANS Institute, "The Twenty Most Critical Internet Security Vulnerabilities (Updated): The Experts' Consensus," *SANS Institute Online* (2 May 2002): available from the World Wide Web http://www.sans.org/top20.html.

31. SANS Institute, "Consensus Roadmap for Defeating Distributed Denial of Service Attacks: A Project of the Partnership for Critical Infrastructure Security," *SANS Institute Online*, (23 February 2000) [Cited 1 February 2002]; available from the World Wide Web http://www.sans.org/ddos_roadmap.html.

32. Paul Brooke, "DDoS: Internet Weapons of Mass Destruction," *Network Computing* 12, no. 1 (January 2001): 67.

33. CERT® Advisory CA-2001-19 'Code Red' Worm Exploiting Buffer Overflow in IIS Indexing Service DLL? CERT, "'Code Red' Worm Exploiting Buffer Overflow in IIS Indexing Service DLL," advisory CA-2001-19.

34. CERT® Advisory CA-1996-21 TCP SYN Flooding and IP Spoofing Attacks, CERT, "TCP SYN Flooding and IP Spoofing Attacks," advisory CA-1996-21.

35. Webopedia, "IP spoofing," *Webopedia Online* (4 June 2002) [Cited 1 February 2002]; available from the World Wide Web http://www.webopedia.com/TERM/I/IP_spoofing.html.

36. Bhavin Bharat Bhansali, "Man-In-The-Middle Attack: A Brief." *SANS Institute Online* (16 February 2001) [Cited 1 February 2002]; available from the World Wide Web http://www.sans.org/threats/middle.php.

37. James Pearce, "Security Expert Warns of MP3 Danger," *ZDNet News Online* (18 March 2002); available from the World Wide Web http://zdnet.com.com/2100-1105-861995.html.

38. Webopedia, "sniffer," *Webopedia Online* (5 February 2002) [Cited 1 February 2002], available from the World Wide Web http://www.webopedia.com/TERM/s/sniffer.html.

39. CERT® Advisory CA-1991-03 Unauthorized Password Change Requests Via Mail Messages, CERT, "Unauthorized Password Change Requests Via Mail Messages," advisory CA-1991-03.

40. Elinor Abreu, "Kevin Mitnick Bares All," *NetworkWorldFusion News Online* (28 September 2000) [Cited 1 February 2002]; available from the World Wide Web http://www.nwfusion.com/news/2000/0928mitnick.html.

41. SearchSecurity.com, "buffer overflow," *SearchSecurity.com Online* (1 May 2001) [Cited 1 February 2002]; available from the World Wide Web http://searchsecurity.techtarget.com/sDefinition/0, sid14_gci549024,00.html.

42. Scott Spanbauer, "Pentium Bug, Meet the IE 4.0 Flaw," *PC World* 16, no. 2 (February 1998): 55.

43. Princeton University, "Standard Feature of Web Browser Design Leaves Opening For Privacy Attacks," *Science Daily Online* (8 December 2000) [Cited 1 February 2002]; available from the World Wide Web http://www.sciencedaily.com/releases/2000/12/001208074325.htm.

44. Gaël Hachez, François Koeune, and Jean-Jacques Quisquater, "Timing attack: what can be achieved by a powerful adversary?" (Proceedings of the 20th symposium on Information Theory in the Benelux, May 1999), 63-70.

45. Dennis Fisher, "MyLife.B Worm Deletes Infected PC's Files," *eWeek Online* (22 March 2002); available from the World Wide Web http://www.eweek.com/article/0,3658,s=712&a=24459,00.asp.

46. *Ibid.*

47. *Ibid.*

48. Andrew Conry-Murray, "Social Engineering: Low-Tech Tools for Virus Writers," *Network Magazine* 16, no. 7 (July 2001): 20.

49. *Ibid.*

50. *Ibid.*

3

Legal, Ethical and Professional Issues in Information Security

HENRY MAGRUDER MADE A MISTAKE. It was a pretty simple mistake as far as mistakes go: he left a CD at the coffee station. But, Iris Majwubu was at the coffee station, topping off her coffee cup in anticipation of another three-hour, deep-coding session back at her cubicle. With a little luck and some hard concentration, she could wrap up the work on the current SQL code module before it was time to go home. As she turned to leave, she saw the unlabeled CD on the counter. Being the helpful sort, she picked it up with the intention of finding the person who had forgotten it.

Thinking it was the latest device drivers, or someone's work from the development team's office, Iris slipped the disk into the drive of her computer and opened the browsing program. What she saw did not make sense. She was correct in assuming the CD contained data files, lots of them. She picked one file at random and names, addresses, and social security numbers scrolled down her screen. These were not the test records she expected, but rather looked more like a critical payroll file. Concerned, she found a readme.txt file and opened it. It read:

> Jill, see files on this disc. Hope they meet your expectations. Wire money to my account as arranged. Rest of data sent on payment.

Iris realized that someone was selling sensitive company data to an outside information broker. She looked back at the directory listing and saw the files spanned the range of every department at Sequential Label and Supply—everything from customer lists to shipping invoices. She saw one file that she knew contained the credit card numbers for every Web customer the company supplied. She opened another file and saw that it stopped about halfway through the data. Whoever did this had split the data into two parts. That made sense, payment on delivery of the first half.

Now, who did this belong to? She opened up the file properties option on the readme file. The file owner was listed as "hmagruder." That must be Henry Magruder, the developer two cubes over in the next aisle. Iris picked up the disc and headed toward his cube.

DISCUSSION QUESTIONS:

1. Was Iris justified in determining who the owner of the CD was?
2. Should Iris approach Henry directly or is there a better action to take?
3. Should Iris have placed the CD back at the coffee station and forgotten the whole thing? Is that an ethical response?

LEARNING OBJECTIVES:

Upon completion of this material you should be able to:

- Use this chapter as a guide for future reference on laws, regulations, and professional organizations.
- Differentiate between laws and ethics.
- Identify major national laws that relate to the practice of information security.
- Understand the role of culture as it applies to ethics in information security.

Introduction

This chapter covers information security law and ethics. Although the two topics are intertwined throughout, the first part of this chapter focuses on relevant legislation and regulation concerning the management of information in an organization. The second part of the chapter presents ethical issues for information security as well as a summary of professional organizations with established ethical codes. Use this chapter both as a reference to the legal aspects of information security and as an aide in planning your professional career.

As a future information security professional, it is vital to understand the scope of an organization's legal and ethical responsibilities. The information security professional plays an important role in an organization's approach to controlling liability for privacy and security risks. In the modern litigious societies of the world, sometimes laws are enforced in civil courts where damages to plaintiffs are assessed at high values against organizations. Sometimes high damages are assessed to set an example. To minimize these liabilities and reduce risks from electronic and physical threats, and to reduce the losses from legal action, information security practitioners must be on their toes. They must understand the current legal environment, stay current with new laws and regulations, and watch for new issues as they emerge. By educating the management and employees of an organization on their legal and ethical obligations and the proper use of information technology and information security, security professionals can help keep an organization focused on its primary objectives.

Law and Ethics in Information Security

As individuals we elect to trade some aspects of personal freedom for social order. As Jean-Jacques Rousseau explains in *The Social Contract Or Principles Of Political Right*[1] (1762), the rules the members of a society create to balance the right of the individual for self-determination with the needs of the whole are called "laws." Laws are needed when individuals choose not to follow social norms. **Laws** are rules adopted for determining expected behavior in modern society and are drawn from **ethics**, which define socially acceptable behaviors. The key difference between laws and ethics is that law carries the sanction of a governing authority and ethics do not. Ethics in turn are based on **cultural mores**: fixed moral attitudes or customs of a particular group. Some ethics are recognized as universal among cultures. For example, murder, theft, assault, and arson are commonly accepted as actions that deviate from ethical and legal codes in the civilized world.

Types Of Law

There are a number of ways to categorize laws. **Civil law** represents a wide variety of laws that are recorded in volumes of legal code available for review by the average citizen. **Criminal law** addresses violations harmful to society and is actively enforced through prosecution by the state. **Tort law** allows individuals to seek recourse against others in the event of personal, physical, or financial injury. Torts are enforced through individual lawsuits rather than criminal prosecutions by the state. When someone brings a legal action under tort law, personal attorneys present the evidence and argue the details rather than representatives of the state who prosecute criminal cases.

The groups of laws that affect the individual in the workplace are called private law and public law. **Private law** regulates the relationship between the individual and the organization, and encompasses family law, commercial law, and labor law. **Public law** regulates the structure and administration of government agencies and their relationships with citizens, employees, and other governments, providing careful checks and balances. Examples of public law include criminal, administrative, and constitutional law.

Relevant U.S. Laws

Historically, the United States has been a leader in the development and implementation of information security legislation to prevent misuse and exploitation of information and information technology. The development of information security legislation promotes the general welfare and creates a stable environment for a solid economy.[2] In this global leadership capacity, the nation has demonstrated a clear understanding of the problems facing the information security field and has identified necessary penalties for the individuals and organizations that fail to follow the requirements set forth in the U.S. civil statutes. The sections that follow present the most important U.S. laws that apply to information security.

General Computer Crime Laws

There are several key laws that impact the field of information security. The **Computer Fraud and Abuse Act of 1986 (CFA Act)** is the cornerstone of many computer-related federal laws and enforcement efforts. It was amended in October 1996 by the **National Information Infrastructure Protection Act of 1996**, which modified several sections of the previous act, and increased the penalties for selected crimes. The punishment for offenses prosecuted under this statute varies from fines to imprisonment for up to 20 years, or both. The penalty depends on the value of the information obtained and whether the offense is judged to have been committed:

1. For purposes of commercial advantage
2. For private financial gain
3. In furtherance of a criminal act

The previous law was further changed when the **U.S.A. Patriot Act of 2001** modified a wide range of existing laws to provide law enforcement agencies with a broader latitude of actions to combat terrorism-related activities. Some of the laws modified by the Patriot Act date from the earliest laws created to deal with electronic technology.

The **Communication Act of 1934** was revised by the **Telecommunications Deregulation and Competition Act of 1996**, which attempts to modernize the archaic terminology of the older act. These much-needed updates of terminology were included as part of the **Communications Decency Act (CDA)**. The CDA was immediately ensnared in a thorny legal debate over the attempt to define indecency, which through major publicity efforts sponsored by the Internet Blue Ribbon Campaign and by the Electronic Freedom Frontier (*www.eff.org*), quickly reached the Supreme Court. Unfortunately, the subsequent Supreme Court ruling left weak and ineffective controls in place of the more aggressive and ambitious law originally intended.

Another key law that is of critical importance for the information security profession is the **Computer Security Act of 1987**. It was one of the first attempts to protect federal computer systems by establishing minimum acceptable security practices. The National Bureau of Standards, in cooperation with the National Security Agency, became responsible for developing these security standards and guidelines.

Privacy

The issue of privacy has become one of the hottest topics in information security at the beginning of the twenty-first century. Many organizations are collecting, swapping, and selling personal information as a commodity, and many individuals are becoming aware of these practices and looking to governments for protection of their privacy. The ability to collect information on an individual, combine facts from separate sources, and merge it with other information has resulted in databases of information that were previously impossible to set up. Figure 3-1 shows a technology that could be used by others to monitor or track private communications. The Clipper Chip, diagrammed in Figure 3-1, was reportedly designed to protect individual communications while allowing the government to decrypt suspect transmissions. The Clipper Chip uses the Skipjack algorithm with a two-part key that was to be managed by two separate government agencies.[3] The Clipper Chip was the target of massive privacy campaigns.

In response to the pressure for privacy protection, the number of statutes addressing an individual's right to privacy has grown. It must be understood, however, that **privacy** in this context is not absolute freedom from observation, but rather is a more precise "state of being free from unsanctioned intrusion."[4] To better understand this rapidly evolving issue, some of the more relevant privacy laws are presented here.

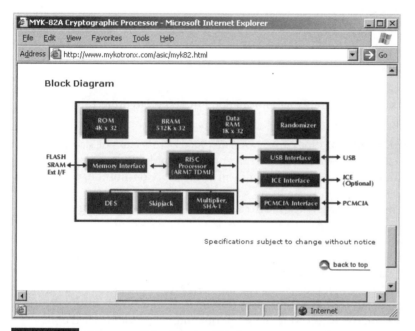

FIGURE 3-1   Diagram of the Clipper Chip

Privacy of Customer Information

Part of the regulations represented in the U.S. legal code specifies the responsibilities of common carriers (organizations that process or move data for hire) to protect the confidentiality of customer information, including that of other carriers. The **Privacy of Customer Information Section** of the common carrier regulation specifies that any proprietary information shall be used explicitly for providing services, and not for any marketing purposes.[5] It also stipulates that carriers cannot disclose this information except when necessary to provide its services. The only other exception is when a customer requests the disclosure of information, and then the disclosure is restricted to that customer's information only. This law does allow for the use of aggregate information, as long as the same information is provided to all common carriers, and the carrier in question conducts business with fair competition. **Aggregate information** is created by combining pieces of data that are not considered private in themselves, but may raise privacy concerns when taken together. This is particularly important for customers whose data is collected in software updates and with cookies.

While the common carrier regulation described above regulates public carriers in the protection of an individual's privacy, **The Federal Privacy Act of 1974** regulates the government in the protection of individual privacy. The Federal Privacy Act was created to insure that government agencies protect the privacy of individuals' and businesses' information and to hold those agencies responsible if any portion of this information is released without permission. The following agencies are exempted from some of the regulations so that they can perform their duties:

- Bureau of the Census
- National Archives and Records Administration
- Congress
- Comptroller General
- Certain court orders
- Credit agencies
- Individuals who demonstrate that information is necessary to protect the health or safety of that individual.

The **Electronic Communications Privacy Act of 1986** is a collection of statutes that regulate the interception of wire, electronic, and oral communications. These statutes work in conjunction with the Fourth Amendment of the U.S. Constitution, which provides protections from unlawful search and seizure.

The **Health Insurance Portability and Accountability Act Of 1996 (HIPAA)** also known as the Kennedy-Kassebaum Act, is an attempt to protect the confidentiality and security of health-care data by establishing and enforcing standards and by standardizing electronic data interchange. HIPAA impacts all health-care organizations including doctors' practices, health clinics, life insurers, and universities, as well as some organizations which have self-insured employee health programs. HIPAA provides stiff penalties for organizations that fail to comply with the law, with up to $250,000 and or 10 years imprisonment for knowingly misusing client information. Organizations had until April 14, 2003, to comply with the act although extensions to this deadline have since been granted.[6]

How does this affect the field of information security? Beyond the basic privacy guidelines, the act requires organizations that retain health-care information to use information security mechanisms to protect this information, as well as policies and procedures to maintain this security. It also requires a comprehensive assessment of the organization's information security systems, policies, and procedures. Electronic signatures have become more prevalent, and HIPAA provides guidelines for the use of these signatures based on security standards that ensure message integrity, user authentication, and nonrepudiation. There is no specification of particular security technologies for each of the security requirements, only that security must be implemented to ensure the privacy of the health-care information.

The privacy standards of HIPAA severely restrict the dissemination and distribution of private health information without documented consent. The standards provide patients the right to know who has access to their information and who has accessed it. The standards also restrict the use of health information to the minimum required for the health-care services required.

HIPAA has five fundamental principles to support these new changes:

1. Consumer control of medical information
2. Boundaries on the use of medical information
3. Accountability for the privacy of private information
4. Balance of public responsibility for the use of medical information for the greater good measured against impact to the individual
5. Security of health information

The **Financial Services Modernization Act** or **Gramm-Leach-Bliley Act of 1999** contains a number of provisions focusing on facilitating affiliation among banks, securities firms, and insurance companies. Specifically this act requires all financial institutions to disclose their privacy policies on the sharing of nonpublic personal information. It also requires due notice to customers, so that they can request that their information not be shared with third parties. The act also ensures that the privacy policies in effect in an organization are fully disclosed when a customer initiates a business relationship, as well as distributed at least annually for the duration of the professional association.

This discussion of computer crime laws is supplemented with additional details regarding each law in Table 3-1.

Table 3-1   Key U.S. Laws of Interest to Information Security Professionals

Act	Subject	Date	Web resource location	Description
Communications Act of 1934, updated by Telecommunications Deregulation and Competition Act of 1996	Telecommunications	1934 (amended 1996 and 2001)	*www.fcc.gov/Reports/ 1934new.pdf*	Regulates interstate and foreign telecommunications
Computer Fraud and Abuse Act (also known as Fraud and Related Activity in Connection with Computers (18 U.S.C. 1030)	Threats to computers	1986 (amended 1994, 1996 and 2001)	*www.usdoj.gov/ criminal/cybercrime/ 1030_new.html*	Defines and formalizes laws to counter threats from computer-related acts and offenses
Computer Security Act of 1987	Federal Agency Information Security	1997	*www.cio.gov/ Documents/ computer_security_ act_Jan_1998.html*	Requires all federal computer systems that contain classified information to have surety plans in place, and requires periodic security training for all individuals who operate, design or manage such systems

Table 3-1   Key U.S. Laws of Interest to Information Security Professionals (continued)

Act	Subject	Date	Web resource location	Description
Economic Espionage Act of 1996	Trade secrets	1996	*www.ncix.gov/pubs/ online/eea_96.htm*	Designed to prevent abuse of information gained by an individual working in one company and employed by another
Electronic Communications Privacy Act Of 1986	Cryptography	1986	*www.itpolicy.gsa.gov/ itpolicy/5.pdf*	Also referred to as the Federal Wiretapping Act; regulates interception and disclosure of electronic information
Federal Privacy Act Of 1974	Privacy	1974	*www.usdoj.gov/foia/ privstat.htm*	Governs federal agency use of personal information
Gramm-Leach-Bliley Act of 1999 (GLB) or Financial Services Modernization Act	Banking	1999	*www.senate.gov/~ banking/conf/*	Focuses on facilitating affiliation among banks, insurance, and securities firms; it has significant impact on the privacy of personal information used by these industries
Health Insurance Portability and Accountability Act (HIPAA)	Health care privacy	1996	*www.hhs.gov/ocr/hipaa/*	Regulates health care, storage, and transmission of sensitive personal information
National Information Infrastructure Protection Act of 1996	Criminal intent	1996	*http://policyworks.gov/ policydocs/14.pdf*	Categorized crimes based on defendant's authority to access computer *and* criminal intent
U.S.A. Patriot Act of 2001 (H.R. 3162) H.R.3162:	Terrorism	2001	*http://thomas.loc.gov/ cgi-bin/bdquery/z?d107:*	Defines stiffer penalties for prosecution of terrorist crimes

Export and Espionage Laws

The discussion up to this point has been focused on domestic laws and issues. There are also considerations to be made for international issues. The protection of national security, trade secrets, and a variety of other state and private assets has led to several laws impacting what information and information management and security resources may be exported from the United States. These laws attempt to stem the theft of information by establishing strong penalties for related crimes. The Economic Espionage Act of 1996 and the Security and Freedom Through Encryption Act of 1999 are two laws that directly affect information security.

In an attempt to protect American ingenuity, intellectual property, and competitive advantage, Congress passed the **Economic Espionage Act (EEA)** in 1996. This law attempts to prevent trade secrets from being illegally shared.

The **Security And Freedom Through Encryption Act of 1999** was an attempt by Congress to provide guidance on the use of encryption, and provided measures of public protection from government intervention. The act's provisions include the following:

- Reinforces an individual's right to use or sell encryption algorithms, without concern for regulations requiring some form of key registration. Key registration is the storage of a cryptographic key (or its text equivalent) with another party to be used to break the encryption of data. This is often called "key escrow."
- Prohibits the federal government from requiring the use of encryption for contracts, grants, and other official documents, and correspondence.
- States that the use of encryption is not probable cause to suspect criminal activity.
- Relaxes export restrictions by amending the Export Administration Act of 1979.
- Provides additional penalties for the use of encryption in the commission of a criminal act.

As illustrated in Figure 3-2, the distribution of many software packages is restricted to only approved organizations, governments, and countries.

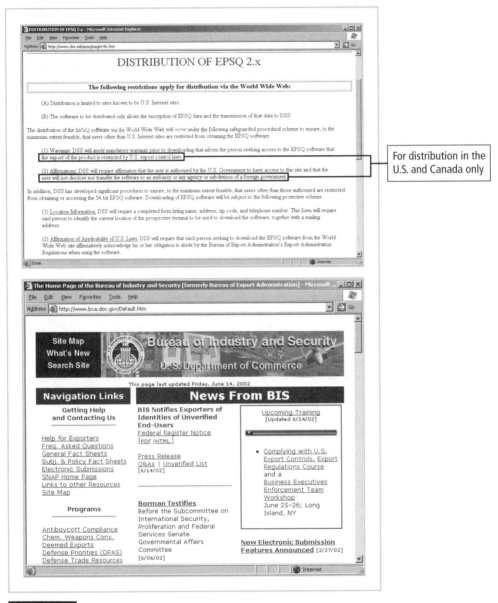

FIGURE 3-2   Export and Espionage

U.S. Copyright Law

Intellectual property is recognized as a protected asset in the United States. The U.S. copyright laws extend this right to the published word, including electronic formats. Fair use of copyrighted materials includes the use to support news reporting, teaching, scholarship, and a number of other related permissions, so long as the use is for educational or library purposes, not for profit, and is not excessive. As long as proper acknowledgement is provided to the original author of such works, including proper description of the location of source materials (citation) and the work is not represented as one's own, it is entirely permissible to include portions of someone else's work as reference. For more detailed information on copyright regulations, visit the Web site pictured in Figure 3-3.

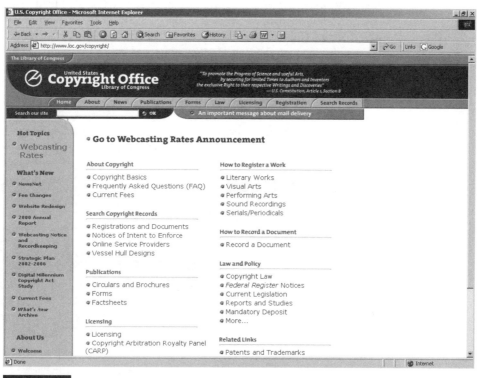

FIGURE 3-3 U.S. Copyright Office Web site

Freedom of Information Act of 1966 (FOIA)

The Freedom of Information Act provides any person with the right to request access to federal agency records or information, not determined to be a matter of national security. Agencies of the federal government are required to disclose any requested information on receipt of a written request. This requirement is enforceable in court. There are exceptions for information that is protected from disclosure, and the act does not apply to state or local government agencies or to private businesses or individuals, although many states have their own version of the FOIA.

State And Local Regulations

In addition to the national and international restrictions placed on an organization in the use of computer technology, each state or locality may have a number of laws and regulations that impact organization. It is the responsibility of the information security professional to understand state laws and regulations and insure the organization's security policies and procedures comply with those laws and regulations.

  For example, the state of Georgia recently passed the Georgia Computer Systems Protection Act. It emphasizes protection of information, and establishes additional penalties for the use of information technology to attack or exploit information systems in organizations.

International Laws and Legal Bodies

It is important for IT professionals and information security practitioners to realize that when their organizations do business on the Internet, they do business globally. As a result, these professionals must be sensitive to the laws and ethical values of many different cultures, societies, and countries. While it may be impossible to please all of the people all of the time, dealing with the laws of other states and nations is one area where it is certainly *not* easier to ask forgiveness than permission.

A number of different security bodies and laws are described in this section. Because of the political complexities of the relationships between nations, and the differences in culture, there are currently few international laws relating to privacy and information security. The laws discussed below are important, but are limited in their enforceability. A typical American institution that deals in international law is shown in Figure 3-4.

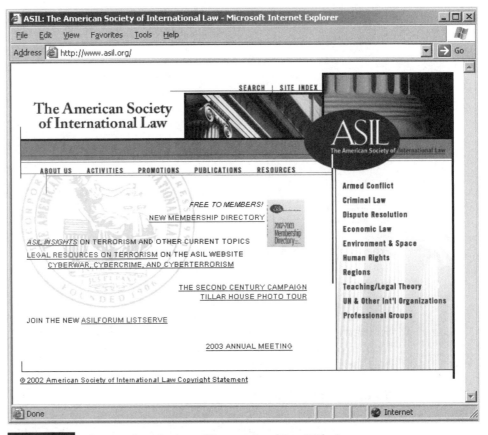

FIGURE 3-4 The American Society of International Law Web site

European Council Cyber-Crime Convention

Recently the Council of Europe drafted the **European Council Cyber-Crime Convention**. It is designed to create an international task force to oversee a range of security functions associated with Internet activities, and to standardize technology laws across international borders. It also attempts to improve the effectiveness of international investigations into breaches of technology law. This convention is well received by advocates of intellectual property rights because of its emphasis on copyright infringement prosecution. See Figure 3-5 for information on the European Union (EU) Law portal.

As with any complex legislation at the international level, the Cyber-Crime Convention lacks any realistic provisions for enforcement. The overall goal of the convention is to simplify the acquisition of information for law enforcement agencies in certain types of international crimes. It also simplifies the extradition process. The convention has more than its share of skeptics who see it as an ambiguous attempt to control a complex problem. Adversaries of the convention are afraid that it could create more problems than it resolves. As the product of a number of governments, the convention tends to favor the interests of national agencies over the rights of businesses, organizations, and individuals.

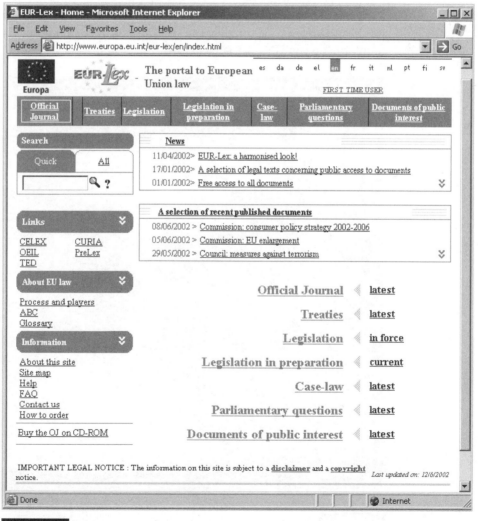

FIGURE 3-5 EU Law Portal

Digital Millennium Copyright Act (DMCA)

The Digital Millennium Copyright Act (DMCA) is the American version of an international effort to reduce the impact of copyright, trademark, and privacy infringement especially through the removal of technological copyright protection measures. In 1995, the European Union also put forward **Directive 95/46/EC** to further protect individuals with regard to the processing of personal data and the free movement of such data. The United Kingdom has already implemented a version of this directive called the **Database Right**.

United Nations Charter

To some degree the **United Nations Charter** provides provisions for information security during information warfare. **Information Warfare (IW)** involves the use of information technology to conduct offensive operations as part of an organized and lawful military operation by a sovereign state. IW is a relatively new application of warfare, although the military has been conducting electronic warfare and counterwarfare operations for decades by jamming, intercepting, and spoofing enemy communications. See Figure 3-6 for information on UN International Law.

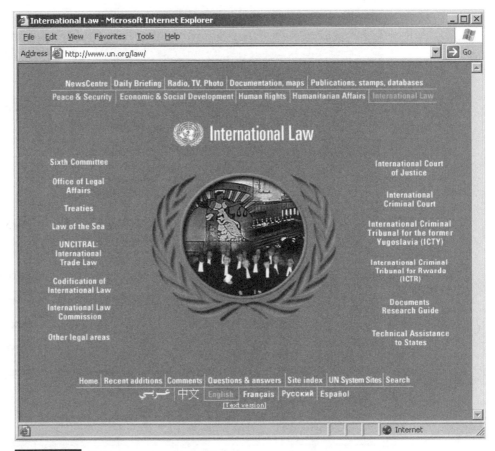

FIGURE 3-6 UN International Law Web site

Policy Versus Law

The sections above discuss the legal issues of information security both in the United States and on the international scene. An information security professional must be informed of the legal regulations that this chapter presents. In addition, a thorough understanding of how information security is maintained within an organization through the establishment of policies is also important. Most organizations develop and formalize a body of expectations that describe acceptable and unacceptable behaviors of employees in the workplace. This body of expectations is called **policy**. Properly executed policies function in an organization as laws, complete with penalties, judicial practices, and sanctions to require compliance. Because these policies function as laws, they must be crafted with the same care to ensure that the policies are complete, appropriate, and fairly applied to everyone in the workplace. The difference between a policy and a law however, is that ignorance of policy is an acceptable defense. For a policy to become enforceable, it must be:

- Distributed to all individuals who are expected to comply with it
- Readily available for employee reference
- Easily understood with multilanguage translations and translations for visually impaired or literacy-impaired employees
- Acknowledged by the employee, usually by means of a signed form.

Only when all of these conditions are met can an organization appropriately penalize, without fear of legal retribution, employees who violate policy.

Ethical Concepts in Information Security

To begin considering the topic of ethical concepts, take a look at the Ten Commandments of computer ethics in the Offline box.

Cultural Differences in Ethical Concepts

Differences in culture causes problems in determining what is ethical and what is not ethical—especially when considering the use of a computer. Studies of ethical sensitivity to computer use reveal that individuals of different nationalities have different perspectives on ethics. Difficulties arise when one nationality's ethical behavior conflicts with that of another national group. For example, Western cultures consider the Asian use of computer technology a hotbed for software piracy.[7] The conflict of ethics between the Western culture and these Asian nations arises out of the Asian tradition of collective ownership. This Eastern tradition clashes with the West's ideological protection of intellectual property. There is also the fundamental problem of "If it's not enforced, it's not a law." Approximately 90 percent of all software is created in the United States. Some countries are more relaxed with intellectual property copy restrictions than others.

OFFLINE

The Ten Commandments of Computer Ethics[8]

From The Computer Ethics Institute

1. Thou shalt not use a computer to harm other people.
2. Thou shalt not interfere with other people's computer work.
3. Thou shalt not snoop around in other people's computer files.
4. Thou shalt not use a computer to steal.
5. Thou shalt not use a computer to bear false witness.
6. Thou shalt not copy or use proprietary software for which you have not paid.
7. Thou shalt not use other people's computer resources without authorization or proper compensation.
8. Thou shalt not appropriate other people's intellectual output.
9. Thou shalt think about the social consequences of the program you are writing or the system you are designing.
10. Thou shalt always use a computer in ways that insure consideration and respect for your fellow humans.

A recent study by Dr. Michael Whitman of Kennesaw State University published in the Journal of International Business Studies has examined computer use ethics among nine countries: Singapore, Hong Kong, United States, England, Australia, Sweden, Wales, and the Netherlands.[9] This study selected a number of computer-use vignettes (see Offline: Use of Scenarios in Computer Ethics Studies) and presented them to students in universities in these nine countries. This study did not categorize or classify the responses as ethical or unethical. Instead the responses only indicated a degree of ethical sensitivity or knowledge about the performance of the individuals in the short case studies. The scenarios were grouped into three categories of ethical computer use: software license infringement, illicit use, and misuse of resources.

Software License Infringement

The topic of software license infringement or piracy routinely fills the popular press. Overall, most of the countries studied had similar attitudes toward software piracy. Statistically speaking, only the United States and the Netherlands had attitudes that differed substantially from all other countries examined. The United States. was significantly less tolerant of piracy, while the Netherlands was significantly more permissive. Although a number of studies have reported that the Pacific Rim countries of Singapore and Hong Kong are hotbeds of pirate activities, this study found their tolerance for copyright infringement to be moderate, as were the attitudes of England, Wales, Australia, and Sweden. What this could mean is that the individuals surveyed *understood* what software license infringement was, but either felt their use was not piracy, or that their society permitted it anyway. Peer pressure, the lack of legal disincentives, the lack of punitive measures, or any one of a number of other reasons could also explain why these alleged piracy centers were not oblivious to intellectual property laws. Even though the Netherlands displayed a more permissive attitude towards piracy, they only ranked third in piracy rates of the countries represented in this study.

Illicit Use

The individuals studied unilaterally condemned viruses, hacking, and other forms of system abuse as unacceptable behavior. There were however, differences in groups as to just how tolerant individuals were. Singapore and Hong Kong proved to be significantly more tolerant than the United States, Wales, England, and Australia. Sweden and the Netherlands were also significantly more tolerant than Wales and Australia but significantly less tolerant than Hong Kong. The low overall degree of tolerance for illicit system use may be a function of the easy association between the common crimes of breaking and entering, trespassing, theft, and destruction of property to their computer-related counterparts.

Misuse of Corporate Resources

The scenarios used to examine the levels of tolerance in this category each represented a different degree of noncompany use of corporate assets, with no indication of established policy toward personal use of company resources. In general, individuals displayed a rather lenient view of personal use of company equipment. Only Singapore and Hong Kong view personal use of company equipment as unethical. There were several substantial differences in this category, with the Netherlands reporting the most lenient view. Regardless of cultural background, with the exceptions of Singapore and Hong Kong, it is apparent that many individuals feel that if an organization does not specifically forbid personal use of its computing resources, such use is acceptable. It is interesting to note that only the two Asian samples, Singapore and Hong Kong, reported generally intolerant attitudes toward personal use of organizational computing resources. The reasons behind this are unknown.

Overall, the researchers found that there is a general agreement among nationalities as to what is acceptable or unacceptable computer use. There is however, a range of views within the acknowledgement of ethical versus unethical behavior as to whether some actions are moderately or severely acceptable or not. "Thus, the results of this study underscore intercultural similarities as much as they describe inter-cultural differences. The study also found little to support, from an ethical perspective, the popular media's portrayal of Asians as 'digital bandits.' In fact, the Hong Kong and Singapore respondents were not consistently the most permissive nationalities among those studied. As noted earlier, the higher piracy rates in Singapore and Hong Kong may be less a function of ethical difference and more a function of the lack of legal and financial disincentive to engage in software copyright infringement. The only country that consistently ranked as 'most tolerant' was the Netherlands. However, this level of tolerance does not seem to have completely manifested itself in action; although the Netherlands has a higher piracy rate than the United States, Australia, Wales, England and Sweden, it still ranks behind Singapore and Hong Kong."[10]

When considering ethical issues of information security, it is useful to judge practical situations. The Offline box on scenarios in computer ethics is designed to challenge your judgement and get you thinking.

OFFLINE

The Use Of Scenarios In Computer Ethics Studies

Adapted from "Cross-National Differences in Computer-Use Ethics: A Nine Country Study" By Michael E. Whitman, Anthony M. Townsend, and Anthony R. Hendrickson, The Journal of International Business Studies.

The following vignettes can be used in an open and frank discussion of computer ethics. Review each scenario carefully and respond to each question using the following statement, choosing the description you feel most appropriate. Then, justify your response. *I feel the actions of this individual were (very ethical / ethical / neither ethical nor unethical / unethical / very unethical).*

Ethical Decision Evaluation

Note: These scenarios are based on published works by Professor Whitman[11] and Professor Paradice.[12]

1. A scientist developed a theory that required proof through the construction of a computer model. He hired a computer programmer to build the model, and the theory was shown to be correct. The scientist won several awards for the development of the theory, but he never acknowledged the contribution of the computer programmer. *The scientist's failure to acknowledge the computer programmer was:*

2. The owner of a small business needed a computer-based accounting system. One day, he identified the various inputs and outputs he felt were required to satisfy his needs. Then he showed his design to a computer programmer and asked the programmer if she could implement such a system. The programmer knew she could implement the system because she had developed much more sophisticated systems in the past. In fact, she felt this design was rather crude and would soon need several major revisions. But, she didn't say anything about her feelings, because the business owner didn't ask her and she thought she might be the one hired to implement the needed revisions later.
The programmer's decision not to point out the design flaws was:

3. A student suspected and found a loophole in the university computer's security system that allowed him access to other students' records. He told the system administrator about the loophole, but continued to access others' record until the problem was corrected two weeks later.
The student's action in searching for the loophole was:
The student's action in continuing to access others' records for two weeks was:
The system administrator's failure to correct the problem sooner was:

4. A computer user called a mail-order software company to order a particular accounting system. When he received his order, he found that the store had accidentally sent him a very expensive word-processing program as well as the accounting package that he had ordered. The invoice listed only the accounting package had been sent. The user decided to keep the word-processing package.
The user's decision to keep the word-processing package was:

continued

5. A programmer at a bank realized that he had accidentally overdrawn his checking account. He made a small adjustment in the bank's accounting system so that his account would not have an additional service charge assessed. As soon as he deposited funds that made his balance positive again, he corrected the bank's accounting system.

   The programmer's modification of the accounting system was:

6. A computer programmer enjoyed building small computer systems (programs) to give his friends. He would frequently go to his office on Saturday when no one was working and use his employer's computer to develop systems. He did not hide the fact that he was going into the building; he had to sign a register at a security desk each time he entered.

   The programmer's use of the company computer was:
   If the programmer sold the programs his actions would have been:

7. A student enrolled in a computer class also was employed at a local business part-time. Frequently her homework in the class involved using popular word-processing and spreadsheet packages. Occasionally she worked on her homework on the office computer at her part-time job, on her coffee or meal breaks.

   The student's use of the company computer was:
   If the student had worked on her homework during "company time" (not during a break), the student's use of the company computer would have been:

8. A student at a university learned to use an expensive spreadsheet program in her accounting class. The student would go to the university microcomputer lab and use the software to complete her assignment. Signs were posted in the lab indicating that copying software was forbidden. One day, she decided to copy the software anyway to complete her work assignments at home.

   If the student destroyed her copy of the software at the end of the term, her action in copying the software was:
   If the student forgot to destroy her copy of the software at the end of the term, her action in copying the software was:
   If the student never intended to destroy her copy of the software at the end of the term, her action in copying the software was:

9. A student at a university found out that one of the local computer bulletin boards contained a "pirate" section (a section containing a collection of illegally copied software programs). He subscribed to the board, and proceeded to download several games and professional programs, which he then distributed to several of his friends.

   The student's actions in downloading the games were:
   The student's actions in downloading the programs were:
   The student's actions in sharing the programs and games with his friends were:

Ethics and Education

Differences in the ethics of computer use are not exclusively international. Differences are found among individuals within the same country, within the same social class, and within the same company. Key studies reveal that the overriding factor in leveling the ethical perceptions within a small population is education. Employees must be trained and kept aware of a number of topics related to information security, not the least of which are the expected behaviors of an ethical employee. This is especially important in areas of information security, as many employees may not have the formal technical training to understand that their behavior is unethical or even illegal. Proper ethical and legal training is vital to creating an informed, well prepared, and low-risk system user.

Deterrence to Unethical and Illegal Behavior

Whatever the cause of illegal, immoral, or unethical behavior, in information security, one thing is certain: it is the responsibility of information security personnel to do everything in their power to deter these acts, using policy, education and training, and technology to protect information and systems. Many security professionals understand the technology aspect of protection, but many underestimate the value of policy. There are three general categories of unethical and illegal behavior:

1. **Ignorance:** As mentioned earlier, ignorance of the law is no excuse, however ignorance of policy and procedures is. The first method of deterrence is education. This is accomplished through the design, publication, dissemination, and agreement to organizational policy and relevant law. Reminders, training, and awareness programs keep the information in front of the individual to better support retention and compliance.
2. **Accident:** Individuals with authorization and privileges to manage information within the organization have the highest chance to cause harm or damage by accident. The careful planning of control helps prevent accidental modification to systems and data.
3. **Intent:** Criminal or unethical intent refers to the state of mind of the individual performing the act. Intent is often the cornerstone of legal defense, whether or not the individual accused of a crime acted from ignorance, accident, or with specific intent to cause harm or damage. Intent is the area best fought through litigation, prosecution, and technical controls. Intent is but one of several characteristics an individual must possess for a computer-related crime to occur. If individuals have the will and the intent to commit crimes, they probably will.

Deterrence

Deterrence is the best method for preventing an illegal or unethical activity. Laws, policies, and technical controls are all examples of deterrents. However, it is generally agreed that laws and policies and their associated penalties only deter if three conditions are present:

1. **Fear of penalty:** The individual desiring to commit the act must fear the penalty. Threats of informal reprimand or verbal warnings may not have the same impact as the threat of imprisonment or forfeiture of pay.
2. **Probability of being caught:** The individual has to know there is a strong possibility of being caught performing the illegal or unethical act. Penalties can be severe, but the penalty will not deter the individual's behavior unless there is an expectation of being caught.
3. **Probability of penalty being administered:** The individual must believe that the penalty is severe, that they will be caught, and that they will actually receive the penalty.

Codes of Ethics, Certifications, and Professional Organizations

A number of professional organizations have established codes of conduct or codes of ethics that members are expected to follow. Codes of ethics can have a positive effect on an individual's judgment regarding computer use.[13] Unfortunately, having a code of ethics is not enough, because many employers do not encourage their employees to join these professional organizations. However, having a code can serve as a deterrent to ethical lapses when an individual has earned some level of certification or professional accreditation. The loss of accreditation or certification due to a violation of the code of conduct can dramatically reduce the individual's marketability and earning power.

It is the responsibility of security professionals to act ethically and according to the policies and procedures of their employers, their professional organizations, and the laws of society. It is likewise the organization's responsibility to develop, disseminate, and enforce its policies. Following is a discussion of organizations with established codes of ethics and where they fit into the ethics landscape. Table 3-2 provides an overview of the following organizations.

Table 3-2   Professional Organizations of Interest to Information Security Professionals

Professional Organization	Web Resource Location	Description	Focus
Association of Computing Machinery	www.acm.org	Code of 24 imperatives of personal ethical responsibilities of security professionals	Ethics of security professionals
Computer Security Division of the National Institute of Standards and Technology	csrc.nist.gov	Raising awareness of information technology security, especially in new and emerging technologies	Promotion of national information on information security
Computer Security Institute	www.gocsi.com	Policy development, risk analysis, security awareness and other vital aspects of information protection; practical insights into the technical problems of network security	Individual training courses and tracks (not certification)
Information Systems Audit and Control Association's Certified Information Systems Auditor (CISA)	www.isaca.org	One process area and six subject areas that focus on auditing, information security, business process analysis, and IS planning	Tasks and knowledge required of the information systems audit professional

| Table 3-2 | Professional Organizations of Interest to Information Security Professionals (continued) |

Professional Organization	Web Resource Location	Description	Focus
Information Systems Security Association	www.issa.org	Professional association of information systems security professionals. Provides education forums, publications, and peer networking for members	Professional security information sharing
Internet Society	www.isoc.org	Professional association of individuals and organizations with an interest in the promotion of the growth and leadership for the Internet	Internet leadership and development
International Information Systems Security Certification Consortium (ISC)2, Systems Security Certified Professional (SCCP)	www.isc2.org	International Consortium dedicated to improving the quality of security professionals	Offers Systems Security Certified Professional (SSCP) and Certified Information Systems Security Professional (CISSP) Certification for security administrators
SANS Institutes Global Information Assurance Certification	www.giac.org	Twelve individual technical certifications that can be tied into six tracks, or culminate in the capstone GIAC Security Engineer certification	Offers GIAC certification for advanced technical subject areas

Association of Computing Machinery (ACM): The ACM (*www.acm.org*, see Figure 3-7) is a respected professional society that was established in 1947 as "the world's first educational and scientific computing society." It is one of the few organizations that strongly promotes education and provides discounts for student members. The ACM's code of ethics requires members to perform their duties in a manner befitting an ethical computing professional. The code contains specific references to protecting the confidentiality of information, causing no harm (with specific references to viruses), protecting the privacy of others, and respecting the intellectual property and copyrights of others. Information security is everyone's responsibility.

The ACM also publishes a wide variety of professional computing publications, including the highly regarded *Communications of the ACM*.

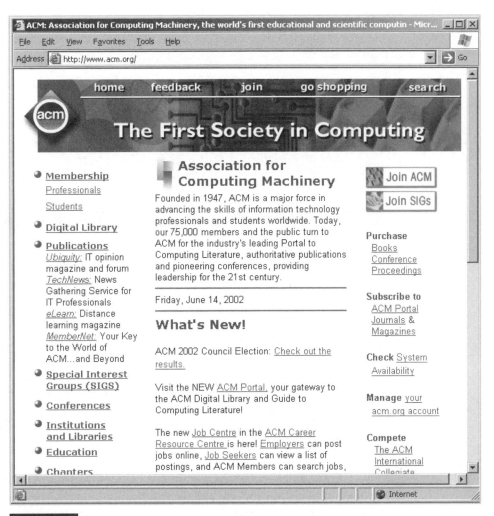

FIGURE 3-7 Association for Computer Machinery Web site

International Information Systems Security Certification Consortium, Inc. (ISC)²: The (ISC)² (*www.isc2.org*), is not a professional organization in the strictest sense, and has no membership services, but is a nonprofit organization that focuses on the development and implementation of information security certifications and credentials. The (ISC)² manages a body of knowledge on information security and administers and evaluates examinations for information security certifications. Currently the (ISC)² offers two professional certifications in the information security arena: the Certification for Information Systems Security Professionals (CISSP), and the Systems Security Certified Professional, or SSCP.

The code of ethics put forth by (ISC)² is primarily designed for information security professionals who have earned a certification from (ISC)². This code, focuses on four mandatory canons: "Protect society, the commonwealth, and the infrastructure; Act honorably, honestly, justly, responsibly, and legally; Provide diligent and competent service to principals; and Advance and protect the profession."[14] Through this code (ISC)² seeks to provide sound guidance that promotes reliance on the ethicality and trustworthiness of the information security professional as the guardian of the information and systems. Figure 3-8 shows the (ISC)² home page.

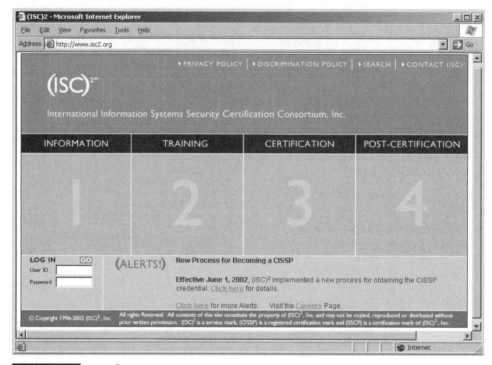

FIGURE 3-8 (ISC)² home page

System Administration, Networking, and Security Institute (SANS): The System Administration, Networking, and Security Institute, or SANS *(www.sans.org)*, is a professional organization with a large membership dedicated to the protection of information and systems. Founded in 1989, SANS is a professional research and education cooperative organization with currently over 156,000 security professionals, auditors, system administrators, and network administrators as members. SANS offers a set of certifications called the Global Information Assurance Certification, or GIAC.

These certifications can be pursued independently or combined into tracks to earn the comprehensive certification known as the GIAC Security Engineer (GSE). The newest GIAC certification is designed to be more along the lines of the CISSP. The GIAC Information Security Officer (GISO) is an overview certification that combines basic technical knowledge with understanding of threats, risks, and best practices. Unlike other certifications, the GIAC certifications require the applicant to complete a written "practical assignment." This assignment requires the applicant to demonstrate his or her abilities and skills by putting them into practice. These assignments are submitted to the SANS Information Security Reading Room for review by security practitioners, potential certificate applicants, and others with an interest in information security. Figure 3-9 shows the SANS and GIAC home pages.

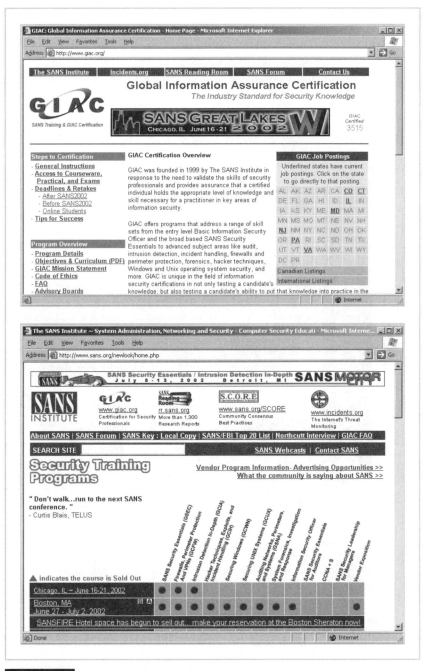

FIGURE 3-9 SANS and the GIAC home pages

Information Systems Audit and Control Association (ISACA): The Information Systems Audit and Control Association or ISACA *(www.isaca.org)* is a professional association with a focus on auditing, control, and security. The membership comprises both technical and managerial professionals. ISACA focuses on providing IT control practices and standards. Although the certification does not focus exclusively on information security, the Certified Information Systems Auditor or CISA certification does contain many information security components.

ISACA also has a code of ethics for its professionals. It requires many of the same high standards for ethical performance as the other organizations and certifications. Figure 3-10 shows the ISACA home page.

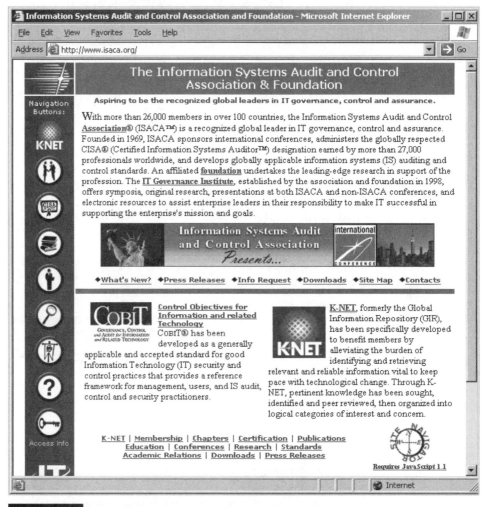

FIGURE 3-10 The Information Systems Audit and Control Association and Foundation home page

Computer Security Institute (CSI): The Computer Security Institute *(www.gocsi.com)* provides information and certification to support the computer, networking, and information security professional. Established in 1974, CSI sponsors a number of conferences. This organization is renowned for its technical expertise and scope. CSI also publishes a newsletter and threat advisory to its membership, and is well known for its annual computer threat survey of threats developed in cooperation with the FBI. Although CSI does not promote a single certification as do CISSP or GISO, it does provide a range of technical training classes in the areas of Internet security, intrusion management, network security, forensics, as well as technical networking.[15] Figure 3-11 shows the CSI home page.

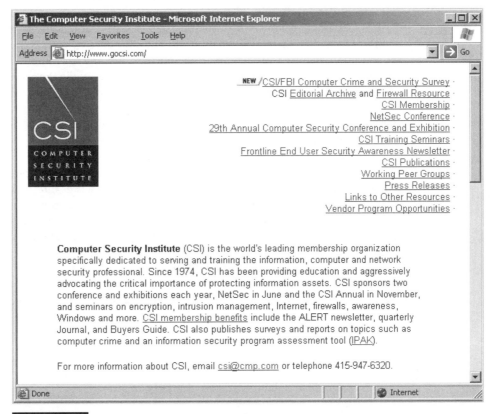

FIGURE 3-11   Computer Security Institute home page

Many of the organizations discussed above combine the ethical elements of their charters with a certification program. In the past these certifications required professional experience in the discipline before the applicant could take the examination. To acquire a certification, the professional must formally subscribe to the ethical code. Upon successfully earning the certification, most professional organizations require some form of continuing education or recertification to maintain the credentials.

The subject of professional certification is covered in more detail in Chapter 11.

Other Security Organizations

There are a number of professional and private societies and organizations that play a key role in the development and dissemination of information security practices and technologies. A few of the more prominent ones are presented here.

The **Information Systems Security Association (ISSA)** *(www.issa.org)* is a nonprofit society of information security professionals. As a professional association, its primary mission is to bring together qualified practitioners of information security for information exchange and educational development. ISSA provides a number of scheduled conferences, meetings, publications, and information resources to promote information security awareness and education.[16] ISSA also holds a code of ethics, similar in content to those of (ISC)[2], ISACA, and the ACM, "promoting management practices that will ensure the confidentiality, integrity, and availability of organizational information resources."[17]

The **Internet Society (ISOC)** *(www.isoc.org)* is a nonprofit, nongovernmental, international organization for professionals. It promotes the development and implementation of education, standards, policy, and education and training to promote the Internet. At the time of this publication, global membership was free. While the general membership does not actively promote education, standards and policy, there are a number of ISOC organizations that do actively review and promote these issues, and one of these is the **Internet Engineering Task Force (IETF)**. The IETF consists of individuals from the computing, networking, and telecommunications industries and is responsible for developing the Internet's technical foundations. Standards developed through the IETF are then reviewed by the Internet Engineering Steering Group (IESG), with appeal to the Internet Architecture Board, and promulgated by the Internet Society as international standards. Standards are reviewed and published through Requests for Comments (RFCs) and may be viewed at *www.rfc-editor.org*, as well as through numerous mirror sites. These RFCs are rich sources of information on the development and standardization of commonly used protocols for both the Internet and related technologies.

The **Computer Security Division (CSD)** of the National Institute for Standards and Technology, or NIST, contains a resource center known as the Computer Security Resource Center (CSRC) which is an almost necessary reference for any current or aspiring information security professional. This Web site *(csrc.nist.gov)* houses one of the most comprehensive sets of publicly available information on the entire suite of information security topics.

The CSD is involved in five major research areas related to information security:

1. Cryptographic standards and applications
2. Security testing
3. Security research and emerging technologies
4. Security management and guidance
5. Outreach, awareness and education

The **CERT Coordination Center** or CERT/CC *(www.cert.org)* is a center of Internet security expertise and is located at the Software Engineering Institute, a federally funded research and development center operated by Carnegie Mellon University. The CERT/CC studies security issues and provides publications and alerts to help educate the public to the threats facing information security. The center also provides training and expertise in the handling of computer incidents. CERT/CC acts both as a research center and outside consultant in the areas of incident response and security practices and programs development.

The **Computer Professionals for Social Responsibility (CPSR)** is a public organization for technologists anyone with a general concern for the impact of computer technology on society. CPSR promotes ethical and responsible development and use of computing, and seeks to inform public and private policy and lawmakers on this subject. It acts as an ethical watchdog for the development of ethical computing.

Key U.S. Federal Agencies

There are a number of key U.S. federal agencies charged with the protection of American information resources and the investigation of threats to, or attacks on, these resources. These include the Federal Bureau of Investigation's National Infrastructure Protection Center, the National Security Administration (see Figure 3-12), and the U.S. Secret Service.

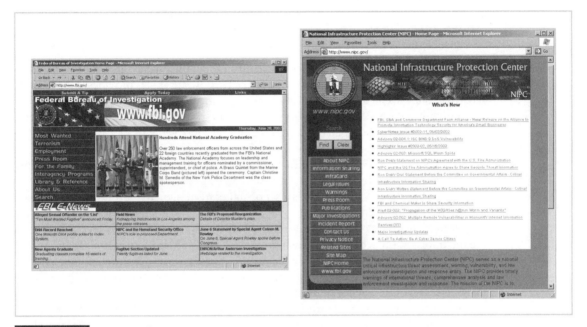

FIGURE 3-12   FBI and NIPC home pages

The Federal Bureau of Investigation's **National Infrastructure Protection Center (NIPC)** *(www.nipc.gov)* was established in 1998 and serves as the U.S. government's center for threat assessment, warning, investigation, and response to threats or attacks against critical U.S. infrastructures.[18] A key part of the NIPC's efforts to educate, train, inform, and involve the business and public sector in information security is the National InfraGard Program. Established in January 2001, the **National InfraGard Program** began as a cooperative effort between the FBI's Cleveland Field Office and local technology professionals. The FBI sought assistance in determining a more effective method of protecting critical national information resources. The resulting cooperative formed the first InfraGard chapter as a formal effort to combat both cyber and physical threats. Since then, every field office has established an InfraGard chapter and collaborates with public and private organizations and the academic community to share information about attacks, vulnerabilities, and threats. The National InfraGard Program serves its members in four basic ways:

1. By maintaining an intrusion alert network using encrypted e-mail
2. By maintaining a secure Web site for communication about suspicious activity or intrusions

3. Through local chapter activities
4. By operating a Help desk for questions

InfraGard's dominant contribution is the free exchange of information to and from the private sector in the areas of threats and attacks on information resources.[19]

Another key federal agency is the **National Security Agency (NSA)**. The NSA is:

> "...the Nation's cryptologic organization. It coordinates, directs, and performs highly specialized activities to protect U.S. information systems and produce foreign intelligence information...It is also one of the most important centers of foreign language analysis and research within the Government."[20]

The NSA (see Figure 3-13) is responsible for signal intelligence and information system security. The NSA's Information Assurance Directorate (IAD) provides information security "solutions including the technologies, specifications and criteria, products, product configurations, tools, standards, operational doctrine, and support activities needed to implement the protect, detect and report, and respond elements of cyber defense."[21] The IAD also develops and promotes an "Information Assurance Framework Forum" developed in cooperation with commercial organizations and academic researchers. This framework provides strategic guidance as well as technical specifications for security solutions. IAD's Common Criteria is a set of standards designed to promote understanding of information security.

Prominent among the NSA's efforts and activities in the information security arena are the Information Security Outreach programs. The NSA recognizes universities that not only offer information security education, but that have also integrated information security philosophies and efforts into the internal operations of the schools. These recognized "Centers of Excellence in Information Assurance Education" receive the prestigious honor of displaying the recognition as well as being displayed on the NSA's Web site. Additionally, the NSA has a program to certify curriculum in information security. The Information Assurance Courseware Evaluation process examines information security courses in an institution, and if accepted, provides a three-year accreditation. Graduates of these programs receive certificates with this recognition indicated.

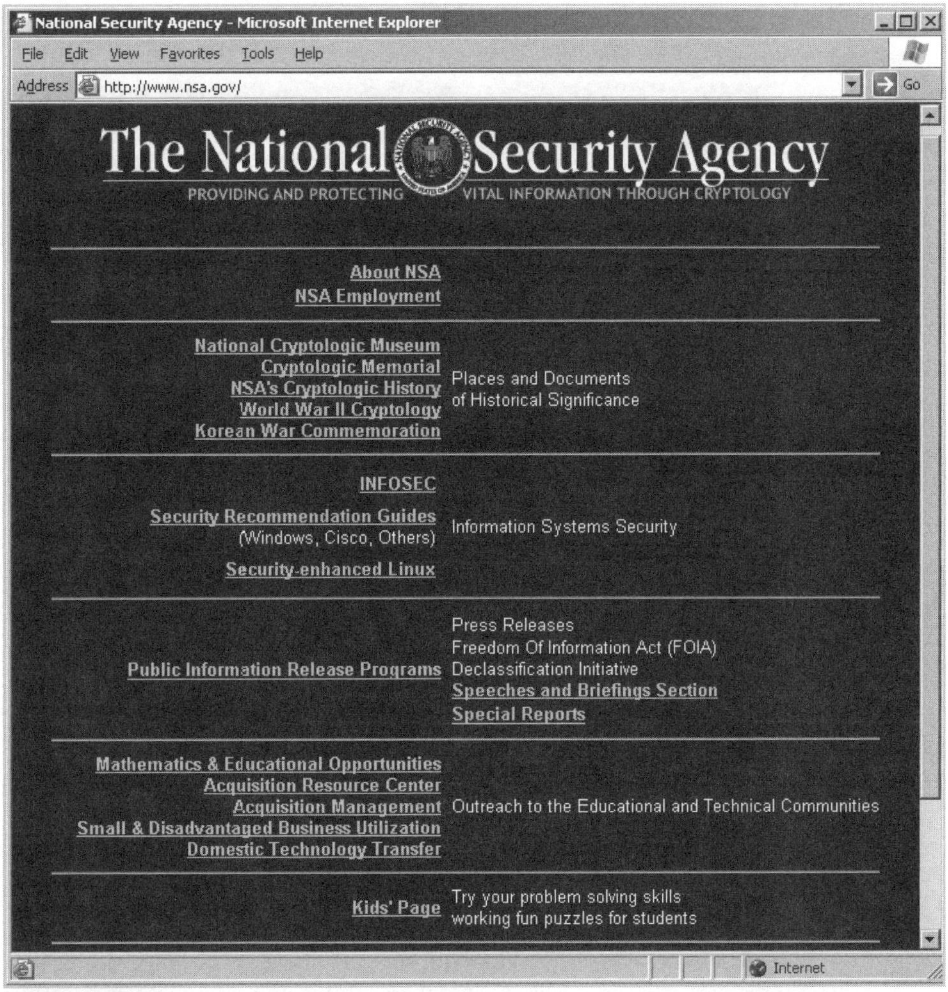

FIGURE 3-13   The National Security Agency home page

The **U.S. Secret Service** is a department within the Department of the Treasury. In addition to the well-known mission of providing protective services for key members of the U.S. government, the Secret Service is also charged with the detection and arrest of any person committing a United States federal offense relating to computer fraud and false identification crimes.[22] This represents an extension of the original mission of protecting U.S. currency to areas of communications fraud and abuse. After all, the communications networks of the U.S. carry more funds than all of the armored cars in the world combined: it's all just electronic data. Protect the networks, protect the data, and you protect the money, stocks, and other financial transactions. For more information on the Secret Service, see Figure 3-14.

FIGURE 3-14 Secret Service Web site

Organizational Liability and the Need for Counsel

What if an organization does not support or even encourage strong ethical conduct on the part of its employees? What if an organization does not behave ethically? Even if there is no breach of criminal law that can be prosecuted under criminal code, there is the issue of liability. **Liability** is the legal obligation of an entity. Liability extends beyond a legal obligation or contract; it includes liability for a wrongful act and the legal obligation to make **restitution**, or compensation for the wrong. The bottom line is that if an employee, acting with or without the authorization of the organization, performs an illegal or unethical act, causing some degree of harm, the organization can be held financially liable for that action. An organization increases its liability if it refuses to take strong measures known as **due care**. Due care is honored when an organization makes sure that every employee knows what is acceptable or not acceptable behavior, and knows the consequences of illegal or unethical actions. **Due diligence** requires that an organization make a valid effort to protect others and continually maintain this level of effort. With the global impact of the Internet, those who could be potentially injured or wronged by an organization's members could be anywhere, in any state, any country around the world. Under the U.S. legal system, any court can impose its authority over an individual or organization if it can establish **jurisdiction**—jurisdiction being the court's right to hear a case in its court if the wrong was committed in its territory or involving its citizenry. This is sometimes referred to as the **long arm jurisdiction,** since the long arm of the law reaches across the country or around the world to pull an accused individual into its court systems. Trying a case in the injured party's home area is usually favorable to the injured party as it creates a home court advantage.[23]

This chapter presents the legal and ethical issues that security professionals deal with, and introduces the professional organizations that set standards for ethical behavior. The chapter is designed to show that the role of an information security professional is vital to keeping organizations and individuals abreast of the most recent changes and additions to legal and ethical codes and regulations.

Chapter Summary

- Laws are formally adopted rules for acceptable behavior in modern society. Ethics are socially acceptable behaviors. The key difference between laws and ethics is that law carries the sanction of a governing authority and ethics do not.

- Organizations formalize desired behaviors in documents called policies. Policies must be read and agreed to before they are binding.

- Civil law represents a wide variety of laws that are written into volumes of legal code available for review by the common man. Criminal law addresses violations that harm society. Tort law is enforced through individual lawsuits rather than criminal prosecution by the state.

- Private law focuses on individual relationships. Public law addresses regulatory agencies. Case law is a published account of the legal decisions of the court system. The legal judgments themselves are referred to as Common law, or more appropriately unwritten law.

- Within the laws currently supported by Congress and enforced by the judicial system, there are a growing number of statutes addressing an individual's right to privacy or freedom from intrusion or observation.

- The desire to protect national security, trade secrets, and a variety of other state and private assets has led to several laws impacting what information and information management and security resources may be exported from the United States.

- Intellectual property is recognized as a protected asset in this country. U.S. copyright law extends this right to the published word, including electronic media.

- Studies of ethical sensitivity to computer use have determined that individuals of differing nationalities have differing perspectives on computer use. Deterrence can prevent an illegal or unethical activity from occurring. Deterrence requires significant penalties, probability of apprehension, and an expectation of enforcement of penalties.

- As part of an effort to sponsor positive ethics, a number of professional organizations have established codes of conduct or codes of ethics that their members are expected to follow.

- There are a number of key U.S. federal agencies responsible for protecting American information resources and investigating threats to, or attacks on, these resources.

Review Questions

1. What is the difference between criminal law and civil law?
2. What is tort law and what does it permit an individual to accomplish?
3. What are the primary examples of public law?
4. Which law amended the Computer Fraud and Abuse act of 1986, and what did it change?
5. Which organization led the efforts to overturn the Computer Decency Act? What happened to the law they opposed?
6. What is privacy as defined in the chapter? You can assume it is not absolute freedom from observation.
7. What is another name for the Kennedy-Kassebaum Act (1996), and why is it important to organizations that are not in the health-care industry?
8. If you work for a financial service organization such as bank or credit union, which law from 1999 affects your use of customer data? What other impacts does it have?
9. Which law from 1999 provides guidance on the use of encryption?
10. What is intellectual property (IP)? Is it offered the same protection in every country of the world? What laws currently protect it in the United States and Europe?
11. What is a policy? How does it differ from a law?
12. What are the three general categories of unethical and illegal behavior?
13. What is the best method for preventing an illegal or unethical activity?
14. Of the organizations listed in this chapter, which has been established for the longest time? When was it founded?
15. Of the organizations listed in this chapter, which is focused on auditing and control? ISACA
16. Of the organizations listed in this chapter, which sponsors a program called Global Information Assurance Certification (GIAC)?
17. Which U.S. federal agency sponsors the InfraGard program?
18. What is due care? Why would an organization want to make sure it exercises due care in its usual course of operations?
19. What can be done to deter someone from committing a crime?
20. How does due diligence differ from due care? Why are both important?

Exercises

1. What does CISSP stand for? Using the Internet, find out what is required for an individual to earn CISSP.
2. For what kind of information security jobs does the NSA recruit? Use the Internet to visit their Web page and find out.
3. Using the resources available in your library, find out what laws your state has passed to prosecute computer crime.
4. Using the Web, go to *www.eff.org*. What are the current top concerns of this organization?
5. Using the ethical scenarios presented in the chapter, answer each question, and bring your answers to class to compare your answers with those of your peers.

Case Exercises

I. "See You In Court"[24]

Adapted from S. Scalet's article, *CIO Magazine*, November 1, 2001.

"Just before 8 a.m. on Feb. 1, 2001, C.I. Host, a Web-hosting company with 90,000 customers, was hit with a crippling denial-of-service attack. By the day after the outage, the CEO, Christopher Faulkner, reported that complaints had come in from 'countless' customers, so the Fort Worth, Texas-based company got its lawyers involved."[25]

In a strange twist of fate, the company hit with this attack dragged not a hacker, but another company, an ISP, and five of its customers into court. The ISP claimed to be the victim not the perpetrator of the attacks and therefore not liable. The suit was referred to a U.S. District Court, but never made it to trial. C.I. Host's attorneys convinced a judge to issue a restraining order shutting down three of the ISP's Web servers until the ISP could prove that the vulnerabilities had been rectified. The attacks lasted a few days; to resolve the issue, the lawsuit took over seven months, and several hundreds of thousands of dollars in legal fees, time, and effort.

The question is, when information security fails, who's to blame? Or in the court's eyes, who's liable? Even though the hacker is the culprit, with the standards of due care and due diligence, the companies that are being hacked and then used in other attacks are becoming increasingly liable for damages to other companies.

"It's not a 'sky is falling' issue," says one CIO when asked about the likelihood of such lawsuits. "This is what an intelligent, forward-thinking company is thinking about. We believe that we've taken every possible precaution, and we're looking at every possible thing on the horizon."[26]

The lawmakers are paying attention as well. A new bill is being drafted in the U.S. Senate that could exempt businesses from the Freedom of Information Act (FOIA), in order to protect businesses from being required to disclose the results of attacks and their information security protection strategies. Another bill in the House, would prohibit the use of voluntarily provided information from being used in a lawsuit in information security related cases.

Although no direct liability lawsuits have been tried yet, it's just a matter of time. What can companies do? "The best defense for the impending legal hassle is a much-advised, often-ignored list of best practices. The question is whether the gathering clouds will have the proverbial silver lining and generate an incentive for companies to act on security best practices. In the process of doing so, they just might prevent hackers from doing damage in the first place."[27] "There's always going to be that rare group of people who want to take advantage of the system," says Bette Walker, CIO of Energy and Chassis Systems for Delphi Automotive Systems in Flint, Michigan. "Security can become a legal problem. I think of it first as preventing a problem from occurring. Then the next step, I don't have to worry about."[28]

1. How can the standards of due care and due diligence protect a company from being sued in this type of situation?

2. Why would a company want to go after an ISP in a situation like this, when clearly the ISP is a victim as much as the attacked organization?

II. Flunking the Feds

Adapted from "Bill Would Extend Federal Information Security Tests"[29]
By E. Chabrow, *Information Week*, March 6, 2002

On Wednesday, March 6, 2002, Rep. Tom Davis, the chairman of the House Subcommittee on Technology and Procurement Policy, introduced the Federal Information Security Management Act. This act permanently reauthorizes a law that expired in the latter part of 2002 and makes federal agencies take steps to ensure that their IT systems are secure. This legislation requires federal agencies to identify risks associated with their systems and to implement appropriate protection. The legislation also requires the Office of Management and Budget to make the standards obligatory, therefore preventing agencies from waiving the standards as the existing law allows.

"Federal information technology continues to be woefully unprotected from malicious attacks and benign interruptions," Rep. Tom Davis, Chairman of the House Subcommittee on Technology and Procurement Policy, said Wednesday. "It's clear that the state of federal information security suffers from a lack of coordinated, uniform management."[30]

The report card for the federal government is somewhat shocking. In 2001, 24 federal agencies had their information security evaluated, and only one agency received a grade higher than a C+. "While these grades are disappointing," Davis said, "they reflect the difficulty of implementing effective security management without sufficient commitment and guidance from an accountable entity within each agency, and for the federal government as a whole."[31]

1. Why can't these federal agencies protect their systems, with clear standards from the National Institute of Standards and Technology (NIST)? What issues complicate the protection of governmental systems?

2. What resources exist within NIST to support the development and implementation of standardized security management? What other agencies can provide support to public and private organizations?

Endnotes

1. John B. Noone, *Rousseau's Social Contract: A Conceptual Analysis* (Athens: University Of Georgia Press, 1981)
2. U.S. Constitution, preamble.
3. *EPIC. "The Clipper Chip" [WWW Document] retrieved 05/02/2002.* http://www.epic.org/crypto/clipper/.
4. American Heritage Dictionary, "privacy," *The American Heritage Dictionary of the English Language Online.* [Cited 12 June 2002]. Available from the World Wide Web *<http://www.bartleby.com/cgi-bin/texis/webinator/ahdsearch?search_type=enty&query= privacy&db=ahd&Submit=Search>.*
5. Legal Information Institute, *Privacy of Customer Information*, title 47, sec. 222. [Cited 12 June 2002]. Available from the World Wide Web *<http://www4.law.cornell.edu/uscode/ 47/222.html.>*
6. HIPAAAdvisory. "HIPAA primer." *HIPAAAdvisory Online.* [Cited 12 June 2002]. Available from the World Wide Web *<http://www.hipaadvisory.com/regs/HIPAAprimer1.htm>.*
7. Inquirer. "Software Piracy in Asia Exposed." *The Inquirer Online.* 27 January 2002. [Cited 12 June 2002]. Available from the World Wide Web *<http://www.theinquirer.net/ piracy1.htm>.*
8. The Computer Ethics Instititute. "The 10 Commandments of Computer Ethics." *CEI Online.* 16 April 2001. [Cited 12 June 2002]. Available from the World Wide Web *<http://www.cpsr.org/program/ethics/cei.html>.*

9. Michael E. Whitman, Anthony M. Townsend, and Anthony R. Hendrickson, "Cross-National Differences in Computer-Use Ethics: A nine Country Study," *The Journal of International Business Studies* 30, no. 4 (1999): 673-687.

10. *Ibid.*

11. *Ibid.*

12. *Ibid.*

13. Susan J. Harrington, "The Effects of Codes of Ethics and Personal Denial of Responsibility on Computer Abuse Judgement and Intentions," *MIS Quarterly* 20, no. 3 (September 1996): 257-278.

14. International Information Systems Security Certification Consortium, Inc. "(ISC)^2 Code of Ethics." *ISC^2 Online.* [Cited 12 June 2002]. Available from the World Wide Web *<http://www.isc2.org/cgi/content.cgi?category=12>*.

15. Computer Security Institute. "CSI Information Security Seminars 2002." *CSI Online.* [Cited 12 June 2002]. Available from the World Wide Web *<http://www.gocsi.com/infosec/wkshop.html>*.

16. ISSA. "Information Systems Security Association." *ISSA Online.* 12 June 2002. [Cited 12 June 2002]. Available from the World Wide Web *<http://www.issa.org>*.

17. ISSA. "ISSA Code of Ethics." *ISSA Online.* 5 December 2000. [Cited 12 June 2002]. Available from the World Wide Web *<http://www.issa.org/codeofethics.html>*.

18. National Infrastructure Protection Center. "Welcome: A Message from Ron Dick, Director of the National Infrastructure Protection Center." *NIPC Online.* [Cited 12 June 2002]. Available from the World Wide Web *<http://www.nipc.gov/about/about.htm>*.

19. U.S. Department of Justice, Federal Bureau of Investigation. *The FBI and the National Infrastructure Protection Center Publically Introduce the National Infragard Program* (Washington D.C., 2001). Available from the World Wide Web *<http://www.fbi.gov/press-rel/pressrel01/infragard.htm>*.

20. The National Security Agency. *About the National Security Agency.* Available from the World Wide Web *<http://www.nsa.gov/about_nsa/index.html>*.

21. The National Security Agency. *About the IAD: Delivering IAD Solutions for Cyber Systems,* August 2001. Available from the World Wide Web *<http://www.nsa.gov/isso/brochure/index.htm>*.

22. U.S. Department of Treasury, United States Secret Service. *Mission Statement,* 2002. Available from the World Wide Web *<http://www.secretservice.gov/mission.shtml>*.

23. Robert J. Alberts, Anthony M. Townsend, and Michael E. Whitman, "The Threat of Long-arm Jurisdiction to Electronic Commerce, *Communications of the ACM* 41, no. 12 (December 1998): 15-20.

24. Sarah D. Scalet. "See You in Court." *CIO.com Online.* 1 November 2001. [Cited 12 June 2002]. Available from the World Wide Web *<http://www.cio.com/archive/110101/court.html>*.

25. *Ibid.*

26. *Ibid.*

27. *Ibid.*

28. *Ibid.*

29. Eric Chabrow. "Bill Would Extend Federal Information Security Tests." *Informationweek.com Online.* 6 March 2002. [Cited 12 June 2002]. Available from the World Wide Web *<http://www.informationweek.com/story/IWK20020306S0004>*.

30. *Ibid.*

31. *Ibid.*

Risk Management: Identifying and Assessing Risk

4

CHARLIE MOODY CLEARED HIS THROAT to call the meeting to order. The conference room was full of developers, systems analysts, IT managers, business users, and business managers.

Charlie raised his voice, "All right everyone, let's get started. Welcome to the kick-off meeting of the Sequential Label and Supply Information Security Task Force. That's the name of our new project team, and we're here today to talk about our objectives and to review the initial work plan."

"Why are all of the users here?" asked the manager of sales. "Isn't this security stuff for you computer types to deal with?"

Charlie answered him, "Well, that used to be the case, but management has realized that information security is a problem for the whole company and needs the participation of people from all departments. Now, I hope everyone has read the packets we sent out last week about the legal requirements we face in our industry and the background articles on threats and attacks from recent trade publications. Today we are going to start the process of identifying and classifying all of the information technology risks that face our organization. This includes everything from fires and floods that could disrupt our business to criminal hackers who might try to steal or destroy our data. Once we identify and classify the risks facing our assets, we can discuss how to eliminate or reduce these risks by establishing controls. What we do will depend on costs and benefits of each control."

"Wow, Charlie! That's going to be a ton of work," said Amy Windahl from the back of the room. "I'm sure we need to do it. I was hit by the last attack, just as everyone here was, but we have hundreds of systems."

"Yes, you're right Amy, and its more like thousands," said Charlie. He went on, "But, that's why we have so many people on this team and why the team includes members of every department."

Charlie continued, "Okay, everyone, please open your packets and take out the project plan with the work list showing teams, tasks, and schedules. Any questions before we start reviewing the work plan?"

DISCUSSION QUESTIONS:

1. Did Charlie effectively organize the work before the meeting? Would it have been better to hold the kick-off meeting until a work plan had been prepared? Why or why not? Make a list of the important issues you think should be covered by a work plan. For each issue, provide a short explanation.
2. Will Charlie and the team get useful information from the team they have assembled? Why or why not?
3. Why might some attendees resist the goals of the meeting? Does it seem that each person invited was briefed on the importance of the event and the issues behind it?

LEARNING OBJECTIVES:
Upon completion of this material you should be able to:

- Define risk management and its role in the SecSDLC
- Understand how risk is identified
- Assess risk based on the likelihood of occurrence and impact on an organization
- Grasp the fundamental aspects of documenting risk identification and assessment

Introduction

As discussed in Chapter 1, the security systems development life cycle (SecSDLC) is a methodology that can be used in a flexible fashion to assist organizations in deploying information security initiatives. The SecSDLC can also be used to improve existing information security programs. In the investigation phase discussed in Chapter 2, analysts examined the organization's business needs for security and explored the environment of threats and possible attacks facing the organization. Continuing the investigation phase, Chapter 3 reviewed relevant laws that currently affect organizations. As shown in Figure 4-1, Chapter 4 initiates the analysis phase and begins the formal process of examining and documenting the security posture of an organization's information technology. This formal process is called **risk identification**. Risk identification is conducted within the larger process of identifying and justifying risk controls, known as **risk management**. Chapter 5 continues the analysis phase and focuses on controlling risk.

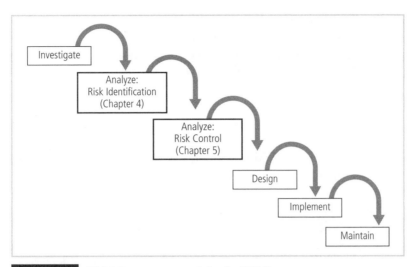

FIGURE 4-1 Risk Management and the SecSDLC

As an aspiring information security professional, you have a key role to play in risk identification. Among the communities of interest, the general management of the organization must structure the IT and information security functions to lead a successful defense of the organization's information assets. Once again, these assets are information and data, hardware, software, procedures, and people. The IT community must serve the information technology needs of the broader organization and at the same time leverage the special skills and insights of the information security community. The information security team must lead the way with skill, professionalism, and flexibility as it works with the other communities of interest to balance the ever present trade-off between the usefulness and security of the information system.

Chapter Organization

Chapters 4 and 5 outline the steps needed to perform risk management, which establishes the overall context for risk identification and assessment. Chapter 4 consists of four sections: risk management, risk identification, risk assessment, and summary documentation as outlined below:

1. Risk management
   - Know your organization.
   - Identify your organization's enemies.
   - Involve relevant groups within the organization.
   - Integrate the steps of the process with the SecDSLC.

2. Risk identification
   - Plan and organize the risk identification process.
   - Categorize system components.
   - Develop an inventory of assets.
   - Categorize assets.
   - Identify threats to the categorized assets.
   - Tie specific threats to specific, vulnerable assets.

3. Risk assessment
   - Assign values to attacks on assets.
   - Assess the likelihood that vulnerable systems will be attacked by specific threats.
   - Calculate the risk to which assets are exposed in their current setting.
   - Conduct a preliminary review of the controls that could be used to protect vulnerabilities.

4. Documentation: Document the findings of risk identification and assessment.

Figure 4-2 outlines the steps in the risk identification and risk assessment described above.

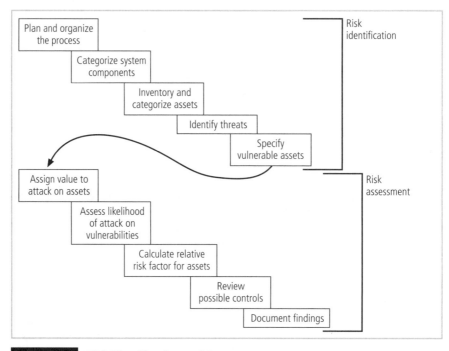

FIGURE 4-2 Risk Identification and Assessment

Risk Management

An observation made over 2,400 years ago by Chinese General Sun Tzu has direct relevance to information security today.

> "If you know the enemy and know yourself, you need not fear the result of a hundred battles. If you know yourself but not the enemy, for every victory gained you will also suffer a defeat. If you know neither the enemy nor yourself, you will succumb in every battle."[1]

Consider for a moment the similarities between information security and warfare. Information security managers and technicians are the defenders of information. The myriads of threats discussed in Chapter 2 are constantly implemented in attacks on the defenses surrounding information assets. Defenses are built in layers, placing safeguard on safeguard. You attempt to prevent, protect, detect, and recover from attack after attack, after attack. Today, an organization's defense is legally prevented from switching to offense, and the offense has no interest in defense, other than to defeat it. So, as Sun Tzu recommends, in order to be victorious, you must know yourself and know the enemy.

Know Yourself

First, you must identify, examine, and understand the information and systems, currently in place within your organization. This is self-evident. To protect **assets**, which are defined here as information and the systems that use, store, and transmit information, you must understand everything about them. Once you know what you have, you can look at what you are already doing to protect the information and systems from threats. Just because you have a control in place to protect an asset, does not necessarily mean that the asset is protected. Frequently, control mechanisms are implemented and then the necessary periodic review, revision, and maintenance are bypassed or simply ignored. Each of the policies, education and training programs, and technologies that protect information must be carefully maintained and administered to ensure that they are still effective.

Know the Enemy

Informed of your organization's assets and weaknesses, you must move to Sun Tzu's second step: know the enemy. For information security, this means identifying, examining, and understanding the *threats* facing the organization. You must determine the aspects of the threats that most directly affect the organization and the security of the organization's information assets. You can then use your understanding of these aspects to create a list of threats prioritized by how important each asset is to the organization.

Risk management defines this journey of discovering an organization's risks and how those risks can be controlled or handled.

All Communities of Interest are Accountable

It is the responsibility of each of the organization's communities of interest to manage the risks the organization encounters. Each community of interest has a role to play as outlined below.

Information Security

Since the members of the information security community best understand the threats and attacks that introduce risk into the organization, they often take a leadership role in addressing risk.

Management and Users

When properly trained and kept aware of the threats the organization faces, this group plays a part in the early detection and response process. Management and users must also ensure that sufficient resources (money and personnel) are allocated to the information security and information technology groups to meet the security needs of the organization. The users work with the systems and the data and are therefore inextricably entwined in its management and protection.

Information Technology

This group must assist in building secure systems and operating them safely. For example, IT operations ensure good backups to control the risk from hard drive failures. All of the communities of interest must work together to address all levels of risk, which range from disasters that can devastate the whole organization to the smallest of employee mistakes.

The owners of the organization count on each community of interest to accomplish the critical steps that lead to success in risk management. This means that general management, IT management, and information security management are accountable for identifying and classifying risk. All three communities of interest are also responsible for the following:

- Evaluating the risk controls
- Determining which control options are cost effective for the organization
- Acquiring or installing the needed controls
- Overseeing that the controls remain effective

It is essential that all three communities of interest conduct periodic management reviews as described below. The first focus of management review is asset inventory. On a regular basis, the asset inventory should be verified as complete and accurate, and the classification and organization of the assets should be verified. In addition, a survey of the threats and vulnerabilities that have been identified as dangerous to the asset inventory must be reviewed and verified as complete and current. Potential controls and mitigation strategies should also be reviewed for completeness. The cost effectiveness of each control should be reviewed as well, and the decisions on deployment of controls revisited. Further, managers of all levels are accountable on a regular schedule for ensuring the ongoing effectiveness of every control deployed. For example, as a test, a sales manager can go through the office before the workday starts and pick up all the papers from every sales desk. When the workers show up, they are told that a fire was simulated and all of those papers were destroyed. Each worker in the sales department must follow the disaster recovery procedures to assess the effectiveness of the procedures and suggest corrections.

Integrating Risk Management into the SecSDLC

As noted in the introduction to the chapter, the security system development life cycle (SecSDLC) is a flexible approach to deploying information security in an organization. The risk management section of the analysis phase is a microcosm of the larger SecSDLC. Note that risk management includes elements of investigation, analysis, design, implementation, and maintenance. While this may be confusing to the beginning project manager or information security professional, note that risk management by itself is not a complete information security program. In a smaller organization, or one with a functioning information security program, a top-to-bottom risk management review, as outlined in this chapter and the next, could meet all of the short-term needs for information security. Those organizations that have no information security program or have a program that is not functioning adequately should consider using the more comprehensive SecSDLC to reengineer the processes.

You now move into the first phase of risk management, risk identification.

Risk Identification

A risk management strategy calls on you to know your organization by identifying, classifying, and prioritizing the organization's information assets. These assets are the targets of various threats and threat agents, and your goal is to protect the assets from the threats. Once you have examined the organizational assets, you move into threat identification. You must assess the circumstances and setting of each information asset. If a threat to an information asset poses one or more vulnerabilities, you must identify and develop controls to limit the impact of the attack on the vulnerability. You begin the process by identifying and assessing the value of the information assets.

Asset Identification and Valuation

This iterative process begins with the identification of assets, including all of the elements of an organization's system: people, procedures, data and information, software, hardware, and networking elements. Then, you classify and categorize the assets adding details as you dig deeper into the analysis.

TABLE 4-1 Categorizing the Components of an Information System

Traditional system components	SecSDLC and risk management system components	
People	Employees	Trusted employees Other staff
	Nonemployees	People at trusted organizations Strangers
Procedures	Procedures	IT and business standard procedures IT and business sensitive procedures
Data	Information	Transmission Processing Storage
Software	Software	Applications Operating systems Security components
Hardware	System devices and peripherals	Systems and peripherals Security devices
	Networking components	Intranet components Internet or DMZ components

Table 4-1 compares the standard components of an information system (people, procedures, data and information, software, and hardware) and an enhanced *risk management* version. As you can see, the SecSDLC categorization introduces a number of new subdivisions:

- People as a group have been subdivided into employees and nonemployees. Each of those categories is further divided into two categories: employees who hold trusted roles and have correspondingly greater authority and accountability, and other staff who have assignments without special privileges. Nonemployees are users at organizations with which your organization has a trust relationship and those who are strangers.

■ Procedures have been split into two categories: IT and business standard procedures, and IT and business sensitive procedures. The sensitive procedures are those that may assist a threat agent in crafting an attack against the organization or that have some other content or feature that may introduce risk to the organization. One example of the loss of a sensitive procedure was the theft of the documentation for the E911 system from Bellsouth.[2] In this case, the documentation revealed certain aspects of the inner workings of a critical phone system.

■ Data components have been expanded to account for the management of information in all states: transmission, processing, and storage. These expanded categories solve the problem posed by the term *data*, which is usually associated with databases, and does not bring to mind the full assessment of all modalities of data and information used by a modern organization.

■ Software components can be assigned to one of three categories: applications, operating systems, or security components. Software components that provide security controls may span the range of operating systems and applications categories, but are differentiated by the fact that they are part of the information security control environment and must be protected more thoroughly than other systems components.

■ Hardware is assigned to one of two categories: the usual systems devices and their peripherals, and the devices that are part of information security control systems. The latter must be protected more thoroughly than the former.

■ Hardware components have been separated into two categories: devices and peripherals; and networks. Since networking subsystems are often the focal point of attacks against the system, they should be considered as special cases rather than combined with general hardware and software components.

People, Procedures, and Data Asset Identification

The asset identification of human resources, documentation, and data information is more elusive than pinning down hardware and software assets. People with knowledge, experience, and judgment should be assigned the task. As the assets of people, procedures, and data are identified, they should also be recorded with a reliable data-handling process. Whatever record keeping mechanism is used, however, be sure it has the flexibility needed to allow attributes to be specified based on the nature of the information asset being tracked. Some attributes are unique to the class of elements. When deciding which information assets to track, you may want to consider including the asset attributes listed below:

■ For people: Position name/number/ID (try to avoid names and stick to identifying positions, roles, or functions); supervisor; security clearance level; special skills.

■ For procedures: Description; intended purpose; relationship to software, hardware, and networking elements; storage location for reference; storage location for update.

- For data: Classification; owner, creator, and manager; size of data structure; data structure used (sequential or relational); online or offline; location; backup procedures employed.

As the data-tracking process is developed, consider carefully how much data should be tracked and for which specific assets. Most large organizations find that that they can only effectively track a few valuable facts about the most critical devices. For instance, a company may only track IP address, server name, and device type for the mission-critical servers used by the company. They may forgo the tracking of more detailed facts on all devices and completely disregard the tracking of desktop or laptop systems.

Hardware, Software, and Network Asset Identification

What attributes of each of these information assets should be tracked? It depends on the needs of the organization and its risk management efforts, as well as the preferences and needs of the management of the information security and information technology communities. When deciding which information assets to track, you may want to consider including the asset attributes listed below:

- **Name:** Use the device or program name that is most common. Organizations may have several names for the same product. For example, a software product might have a nickname that people within the company use while the product is in development, as well as a formal name used by marketing and vendors. No matter how many names you track and how you select a name, always define what each name means for each group that uses the information. You should to adopt naming standards that do not convey information to potential system attackers. For instance, a server named CASH1 or HQ_FINANCE may entice attackers to take a shortcut to those systems and go for the valuables first.

- **IP address:** Useful for network devices and servers, but does not usually apply to software. You can, however, use a relational database and track software instances on specific servers or networking devices. Also note that larger organizations use the **dynamic host control protocol (DHCP)** within TCP/IP that reassigns IP numbers to devices as needed, making the use of IP numbers as part of the asset identification process problematic.

- **Media access control (MAC) address:** MAC addresses are sometimes called electronic serial numbers or hardware addresses. As part of the TCP/IP standard, all network interface hardware devices have a unique number. The number is used by the network operating system as a mechanism to identify a specific network device. It is used by the client's network software to recognize traffic that it must process. In most settings, MAC addresses can be a useful way to track connectivity. They can, however, be spoofed by some hardware and software combinations.

- **Element type:** Document the function of each element by listing its type. For hardware, you can develop a list of possible element types, such as servers, desktops, networking devices, or test equipment, to whatever degree of granularity you require. For software elements, you may choose to develop a list of types that includes operating systems, custom applications by type (accounting, HR, or payroll to name a few), packaged applications, and specialty applications, such as firewall programs.

The needs of the organization determine the degree of specificity. Types may, in fact, be recorded at two or more levels of specificity. Record one attribute that classifies the asset at a high level and then add attributes for more detail. For example, one server might be listed as:

- DeviceClass = S (server)
- DeviceOS = W2K (Windows 2000)
- DeviceCapacity = AS (advanced server)

- **Serial number:** For hardware devices, the serial number can uniquely identify a specific device. Some software vendors also assign a software serial number to each instance of the program licensed by the organization.

- **Manufacturer name:** Record the manufacturer of the device or software component. This can be useful when analyzing threat outbreaks when certain manufacturers announce specific vulnerabilities.

- **Manufacturer's model number or part number:** Record the model or part number of the element. This record of exactly what the element is can be very useful in later analysis of vulnerabilities, because some vulnerability instances only apply to specific models of certain devices and software components.

- **Software version, update revision, or FCO number:** Whenever possible, document the specific software or firmware revision number and, for hardware devices, the current **field change order** (**FCO**) number. An FCO is an authorization issued by an organization for the repair, modification, or update of a piece of equipment. The equipment is not returned to the manufacturer, but usually repaired at the customer's location, often by a third party. Documenting the revision number and FCO is particularly important for networking devices that function mainly through the software running on them. For example, firewall devices often have three versions: an operating system (OS) version, a software version, and a basic input/output system (BIOS) firmware version. Depending on your needs, you may have to track each of those version numbers.

- **Physical location:** Note where this element is located physically. This may not apply to software elements, but some organizations have license terms that specify where software can be used.

- **Logical location:** Note where this element can be found on the organization's network. The logical location is most useful for networking devices and indicates the logical network where the device is connected.

- **Controlling entity:** Identify which organizational unit controls the element. A remote location's onsite staff sometimes controls a networking device, and at other times the central networks team controls other devices of the same make and model. You should try to differentiate which group or unit controls each specific element, because the group may want a voice in how much risk that device can tolerate and how much expense they can sustain to add controls.

Automated Risk Management Tools

Automated tools can sometimes uncover the system elements that make up the hardware, software, and network components. For example, many organizations use automated asset inventory systems. The inventory listing is usually available in a database, or can be exported to a database for custom information on security assets. Once stored, the inventory listing must be kept current, often through a tool that periodically refreshes the data.

When you move to later steps of risk management involving calculations of loss and projections of costs, the case for the use of automated risk management tools for tracking information assets becomes stronger. At this point in the process, simple word-processing, spreadsheet, and database tools can provide adequate record keeping. You revisit the capabilities and usefulness of automated risk management software in Chapter 5.

Information Asset Classification

Some organizations further subdivide the categories listed in Table 4-1. For example, the category of Internet components can be subdivided into servers, networking devices (routers, hubs, switches), protection devices (firewalls, proxies), and cabling. Each of the other categories can be further subdivided as needed by the organization.

In addition to the expanded categories used to classify the SecSDLC system components, you also add another dimension to represent the sensitivity and security priority of the data and the devices that store, transmit, and process the data. Many organizations already have a classification scheme. Examples of these kinds of classifications are confidential data, internal data, and public data. Informal organizations may have to organize themselves to create a useable data classification model. The other side of the data classification scheme is the personnel security clearance structure, identifying the level of information each individual is authorized to view, based on what they need to know.

No matter how an organization chooses to identify the various components of systems, it is most important that the classification of components be specific enough to allow determination of the various priority levels. This is necessary because the next step is to rank the components based on criteria established by the categorization. It is also important that the categories be comprehensive and mutually exclusive. *Comprehensive* means that all information assets must fit in the list somewhere, and *mutually exclusive* means that the best fit of an information asset should be in only one category. For example, an organization has a **public key infrastructure certificate authority**, which is a software application that provides cryptographic key management services. Using a purely technical standard, an analysis team could categorize the authority in the asset list of Table 4-1 as software, and within the software category as either an application or as security component. It should actually be categorized as software security components, since a certificate authority must be carefully protected as part of the security infrastructure. It is essential to establish a clear and comprehensive set of categories to simplify decisions on the categorization of elements that could be placed in a number of slots.

Information Asset Valuation

As each asset of the organization is assigned to its category, posing a number of questions assists in developing the weighting criteria to be used for information asset valuation or impact evaluation. As each question is asked and answered, you should prepare a worksheet such as that shown in Figure 4-3 to collect your answers for later analysis. The data gathering questions are:

■ **Which information asset is the most critical to the success of the organization?**
   When determining the relative importance of each asset, refer to the organization

mission statement or statement of objectives. From that source, determine what elements of the organization are essential to meeting the organization's objectives, which elements support the objectives, and which are merely adjuncts. For example, a manufacturing company that makes aircraft engines finds that the process control systems controlling the machine tools on the assembly line are of the first order of importance. Although shipping and receiving data-entry consoles are important to those functions, they may be less critical if alternatives are available or can be easily arranged. Another example is an online organization such as Amazon.com. The Web servers that advertise their products and receive their orders 24 hours a day are essential to the critical success of the business, whereas the desktop systems used by the Customer Service Department to answer customer e-mails are not nearly as important.

System Name: ___SLS E-Commerce___

Date Evaluated: ___February 2003___

Evaluated By: ___D. Jones___

Information assets	Data classification	Impact to profitability
Information Transmitted:		
EDI Document Set 1 —Logistics BOL to outsourcer (outbound)	Confidential	High
EDI Document Set 2—Supplier orders (Outbound)	Confidential	High
EDI Document Set 2—Supplier fulfillment advice (inbound)	Confidential	Medium
Customer order via SSL (inbound)	Confidential	Critical
Customer service Request via e-mail (inbound)	Private	Medium
DMZ Assets:		
Edge Router	Public	Critical
Web server #1—home page and core site	Public	Critical
Web server #2—Application server	Private	Critical

Notes: BOL: Bill of Lading:
DMZ: Demilitarized Zone
EDI: Electronic Data Interchange
SSL: Secure Sockets Layer

FIGURE 4-3 Example Worksheet for the Asset Identification of Information Systems

■ **Which information asset generates the most revenue?** You can also determine which information assets are critical by evaluating how much of the organization's revenue depends on a particular asset. Nonprofit organizations determine which information assets are most critical to service delivery. In some organizations, different systems are in place for each line of business or service offering. Which of these play the biggest role in generating revenue or delivering services?

- **Which information asset generates the most profitability?** Organizations should evaluate how much of the organization's profitability depends on a particular asset. For instance, at Amazon.com, some servers support the book sales operations and other servers support the auction process, while yet other servers support the customer book review database. Which of these servers contribute most to the profitability of the business? Although important, the review database server really does not directly add to profitability. Note that some services may have large revenue values, but are operating on such thin or nonexistent margins that they do not generate a profit. In the case of nonprofit organizations, another way to look at this issue is to determine what percentage of the agency's clientele receives services from the information asset being evaluated.

- **Which information asset would be the most expensive to replace?** Sometimes an information asset acquires special value because it is unique. If an enterprise still uses a Model-129 keypunch machine, for example, to create special punch card entries for a critical batch run, that machine may be worth more than its cost, since there may no longer be spare parts or service providers available for it. Another example is a specialty device with a long leadtime to acquire because of manufacturing or transportation requirements. This device has a unique value to the organization. After the organization has identified this unique value, it can address ways to control the risk of losing access to the unique asset. An organization can also control the risk of loss for this kind of asset by buying and storing a backup device.

- **Which information asset would be the most expensive to protect?** In this case, you are looking at the cost of providing controls. Some assets are by their nature difficult to protect. Finding a complete answer to this factor may have to be delayed beyond the risk identification phase of the process, because the costs of controls cannot be computed until the controls are identified, and that is a later step in this process. But, information about the difficulty of establishing controls should be collected in this identification phase.

- **Which information asset would be the most embarrassing or cause the greatest liability if revealed?** Almost every organization is aware of their *image* in the local, national, and international spheres. Some assets would prove especially embarrassing if they were compromised. The image of Microsoft, for example, was tarnished when one of its employees became a victim of the QAZ Trojan capability and the latest version of Microsoft Office was stolen.[3]

In addition to those listed above, there are other company-specific questions that may add value to the evaluation process. They should be identified, documented, and added to the process. To finalize this step of the information asset identification process, each organization should weight each asset based on the answers to the chosen questions.

Listing Assets in Order of Importance

Once each question, or criterion, has been weighted, calculating the importance of each asset is straightforward. The final step is to list the assets in order of importance. This can be achieved by using a weighted factor analysis worksheet similar to the one shown in Table 4-2. In this process, each information asset is assigned a score for each critical factor.

In the example shown in Table 4-2, the NIST SP800-30 recommended values of 0.1 to 1.0 are used. NIST SP800-30 is a document which is published by the National Institute of Standards and Technology and is entitled *Risk Management for Information Technology Systems*. Chapter Eight covers this document in greater detail. (Your organization may choose to use other weighting factors). Each critical factor has a weight assigned, showing that criteria's assigned importance for the organization.

TABLE 4-2   Example of a Weighted Factor Analysis Worksheet

Information asset	Criteria 1: impact to revenue	Criteria 2: impact to profitability	Criteria 3: public image impact	Weighted score
Criterion Weight (1-100) *Must total 100*	30	40	30	
EDI Document Set 1— Logistics BOL to outsourcer (outbound)	0.8	0.9	0.5	75
EDI Document Set 2— Supplier orders (outbound)	0.8	0.9	0.6	78
EDI Document Set 2— Supplier fulfillment advice (inbound)	0.4	0.5	0.3	41
Customer order via SSL (inbound)	1.0	1.0	1.0	100
Customer service request via e-mail (inbound)	0.4	0.4	0.9	55

Notes: EDI: Electronic Data Interchange
        SSL: Secure Sockets Layer

A quick review of Table 4-2 shows that the Customer order via SSL (inbound) data flow is the most important asset on this worksheet, and that the EDI Document Set 2–Supplier fulfillment advice (inbound) is the least critical.

Data Classification and Management

Corporate and military organizations use a variety of classification schemes. Georgia-Pacific Corporation (G-P) uses a corporate **data classification scheme** throughout the company that helps secure confidentiality and integrity of information.

The G-P information classification scheme has three categories: confidential, internal, and external. Information owners are responsible for classifying the information assets for which they are responsible. At least once a year, information owners must review information classifications to ensure the information is still classified correctly and the appropriate access controls are in place.

The information classifications are defined as follows:

- **Confidential:** Used for the most sensitive Georgia-Pacific information that must be tightly controlled, even within the company. Access to information with this classification is strictly on a need-to-know basis or as required by the terms of a contract. Information with this classification may also be referred to as "sensitive" or "proprietary."

- **Internal:** Used for all internal information that does not meet the criteria for the confidential category and is to be viewed only by G-P employees, authorized contractors, and other third parties.
- **External:** All information that has been approved by management for public release.[4]

As you might expect, the U.S. military classification scheme has a more complex categorization system than required by most corporations. The military is perhaps the best-known user of data classifications schemes. Primarily concerned with the protection of the confidentiality of information, the military has invested heavily in INFOSEC (information security), OPSEC (operations security), and COMSEC (communications security). In fact, many of the developments in data communications and information security are the result of military-sponsored research and development. For most information, the military uses a five-level classification scheme: Unclassified, Sensitive But Unclassified (i.e., For Official Use Only), Confidential, Secret, And Top Secret. Each of these is defined below.[5]

1. **Unclassified Data:** Information that can generally be distributed to the public without any threat to U.S. national interests.
2. **Sensitive But Unclassified (SBU) Data:** "Any information of which the loss, misuse, or unauthorized access to, or modification of might adversely affect U. S. National interests, the conduct of Department of Defense (DoD) programs, or the privacy of DoD personnel." Common classifications in this category include For Official Use Only, Not for Public Release, or For Internal Use Only.
3. **Confidential Data:** "Any information or material the unauthorized disclosure of which reasonably could be expected to cause damage to the national security. Examples of damage include the compromise of information that indicates strength of ground, air, and naval forces in the United States and overseas areas; disclosure of technical information used for training, maintenance, and inspection of classified munitions of war; revelation of performance characteristics, test data, design, and production data on munitions of war."
4. **Secret:** "Any information or material the unauthorized disclosure of which reasonably could be expected to cause serious damage to the national security. Examples of serious damage include disruption of foreign relations significantly affecting the national security; significant impairment of a program or policy directly related to the national security; revelation of significant military plans or intelligence operations; compromise of significant military plans or intelligence operations; and compromise of significant scientific or technological developments relating to national security."
5. **Top Secret Data:** "Any information or material the unauthorized disclosure of which reasonably could be expected to cause exceptionally grave damage to the national security. Examples of exceptionally grave damage include armed hostilities against the United States or its allies; disruption of foreign relations vitally affecting the national security; the compromise of vital national defense plans or complex cryptologic and communications intelligence systems; the revelation of sensitive intelligence operations; and the disclosure of scientific or technological developments vital to national security." This classification comes with the general expectation of "crib-to-grave" protection, meaning that any individual entrusted with top-secret information is expected to retain this level of confidence for their lifetime.

The military also has some specialty classification ratings such as Personnel Information and Evaluation Reports, to protect related areas of information. Federal agencies as the FBI and CIA also use specialty classification schemes, like Need-to-Know, and Named Projects. Obviously, Need-to-Know allows access to information by individuals who need the information to perform their work. Named Projects are clearance levels based on a scheme similar to Need-to-Know. When an operation, project, or set of classified data is created, the project is assigned a code name, such as Phoenix. Next, a list of authorized individuals is created and assigned to either the Need-to-Know or Named Projects category, and the list is maintained to enable the restriction of access to these categories of material.

Most organizations do not need the detailed level of classification used by the military or federal agencies. However, organizations may find it necessary to classify data to provide protection. A simple scheme can allow an organization to protect such sensitive information as marketing or research data, personnel data, customer data, and general internal communications. Or, a scheme such as the following could be adopted:

Public: Information for general public dissemination, such as an advertisement or public release.

For Official Use Only: Information that is not particularly sensitive, but not for public release, such as internal communications.

Sensitive: Information important to the business that could embarrass the company or cause loss of market share if revealed.

Classified: Information of the utmost secrecy to the organization, disclosure of which could severely impact the well-being of the organization.

Security Clearances

The other side of the data classification scheme is the personnel **security clearance** structure. For organizations that require security clearances for their employees, each user of data in the organization must be assigned a single level of authorization that indicates the level of classification he or she is authorized to view. This is usually accomplished by assigning each employee to a named role, such as data entry clerk, development programmer, information security analyst, or even CIO. Most organizations have developed a set of roles and the accompanying security clearances associated with each role. The result is that individuals are assigned security labels that correlate with the security labels of the data or information. Overriding this security clearance is the fundamental principle of **need-to-know**. Regardless of one's security clearance, an individual is not allowed to view data simply because it falls within that individual's level of clearance. Before an individual is allowed access to a specific set of data, he must meet the need-to-know requirement. This extra level of protection ensures that the confidentiality of information is properly maintained.

Management of Classified Data

Once data is classified, it must also be managed. Requirements for the management of information include the storage, distribution, portability, and destruction of classified information. Information that has a classification designation other than unclassified or public must be clearly marked as such. The military uses color-coordinated cover sheets to protect classified information from the casual observer. Take a look at the examples shown in Figure 4-4. In addition, each classified document should contain the appropriate designation at the top and bottom of each page. When classified data is stored, it must be available only to authorized individuals. This usually requires locking file cabinets, safes, or other such protective devices for hard copies and systems. When an individual carries classified information, it should be inconspicuous, as in a locked briefcase or portfolio.

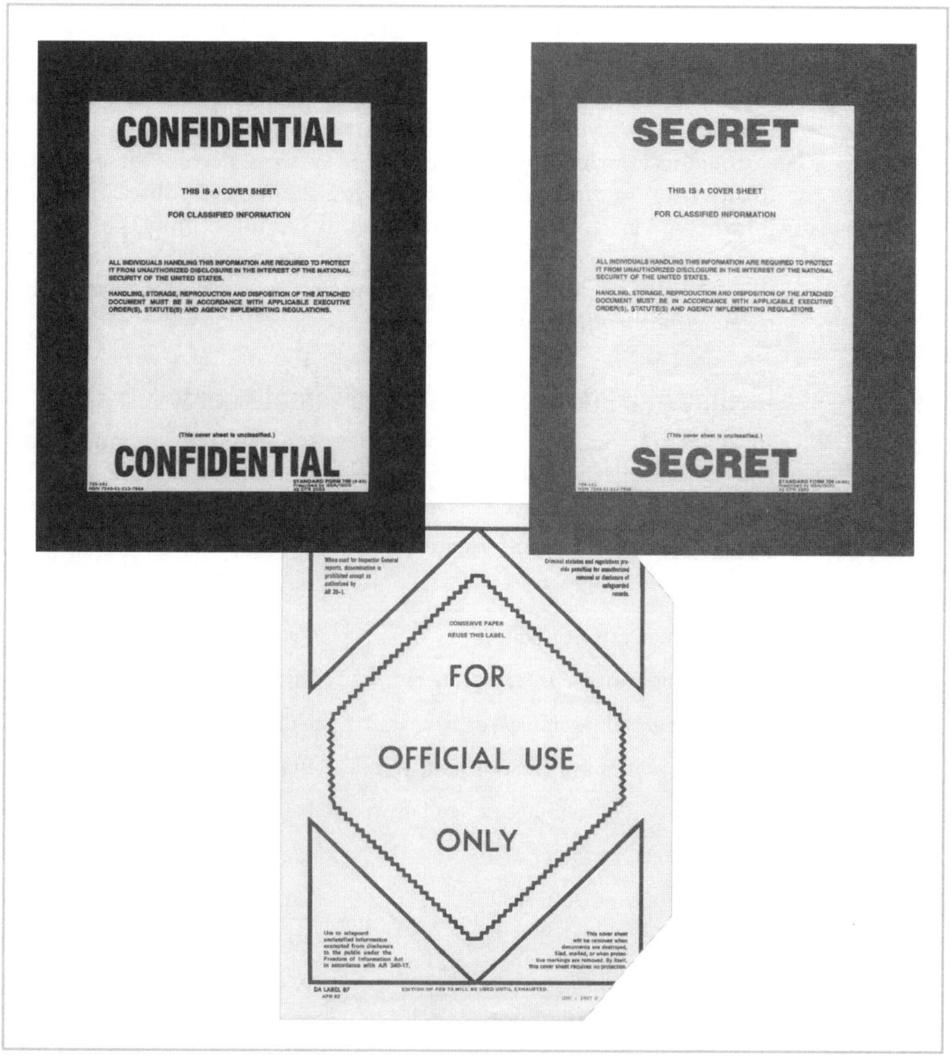

FIGURE 4-4 Military Data Classification Cover Sheets

One control policy that usually meets with difficulty in the organization is the **clean desk policy**. A clean desk policy requires each employee to secure all information in its appropriate storage container at the end of each day. When copies of classified information are no longer valuable or excessive copies exist, proper care should be taken to destroy unneeded copies, usually after double signature verification. Destruction is often through shredding, burning, or transfer to a service offering authorized document destruction. One area of particular concern in the destruction of classified information is the enforcement of policies to ensure that no classified information is inappropriately disposed of in trash or recycling areas. As indicated earlier, there are individuals who engage in **dumpster diving** to retrieve information that could prove embarrassing to the company or could compromise the security of information.

Threat Identification

After identifying and performing a preliminary classification of an organization's information assets, the analysis phase moves on to an examination of the threats facing the organization. As you discovered in Chapter 2, a wide variety of threats face an organization and its information and information systems. Each of these threats has the potential to attack any of the assets protected. If you assume every threat can and will attack every information asset, the project scope quickly becomes complex enough to overwhelm the ability to plan. To make this part of the process manageable, each step in the threat identification and vulnerability identification process is managed separately and then coordinated at the end of the process.

Identify And Prioritize Threats and Threat Agents

In Chapter 2, you identified 12 categories of threats to information security. These are listed alphabetically in Table 2-1 and are repeated here in Table 4-3.

TABLE 4-3   Threats to Information Security

Threat	Example
Act of human error or failure	Accidents, employee mistakes
Compromises to intellectual property	Piracy, copyright infringement
Deliberate acts of espionage or trespass	Unauthorized access and data collection
Deliberate acts of information extortion	Blackmail for information disclosure
Deliberate acts of sabotage or vandalism	Destruction of systems or information
Deliberate acts of theft	Illegal confiscation of equipment or information
Deliberate software attacks	Viruses, worms, macros, denial of service
Forces of nature	Fire, flood, earthquake, lightning
Quality of service deviations from service providers	Power and WAN quality of service issues
Technical hardware failures or errors	Equipment failure
Technical software failures or errors	Bugs, code problems, unknown loopholes
Technological obsolescence	Antiquated or outdated technologies

©2003 ACM, Inc., Included here by permission.

Each of these threats presents a unique challenge to information security and must be handled with sets of specific controls that directly address the particular nature of each threat and the threat agent's attack strategy.

But before threats can be used in the information security process, each threat must be further examined to assess its potential to impact the specific targeted organization. In general this is referred to as a **threat assessment**. To frame the discussion of threat assessment, you can address each threat with a few basic questions. The answer to each question is then used in the next question to further refine the understanding of these threats. These questions are:

- **Which threats present a danger to an organization's assets in the given environment?** Not all threats face every organization. Beginning with the general categories of threats presented in Table 4-3, the organization examines each category and determines if any of the categories do not apply to it. While it is unlikely that an entire category of threats can be eliminated, if it is possible, such elimination speeds up later steps of the process. Take a look at the Offline entitled "Threats to Information Security" to see what threats leading CIOs identified for their organizations. Once an organization has determined which threats apply to its business, the security team brainstorms for particular examples of threats within each category. These specific threats are examined to determine if any do not apply to the organization. For example, a company with offices in the 12th floor of a high-rise in Denver, Colorado, might not be subject to the threat of floods.Similarly, a firm with an office in Oklahoma City, Oklahoma, might not be concerned with landslides. With this methodology, specific threats may be eliminated because of very low probability.

- **Which threats represent the most danger to the organization's information?** Danger of a threat is something difficult to assess. Danger may be simply the probability of a threat attacking the organization, or it can represent the amount of damage the threat could create. It can also represent the frequency with which an attack can occur. Since this is a preliminary assessment, the analysis is limited to examining the existing level of preparedness, as well as improving the strategy of information security. The results represent a quick overview of the components involved.

As you will discover in Chapter 5, you can use both quantitative and qualitative measures to rank values. Since information in this case is preliminary, the security team may wish to subjectively rank threats in order of danger. Alternatively, the organization may simply rate each of the threats on a scale of one to five, with one indicating threats that are not significant and five indicating threats that are highly significant.

OFFLINE

Threats to Information Security—Survey of Industry

Adapted from "Enemy at the Gates: Threats to Information Security"[7]
By Michael E. Whitman, Communications of the ACM, 2003, forthcoming.

What are the threats to information security according to top computing executives? A recent study by Professor Mike Whitman asked that very question. Based on the categories of threats presented earlier, over 1000 top computing executives were asked to rate each threat category on a scale of not significant to very significant. The data was converted to a five-point scale with five representing very significant. You can see in the table below that the mean of the threats ranged from 3.99 to 2.45. CIOs were also asked to identify the top five threats to their organizations. This was converted into a weight with five points for a first place vote, and so on to one point for a fifth place vote. The sum of weights is presented under the Weight heading in the table below. The two ratings were combined into a weighted rank.

continued

Weighted Ranks to Threats to information Security

Threat	Mean	Std. Dev	Weight	Weighted Rank
1. Deliberate software attacks	3.99	1.03	546	2178.3
2. Technical software failures or errors	3.16	1.13	358	1129.9
3. Act of human error or failure	3.15	1.11	350	1101.0
4. Deliberate acts of espionage or trespass	3.22	1.37	324	1043.6
5. Deliberate acts of sabotage or vandalism	3.15	1.37	306	962.6
6. Technical hardware failures or errors	3.00	1.18	314	942.0
7. Deliberate acts of theft	3.07	1.30	226	694.5
8. Forces of nature	2.80	1.09	218	610.9
9. Compromises to intellectual property	2.72	1.21	181	494.8
10. Quality of service deviations from service providers	265	1.06	164	433.9
11. Technological obsolescence	2.71	1.11	158	427.9
12. Deliberate acts of information extortion	2.45	1.42	92	225.2

Another popular study also examines threats to information security. The Computer Security Institute in cooperation with the Federal Bureau of Investigation conducts an annual study of computer crime. The CSI/FBI Survey table presented below shows their results from the last five years.

The number of attacks is increasing. In the CSI/FBI study, the average company reported between 10 to 15 attacks per year. This represents a steady rise each year from an average of 5 to 10 in 1996. Unfortunately the number of organizations reporting that they just don't know is also rising. The fact is, almost every company has been attacked. Whether or not that attack was successful depends on the company's security efforts. Whether a company catches an attack and is then willing to report the attack is another matter entirely.

continued

CSI/FBI Survey Results for Types of Attack or Misuse (1997-2001)[8]

Types of attack or misuse	2001:	2000:	1999:	1998:	1997:
1. Virus	94%	85%	90%	83%	82%
2. Insider abuse of net access	91%	79%	97%	77%	68%
3. Laptop	64%	60%	69%	64%	58%
4. Unauthorized access by insiders	49%	71%	55%	44%	40%
5. System penetration	40%	25%	30%	23%	20%
6. Denial of service	36%	27%	31%	24%	
7. Theft of proprietary info	26%	20%	25%	18%	20%
8. Sabotage	18%	17%	13%	14%	14%
9. Financial fraud	12%	11%	14%	14%	12%
10. Telecom fraud	10%	11%	17%	16%	27%
11. Telecom eavesdropping	10%	7%	14%	9%	11%
12. Active wiretap	2%	1%	2%	1%	3%

All text, excluding the "CSI/FBI Survey Results for Attack of Misuse,"
©2003 ACM, Inc., Included here by permission.

■ **How much would it cost to recover from a successful attack?** One of the calculations that guides corporate spending on controls is the cost of recovery operations if an attack occurs and is successful. At this preliminary phase, it is not necessary to conduct a detailed assessment of the costs associated with recovering from a particular attack. One of the following techniques may be quite sufficient to allow investigators to continue with the process. You could subjectively rank or list the threats based on the cost to recover. Or you could assign a rating for each of the threats on a scale of one to five, with one representing not expensive at all and five representing extremely expensive. You could, if the information were available, assign a raw value to the cost, e.g., $5K, $10K, or $2M. In other words, the goal at this phase is to provide a rough assessment of the cost to recover operations should the attack interrupt normal business operations and require recovery. It may not be possible to assign a specific value, which is why the ranking or rating options are currently so popular.

■ **Which of the threats would require the greatest expenditure to prevent?** Just as in the previous question, another factor that impacts the level of danger associated with a particular threat is the amount it would cost to protect against the particular threat. Some threats have nominal costs of protection, as in malicious code. Some threats have extreme levels of costs for prevention, as in forces of nature. As a result, the amount of time and money invested in protecting against a particular threat is moderated by the amount of time and money required to fully protect against that particular threat. Here again you can begin by ranking, rating, or attempting to quantify the level of danger associated with protecting against a particular threat, by using the same techniques outlined above in calculating recovery costs. Take a look at the Offline on expenditure for threats to see how some top executives recently handled this issue.

By posing and answering the questions stated above, you have established a framework for the discussion of threat assessment. This list of questions may not cover everything that affects the information security assessment of the threats. If an organization has specific guidelines or policies, they should influence the process and require the posing of additional questions. This list can be easily expanded to include additional requirements.

OFFLINE

Expenditures For Threats To Information Security

Adapted from "Enemy at the Gates: Threats to Information Security"[9]
By Michael E. Whitman, Communications of the ACM, 2003, forthcoming.

The recent study by Professor Mike Whitman asked top computing executives to determine the priorities for expenditures for threats to information security. The respondents indicated their top five expenditures. These ratings were used to create a rank order of the expenses. The results are presented in the following table:

Weighted Ranking of Top Threat-Driven Expenditures

Threats	Weighted ranking
1. Deliberate software attacks	12.7
2. Act of Human Error or Failure	7.6
3. Technical software failures or errors	7.0
4. Technical hardware failures or errors	6.0
5. Quality of service deviations from service providers	4.9
6. Deliberate acts of espionage or trespass	4.7
7. Deliberate acts of theft	4.1
8. Deliberate acts of sabotage or vandalism	4.0
9. Technological obsolescence	3.3
10. Forces of nature	3.0
11. Compromises to intellectual property	2.2
12. Deliberate acts of information extortion	1.0

Vulnerability Identification

At this point in the risk identification process, you have identified the information assets of the organization and documented some criteria for beginning to assess the threats they face. You now proceed to reviewing each information asset for each threat it faces and creating a list of the **vulnerabilities** that remain viable risks to the organizations. What are vulnerabilities? They are specific avenues that threat agents can exploit to attack an information asset. They are chinks in the armor of the information asset—a flaw or weakness in an information asset, security procedure, design, or control that could be exercised either accidentally or on purpose to breach security. For example, if the edge router in an organization's DMZ is the asset, the threats to the possible vulnerabilities are analyzed Table 4-4.

TABLE 4-4   Vulnerability assessment of a hypothetical DMZ router

Threat	Possible vulnerabilities
Deliberate software attacks	■ Internet protocol is vulnerable to denial of service ■ Outsider IP fingerprinting activities can reveal sensitive information unless suitable controls are implemented
Act of human error or failure	■ Employees or contractors may cause outage if configuration errors are made
Technical software failures or errors	■ Vendor-supplied routing software could fail and cause an outage
Technical hardware failures or errors	■ Hardware can fail and cause an outage ■ Power system failures are always possible
Quality of service deviations from service providers	■ Unless suitable electrical power conditioning is provided, failure is probable over time
Deliberate acts of espionage or trespass	■ This information asset has little intrinsic value, but other assets protected by this device could be attacked if it compromised
Deliberate theft	■ This information asset has little intrinsic value, but other assets protected by this device could be attacked if it is compromised
Deliberate acts of sabotage or vandalism	■ Internet protocol is vulnerable to denial of service ■ This devise may be subject to defacement or cache poisoning
Technological obsolescence	■ If this asset is not reviewed and periodically updated, it may fall too far behind its vendor support model to be kept in service
Forces of nature	■ All information assets in the organization are subject to forces of nature, unless suitable controls are provided
Compromises to intellectual property	■ This information asset has little intrinsic value, but other assets protected by this device could be attacked if it is compromised
Deliberate acts of information extortion	■ This information asset has little intrinsic value, but other assets protected by this device could be attacked if it is compromised

Now, you examine how each of the threats that are possible or likely could be perpetrated and list the organization's assets and their vulnerabilities. The list is usually long and shows all the vulnerabilities of the information asset. Some threats are manifested in multiple ways, yielding multiple vulnerabilities for that threat. The process of listing vulnerabilities is somewhat subjective and is based on the experience and knowledge of the people creating the list. Therefore, the process works best when groups of people with diverse backgrounds within the organization work iteratively in a series of brainstorming sessions. For instance, the team that reviews the vulnerabilities for networking equipment should include the networking specialists, the systems management team that operates the network, the information security risk specialist, and even technically proficient users of the system.

At the end of the process, a list of assets and their vulnerabilities list has been developed. This list is the starting point (with its supporting documentation from the identification process) for the next step, risk assessment.

Risk Assessment

Now that you have identified the information assets of the organization, their threats and vulnerabilities, you can assess the relative risk for each of the vulnerabilities. This is accomplished by a process called **risk assessment**. Risk assessment assigns a risk rating or score to each specific information asset. While this number does not mean anything in absolute terms, it is useful in gauging the relative risk introduced by each vulnerable information asset and facilitates making comparative ratings later in the risk control process.

Introduction to Risk Assessment

Figure 4-5 represents the factors that go into the risk-rating estimate for each of the vulnerabilities.

FIGURE 4-5   Risk Identification Estimate Factors

It is important to note that the goal at this point is to create a method to evaluate the relative risk of each of the listed vulnerabilities. Chapter 5 describes methods to determine more accurate and detailed costs of each of the vulnerabilities, as well as projected expenses for the variety of controls that can reduce the risk for each of them.For now, you use the simpler risk model of Figure 4-5 to evaluate the risk for each information asset. The next section presents the factors that are used to calculate the relative risk for each vulnerability.

Likelihood

Likelihood is the overall rating of the probability that a specific vulnerability within an organization will be successfully attacked.[10] In common usage, you assign a numeric value for the likelihood of a vulnerability being successfully exploited. The National Institute of Standards and Technology recommends in Special Publication 800-30 that likelihood vulnerabilities be assigned a number between 0.1 for low and 1.0 for high. Being struck by a meteorite while indoors would be rated 0.1. At the other extreme, receiving at least one e-mail containing a virus or worm in the next year would be rated 1.0. You could also choose to use a number between 1 and 100, but there is no option to use zero, since those vulnerabilities with a zero likelihood have already been removed from the asset/vulnerability list. Whatever rating system you decide on for assigning likelihood, use professionalism, experience, and judgment use it consistently. Whenever possible, use external references for likelihood values that have been reviewed and adjusted for your specific circumstances. Many asset/vulnerability combinations have sources for likelihood such as the following:

- The likelihood of a fire has been estimated actuarially for each type of structure.
- The likelihood that any given e-mail contains a virus or worm has been researched.
- The number of network attacks can be forecast based on how many network addresses the organization has assigned.

Valuation of Information Assets

Using the information documented during the information asset identification steps, you can now assign weighted scores for the value to the organization of each information asset. The actual number used can vary with the needs of the organization. Some groups use a scale of 1 to 100, with 100 reserved for those information assets the loss of which would stop company operations within a few minutes. Other recommendations, including NIST SP 800-30, use assigned weights in broad categories, assigning all-important assets to a value of 100, all low-criticality assets to a value of 1, and all others a medium value of 50. Still other groups use weights from 1 to 10 in a scale or use assigned values of 1, 3, and 5 to represent low, medium, and high-valued assets. You can also create weight values for your specific needs. To be effective, the values must be assigned by asking the questions listed above in the section entitled, "Identify and Prioritize Threats and Threat Agents." These questions are restated below:

- Which threats present a danger to an organization's assets in the given environment?
- Which threats represent the most danger to the organization's information?
- How much would it cost to recover from a successful attack?
- Which of the threats would require the greatest expenditure to prevent?

After reevaluating these questions, you must use the background information from the risk identification process and illuminate that information by posing one additional question:

- Which of the questions posed above for each information asset is the most important to the protection of information of the organization?

This question helps to set priorities in the assessment of vulnerabilities. Which is the most important to the organization, the cost to recover from a threat attack, the cost to protect against a threat attack, or generally, which of the threats has the highest probability of successful attack? Additional questions, if helpful, may also be asked. Again, you are looking at threats the organization faces in its current state; however, this information will be valuable in later stages as you begin to design the final security solution. Once these questions are answered, you move to the next step in the process: examining how current controls can reduce the risk faced by specific vulnerabilities.

Percentage of Risk Mitigated by Current Controls

If a vulnerability is fully managed by an existing control, it no longer needs to be considered for additional controls and can be set aside. If it is partially controlled, estimate what percentage of the vulnerability has been controlled.

Uncertainty

It is not possible to know everything about each vulnerability, such as how likely it is to occur or how great an impact a successful attack would have. The degree that a current control can reduce risk is also subject to estimation error. You must now apply judgment to add a factor into the equation to allow for an estimation of the uncertainty of the information.

Risk Determination

For the purpose of relative risk assessment, risk *equals* likelihood of vulnerability occurrence *times* Value (or impact) *minus* percentage risk already controlled *plus* an element of uncertainty. For example:

- Information asset A has an value score of 50 and has one vulnerability: Vulnerability 1 has a likelihood of 1.0 with no current controls; and you estimate that assumptions and data are 90 percent accurate.
- Information asset B has an value score of 100 and has two vulnerabilities: Vulnerability 2 has a likelihood of 0.5 with a current control that addresses 50 percent of its risk; vulnerability 3 has a likelihood of 0.1 with no current controls. You estimate that assumptions and data are 80 percent accurate.
  The resulting ranked list of risk ratings for the three vulnerabilities is:

- Asset A: Vulnerability 1 rated as $55 = (50 \times 1.0) - 0\% + 10\%$
- Asset B: Vulnerability 2 rated as $35 = (100 \times 0.5) - 50\% + 20\%$
- Asset B: Vulnerability 3 rated as $12 = (100 \times 0.1) - 0\% + 20\%$

Identify Possible Controls

For each threat and its associated vulnerabilities that have residual risk, create a preliminary list of control ideas. **Residual risk** is the risk that remains to the information asset even after the existing control has been applied.

As you discovered in Chapter 1, controls, safeguards, and countermeasures are terms used to represent security mechanisms, policies, and procedures. These mechanisms, policies, and procedures counter attacks, reduce risk, resolve vulnerabilities, and otherwise improve the general state of security within an organization.

As was presented in the NSTISSC model in Chapter 1, there are three general categories of controls: policies, programs, and technologies.

Policies are documents that specify an organization's approach to security. There are four types of security policies: general security policy, program security policy, issue-specific policies, and systems-specific policies. Each of these types of policy is outlined in this section, and covered in additional detail in Chapter 6. The **general security policy** is an executive-level document that outlines the organization's approach and attitude towards information security and relates the strategic value of information security within the organization. This document, typically created by the CIO in conjunction with the CEO and CISO, sets the tone for all subsequent security activities. The **program security policy** is a planning document that outlines the process of implementing security in the organization. This policy is the blueprint for the analysis, design, and implementation of security. **Issue-specific policies** address the specific implementations or applications of which users should be aware. These policies are typically developed to provide detailed instructions and restrictions associated with security issues. Examples include policies for Internet use, e-mail, and access to the building. Finally, **systems-specific policies** address the particular use of certain systems. This could include firewall configuration policies, systems access policies, and other technical configuration areas. **Programs** are activities performed within the organization to improve security. These include security education, training, and awareness programs. Chapter 6 covers the details of these types of programs. Security **technologies** are the technical implementations of the policies defined by the organization. Chapter 8 presents a more detailed examination of the various technologies used in security implementations.

Access Controls

One particular application of controls is **access controls**, which specifically address admission of a user into a trusted area of the organization. These areas can include information systems, physically restricted areas such as computer rooms, and even the organization in its entirety. Access controls usually consist of a combination of policies, programs, and technologies.

Types of Access Controls

There are a number of approaches to, and categories of, controlling access. Access controls can be mandatory, nondiscretionary, or discretionary. Each of these approaches addresses a group of controls used to regulate access to a particular type or collection of information as explained below.

Mandatory access controls (MACs): MACs are required, obviously, and they are also structured and coordinated with a data classification scheme. With **mandatory access controls**, the users and data owners have limited control over the access to information resources. In a data classification scheme, each collection of information is rated. Next, each user is rated to specify the level of information the user may access. These ratings are often referred to as sensitivity levels, and these sensitivity levels indicate the level of confidentiality the information requires. A variation of this form of access control is called **lattice-based access control**, in which users are assigned a matrix of authorizations for particular areas of access. The level of authorization may vary between levels depending on the classification authorizations individuals possess for each group of information or resources. The lattice structure contains subjects and objects, and the boundaries associated with each pair are demarcated. Lattice-based control specifies the level of access each subject has to each object, if any. With this type of control, the column of attributes associated with a particular object (such as a printer) is referred to as an **access control list (ACL)**. The row of attributes associated with a particular subject (such as a user) is referred to as a **capabilities table**.

Nondiscretionary controls: These controls are determined by a central authority in the organization and can be based on an individual's role, and are called **role-based controls**, or a specified set of tasks the individual is assigned, which are called **task-based controls**. Task-based controls can also be based on lists maintained on subjects or objects. Role-based controls are tied to the role a particular user performs in an organization, and task-based controls are tied to a particular assignment or responsibility. The role and task controls make it easier to maintain the controls and restrictions associated with a particular role or task, especially if the individual performing the role or task changes often. Instead of constantly assigning and revoking the particular privileges of individuals who come and go, the administrator simply assigns the associated access rights to the role or task, and then whenever individuals are associated with those roles or tasks, they automatically receive the corresponding access. When their turns are over, they are removed from the role or task, and the access is revoked.

Discretionary access controls (DAC): These controls are implemented at the discretion or option of the data user. The ability to share resources in a peer-to-peer configuration allows users to control and possibly provide access to sets of information or resources at their disposal. The users can allow general, unrestricted access, or they can allow specific individuals or sets of individuals to access these resources. For example, a user has a hard drive containing information to be shared with office coworkers. This user can elect to allow access to specific individuals by providing access, by name, in the share control function. Figure 4-6 shows an example of a **discretionary access control** from a peer-to-peer network using Microsoft Windows.

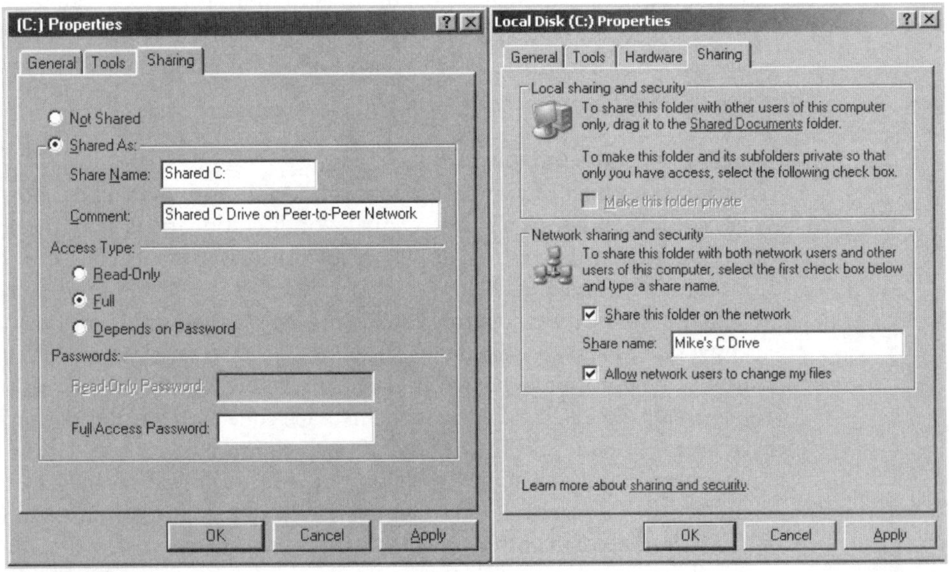

FIGURE 4-6 Discretionary Access Control Examples

Documenting Results of Risk Assessment

By the end of the risk assessment process, you probably have in hand a collection of long lists of information assets with data about each of them. The goal of this process so far has been to identify the information assets of the organization that have specific vulnerabilities and list them, ranked according to those most needing protection. In preparing this list, you have collected and preserved a wealth of factual information about the assets, the threats they face, and the vulnerabilities they expose. You should also have collected some information about the controls that are already in place. The final summarized document is the ranked vulnerability risk worksheet, as pictured in Table 4-5. A review of this worksheet shows similarities to the weighted factor analysis worksheet shown in Table 4-2. The worksheet shown in Table 4-5 is used as follows:

- Asset: List each vulnerable asset.
- Asset impact: Show the results for this asset from the Weighted Factor Analysis Worksheet. In the example, this is a number from 1 to 100.
- Vulnerability: List each uncontrolled vulnerability.
- Vulnerability likelihood: State the likelihood of the realization of the vulnerability by a threat-agent as noted in the vulnerability analysis step. In the example, the number is from 0.1 to 1.0.
- Risk-rating factor: Enter the figure calculated from the asset impact multiplied by likelihood. In the example, the calculation yields a number from 0.1 to 100.

TABLE 4-5   Ranked Vulnerability Risk Worksheet

Asset	Asset impact	Vulnerability	Vulnerability likelihood	Risk-rating factor
Customer service request via e-mail (inbound)	55	E-mail disruption due to hardware failure	0.2	11
Customer order via SSL (inbound)	100	Lost orders due to web server hardware failure	0.1	10
Customer order via SSL (inbound)	100	Lost orders due to Web server or ISP service failure	0.1	10
Customer service request via e-mail (inbound)	55	E-mail disruption due to SMTP mail relay attack	0.1	5.5
Customer service request via e-mail (inbound)	55	E-mail disruption due to ISP service failure	0.1	5.5
Customer order via SSL (inbound)	100	Lost orders due to Web server denial-of-service attack	0.025	2.5
Customer order via SSL (inbound)	100	Lost orders due to Web server software failure	0.01	1

SSL: Secure sockets layer

If you look at the sample results shown in Table 4-5, you may not have guessed that the environment shows that the most pressing risk requires making the mail server or servers more robust. Even though the impact of the information asset represented by the customer service e-mail has an impact rating of only 55, the relatively high likelihood of a hardware failure makes it the most pressing problem.

Now that you have completed the risk identification process, what should the documentation package for this process look like? In other words, what are the deliverables from this phase of the project SecSDLC? The process you develop for risk identification should include designating what function the reports serve, who is responsible for preparing the reports, and who reviews them. The ranked vulnerability risk worksheet is the initial working document for the next step in the risk management process: assessing and controlling risk. Table 4-6 shows a sample list of the worksheets that have been prepared by the information security project team.

TABLE 4-6   Risk Identification and Assessment Deliverables

Deliverable	Purpose
Information asset classification worksheet	Assembles information about information assets and their impact on or value to the organization
Weighted criteria analysis worksheet	Assigns ranked value or impact weight to each information asset
Ranked vulnerability risk worksheet	Assigns ranked value of risk rating for each uncontrolled asset-vulnerability pair

The goal of this chapter has been to identify risks facing an organization and to understand how to assign a preliminary relative ranking. The next step in the risk management process is to control the risks identified. This is done by first exploring the ways that risk can be mitigated or controlled. Then controls should be applied, evaluating and assessing them to be sure they are effective and applied in economically feasible ways. Once implemented, controls need to be kept current and verified as effective.

The risk management process comprises the analysis phase of the SecSDLC. This may be confusing, since the phase itself covers activities that could be attributed to other phases, such as design, implementation, and maintenance. You need to understand that some organizations do not use a fully formed SecSDLC, and instead rely on an approach that focuses exclusively on risk management for achieving all information security goals.

Chapter Summary

- Risk management examines and documents the current information technology security being used in an organization. Management is responsible for identifying and controlling the risks the organization encounters. In the modern organization, the information security group often plays a leadership role in risk management.

- A key component of a risk management strategy is the identification, classification, and prioritization of the information assets in the organization.

- Assessment is the identification of assets, including all of the elements of an organization's system: people, procedures, data and information, software, hardware, and networking elements.

- The human resources, documentation, and data information assets of an organization are not as easily identified and documented as tangible assets, such as hardware and software. These more elusive assets should be identified, described, and evaluated by people using knowledge, experience, and judgment.

- A number of questions can be used to develop weighting criteria for information assets, including: Which information asset is the most important to the critical success of the organization? Which information asset generates the most revenue? Which information asset generates the most profitability? Which information asset would be the most expensive to replace? Which information asset would be the most expensive to protect? Which information asset would be the most embarrassing if revealed? What questions should be added to cover the needs of a specific organization and its environment?

- After identifying and performing a preliminary classification of information assets, the threats facing an organization should be examined. There are 12 categories of threats to information security noted in the text.

- To fully understand each threat and the impact it can have on the organization, each identified threat must be examined through a threat assessment process that addresses the following questions; Which of these threats: Exist in this organization's environment? Are most dangerous to the organization's information? Require the greatest expenditure for recovery? Require the greatest expenditure for protection?

- An organization may have specific guidelines or policies that should influence the threat assessment process and require the posing of additional questions.

- Each information asset is evaluated for each threat it faces; the resulting information is used to create a list of the vulnerabilities that remain as risks to the organization. The process results in an information asset and vulnerability list, which becomes the starting point for risk assessment.

- The goal of risk assessment is the assignment of a risk rating or score that represents the relative risk for a specific vulnerability of a specific information asset.

- Likelihood is of the probability that a potential vulnerability may be exploited within the organization's threat environment.

- If any specific vulnerability is completely managed by an existing control, it no longer need be considered for additional controls.

- For each identified threat and its associated vulnerabilities that have any uncontrolled risk, a preliminary list of control ideas should be created. Controls, safeguards, and countermeasures are terms for security mechanisms, policies, and procedures that counter attacks, reduce risk, resolve vulnerabilities, and otherwise improve the general state of security within an organization.

- In general there are three categories of controls: policies, programs, and technologies.
- Access controls can be categorized as mandatory, discretionary, and nondiscretionary.

Review Questions

1. What is risk management?
2. List and describe the key areas of risk management.
3. Why is identification of risks, by listing assets and their vulnerabilities, so important to the risk management process?
4. According to Sun Tzu, what two key understandings must you achieve to be successful?
5. Who is responsible for risk management in an organization?
6. Which community of interest usually takes the lead in information security risk management?
7. In risk management strategies, why does periodic review have to be a part of the process?
8. In which phase of the SecSDLC does risk management occur?
9. Why can't you use the standard list of system components when doing risk identification in the SecSDLC?
10. Why do networking components need more examination from an information security perspective than from a systems development perspective?
11. What value would an automated asset inventory system have for the risk identification process?
12. What information attributes would seldom or never be applied to software elements?
13. What information attribute is often of great value for networking equipment when DHCP is not used?
14. When you document procedures, why is it useful to know where the electronic versions are stored?
15. Which is more important to the systems components classification scheme, that the list be comprehensive or mutually exclusive?
16. What's the difference between an asset's ability to generate revenue and its ability to generate profit?
17. How many categories must be in a data classification scheme? Why?
18. How many threat categories are listed in the textbook? Which do you think is the most common and why?
19. What are vulnerabilities? How do you identify them?
20. Examine both the simplest risk formula and the one presented in this chapter? Are there other formulas? If so, when are they used?

Exercises

1. If an organization has three information assets to evaluate for risk management as shown in the accompanying data, which vulnerability should be evaluated for additional controls first? Which one should be evaluated last?

   Data for Exercise 1:
   - Switch L47 connects a network to the Internet. It has two vulnerabilities: it is susceptible to hardware failure at a likelihood of 0.2, and it is subject to an SNMP buffer overflow attack at a likelihood of 0.1. This switch has an impact rating of 90 and has no current controls in place. You are 75 percent certain of the assumptions and data.

- Server WebSrv6 hosts a company Web site and performs e-commerce transactions. It has a Web server version that can be attacked by sending it invalid Unicode values. The likelihood of that attack is estimated at 0.1. The server has been assigned an impact value of 100 and a control has been implanted that reduces the impact of the vulnerability by 75 percent. You are 80 percent certain of the assumptions and data.

- Operators use a MGMT45 control console to monitor operations in the server room. It has no passwords and is susceptible to unlogged misuse by the operators. Estimates show the likelihood of misuse is 0.1. There are no controls in place on this asset; it has an impact rating of 5. You are 90 percent certain of the assumptions and data.

2. Using the Web, search for tools to automate risk assessment. (Chapter 5 addresses risk management in more detail.) Collect information on automated risk assessment tools for use in the discussions of Chapter 5. What do they cost? What features do they provide?

3. Take the list of threats to information security presented in Table 4-3 and find three examples of each threat not covered in this chapter.

4. Using the data classification scheme presented in this chapter, identify and classify the information contained in your personal computer or personal digital assistant. Based on the potential for misuse or embarrassment, what information would be confidential, sensitive but unclassified, or for public release?

5. Using the asset valuation method presented in this chapter, conduct a preliminary risk assessment of the information contained in your home. Answer each of the questions covered in the chapter. What would it cost if you lost all your data?

Case Exercises

I. The Question of Risk Management

Adapted from "Hackers and Other Hazards"[11]

By Emily Q. Freeman, *Financial Executive*, May/June, 2000.

"Risk management has always concerned itself with critical enterprise infrastructures—processes and assets essential to basic business operations. In a technology-based environment, an enterprise's core operations depend on electronic information and computer networks. Everything a business knows and has besides its creative people resides on its databases and systems. Information technology risk management now should involve the identification, assessment, control, mitigation and financing and probable risks commensurate with the enterprise's brand, reputation, assets and operations."[12]

Identifying and understanding threats is an important first step in risk management. Since the explosion of the Internet, these threats have increased in probability of attack and in magnitude. Internet technologies have affected the management of liability risks and exposure, so that we see:

- "A rise in the number of claims

- "An upsurge in the severity of claims

- "Increases in the number of defendants

- "Increases in the complexity of traditional claims and procedural issues

- "New claims and remedies"[13]

Businesses must analyze their systems and processes to identify vulnerabilities and exposure. This analysis can be performed by in-house or contracted experts and can include ethical hacking, policy evaluations, and monitoring. "One consulting service many businesses want is risk identification and mapping by frequency and severity… The results will yield a more efficient use of resources for adopting risk control and risk mitigation strategies."[14]

Barriers to risk management include the funding chasm in technology, and the misperception that technology alone can solve the problem. Information Security risks need to be managed as business risks, as they will emerge on financial statements and will be the focal point of legal action.

1. Why has the Internet so negatively affected the management of risk and liability?

2. How does the increase in legal action impact the security risk management of an organization? How does it affect the expenditures on security? Research this article on the Internet and examine the pressing questions associated with risk management.

II. Risk Assessment as a Project Management Tool

Adapted from "Risky Business: Beyond TCO and ROI"[15]
By Adrian Mello, *ZDNet Tech Update Online*, June, 2002.

"Times are tough in the current economic climate. Enterprises are increasingly scrutinizing their IT spending, and proponents of e-business projects must go to much greater lengths to justify any spending. Two metrics are primarily used to do this: total cost of ownership (TCO) and return on investment (ROI). These metrics are certainly useful but they fall short of providing a complete financial picture for business planning."[16]

The concept of total cost of ownership allows a more complete understanding of the costs associated with an IT project. In addition to the costs associated with the purchase (or creation) of software and hardware upgrades, there are hidden costs such as consultation fees, personnel training, preparation of data, software integration, documentation, and the management of change and the project itself. This provides a much more realistic view of the total cost of ownership (TCO), as the name suggests. Unfortunately TCO doesn't provide the answer to the question, "If you pay for all this, what do you get for your money?"

The answer to this question is return on investment. ROI attempts to determine the improvement in bottom-line dollars that can be directly attributable to a particular expenditure. ROI too has faults, as it cannot paint the whole picture. "TCO and ROI are useless when it comes to evaluating risk, flexibility, and intangible benefits—factors that have a critical impact on business and should be factored into spending decisions."[17]

The missing piece of the picture is risk assessment. Risks don't lend themselves to easy or precise quantification. General frameworks do provide enough insight to make the process work.

There are a number of common risk factors to consider when performing risk assessment on a project. These include project size, technology, vendors, resources, management, market conditions, and culture.

1. How is a study of project management related to the management of security? Can the implementation of security be construed as a project to be managed?

2. What areas of risk assessment work with TCO and ROI to fill in the missing pieces?

Endnotes

1. Sun Tzu, *The Art of War,* trans. Samuel B. Griffith (Oxford: Oxford University Press, 1988) p. 84.

2. Mike Godwin, "When Copying Isn't Theft," *Electronic Frontier Foundation Online,* [Cited 17 June 2002]; available from the World Wide Web *http://www.eff.org/IP/phrack_riggs_neidorf_godwin.article*

3. Ted Bridis and Rebecca Buckman, "Microsoft Hacked! Code Stolen?" *ZDNet News Online,* 26 October 2000, [Cited 17 June 2002]; available from the World Wide Web *http://zdnet.com.com/2100-11-525083.html.*

4. Adapted from the Georgia-Pacific Corporation Practices Guide.

5. U.S. Army, Fort Gordon, *School of Information Technology* AR 350-1. [Cited 5 March 2002]; available from the World Wide Web *http://atzhssweb.gordon.army.mil/otd/ c2protect/iaso/Army/AR%20380-5/chapter1.htm*

6. Michael E. Whitman, "Enemy at the Gates: Threats to Information Security" (*Communications of the ACM,* 2003, forthcoming).

7. *Ibid.*

8. Richard Power, "2001 CSI/FBI Computer Crime and Security Survey," *Computer Security Issues and Trends* 7, no. 1 (2001): 1-20.

9. Michael E. Whitman, "Enemy at the Gates: Threats to Information Security" (*Communications of the ACM,* 2003, forthcoming).

10. National Institute of Standards and Technology, *Risk Management Guide for Information Technology Systems,* SP 800-30, (January 2002).

11. Emily Q. Freeman, "Hackers and Other Hazards," *Financial Executive* 16, no. 3 (May/June 2000): 30-32.

12. *Ibid.*

13. *Ibid.*

14. *Ibid.*

15. Adrian Mello, "Risky Business: Beyond TCO and ROI," *ZDNet Tech Update Online,* (13 February 2002) [Cited 17 June 2002]; available from the World Wide Web *http://techupdate.zdnet.com/techupdate/stories/main/0,14179,2847269,00.html*

16. *Ibid.*

17. *Ibid.*

Risk Management: Assessing and Controlling Risk

> If this is the information superhighway, it's going through a lot of bad, bad, neighborhoods.
>
> **DORIAN BERGER, 1997**

CHARLIE OPENED THE DOOR TO the coffee shop and walked up to the counter to place his order. He ordered a soda and picked it up at the delivery counter. Turning to leave the store, he saw Jane Harris, the accounting supervisor of Sequential Label and Supply, at a table by the window. She was pouring over a spreadsheet that Charlie recognized.

"Hi Jane," he said. "Can I join you?"

"Sure Charley," she said. "Perhaps you can help we with this form you want us to fill out."

He saw she was working on the asset valuation worksheet he had sent to all of the managers of the company. On this form, he had listed all the information assets that everyone in his department could think of. Each manager of the company was asked to provide four figures for each item: how much it had cost, how much it would cost to replace, how important it is to the company, and a force-rank number with the most important item as number one, the second as number two, and so on. He hoped these numbers could be used to build a consensus about the relative importance of various assets to the company.

"What's the problem?" he asked.

"I understand these first two columns. But, how am I supposed to decide what's the most important?" she complained.

"Well," he began, "with your accounting background, you could base your answer on some of the data you collect about each of these information assets. For this quarter, what's more important to senior management, revenue or profitability?"

"Profitability is almost always more important. We have some systems that have lots of revenue, but operate at a loss," she said.

"Well, there you go," he said. "Why not calculate the profitability margin for each listed item and use that to rate and rank them?"

"Oh, okay, Charlie. Thanks for the idea." She started to make notes on her copy of the form. Charlie got up and headed for the door. He recalled his earlier meeting with the manager of the Shipping Department. Charlie had recommended ranking how each asset affected the Shipping Department's effectiveness. He had also suggested to the manager of marketing that he might want to use the percentage of sales that each listed asset generates. As he walked off to a meeting with the payroll manager, Charlie tried to think up an answer for that manager.

DISCUSSION QUESTION:

1. Is Charlie influencing the ranking process in inappropriate ways?

LEARNING OBJECTIVES:

Upon completion of this material you should be able to:

- Recognize why risk control is needed in today's organizations.
- Know the risk mitigation strategy options for controlling risks.
- Identify the categories that can be used to classify controls.
- Be aware of the conceptual frameworks that exist for evaluating risk controls, and be able to formulate a cost benefit analysis when required.
- Understand how to maintain and perpetuate risk controls.

Introduction

In the early days of information technology, corporations used IT systems mainly to gain a definitive advantage over the competition. Establishing a competitive business model, method, or technique allowed an organization to provide a product or service that was superior and created a **competitive advantage**. But, this is no longer true. The current IT industry has evolved from this earlier model to one in which all competitors have met an expected level of automation. IT is now readily available to all organizations that make the investment, allowing them to react quickly to changes in the market. In this highly competitive environment, organizations realize investing in IT systems to obtain a sustainable competitive advantage is no longer sufficient. This means that it is naive to expect that the implementation of new technologies enables an organization to maintain a competitive lead over others in the industry. Instead, the concept of **competitive disadvantage** has emerged, which is the need to avoid falling behind the competition. Effective IT-enabled organizations now quickly absorb emerging technologies, not to gain or maintain competitive advantage, but to avoid loss of market because of an inability to maintain the standard of highly responsive services required in today's marketplaces.

To keep up with the competition, organizations must design and create a safe environment in which business processes and procedures can function. This environment must maintain confidentiality and privacy and assure the integrity of organizational data. These objectives are met through the application of the principles of risk management.

Risk management is the process of identifying vulnerabilities in an organization's information systems and taking carefully reasoned steps to assure the confidentiality, integrity, and availability of all the components in the organization's information system. Each of the three components in the C.I.A. triangle, introduced in Chapter 1, is an essential component in every IT organization's ability to sustain long-term competitiveness. When an organization depends on IT-based systems to remain viable, information security and the discipline of risk management move beyond theoretical discussions and become an integral part of the economic basis for making business decisions. These decisions are based on trade-offs between the costs of applying information systems controls and the benefits realized from the operation of secured, available systems.

The concepts in this chapter build on those developed in Chapter 4. That chapter focused on the identification of risk and the assessment of its relative impact from all identified vulnerabilities. The primary result from that effort was a list of documented vulnerabilities, ranked by criticality of impact. In this chapter, working from that list, the goal is to assess options, estimate costs, weigh the relative merits of options, and gauge the benefits from various control approaches.

The discussion of controlling risk begins with risk mitigation strategies and how to formulate them. The chosen strategy may include applying controls to some or all of the vulnerabilities from the ranked vulnerability worksheet prepared in Chapter 4. This chapter explores a variety of control approaches, and follows with a discussion of how controls can be categorized to better understand control processes and details. The critical concept of cost benefit analysis is explained along with the topic of residual risk.

From there the chapter moves into examining how to evaluate the effectiveness of a control strategy through the process of assessment. The chapter finishes with a section on maintaining effective controls in the modern IT organization.

Risk Control Strategies

When organizational management has determined that risks from information security threats are creating a competitive disadvantage, they empower the information technology and information security communities of interest to control the risks. Once the project team for information security development has created the ranked vulnerability worksheet (see Chapter 4), the team must choose one of four basic strategies to control the risks that result from these vulnerabilities. The four strategies listed below guide an organization to:

1. Apply safeguards that eliminate or reduce the remaining uncontrolled risks for the vulnerability (avoidance)
2. Transfer the risk to other areas or to outside entities (transference)
3. Reduce the impact should the vulnerability be exploited (mitigation)
4. Understand the consequences and accept the risk without control or mitigation (acceptance)

Avoidance

Avoidance is the risk control strategy that attempts to prevent the exploitation of the vulnerability. This is the preferred approach, as it seeks to avoid risk in its entirety rather than dealing with it after it has been realized. Avoidance is accomplished through countering threats, removing vulnerabilities in assets, limiting access to assets, and adding protective safeguards.

There are three common methods of risk avoidance: avoidance through application of policy, avoidance through application of training and education, and avoidance through application of technology.

Avoidance Through Application of Policy

This approach allows management to mandate that certain procedures are always followed. For example, if the organization needs to control password use more tightly, a policy requiring passwords on all IT systems can be implemented. Note that policy alone may not be enough, and effective management always couples changes in policy with training and education or an application of technology, or both.

Implementing Training and Education

As explained in earlier chapters, policy must be communicated to employees. In addition, new technology often requires training. Awareness, training, and education are essential if employees are to exhibit safe and controlled behavior.

Applying Technology

In the real world of information security, technical solutions are often required to assure that risk is reduced. To continue the earlier example, passwords can be used with most modern operating systems. Some system administrators may not configure systems to use passwords. If, however, policy requires passwords, and the administrators are both aware of the requirement and trained to implement it, the technical control is successfully used.

Countering Threats

Risks are avoided by countering the threats facing an asset or by eliminating the exposure of a particular asset. Eliminating a threat is a difficult proposition, but it is possible. For example, when an organization becomes susceptible to **cyberactivism** (the use of computer-related technologies to advance a political agenda), it must take steps to avoid potential attacks. Recently McDonald's Corporation sought to reduce risks to its image by imposing stricter conditions on egg suppliers regarding the health and welfare of chickens.[1] This had been a source of contention between animal rights activists and the corporation for many years. This strategy accords with other changes made by McDonald's to meet demands from animal rights activists to improve relationships with these groups.

Implementing Security Controls and Safeguards

Another method of risk management that falls under the category of avoidance is the implementation of security controls and safeguards to deflect attacks on systems and therefore minimize the probability that an attack will be successful. An organization with dial-in access vulnerability, for example, may choose to implement a control or safeguard for those services. An authentication procedure based on a cryptographic technology, such as RADIUS (Remote Authentication Dial-In User Service) or another protocol or product, would provide sufficient control.[2] On the other hand, the organization may choose to eliminate this system and service to avoid the potential risk.

OFFLINE

The Human Firewall Project[3]

By The Human Firewall Council, July 2002

"A consortium of security experts from government, private industry, associations and nonprofit organizations known as the Human Firewall Council is directing the Human Firewall campaign. The goal of the Council is to help educate people in organizations on how to better protect information assets from the perspective of changing human behavior. The creation of a "human firewall" complements the usual technical firewalls and other network security devices and software designed to safeguard the enterprise.

"Eight Essential Steps to Building a Human Firewall

"1. Get top management buy-in and commitment. The Gartner Group has identified three major questions that executives and boards of directors need to answer when confronting information security issues:

- Is our security policy enforced fairly, consistently, and legally across the organization?
- Would our employees, contractors, and partners know if a security violation were being committed?
- Would they know what to do about it if they did recognize a security violation?

"2. Assign and clarify roles and responsibilities.

"3. Create an Action Plan with a budget.

"4. Develop and/or update information security policies."

"5. Develop an organization-wide Security Awareness/Education program.

"6. Measure the progress of your Security Awareness/Education efforts.

"7. Adapt and improve your Security Awareness/Education programs according to progress/feedback.

"8. Develop an information security incident response team and plan."

To see where the Human Firewall Council places people in the layers of defenses surrounding information, examine Figure 5-1.

continued

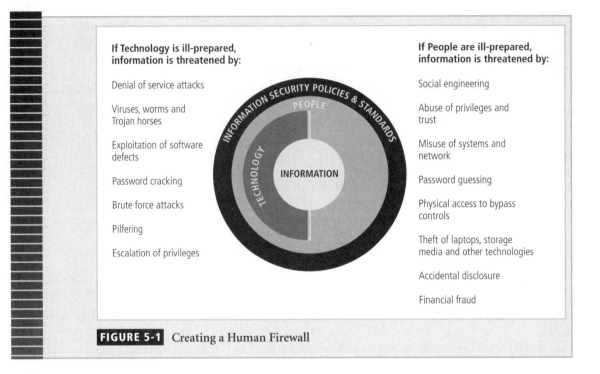

If Technology is ill-prepared, information is threatened by:

Denial of service attacks

Viruses, worms and Trojan horses

Exploitation of software defects

Password cracking

Brute force attacks

Pilfering

Escalation of privileges

If People are ill-prepared, information is threatened by:

Social engineering

Abuse of privileges and trust

Misuse of systems and network

Password guessing

Physical access to bypass controls

Theft of laptops, storage media and other technologies

Accidental disclosure

Financial fraud

INFORMATION SECURITY POLICIES & STANDARDS

PEOPLE

TECHNOLOGY

INFORMATION

FIGURE 5-1 Creating a Human Firewall

Transference

Transference is the control approach that attempts to shift the risk to other assets, other processes, or other organizations. This may be accomplished through rethinking how services are offered, revising deployment models, outsourcing to other organizations, purchasing insurance, or by implementing service contracts with providers.

In the popular book *In Search of Excellence* management consultants Tom Peters and Robert Waterman present a series of case studies of high-performing corporations. One of the eight characteristics of excellent organizations is that they "Stick to their knitting. They stay reasonably close to the business they know."[4] What does this mean? It means that a company such as Kodak, a manufacturer of photographic equipment and chemicals, focuses on photographic equipment and chemicals. A company such as General Motors focuses on the design and construction of cars and trucks. Neither company spends strategic energies on the technology of developing of Web sites. They focus energy and resources on what they do best while relying on consultants or contractors for other types of expertise.

These lessons should be taken to heart whenever an organization begins to expand its operations, including information and systems management, and even information security. If an organization does not already have quality security management and administration experience, it should hire individuals or firms that provide such expertise. For example, many organizations want Web services, including Web presences, domain name registration, domain, and Web hosting. Rather than implementing their own servers, hiring their own Webmasters, Web systems administrators, and even specialized security experts, savvy organizations hire an ISP or a consulting organization to provide these products and services for them.

This allows the organization to transfer the risk associated with the management of these complex systems to another organization that has experience in dealing with those risks. A side benefit of specific contract arrangements is that the provider is responsible for disaster recovery and through service level agreements is responsible for guaranteeing server and Web site availability.

Outsourcing, however, it not without its own risks. It is up to the owner of the information asset, IT management, and the information security team to ensure that the disaster recovery requirements of the outsourcing contract are sufficient and have been met *before* they are needed for recovery efforts. If the outsourcer has failed to meet the contract terms, the consequences may be far worse than expected.

OFFLINE

Top Ten Information Security Mistakes Made By Individuals

Adapted from "Top 10 Security Mistakes"[5]
By Alan S. Horowitz, *Computerworld*, July 9, 2001.

The following compilation was developed by security experts to represent mistakes most commonly made by employees—often unknowingly—which put their organization's information assets at risk:

"1. Passwords on Post-it Notes
"2. Leaving unattended computers on
"3. Opening e-mail attachments from strangers
"4. Poor password etiquette
"5. Laptops on the loose (unsecured laptops that are easily stolen)
"6. Blabbermouths (people who talk about passwords)
"7. Plug and play (technology that enables hardware devices to be installed and configured without the protection provided by people who perform installations)
"8. Unreported security violations
"9. Always behind the times (the patch procrastinator)
"10. Not watching for dangers *inside* the organization"

Mitigation

Mitigation is the control approach that attempts to reduce the impact caused by the exploitation of vulnerability through planning and preparation. This approach includes three types of plans: the disaster recovery plan (DRP), incident response plan (IRP), and business continuity plan (BCP). Each of these strategies depends on the ability to detect and respond to an attack as quickly as possible. Mitigation begins with the early detection that an attack is in progress.

Disaster Recovery Plan

The most common of the mitigation procedures is the **disaster recovery plan (DRP)**. Although media backup strategies are an integral part of the disaster recovery plan, the overall program includes the entire spectrum of activities to recover from an incident. DRP can include strategies to limit losses before and during the disaster. These strategies are fully deployed once the disaster has stopped. DRPs usually include all preparations for the recovery process, strategies to limit losses during the disaster, and detailed steps to follow when the smoke clears, the dust settles, or the floodwaters recede.

Incident Response Plan

The actions an organization can and perhaps should take while the incident is in progress should be defined in a document referred to as the **incident response plan (IRP)**. The IRP provides answers to questions victims might pose in the midst of a disaster, such as, "What do I do *now*!" For example, a systems administrator may notice that someone is copying information from the server without authorization, signaling violation of policy by a potential hacker or an unauthorized employee. What should the administrator do first? Whom should they contact? What should they document? The IRP supplies the answers.

DRP and IRP planning overlap to a degree. In many regards, the DRP is the subsection of the IRP that covers disastrous events. The IRP is also flexible enough to be useful in situations that are near disasters but still require coordinated, planned actions. While some DRP and IRP decisions and actions are the same, their urgency and results can differ dramatically. The DRP focuses more on preparations completed before and actions taken after the incident, whereas the IRP focuses on intelligence gathering, information analysis, coordinated decision making, and urgent, concrete actions.

For example, in the event of a serious virus or worm outbreak, the IRP may be used to assess the likelihood of imminent damage and to inform key decision makers in the various communities of interest (IT, Information Security, Organization Management, and users). The IRP also enables the organization to take coordinated action that is either predefined and specific, or *ad hoc* and reactive.

Business Continuity Plan

The third type of planning document under mitigation is the **business continuity plan (BCP)**. The BCP is the most strategic and long term of the three plans. It encompasses the continuation of business activities if a catastrophic event occurs, such as the loss of an entire database, building, or operations center. The BCP includes planning the steps necessary to ensure the continuation of the organization when the scope or scale of a disaster exceeds the ability of the DRP to restore operations. This can include preparation steps for activation of secondary data centers or hot sites. A **hot site**, also known as a **business recovery site**, is a remote location with systems identical or similar to the home site. These systems enable the organization to continue operations with minimal disruption of service. Many companies offer this service as a contingency against disastrous events such as fires, floods, earthquakes, and most natural disasters.

As an aid to comparing and learning the three types of mitigation plans, Table 5-1 summarizes each of their characteristics and supplies examples.

TABLE 5.1 Summaries of Mitigation Plans

Plan	Description	Example	When deployed	Time frame
Incident response plan (IRP)	Actions an organization takes during incidents (attacks)	▪ List of steps to be taken during disaster ▪ Intelligence gathering ▪ Information analysis	As incident or disaster unfolds	Immediate and real-time reaction
Disaster recovery plan (DRP)	Preparations for recovery should a disaster occur; strategies to limit losses before and during disaster; step-by-step instructions to regain normalcy	▪ Procedures for the recovery of lost data ▪ Procedures for the reestablishment of lost services ▪ Shut-down procedures to protect systems and data	Immediately after the incident is labeled a disaster	Short-term recovery
Business recovery plan (BCP)	Steps to ensure continuation of the overall business when the scale of a disaster requires relocation	▪ Preparation steps for activation of secondary data centers ▪ Establishment of a hot site in a remote location	Immediately after it is determined that the disaster affects the continued operations of the organization	Long-term recovery

Acceptance

As described above, mitigation is a control approach that attempts to reduce the impact of an exploited vulnerability. In contrast, acceptance of risk is the choice to do nothing to protect vulnerability and to accept the outcome of its exploitation. This may or may not be a conscious business decision. The only use of the acceptance strategy that industry practices recognize as valid occurs when the organization has:

▪ Determined the level of risk
▪ Assessed the probability of attack
▪ Estimated the potential damage that could occur from attacks
▪ Performed a thorough cost benefit analysis
▪ Evaluated controls using each appropriate type of feasibility
▪ Decided that the particular function, service, information, or asset did not justify the cost of protection

This control, or rather lack of control, is based on the assumption that it may be a prudent business decision to examine the alternatives and determine that the cost of protecting an asset does not justify the security expenditure. For example, it would cost an organization $100,000 per year to protect a server. The security assessment determined that for $10,000 it could replace the information contained in the server, replace the server itself, and cover associated recovery costs. Therefore, management may be satisfied with taking its chances and saving the money that would normally be spent on protecting this particular asset.

On a cautionary note, if every vulnerability identified in the organization is handled through acceptance, it may reflect an organization's inability to conduct proactive security activities and an apathetic approach to security in general. It is not acceptable for an organization to assume the policy that ignorance is bliss and hope to avoid litigation by pleading ignorance of the requirements of protecting employees' and customers' information. It is also unacceptable for management to hope that if they don't try to protect information, the opposition will imagine that there is little to be gained by an attack. The risks far outweigh the benefits of this approach, which usually ends in regret, as the exploitation of the vulnerabilities causes a seemingly unending series of information security lapses.

Now that you understand the four strategies that are used to control risk, you need to learn the next step in the process: selection of the proper strategy to defend the specific vulnerability of a specific information asset.

Risk Mitigation Strategy Selection

Risk mitigation involves selecting one of the four mitigation strategies for each vulnerability identified. The flowchart shown in Figure 5-2 guides you through the process of deciding if you need to proceed with one of the four strategies. As shown in the diagram, after the information system is designed, you question whether the protected system has vulnerabilities and can be exploited. If the answer is yes, and a viable threat exists, you begin to examine what the attacker would gain from a successful attack. Then to determine if the risk is acceptable or not, you estimate the expected loss the organization will incur if the risk is exploited.

For further guidance, some rules of thumb on strategy selection are presented below. When weighing the benefits of the different strategies that are listed below, keep in mind that the level of threat and value of the asset should play a major role in strategy selection.

- **When a vulnerability (flaw or weakness) exists:** Implement security controls to reduce the likelihood of a vulnerability being exercised.
- **When a vulnerability can be exploited:** Apply layered protections, architectural designs, and administrative controls to minimize the risk or prevent occurrence.
- **When the attacker's cost is less than his potential gain:** Apply protections to increase the attacker's cost (e.g., use system controls to limit what a system user can access and do, thereby significantly reducing an attacker's gain).
- **When potential loss is substantial:** Apply design principles, architectural designs, and technical and nontechnical protections to limit the extent of the attack, thereby reducing the potential for loss.[6]

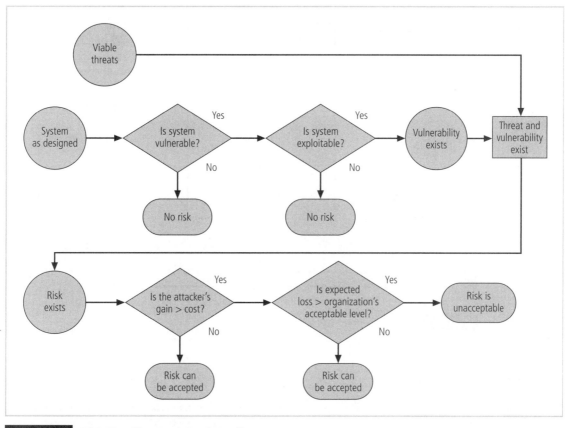

 **FIGURE 5-2** Risk Handling Decision Points[7]

Evaluation, Assessment, and Maintenance of Risk Controls

Once a control strategy has been implemented, the effectiveness of controls should be monitored and measured on an ongoing basis to determine the effectiveness of the security controls and the accuracy of the estimate of the residual risk. Figure 5-3 shows how this cyclical process is continuously used to assure risks are controlled.

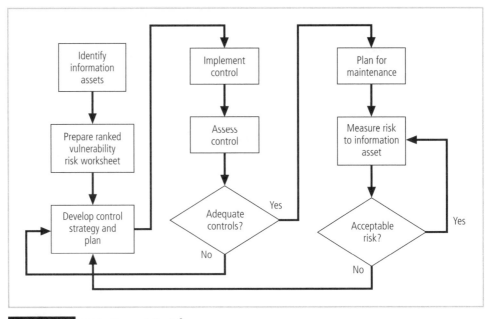

FIGURE 5-3   Risk Control Cycle[8]

Categories of Controls

Controlling risk through avoidance, mitigation, or transference may be accomplished by implementing controls or safeguards. To help you approach this topic, four ways to categorize controls have been identified:

1. Control function
2. Architectural layer
3. Strategy layer
4. Information security principle

While there are certainly additional ways to categorize controls and safeguards, these effectively introduce the process and provide an opportunity to present information about the varieties of controls currently in use.

Control Function

Controls or safeguards designed to defend the vulnerability are either preventive or detective. **Preventive controls** stop attempts to exploit a vulnerability by implementing enforcement of an organizational policy or a security principle, such as authentication or confidentiality. Preventive controls use a technical procedure, such as encryption, or some combination of technical means and enforcement methods. **Detective controls** warn organizations of violations of security principles, organizational policies, or attempts to exploit vulnerabilities. Detective controls use techniques such as audit trails, intrusion detection, and configuration monitoring.

Architectural Layer

Some controls apply to one or more layers of an organization's technical architecture. Controls can be classified by the layer or layers in which they provide control. Some controls, such as firewalls, operate at the interface between architectural layers, such as between the external network and the extranet, or between the organization's WAN and the LAN for a specific facility. Other controls, such as an organizational policy to always use nine or more characters for all passwords and SNMP shared-device passwords(or community strings), operate at all of the architectural layers, from external networks through and including specific applications. Architectural layer designators include the following:

- Organizational policy
- External networks
- Extranets (or demilitarized zones)[9]
- Intranets (WANs and LANs)
- Network devices that interface network zones (switches, routers, firewalls, and hubs)
- Systems (computers for mainframe, server, and desktop use)
- Applications

Strategy Layer

Controls are sometimes classified by the risk control strategy they operate within: avoidance, mitigation, or transference.

Information Security Principles

Controls operate within one or more of the commonly accepted information security principles:

- **Confidentiality:** This principle is in use when the control provides assurance of the confidentiality of organizational data when it is stored, processed, or transmitted. An example is the use of Secure Sockets Layer (SSL) encryption technology to secure Web content as it moves from Web server to browser.

- **Integrity:** This principle is in use when the control provides assurance that the information asset properly, completely, and correctly receives, processes, stores, and retrieves data in a consistent and correct manner. An example is the use of parity or cyclical redundancy checks in data transmission protocols. Another example is the use of a product, such as Tripwire, that monitors the contents and structure of critical system files for unauthorized change.

- **Availability:** This principle is in use when the control provides assurance of ongoing access to critical information assets. An example of this kind of control is the deployment of a network operations center using a sophisticated network monitoring tool set, such as Tivoli or OpenView to assure optimum availability of network resources.

- **Authentication:** This principle is in use when the control provides assurance that users of information assets are in fact the entity (person or computer) they claim to be. Examples of this include the use of cryptographic certificates to establish SSL connections, or the use of cryptographic hardware tokens such as SecurID cards as a second authentication of identity.

- **Authorization:** This principle is in use when the control provides assurance that a specific user (person or computer) has been specifically and explicitly authorized by the proper authority to access, update, or delete the contents of an information asset. An example of this control is the activation and use of access control lists and authorization groups in the Windows networking environment. Another example is the use of a database authorization scheme to verify users of an application are the designated users for each function.

- **Accountability:** This principle is in use when the control provides assurance that every activity undertaken can be attributed to a specific named person or automated process. An example of this control is the use of audit logs to track when each user logged in and logged out of each computer.

- **Privacy:** This principle is in use when the control provides assurance that the procedures to access, update, or remove personally identifiable information comply with the applicable laws and policies for that kind of information.

Feasibility Studies

Before deciding on the strategy (avoidance, transference, mitigation, or acceptance) for a specific vulnerability, all information about the economic and noneconomic consequences of the vulnerability facing the information asset must be explored. This is an attempt to answer the question, "What are the actual and perceived advantages of implementing a control as opposed to the actual and perceived disadvantages of implementing the control?"

There are a number of ways to determine the advantage of a specific control. The primary means is to determine the value of the information assets to be protected from the vulnerability in question. There are also many choices when faced with the daunting task of determining the disadvantages associated with specific controls for avoidance, transference, or mitigation of risk. The following sections discuss some of the more commonly used techniques for making these choices. Note that some of these discussions involve dollar expenses and savings implied from economic cost avoidance, and other discussions deal with noneconomic feasibility criteria. **Cost avoidance** is the money saved from avoiding the financial impact of an incident prevented by a control.

Cost Benefit Analysis (CBA)

The approach most commonly considered for a project of information security controls and safeguards is the economic feasibility of implementation. While a number of alternatives may exist to solve a particular problem, they may not all have the same economic feasibility. Most organizations can spend only a reasonable amount of time and money on information security, and the definition of reasonable differs from organization to organization, and even from manager to manager. Organizations are urged to begin the cost benefit analysis by evaluating the worth of the information assets to be protected and the loss in value if those information assets are compromised by the exploitation of a specific vulnerability. It is only common sense that an organization should not spend more to protect an asset than it is worth. The formal process to document this decision-making process is called a **cost benefit analysis** or an **economic feasibility study**.

Cost

Just as it is difficult to determine the value of information, it is difficult to determine the **cost** of safeguards. Some of the items that impact the cost of a control or safeguard include:

- Cost of development or acquisition (purchase cost) of hardware, software, and services
- Training fees (cost to train personnel)
- Cost of implementation (cost to install, configure, and test hardware, software, and services)
- Service costs (vendor fees for maintenance and upgrades)
- Cost of maintenance (labor expense to verify and continually test, maintain, and update)

Benefit

Benefit is the value that the organization recognizes by using controls to prevent losses associated with a specific vulnerability. This is usually determined by valuing the information asset or assets exposed by the vulnerability and then determining how much of that value is at risk, and how much risk there is for the asset. This is expressed as the annualized loss expectancy, defined below.

Asset Valuation

Asset valuation is the process of assigning financial value or worth to each information asset. Some argue that it is virtually impossible to accurately determine the true value of information and information-bearing assets. Perhaps this is one reason why insurance underwriters currently have no definitive valuation tables for assigning worth to information assets. As discussed in Chapter 4, the value of information differs within organizations and between organizations, based on the characteristics of information and the perceived value of that information to each organization. Much of the work of assigning value can draw on the preparations made in assessing the information assets done in the risk identification process completed in Chapter 4.

Assessing information assets is among the most challenging activities in the security systems development life cycle (SecSDLC). The valuation of assets involves estimation of real and perceived costs associated with the design, development, installation, maintenance, protection, recovery, and defense against loss and litigation. These estimates are calculated for every set of information-bearing systems or information assets. Some component costs are simple to determine, such as the cost to replace a network switch or the hardware needed for a specific class of server. Other costs are almost impossible to accurately determine, such as the dollar value of the loss in market share if information on new product offerings were released prematurely and a company lost its competitive edge. A further complication is the value that some information assets acquire over time that is beyond the **intrinsic value** of the asset under consideration. The higher **acquired value** is, the more appropriate value in most cases.

Some of the components of asset valuation include:

- **Value retained from the cost of creating the information asset:** Information is created or acquired at some cost to the organization. The cost can be calculated or estimated. One category of the cost of creating an asset is software development and another is data collection and processing. Many organizations have developed extensive cost-accounting practices to capture the costs associated with the collection and processing of data, as well as the costs of the software development and maintenance activities. For software development, cost includes the cost of the blood, sweat, and tears of many people designing, testing, and resolving problems in the systems development life cycle for each application and system. The effort draws mainly on IT personnel but includes the user and general management community and sometimes the information security staff. In today's marketplace, with average programmer salaries of almost $29 per hour and contractor expenses even higher, the average cost to complete even a moderately sized application quickly escalates.[10] For example, multimedia-based training averages 350 hours of development for each hour of training.[11] That's over $10,000 per hour for multimedia-based training software.

- **Value retained from past maintenance of the information asset:** It is estimated that for every dollar spent to develop an application or to acquire and process data stored by the organization, many more dollars are spent on maintenance over the useful life of the data or software. If actual costs have not been recorded, the cost can be estimated in terms of the amount and level of the human resources necessary to continually update, support, modify, and service the applications and systems associated with a particular set of information.

- **Value implied by the cost of replacing the information:** Another important cost associated with the loss or damage to information is the cost associated with replacing or restoring the information. This includes the human resource time needed to reconstruct, restore, or regenerate the information from backups, independent transactions logs, or even hardcopies of data sources. Most organizations rely on routine media backups to protect their information. If you find yourself estimating recovery costs, keep in mind that employees are occupied with routine work, and you may have to hire contractors for this effort. Also, loss of real-time information may not be recoverable from a previous tape backup, unless journaling capabilities were built into the system process. To replace information in the system, the various sources of the information may have to be reconstructed, and the data reentered into the system and validated for accurate representation of the original data. This restoration can take longer than the time it took to create the data, not to mention the need for simultaneous entry of new data.

- **Value from providing the information:** Different from the cost of developing or maintaining the information is the cost of providing the information to the users who need it. These costs include the values associated with the delivery of the information through databases, networks, and hardware and software systems. It also includes the cost of the infrastructure necessary to provide access and control of the information.

- **Value incurred from the cost of protecting the information:** Here there is a recursive dilemma: the value of an asset is based in part on the cost to protect it. The amount of money spent to protect an asset is based in part on the value of the asset. While this is a seemingly unsolvable circle of logic, it is possible to estimate the value of the protection for an information asset to better understand the value associated with its potential loss. For the values listed above, it was easy to calculate a specific value. With this and the following values, the result is likely be an estimate of cost.

- **Value to owners:** How much is your social security number worth to you? Or your telephone number? It can be quite a daunting task to place a value on information. In addition to the costs associated with the information described above, what is the increase in the value of information above and beyond its cost? A market researcher collects data from a company's sales figures and determines that there is a strong market potential for a certain age group with a certain demographic value for a new product offering. While the cost associated with the creation of this new information may be small, how much is the new information actually worth? It could be worth millions if it successfully defines a new market share. The value of information to an organization, or how much of the organization's bottom line is directly attributable to the information, may be impossible to estimate. However, it is vital to understand the overall cost of protecting this information in order to understand its value. Here again, estimating value may be the only method possible.

- **Value of intellectual property:** Related to the value of information is the specific consideration of the value of intellectual property. The value of a new product or service to a customer may be unknowable. How much would a cancer patient pay for a cure? How much would a shopper pay for a new flavor of cheese? What is the value of a poem? All of these could represent the intellectual property of an organization, yet their valuation is complex. A related but separate consideration is intellectual properties known as trade secrets. These intellectual information assets are so valuable that they are literally the primary assets of some organizations.

- **Value to adversaries:** Also related to this analysis is the value of information to the organization's competition or adversaries. How much would it be worth to an organization to know what the competition is up to? Many organizations now have established departments that deal in competitive intelligence, tasked with the assessment and estimation of the activities of the organization's competition or opposition. Even organizations in traditionally non-profit or not-for-profit industries can benefit from understanding what is going on in political, business, and competitive organizations. Stories of industrial espionage abound, including the urban legend of Company A encouraging its employees to hire on as janitors at Company B. As custodians, the employees could snoop through open terminals, photograph and photocopy key unsecured documents, and rifle through internal trash and recycling bins. Such legends highlight the value information can have to the right individuals. Similarly, stories of how disgruntled employees, soon to be terminated, steal information and present it to competitive organizations to gain favor and new employment. Those considering such a tactic should reflect on this: would you trust someone who stole from your competition to gain a job with your company? Most everyone assumes that saboteurs repeat their activities when they become disgruntled.

- **Loss of productivity while the information assets are unavailable:** Many times, electrical power may be interrupted. Although effective use of UPS equipment can prevent the loss of the data, system users are unable to continue work that would create additional information. Workers resort to other activities until power is restored. Although this is not an example of an attack that damages information, it is an instance in which a threat (deviations in quality of service from service providers) impacts the productivity of an organization. The hours of wasted employee time, the cost of using alternatives, and the general lack of productivity can severely set back a critical operation or process.

- **Loss of revenue while information assets are unavailable:** Have you ever been in a retail store when your credit card wouldn't scan? How many times did salespeople rescan before resorting to manually entering the numbers? How long did it take to enter the numbers manually in contrast to the quick swipe? What if the credit card verification process was offline? Did the organization have a manual process to validate or process credit card payment in the absence of the familiar approval system? Many organizations have all but abandoned manual backups for automated processes. There are situations in which businesses turn away customers because their automated payments systems are inoperative. While this is typically a failure of management to prepare (disaster recovery planning), it clearly illustrates the potential loss of revenue when information and information systems are unavailable. In today's grocery markets, most stores no longer label each item with the price, because the UPC scanners and the related databases calculate the costs and inventory levels dynamically. Without these systems, could your grocery store sell goods? How much would they lose if they could not? It has been estimated that "43 percent of all businesses that close their doors due to a disaster or crisis, even for one day, never reopen them again. An additional 28 percent fail during the next three to five years."[12] Now, imagine, instead of a grocery store, an online book retailer such as Amazon.com suffering a power outage. The entire operation is instantly closed. Even if Amazon's offering system were operational, what if the payment systems were offline? Customers could make selections, but not check out. While the dot com businesses may be more susceptible to loss of information as a loss of revenue, most organizations would be unable to conduct business if certain pieces of information were unavailable.

The organization must be able to place a dollar value on each collection of information and the information assets it owns. This value is based on the answers to these questions:

- How much did it cost to create or acquire this information?
- How much would it cost to recreate or recover this information?
- How much does it cost to maintain this information?
- How much is this information worth to the organization?
- How much is this information worth to the competition?

Once an organization has estimated the worth of various assets, it can begin to examine the potential loss that could occur from the exploitation of vulnerability or a threat occurrence. This process results in the estimate of potential loss per risk. The questions that must be asked here include:

- What damage could occur, and what financial impact would it have?
- What would it cost to recover from the attack, in addition to the financial impact of damage?
- What is the single loss expectancy for each risk?

A **single loss expectancy**, or **SLE**, is the calculation of the value associated with the most likely loss from an attack. It is a calculation based on the value of the asset and the expected percentage of loss that would occur from a particular attack, as shown below.

$$\text{SLE} = \text{asset value x exposure factor (EF)}$$

Where EF equals the percentage loss that would occur from a given vulnerability being exploited.

For example, if a Web site has an estimated value of $1,000,000 (value determined by asset valuation), and a deliberate act of sabotage or vandalism (hacker defacement) scenario indicates that 10 percent of the Web site would be damaged or destroyed, then the

SLE for this Web site would be $1,000,000 x .10 = $100,000. This estimate is then used to calculate another value, annual loss expectance, discussed below.

As difficult as it is to estimate the value of information, the estimation of the probability of a threat occurrence or attack is even more difficult. There are not always tables, books, or records that indicate the frequency or probability of any given attack. There are sources available for some asset-threat pairs. For instance, the likelihood of a tornado or thunderstorm destroying a building of a specific type of construction within a specified region of the country is available to insurance underwriters. In most cases, however, an organization can rely only on its internal information to calculate the security of its information assets. Even if the network, systems, and security administrators have been actively and accurately tracking these occurrences, the organization's information is sketchy at best. As a result, this information is usually estimated. In most cases, the probability of a threat occurring is usually a loosely derived table indicating the probability of an attack from each threat type within a given time frame (for example once every ten years). This value is commonly referred to as the **ARO**, or **annualized rate of occurrence**. ARO is simply how often you expect a specific type of attack to occur. As discovered in Chapter 4, many of these attacks occur much more frequently than every year or two. For example, if a successful deliberate act of sabotage or vandalism occurs about once every two years, then the ARO would be 50 percent (.50), whereas some kinds of network attacks can occur multiple times per second. To be useful for standardization of calculations, you convert the rate to a yearly (annualized) value. This is expressed as the probability of a threat occurrence.

Once each asset's worth is known, the next step is to ascertain how much loss is expected from a single expected attack, and how often these attacks occur. Once those values are determined, the equation can be completed to determine the overall lost potential per risk. This is usually determined through an **annualized loss expectancy**, or **ALE**, using the values for the ARO and SLE from previous sections.

$$ALE = SLE \times ARO$$

To use the previous example, with an SLE of $100,000 and an ARO of .50, then:

$$ALE = \$100,000 \times .50$$
$$ALE = \$50,000$$

This indicates that unless you increase the level of security on your Web site, the organization can expect to lose $50,000 per year, every year. Now, armed with a figure to justify expenditure for controls and safeguards, the information security design team can deliver a budgeted value for planning purposes. Note that sometimes noneconomic factors are considered in this process, so that in some cases even when ALE amounts are not huge, control budgets can be justified.

The Cost Benefit Analysis or CBA Formula

In its simplest definition, CBA (or economic feasibility) is whether or not the control alternative being evaluated is worth the associated cost incurred to control the specific vulnerability. CBAs may be calculated before a control or safeguard is implemented, to determine if the control is worth implementing. As an alternative, CBAs can be calculated after controls have been implemented and have been functioning for a time. Observation over time adds precision to the evaluation of the benefits of the safeguard and the determination of whether the safeguard is functioning as intended. While many CBA techniques exist, the CBA is most easily calculated using the ALE from earlier assessments.

$$CBA = ALE(prior) - ALE(post) - ACS$$

ALE (prior) is the annualized loss expectancy of the risk before the implementation of the control.

ALE (post) is the ALE examined after the control has been in place for a period of time.

ACS is the annual cost of the safeguard.

Once the controls are implemented, it is crucial to continue to examine their benefits, to determine when the controls must be upgraded, supplemented, or replaced. As Frederick Avolio states in his article "Best Practices in Network Security:"

> "Security is an investment, not an expense. Investing in computer and network security measures that meet changing business requirements and risks makes it possible to satisfy changing business requirements without hurting the business' viability."[13]

Benchmarking

Rather than using the cost benefit analysis to placing a dollar figure on each information asset, you can approach risk management from a different angle. Instead of determining the financial value of information and then implementing security as an acceptable percentage of that value, an organization could look to peer organizations for benchmarks. **Benchmarking** is the process of seeking out and studying the practices used in other organizations that produce the results you desire in your organization. An organization typically benchmarks by selecting a measure with which to compare itself with the other organizations in its market. The organization then measures the difference in the way it conducts business and the way the other organizations conduct business. The industry Website Best Practices Online puts it this way:

> "Benchmarking can yield great benefits in the education of executives and the realized performance improvements of operations. In addition, benchmarking can be used to determine strategic areas of opportunity. In general, it is the application of what is learned in benchmarking that delivers the marked and impressive results so often noted. The determination of benchmarks allows one to make a direct comparison. Any identified gaps are improvement areas. Benchmarking can take several forms. Internal benchmarking studies the practices and performance within the client organization. External benchmarking determines the performance of other, preferably world-class, companies."[14]

When benchmarking, an organization typically uses one of two measures to compare practices: metrics-based measures or process-based measures.

Metrics-based measures are comparisons based on numerical standards, such as:

- Numbers of successful attacks
- Staff-hours spent on systems protection
- Dollars spent on protection
- Numbers of security personnel
- Estimated value in dollars of the information lost in successful attacks
- Loss in productivity hours associated with successful attacks

An organization uses this information by ranking competing organizations with a similar size or market to its own and then determining how it measures up to the others. The difference between an organization's measures and those of others is often referred to as a **performance gap**. Performance gaps provide insight into the areas that an organization should work on to improve its security postures and defenses.

The other measures commonly used are **process-based measures**. Process-based measures are generally less focused on numbers and more strategic than metrics-based measures. For each of the areas the organization is interested in benchmarking, process-based measures enable the companies to examine the activities an individual company performs in pursuit of its goal, rather than the specifics of how goals are attained. The primary focus is *the method* the organization uses to accomplish a particular process, rather than the outcome.

In information security, two categories of benchmarks are used: standards of due care and due diligence, and best practices. Within best practices, the **gold standard** is a subcategory of practices that are typically viewed as "the best of the best." Each of these is described in the following sections:

Due Care and Due Diligence: For legal reasons, an organization may be forced to adopt a certain minimum level of security, as discussed in Chapter 3. When organizations adopt levels of security for a legal defense, they may need to show that they have done what any *prudent* organization would do in similar circumstances. This is referred to as a **standard of due care**. It is insufficient to implement these standards and then ignore them. The application of controls at or above the prescribed levels and the maintenance of those standards of due care show that the organization has performed due diligence. **Due diligence** is the demonstration that the organization is diligent in ensuring that the implemented standards continue to provide the required level of protection. Failure to support a standard of due care or due diligence can open an organization to legal liability, provided it can be shown that the organization was negligent in its application or lack of application of information protection. This is especially important in areas in which the organization maintains information about customers, including medical, legal, or other personal data.

The security protection an organization is expected to maintain is complex and broad in scope. It may, therefore, be physically impossible to be the "best in class" in any or all categories. Based on the budgets assigned to the protection of information, it may also be financially impossible to provide a level of security equal to organizations with greater revenues. "Good security now is better than perfect security never."[15] Sometimes organizations want to implement the best, most technologically advanced, most secure levels of protection, but for financial or other reasons cannot. It would also be counter productive to establish costly, state-of-the-art security in one area, only to leave other areas exposed. Organizations must make sure they have met a reasonable level of security across the board, protecting all information, before beginning to improve individual areas to reach a higher standard, such as best practices.

Best Business Practices: Security efforts that seek to provide a superior level of performance in the protection of information are referred to as **best business practices (BSPs)** or simply **best practices** or **recommended practices**. Even the standards promoted on the Internet as requests for comments (RFCs) have best practices (see *www.rfc-editor.org/categories/rfc-best.html*). Best security practices are those security efforts that are among the best in the industry, balancing the need to access information with the need to provide adequate protection. Best practices seek to provide as much security as possible for information and systems while maintaining a solid degree of fiscal responsibility. Companies with best practices may not be the best in every area, but may simply have established an extremely high quality or successful security effort in one or more area. Benchmarking best practices is accomplished through metric-based or process-based measures described earlier. The federal government has established a Web site for government agencies to share best security practices with other agencies (see *http://fasp.nist.gov*). This project is known as the Federal Agency Security Project (FASP). It was the result of

> "the Federal Chief Information Officer Council's Federal Best Security Practices (BSP) pilot effort to identify, evaluate, and disseminate best practices for computer information protection and security… The FASP site contains agency policies, procedures and practices; the CIO pilot BSPs; and, a Frequently-Asked-Questions (FAQ) section."[16]

While few commercial equivalents exist at this time, many of the BSPs are applicable to the areas of security in both the public and the private sector. The FASP has collected sample policies, strategies, and other practice-related documents, which are presented for use as guidelines.

The Gold Standard: Even the best business practices are not sufficient for some organizations. These organizations prefer to set the standard by implementing the most protective, supportive, and yet fiscally responsible standards they can. They strive toward the gold standard. The gold standard is a defining level of performance that shows other organizations one company's industrial leadership, quality, and concern for the protection of information. The implementation of this level of security requires a great amount of support, both in financial and personnel resources. While there is limited public information on best practices, there is virtually no true published criteria for the gold standard. The gold standard represents an almost unobtainable level of security, unsurpassed in industry. Many vendors claim to offer a gold standard in one product or service, but this is predominantly marketing hype.

Government Recommendations and Best Practices: You can sometimes get advice about how to select control strategies from government sources. For some organizations that operate in industries that are regulated by governmental agencies, government recommendations are, in effect, requirements. For other organizations, government regulations are excellent sources for information about what other organizations may be doing or are required to do in controlling information security risks.

Applying Best Practices

The preceding sections have presented a number of sources you can consider when applying standards to your organization. You can study the documented best practice processes or procedures that have been shown to be effective and are thus recommended by a person or organization and evaluate how they apply to your organization. When considering best practices for adoption, consider the following:

- Does your organization resemble the identified target organization with the best practice under consideration? Is your organization in a similar industry as the target? For example, a strategy that works well in manufacturing organizations often has little bearing in a nonprofit organization. Does your organization face similar challenges as the target? If your organization has no functioning information security program, a best practice target that assumes you start with a functioning program is not useful. Is your organizational structure similar to the target? Obviously, a best practice proposed for a small home office setting does not help to design control strategies for a multinational company.

■ Are the resources your organization can expend similar to those identified with the best practice? If your approach is significantly limited by resources, it is not useful to submit a best practice proposal that assumes unlimited funding and does not specify items that are too expensive to implement.

■ Is your organization in a similar threat environment as that proposed in the best practice? A proposal of best practice from months and even weeks ago may not be appropriate for the current threat environment. Think of the best practice for Internet connectivity required in the modern organization at the opening of the twenty-first century and compare it to best practices of five years ago.

Another source for best practices information is the CERT Web site (*www.cert.org/ security-improvement/*) that presents a number of security improvement modules and practices in HTML and PDF format. Similarly, Microsoft has published a set of best security practices at its Web site (*www.microsoft.com/privacy/safeinternet/security/best_ practices/default.htm*). Microsoft focuses on seven key areas for their best practices:

1. Use antivirus software
2. Use strong passwords
3. Verify your software security settings
4. Update product security
5. Build personal firewalls
6. Back up early and often
7. Protect against power surges and loss

In support of security efforts, Microsoft offers "The Ten Immutable Laws of Security"[17] as follows:

"Law #1: If a bad guy can persuade you to run his program on your computer, it's not your computer anymore.
"Law #2: If a bad guy can alter the operating system on your computer, it's not your computer anymore.
"Law #3: If a bad guy has unrestricted physical access to your computer, it's not your computer anymore.
"Law #4: If you allow a bad guy to upload programs to your Web site, it's not your Web site anymore.
"Law #5: Weak passwords trump strong security.
"Law #6: A machine is only as secure as the administrator is trustworthy.
"Law #7: Encrypted data is only as secure as the decryption key.
"Law #8: An out-of-date virus scanner is only marginally better than no virus scanner at all.
"Law #9: Absolute anonymity isn't practical, in real life or on the Web.
"Law #10: Technology is not a panacea."

Problems with Applying Benchmarking and Best Practices
The biggest problem with benchmarking and best practices in information security is that organizations don't talk to each other. A successful attack is viewed as an organizational

failure. Because valuable lessons are not recorded, disseminated and evaluated, the entire industry suffers. However, with the increased attention paid to security, more and more security administrators are joining professional associations and societies (such as the Information Systems Security Association) and sharing stories and publishing the lessons learned. Individual security administrators are more often submitting sanitized versions of attacks to security journals. Again, most organizations refuse to even acknowledge, much less publicize, the occurrence of successful attacks.

Another problem with benchmarking is that no two organizations are identical. Even if two organizations are producing products or services in the same market, their size, composition, management philosophies, organizational culture, technological infrastructure, and budgets for security may differ dramatically. Even if they would exchange information, it may be a case of apples and oranges. What organizations seek most are lessons they can apply, rather than specific technologies they should adopt. This goes back to the expression that "security is a managerial problem, not a technical one." If it were a technical problem, implementing the same technology would solve the problem regardless of industry or organizational composition. As a managerial and people problem, the number and types of variables that impact the security of the organization can differ radically in any two businesses.

A third problem is that best practices are a moving target. What worked well two years ago may be completely worthless against today's threats. Security has to keep abreast of new threats in addition to the methods, techniques, policies, guidelines, educational and training approaches, and technologies used to combat the threats.

One last issue to consider is that simply knowing what was going on a few years ago, as in benchmarking, doesn't necessarily indicate what to do next. It is said, that "those who cannot remember the past are condemned to repeat it." In security, those who do not prepare for the attacks of the past see them repeat again and again. However, preparing for past threats does not safeguard against new and different challenges ahead. It is important to be as prepared as possible and then focus efforts on monitoring the communications and new listings that are popular among systems and security administrators to determine what is new and how to prepare for it.

Baselining

Related to the concept of benchmarking is the process of baselining. A **baseline** is a "value or profile of a performance metric against which changes in the performance metric can be usefully compared."[18] An example is the ability to establish a baseline for the number of attacks per week the organization is experiencing. In the future, this baseline can serve as a reference point to determine if the average number of attacks is increasing or decreasing. **Baselining** is the analysis of measures against established standards. In information security, baselining is the comparison of security activities and events against the organization's future performance. In a sense, baselining can provide the foundation for internal benchmarking. The information gathered for an organization's first risk assessment becomes the baseline for future comparisons. Therefore, the initial baseline must be carefully established.

When baselining, it is useful to have a guide to the overall process. The National Institute of Standards and Technology has two publications specifically written to support these activities:

1. Security SP 800-27 Engineering Principles for Information Technology Security (A Baseline for Achieving Security), June 2001

2. SP 800-26 Security Self-Assessment Guide for Information Technology Systems, November 2001

Both of these documents are available at *http://csrc.nist.gov/publications/nistpubs/index.html*.

Other Feasibility Studies

In addition to the methods discussed above, which are frequently used to document feasibility, there are other approaches to be considered. In the previous sections the concepts of economic feasibility or using baselines or benchmarks were used to justify proposals for information security controls. When the analyst moves to the next step of measuring how ready an organization is for these controls, he can determine the proposal's organizational, operational, technical, and political feasibility. The methods to accomplish these types of feasibility evaluations are discussed below.

Organizational Feasibility

Organizational feasibility examines how well the proposed information security alternatives will contribute to the efficiency, effectiveness, and overall operation of an organization. In other words, the proposed control approach for the vulnerability must contribute to the organization's strategic objectives. Above and beyond the impact on the bottom line, the organization must determine how the proposed alternatives contribute to the business objectives of the organization. Does the implementation align with the strategic planning for the information systems? Or does it require deviation from the planned expansion and management of the current systems? The organization should not invest in technology that changes the fundamental ability of the organization to explore certain avenues and opportunities. For example, imagine that without considering the organizational feasibility, a university decides to implement a new firewall, and it takes a few months for the technology group to learn enough about the firewall to completely configure it. A few months after the implementation begins, it is discovered that the firewall in its current configuration does not permit outgoing Web-streamed media. If one of the business goals of the university is the pursuit of distance-learning opportunities, and the firewall prevents the pursuit of that goal, the firewall has failed the organizational feasibility measure and should be modified or replaced.

Operational Feasibility

Operational feasibility addresses several key areas not covered in the other feasibility measures. **Operational feasibility** addresses user acceptance and support, management acceptance and support, and the overall requirements of the organization's stakeholders. Operational feasibility is also known as **behavioral feasibility**, because it measures the behavior of users. One of the fundamental principles of systems development is obtaining user buy-in on a project. If the users do not accept a new technology, policy, or program, it will fail. Users may not openly oppose a change, but the result may be the same. If users do not support a control, they will find ways of disabling or otherwise circumventing it, creating yet another vulnerability. One of the most common methods for obtaining user acceptance and support is through **user involvement**. User involvement can be obtained through three simple steps: communicate, educate, and involve.

Organizations *communicate* with system users throughout the SecSDLC process, letting them know that change is occurring. This includes the timetables and schedules of implementation, plus the dates, times, and locations of upcoming briefings and training. Those making the changes let those being affected know the purpose of the proposed changes, and how these changes will enable everyone to work more securely. Education should be designed to instruct trainees to work under the new constraints while avoiding any negative impact on performance. One of the most frustrating things from a user's perspective is the implementation of a new program that prevents them from accomplishing their duties, with only a promise of eventual training. Those making changes *involve* users by asking them what they want from the new systems, what they will tolerate from the new systems, and by including selected representatives from the various constituencies in the development process. Adherence to these three simple steps of communication, education, and involvement can reduce *resistance* to change and build *resilience* for change—that ethereal quality that allows workers to not only tolerate constant change but also accept it as a necessary part of the job.

Technical Feasibility

In addition to the straightforward feasibilities associated with the economic costs and benefits of the controls, the project team must also consider the **technical feasibilities** associated with the design, implementation, and management of controls. Some safeguards, especially technology-based safeguards, are extremely complex to implement, configure, and manage. Technical feasibility examines whether or not the organization has or can acquire the technology necessary to implement and support the control alternatives. Does the organization have the hardware and software necessary to support a new firewall system? If not, can it be obtained? Technical feasibility also examines whether the organization has the technological expertise to manage the new technology. Does the organization have a staff of individuals qualified (and possibly certified) to install and manage a new firewall system? If not, can staff be spared from their current obligations to attend formal training and education programs to prepare them to administer the new systems? Or must personnel be hired? In the current job environment, how difficult is it to find qualified personnel? These issues must be examined in detail before acquiring a new set of controls. Many organizations rush into the acquisition of new safeguards, without completely examining the requirements of these complex controls.

Political Feasibility

For some organizations, the most significant feasibility evaluated may be political. Politics is often defined as "the art of the possible".[19] Within organizations, **political feasibility** defines what can and cannot occur based on the consensus and relationships between the communities of interest. The limits placed on an organization's actions or behaviors by the information security controls must fit within the realm of the possible before they can be effectively implemented, and that realm includes the availability of staff resources.

In some cases, resources are provided to the information security community directly under a budget apportionment model. The management and professionals involved in information security then allocate the resources to activities and projects using processes of their own design.

In other organizations, resources are first allocated to the IT community of interest. The information security team then must compete for resources in that context. In some of these cases, the cost benefit analysis and the other forms of justification discussed here are used in an allocation process to make rational decisions about the relative merit for funding activities and projects. Unfortunately in some settings, these decisions are politically charged and do not focus on the pursuit of the greater organizational goals.

Another methodology for budget allocation requires the information security team to propose and justify use of the resources for activities and projects in the context of the entire organization. This requires that arguments for information security spending articulate the benefit of the expense for the whole organization, so that members of the organizational communities of interest can understand and perceive their value.

Risk Management Discussion Points

Not every organization has the collective will or budget to manage each vulnerability through the application of controls, and therefore each organization must define the level of risk it is willing to live with.

Risk Appetite

Risk appetite defines the quantity and nature of risk that organizations are willing to accept, as they evaluate the trade-offs between perfect security and unlimited accessibility. For instance, a financial services company, regulated by government and conservative by nature, seeks to apply every reasonable control and even some invasive controls to protect its information assets. Other, nonregulated organizations may also be conservative by nature, seeking to avoid negative publicity associated with the perceived loss of integrity from the exploitation of a vulnerability. Perhaps a firewall vendor installs a set of firewall rules that are far more onerous than necessary, because the negative consequence of being hacked would be catastrophic in the eyes of its customers. Other organizations may take on dangerous risks through ignorance. The reasoned approach to risk is one that balances the expense (in terms of finance and the usability of information assets) against the possible losses if exploited.

It may be helpful to reexamine a quotation from Chapter 1 within the context of this chapter to see how its meaning has deepened. As stated previously, James Anderson, vice president of information security at Inovant, the world's largest commercial processor of financial payment transactions believes: Information security in today's enterprise is a 'well-informed sense of assurance that the information risks and controls are in balance."

As this statement shows, the key for the organization is to find the balance in its decision-making processes and in its feasibility analyses, therefore assuring that an organization's risk appetite is based on experience and facts and not on ignorance or wishful thinking.

Residual Risk

When vulnerabilities have been controlled as much as possible, there is often risk that has not been completely removed or has not been completely shifted or planned for. This remainder is called residual risk. To express it another way, "**Residual Risk** is a combined function of (1) a threat less the effect of threat-reducing safeguards; (2) a vulnerability less the effect of vulnerability-reducing safeguards, and (3) an asset less the effect of asset value-reducing safeguards."[20] Figure 5-4 illustrates how residual risk remains after safeguards are implemented.

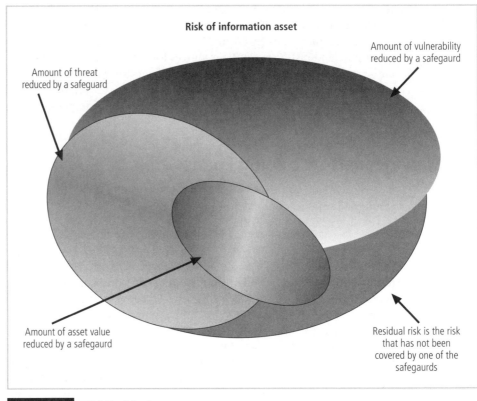

FIGURE 5-4 Risk Residual

The significance of residual risk must be judged within the context of an organization. Although it is counterintuitive, the goal of information security is not to bring residual risk to zero; it is to bring residual risk into line with an organization's comfort zone or risk appetite. If decision makers have been informed of uncontrolled risks and the proper authority groups within the communities of interest have decided to leave residual risk in place, the information security program has accomplished its primary goal.

Documenting Results

When the risk management program of an organization has weighed in, a series of proposed controls are prepared, each of which has been justified by one or more feasibility or rationalization approaches. At a minimum, each information asset-threat pair should have a documented control strategy that clearly identifies any residual risk remaining after the proposed strategy has been executed. This control strategy articulates which of the four fundamental risk-reducing approaches will be used, how they might be combined, and justifies the findings by referencing the feasibility studies.

Some organizations document the outcome of the control strategy for each information asset-threat pair in an action plan. This action plan includes concrete tasks, each with accountability assigned to an organizational unit or to an individual. It may include hardware and software requirements, budget estimates, and detailed timelines.

Recommended Practices in Controlling Risk

To put concept into practice, let's assume a $50,000 maximum budget from the action plan mentioned above. The expenditures must be justified and budget authorities must be convinced to spend up to $50,000 to protect a particular asset from an identified threat. Unfortunately it is the *up to* that most budget authorities focus on and then try to cut a percentage of the total figure to save the organization money. This underlines the importance for developing strong justifications for specific action plans and providing concrete estimates in those plans.

Another factor to consider is that each control or safeguard implemented impacts more than one asset-threat pair. If a new $50,000 firewall is installed to protect the Internet connection infrastructure from the threat posed by hackers launching port-scanning attacks, the same firewall may protect this Internet connection infrastructure from other threats and attacks. In addition, the firewall may protect other information assets from other threats and attacks. The final choice of proposed controls may be a balanced mixture of controls that provide the greatest value to as many asset-threat pairs as possible. This reveals another facet of the problem: information security professionals manage a dynamic matrix covering a broad range of threats, information assets, controls, and identified vulnerabilities. Each time a control is added to the matrix, it undoubtedly changes the ALE for the information asset vulnerability for which it has been designed, and it also may alter the ALE for other information asset vulnerabilities. To put it more simply, if you put in one safeguard, you decrease the risk associated with all subsequent control evaluations. To make it worse, the action of implementing a control may change the values assigned or calculated in a prior estimate.

Between the impossible task associated with the valuation of information assets and the dynamic nature of the ALE calculations, it's no wonder organizations are looking for a more straightforward method of implementing controls that doesn't involve such complex, inexact, and dynamic calculations. This leads to an ongoing search for ways to design security architectures that go beyond the direct application of specific controls, in which each is justified specifically for information asset vulnerability. Some of the alternatives that have been and continue to be developed are discussed below.

Qualitative Measures

The spectrum of steps described above was performed with actual values or estimates. This is known as a **quantitative assessment**. However, an organization could determine that it cannot put specific numbers on these values. Fortunately, it is possible to repeat these steps using estimates based on a qualitative assessment. For example instead of placing a value of once every ten years for the ARO, the organization could list all possible attacks on a particular set of information and rate each by the probability of occurrence. This could be accomplished using scales, rather than specific estimates. A sample scale can range from zero, representing no chance of occurrence, to ten, representing almost certain occurrence. Organizations may, of course, prefer other scales: 0-10, 1-5, 0-20. Using scales also relieves the organization from the difficult determination of exact values. These same scales can be used in any situation requiring a value, even in asset valuation. For example, instead of estimating that a particular piece of information is worth $1,000,000, you can value information on a scale of 1-20, with 1 indicating relatively worthless information, and 20 indicating extremely critical information, such as a certain soda manufacturer's secret recipe or those special 11 herbs and spices of a popular chicken vendor.

Delphi Technique

How do you calculate the values and scales of either qualitative or quantitative assessment? An individual can pull the information together based on personal experience, but "two heads are better than one." And a team of heads is better than two. One technique for accurately estimating scales and values is the Delphi technique. The **Delphi technique**, named for the oracle at Delphi, is a process whereby a group rates or ranks a set of information. The individual responses are compiled and then returned to the group for another iteration. This process continues until the entire group is satisfied with the result. This technique can be applied to the development of scales, asset valuation, asset or threat ranking, or any decision that can benefit from the input of more than one decision maker.

Risk Management and the SecSDLC

Risk control systems follow the pattern of the security systems development life cycle. The risk control effort is at once part of the analysis phase of the SecSDLC and also a microcosm of the entire cycle. The relationship of risk management to the SecSDLC is shown in Figure 5-5 and has been briefly discussed in Chapter 4. As you see in the diagram, the implementation phase occurs after analysis and design. Implementation encompasses the finer points of building control systems and then exploring the maintenance activities required to keep the entire information security system operating correctly. Subsequent chapters of this book examine the need for assessment of risk control systems by external and internal monitoring (activities such as penetration testing and platform policy validation), as well as the specific requirements to be deployed for the maintenance of risk controls. To be effective these practices include refreshing information asset inventories, continuous revaluation of threats and vulnerabilities, and ongoing confirmation of the effectiveness of the control systems built.

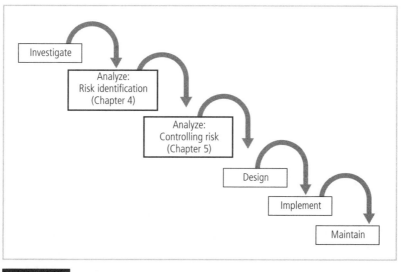

FIGURE 5-5 Risk Management and the SecSDLC

Chapter Summary

- Risk management is the process of identifying vulnerabilities in an organization's information systems and taking carefully reasoned steps to assure the confidentiality, integrity, and availability of all of the components in the information system.

- Once the vulnerabilities are identified and ranked, the organization must choose a strategy to control the risks resulting from these vulnerabilities. Four control strategies are covered: Avoidance, which attempts to prevent the realization or exploitation of the vulnerability, is the preferred approach. Transference attempts to shift the risk to other assets, other processes, or other organizations. Mitigation attempts to reduce the impact of vulnerability exploitation through planning and preparation, and includes disaster recovery planning, business continuity planning, and incident response planning. Acceptance allows the vulnerability to exist as is and accepts whatever outcome arises.

- The economic feasibility study is used to determine the costs associated with protecting an asset. The formal documentation process of feasibility is called a cost benefit analysis.

- Single loss expectancy is a calculation based on the value of the asset and the expected percentage of loss that would occur from a particular attack.

- Annualized loss expectancy provides a single figure to represent the potential loss per risk.

- Benchmarking is the process of seeking out and studying the practices used in other organizations that produce the results desired in an organization.

- Due diligence is the demonstration that the organization acts rigorously to ensure that the implemented standards continue to function at the required level.

- Organizational feasibility studies examine how well the proposed alternatives contribute to efficiency, effectiveness, and overall operation.

- Operational feasibility addresses user acceptance and support, management acceptance and support, and the overall requirements of the organizations' stakeholders.

- Technical feasibility examines whether or not the organization has or can acquire the technology necessary to implement and support the technical alternatives.

- Political feasibility defines what can and cannot occur based on the consensus and relationships between the communities of interest.

- The goal of information security is to bring residual risk, the amount of risk unaccounted for after the application of controls and other risk management strategies, to an acceptable level. A reasoned approach to information security risk is one that balances the expense of implanting controls against the possible losses.

- Once a control strategy has been implemented, the effectiveness of controls should be monitored and measured to determine the effectiveness of the security controls and the accuracy of the estimate of the residual risk.

Review Questions

1. What is competitive advantage? How has it changed over the years since the IT industry began?
2. What is competitive disadvantage? Why has it emerged as a factor?
3. What is risk management? How does it tie to the C.I.A. triangle?
4. What are the four risk strategies for controlling risk?
5. Describe risk avoidance.
6. Describe risk transference.
7. Describe risk mitigation.
8. Describe risk acceptance.
9. Name three common methods of risk avoidance.
10. Describe how outsourcing can be used for risk transference.
11. What three planning approaches are discussed in the text as opportunities to mitigate risk?
12. How is a disaster recovery plan different from a business continuity plan?
13. How is an incident response plan different from a disaster recovery plan?
14. What conditions must be met to assure that risk acceptance has been used properly?
15. What is risk appetite? Explain why risk appetite varies from organization to organization.
16. List four ways to categorize risk controls.
17. What is the difference between a detective control and a preventive control?
18. In which architectural layers are controls implemented?
19. What is a cost benefit analysis?
20. What is the difference between intrinsic value and acquired value?
21. What is the definition of single loss expectancy?
22. What is annual loss expectancy?

23. What is the difference between benchmarking and baselining?
24. What is the difference between organizational feasibility and operational feasibility?
25. What is residual risk?
26. What is the difference between qualitative measurement and quantitative measurement?

Exercises

1. Using the following table, calculate the SLE, ARO, and ALE for each threat category listed:

XYZ Software Company, major threat categories for new applications development asset value: $1,200,000 in projected revenues	Cost per incident	Frequency of occurrence
Programmer mistakes	$5,000	1 per week
Loss of intellectual property	$75,000	1 per year
Software piracy	$500	1 per week
Theft of information (hacker)	$2,500	1 per quarter
Theft of information (employee)	$5,000	1 per 6 months
Web defacement	$500	1 per month
Theft of equipment	$5,000	1 per year
Virus, worms, Trojan horses	$1,500	1 per week
Denial-of-service attacks	$2,500	1 per quarter
Earthquake	$250,000	1 per 20 years
Flood	$250,000	1 per 10 years
Fire	$500,000	1 per 10 years

2. How might the XYZ Software Company arrive at the values in the above table? For each entry, describe the process of determining the cost per incident and frequency of occurrence.

3. How do the values in the table differ from the calculations presented in the text? How can you determine SLE if there is no percentage given? Which method is easier for determining the SLE, a percentage of value lost or cost per incident?

4. Assume a year has passed and XYZ has improved security. Using the following table, calculate the SLE, ARO, and ALE for each threat category listed:

XYZ Software Company, major threat categories for new applications development asset value: $1,200,000 in projected revenues	Cost per incident	Frequency of occurrence	Cost of controls	Type of control
Programmer mistakes	$5,000	1 per month	$20,000	Training
Loss of intellectual property	$75,000	1 per 2 years	$15,000	Firewall/IDS
Software piracy	$500	1 per month	$30,000	Firewall/IDS
Theft of information (hacker)	$2,500	1 per 6 months	$15,000	Firewall/IDS
Theft of information (employee)	$5,000	1 per year	$15,000	Physical security
Web defacement	$500	1 per quarter	$10,000	Firewall
Theft of equipment	$5,000	1 per 2 year	$15,000	Physical security
Virus, worms, Trojan horses	$1,500	1 per month	$15,000	Anti-virus
Denial-of-service attacks	$2,500	1 per 6 months	$10,000	Firewall
Earthquake	$250,000	1 per 20 years	$5,000	Insurance/backups
Flood	$50,000	1 per 10 years	$10,000	Insurance/backups
Fire	$100,000	1 per 10 years	$10,000	Insurance/backups

Why have some values changed in the following columns: cost per incident, and frequency of occurrence? How could a control affect one, but not the other?

Assume the costs of controls presented in the table for exercise 3 were those unique costs directly associated with protecting against that threat. In other words, don't worry about overlapping costs between threats. Calculate the CBA for each control. Are the controls worth the costs listed?

5. Using the Web, research the costs associated with the following items:
   - Managed antivirus software licenses for 500 workstations
   - A Nokia firewal?
   - A Tripwire host-based IDS for 10 servers
   - A continuing education program for ten employees to learn Java programming
   - Check-point FireWall solutions

Case Exercises

I. Risk Management or Risk Analysis?

Adapted from "Risk Management or Risk Analysis?"[21]
By Fred Cohen, *Managing Network Security Online*, March 1997.

Decisions on the protection of information cannot be made exclusively on the basis of quantitative risk analysis. However, there is a way to develop a framework for improved analysis. "Standard risk analysis asserts that we calculate an expected loss (L) by multiplying the probability of each event (p(e)) that can cause a loss by the expected loss from that event (l(e)) and adding these results for all of the events (all e in E)."[22] The selection of a mitigation strategy can then be improved by "examining each proposed mitigation technique to derive the reduction in expected loss associated with the technique's use, dividing by the cost of the mitigation technique to derive a return on investment (ROI), and applying the most cost-effective (i.e., the highest ROI) method first. Apply methods until no technique with a high enough ROI for the organization is left, and you are done."[23] This sounds simple enough; however, there are a number of factors that influence this calculation, including:

- **The list of events:** It's impossible to list all possible events.
- **The probability of events:** It's impossible to accurately model event probabilities.
- **Event independence:** Events may or may not be independent.
- **Expected loss of events:** Loss is as impossible to accurately calculate as asset value.
- **Mitigation techniques:** Techniques are wide and varied; one cannot know them all.
- **Reduction in expected loss:** It is equally difficult to calculate how much a safeguard reduces the expected loss in an asset.
- **Sensitivity:** The analysis is sensitive to many unknown and unpredictable factors.
- **Network complexity:** A system is substantially more complex than the sum of its parts; networks are very complex systems.

This having been said, there are professionals who claim to be able to make reasonable estimates and have done so.

Risk management works on the assumption that not all risk can be averted, avoided, or mitigated. So the best you can do is to minimize the losses. The task, therefore, is to determine how much to spend to reduce risk to an acceptable level. The possible answers range from spending nothing and risking everything, to spending everything and risking nothing. Neither extreme is acceptable. A common technique referred to as the "covering approach" works by identifying possible attacks, identifying possible defenses, and then matching the two lists. In this process each manager uses his department's priorities to determine the attacks against which he will set protections. Costs may be associated with defenses, but losses cannot be associated with attacks (e.g., no loss equals no attack).

Managers can ask: "What can reasonably be ignored for now? What decisions can reasonably be delayed? What can be managed if and when it occurs rather than planned in advance? What sorts of contingency planning should be considered over time? What can I ensure against? What expertise should I bring into the organization to help in these areas? How does this impact other operational decisions? Answering these types of questions can result in a more intuitive approach to selection of defenses. For example, a manager might think, "Defense B covers important assets, C and D, and less important assets, E and F, and will only cost X dollars. On the other hand, defense A is expensive, and I think that we can manage our way out of trouble with some temporary emergency measures, if threats ever materialize."[24]

The downside of risk management approaches such as the covering approach, include the following: 1) decision makers need to understand the implications of their decisions, and 2) risk management requires management awareness and consideration. There is one success factor that is critical to both risk analysis and the covering approach: the individual in charge must have the experience and wisdom to make the approach work in any given situation. It would then be logical to state that perhaps the most important risk management or risk analysis decision to be made is who is put in charge.

1. How does the covering approach differ from techniques discussed in this chapter?
2. What distinguishes the covering approach from simply stating that risk assessment is a quantitative approach, while risk management is a qualitative approach?

II. Balancing Risk: A Due Care Approach

Adapted from "Balancing Risk"[25]

By Fred Cohen, *Managing Network Security Online*, March 1997.

It is well understood that security is like a balancing act on a tightrope. Unfortunately, it is seldom a fair act, with demands on one side outweighing resources on the other. Similarly, arguments for one particular approach to protecting a system frequently overwhelm arguments for a different approach. Consider this case in point: cryptography versus host security.

There are those who enjoy the ongoing debate over the strength of the various cryptographic tools used to protect information on a system. They frequently bicker and growl over how quickly a standard can be cracked and how long a key size should be. The problem is that debate should center on whether or not cryptography is a valid alternative to other protection schemes, especially on systems that have so many other vulnerabilities and weaknesses that cryptography alone cannot protect it. The imbalance is in the demand for strong cryptography and the expectation that it can serve as a panacea. The other side of the imbalance is the lack of mechanisms, such as enhanced security-rated operating systems, host-based intrusion detection systems, and effective configuration management practices. These host server improvements are rarely used because of the costs and the complications associated with the interaction between hardware, host operating system, and various applications. This imbalance is present because people say that it is generally easy to increase cryptographic protection, whereas it is usually difficult to increase host protection. Cryptography systems are simple to implement and easy to justify, while hours and hours configuring and reconfiguring and then adding security to a host system seem too big an undertaking.

Ironically, many organizations have chosen the solution of host security hardening by dedicating the necessary time and effort to preparing the host and foregoing the cryptographic solution for now.

Underlying this trade-off decision of cryptography versus host security hardening is the fundamental notion of using risk management is the fundamental notion of using risk management methods to make prudent decisions about relative levels of protection. Unfortunately, modern risk management techniques in information protection are inadequate to the task, and there are no clear-cut quantitative measures for making prudent decisions about these trade-offs. In fact, there isn't even a widely accepted list of these tradeoffs. It's hard to conduct risk management when you lack a comprehensive list of options.

As a holdover from the days when the number one focus in security was the protection of the confidentiality of information, information security tends to lean heavily on protection mechanisms that promise irrefutable secrecy. The assumption that secrecy is the greatest protection is wrong in most cases. It is wrong to conclude that better encryption is always worthwhile, because even relatively trivial encryption can divert most attackers from reading messages and from subverting the operating environment.

The solution? Here is a simple approach to risk management:

"**Step 1:** With few exceptions, all aspects of protection need to meet some standard of due care.

"**Step 2:** Higher consequences lead to more attention.

"**Step 3:** Revisit everything often."[26]

For this case exercise, imagine a common application, an e-commerce site using online servers. The company advertises, conducts sales, processes credit cards, and handles deliveries all over the Web. Apply the steps listed above to the e-commerce site:

Step 1: Due diligence: List areas to be covered and perform a review. Areas can include "management, policy, standards, procedures, documentation, audit, testing, technical safeguards, personnel, incident handling, legal, physical, awareness, training, education, and organization." You can also use such external standards as ISO17799 or GASSP. Identify the areas that are strong, moderate, and weak. Update all weak ratings to at least moderate.

Step 2: High consequences: Identify the high consequences, validate that the threats and vulnerabilities are such that these consequences can reasonably happen, and determine whether these possibilities are adequately covered by the protection in place or planned. Where protection is not adequate and budget is available to mitigate the threats, implement protections.

Step 3: Revisit: Keep abreast of the industry and of new security threats by monitoring electronic mailing lists, security publications, and visiting security Web sites providing such information. Update systems routinely with new information.

Where's the balance between cryptography and host security? In Step 1, you examine technical safeguards, both cryptographic protection and host security. Both should be addressed equally. In Step 2, you evaluate host security versus cryptography, and determine there is a greater consequence if someone hacks your system and modifies the prices than if someone cracked your SSL commerce link. You focus mitigation on host security? In Step 3, you update both approaches constantly, reviewing and resolving known vulnerabilities. Balance is achieved by strengthening what is weak. The ultimate resolution is eternal vigilance. You have to constantly rebalance the risk to maintain protection.

Use your imagination and common sense to answer these questions:

1. How can the standards of the due care approach be considered a valid risk management approach? What benefits are derived from this approach?

2. Using the due care approach, evaluate the strengths and weaknesses of another imbalance: physical security versus systems security. How can an imbalance between the protection of physical assets and online assets be resolved? Which way is the imbalance currently skewed?

Endnotes

1. Jack M. Greenberg, "Corporate Press Release: First Worldwide Social Responsibility Report," *McDonald's Corporation Online* (15 April 2002) [Cited 19 June 2002]; available from the World Wide Web *http://www.mcdonalds.com/corporate/press/corporate/2002/04152002/index.html.*

2. 37th IETF, "Remote Authentication Dial-In User Service (RADIUS) Charter" (proceedings at the 37th IETF meeting, San Jose, Calif., December 1996); available from the World Wide Web *http://www.ietf.org/proceedings/96dec/charters/radius-charter.html.*

3. HumanFirewall.org, "Building a Human Firewall," *Human Firewall Online 2001* [Cited 19 June 2002]; available from the World Wide Web *http://www.humanfirewall.org.*

4. Thomas J. Peters and, Robert H. Waterrman, *In Search of Excellence: Lessons from America's Best Run Companies* (New York: Harper and Row, © 1982)

5. Alan S. Horowitz, "Top 10 Security Mistakes," *ComputerWorld* (Framingham) 35, no. 28 (9 July 2001): 38.

6. National Institute of Standards and Technology, *Risk Management Guide for Information Technology Systems*, SP 800-30 (January 2002).

7. *Ibid.*

8. *Ibid.*

9. Webopedia, "DMZ," *Webopedia Online* (18 November 1999) [Cited 19 June 2002]; available from the World Wide Web *http://www.webopedia.com/TERM/D/DMZ.html*.

10. Shannon Cochran, "The Top Ten Cities for Programmers," *Dr. Dobb's Journal Online* (October 2000) [Cited 19 June 2002]; available from the World Wide Web *http://www.ddj.com/documents/s=880/ddj0010l/*.

11. Shelley Hesse, "Guidelines for Your First Authorware Project," *Multimedia Enterprise Online* [Cited 19 June 2002]; available from the World Wide Web *http://www.media-enterprise.com/articles/aw_guidelines.htm*.

12. Peter Gourlay, "Playing it Safe," *U.S. Business Review Online* (December 2001) [Cited 19 June 2002]; available from the World Wide Web *http://www.usbusiness-review.com/0112/02.html*.

13. Frederick M. Avolio, "Best Practices in Network Security," *Network Computing* 11, no. 5 (20 March 2000): 60-66.

14. Best Practices, LLC. "What is Benchmarking?" *Best Practices Online*. [Cited 19 June 2002]. Available from the World Wide Web *<http://www.best-in-class.com/site_tools/faq.htm#benchmarking>*.

15. Frederick M. Avolio, "Best Practices in Network Security," *Network Computing* 11, no. 5 (20 March 2000): 60-66.

16. National Institute of Standards and Technology, *Computer Security Resource Center* (Gaithersburg, June 2002); available from the World Wide Web *http://fasp.nist.gov*.

17. The Microsoft Security Response Center, *The Ten Immutable Laws of Security*? (Redmond, July 2002); available from the World Wide Web *http://www.microsoft.com/technet/treeview/default.asp?url=/technet/columns/security/10imlaws.asp*.

18. Philip Carden, "Network Baselining and Performance Management," *Network Computing Online* [Cited 19 June 2002]; available from the World Wide Web *http://www.networkcomputing.com/netdesign/base1.html*.

19. Thomas Mann, "Politics is often defined as the art of the possible." (speech in the Library of Congress, Washington, D.C., 29 May 1945).

20. Gamma Secure Systems Limited, "First Measure Your Risk," *Gamma Online. 2 January 2002* [Cited 19 June 2002]; available from the World Wide Web *http://www.gammassl.co.uk/inforisk/*.

21. Fred Cohen, "Risk Analysis," *Managing Network Security Online* (March 1997) [Cited 19 June 2002]; available from the World Wide Web *http://www.all.net/journal/netsec/1998-12.html*.

22. *Ibid.*

23. *Ibid.*

24. *Ibid.*

25. Fred Cohen, "Balancing Risk," *Managing Network Security Online* (December 1998) [Cited 19 June 2002]; available from the World Wide Web *http://www.all.net./journal/netsec/1998-12.html*.

26. *Ibid.*

Blueprint For Security

6

CHARLIE MOODY CLOSED THE DOOR of his office behind Kelvin Urich.

"Sit, please," Charlie said as he gestured to the one of the chairs at the small table. "Welcome to Sequential Label and Supply," he said grimly.

"Thanks," said Kelvin, looking green but enthusiastic. "I'm glad to be here. It's been a few weeks since we met at my interview, and I'm anxious to get started. We talked about the information security project a lot, and I'm really looking forward to the kickoff."

"Good and bad news there, Kelvin. We've been underway since your interview. Now let me get you up to speed," said Charlie ponderously.

"Oh, okay," said Kelvin, looking a little surprised.

Charlie dropped a heavy, four-inch thick, three-ring binder on the table with a thud. "This is what we have so far," he said. Charlie began to meander on and on about the process which had been followed to assess the need for the security program. He pontificated on the efforts taken by the legal department to identify the legal and privacy requirements the company needed to meet. He went on for 15 minutes about the threat and vulnerability analysis already completed and described the more detailed work to come. He outlined future work that would identify controls and create feasibility reports and cost-benefit analysis reports. As he talked, Charlie pulled one voluminous document after another out of the notebook to point at the graphs and statistics.

Kelvin eyed the pile of documents with some trepidation.

Charlie continued, "Now, you get the really difficult task of trying to make an overall plan out of this." He looked at Kelvin over the top rim of his glasses. "Got any ideas on how you plan to start?"

DISCUSSION QUESTIONS:

1. Given what you've learned so far about information security, what are some of the issues you think Kelvin faces in this kind of scenario?
2. If you were Kelvin, what questions would you ask Charlie about the project?
3. What should be Kelvin's first task when Charlie sends him to his new office?

LEARNING OBJECTIVES:

Upon completion of this material you should be able to:

- Understand management's role in the development, maintenance, and enforcement of information security policy, standards, practices, procedures, and guidelines.
- Understand the differences between the organization's general information security policy and the requirements and objectives of the organization's issue-specific and system-specific policies.
- Know what an information security blueprint is and what its major components are.
- Understand how an organization institutionalizes its policies, standards, and practices using education, training, and awareness programs.
- Become familiar with what viable information security architecture is, what it includes, and how it is used.

Introduction

Where to begin? This is the question that Kelvin faces in the chapter scenario. Looking at all the work that has led to this juncture can be daunting; however, it is important that an organization work in a systematic fashion to design an information security program. The creation of an information security program begins with an information security blueprint, and before examining blueprints, it is important to look at management's responsibility in shaping policy. It is prudent for information security professionals to know the information security polices and how these policies contribute to the overall objectives of the organization.

Information Security Policy, Standards, and Practices

Management from all communities of interest, including general staff, information technology, and information security, must consider policies as the basis for all information security planning, design, and deployment. In general, policies direct how issues should be addressed and technologies used. Policies should not cover the specifics on the proper operation of equipment or software, which are more appropriately placed in the standards, procedures, and practices of users' manuals and systems documentation. Policies, on the other hand, provide instructions on what the technologies can and cannot be used for, that is, the personal or private use of organizational equipment and the viewing of certain types of materials. In addition, *policy should never contradict law*, because this can create a significant liability for the organization. For a sidebar discussion of this issue, see the Offline box regarding Arthur Andersen.

OFFLINE

"Andersen Trial Heats Up"[1]

By Claire Poole, *Law.com Online*, May 20, 2002.

"Tensions ran high at the Arthur Andersen LLP obstruction of justice trial in Houston as defense attorney Rusty Hardin continued to question the government's star witness—fired auditor David Duncan—in an attempt to show that he was neither actively shredding paper nor worried about a Securities and Exchange Commission investigation the week after getting a reminder from the firm's attorney about its document retention policy.

"After the jury was let in, Hardin questioned Duncan about a long conference call between Enron officials and Andersen partners on October 23. Duncan said the Andersen participants agreed the call had not gone well, and one partner suggested they meet with the entire Enron engagement team that afternoon to discuss the Enron matter.

"Duncan's executive assistant sent an e-mail about the meeting titled 'urgent.' Duncan characterized the meeting as part 'pep talk' of where Andersen stood and 'part discussion' of the document retention policy, repeating his earlier testimony to 'do no more nor less than what was in the policy.' Duncan said even though the SEC had launched a formal inquiry into Enron's accounting practices, Andersen officials were not worried that it would involve their firm.

"Hardin repeatedly asked Duncan about whether Duncan was destroying documents during this time. He generally responded that he was not. He also repeatedly denied ever using the word 'destroy.'

"'I did not intend for anyone to get rid of . . . important documents,' he said.

"Hardin then asked Duncan about all the things his staff was working on at the time, trying to prove that the document retention policy was not his top priority. Prosecutors began to object when Hardin tried to cover old ground, including asking about whether the document retention policy was discussed and whether there were worries the SEC was looking at Andersen.

"Hardin was clearly trying to hit home the idea that those issues, which the government has offered as cause and effect, were not at the top of Duncan's mind at that time.

"At one point when Hardin asked whether there was any shredding during October, which prosecutors objected to as asked and answered, Hardin retorted before the judge could rule, 'that has not been asked.' When the judge motioned the attorneys to the

continued

bench, Hardin said, 'I beg you, I don't want to come back up there. Nothing good happens up there.' A 10-minute sidebar followed. The tedious third day of Duncan's cross-examination was peppered with a few funny incidents from the famously flamboyant Hardin. Before beginning his questioning, Hardin asked if he could be excused from the courtroom (he told a U.S. marshal that his fly was down). At another point, he turned his back to the judge and jury and counted to 10 after yet another objection from the prosecution."

Quality security programs begin and end with policy.[2] Because information security is primarily a management problem, not a technical one, policy guides personnel to function in a manner that adds to the security of information assets, rather than as a threat to those assets. It is interesting to note that security policies are the least expensive control to execute, but the most difficult to *properly* implement. They are the lowest cost in that they involve only the time and effort of the management team to create, approve, and communicate. Even if the management team decides to hire an outside consultant to assist in the development of policy, the costs are minimal compared to technical controls. Shaping policy is difficult because it must:

1. Never conflict with laws
2. Stand up in court, if challenged
3. Be properly administered through dissemination and documented acceptance

Definitions

Before examining the various types of information security policies, it is important to understand exactly what policy is and how it can and should be used.

A **policy** is "a plan or course of action, as of a government, political party, or business, intended to influence and determine decisions, actions, and other matters."[3] As discussed in Chapter 3, policies specify acceptable and unacceptable behavior. Policies are organizational laws, in that they dictate acceptable and unacceptable behavior within the context of the organization's culture. Like laws, policies must define what is right, and what is wrong, what the penalties are for violating policy, and what the appeal process is. These topics are explored further in the following sections. **Standards**, on the other hand, are more detailed statements of what must be done to comply with policy. They have the same requirements for compliance as policies. The level of acceptance of standards may be informal, as in *de facto* **standards**. Or standards may be published, scrutinized, and ratified by a group, as in formal or *de jure* **standards**. Finally, practices, procedures, and guidelines effectively explain how to comply with policy. Figure 6-1 shows policies as the force that drives standards, which in turn drive practices, procedures, and guidelines.

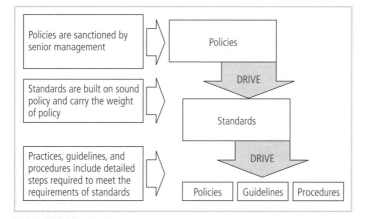

FIGURE 6-1 Policies, Standards, and Practices

Policies are written to support the mission, vision, and strategic planning of an organization. The **mission** of an organization is a written statement of an organization's purpose. The **vision** of an organization is a written statement about the organization's goals. Where will the organization be in five years? In ten? **Strategic planning** is the process of moving the organization towards its vision by accomplishing its mission. To be effective, a policy must be disseminated by all means possible, including printed personnel manuals, organization intranets, and periodic supplements. All members of the organization must read, understand, and agree to the policies. At the same time, policies should be considered living documents, in that they require constant modification and maintenance as the needs of the organization evolve.

The meaning of the term, **security policy**, depends on its context. Governmental agencies discuss security policy in terms of national security and national policies to deal with foreign states. A security policy can also represent a credit card agency's policy for processing credit card numbers. In general, a security policy is a set of rules that protect an organization's assets. An **information security policy** provides rules for the protection of the information assets of the organization. As stated in Chapter 1, the task of information security professionals is to protect the confidentiality, integrity, and availability of information and information systems, whether in the state of transmission, storage, or processing. This is accomplished by applying policy, education and training programs, and technology.

Management must define three types of security policy, based on The National Institute of Standards and Technology's Special Publication 800-14 (this publication is discussed later in this chapter in much greater detail):

1. General or security program policies
2. Issue-specific security policies
3. Systems-specific security policies

Each of these management policies is examined in greater detail below.

Security Program Policy (SPP)

A **security program policy** is also known as a general security policy, IT security policy, and information security policy. The SPP is based on and directly supports the mission, vision, and direction of the organization and sets the strategic direction, scope, and tone for all security efforts within the organization. The SPP is an executive-level document, usually drafted by, or in cooperation with, the chief information officer of the organization. This policy is usually two to ten pages long and shapes the philosophy of security in the IT environment. The SPP does not usually require continuous modification, unless there is a change in the strategic direction of the organization.

The SPP guides the development, implementation, and management of the security program. It contains the requirements to be met by the information security blueprint or framework. It defines the purpose, scope, constraints, and applicability of the security program in the organization. It also assigns responsibilities for the various areas of security, including systems administration, maintenance of the information security policies, and the practices and responsibilities of the users. Finally, it addresses legal compliance. According to the National Institute of Standards, the SPP typically addresses compliance in two areas:

> "1) General compliance to ensure meeting the requirements to establish a program and the responsibilities assigned therein to various organizational components and 2) the use of specified penalties and disciplinary action."[4]

When the SPP has been developed, the CISO (the chief information security officer, Charlie Moody in the opening scenario) begins forming the security team and initiates the SecSDLC process.

Issue-Specific Security Policy (ISSP)

As an organization executes various technologies and processes to support routine operations, certain guidelines are needed to instruct employees to use these technologies and processes properly. In general, the **issue-specific security policy** 1) addresses specific areas of technology as listed below, 2) requires frequent updates, and 3) contains a statement on the organization's position on a specific issue.[5] An ISSP may cover the following topics among others:

- Electronic mail
- Use of the Internet
- Specific minimum configurations of computers to defend against worms and viruses
- Prohibitions against hacking or testing organization security controls
- Home use of company-owned computer equipment
- Use of personal equipment on company networks
- Use of telecommunications technologies (FAX and phone)
- Use of photocopy equipment

There are a number of approaches toward creating and managing ISSPs within an organization. Three of the most common are to create the following types of ISSP documents:

1. Independent ISSP documents, each tailored to a specific issue
2. A single comprehensive ISSP document covering all issues
3. A modular ISSP document that unifies policy creation and administration, while maintaining each specific issue's requirements

The independent document approach to creating and managing ISSPs typically has a shotgun effect. Each department responsible for a particular application of technology creates a policy governing its use, management, and control. This approach to creating ISSPs may fail to cover all of the necessary issues, and it can suffer from poor policy distribution, management, and enforcement.

The single comprehensive policy approach is centrally managed and controlled. With formal procedures for the management of ISSPs in place, the comprehensive policy approach establishes guidelines for overall coverage of necessary issues and clearly identifies processes for the dissemination, enforcement, and review of these guidelines. Usually, technology providers within the organization that centrally manages the information technology resources develop these policies. Unfortunately, these policies tend to overgeneralize the issues and skip over vulnerabilities.

The optimal balance between the independent and comprehensive ISSP approaches is the modular approach. It is also centrally managed and controlled but tailored to the individual technology issues. The modular approach provides a balance between issue orientation and policy management. The policies created with this approach comprise individual modules, each created and updated by individuals responsible for the issues addressed. These individuals report to a central policy administration group that incorporates specific issues into an overall comprehensive policy.

Figure 6-2 is an outline of a sample ISSP, which can be used as a model. Each organization adds to this structure the specific details that dictate security procedures for individual issues not covered by these general guidelines.

Considerations for an Effective Telecommunications Use Policy

1. Statement of policy
   a. Scope and applicability
   b. Definition of technology addressed
   c. Responsibilities
2. Authorized access and usage of equipment
   a. User access
   b. Fair and responsible use
   c. Protection of privacy
3. Prohibited usage of equipment
   a. Disruptive use or misuse
   b. Criminal use
   c. Offensive or harassing materials
   d. Copyrighted, licensed, or other intellectual property
   e. Other restrictions
4. Systems management
   a. Management of stored materials
   b. Employer monitoring
   c. Virus protection
   d. Physical security
   e. Encryption
5. Violations of policy
   a. Procedures for reporting violations
   b. Penalties for violations
6. Policy review and modification
   a. Scheduled review of policy and procedures for modification
7. Limitations of liability
   a. Statements of liability or disclaimers

©2003 ACM, Inc., Included here by permission.

FIGURE 6-2 Example of an Issue-Specific Policy Statement[6]

The components for each of the major categories presented in the sample issue-specific policy shown in Figure 6-2 are discussed below. Even though the details may vary from policy to policy and some sections of a modular policy may be combined, it is essential for management to address and complete each section.

Statement of Policy

Well begun is half done. The policy should begin with a clear statement of purpose. As a sample policy, consider one entitled "Fair and Responsible Use of the WWW and Internet in XYZ Company." The introductory section should outline these topics: What is the scope of this policy? Who is responsible and accountable for policy implementation? What technologies and issues does it address?

Authorized Access and Usage of Equipment

This section of the policy statement addresses *who* can use the technology governed by the policy, and *what* it can be used for. Remember that an organization's information systems are the exclusive property of an organization, and users have no particular rights of use. Each technology and process is provided for business operations. Use for any other purpose constitutes misuse of equipment. This section defines "fair and responsible use" of equipment and other organizational assets, and should also address key legal issues, such as protection of personal information and privacy.

Prohibited Usage of Equipment

Although the policy section described above detailed what the issue or technology *can* be used for, this section outlines what it *cannot* be used for. Unless a particular use is clearly prohibited, the organization cannot penalize its employees for misuse. The following actions can be prohibited: personal use, disruptive use or misuse, criminal use, offensive or harassing materials, and infringement of copyrighted, licensed, or other intellectual property.

Appropriate Use

As an alternative approach, categories two and three of Figure 6-2 can be collapsed into a single category, appropriate use. Many organizations use an ISSP with that name to cover both categories.

Systems Management

There may be some overlap between an ISSP and a systems-specific policy (SysSP), but the systems management section of the ISSP policy statement focuses on the users' relationship to systems management. Specific rules from management include regulating the use of e-mail, the storage of materials, authorized monitoring of employees, and the physical and electronic scrutiny of e-mail and other electronic documents. It is important that all responsibilities are designated as belonging to either the systems administrator or the users. Otherwise both parties may infer that the responsibility belongs to the other parties.

Violations of Policy

Once guidelines on equipment use have been outlined and responsibilities have been assigned, the individuals to whom the policy applies must understand the penalties and repercussions of violating the policy. Violations of policy should carry appropriate, not draconian, penalties. This section of the policy statement should contain not only the specifics of the penalties for each category of violation but also instructions on how individuals in the organization can report observed or suspected violations. Many individuals feel that powerful individuals in the organization can discriminate, single out, or otherwise retaliate against someone who reports violations. Anonymous submissions are often the only way to convince individual users, especially the staff who lay people off, to report the unauthorized activities of other, more influential employees.

Policy Review and Modification

Because any document is only as good as its frequency of review, each policy should contain procedures and a timetable for periodic review. As the needs and technologies change in the organization, so must the policies that govern their use. This section should contain a specific methodology for the review and modification of the policy, to ensure that users do not begin circumventing it as it grows obsolete.

Limitations of Liability

The final section covered by Figure 6-2 is a general statement of liability or set of disclaimers. If an individual employee is caught conducting illegal activities with organizational equipment or assets, management does not want the organization held liable. So the policy should state that if employees violate a company policy or any law using company technologies, the company will not protect them, and the company is not liable for their actions. It is inferred that such a violation would be without knowledge or authorization by the organization.

Systems-Specific Policy (SysSP)

To this point, the chapter has covered two of the three levels of security policy: security program policies and issue-specific security policies. This section covers the third type: **systems-specific security policies**.

While issue-specific policies are formalized as written documents, distributed to users, and agreed to in writing, SysSPs are frequently codified as standards and procedures used when configuring or maintaining systems. An example of a systems-specific policy is an access control list that defines which users may and may not access a particular system, complete with the levels of access for each authorized user. Systems-specific policies can be organized into two general groups:

1. **Access control lists (ACLs)** are lists, matrices, and capability tables governing the rights and privileges of a particular user to a particular system. As indicated earlier, an ACL is a list of access rights used by file storage systems, object brokers, or other network communications devices to determine which individuals or groups may access an object that it controls. (As you probably know from previous coursework, object brokers are system components that handle message requests between the software components of a system.) A similar list, which is also associated with users and groups, is called a **capability table**. This specifies which subjects and objects a user or group can access. Capability tables are frequently complex matrices, rather than simple lists or tables.

2. **Configuration rules** comprise the specific configuration codes entered into security systems to guide the execution of the system when information is passing through it. Each of these is examined below in more detail.

ACL Policies

As illustrated in the figures below, both Microsoft Windows NT/2000 and Novell Netware 5.x/6.x families of systems translate ACLs into sets of configurations that administrators use to control access to their respective systems. The level of detail may differ from system to system, but in general ACLs allow configuration to restrict access from anyone and anywhere. Restrictions can be set for a particular user, computer, time, duration, and even a particular file. This specificity provides powerful control to the administrator. In general ACLs regulate the who, what, when, where, and how of access:

- *Who* can use the system
- *What* authorized users can access
- *When* authorized users can access the system
- *Where* authorized users can access the system from
- *How* authorized users can access the system

Restrictions on who can use the system require no explanation. Restrictions on what users can access require some detailing. ACLs can restrict any number of the attributes of the system resources, such as printers, files, communications, and applications by setting privileges to one of the following:

- Read
- Write
- Create
- Modify
- Delete
- Compare
- Copy

The list above is not exhaustive, but represents the key ACL items. In some systems, capability tables are referred to as user profiles or user policies, specifying what the user can and cannot do on the resources within that system. Figures 6-3 and 6-4 show how the ACL security model has been implemented by Novell and Microsoft operating systems.

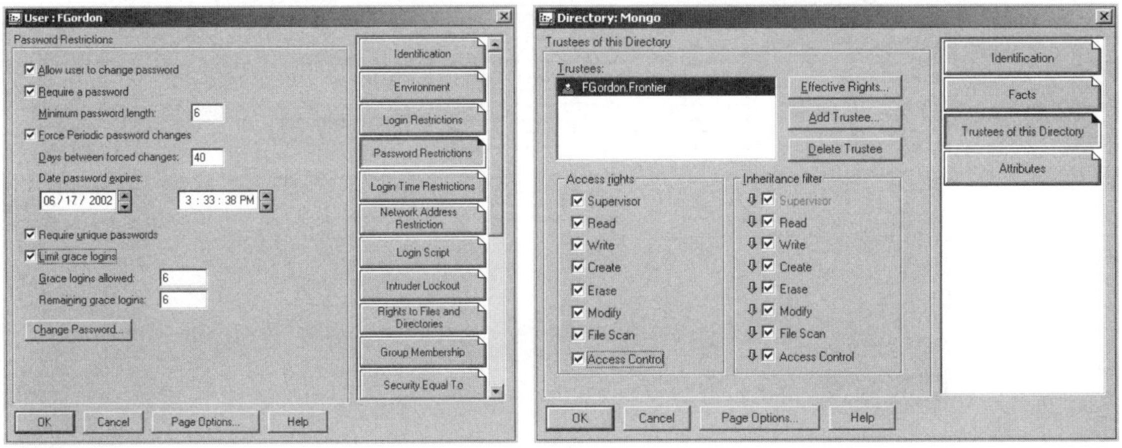

FIGURE 6-3 Novell Configuration Screens

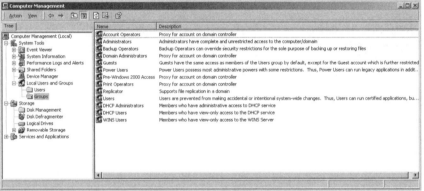

FIGURE 6-4   Windows 2000 Configuration Screens

Rule Policies

Rule policies are more specific to the operation of a system than ACLs and may or may not deal with users directly. Many security systems require specific configuration scripts telling the systems what actions to perform on each set of information they process. Examples include firewalls, intrusion detection systems, and proxy servers. The examples in Figures 6-5 and 6-6 show how this security model has been implemented by Checkpoint in a firewall rule set and by TripWire in an IDS rule set.

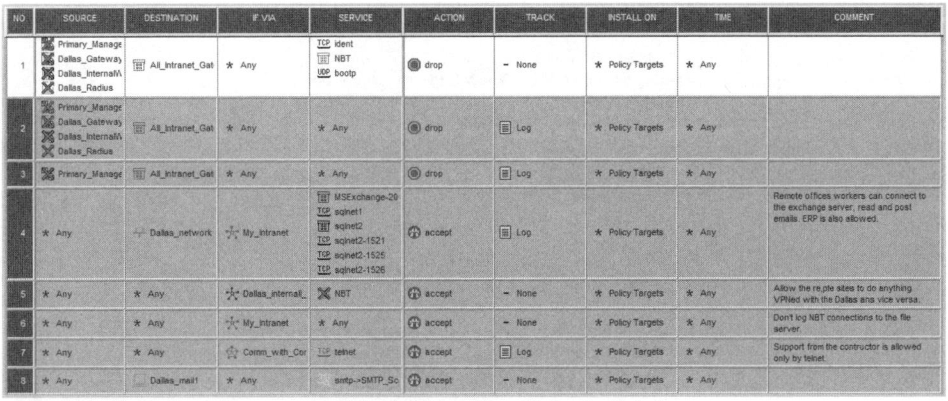

NO	SOURCE	DESTINATION	IF VIA	SERVICE	ACTION	TRACK	INSTALL ON	TIME	COMMENT
1	Primary_Manage Dallas_Gateway Dallas_Internal\\ Dallas_Radius	All_Intranet_Gat	✶ Any	TCP ident NBT UDP bootp	drop	– None	✶ Policy Targets	✶ Any	
2	Primary_Manage Dallas_Gateway Dallas_Internal\\ Dallas_Radius	All_Intranet_Gat	✶ Any	✶ Any	drop	Log	✶ Policy Targets	✶ Any	
3	Primary_Manage	All_Intranet_Gat	✶ Any	✶ Any	drop	Log	✶ Policy Targets	✶ Any	
4	✶ Any	Dallas_network	My_Intranet	MSExchange-20 sqlnet1 sqlnet2 TCP sqlnet2-1521 TCP sqlnet2-1526 TCP sqlnet2-1526	accept	Log	✶ Policy Targets	✶ Any	Remote offices workers can connect to the exchange server, read and post emails. ERP is also allowed.
5	✶ Any	✶ Any	Dallas_internal_	NBT	accept	– None	✶ Policy Targets	✶ Any	Allow the repte sites to do anything VPNed with the Dalles ans vice versa.
6	✶ Any	✶ Any	My_Intranet	✶ Any	accept	– None	✶ Policy Targets	✶ Any	Don't log NBT connections to the file server.
7	✶ Any	✶ Any	Comm_with_Cor	TCP telnet	accept	Log	✶ Policy Targets	✶ Any	Support from the contractor is allowed only by telnet
8	✶ Any	Dallas_mail1	✶ Any	smtp->SMTP_Sc	accept	– None	✶ Policy Targets	✶ Any	

VPN-1/Firewall-1 Policy Editor courtesy of Check Point Software Technologies Ltd.

FIGURE 6-5 Checkpoint VPN-1/Firewall-1 Policy Editor

```
################################################################## #
# This Policy was created by the Tripwire Policy Resource Center # #
# Created on: Mon Mar 25 21:54:27 GMT 2002                       # #
# Copyright (C) 2001, Tripwire Inc. Reprinted with permission    #
################################################################
@@section global
SYSTEMDRIVE="C:" ;
BOOTDRIVE="C:" ;
SYSTEMROOT="C:\\Winnt" ;
PROGRAMFILES="C:\\Program Files" '
IE5="C:\\Program Files\\Plus!\\Microsoft Internet" ;
# Email Recipients # #
SIG_HIGHEST_MAILRECIPIENTS  = "Administrator" ;
SIG_HIGH_MAILRECIPIENTS     = "Administrator" ;
SIG_MED_MAILRECIPIENTS      = "Administrator" ;
SIG_LOW_MAILRECIPIENTS      = "Administrator" ;
# Security Levels # #
SIG_LOW      = 33 ;     # Non-critical files that are of minimal security impact
SIG_MED      = 66 ;     # Non-critical files that are of segnificant security impact
SIG_HIGH     = 100;     # Critical files that are significant points of vulnerability
SIG_HIGHEST  = 1000;    # Super-critical files. Mostly used for the TCB section.
@@section NTFS
{
 rulename = "IE 5.01 Registry keys",
 severity = $ (SIG_HIGHEST),
 emailto  = $ (SIG_HIGHEST_MAILRECIPIENTS),
 recurse  = true
}
{
 $ (HKLM_CCS_SM_CBadApps)                            -> $ (REG_SEC_HIGHEST) ;
 $ (HKLM_CRYPT)                                      -> $ (REG_SEC_HIGHEST) ;
 $ (HKLM_CRYPTINIT)                                  -> $ (REG_SEC_HIGHEST) ;
 $ (HKLMCRYPTMSG)                                    -> $ (REG_SEC_HIGHEST) ;
 $ (HKLM_CRYPTSIGN)                                  -> $ (REG_SEC_HIGHEST) ;
 $ (HKLM_EventSystem)                                -> $ (REG_SEC_HIGHEST) ;
 $ (HKLM_SW_IE_Setup)                                -> $ (REG_SEC_HIGHEST) ;
 $ (HKLM_WHM)                                        -> $ (REG_SEC_HIGHEST) ;
 $ (HKLM_WIE)                                        -> $ (REG_SEC_HIGHEST) ;
 $ (HKLM_WIE_INF_Setup)                              -> $ (REG_SEC_HIGHEST) ;
 $ (HKLM_WMM)                                        -> $ (REG_SEC_HIGHEST) ;
}
```

FIGURE 6-6 IDS Rules

```
#       Snippet Name: A Nimda Virus Rule                          # #
#       Snippet Author: support@tripwire.com                      # #
#      Snippet Version: 1.0.0      # #
#               Nimda#    # #
@@section NTFS
{
rulename = "Nimda File Scan",
Severity = 100
}
{
$ (SYSTEMROOT)\ZaCker.vbs -> $ (IgnoreNone);
$ (SYSTEMROOT)\MixDaLaL.vbs -> $ (IgnoreNone);
$ (SYSTEMDIR)\ZaCker.vbs -> $ (IgnoreNone);
$ (SYSTEMDIR)\MixDaLaLa.vbs -> $ (IgnoreNone);
}
```

Courtesy of Tripwire®, Inc.

FIGURE 6-6 IDS Rules (continued)

Policy Management

As indicated throughout this chapter, policies are living documents that must be managed and nurtured, as they constantly change and grow. It is unacceptable to simply create such an important set of documents and then shelve them. These documents must be properly disseminated (distributed, read, understood, and agreed to), and managed. How they are managed relates directly to the policy management section of the issue-specific policy indicated earlier. Good management practices for policy development and maintenance make for a more resilient organization. For example, all policies, including security policies, undergo tremendous stress when corporate mergers and divestitures occur. These situations induce high rates of change and create settings in which employees undergo uncertainty and are faced with many distractions. Organizations faced with this degree of change reveal any weaknesses in the process designed to manage security policies. When two companies merge but retain separate policies, it can be difficult to implement security controls. Likewise, when one company with unified policies splits in two, each new company may require different policies.

To remain viable, these policies must have: an individual responsible for reviews, a schedule of reviews, a method for making recommendations for reviews, and a specific policy and revision date. Each of these is examined in additional detail below.

Responsible Individual

Just as information systems and information security projects must have a champion and manager, so must policies. The policy champion and manager is called the **policy administrator**. Typically the policy administrator is a mid-level staff member and is responsible for the creation, revision, distribution, and storage of the policy. Note that the policy administrator does not necessarily have to be a technically oriented person. While much of the background for practicing information security professionals requires extensive technical knowledge, the particular area of policy management and policy administration requires only a moderate level technical background. Good practice requires that for revisions and improvements of security policies, this individual should actively solicit input both from the technically adept information security experts and from the business-focused managers in each community of interest. This individual also notifies all affected members of the organization when the policy is modified.

It is disheartening if a policy that required hundreds of staff-hours to develop and document is ignored. Someone must be responsible for making sure that the policy and all subsequent revisions are placed into the hands of those individuals who are held accountable for their implementation. The policy administrator must be clearly identified on the policy document as the primary point of contact for additional information or for suggesting revisions to the policy.

Schedule of Review

Policies can only retain their effectiveness in a changing environment if they are periodically reviewed for currency and accuracy and modified to reflect these changes. Policies that are not kept current can become liabilities for the organization, as outdated rules are enforced (or not), and new requirements are ignored. As stated in Chapter 3, for the organization to demonstrate due diligence, it must demonstrate that it is actively trying to meet the requirements of the market in which it operates. This applies equally to both public (government, academic, and nonprofit) and private (commercial and for-profit) organizations. A properly organized schedule of reviews should be defined and published as part of the document. Typically a policy should be reviewed at least annually to ensure that it is still an effective control.

Review Procedures and Practices

To facilitate policy reviews, the policy manager should implement a mechanism by which individuals can comfortably make recommendations for revisions to the policies and the other related documentation. Recommendation methods can include e-mail, office mail, and an anonymous drop box. If the policy is controversial, the policy administrator may feel that anonymous submission of information is the best way to determine staff opinions. Many employees feel intimidated by management and hesitate to voice honest opinions about a policy, unless they can do so anonymously. Once the policy has come up for review, all comments should be examined and management-approved improvements should be implemented. Additional review methods can involve including representative users in the revision process and allowing direct comment on the revision of the policy. In reality, most policies are drafted by a single responsible individual and are then reviewed by a higher-level manager. This method should not preclude the collection and review of employee input.

Policy and Revision Date

The simple action of dating the policy is often skipped over. When policies are drafted and published without a date, confusion can arise when users of the policy are unaware of the policy's age or status. If policies are not reviewed and kept current, or if members of the organization are following undated versions, disastrous results and legal headaches can occur. These problems are particularly common in a high-turnover environment. It is, therefore, important that the policy contain the date of origin, along with the date(s), if any, of revisions. Some policies may need a sunset clause indicating their expiration date. This can be particularly important for policies governing information use in cooperation with other businesses or agencies that are involved in a short-term association. A **sunset clause** prevents a temporary policy from becoming a permanent mistake.

Automated Policy Management

A final topic for this section is the emergence of a new category of software for managing information security policies. In recent years, this category has emerged in response to needs articulated by information security practitioners. While there have been many software products that meet the need for a specific technical control, there is now a need for software to automate some of the busywork of policy management. Automation can streamline the repetitive steps of writing policy, tracking the workflow of policy approvals, publishing policy once it is written and approved, and tracking when individuals have read the policy. Using techniques from computer-based training and testing, organizations can train staff members and also improve the organization's awareness program. To quote the marketing literature from PentaSafe Corporation:

> "SOFTWARE THAT PUTS YOU IN CONTROL OF SECURITY POLICY CREATION, DISTRIBUTION, EDUCATION AND TRACKING FOR COMPLIANCE.
>
> "VigilEnt Policy Center now makes it possible to manage security policy dynamically so that you can create, distribute, educate, and track understanding of your information security policies for all employees in your organization. It enables you to keep policies up-to-date, change them quickly as needed, and ensure that they are being understood properly, all through a new automated, interactive, Web-based software application."[7]

Information Classification

This section delves further into **information classification**, a topic that has been discussed earlier. The classification of information is an important facet of policy and is also a control for the protection of information in general. In other words, policies are classified. The same protection scheme created to prevent production data from accidental release to the wrong party should be applied to policies, in order to keep them freely available, but only within the organization. Many company policies are at least classified as "for internal use only." As such, they should not be left where they could be inadvertently thrown away, picked up, or observed by unauthorized individuals outside the organization. With the increase in incidences of shoulder surfing and dumpster diving, organizations should pay increased attention to securing access to sensitive policy materials. For example, if an individual can determine from an unsecured copy of the policy document that tape backups are made at midnight and then carried off-site to an administrator's home, the intruder could obtain valuable data without even setting foot in the organization or accessing the organization's systems directly.

Related to document classification and the requirement to protect policies is the idea of the clean desk policy. If an organization has properly implemented a data classification scheme, an average administrator may be dealing with a number of types of information throughout a busy day. At the end of the day, an administrator may gladly run for the exit, leaving various types of information strewn throughout his office. This could open an opportunity for the accidental or intentional disclosure of information by individuals still in the building. In today's open office environments, most employees work from cubicles and do not have a door to secure their workspaces, so it may be beneficial to implement a clean desk policy. A **clean desk policy** stipulates that at the end of the business day, all classified information must be properly stored and secured. Secure storage could include file cabinets, desk drawers, or other controlled access areas. As is evident from the photograph of the desk of one of the authors (Figure 6-7), this is not a requirement in academia.

Once an organization has developed its information security policies and standards, it is time for the information security community to begin developing the blueprint for the information security program. It should be noted that if one or more components of policies, standards, or practices are missing before or during development of the blueprint, management must determine if such omission is acceptable to the organization.

FIGURE 6-7   Professor Whitman's Desk

Systems Design

At this point in the Security SDLC, the analysis phase is complete and the design phase begins. At the end of the analysis phase, the security team has assessed the threats to the information and systems and has prioritized those threats. The team has also developed a prioritized inventory of the organization's information assets, as well as an evaluation of the current asset-threat-vulnerability environment with all the existing controls and safeguards in place. The current state of the information assets, protected or not, forms the background for the development steps to follow.

In addition, the team has completed risk assessments with either a quantitative or qualitative analysis of each asset's protection level and has prepared a benchmark comparison of security standards from similarly structured organizations. Finally, the team has completed a set of feasibility studies, including cost benefit analyses, identifying whether or not any given control should proceed as planned, and in aggregate, whether the project should continue as originally planned.

Armed with a general idea of the vulnerabilities present in the information technology systems of the organization, the security team can move to the next phase of the security systems development life cycle (the SecSDLC). Figure 6-8 illustrates the two components of the design phase and shows how they are covered in this and the following chapter. This chapter covers the design blueprint for security, which is used to implement the security program. Chapter 7 continues the SecSDLC design effort by covering the planning efforts needed to assure the continuity of the organization.

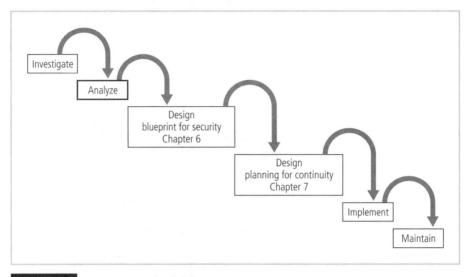

FIGURE 6-8 SecSDLC Methodology

Designing a working plan for securing the organization's information assets begins by creating or validating an existing **security blueprint** for the implementation of needed security controls to protect the information assets. The terms "blueprint" and "framework" are closely related. A **framework** is the outline from which a more detailed blueprint evolves. The blueprint is the basis for the design, selection, and implementation of all subsequent security policies, education and training programs, and technologies. The blueprint provides scalable, upgradeable, and comprehensive security for the coming years. However, the team still may not fully understand how to proceed until it sets priorities for analysis. An awareness of the problems associated with the system and how to solve them is vital to the resolution of information security problems. The benchmarking of other organizations may provide details on *what* controls should be considered, but this method does not provide the details on how to implement them, and in what order.

Thus, the next step is to use the blueprint to plan the tasks to be accomplished and the order in which to proceed. The prioritization of activities in the analysis phase provides helpful insights into the order in which these tasks must be accomplished. The priorities serve as a guideline during the implementation phase.

Setting priorities can follow the recommendations of published sources, such as this textbook, or from published standards provided by government agencies or private consultants. If the organization hires consultants to conduct the security assessment and implementation, they bring their own methodologies.

So, where to begin? First, a number of approaches to blueprint development are discussed. Finally, a hybrid methodology is presented that takes into account the best current alternatives available.

Information Security Blueprints

One approach to selecting a methodology is to adapt or adopt a published model or framework for information security. As stated above, a framework is the basic skeleton for planning the blueprint. The framework can be an outline of steps involved in designing and later implementing information security in the organization. There are a number of published information security frameworks, such as those from government organizations presented later in this chapter. Each framework focuses on differing levels of detail. Because of the unique nature of each information security environment, the security team may need to modify or adapt pieces from several frameworks. Experience teaches you that what works well for one organization may not precisely fit another. As a result, each implementation may need modification or even redesign before it suits the needs of a particular asset-threat problem.

ISO 17799/BS 7799

One of the most widely referenced and often discussed security models is the *Information Technology – Code of Practice for Information Security Management*, which was originally published as the British Standard BS 7799. In 2000, this Code of Practice was adopted as an international standard framework for information security by the International Organization for Standardization (ISO) and the International Electrotechnical Commission (IEC) as ISO/IEC 17799. While the details of ISO/IEC 17799 are available only through purchase of the standard, the structure and general organization are well known. For a summary description, see Figure 6-9, which is entitled Ten Sections of ISO/IEC 17799. For more details on ISO/IEC Sections, see *http://www.iso17799software.com/what.htm*.

Content Outline

1. Organizational Security Policy
2. Organizational Security Infrastructure
3. Asset Classification and Control
4. Personnel Security
5. Physical and Environmental Security
6. Communications and Operations Management
7. System Access Control
8. System Development and Maintenance
9. Business Continuity Planning
10. Compliance

FIGURE 6-9 Ten Sections of ISO/IEC 17799[8]

The stated purpose of ISO/IEC 17799 is to "give recommendations for information security management for use by those who are responsible for initiating, implementing or maintaining security in their organization. It is intended to provide a common basis for developing organizational security standards and effective security management practice and to provide confidence in inter-organizational dealings."[9]

The International Standards is actually the first volume of the two volume British standard, BS 7799:2. This document picks up where ISO/IEC 17799 leaves off. In ISO/IEC 17799, the focus is on a broad overview of the various areas of security, providing information on 127 controls over ten broad areas. Volume 2 provides information on how to implement Volume 1 (17799) and how to set up an information security management system (ISMS). The overall methodology for this process and its major steps are presented in Figure 6-10.

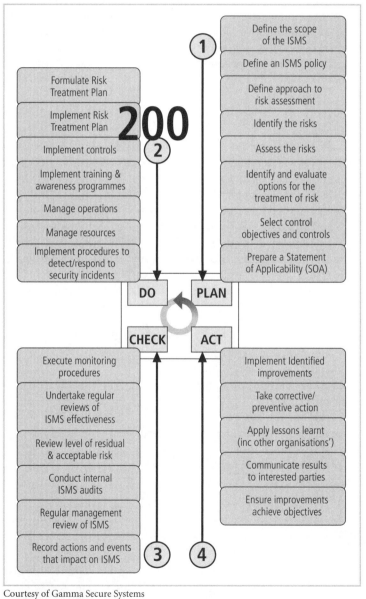

Courtesy of Gamma Secure Systems

FIGURE 6-10   BS7799:2 Major Process Steps[10]

In the United Kingdom, these standards are used to obtain system (ISMS) certification and accreditation if implemented in accordance with both volumes of the standard and evaluated by a BS 7799 certified evaluator.

Several countries including the United States, Germany, and Japan have not adopted 17799. They claim that there are several fundamental problems, which include:

1. The global information security community has not defined any justification for a code of practice as identified in the ISO/IEC 17799.
2. ISO/IEC 17799 lacks "the necessary measurement precision of a technical standard." [11]
3. There is no reason to believe that ISO/IEC 17799 is more useful than any other approach currently available.
4. ISO/IEC 17799 is not as complete as other frameworks available.
5. ISO/IEC 17799 is perceived to have been hurriedly prepared given the tremendous impact its adoption could have on industry information security controls. [12]

Although ISO/IEC 17799 is an interesting framework for information security, small and medium-sized organizations in the United States would not be required to adopt it as a standard, except those relatively few organizations that operate in the European Union or are otherwise obliged to comply with it.

NIST Security Models

Another possible approach is described in the many documents available from the Computer Security Resource Center of the National Institute for Standards and Technology (*csrc.nist.gov*). These are among the references cited by the federal government when deciding not to select the ISO/IEC 17799 standards. These documents are publicly available at no charge and have been available for some time and therefore have been broadly reviewed by government and industry professionals. The following documents can assist in the design of a security framework:

- SP 800-12: *Computer Security Handbook*
- SP 800-14: *Generally Accepted Security Principles & Practices*
- SP 800-18: *Guide for Developing Security Plans*
- SP 800-26: *Security Self-Assessment Guide for Information Technology Systems*
- SP 800-30: *Risk Management for Information Technology Systems*

Many of these documents have been referenced in earlier chapters as sources of information for the management of security. The following sections examine these documents in more detail as they apply to the blueprint for information security.

NIST Special Publication SP 800-12

SP 800-12, *The Computer Security Handbook*, is an excellent reference and guide for the security manager or administrator in the routine management of information security. It provides little guidance, however, on design and implementation of new security systems and should be used as a valuable precursor to understanding an information security blueprint, but should not be considered as a model.

NIST Special Publication 800-14

Generally Accepted Principles and Practices for Securing Information Technology Systems provides best practices and security principles that can direct the security team in the development of a security blueprint. In addition to detailing security best practices across the spectrum of security areas, it provides philosophical principles that the security team should integrate into the entire information security process. Figure 6-11 presents the table of contents of the NIST SP 800-14. The document can guide the development of the security framework and should be combined with other NIST publications providing the necessary structure to the entire security process.

NIST SP 800-14 Generally Accepted Principles and Practices for Securing Information Technology Systems
Table of Contents

2. Generally Accepted System Security Principles
   2.1 Computer Security Supports the Mission of the Organization
   2.2 Computer Security is an Integral Element of Sound Management
   2.3 Computer Security Should Be Cost-Effective
   2.4 Systems Owners Have Security Responsibilities Outside Their Own Organizations
   2.5 Computer Security Responsibilities and Accountability Should Be Made Explicit
   2.6 Computer Security Requires a Comprehensive and Integrated Approach
   2.7 Computer Security Should Be Periodically Reassessed
   2.8 Computer Security is Constrained by Societal Factors
3. Common IT Security Practices
   3.1 Policy
       3.1.1 Program Policy
       3.1.2 Issue-Specific Policy
       3.1.3 System-Specific Policy
       3.1.4 All Policies
   3.2 Program Management
       3.2.1 Central Security Program
       3.2.2 System-Level Program
   3.3 Risk Management
       3.3.1 Risk Assessment
       3.3.2 Risk Mitigation
       3.3.3 Uncertainty Analysis
   3.4 Life Cycle Planning
       3.4.1 Security Plan
       3.4.2 Initiation Phase
       3.4.3 Development/Acquisition Phase
       3.4.4 Implementation Phase
       3.4.5 Operation/Maintenance Phase
       3.4.6 Disposal Phase
   3.5 Personnel/User Issues
       3.5.1 Staffing
       3.5.2 User Administration
   3.6 Preparing for Contingencies and Disasters
       3.6.1 Business Plan
       3.6.2 Identify Resources
       3.6.3 Develop Scenarios
       3.6.4 Develop Strategies
       3.6.5 Test and Revise Plan
   3.7 Computer Security Incident Handling
       3.7.1 Uses of a Capability
       3.7.2 Characteristics
   3.8 Awareness and Training
   3.9 Security Considerations in Computer Support and Operations
   3.10 Physical and Environmental Security
   3.11 Identification and Authentication
       3.11.1 Identification
       3.11.2 Authentication
       3.11.3 Passwords
       3.11.4 Advanced Authentication
   3.12 Logical Access Control
       3.12.1 Access Criteria
       3.12.2 Access Control Mechanisms
   3.13 Audit Trails
       3.13.1 Contents of Audit Trail Records
       3.13.2 Audit Trail Security
       3.13.3 Audit Trail Reviews
       3.13.4 Keystroke Monitoring
   3.14 Cryptography

FIGURE 6-11   Table of contents of NIST SP 800-14[13]

The scope of NIST SP 800-14 is broad. It is important to consider each of the security principles it presents, and therefore the following sections examine some of the more significant points in more detail:

2.1 Security Supports the Mission of the Organization: As stated earlier in this chapter, failure to develop an information security system based on the organization's mission, vision, and culture guarantees the failure of the information security program.

2.2 Security is an Integral Element of Sound Management: Effective management includes planning, organizing, leading, and controlling. Security enhances these areas by supporting the planning function when information security policies provide input into the organization initiatives. Information security specifically supports the controlling function, as security controls support sound management through the enforcement of both managerial and security policies.

2.3 Security Should Be Cost-Effective: The costs of information security should be considered part of the cost of doing business, much like the cost of the computers, networks, and voice communications systems. These are not profit-generating areas of the organization and may not lead to competitive advantages. As discussed in Chapter 5, however, information security should justify its own costs. Security measures that do not justify cost benefit levels must have a strong business case (such as a legal requirement) to warrant their use.

2.4 Systems Owners Have Security Responsibilities Outside Their Own Organizations: Whenever systems store and use information from customers, patients, clients, partners, and others, the security of this information becomes a serious responsibility for the owner of the systems. In addition to the requirement for the protection of others' data, it is the general responsibility of the systems owners to protect their information assets for all of the stakeholders of the organization. Stakeholders include shareholders in the case of publicly held organizations, and the government and taxpayers in the case of public agencies and institutions.

2.5 Security Responsibilities and Accountability Should Be Made Explicit: Policy documents should clearly identify the security responsibilities of users, administrators, and managers. To be legally binding, this information must be documented, disseminated, read, understood, and agreed to. As noted in Chapter 3, ignorance of the law is no excuse, but ignorance of policy is. Regarding the law, the organization should also detail the relevance of laws to issue-specific security policies. These details should be distributed to users, administrators, and managers to assist them in complying with their responsibilities.

2.6 Security Requires a Comprehensive and Integrated Approach: Security personnel alone cannot effectively implement security. As emphasized throughout this textbook, *security is everyone's responsibility*. Throughout each stage of the SecSDLC, the three communities of interest (information technology management and professionals, information security management and professionals, as well as the users, managers, administrators, and other stakeholders of the broader organization) should participate in all aspects of the information security program.

2.7 Security Should Be Periodically Reassessed: In connection with the legal concept of due diligence, information security that is implemented and then ignored is considered negligent. Security is an ongoing process. It cannot be started and then expected to function independently without constant maintenance and change. To be effective against a constantly shifting set of threats and constantly changing user base, the security process must be periodically repeated. Continuous analyses of threats, assets, and controls must be conducted and new blueprints developed. Only through thorough preparation, design, implementation, eternal vigilance, and ongoing maintenance can the organization's information assets be considered truly secure.

2.8 Security is Constrained by Societal Factors: There are a number of factors that influence the implementation and maintenance of security. Legal demands, shareholder requirements, even business practices impact the implementation of security controls and safeguards. While security professionals would prefer to isolate information assets from the Internet, which is the leading avenue of threats to the assets, the business requirements of the organization may preclude this control measure.

Figure 6-12 presents the "Principles for Securing Information Technology Systems," which is a document from NIST SP 800-14. This document covers many factors and each of them may have been identified in part during the analysis phase. This figure serves as a checkpoint for the blueprint process and provides a method to make sure all key elements are factored into the design of an information security program and to produce a blueprint for an effective security architecture.

Principles for Securing Information Technology Systems
NIST SP 800-14 Generally Accepted Principles and Practices
for Securing Information Technology Systems

Principle 1.   Establish a sound security policy as the foundation for design.

Principle 2.   Treat security as an integral part of the overall system design.

Principle 3.   Clearly delineate the physical and logical security boundaries governed by associated security policies.

Principle 4.   Reduce risk to an acceptable level.

Principle 5.   Assume that external systems are insecure.

Principle 6.   Identify potential trade-offs between reducing risk and increased costs and decrease in other aspects of operational effectiveness.

Principle 7.   Implement layered security (ensure no single point of vulnerability).

Principle 8.   Implement tailored system security measures to meet organizational security goals.

Principle 9.   Strive for simplicity.

Principle 10.   Design and operate an IT system to limit vulnerability and to be resilient in response.

Principle 11.   Minimize the system elements to be trusted.

Principle 12.   Implement security through a combination of measures distributed physically and logically.

Principle 13.   Provide assurance that the system is, and continues to be, resilient in the face of expected threats.

Principle 14.   Limit or contain vulnerabilities.

Principle 15.   Formulate security measures to address multiple overlapping information domains.

Principle 16.   Isolate public access systems from mission critical resources (e.g., data, processes, etc.).

Principle 17.   Use boundary mechanisms to separate computing systems and network infrastructures.

Principle 18.   Where possible, base security on open standards for portability and interoperability.

Principle 19.   Use common language in developing security requirements.

Principle 20.   Design and implement audit mechanisms to detect unauthorized use and to support incident investigations.

Principle 21.   Design security to allow for regular adoption of new technology, including a secure and logical technology upgrade process.

Principle 22.   Authenticate users and processes to ensure appropriate access control decisions both within and across domains.

Principle 23.   Use unique identities to ensure accountability.

Principle 24.   Implement least privilege.

Principle 25.   Do not implement unnecessary security mechanisms.

Principle 26.   Protect information while being processed, in transit, and in storage.

Principle 27.   Strive for operational ease of use.

Principle 28.   Develop and exercise contingency or disaster recovery procedures to ensure appropriate availability.

Principle 29.   Consider custom products to achieve adequate security.

Principle 30.   Ensure proper security in the shutdown or disposal of a system.

Principle 31.   Protect against all likely classes of "attacks."

Principle 32.   Identify and prevent common errors and vulnerabilities.

Principle 33.   Ensure that developers are trained in how to develop secure software.

FIGURE 6-12 Principles of NIST SP 800-14[14]

NIST Special Publication 800-18

The Guide for Developing Security Plans for Information Technology Systems is considered the foundation for a comprehensive security blueprint and framework. This publication provides detailed methods for assessing, designing, and implementing controls and plans for applications of varying size. SP 800-18 is designed to guide the activities described in this chapter and to aid in the planning process. It also includes templates for major application security plans. As with any publication of this scope and magnitude, SP 800-18 must be customized to fit the particular needs of an organization. The table of contents for Publication 800-18 is presented in Figure 6-13.

Guide for Developing Security Plans for Information Technology Systems
Table of Contents

2. System Analysis
    2.1 System Boundaries
    2.2 Multiple Similar Systems
    2.3 System Category
        2.3.1 Major Applications
        2.3.2 General Support System
3. Plan Development – All Systems
    3.1 Plan Control
    3.2 System Identification
        3.2.1 System Name/Title
        3.2.2 Responsible Organization
        3.2.3 Information Contact(s)
        3.2.4 Assignment of Security Responsibility
    3.3 System Operational Status
    3.4 General Description/Purpose
    3.5 System Environment
    3.6 System Interconnection/Information Sharing
    3.7 Sensitivity of Information Handled
        3.7.1 Laws, Regulations, and Policies Affecting the System
        3.7.2 General Description of Sensitivity
4. Management Controls
    4.1 Risk Assessment and Management
    4.2 Review of Security Controls
    4.3 Rules of Behavior
    4.4 Planning for Security in the Life Cycle
        4.4.1 Initiation Phase
        4.4.2 Development/Acquisition Phase
        4.4.3 Implementation Phase
        4.4.4 Operation/Maintenance Phase
        4.4.5 Disposal Phase
    4.5 Authorize Processing
5. Operational Controls
    5.MA. Major Application – Operational Controls
    5.MA.1 Personnel Security
    5.MA.2 Physical and Environmental Protection
        5.MA.2.1 Explanation of Physical and Environment Security
        5.MA.2.2 Computer Room Example
    5.MA.3 Production, Input/Output Controls
    5.MA.4 Contingency Planning
    5.MA.5 Application Software Maintenance Controls
    5.MA.6 Data Integrity/Validation Controls
    5.MA.7 Documentation
    5.MA.8 Security Awareness and Training
6.MA Major Application - Technical Controls
    6.MA.1 Identification and Authentication
        6.MA.1.1 Identification
        6.MA.1.2 Authentication
    6.MA.2 Logical Access Controls (Authorization/Access Controls)
    6.MA.3 Public Access Controls
    6.MA.4 Audit Trails
5.GSS General Support System – Operational Controls
    5.GSS.1 Personnel Controls
    5.GSS.2 Physical and Environmental Protection
        5.GSS.2.1 Explanation of Physical and Environment Security
        5.GSS.2.2 Computer Room Example
    5.GSS.3 Production, Input/Output Controls
    5.GSS.4 Contingency Planning (Continuity of Support)
    5.GSS.5 Hardware and System Software Maintenance Controls
    5.GSS.6 Integrity Controls
    5.GSS.7 Documentation
    5.GSS.8 Security Awareness and Training
    5.GSS.9 Incident Response Capability
6.GSS General Support System - Technical Controls
    6.GSS.1 Identification and Authentication
        6.GSS.1.1 Identification
        6.GSS.1.2 Authentication
    6.GSS.2 Logical Access Controls (Authorization/Access Controls)
    6.GSS.3 Audit Trails

FIGURE 6-13 NIST SP 800-18[15]

IETF Security Architecture

While no specific architecture is promoted through the Internet Engineering Task Force (IETF), the Security Area Working Group acts as an advisory board for the protocols and areas developed and promoted through the Internet Society. One request for comment (RFC) in particular provides a good functional discussion of important security issues. RFC 2196: *Site Security Handbook* covers five basic areas of security with detailed discussions on development and implementation. There are also chapters on such important topics as security policies, security technical architecture, security services, and security incident handling.

The chapter on architecture begins with a discussion of the importance of security policies, and expands into an examination of services, access controls, and other relevant areas. The Table of Contents for the RFC 2196: *Site Security Handbook* is represented in the Figure 6-14.

RFC 2196: Site Security Handbook
Table of Contents

1. Introduction
   1.1   Purpose of this Work
   1.2   Audience
   1.3   Definitions
   1.4   Related Work
   1.5   Basic Approach
   1.6   Risk Assessment
2. Security Policies
   2.1   What is a Security Policy and Why Have One?
   2.2   What Makes a Good Security Policy?
   2.3   Keeping the Policy Flexible
3. Architecture
   3.1   Objectives
   3.2   Network and Service Configuration
   3.3   Firewalls
4. Security Services and Procedures
   4.1   Authentication
   4.2   Confidentiality
   4.3   Integrity
   4.4   Authorization
   4.5   Access
   4.6   Auditing
   4.7   Securing Backups
5. Security Incident Handling
   5.1   Preparing and Planning for Incident Handling
   5.2   Notification and Points of Contact
   5.3   Identifying an Incident
   5.4   Handling an Incident
   5.5   Aftermath of an Incident
   5.6   Responsibilities
6. Ongoing Activities
7. Tools and Locations
8. Mailing Lists and Other Resources
9. References

FIGURE 6-14 RFC 2196: Site Security Handbook[16]

VISA International Security Model

VISA International promotes strong security measures in its business associates and has established guidelines for the security of its information systems. VISA has developed two important documents that improve and regulate its information systems: "Security Assessment Process" and "Agreed Upon Procedures." Both documents provide specific instructions on the use of the VISA Cardholder Information Security Program.[17] The "Security Assessment Process" document is a series of recommendations for the detailed examination of an organization's systems with the eventual goal of integration into the VISA systems. The "Agreed Upon Procedures" document outlines the policies and technologies necessary to security systems that carry the sensitive cardholder information to and from VISA systems. Using the two documents, a security team can develop a sound strategy for the design of good security architecture. The only downside to this approach is the specific focus on systems that can or do integrate with VISA's systems with the explicit purpose of carrying the aforementioned cardholder information.

Baselining and Best Business Practices

As presented in Chapter 5, baselining and best practices are solid methods for collecting security practices. Baselining and best practices can have the drawback, however, of lacking a complete methodology for the design and implementation of all the practices needed by an organization. However, it is possible to gain information by baselining and using best practices, to piece together the desired outcome of the security process, and to therefore work backwards to an effective design. The Federal Agency Security Practices (FASP) Site (*fasp.nist.gov*) is a popular place to look up best practices. FASP is designed to provide best practices for public agencies, but these practices can be adapted easily to private institutions. The documents found in this site include specific examples of key policies and planning documents, implementation strategies for key technologies, and position descriptions for key security personnel. Of particular value is the section on program management, which includes the following information:

- A summary guide: public law, executive orders, and policy documents, Department of the Treasury
- Position description for computer system security officer
- Position description for information security officer
- Position description for computer specialist
- Sample of an information technology (IT) security staffing plan for a large service application (LSA)
- Sample of XX agency large service application (LSA) information technology (IT) security program policy
- Security handbook and standard operating procedures
- Telecommuting and mobile computer security policy

In the later stages of creating an information security blueprint, these policy documents are particularly useful.

Other public and semipublic institutions that provide information on best practices include the Internet Security Task Force (*www.ca.com/ISTF*). This task force is a collection of interested parties, both public and private, with a shared interest in the security of the

Internet. They provide recommendations for security implementations. Another widely referenced source is the Computer Emergency Response Team (CERT) at Carnegie Mellon University (*www.cert.org*). Although detailed and specific, CERT promotes a series of security modules with links to practices and implementation that represent a security methodology.

It is often worthwhile for a security professional to join professional societies that provide information on best practices for their members. The Technology Manager's Forum (*www.techforum.com*) has an annual best practice award in a number of areas including information security. The Information Security Forum (*www.isfsecuritystandard.com*) has a free publication titled "Standard of Good Practice." This publication outlines information security best practices.

Many organizations have seminars and classes on best practices for implementing security. For example, the Information Systems Audit and Control Association (*www.isaca.com*) hosts a seminar on a routine basis. Similarly, the International Association of Professional Security Consultants (*www.iapsc.org*) has a listing of best practices, as does the Global Grid Forum (*www.gridforum.org*). At minimum, information security professionals can peruse Web portals for posted security best practices. There are several free portals dedicated to security that have collections of practices, such as SearchSecurity.com, and NIST's Computer Resources Center. These are but a few of the many public and private organizations that promote solid best security practices. Investing a few hours searching the Web reveals dozens of locations for additional information.

Finding information on security design is the easy part. Sorting through the collected mass of information, documents, and publications can take a substantial investment in time and human resources. In the end, each organization needs a clear methodology for the creation of the framework leading to a blueprint for the development of a security system. The hybrid framework outlined in the following section fulfills that need.

Hybrid Framework for a Blueprint of an Information Security System

This section identifies a hybrid framework for a methodology that organizations can use to fill in the implementation details to create a security system blueprint and address almost all of the components of a solid information security plan.

Each of the topics in the Self-Assessment Guide shown in Figure 6-15 emerged out of documents discussed earlier which were filtered with the current knowledge and experience of information security professionals. This framework of security also includes philosophical components of the Human Firewall Project,[18] indicating that people, not technology, are the primary defenders of information assets in an information security program, and are uniquely responsible for their protection.

NIST SP 800-26 Security Self-Assessment Guide
for Information Technology Systems

Management Controls

1. Risk Management
2. Review of Security Controls
3. Life Cycle Maintenance
4. Authorization of Processing (Certification and Accreditation)
5. System Security Plan

Operational Controls

6. Personnel Security
7. Physical Security
8. Production, Input/Output Controls
9. Contingency Planning
10. Hardware and Systems Software
11. Data Integrity
12. Documentation
13. Security Awareness, Training, and Education
14. Incident Response Capability

Technical Controls

15. Identification and Authentication
16. Logical Access Controls
17. Audit Trails

FIGURE 6-15 Self-Assessment Guide[19]

Figure 6-16, showing the sphere of security, is the foundation of the security framework. Generally speaking, the sphere of security represents the fact that information is under attack from a variety of sources. The sphere of use, at the left of the figure, illustrates the ways in which people can directly access information: for example, people read hard copies of documents; they also access information through systems, such as the electronic storage of information. Information, as the most important asset to security, is illustrated at the core of the sphere. Information is always at risk from attacks through the people and computer systems that have direct access to the information. Networks and the Internet represent indirect threats, as exemplified by the fact that a person attempting to access information from the Internet must first go through the local networks and then access systems that contain the information. The sphere of protection, at the right of the figure, illustrates that between each layer of the sphere of use there must exist a layer of protection to prevent access to the inner layer from the outer layer. Each shaded band is a layer of protection and control. For example, the layer labeled "policy education and training" is located between people and the information. Controls are also implemented between systems and the information, between networks and the computer systems, and between the Internet and internal networks. This reinforces the concept of defense in depth. As illustrated in the sphere of protection portion of Figure 6-16, a variety of controls can be used to protect the information. The list in the figure is not intended to be comprehensive but illustrates individual safeguards that protect the various systems that are located closer to the center of the sphere. However, as people can directly access each ring as well as the information at the core of the model, people require unique approaches to security. In fact, the resource of people must become a layer of security, a **human firewall** that protects the information from unauthorized access and use. The members of the organization must become a safeguard, which is effectively trained, implemented, and maintained, or else they, too, become a threat to the information.

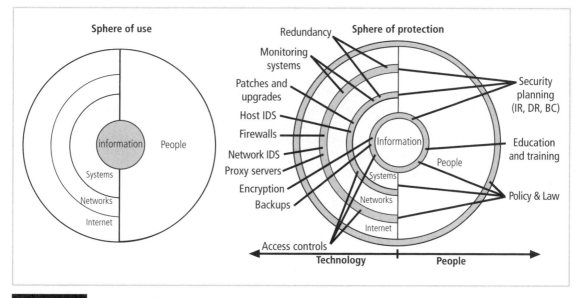

FIGURE 6-16 Spheres of Security

As stated earlier in this chapter, information security is designed and implemented in three layers: policies, people (education, training, and awareness programs), and technology. While the design and implementation of the people layer and the technology layer overlap, both must follow sound management policies discussed earlier in this chapter. Each of the layers constitutes controls and safeguards that are put into place to protect the information and information system assets that the organizations values. The order of the controls within the layers follows the prioritization scheme developed in Chapter 4. But before any controls and safeguards are put into place, the policies defining management philosophies that guide the security process must already be in place.

As represented in Figure 6-15, safeguards provide three levels of control: managerial, operational, and technical. Each of these is examined in detail below.

Management controls cover security processes that are designed by strategic planners and implemented by the security administration of the organization. The topics listed under management controls set the direction and scope of the security process and provide detailed instructions for its conduct. Management controls address the design and implementation of the security planning process and security program management. They also address risk management and security control reviews discussed in Chapters 4 and 5. Management controls further describe the necessity and scope of legal compliance and the maintenance of the entire security life cycle.

Operational controls deal with the operational functionality of security in the organization. They cover management functions and lower-level planning, such as disaster recovery and incident response planning. Operational controls also address personnel security, physical security, and the protection of production inputs and outputs. Operational controls also structure the development of education, training and awareness programs for users, administrators, and management. Finally, they address hardware and software systems maintenance and the integrity of data.

Technical controls address the tactical and technical issues related to designing and implementing security in the organization, as well as issues related to examining and selecting the technologies appropriate to protecting information. While operational controls address specific operational issues, such as developing and integrating controls into the business functions, technical controls address the specifics of technology selection and the acquisition (make or buy) of certain technical components. They also cover logical access controls, such as identification, authentication, authorization, and accountability. Technical controls also address the development and implementation of audit trails for accountability. These controls also cover cryptography to protect information in storage and transit. Finally, they cover the classification of assets and users, to facilitate the authorization levels needed.

Using the three sets of controls just described, the organization should be able to specify controls to cover the entire spectrum of safeguards, from strategic to tactical, from managerial to technical.

When your organization has outlined its plan in a framework and fleshed it out into a blueprint for implementation, it is important to create a training program that increases information security awareness and enables members of the organization to work in ways that secure the organization's information assets.

Security Education, Training, and Awareness Program

As soon as the general security policy and its approach to security in the organization has been drafted, policies to implement **security education, training, and awareness (SETA)** programs should naturally follow. The SETA program is the responsibility of the CISO and is a control measure designed to reduce the incidences of accidental security breaches by employees. As indicated in Chapter 2, employee errors are among the top threats to information assets. As a result, it is worth expending the organization's resources to develop programs to combat this threat. SETA programs are designed to supplement the general education and training programs that many organizations have in place to educate staff on information security. For example, if an organization detects that many employees are opening e-mail attachments inappropriately, those employees must be retrained. As a matter of good practice, systems development life cycles must include user training during the implementation phase. Employee training should be managed so that there is some assurance that all employees are trained properly. Security education and training is designed to build on the general knowledge that employees possess to do their jobs and to focus on ways to work securely.

The SETA program consists of three elements: security education, security training, and security awareness. The organization may not be capable of or willing to undertake all three of these elements, but may outsource them to local educational institutions. The purpose of SETA is to enhance security by:

- Improving awareness of the need to protect system resources
- Developing skills and knowledge so computer users can perform their jobs more securely
- Building in-depth knowledge, as needed, to design, implement, or operate security programs for organizations and systems[20]

Table 6-1 compares the features of security education, training, and awareness within the organization.

Table 6-1   Comparative Framework of SETA: NIST SP800-12[21]

	Education	Training	Awareness
Attribute	Why	How	What
Level	Insight	Knowledge	Information
Objective	Understanding	Skill	
Teaching method	Theoretical instruction ■ Discussion seminar ■ Background reading	Practical instruction ■ Lecture ■ Case study workshop ■ Hands-on practice	Media ■ Videos ■ Newsletters ■ Posters
Test measure	Essay (interpret learning)	Problem solving (apply learning)	■ True or false ■ Multiple choice (identify learning)
Impact timeframe	Long-term	Intermediate	Short-term

Security Education

Everyone in an organization needs to be trained and aware of information security, but not every member of the organization needs a formal degree or certificate in information security. When formal education for appropriate individuals in security is needed, with the support of management, an employee can identify curriculum available from local institutions of higher learning or continuing education. A number of universities have formal coursework in information security. For those interested in researching formal information security programs, there are resources available, such as Avi Rubin's page on cryptography and security courses (*http://avirubin.com/courses.html*), or the NSA identified Centers of Excellence in Information Assurance Education (*www.nsa.gov/isso/programs/nietp/newspg1.htm*). The Centers of Excellence program identifies outstanding universities with both coursework in information security and an integrated view in information security in the institution itself. Other local resources can also provide security education information, such as Kennesaw State's Center for Information Security Education and Awareness (*http://infosec.kennesaw.edu*).

Security Training

Security training involves providing members of the organization with detailed information and hands-on instruction designed to prepare them to perform their duties securely. Management of information security can develop customized in-house training or outsource the training program.

Another option to formal training programs are industry training conferences and programs offered through professional agencies such as SANS *(www.sans.org)*, ISC2 *(www.isc2.org)*, ISSA *(www.issa.org)*, and CSI *(www.gocsi.org)*. Many of these programs may be too technical for the average employee, but may be perfect for the continuing education requirements of information security professionals.

There are a number of available resources for conducting SETA programs, including sample topics and structures for security classes. For organizations, the Computer Security Resource Center at NIST provides several useful documents free of charge in their special publications area *(http://csrc.nist.gov)*.

Security Awareness

One of the least frequently implemented, but the most beneficial programs is the security awareness program. A security awareness program is designed to keep information security at the forefront of the users' minds as they work day to day. These programs don't have to be complicated or expensive. Good programs can include newsletters, security posters (see Figure 6-17 for an example), videos, bulletin boards, flyers, and trinkets, or they can be included with other training programs. Trinkets can include security slogans printed on mouse pads, coffee cups, T-shirts, pens, or any object frequently used during the workday that reminds employees of security. In addition, a good security awareness program requires a dedicated individual willing to invest the time and effort into promoting the program, and a champion willing to provide the needed financial support.

The security newsletter is the most cost-effective method of disseminating security information and news to the employee. Newsletters can be hard copy, e-mail, or Intranet based. Newsletter topics can include new threats to the organization's information assets, the schedule for upcoming security classes, and the addition of new security personnel. The goal is to keep the idea of information security in the users' minds and to stimulate them to care about security. If the program is not actively implemented, employees begin to tune out, and the risk of employee accidents and failures increases.

FIGURE 6-17 Information Security Awareness at KSU

As a final component for the discussion of blueprints, it is important to present the entire information security systems design, whether expressed as a framework (outline) or blueprint (plan) as a unified proposal. This requires the preparation of a complete and concise explanation of the information security program and its technical controls. The proposal must communicate its business function as well as its technical impact on each of the communities of interest.

Design of Security Architecture

To add some background to the discussion of information security program architecture and to illustrate industry best practices, the following discussion outlines a few key security architectural components. Many of these components are examined in detail in Chapter 8. However it is important to have a working knowledge of the areas discussed in order to ensure the framework and/or blueprint are on target to meet organization needs at this stage of the SecSDLC.

Defense in Depth

As indicated earlier, one of the foundations of security architectures is the requirement to implement security in layers. This layered approach is referred to as **defense in depth**. Defense in depth requires that the organization establish sufficient security controls and safeguards, so that an intruder faces multiple layers of control. These layers of control can be organized into policy, training and education, and technology, as per the NSTISSC model presented in Chapter 1. While policy itself may not prevent attacks, it certainly prepares the organization to handle attacks. Coupled with other layers, policy can deter attacks. Training and education are similar. Technology is also implemented in layers, with detection equipment working in tandem with reaction technology, all operating behind access control mechanisms. Implementing multiple types of technology and thereby preventing failure of one system from compromising the security of the information is referred to as **redundancy**. Redundancy can be implemented in a number of points throughout the security architecture, such as firewalls, proxy servers, and access controls. Figure 6-18 illustrates the concept of building controls in multiple, sometimes redundant layers. The figure shows the use of firewalls and intrusion detection systems (IDS) that use both packet-level rules (shown as the header in the diagram) and data content analysis (shown as 0100101011 in the diagram).

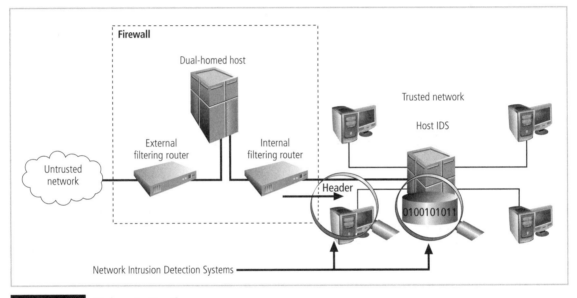

FIGURE 6-18   Defense in Depth

Security Perimeter

A perimeter is the boundary of an area. A **security perimeter** defines the edge between the outer limit of an organization's security and the beginning of the outside world. A security perimeter is the first level of security that protects all internal systems from outside threats, as pictured in Figure 6-19. Unfortunately the perimeter does not apply to internal attacks from employee threats or on-site physical threats. There can be both an electronic security perimeter, usually at the organization's exterior network or Internet connection, and a physical security perimeter, usually at the gate to the organization's offices. Both require perimeter security. Security perimeters can effectively be implemented as multiple technologies that segregate the protected information from those who would attack it. Within security perimeters the organization can establish **security domains**, or areas of trust within which users can freely communicate. The assumption is that if individuals have access to one system within a security domain, they have authorized access to all systems within that particular domain.

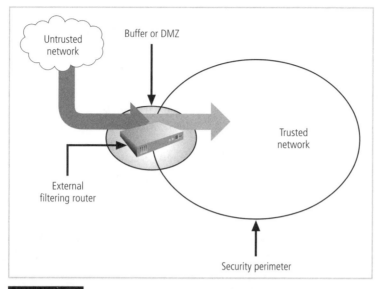

FIGURE 6-19   Security Perimeters and Domains

Key Technology Components

A few other key technology components that are important to understand during the design phase of a security architecture are the firewall, proxy server, intrusion detection systems, and DMZs. Again, additional technical discussion of these controls will be presented in Chapter 8 and only a cursory overview is provided here.

Firewalls

A **firewall** is a device that selectively discriminates against information flowing into or out of the organization. A firewall is usually a computing device, or specially configured computer that allows or prevents information from entering or exiting the defined area based on a set of predefined rules. Firewalls are usually placed on the security perimeter, just behind or as part of a **gateway router**. While the gateway router is primarily designed to connect the organization's systems to the outside world, it too can be used as the front-line defense against attacks, as it can be configured to allow only a few types of protocols to enter. There are a number of types of firewalls, usually classified by the level of information they can filter. Firewalls can be packet filtering, stateful packet filtering, proxy, or application level. A firewall can be a single device or a **firewall subnet** that consists of multiple firewalls creating a buffer between the outside and inside networks. See Figure 6-19 for an illustration of a security perimeter.

DMZs

A buffer against outside attacks is frequently referred to as a **demilitarized zone (DMZ)**. The DMZ is a no-man's-land between the inside and outside networks where some organizations place Web servers. These servers provide access to organizational Web pages, without allowing Web requests to enter the interior networks.

Proxy Servers

An alternative approach to this strategy is to use a **proxy server**, or **proxy firewall**. A proxy server performs actions on behalf of another system. When deployed, a proxy server is configured to look like a Web server and is assigned the domain name that users would be expecting to find for the system and its services. When an outside client requests a particular Web page, the proxy server receives the request as if it were the subject of the request, then asks for the same information from the true Web server (acting as a proxy for the requestor), and then responds to the request as a proxy for the true Web server. This gives requestors the response needed without allowing them to gain direct access to the internal and more sensitive server. For more frequently accessed pages, proxy servers can cache or temporarily store the page, earning them the name **cache servers**. Figure 6-20 shows a number of options for proxy server configuration.

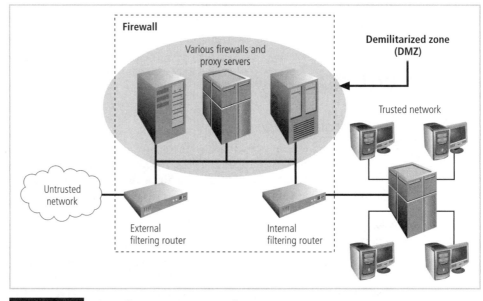

FIGURE 6-20 Firewalls, Proxy Servers, and DMZs

Intrusion Detection Systems (IDSs)

In an effort to detect unauthorized activity within the inner network or on individual machines, an organization may wish to implement **Intrusion Detection Systems (IDSs)**. IDS come in two versions, with hybrids possible. **Host-based IDS** are usually installed on the machines they protect to monitor the status of various files stored on that system (see Figure 21). The IDS learn the configuration of the system, assigns priorities to various files depending on their value, and can then alert the administrator of suspicious activity. **Network-based IDS** look at patterns of network traffic and attempt to detect unusual activity based on previous baselines. This could include packets coming into the organization's networks with addresses from machines already within the organization (IP spoofing). IDS can also detect high volumes of traffic going to outside addresses (data theft) or coming into the network (denial of services). Both host- and network-based IDS require a database of previous activity. In the case of host-based IDS, the system can create a database of file attributes, as well as maintain a catalog of common attack signatures.

Network-based IDS can use a similar catalog of common attack signatures and develop databases of "normal" activity for comparison with future activity. IDSs can be used together for the maximum level of security for a particular network and set of systems.

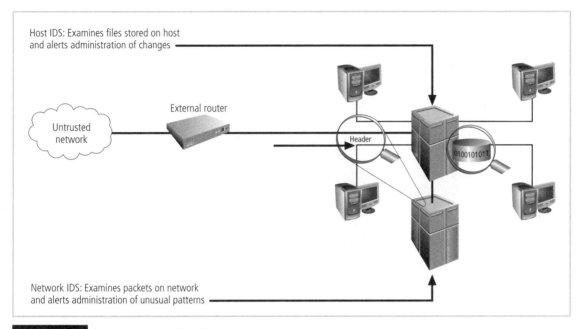

Host IDS: Examines files stored on host and alerts administration of changes

External router

Untrusted network

Header

0100101011

Network IDS: Examines packets on network and alerts administration of unusual patterns

FIGURE 6-21   Intrusion Detection Systems

The overview of technologies just presented was purposely cursory. It was meant to provide sufficient understanding of the various technologies to allow a decision maker to determine where the technologies should be implemented and when to bring in additional expertise to better craft the security design. Once the organization is ready to move to the next stage, the policies and programs outlined here are coupled with specific planning from Chapter 7. Chapter 8 examines in detail the implementation of the chosen technologies as well as other technologies.

Chapter Summary

- Management from all communities of interest (general staff, information technology, and information security) must consider policies as the basis for all information security planning, design, and deployment. Policies direct how issues should be addressed and technologies used. Information security is primarily a management problem, not a technical one.

- Standards are more detailed than policies and describe steps to be taken for an organization to conform to policies.

- Management must define three types of security policy: general or security program policy, issue-specific security policies, and systems-specific security policies.

- Policy documents must be properly managed. Good management practices for policy development and maintenance require: an individual responsible for reviews; a schedule of reviews; a method for making recommendations for reviews; and a policy issuance and revision date.

- Once an organization has developed its information security policies and standards, it is time for the information security community to begin to adopt or develop the framework and then complete the blueprint for the information security program.

- There are a number of published information security frameworks, such as those from government organizations. One of the most widely referenced and often discussed security models is the *Information Technology – Code of Practice for Information Security Management*, which was originally published as the British Standard BS 7799. Another approach available is described in the many documents available from the Computer Security Resource Center of the National Institute for Standards and Technology (*csrc.nist.gov*). Key NIST documents include the following: NIST Special Publication SP 800-12 is the *Computer Security Handbook*, and is an excellent tool for the security manager or administrator as a routine guide to the management of information security; NIST Special Publication 800-14 titled *Generally Accepted Principles and Practices for Securing Information Technology Systems* provides best practices and security principles that can direct the security team in the development of a security blueprint; NIST Special Publication 800-18 titled *The Guide for Developing Security Plans for Information Technology Systems* is considered the foundation for a comprehensive security blueprint and framework; the "VISA International Security Model" from VISA International promotes strong security measures in its business associates and has established guidelines for these measures.

- It is often worthwhile for security professionals to join professional societies that supply information on best practices for their members.

- The hybrid framework is a methodology that organizations can use to fill in the implementation details to create a security system blueprint and address almost all of the components of a solid information security plan.

- When your organization has outlined its plan in a framework and fleshed it out as a blueprint, it is important to create a security education, training, and awareness (SETA) program. One of the least frequently implemented but the most beneficial programs is the security awareness program. A security awareness program is designed to keep information security at the forefront of the users' minds at they work day to day. The security newsletter is the most cost-effective method of disseminating security information and news to the employee.

- It is important to present to management the entire information security systems design, whether expressed as a framework (outline) or blueprint (plan), as a unified proposal.

- One of the foundations of security architectures is the requirement to implement security in layers. This layered approach is referred to as defense in depth.

- A security perimeter defines the edge between the outer limit of an organization's security and the beginning of the outside world.
- In an effort to detect unauthorized activity within the inner network or on individual machines, an organization may wish to implement Intrusion Detection Systems (IDS).

Review Questions

1. How can a security framework assist in the design and implementation of a security infrastructure?
2. Where can a security administrator go to find information on established security frameworks?
3. What are the inherent problems with ISO 17799, and why hasn't the U.S. adopted it? What are the recommended alternatives?
4. Why wouldn't the IETF have a security framework? What benefit can be derived from RFC 2196?
5. What documents are available from the NIST Computer Resource Center, and how can they support the development of a security framework?
6. Can an organization that does not use the VISA cardholder protection system in conjunction with the processing of credit cards benefit from VISA's security framework? How?
7. What benefit can a private, for-profit agency derive from best practices designed for federal agencies?
8. What resources are available on the Web to aid an organization in developing best practices as part of a security framework?
9. What is the difference between a management, an operational, and a technical control, and when would each be applied as part of a security framework?
10. What are the two major components of the "sphere of security?"
11. Why can't technology provide a comprehensive solution to security? What else is needed?
12. What are the three types of security policies? Where would each be used?
13. What type of policy would be needed to guide use of the Web? E-mail? Office equipment for personal use?
14. What is the difference between a policy, a standard, and a practice?
15. How is a good issue-specific policy begun? Ended?
16. Why must management define what is and is not acceptable in great detail? What would happen if they did not and an employee violated the policy?
17. What is the difference between an ACL and a configuration rule? Where is each used?
18. Who is ultimately responsible for managing a technology? Who is responsible for enforcing it?
19. What is the difference between security education and security training? Which is preferable for employees already in security positions?
20. What are the components of an effective security awareness program? What can the organization do to stimulate security awareness in its employees?

Exercises

1. Using the Web, search for sites with information on security best practices. Bring the list to class to discuss. What categories can you determine?
2. Search the Web for examples of issue-specific security policies. What types of policies can you find?

3. Using a graphics program, design a number of security awareness posters on the following themes: updating antivirus signatures, protecting sensitive information, watching out for e-mail viruses, prohibiting use of company equipment for personal matters, changing and protecting passwords, avoiding social engineering, and protecting software copyrights. What other areas can you come up with?

4. Search the Web for a listing of security education and training programs in your area. Keep a list and see which category has the most examples. See if you can determine the costs associated with each example. Which do you feel would be more cost effective in terms of both time and money?

5. Draft a simple issue-specific policy, using the format provided in the text, outlining "Fair and Responsible Use of College Computers," based on the rules and regulations you have been provided in your institution. Does your school have a similar policy? Does it contain all the elements listed in the text?

Case Exercises

I. Enterprise Security

Adapted from "The Slippery Slope of Enterprise Security" *Information Executive*, March/April 2002.[22]

In the field of information security, being good falls short of being good enough. Security isn't a project, it's a process and cannot be implemented and then forgotten. At the root of the problem is the proliferation of script kiddies, who are inexperienced and relatively unskilled computer hackers using the latest generation of hacking tools to exploit security vulnerabilities.

No longer is a simplistic security profile sufficient to protect an organization's information, and on the other hand, there is no such thing as perfect security. An organization can only hope to establish a defense that is complex enough to make the attackers look for easier targets. The solution is defense in depth, which means a series of protective strategies that work together in layers to protect information assets. RedSiren security (*www.redsiren.com*) refers to this as security wellness.

"Security wellness can be compared to a castle, where you have the moat, the castle wall, guards, vaults, et cetera. In other words, security needs to be less of a technical solution and more of an integrated business process,"[23] says Matt Miller, director of mid-tier consulting at RedSiren.

Foremost in the RedSiren security wellness continuum is security policy. The security policy provides the front-line defense for internal security protection. An effective, well-written, and appropriately implemented security policy provides guidance and structure to all other security efforts. A number of policies may be needed from strategic planning policies to fair and responsible use policies. "The security policy should be written in pencil, not pen," said Miller. "It's not something you write up, put away in a binder and never use again. It needs to constantly be refreshed and adapted as new software, technology, or procedures are added."[24]

Only after policy is developed and implemented, should the organization consider technology, which can range from the familiar firewall implementations to intrusion detection systems, security services with external monitoring, and planned security responses. Unfortunately these devices are not sufficient to stop the most common attacks: those from inside the company's security perimeter. Inside attackers can be contractors, temporary employees, or simply discontented employees.

What can companies do to protect their vital assets? First, they must develop strong security policies and enforce them. This approach is supplemented with technologies, such as placing antivirus software on every system and with daily signature updates. Third, companies can subscribe to security advisory mailing lists, such as *www.cert.org* to receive up-to-the-minute information. Last, they must keep up with systems patches and upgrades. Vigilance is the key to security success.

"Enterprise security is a slippery slope," said Miller. "No one wants to be known as `the company that got hacked.' Many people do not want to report breaches for fear of losing their jobs, or causing embarrassment to the company. But the simple fact is, Code Red might have disappeared a lot more quickly if businesses had initiated simple preventative security measures to secure their networks.'"[25]

1. How could Code Red have disappeared more quickly if businesses had initiated simple preventative security measures to secure their networks?

2. Why must policy come first? Why can't the technology come first, and then policy fill in the gaps?

II. Undergraduate InfoSec Education

Kennesaw State University Leads Georgia in Undergraduate Information Security Education"[26]
By Dr. Michael Whitman, TechLinks Online, February 2002.

Kennesaw State University offers Georgia's first Certificate in Information Security and Assurance beginning in the fall of 2002. This certificate is a five-course, for-credit concentration at the undergraduate level in the College of Science and Mathematics.

In response to metropolitan Atlanta's need for more graduates with education and training in information security, the Computer Science and Information Systems Department, in cooperation with state and federal law enforcement agencies, state security officials, and local businesses, has put forward this expansive security education program.

The Certificate in Information Security and Assurance consists of three core courses focusing on principles, technical applications and administration, and policy in information security. Students build on this core by selecting one of five tracks: technical security, consisting of a UNIX administration course and a communications protocols course; auditing, consisting of accounting information systems and auditing courses; computer law and ethics; computer forensics, which includes criminal justice or political science courses; or applied security centered on an applied internship or cooperative study.

According to Dr. Michael Whitman, designer and coordinator of the certificate, this program places KSU at the forefront of information security education in the Southeast and around the country. Kennesaw intends to make itself known as the undergraduate information security education hub of the Southeast.

Information security is one of the hottest job markets in computing. The university has also established a Center for Information Security Education and Awareness, a virtual center designed for those interested in information security education, training and awareness in the region.

The Web site, *http://infosec.kennesaw.edu,* provides information on for-credit courses at Kennesaw, continuing education and training opportunities at Kennesaw's Southeast Cybercrime Institute, and various information security awareness programs. The center will also showcase student and faculty research, teaching and service activities, and provide a central point of reference for other information security activities and agencies in the United States.

1. What value can the stakeholders mentioned in this case derive from this type of program? How can a program such as this effectively serve its target market?

2. What can a company with a dire need for properly educated and trained information security employees do to fill their need by using this type of program?

Endnotes:

1. Claire Poole, "Andersen Trial Heats Up," *Law.com Online* (20 May 2002) [Cited 24 June 2002]; available from the World Wide Web *http://www.law.com/servlet/ContentServer?pagename=OpenMarket/Xcelerate/View&c= LawArticle&cid=1022761088013&live=true&cst=1&pc=0&pa=0.*

2. Charles Cresson Wood, "Integrated Approach Includes Information Security," *Security* 37, no. 2 (February 2000): 43-44.

3. Merriam-Webster, "policy," *Merriam-Webster Online* [Cited 24 June 2002]; available from the World Wide Web *http://www.m-w.com/cgi-bin/dictionary.*

4. National Institute of Standards and Technology, *An Introduction to Computer Security: The NIST Handbook.* SP 800-12.

5. *Ibid.*

6. Robert J. Aalberts, Anthony M. Townsend, and Michael E. Whitman, "Considerations for an Effective Telecommunications-Use Policy," *Communications of the ACM* 42, no. 6 (June 1999): 101-109.

7. Pentasafe Security Technologies, Inc, "Enterprise Security Infrastructure Solution," *Pentasafe Online* [Cited 24 June 2002]; available from the World Wide Web *http://www.pentasafe.com/products/.*

8. National Institute of Standards and Technology, *Information Security Management, Code of Practice for Information Security Management.* ISO/IEC 17799. (6 December 2001).

9. *Ibid.*

10. *Ibid.*

11. *Ibid.*

12. *Ibid.*

13. National Institute of Standards and Technology, *Generally Accepted Principles and Practices for Securing Information Technology Systems.* SP 800-14. (September 1996).

14. *Ibid.*

15. National Institute of Standards and Technology, *Guide for Developing Security Plans for Information Technology Systems.* SP 800-18. December 1998.

16. B. Fraser, *Site Security Handbook - RFC 2196,* (September 1997) [WWW Document]; accessed 01/10/2002, *http://www.ietf.org/rfc/rfc2196.txt.*

17. *Visa,* "Cardholder Information Security Program," Visa Online, [Cited 24 June 2002]; available from the World Wide Web *http://www.usa.visa.com/business/merchants/ cisp_index.html.*

18. HumanFirewall.org, "Building a Human Firewall," *Human Firewall Online,* (2001) [Cited 24 June 2002]; available from the World Wide Web *http://www.humanfirewall.org/.*

19. Marianne Swanson, *Security Self-Assessment Guide for InformationTechnology Systems - NIST Special Publication 800-26,* (November 2001) WWW Document, Accessed 2/11/2002, *http://csrc.nist.gov/publications/nistpubs/800-26/sp800-26.pdf*

20. *National Institute of Standards and Technology,* An Introduction to Computer Security: The NIST Handbook. SP 800-12.

21. *Ibid.*

22. Anonymous, "The Slippery Slope of Enterprise Security," *Information Executive* 6, no. 2 (March/April 2002): 6.

23. *Ibid.*

24. *Ibid.*

25. *Ibid.*

26. TechLinks, "Kennesaw State University Leads Georgia in Undergraduate Information Security Education," *TechLinks Online,* (5 February 2002) [Cited 24 June 2002]; available from the World Wide Web *http://www.jaye.com/showtechlinks.cfm?prid=1657.*

Planning for Continuity

7

CHARLIE MOODY FLIPPED HIS JACKET collar up to cover his ears. The spray blowing over him from the fire hoses was cold and was icing the cars that lined the street where he stood watching his office building burn to the ground. The warehouse and shipping dock were not gone, only severely damaged by smoke and water. He tried to hide his dismay by turning to speak to Fred Chin.

"Look at the bright side, boss," said Charlie. "At least we can get the new server that we have been putting off."

Fred cleared his throat and said, "Charlie, you must be dreaming. We don't have enough insurance for a full replacement of everything we've lost today."

Charlie was stunned. It was bad enough that the offices were gone, and all the computer systems, servers, and desktops were melted slag soaking in the water that almost filled what used to be the basement. Now Charlie was going to have to try to rebuild without all the resources he needed. At least he had good backups, or so he hoped. He thought hard trying to remember the last time the off-site backup tapes had been tested.

He wondered where all the network design diagrams were. He knew he could call his network provider to order new circuits as soon as Fred found some new office space. But wait, where were all the circuit specs? The only copy had been in a drawer in his office, the office that wasn't there anymore. This was not going to be fun. He would have to call directory assistance just to get the phone number for his boss, Gladys Williams, the CFO.

235

Charlie heard a buzzing noise off to his left. He turned to see the flashing numbers of his alarm clock. Relief flooded over him as he realized it was just another nightmare and Sequential Label and Supply had not really burned down. He turned on the light to make himself some notes to go over with Kelvin later in the morning. Charlie was going to make some changes to the company contingency plans *today*.

DISCUSSION QUESTIONS:

1. What would be the first note you would write down if you were Charlie?
2. What else should be on Charlie's list?

LEARNING OBJECTIVES:

Upon completion of this material you should be able to:

- Know what contingency planning is and how incident response planning, disaster recovery planning, and business continuity plans are related to contingency planning.
- Understand the elements that comprise a business impact analysis and the information that is collected for the attack profile.
- Recognize the components of an incident response plan.
- Understand the capabilities and limitations of current incident response systems.
- Understand the steps involved in incident reaction and incident recovery.
- Define the disaster recovery plan and its parts.
- Define the business continuity plan and its parts.
- Grasp the reasons for and against involving law enforcement officials in incident responses.

Introduction

Since this is the midpoint of this textbook, it may help to review what you've covered. The security systems development life cycle (SecSDLC) has brought you to the next step in the process of planning and building an information security system. So far you have:

- Identified the problems facing the organization
- Assessed the value of the organization's information assets
- Analyzed the threats associated with the organization's environment
- Identified potential vulnerabilities
- Assessed the risks associated with current levels of the organization's exposure
- Prepared solid business reasons to support the risk strategy the organization should adopt for each information asset
- Begun to develop a security blueprint for future actions
- Outlined information security architecture or the necessary policies and technologies to guide the organization's next steps

To continue with the logical design process, the next step is to examine the topic of contingency planning within the information security context. For a mapping of SecSDLC phases with this textbook's structure, see Figure 7-1.

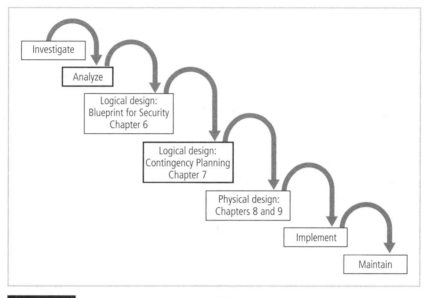

FIGURE 7-1 Contingency Planning and the SecSDLC

Continuity Strategy

A key role for all managers is planning. Managers in the IT and information security communities are usually called on to provide strategic planning to assure the continuous information systems availability.[1] The probability is that some form of attack will occur, whether from the inside or outside, intentional or accidental, human or nonhuman, annoying or catastrophic. The managers from each community of interest within the organization must be ready to act when a successful attack occurs.

Plans for events of this type are referred to in a number of ways: business continuity plans (BCPs), disaster recovery plans (DRPs), incident response plans (IRPs), and contingency plans. In some organizations, these plans may be viewed as one and the same, or simply extensions of the same idea. The organizations consider them as facets of the planning necessary for an organization to react to and recover from some form of attack on their information assets. In large, complex organizations, each of these named plans may represent separate but related planning functions, differing in scope, applicability, and design. In a small organization, the security administrator (or systems administrator) may have one simple plan that consists of a straightforward set of media backup and recovery strategies, and a few service agreements from the company's service providers. The sad reality is that many organizations have a level of planning that is woefully deficient.

For the purposes of this chapter, one can classify incident response, disaster recovery, and business continuity planning, as components of contingency planning, as shown in Figure 7-2. **Contingency planning (CP)** is the entire planning conducted by the organization to prepare for, react to, and recover from events that threaten the security of information and information assets in the organization, and the subsequent restoration to normal modes of business operations. The discussion of CP begins with an explanation of the difference between the various elements, and an examination of the points at which each is brought into play. Organizations need to develop disaster recovery plans, incident response plans, and business continuity plans as subsets of the overall CP. An **incident** is any clearly identified attack on the organization's information assets that would threaten the assets' confidentiality, integrity, or availability. **Incident response planning (IRP)** is planning for the identification, classification, response, and recovery from an incident. **Disaster recovery planning (DRP)** is planning the preparation for and recovery from a disaster, whether natural or man-made. **Business continuity planning (BCP)** is the planning to ensure that critical business functions continue, if a catastrophic incident or disaster occurs. The primary functions of these three types of planning are as follows:

1. IRP focuses on immediate response, but if the attack escalates or is disastrous (e.g., fire, flood, earthquake, or total blackout) the process changes to disaster recovery and BCP.
2. DRP typically focuses on restoring systems at the original site after disasters occur, and as such is closely associated with BCP.
3. BCP occurs concurrently with DRP when the damage is major or long term, requiring more than simple restoration of information and information resources. The BCP reestablishes critical business functions at an alternate site.

Some experts argue that the three plans are so closely linked that they are indistinguishable. However, each has a distinct place, role, and planning requirement. The following sections detail the tasks necessary for each of these three types of plan.

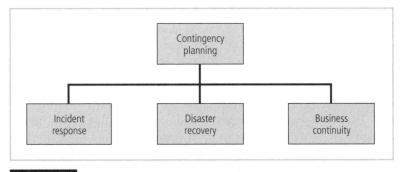

FIGURE 7-2 Contingency Planning Hierarchy

You can also further distinguish between the three types of plan by examining when each comes into play during the life of an incident. Figure 7-3 illustrates a sample sequence of events and the overlap between the times each plan comes into play. Disaster recovery activities typically continue even after the organization has resumed operations at the original site.

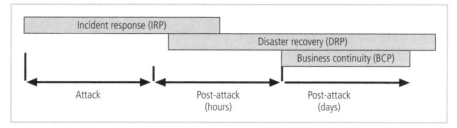

FIGURE 7-3 Contingency Planning Timeline

As the individual components of contingency planning are described, you may notice that contingency planning has many similarities with the risk management process, and the overall methodology represented by the Security SDLC. This is intentional and necessary. The CP is a microcosm of the risk management and SecSDLC activities and it focuses on the specific steps required to return all information assets to the level at which they were functioning before the incident or disaster. As a result the planning process closely emulates the risk management and SecSDLC activities.

Before any planning can begin, an assigned person or a planning team has to be developed to plan the effort and prepare the resulting documents. In this case, a contingency planning team is constructed. A roster for this team can consist of the following members:

- **Champion:** As with any strategic function, the CP project must have a high-level manager to support, promote, and endorse the findings of the project. In a CP project this could be the CIO, or ideally the CEO.
- **Project Manager:** A champion provides the strategic vision and the linkage to the power structure of the organization, but someone has to manage the project itself. A project manager, possibly a midlevel manager or even the CISO, must lead the project and make sure a sound project planning process is used, a complete and useful project plan is developed, and project resources are prudently managed to reach the goals of the project.
- **Team Members:** The team members for this project should be the managers or their representatives from the various communities of interest: business, information technology, and information security. Representative business managers, familiar with the operations of their respective functional areas, supply details on their activities and provide insight into the criticality of their functions to the overall sustainability of the business. Information technology managers on the project team should be familiar with the systems that could be at risk and with the IRPs, DRPs, and BCPs that are needed to provide technical content within the planning process. Information security managers are needed to oversee the security planning of the project and to provide information on the threats, vulnerabilities, attacks, and recovery requirements needed in the planning process.

The major project work modules performed by the contingency planning project team are shown in Figure 7-4. As you read much of the remainder of this chapter, it may help you to look back at this diagram, since the sections correspond to the steps the diagram depicts.

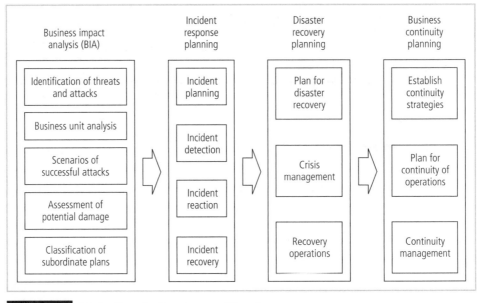

FIGURE 7-4 Major Steps in Contingency Planning

Business Impact Analysis

The first phase in the development of the CP process is the **business impact analysis** or **BIA**. A BIA is an investigation and assessment of the impact that various attacks can have on the organization. BIA takes up where the risk assessment process leaves off. It begins with the prioritized list of threats and vulnerabilities identified in Chapters 2, 4, and 5, and adds critical information. The BIA is a crucial component of the initial planning stages, as it provides detailed scenarios of the potential impact each attack could have on the organization. The BIA therefore adds insight into what the organization must do to respond to attack, minimize damage from the attack, recover from the effects, and return to normal operations. One of the fundamental differences between a BIA and the risk management processes discussed in Chapters 4 and 5 is that the risk management approach identifies the threats, vulnerabilities, and attacks to determine what controls can protect the information. The BIA assumes that these controls have been bypassed, have failed, or are otherwise ineffective in stopping the attack, and that the attack is successful. The question asked at this point is, *if* the attack succeeds, *what* do you do then? Obviously the organization's security team does everything in its power to stop these attacks, but as you have seen, some attacks may be unstoppable, such as natural disasters, deviations from service providers, acts of human failure or error, and deliberate acts of sabotage and vandalism.

The CP team conducts the BIA in the following stages that are shown in Figure 7-4 and described in the sections that follow:

1. Threat attack identification
2. Business unit analysis
3. Attack success scenarios
4. Potential damage assessment
5. Subordinate plan classification

Threat Attack Identification and Prioritization

If this section sounds familiar, it is. Most organizations that have followed the SecSDLC as outlined in Chapters 2, 4, and 5 have already performed the tasks of identifying and prioritizing the threats facing the organization. For those organizations, all that is required now is to update the threat list with the latest developments and add one additional piece of information, the attack profile. An **attack profile** is a detailed description of the activities that occur during an attack. The content items in an attack profile, shown in Table 7-1, include preliminary indications of an attack, as well as the actions and outcomes involved in the attack. These profiles must be developed for every serious threat the organization faces, natural or man-made, deliberate or accidental. It is as important to know what the typical hacker's profile is as it is to know how employees make errors in data entry, or what weather conditions indicate the threat of an imminent tornado or hurricane. The attack profile is useful in later planning stages to provide indicators of attacks. It is used here to determine the extent of damage that could result to a business unit if the attack is successful.

TABLE 7-1 Attack Profile

Date of analysis	
Attack name and description	
Threat and probable threat agent	
Known or possible vulnerabilities	
Likely precursor activities or indicators	
Likely attack activities or indicators of attack in progress	
Information assets at risk from this attack	
Damage or loss to information assets likely from this attack	
Other assets at risk from this attack	
Damage or loss to other assets likely from this attack	

Business Unit Analysis

The second major task within the BIA is the analysis and prioritization of business functions within the organization. The intent of this task is to identify the functional areas of the organization and prioritize them to determine which are most vital to the continued operations of the organization. Each business department, unit, or division must be independently evaluated for insight into its functions and how important the functions are to the organization as a whole. For example, recovery operations would probably focus on the IT Department and network operation before addressing the Personnel Department and hiring activities. Likewise, a manufacturing company assembly line function is more urgent to reinstate than the maintenance tracking system for that assembly line. This is not to say that personnel functions and assembly line maintenance are not important to the business, but that unless the organization's main revenue-producing operations can be restored quickly, there may be no need for other functions. This is why efforts in function analysis focus on the result of a prioritized list of the various functions the organization performs.

Attack Success Scenario Development

Once the threat attack profiles have been developed and the business functions prioritized, the business impact analysis team must create a series of scenarios depicting the impact of a successful attack from each threat on each prioritized functional area. This can be a long and detailed process, as threats that succeed can impact many functions. Attack profiles should include scenarios depicting a typical attack with details on the method of attack, the indicators of attack, and the broad consequences. Once the attack profiles are completed, the business function details can be integrated with the attack profiles. Then attack success scenarios with more detail are added to the attack profile, including alternate outcomes. These alternate outcomes should describe a best, worst, and most likely case that could result from each type of attack on a particular business functional area. This level of detail allows planners to address each in turn.

Potential Damage Assessment

From the attack success scenarios developed above, the BIA planning team must estimate the cost of the best, worst, and most likely cases. At this stage, you are *not* determining how much to spend on the protection of information assets, since this was analyzed during the risk management activities. Instead, you are identifying what must be done to recover from each possible case. These costs include the actions of the response team(s), which are described in subsequent sections, as they act to quickly and effectively recover from an incident or disaster. These cost estimates can also inform management representatives from all the organization's communities of interest of the importance of the planning and recovery efforts. This final result is referred to as an **attack scenario end case**.

Subordinate Plan Classification

Once the potential damage has been assessed, and each scenario and attack scenario end case has been evaluated, a subordinate plan must be developed or identified from among existing plans already in place. These subordinate plans take into account the identification of, reaction to, and recovery from each attack scenario. Most attacks are not disastrous and therefore fall into the category of incident response. Those scenarios that do qualify as disastrous are addressed in the disaster recovery plan.

An attack scenario end case is categorized either as disastrous or not disastrous. The qualifying difference is whether or not an organization is able to take effective action during the event to combat the effect of the attack. Attack end cases that are disastrous find members of the organization waiting out the attack with hopes to recover effectively after it is over. In a typical disaster recovery operation, the lives and welfare of the employees are the most important priority *during* the attack, as most disasters are fires, floods, hurricanes, and tornadoes. Please note that there are attacks that are not natural disasters that fit this category as well:

- Electrical blackouts that have plagued major cities in the past
- Attacks on service providers that result in a loss of communications to the organization (either telephone or Internet)
- Massive, malicious code attacks that sweep through an organization before they can be contained

The bottom line is that each scenario should be classified as a probable incident or a disaster, and then the corresponding actions to respond to the scenario are built into either the IRP or DRP.

Incident Response Planning

Incident response planning covers the identification of, classification of, and response to an incident as described in the sections below. The IRP is made up of activities that are to be performed when an incident has been identified. Before developing such a plan, you should understand the philosophical approach to incident response planning:

What is an incident? What is incident response? As stated earlier, an incident is an attack against an information asset that poses a clear threat to the confidentiality, integrity, or availability of information resources. If an action that threatens the C.I.A. of information occurs and is completed, the action is classified as an incident. All of the threats identified in Chapter 2 could result in attacks that would be classified as information security incidents. For purposes of this discussion, these attacks are only classified as incidents if they have the following characteristics:

- They are directed against information assets
- They have a realistic chance of success
- They could threaten the confidentiality, integrity, or availability of information resources

Incident response (IR) is therefore the set of activities taken to plan for, detect, and correct the impact of an incident on information assets. Prevention is purposefully omitted, as that is more a function of information security in general than IR. IR is more reactive, than proactive, with the exception of the planning that must occur to prepare the IR teams to be ready to react to an incident.

IR consists of the following four phases of an incident:

1. Planning
2. Detection
3. Reaction
4. Recovery

Before examining each of these phases, consider the following scenario from the not too distant past:

The Second Armored Cavalry Regiment was the oldest cavalry regiment on continuous active duty until it was decommissioned in 1994. The IInd ACR served as the vanguard of the first Armored Division in the sweep of Iraqi forces during the Gulf War. But, before Desert Shield, the IInd ACR served for many years tasked with the patrol and protection of the West Germany, East Germany, and the Czechoslovakian border. This mission was carried out by placing one troop from each of the three front line squadrons in various border patrol camps along the border. Each of these border troops conducted constant surveillance of the border, ready to give early warning of potential border violations, political incidents, and even hostile invasions. Within the border camp, the border troop consisted of either a cavalry troop with 12 M3A1 Bradley fighting vehicles and 9 M1A1 Abrams Main Battle tanks, or a tank company, with 14 M1A1s.

Occasionally, units from outside the ACR took a shift on the border, but it was ultimately the IInd ACR's responsibility to guard this stretch of territory.

The unit occupying the border camp was required to organize a series of reaction elements capable of deploying in reaction to an incident on the border, be it a border crossing by a political defector or an invasion by a military force. The smallest group was the "reaction force" made up of eight to 10 soldiers manning two battle vehicles (Bradleys or Abrams) required to deploy to an area outside the base within 15 minutes, ready to combat a foe or report on the incident. While the routine patrols were conducted in HMMWVs (Hummers), the reaction elements had to deploy in battle vehicles. The next larger element was the "reaction platoon," the remainder of the reaction force's platoon (two additional Abrams, or four additional Bradleys, and eight to 20 additional troops) that had to be ready to deploy within 30 minutes. Had the incident warranted it, the entire troop had to be prepared to depart base within one hour. This deployment was rehearsed daily for the reaction force, weekly for the reaction platoon, and at least twice during border camp for the entire troop.

What does this scenario illustrate? An incident is an incident. The employees in an organization responding to a security incident are of course not expected to deploy fully armed to engage in combat against a physical threat. The preparation and planning for an incident, however, is not that different than that of a military response. The same careful attention to detail must be paid, examining each potential threat scenario, and developing a number of responses commensurate with the level of the incident.

Incident Planning

Planning for incidents is the first step in the overall process of incident response planning. Planning for an incident requires a detailed understanding of the scenarios developed for the BIA. With this information in hand, the planning team can develop a series of predefined responses that guide the organization's incident response (IR) team and information security staff. The predefined responses enable the organization to react quickly and effectively to the detected incident. This assumes two things: first, the organization has an IR team, and second, the organization can detect the incident.

The IR team consists of those individuals who must be present to handle the systems and functional areas that can minimize the impact of an incident as it takes place. Picture the military movies you have seen in which some form of attack has occurred on the United States. The designated teams act to verify the threat, determine the appropriate response, and coordinate the actions necessary to deal with the situation.

Incident Response Plan

The military process of planned team responses can be used in an incident response. The planners should develop a set of documents that guide the actions of each involved individual who reacts to and recovers from the incident. These plans must be properly organized and stored to be available when, where, and in a format supportive of the incident response. An example of such a document is presented later in the chapter.

Format and Content. The IR plan must be organized so that, its organization supports, rather than impedes, quick and easy access to the information needed. This can be accomplished through a number of measures, the simplest of which is to create a directory of incidents, with tabbed sections for each one. When an individual needs to respond to an incident, he or she simply opens the binder, flips to the appropriate section, and follows the clearly outlined procedures for an assigned role. This requires the planners to eventually develop the detailed procedures necessary to respond to each incident that include both actions to take *during* the incident, as well as actions to take *after* the incident. In addition, the document should contain information to prepare the staff for the incident by providing procedures to perform *before* the incident.

Storage. Where is the IR plan stored? Note that the information in the IR plan should be protected as sensitive information. If attackers gain knowledge of how a company responds to a particular incident, they can improve their chances of success in the attack. On the other hand, the organization needs to have this information readily available to the individuals who must respond to the incident. This typically means storing the IR plan within arm's reach of the information assets that must be modified or manipulated during or immediately after the attack. The binder could be stored adjacent to the administrator's workstation, or in a bookcase in the server room. The bottom line is that the individuals responding to the incident should not have to search frantically for the needed information, especially under high stress.

Testing. A plan untested is not a useful plan. Or in the military vernacular, "Train as you fight, and fight as you train." If an organization has an effective IR plan, the plan may be ineffective unless its procedures have been practiced. The levels of testing strategies can vary. Five testing strategies are presented here.[2]

1. **Checklist:** Copies of the IR plan are distributed to each individual who has a role during an actual incident. Each individual reviews the plan and creates a checklist of correct and incorrect components. While not a true test, it is an important step in reviewing the document before it is actually needed.

2. **Structured walk-through:** In a walk-through, each involved individual practices the steps he or she will take during an actual event. This can consist of an "on-the-ground" walk-through, in which everyone discusses their actions at each particular location and juncture, or it can be more of a "talk-through," in which all involved individuals sit around a conference table and discuss in turn how they would act as the incident unfolded.

3. **Simulation:** The next step up is a simulation of an incident. Here each involved individual works individually, rather than in conference, simulating the performance of each task required to react to and recover from a simulated incident. The simulation stops short of the actual physical tasks required, such as installing the backup, or disconnecting a communications circuit. The major difference between a walk-through and a simulation, is the independence of the individual performers in a simulation, as they work on their own tasks and assume responsibility for identifying the faults in their own procedures.

4. **Parallel:** Yet another test, larger in scope and intensity, is the parallel test. In the parallel test, individuals act as if an actual incident occurred, performing their required tasks and executing the necessary procedures. The difference is that the normal operations of the business do not stop. The business continues to function, even though the IR team acts to contain the test incident. Great care must be taken to ensure that the procedures performed do not halt the operations of the business functions, creating an actual incident.

5. **Full interruption:** The final, most comprehensive and realistic test is to react to an incident as if it were real. In a full interruption, the individuals follow each and every

procedure, including the interruption of service, restoration of data from backups, and notification of appropriate individuals as discussed in subsequent sections. This is often performed after normal business hours in organizations that cannot afford to disrupt or simulate the disruption of business functions for the purposes of the test. This is the best practice the team can get, but is unfortunately too risky for most businesses.

At a minimum, organizations should conduct periodic walk-throughs (or talk-throughs) of the IR plan. As quickly as business and information resources change, a failure to update the IR plan can result in an inability to react effectively to an incident, or possibly cause greater damage than the incident itself. If this sounds like a major training effort, note the sayings below from the author Richard Marcinko, a former Navy SEAL, which have been paraphrased and cleaned up for your edification.[3]

- The more you sweat in training, the less you bleed in combat.
- Training and preparation hurt.
- Lead from the front, not the rear.
- You don't have to like it, just do it.
- Keep it simple.
- Never assume.
- You are paid for your results, not your methods.

Incident Detection

Individuals sometimes notify systems administrators, security administrators, or their managers of an unusual occurrence. This is most often a complaint to the help desk from one or more users about a technology service. These complaints are often collected by the help desk and can include reports, such as "the system is acting unusual," "programs are slow," "my computer is acting weird," or "data is not available." Incident detection relies on either a human or automated system, which is often the help desk staff, to identify an unusual occurrence and to properly classify it as an incident. The mechanisms that could potentially detect an incident include intrusion detection systems (both host-based and network-based), virus detection software, systems administrators, and even end users. Intrusion detection systems and virus detection software are examined in detail in Chapter 8. In this chapter, the focus is on the human element.

In defining an incident as any clearly identified attack on the organization's information assets, the emphasis is on *clearly identified*. An ambiguously identified attack could be an actual attack, a problem with heavy network traffic, or even the client's computer malfunctioning. Only by carefully training the user, the help desk, and all security personnel on the analysis and identification of attacks can the organization hope to quickly identify and classify an incident. Once an attack is properly identified, the organization can effectively execute the corresponding procedures from the IR plan. **Incident classification** is the process of examining a potential incident, or incident candidate, and determining whether or not the candidate constitutes an actual incident. Who does this? Anyone with the appropriate level of knowledge can classify an incident. Typically a help desk operator brings the issue forward to a help desk supervisor, the security manager, or a designated incident watch manager. Once the candidate has been determined as a valid incident, the responsible manager must decide whether to implement the incident response plan.

Incident Indicators

There are a number of occurrences that could signal the presence of an incident candidate. Unfortunately many of these are similar to the actions of an overloaded network, computer or server, and some are similar to the normal operation of these information assets. Other incident candidates are similar to the actions of a misbehaving computing system, software package, or other less serious threat. Donald Pipkin, an IT security expert, identified three categories of incident indicators: possible, probable, and definite.[4]

Possible indicators. The four types of events described below are possible indicators of incidents:

1. **Presence of unfamiliar files:** Users can report discovering files in their home directories or on their office computers. Administrators can also find files that do not seem to have been placed in a logical location or by an authorized user.
2. **Presence or execution of unknown programs or processes:** Similar to the presence of unfamiliar files, if users or administrators detect unfamiliar programs running, or processes executing on office machines or network servers, this could be an incident.
3. **Unusual consumption of computing resources:** Many computer operating systems provide the ability to monitor the consumption of resources. Windows 2000 and XP, as well as many UNIX variants, allow users and administrators to monitor CPU and memory consumption. Most computers have the ability to monitor hard drive space. Servers maintain logs of file creation and storage. The sudden consumption of resources, spikes, or drops, can be indicators of candidate incidents, or, on the other hand, a user may have finally cleaned out some shared drives.
4. **Unusual system crashes:** Some computer systems crash on a regular basis. Older operating systems, running newer programs are notorious for locking up or rebooting, whenever the OS is unable to execute a requested process or service. Many people are familiar with these systems error messages: "Unrecoverable Application Error," "General Protection Fault," and the infamous NT "Blue Screen of Death." But, if a computer-based system seems to be crashing, hanging, rebooting, or freezing more than usual, it could be a candidate incident.

Probable indicators. The four types of events described below are probable indicators of incidents:

1. **Activities at unexpected times:** If traffic levels on the organization's network exceed the measured baseline values, there is a probability that a candidate incident is underway. If this surge in activity occurs at times when few members of the organization are at work, the probability that it actually is an incident is much higher. Similarly if systems are accessing drives, such as floppies and CD-ROMs when the end user is not using them, an incident may be occurring.
2. **Presence of new accounts:** Periodic review of user accounts can reveal an account (or accounts) that the administrator does not remember creating, or accounts that are not logged in the administrator's journal. Even one unlogged new account is a candidate incident. An unlogged new account with root or other special privileges has an even higher probability of being an actual incident.
3. **Reported attacks:** If users of the system report a suspected attack, there is a high probability that an attack has occurred and constitutes an incident. When considering the probability of an attack, you should consider the technical sophistication of the person making the report.

4. **Notification from IDS:** If the organization has installed host-based, or network-based Intrusion Detection Systems, and if they are correctly configured, the notification from the IDS could indicate a strong likelihood that an incident is in progress. The problem with most IDS is that they are seldom configured optimally, and even when they are, they tend to issue high levels of false positives or false alarms. It is then up to the administrator to determine if the notification is real, or the result of a routine operation by a user or other administrator.

Definite indicators. The five types of events described below are definite indicators of incidents. Definite indicators of incidents are those activities which clearly signal that an incident is in progress or has occurred.

1. **Use of dormant accounts:** Many network servers maintain default accounts that came with the system from the manufacturer. Although industry best practices indicate that these accounts should be changed or removed, some organizations ignore these practices by making the default accounts inactive. In addition, systems may have any number of accounts that are not actively used, such as those of previous employees, employees on extended vacation or sabbatical, or dummy accounts set up to support system testing. If any of these dormant accounts suddenly becomes active without a change in status for the underlying user, it most probably indicates that an incident occurred.

2. **Changes to logs:** The smart administrator backs up systems logs as well as systems data. These logs may be compared to the online version to determine if they have been modified, as part of a routine incident scan. If they have been modified, and the systems administrator cannot determine explicitly that an authorized individual modified them, an incident has occurred.

3. **Presence of hacker tools:** The authors of this textbook have had a number of hacker tools installed or stored on their office computers. These are used to periodically scan internal computers and networks to determine what the hacker can see. They are also used to support research into attack profiles. Every day when the computers are booted, the antivirus program detects these tools as threats to the systems. If the authors did not positively know that they themselves installed the tools, this would be an incident. Many organizations have policy statements that explicitly state that tools of this nature cannot be placed on computers without explicit written permission from the CISO. The act of installing these tools without the proper authorization is a policy violation and subject to discipline. Most organizations that have sponsored and approved penetration-testing operations require that all tools in this category be confined to specific systems that are not used on the general network unless active penetration testing is underway.

4. **Notifications by partner or peer:** Not all incidents can be directly detected. Many organizations have business partners, upstream and downstream value chain associations, and even hierarchical superior or subordinate organizations. If one of these organizations indicates that they are being attacked, and that the attackers are using your computing systems, this is a direct indication of an incident.

5. **Notification by hacker:** Some hackers enjoy taunting their victims. If your Web page suddenly begins displaying a "gotcha" from a hacker, it's an incident. If you receive an e-mail from a hacker containing information from your "secured" corporate e-mail, it's an incident. If you receive an extortion request for money in exchange for your customers' credit card files, it's an incident.

Predefined situations.   There are also several predefined situations that signal an automatic incident. These include:

1. **Loss of availability:** Information or information systems become unavailable.
2. **Loss of integrity:** Users report corrupt data files, garbage where data should be, or the data just looks wrong.
3. **Loss of confidentiality:** You are notified of sensitive information leaks, or that information you thought was protected has been disclosed.
4. **Violation of policy:** If organizational policies addressing information or information security have been violated, an incident has occurred.
5. **Violation of law:** If the law has been broken, and the organization's information assets were involved, an incident has occurred.

When Does an Incident Become a Disaster?

An event can be categorized as a disaster when the following events happen: 1) the organization is unable to mitigate the impact of an incident during the incident, and 2) the level of damage or destruction is so severe that the organization is unable to quickly recover. The difference may be subtle. It is up to the organization to decide which incidents are classified as disasters and therefore receive the appropriate level of response.

Incident Reaction

Once an incident has been classified as such, the organization moves from detection to reaction. **Incident reaction** consists of actions outlined in the IRP that guide the organization in attempting to stop the incident, mitigate the impact of the incident, and provide information for recovery from the incident. These actions take place as soon as the incident itself is over. In reacting to the incident there are a number of actions that must occur quickly. These must have been prioritized and documented in the IRP for quick use in the heat of the moment. These include notification of key personnel, assignment of tasks, and documentation of the incident.

Notification of Key Personnel

As soon as the help desk, end user, or system administrator determines that an incident is in progress, he or she must immediately notify the right people in the right order. Most organizations, including the military, maintain an alert roster for just such an emergency. An **alert roster** is a document containing contact information for the individuals to be notified in the event of an incident. There are two ways to activate an alert roster: sequential and hierarchical. A **sequential roster** is activated as a contact person calls each person on the roster. A **hierarchical roster** is activated as the first person calls a few other people on the roster, who in turn call a few other people. Each has its advantages and disadvantages. The hierarchical is quicker, with more people calling at the same time, but the message may get distorted, as it is passed from person to person. The sequential is more accurate, as the contact person provides each person with the same message, but takes longer, and may be critical.

The **alert message** is a scripted description of the incident, usually just enough information so that each individual knows what portion of the IRP to implement, and not enough to slow down the notification process. It is important to mention that not everyone is on the alert roster, only those individuals necessary to respond to the incident. The alert roster, as with any document, must be maintained and tested to ensure accuracy. The notification process must be periodically rehearsed to assure it is effective and efficient.

There are other personnel that must also be notified. They may not be part of the scripted alert notification process, since the individuals involved are not needed until preliminary information has been collected and analyzed. Management must be notified, but not so early as to cause a panic should the incident prove to be a false or minor alarm. However, the notification can't be so late that it causes embarrassment if the media or other external sources learn of the incident before management. Some incidents are disclosed to the employees in general, as a lesson in security, and some are not, as a measure of security. Other organizations may need to be notified, if it is determined that the incident is not confined to the organization's information resources, or if the incident is part of a larger-scale assault. An example is Mafiaboy's DDoS attack on multiple Web-based vendors in late 1999. It is up to the IRP development team to determine whom to notify and when to offer guidance about additional notification steps to be taken.

Documenting an Incident

As soon as an incident, or disaster, has been declared, key personnel must be notified and documentation of the unfolding event begun. There are many reasons for documenting the event. First, it is important to ensure that the event is recorded for the organization's records, to know what happened, and how it happened, and what actions were taken. The documentation should record the who, what, when, where, why, and how of the event. This documentation serves as a case study after the fact to determine if the right actions were taken, and if they were effective. Second, it is important to prove, should it ever be questioned, that the organization did everything possible to prevent the spread of the incident. From a legal standpoint, the standards of due care protect the organization, should an incident impact individuals inside and outside the organization. The protection of the organization is also important if the incident impacts information and information systems of other organizations that use the attacked organization's systems. The recorded incident can also be used as a simulation in future training sessions on future versions of the IRP.

Incident Containment Strategies

One of the most critical components of incident reaction is to stop the incident or contain its scope or impact. However, sometimes situations prevent the most direct measures, or simply "cutting the wire." Incident containment strategies vary depending on the incident, and on the amount of damage caused by the incident. However, before an incident can be contained, the affected areas of the information and information systems must be determined. This is not the time to conduct a detailed analysis of the affected areas; that type of analysis is typically performed after the fact, in the forensics process. In determining areas affected by the incident, you need to identify simply what information and systems have been involved in the incident to determine the need for system interruption for containment. In general, incident containment strategies focus on two tasks: stopping the incident and recovering control of the systems.

The organization can stop the incident and attempt to recover control through a number of strategies:

- If the incident originates outside the organization, the simplest and most straightforward approach is to sever the affected communication circuits. This may not always be advisable. If the organization's lifeblood runs through that circuit, it may not be feasible to take so drastic a measure. If the incident does not threaten the most critical functional areas, it may be more feasible to simply monitor the incident and contain it in another way. One approach used by some organizations is to dynamically apply filtering rules to limit certain types of network access. For example, if a threat agent is attacking a network by exploiting a vulnerability in the Simple Network Management Protocol (SNMP), applying a blocking filter for the commonly used IP ports for that vulnerability stops the attack without compromising other services on the network. Depending on the nature of the attack and the technical capabilities of the organization, *ad hoc* controls can sometimes gain valuable time to devise a more permanent control strategy.
- If the incident is using compromised accounts, those accounts can be disabled.
- If the incident is coming in through a firewall, the firewall can be reconfigured to block that particular traffic.
- If the incident is using a particular service or process, that process or service can be disabled temporarily.
- If the incident is using the organization's e-mail system to propagate itself, it may be feasible to take down that particular application or server that supports e-mail.
- The ultimate containment option, reserved for only the most drastic of scenarios, involves a full stop of all computers and network devices in the organization. Obviously, this step is taken only when all control of the infrastructure has been lost, and the only hope is to preserve the data stored on the computers with the hope of using the data in the future to restore operations.

The bottom line is that containment consists of isolating the affected channels, processes, services, or computers, and removing the losses. Taking down the entire system, servers, and network may accomplish this. The incident response manager informed by the guidance of the IRP determines the length of the interruption.

Incident Recovery

Once the incident has been contained and control of the systems regained, the next stage of the IRP must be immediately executed. This is recovery from the incident. As with reaction to the incident, the first task is to identify the human resources needed for the recovery and launch them into action. Almost simultaneously with identifying and notifying the staff, the full extent of the damage must be assessed. Assessment provides the information necessary to determine what must be done to restore the system to a fully functional state. Next, the process of computer forensics entails determining how the incident occurred and what happened. These facts emerge as the incident is reconstructed from the data recorded before and during the incident. Next the organization repairs vulnerabilities, addresses any shortcomings in safeguards, and restores the data and services of the systems.

Prioritization of Efforts

As the dust from the incident settles, a natural state of confusion and disbelief follows. This is often referred to as post-traumatic stress disorder or PTSD. One does not have to be involved in a military battle to suffer from this ailment. Emergency workers and civilians involved in the September 11, 2001 tragedy still suffer from it. Attacks of all kinds can affect anyone. The important thing is to get everyone moving and focused on the task ahead: the restoration of the systems. Each individual involved should begin recovery operations based on the appropriate section of the IRP.

Damage Assessment

The military calls it "battlefield damage assessment." The medical field calls it "triage." Whatever the terminology used, **incident damage assessment** is the immediate determination of the scope of the breach of confidentiality, integrity, and availability of information and information assets immediately following an incident. The process of damage assessment can take days or weeks depending on the extent of the damage. The damage caused by an incident can range from minor—a curious hacker snooped around—to extremely severe—a credit card number theft, or the infection of hundreds of computer systems by a worm or virus.

There are several sources of information on the type, scope, and extent of damage. These include system logs, intrusion detection logs, configuration logs and documents, the documentation from the incident response, and the results of a detailed assessment of systems and data storage. Based on these logs and documentation, the IR team must begin to examine the current state of the information and systems and compare them to a known state. Related to the task of incident damage assessment is the field of computer forensics. **Computer forensics** is the process of collecting, analyzing, and preserving computer-related evidence. **Evidence** proves an action or intent. Computer evidence must be carefully collected, documented, and maintained to be acceptable in formal or informal proceedings. Organizations may have informal proceedings when dealing with internal violations of policy or standards of conduct. They may also need to use evidence in formal administrative or legal proceedings, should a perpetrator be brought to justice. Sometimes the fallout from an incident lands in a courtroom for a civil trial. Each of these circumstances requires that individuals who examine the damage incurred receive special training, so that if an incident becomes part of a crime or results in a civil action, the individuals are adequately prepared to participate.

Recovery

Once the extent of the damage has been determined, the recovery process can begin in earnest. The recovery process involves much more than the simple restoration of stolen, damaged, or destroyed data files. It involves the following steps:[5]

1. Identify the vulnerabilities that allowed the incident to occur and spread. Resolve them.
2. Address the safeguards that failed to stop or limit the incident, or were missing from the system in the first place. Install, replace, or upgrade them.
3. Evaluate monitoring capabilities (if present). Improve their detection and reporting methods, or simply install new monitoring capabilities.

4. Restore the data from backups. See the Technical Details boxes on the following topics for more information: 1) data storage and management, 2) system backups and recovery, and 3) RAID. Restoration requires the IR team to understand the backup strategy used by the organization, restore the data contained in backups, and then recreate the data that was created or modified since the last backup.

5. Restore the services and processes in use. Should services and processes be compromised, they must be examined, cleaned, and then restored. If services or processes were interrupted during the process of regaining control of the systems, they need to be brought back online.

6. Continuously monitor the system. If it happened once, it could easily happen again. Just because the current incident is over, doesn't mean the organization is in the clear. Hackers frequently boast of their abilities in chat rooms and dare their peers to match their efforts. If word gets out, others may be tempted to try their hands at the same or different attacks. It is therefore important to maintain vigilance during the entire IR process.

7. Restore the confidence of the members of the organization's communities of interest. It may be advisable to issue a short memorandum outlining the incident, and assuring everyone that the incident was handled and the damage controlled. If the incident was minor, say so. If the incident was major or severely damaged systems or data, reassure the users that they can expect operations to return to normal shortly. The objective is not to placate or lie, but to prevent panic or confusion from causing additional disruption to the operations of the organization.

Before returning to routine duties, the IR team must conduct an **after-action review** or AAR. The after-action review is a detailed examination of the events that occurred from first detection to final recovery. All key players review their notes, and verify that the IR documentation is accurate and precise. All team members review their actions during the incident and identify areas in which the IR plan worked, didn't work, or should improve. This allows the team to update the IRP while the needed changes are fresh in their minds. The AAR is documented and can serve as a training case for future staff. It also brings to a close the actions of the IR team.

TECHNICAL DETAILS

Data Storage and Management

To better understand what goes on during incident response or disaster recovery data restoration, it is important to understand what goes on in computing systems to create the backup in the first place.

Data backup is a complex operation and involves selecting the backup type, establishing backup schedules, and even duplicating data automatically using a variety of redundant array of inexpensive drives (RAID) structures. For more details, see the Technical Details box on RAID.

Each RAID structure is examined in detail here:
There are three basic types of backups: full, differential, and incremental. A **full backup** is just that, a full and complete backup of the entire system, including all applications,

continued

operating systems components, and data. The advantage of a full backup is that it takes a comprehensive snapshot of the organization's system. The primary disadvantages are that it requires large media to store such a large file, and the backup can be time consuming. A **differential backup** is the storage of all files that have changed or been added since the last full backup. The differential backup works faster and uses less storage space than the full backup. The downside to differential backups is that each daily differential backup is larger and slower than that of the day before. For example, if you conduct a full backup on Sunday, then Monday's backup contains all the files that have changed since Sunday, and Tuesday's backup contains all the files that have changed since Sunday as well, including Monday. By Friday, the file size has grown substantially. If one backup is corrupt, the previous day's backup contains almost all of the same information. The third type of backup is the incremental backup. The **incremental backup** only archives the files that have been modified that day, and thus requires less space and time than the differential. The downside to incremental backups is that if an incident occurs, multiple backups would need to be restored to restore the full system.

The first component of a backup and recovery system is the scheduling of the backups, coupled with the storage of these backups. The most common schedule is a daily on-site, incremental or differential backup, with a weekly off-site full backup. Most backups are conducted during twilight hours, when systems activity is lowest, and the probability of user interruption is limited. There are also some other popular methods for selecting the files to back up. These include grandfather/father/son and Towers of Hanoi (see the Technical Details box on the general strategies of backups and recovery).

Regardless of the strategy employed, some fundamental advice must be heeded: first, all on-site and off-site storage must be secured. It is common practice to use fireproof safes or filing cabinets to store tapes. The off-site storage in particular must be in a safe location, such as a safety deposit box in a bank or a professional backup and recovery service. The trunk of the administrator's car is not considered secure off-site storage. It is also important to provide a conditioned environment for the tapes, preferably in an airtight, humidity-free, static-free storage container. Each tape must be clearly labeled, and write-protected. Because tapes frequently wear out, it is important to retire them periodically and introduce new media.

TECHNICAL DETAILS

System Backups and Recovery—General Strategies

Some of the most popular methods for selecting the files to back up are outlined below.

1. **Grandfather, father, son:** Assuming that backups are taken every night, with five tapes used every week, this method is based on a 15-tape strategy.

   The first week uses the first five tapes (set A).

   The second week uses the second five tapes (set B).

   The third week uses a third set of five tapes (set C).

   The fourth week, the set A tapes are reused.

continued

The fifth week, the set B tapes are reused.

The sixth week, the set C tapes are reused.

Every second or third month, a set of tapes is taken out of the cycle for permanent storage and a new set is brought in. This method equalizes the wear and tear on the tapes, and helps to prevent tape failure.

2. **Towers of Hanoi:** The Towers of Hanoi is more complex and is actually based on mathematical principles. With this method, different tapes are used with different frequencies. This strategy assumes a five-tape per week strategy, with a backup each night.

The first night tape A is used.

The second night tape B is used.

The third night tape A is reused.

The fourth night tape C is used.

The fifth night tape A is reused.

The sixth night tape B is reused.

The seventh night tape A is reused.

The eighth night tape D is used.

The ninth night tape A is reused.

The tenth night tape B is reused.

The eleventh night tape A is reused.

The twelfth night tape C is reused.

The thirteenth night tape A is reused.

The fourteenth night tape B is reused.

The fifteenth night tape A is reused.

The sixteenth night tape E is used.

Tape A is used for incremental backups after its first use and must be monitored closely as it tends to wear out faster than the other tapes.

Backup Media

The brief overview of backup media in this section provides additional insight into the backup management process. Most common types of backup media include digital audio tapes (DAT), quarter-inch cartridge drives (QIC), 8mm tape, and digital linear tape (DLT). Each type of tape has its restrictions and advantages. Backups can also be performed to CD-ROM and DVD options (CD-R, CD-RW, and DVD-RW), specialized drives (Zip, Jaz, and Bernouli) or tape arrays.

TECHNICAL DETAILS

System Backups and Recovery—RAID

One form of data backup for online usage is the **Redundant Array of Inexpensive Drives (RAID)** system. Unlike tape backups, RAID uses a number of hard drives to

continued

store information across multiple drive units. This spreads out data and minimizes the impact of a single drive failure. There are nine established RAID configurations:

RAID Level 0. This is not a form of redundant storage. RAID 0 creates one larger logical volume across several available hard disk drives and stores the data in segments, called stripes, across all the disk drives in the array. This is also often called **disk striping** without parity and is frequently used to combine smaller drive volumes into fewer, larger volumes. Unfortunately, failure of one drive may make all data inaccessible.

RAID Level 1. Commonly called **mirroring**, RAID Level 1 uses twin drives in a computer system. The computer records all data to both drives simultaneously, providing a backup if the primary drive fails. It's a rather expensive and inefficient use of media. A variation of mirroring is called **duplexing**. With mirroring, the same drive controller manages both drives, but with duplexing each drive has its own controller. Mirroring is often used to create duplicate copies of operating system volumes for high-availability systems.

RAID Level 2. This is a specialized form of disk striping with parity that is not widely used. It uses a specialized parity coding mechanism known as the Hamming Code to store stripes of data on multiple data drives and corresponding redundant error correction on separate error correcting drives. This approach allows the reconstruction of data in the event some of the data or redundant parity information is lost. There are no commercial implementations of RAID Level 2.

RAID Levels 3 and 4. RAID 3 is byte-level and RAID 4 is block-level striping of data in which the data is stored in segments on dedicated data drives, and parity information is stored on a separate drive. Similar to RAID 0, one large volume is used for the data, but the parity drive operates independently to provide error recovery.

RAID LEVEL 5. This form of RAID is most commonly used in organizations that balance safety and redundancy against the costs of acquiring and operating the systems. It is similar to RAID 3 and 4 in striping the data across multiple drives, except that there is no dedicated parity drive. Instead segments of data are interleaved with parity data and are written across all of the drives in the set. RAID 5 drives can also be **hot swapped**, meaning they can be replaced without taking the entire system down.

RAID Level 6. This is a combination of RAID 1 and RAID 5.

RAID Level 7. This is a variation on RAID 5 in which the array works as a single virtual drive. RAID Level 7 is sometimes performed by running special software over RAID 5 hardware.

RAID Level 10. This is a combination of RAID 1 and RAID 0.

Additional redundancy can be provided by mirroring entire servers called redundant servers or **server fault tolerance** (SFTIII in Novell).

Automated Response

New series of technologies and capabilities are emerging in the field of incident response. Some of these build on traditional strategies and extend their capabilities and functions. Although traditional systems were configured to detect incidences and then notify the human administrator, new systems can respond to the incident threat autonomously, based on preconfigured options.

These systems, referred to as **trap and trace**, use a combination of resources to detect an intrusion, and then to trace incidents back to their sources. On the surface this seems like an ideal solution. Security is no longer limited to defense. Now the security administrators can take the offense. They can track down the perpetrators and turn them over to the appropriate authorities. Under the guise of justice, some less scrupulous administrators might even be tempted to **back hack** or hack into a hacker's system to find out as much as possible about the hacker. Vigilante justice would be a more appropriate term, and activities in this vein are deemed unethical by most codes of professional conduct. The problem is that to access an organization's computer systems, the hacker may actually move into and out of a number of other organizations' systems. By tracking the hacker, administrators may wander through other organizations' systems. The wily hacker may use IP spoofing, compromised systems, or a myriad of other techniques to throw trackers off the trail. The result is that the administrator becomes a hacker himself, and therefore defeats the purpose of catching hackers.

There are more than legal drawbacks to trap and trace. The trap portion frequently involves the use of honeypots or honeynets. **Honeypots** are computer servers configured to resemble production systems, containing rich information just begging to be hacked. If a hacker stumbles into the system, alarms are set off, and the administrator notified. **Honeynets** operate similarly, except that they consist of networks or subnets of systems, representing a much richer target. When using honeypots and honeynets, administrators should be careful not to cross the line between enticement and entrapment. **Enticement** is the process of attracting attention to a system by placing tantalizing bits of information in key locations. **Entrapment** is the action of luring an individual into committing a crime to get a conviction. Enticement is legal and ethical, whereas entrapment is not. It is difficult to gauge the effect such a system can have on the average user, especially if the individual has been nudged into looking at the information. There is also the "wasp trap syndrome." A concerned homeowner may install a wasp trap in the backyard to trap the few insects he sees flying about. These traps use scented bait and may result in attracting far more wasps than originally present. Security administrators should keep the wasp trap syndrome in mind and seek appropriate council before implementing honeypots and honeynets.

The downsides of current automated response systems may outweigh their benefits. Legal issues associated with tracking individuals through the systems of others have yet to be resolved. What if the hacker that is backtracked is actually a compromised system running an automated attack? What are the legal liabilities of a counterattack? How can security administrators condemn a hacker, when they themselves may have illegally hacked systems to track the hacker? These issues are complex but must be resolved to give the security professionals better tools to combat incidents.

Disaster Recovery Planning

As discussed in the beginning of this chapter, disaster recovery planning (DRP) is planning the preparation for and recovery from a disaster, whether natural or man-made. The contingency planning team must decide which actions constitute disasters and which constitute incidents. This determination may be impossible until the attack occurs, and an initial classification of an incident is escalated to that of a disaster. At the time that a decision is made and the situation is classified as a disaster, the organization may change how it is responding and take action to secure its most valuable assets to preserve value for the longer term even at the risk of more disruption in the immediate term. Again, the key emphasis of a DRP is to reestablish operations at the primary site, the location at which the organization performs its business. The goal is to make things whole or as they were before the disaster.

The Disaster Recovery Plan

Similar in structure to the IRP, the DRP provides detailed guidance in the event of a disaster. It is organized by disaster and provides procedures to execute during and after a disaster. It also provides details on the roles and responsibilities of the various individuals involved in the disaster recovery effort, and identifies the personnel and agencies that must be notified. Just as the IRP must be tested, so must the DRP, using the same testing mechanisms. At a minimum, the DRP must be reviewed during a walk-through or talk-through on a periodic basis.

"When disaster strikes" is a key phrase that causes disaster recovery participants to swing into action. Many of the same planning actions performed in incident response apply to disaster recovery.

1. There must be a clear establishment of priorities. The first priority is always the preservation of human life. Data and systems immediately fall to the wayside if the disaster threatens the lives, health, or welfare of the employees of the organization or members of the community in which the organization operates. Only after all employees and neighbors have been safeguarded can the disaster recovery team attend to nonhuman asset protection.
2. There must be a clear delegation of roles and responsibilities. Everyone who is assigned to the DR team should be aware of his or her expected actions during a disaster. Some people are responsible for coordinating with local authorities, such as fire, police, and medical staff. Others are responsible for the evacuation of personnel, if required. And still others are tasked to simply pack up and leave.
3. Someone must initiate the alert roster and notify key personnel. Those to be notified may well be the fire, police, or medical authorities mentioned earlier. They may also include insurance agencies, disaster teams like the Red Cross, and management teams.
4. Someone must be tasked with the documentation of the disaster. Just as in an IR reaction, someone must begin recording what happened to serve as a basis for later determination of why and how the event occurred.
5. If and only if it is possible, attempts must be made to mitigate the impact of the disaster on the operations of the organization. If everyone is safe, and all needed authorities have been notified, some individuals can be tasked with the evacuation of physical assets. Some can be responsible for making sure all systems are securely shut down to prevent further loss of data.

Crisis Management

In many cases, incidents and disasters only differ in scope. Disasters are, of course, larger in scale and less manageable than incidents. In any case the planning processes are the same, and in many cases conducted simultaneously. What may truly distinguish the incident from the disaster are the actions of the response teams. An incident response team typically rushes to duty stations or to the office from home. The first act is to reach for the IRP to begin reacting. A disaster recovery team may not have the luxury of flipping through a binder to see what must be done. The disaster recovery personnel must know their responses without any supporting documentation. This is a function of preparation, training, and rehearsal. You probably all remember the frequent fire drills, tornado, or hurricane drills, and even the occasional nuclear blast drills from your public school days. Just because you move from school to the business world doesn't lessen the threat of a fire or other disaster. As a result, DRP rehearsals are just as important now as then.

The actions taken during and after a disaster are referred to as **crisis management**. Crisis management differs dramatically from incident response, as it focuses first and foremost on the people involved. Secondly, it addresses the viability of the business. The disaster recovery team works closely with the crisis management team. According to Gartner Research, the crisis management team is

> "responsible for managing the event from an enterprise perspective and covers the following major activities:
>
> - Supporting personnel and their loved ones during the crisis
> - Determining the event's impact on normal business operations and, if necessary, making a disaster declaration
> - Keeping the public informed about the event and the actions being taken to ensure the recovery of personnel and the enterprise
>
> Communicating with major customers, suppliers, partners, regulatory agencies, industry organizations, the media, and other interested parties."[6]

The crisis management team should establish a base of operations or command center to support communications until the disaster has ended. The crisis management team includes individuals from all functional areas of the organization to facilitate communications and cooperation. Some key areas of crisis management include:

1. **Verifying personnel head count:** Everyone must be accounted for, including those on vacations, leaves of absence, and on business trips.
2. **Checking the alert roster:** Alert rosters and general personnel phone lists are used to notify individuals whose assistance may be needed, or to simply tell employees not to report to work, until the disaster is over.
3. **Checking emergency information cards:** It is important that each employee has in his possession two types of emergency information cards. The first is personal emergency information that lists whom to notify in case of an emergency (next of kin), medical conditions, and a form of identification. The second type is a set of instructions on what to do in the event of an emergency. This minisnapshot of the disaster recovery plan should contain, at a minimum, a contact number or hot line, emergency services numbers (fire, police, medical), evacuation and assembly locations (storm shelters for example), the name and number of the disaster recovery coordinator, and any other needed information.

Crisis management must balance the needs of the employees with the needs of the business in providing personnel with support for personal and family issues during disasters.

Recovery Operations

Reaction to a disaster can vary so widely that it is impossible to describe the process with any accuracy. As a result it is up to each organization to examine its scenarios, developed during the initial contingency planning, and determine how to respond to various disasters.

Should the physical facilities be spared after the disaster, the disaster recovery team should begin the restoration of systems and data to reestablish full operational capability. If the organization's facilities do not survive, alternative actions must be taken until new facilities can be acquired. When a disaster threatens the viability of the organization at the primary site, the disaster recovery process transitions into the process of business continuity planning.

Business Continuity Planning

Business continuity planning outlines the reestablishment of critical business operations during a disaster that impacts operations at the primary site. If a disaster has rendered the current location of the business unusable for continued operations, there must be a plan to allow the business to continue to function. Not every business needs such a plan or such facilities. Small companies or fiscally sound organizations may have the latitude to simply cease operations, until the physical facilities can be restored. Organizations such as manufacturing and retail may not have this option, because they depend on physical types of commerce and may not be able to relocate operations.

Developing Continuity Programs (BCPs)

The business continuity program, as documented in the BCP, is a function of the contingency planning process. Once the incident response plans and disaster recovery plans are in place, the organization needs to address the possibility of finding temporary facilities to support the continued viability of the business. The development of the BCP is somewhat simpler that of the IRP or DRP, in that it consists primarily of selecting a continuity strategy and integrating the off-site data storage and recovery functions into this strategy. Some of the components of the BCP could already be integral to the normal operations of the organization, such as an off-site backup service. Others require special consideration and negotiation. The first part of the BCP is performed when the joint DRP/BCP plan is developed. The identification of critical business functions and the resources needed to support them is the cornerstone of BCP. When a disaster strikes, these functions are the first to be reestablished at the alternate site. The contingency planning team needs to appoint a group of individuals to evaluate and compare the various alternatives available, and recommend which strategy should be selected and implemented. The strategy selected usually involves some form of off-site facility, which should be inspected, configured, secured, and tested on a periodic basis. The selection should be reviewed periodically to determine if a superior alternative has emerged or if the organization needs a different solution.

Continuity Strategies

There are a number of strategies from which an organization can choose when planning for business continuity. The determining factor in selection between these options is usually cost. The options can be extremely expensive and depend on the criticality of restoring functions and the speed with which they need to be restored. In general there are three exclusive options: hot sites, warm sites, and cold sites, and three shared functions: time-share, service bureaus, and mutual agreements.

Hot Sites

A **hot site** is a fully configured computer facility, with all services, communications links, and physical plant operations including heating and air conditioning. Hot sites duplicate computing resources, peripherals, phone systems, applications, and workstations. A hot site is the epitome of contingency planning, a duplicate facility that needs only the latest data backups and the personnel to function as a fully operational twin of the original. If the organization uses one of the data services listed in the following sections, it can be fully functional within minutes. It is therefore the most expensive alternative available. The other disadvantages include the need to provide maintenance for all the systems and equipment in the hot site, as well as physical and information security. However, if the organization desires a 24/7 capability for near real-time recovery, the hot site is the way to go.

Warm Sites

The next step down from the hot site is the warm site. A **warm site** provides many of the same services and options of the hot site. However, it typically does not include the actual applications the company needs, or the applications may not yet be properly installed and configured. A warm site frequently includes computing equipment and peripherals with servers but not client workstations. A warm site has many of the advantages of a hot site, but at a lower cost. The down side is that it requires several hours if not days to make a warm site fully functional.

Cold Sites

The final dedicated site option is the cold site. A **cold site** is the next step down from the warm site, providing only rudimentary services and facilities. No computer hardware or peripherals are provided. All communications services must be installed after the site is occupied. Basically a cold site is an empty room with heating, air conditioning, and electricity. Everything else is an option. Although the obvious disadvantages may preclude selection, a cold site is better than nothing. The advantages of cold sites over hot and warms sites include cost and the not having to contend with organizations sharing space and equipment should a widespread disaster occur. In spite of these advantages, some organizations feel it would be easier to lease a new space than pay maintenance fees on a cold site.

Time-shares

The first of the three sharing options is the time-share. Just as the name indicates, a **time-share** is a hot, warm, or cold site but is leased in conjunction with a business partner or sister organization. The time-share allows the organization to provide a disaster recovery and business continuity option, while reducing the overall cost. The advantages are identical to the type of site selected (hot, warm, or cold). The primary disadvantage is the possibility that more than one organization involved in the time-share may need the facility simultaneously. Other disadvantages include the need to stock the facility with the equipment and data from all organizations involved, the negotiations for arranging the time-share, and associated agreements should one or more parties decide to cancel the agreement or to sublease its options. It's much like agreeing to co-lease an apartment with a group of friends. One can only hope the organizations remain on amiable terms, as they would all have physical access to each other's data.

Service Bureaus

A **service bureau** is a service agency that provides a service for a fee. In the case of disaster recovery and continuity planning, the service is the agreement to provide physical facilities in the event of a disaster. These types of agencies also frequently provide off-site data storage for a fee. With service bureaus, contracts can be carefully created, specifying exactly what the organization needs, without the need to reserve dedicated facilities. A service agreement usually guarantees space when needed, even if the service bureau has to acquire additional space in the event of a widespread disaster. It's much like the rental car clause in your car insurance policy. The disadvantage is that it is a service, and must be renegotiated periodically as rates increase with the success and viability of a particular bureau. It can also be quite expensive.

Mutual Agreements

The last option discussed here is the mutual agreement. A **mutual agreement** is a contract between two or more organizations that specifies how each to assist the other in the event of a disaster. It stipulates that each organization is obligated to provide the necessary facilities, resources, and services until the receiving organization is able to recover from the disaster. This type of arrangement, however, is much like moving in with relatives or even friends: it doesn't take long to outlive your welcome. While this may seem like a viable solution, many organizations balk at the idea of having to fund (even in the short term) duplicate services and resources, should the other agreeing parties need them. The arrangement is ideal if you need the assistance, but not if you are the host. Still, mutual agreements between divisions of the same parent company, between subordinate and superior organizations, or between business partners may be a cost-effective solution.

Other Options

There are also some specialized alternatives available, such as a rolling mobile site configured in the payload area of a tractor or trailer, or externally stored resources. These can consist of a rental storage area containing duplicate or second-generation equipment to be extracted in the event of an emergency. These alternatives are similar to the POM-CUS (Prepositioning of Overseas Materiel Configured to Unit Sets) sites of the Cold War era (caches of materials to be used in the event of an emergency or war). An organization can also contract with a prefabricated building contractor for immediate, temporary facilities (mobile offices) to be placed on site in the event of a disaster. At any rate, these alternatives should be considered when evaluating strategy options.

Off-Site Disaster Data Storage

For these types of sites to be up and running quickly, the organization must have the ability to move data into the new site's systems. There are a number of options for getting operations up and running quickly, and some of these options can be used for purposes other than restoration of continuity. These include electronic vaulting, remote journaling, and database shadowing. These options are discussed in detail below and, of course, are measures additional to the traditional backup methods mentioned earlier.

- **Electronic vaulting:** The transfer of large batches of data to an off-site facility is called **electronic vaulting**. This transfer is usually conducted through leased lines, or services provided for a fee. The receiving server archives the data until the next received electronic-vaulting process is received. Some disaster recovery companies specialize in electronic vaulting services.

- **Remote journaling:** The transfer of live transactions to an off-site facility is **remote journaling**. It differs from electronic vaulting in that 1) only transactions are transferred not archived data, and 2) the transfer is in real-time. Electronic vaulting is much like a traditional backup, with a dump of data to the off-site storage, but remote journaling involves activities on a systems level, much like server fault tolerance, with the data written to two locations simultaneously.
- **Database shadowing:** An improvement to the process of remote journaling, **database shadowing** not only processes duplicate, real-time data storage, but also duplicates the databases at the remote site to multiple servers. It combines the server fault tolerance mentioned earlier with remote journaling, writing three or more copies of the database simultaneously.

Model for a Consolidated Contingency Plan

To facilitate understanding of the structure and use of the incident response and disaster recovery plan, a comprehensive model is presented that incorporates the basics of each type of planning in a single document. It is not uncommon for the small-to-medium sized organization to use such a document. The single document set supports concise planning and encourages smaller organizations to develop, test, and use IR and DR plans. The model presented is based on analyses of disaster recovery and incident response plans of dozens of organizations.

The Planning Document

The first document created for the IR and DR document set is the incident reaction document. The key players in an organization, typically the top computing executive, systems administrators, security administrator, and a few functional area managers get together to develop the IR and DR Plan. The first task is to establish the responsibility for managing the document, which typically falls to the security administrator. A secretary is appointed to document the activities and results of the planning session. First, independent incident response and disaster recovery teams are formed. For this model, the two groups include the same individuals as the planning committee, plus additional systems administrators. Next, the roles and responsibilities are outlined for each team member. At this point general responsibilities are being addressed, not procedural activities. The alert roster is developed as are lists of critical agencies, should they be needed.

Next, the group identifies and prioritizes threats to the organization's information and information systems. Because of the integrated nature of the IR and DR and the BCP, the overall contingency planning process addresses areas within each. These are the six steps in the consolidated contingency planning process:[7]

1. **Identifying the mission- or business-critical functions:** Each organization must identify those areas of operation that must continue in a disaster to enable the organization to operate. These must be prioritized from most critical to least critical to allow optimal allocation of resources (time, money, and personnel) in the event of a disaster.

2. **Identifying the resources that support the critical functions:** For each function, the organization must identify the resources required by that function to be successful These resources can include people, computing capability, applications, data, services, physical infrastructure, and documentation.

3. **Anticipating potential contingencies or disasters:** Organizations brainstorm potential disasters and determine what functions they would affect.

4. **Selecting contingency planning strategies:** Organizations identify methods of dealing with each anticipated scenario and outline a plan to prepare for and react to the disaster.

Armed with this information, the actual consolidated plan begins to take shape. For each incident scenario, three sets of procedures are created:

- The group develops and documents the procedures that must be performed *during the incident*. These procedures are grouped and assigned to individuals. The planning committee begins to draft a set of these function-specific procedures.

- Once the procedures for handling an incident have been drafted, the second set of procedures is developed, which are those that must be performed immediately *after the incident has ceased*. Again, separate functional areas may be assigned different procedures.

- The group drafts a third set of procedures, which are those tasks that must be performed to *prepare for the incident*. These are the details of the data backup schedules, the disaster recovery preparation, training schedules, testing plans, copies of service agreements, and business continuity plans if any.

At this level the business continuity plan can consist simply of additional material about a service bureau that can store off-site data via electronic vaulting with an agreement to provide office space and lease equipment as needed.

Finally, the IR portion of the plan is assembled. Sections detailing the organization's DRP and BCP efforts are placed after the incident response sections. Critical information as outlined in these planning sections is recorded, including information on alternate sites. Figure 7-5 overviews some specific formats for the contingency plan. Multiple copies for each functional area are created, cataloged, and signed out to responsible individuals.

5. **Implementing the contingency strategies.** At this stage the organizaton signs contracts, acquires services, and implements backup programs that integrate the new strategy into the organization's routine operations.

6. **Testing and revising the strategy.** Again, practice, practice, practice.

These are the words that all contingency planners live by: plan for the worst and hope for the best.

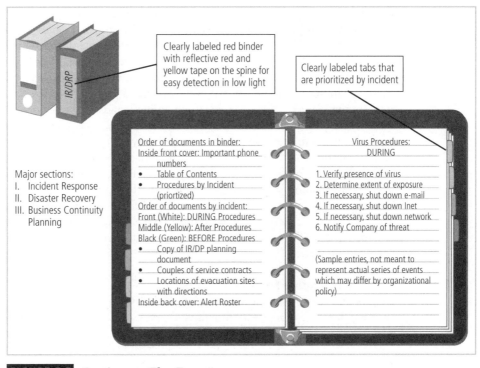

Clearly labeled red binder with reflective red and yellow tape on the spine for easy detection in low light

Clearly labeled tabs that are prioritized by incident

IR/DRP

Major sections:
I. Incident Response
II. Disaster Recovery
III. Business Continuity
  Planning

Order of documents in binder:
Inside front cover: Important phone numbers
• Table of Contents
• Procedures by Incident (priortized)
Order of documents by incident:
Front (White): DURING Procedures
Middle (Yellow): After Procedures
Black (Green): BEFORE Procedures
• Copy of IR/DP planning document
• Couples of service contracts
• Locations of evacuation sites with directions
Inside back cover: Alert Roster

Virus Procedures:
DURING

1. Verify presence of virus
2. Determine extent of exposure
3. If necessary, shut down e-mail
4. If necessary, shut down Inet
5. If necessary, shut down network
6. Notify Company of threat

(Sample entries, not meant to represent actual series of events which may differ by organizational policy)

FIGURE 7-5   Contingency Plan Format

Law Enforcement Involvement

There may come a time, when it has been determined that an incident has exceeded the violation of policy and actually constitutes a violation of law. Perhaps what was originally assumed to be an accidental violation of policy turns out to be an attempt at corporate espionage, sabotage, or theft. When an organization considers involving law enforcement, there are several questions that must be answered. When should the organization get law enforcement involved? What level of law enforcement agency should be involved: local, state, or federal? What happens when a law enforcement agency is involved? Some of these questions are best answered by the organization's legal department. But what if the organization doesn't have a legal department or if in the middle of an attack the security administrators are all unable to contact the legal department? The following sections provide some guidance in these situations.

Local, State, or Federal Authorities

Selecting the level of law enforcement to involve depends in part on the level and type of crime discovered. The Federal Bureau of Investigation deals with many computer crimes that are categorized as felonies. There are other federal agencies available to deal with various criminal incidents, including the U.S. Secret Service for crimes involving U.S. currency, counterfeiting, credit cards, identity theft, and other crimes. The U.S. Treasury Department has a bank fraud investigation unit and the Securities and Exchange Commission has investigation and fraud control units as well. However, because of the heavy load of cases these agencies must handle, they typically give preference to incidents that address the national critical infrastructure or that have significant economic impact. The FBI Web site states that the FBI Computer Intrusion Squad pursues "the investigation of cyber-based attacks, primarily unauthorized access (intrusion) and denial-of-service, directed at the major components of this country's critical information, military and economic infrastructures. Critical infrastructure includes the nation's power grids and power-supply systems, transportation control systems, money transfer and accounting systems, defense-related systems, and telecommunications networks. Additionally, the Squad investigates cyber attacks directed at private industry and public institutions that maintain information vital to national security and/or the economic success of the nation."[8] In other words, if the crime isn't directed at or doesn't affect the national infrastructure, the FBI may not be able to assist as effectively as state or local agencies. As a rule of thumb, however, if the crime crosses state lines, it's a federal matter. The FBI may also become involved at the request of a state agency, if it has the manpower to spare.

State Investigative Services

Many states have their own version of the FBI. In Georgia, it's called the Georgia Bureau of Investigation. The GBI arrests individuals, serves warrants, and generally enforces laws that regulate property that is owned by the state or any state agency. The GBI also assists local law enforcement officials in pursuing criminals and enforcing state laws. The state investigative office may not have a special agency dedicated to computer crime. If, however, there is a law within the state that impacts computer crimes, the state agency handles the case. The state agency also comes in when requested by a local law enforcement office.

Local Law Enforcement

Each county and city has its own law enforcement agency. These agencies enforce all local and state laws and handle suspects and security crime scenes for state and federal cases. Local law enforcement agencies seldom have a computer crimes task force, but the investigative (detective) units are quite capable of processing crime scenes, and handling most common criminal activities, such as physical theft or trespassing, damage to property, and the apprehension and processing of suspects of computer related crimes.

Benefits and Drawbacks of Law Enforcement Involvement

Involving law enforcement agencies has both advantages and disadvantages. The agencies may be much better equipped at processing evidence than a particular organization. Unless the security forces in the organization have been trained in processing evidence and computer forensics, they may do more harm than good in extracting the necessary information to legally convict a suspected criminal. Law enforcement agencies are also prepared to handle the warrants and subpoenas necessary to documenting a case. They are also adept at obtaining statements from witnesses, affidavits, and other required documents. Law enforcement personnel can be a security administrator's greatest ally in the war on computer crime. It is therefore important to get to know your local and state officials charged with enforcing information security laws, before you have to make a call announcing a suspected crime. Most state and federal agencies even offer awareness programs, including guest speakers at conferences, and programs like the InfraGard program of the FBI's National Information

Protection Center (*www.infragard.net/*). These agents appreciate the challenges facing security administrators, who often have a law enforcement background.

On the downside, once a law enforcement agency takes over a case, it really takes over the case. The organization loses complete control over the chain of events, the collection of information and evidence, and the prosecution of suspects. An individual the organization may want only to censure and dismiss may face criminal charges, through which the intricate details of their crimes become matters of public record. The organization may not be informed about the progress of the case for weeks or even months. Equipment vital to the organization's business may be tagged as evidence, to be removed, stored, and preserved until it can be examined for possible support for the criminal case. However, if the organization detects a criminal act, it has a legal obligation to involve the appropriate law enforcement officials. Failure to do so can subject the organization and its officers to prosecution as accessories to the crimes, or as impeding the course of an investigation. It is up to the security administrator to ask questions of their law enforcement counterparts to determine when each agency wishes to be involved, and specifically which crimes are to be addressed by each agency.

Chapter Summary

- Contingency planning (CP) comprises a set of plans conducted by the organization. It is designed to ensure the effective reaction to and recovery from an attack on the organization and the subsequent restoration to normal modes of business operations.

- There are six steps to contingency planning:
    1. Identifying the mission- or business-critical functions
    2. Identifying the resources that support the critical functions
    3. Anticipating potential contingencies or disasters
    4. Selecting contingency planning strategies
    5. Implementing the contingency strategies
    6. Testing and revising the strategy

- Organizations need to develop disaster recovery plans, incident response plans, and business continuity plans as subsets of the overall CP. The first phase in the development of the CP process is the business impact analysis, an investigation and assessment of the impact that various attacks can have on the organization. The BIA consists of five stages:
    1. Identification and prioritization of the threat attack
    2. Business unit analysis and prioritization
    3. Attack success scenario development
    4. Potential damage assessment
    5. Subordinate plan classification

- Incident response planning covers the identification, classification, and response to an incident, and comprises activities to be performed when an incident is identified. An incident is an attack against an information asset that poses a clear threat to the confidentiality, integrity, or availability of information resources. IR consists of four phases:
  1. Incident planning
  2. Incident detection
  3. Incident reaction
  4. Incident recovery

- Disaster recovery planning outlines the response to and recovery from a disaster, whether natural or man-made.

- The actions taken during and after a disaster are referred to as crisis management, which focuses first and foremost on the people involved.

- Business continuity planning outlines recovery from catastrophic incidents and disasters, focusing on long-term continuation of business operations. Organizations can choose from the following business continuity strategies:
  1. Hot sites
  2. Warm sites
  3. Cold sites

  They can also choose to share functions by using the following:
  1. Time-share
  2. Service bureaus
  3. Mutual agreements

- When the incident at hand exceeds the violation of policy and constitutes a violation of law, involving law enforcement may be a necessary.

- It is important to get to know your local and state officials charged with enforcing information security laws before you have to make a call announcing a suspected crime.

Review Questions

1. What is contingency planning? How is it different from routine management planning?
2. What are the components of contingency planning as defined by the text?
3. What are the differences among the IRP, DRP, and BCP?
4. When is IRP used?
5. When is DRP used?
6. When is BCP used?
7. How do you determine when to use IRP, DRP, or BCP plans? *P 238*
8. What are the five elements of a business impact analysis? *P 240*
9. What questions should an attack profile answer? *P 241*
10. Why are some business functions more important than others? *some are more crushal*
11. What three outcomes or end cases should you prepare when creating attack success scenarios? *best worst mostlikly*
12. What measurement do you use when preparing potential damage assessments? Why? *P 242 cost*
13. What are the four phases of an incident response? *247*

14. What are Pipkin's three categories of incident indicators? *possible, probable, definite*

15. When does an incident become a disaster? *P24 G*

16. What is containment and why is it part of the planning process? *stop*

17. What is computer forensics? When are the results of computer forensics used? *P252*

18. What is an after-action review? When is it performed? Why is it done?

19. What is crisis management?

20. List the six continuity strategies identified in the text.

Exercises

1. Use your library or the Web to find a natural disaster reported in the past 60 days. From the news accounts determine if local or national officials had prepared disaster plans and if they were used.

2. Use your library or the Web to find a reported natural disaster that occurred at least 180 days ago. From the news accounts determine if local or national officials had prepared disaster plans and if they were used. See if you can determine how the plans helped the officials improve the response to the disaster. How do the plans help the recovery?

3. Use your library or the Web to find a company that has folded because of a disaster, natural or man-made. Would incident, disaster, or business continuity planning have kept the company in business? Why or why not?

4. Classify each of the following occurrences as an incident or disaster. If an occurrence is a disaster, determine whether or not business continuity plans would be called into play.

   a. A hacker gets into the network and deletes files from a server.
   b. A fire breaks out in the storeroom and sets off sprinklers on that floor. Some computers are damaged, but the fire is contained before it moves out of the area.
   c. A tornado hits a local power company, and the company will be without power for three to five days.
   d. Employees go on strike, and the company could be without critical workers for weeks.
   e. A disgruntled employee takes a critical server home, sneaking it out after hours.

5. For each of the scenarios presented in the previous question, describe the steps necessary to restore operations. Indicate whether or not law enforcement would be involved.

Case Exercises

I. DoD Gets a "D" in Security

Adapted from "Defense faces cyber-challenges"[9]
By P. Piazza, *Security Management*, July 2001.

The U.S. General Accounting Office (GAO) released a report in July of 2001 indicating that the Department of Defense (DoD) still has substantial work to do to secure its networks. The DoD uses "over 2.5 million unclassified computer systems, 10,000 local area networks, and hundreds of long-distance networks for mission-critical operations." These systems use virtually every operating system, software, and hardware configuration available, and incorporate both Internet and public phone connections. The GAO outlined six areas the DoD needs to concentrate on:

- Synchronize and coordinate incident response priorities and requirements across the armed services, to prevent a successful intrusion on one network from compromising all.

- Integrate collected intrusion data across all DoD systems. This requires classification and reporting standards for incidents, including what to report and what not to report. This will assist all services to identify potential and future attacks.

- Establish a process for prioritizing and conducting vulnerability assessments. This requires standards and methodologies for conducting the penetration testing and assessments, which are currently performed on an ad hoc basis. Share information learned about these tests with the corresponding classification levels.

- Establish procedures to fix well-known vulnerabilities published in the Information Assurance Vulnerability Alerts (IAVA). It has been estimated that almost 95% of confirmed intrusions could have been averted if this had been done.

- Improve the DoD Information Operations Condition (INFOCON), the DoD guidelines for incident response and defense postures. This also requires standardization of procedures during attacks. "When the ILOVEYOU virus struck, some commands made few changes to their daily operational procedures, while others cut off all electronic mail communications and therefore became isolated from outside contact regarding the status of the attack."

- Improve the incident response performance measures and goals, to allow DoD to determine how effective and efficient incident response activities are. Unless DoD assesses its activities, it cannot learn from its mistakes and improve the general level of readiness.

DoD agreed. Even though progress had been made, there was still a long way to go. But forewarned is forearmed. Change is on the way.

1. How do the problems in the DoD's incident response readiness impact an individual organization, or do they? How can an individual organization learn from the problems associated with the DoD systems?

2. How does the scope and scale of the DoD systems impact their ability to perform incident response planning? If you were the Secretary of Defense reading the July 2001 report, what would your first actions have been?

II. Planning for the Worst

Adapted from "Strategic planning said to ensure continuity in business operations"[10]
By Staff, *Businessworld*, May 21, 2002.

One might think that business continuity and disaster recovery are technology issues. Those in the know realize that the issue is much broader, requiring personnel, facility, and strategy components, as well as technology to address "the single point of failure" or any collection of items that can contribute to this failure. In the big picture, disasters prevent businesses from operating and transactions from occurring. Technology can be used to reduce or eliminate single point of failures. While disaster recovery deals with the loss of a computing center, business continuity addresses preparedness, a readiness to react to disastrous circumstances.

When considering a disaster recovery scenario, start first with the most important asset—people. Will you have enough manpower and organizational knowledge to restore business operations? This requires the organization to have distributed its knowledge base to ensure continuity of effort should one site be severely impacted. Of the utmost importance is the rapid restoration of operations, to restore a sense of normalcy. For this to happen, disaster recovery requires planning and procedures, documented and tested, implemented by individuals who are well versed in the plan and well trained in its execution. It also requires predetermined prioritizations of efforts. Which systems need to be restored first? Then what? What physical facilities are needed?

Disaster recovery strategies must also include alternative implementations for the various systems components, should primary versions be unavailable. This includes standby equipment, either purchased, leased, or under contract with a disaster recovery service agency. Developing systems with excess capacity, fault-tolerance, autorecovery, and fail-safe features facilitates a quick rebounding. Something as simple as Dynamic Host Configuration Protocol (DHCP) clients instead of static addresses allow systems to quickly and easily regain connectivity without technical support. Networks should support dynamic reconfiguration; restoration of network connectivity should be planned. Data recovery requires effective backup strategies and flexible hardware configurations. System management should be a top priority. All solutions should be tightly integrated and developed in a strategic plan to provide continuity. Piecemeal construction can result in a disaster after the disaster, as incompatible systems are thrust together.

Failure is not an option.

1. Examine the concept of organizational knowledge. What is organizational knowledge? How can organizational knowledge be distributed? How can the distribution of organization knowledge aid in disaster recovery?

2. Explain the statement "piecemeal construction can result in disaster after the disaster." What does this mean, and how can this be prevented?

Endnotes

1. William R. King and Paul Gray, *The Management of Information Systems* (Chicago: Dryden Press, 1989), 359.

2. Ronald L. Krutz and Russell Dean Vines, *The CISSP Prep Guide: Mastering the Ten Domains of Computer Security* (New York: John Wiley and Sons Inc., 2001), 288.

3. Richard Marcinko and John Weisman, *Designation Gold* (New York: Pocket Books, 1998), preface.

4. D. L. Pipkin, *Information Security: Protecting the Global Enterprise*, Upper Saddle River, NJ: Prentice Hall 2000) 256.

5. Donald L. Pipkin, *Information Security: Protecting the Global Enterprise* (Upper Saddle River, NJ: Prentice Hall PTR, 2000), 285.

6. Roberta Witty, "What is Crisis Management?" *Gartner Online* (19 September 2001) [Cited 26 June 2002]; available from the World Wide Web *http://security1.gartner.com/story.php.id.152.jsp.*

7. NIST, "Special Publication 800-12 An Introduction to Computer Security: The NIST Handbook," (October 1995); accessed 02/10/2002. *http://csrc.nist.gov/publications/nistpubs/800-12/*

8. Federal Bureau of Investigation, *Technology Crimes,* (San Francisco); available from the World Wide Web *http://www.fbi.gov/contact/fo/sanfran/sfcomputer.htm.*

9. Peter Piazza, "Defense Faces Cyber-Challenges," *Security Management* 45, no. 7 (July 2001): 38.

10. Staff, "Strategic Planning Said to Ensure Continuity in Business Operations," *Businessworld,* (21 May 2002): 1.

Security Technology

> People are the missing link to improving Information Security.
> Technology alone can't solve the challenges of Information Security.
>
> **THE HUMAN FIREWALL COUNCIL**

KELVIN CAME INTO THE MEETING ROOM a few minutes late. He took an empty chair at the conference table, flipped open his notepad, and went straight to the point. "Okay, folks, what seems to be the problem? We aren't scheduled for the Network Intrusion Deployment Team meeting until next Tuesday."

"Uh," stammered Laverne Ngyuen. "We seem to be a little confused about the rules for configuring the correlation engine. We could use a little clarification."

Miller Harrison cleared his throat. "We don't seem to agree on how to plan the deployment of the intrusion sensors. It seems obvious to me that we want sensors on every piece of equipment in the DMZ. But, Laverne seems uncertain of that strategy."

Kelvin looked at each of the technical specialists in turn. Knowing the answer already, he said, "Laverne, what does the project plan call for?"

Laverne knew the answer to this one. "We are to deploy an intrusion detection system in the DMZ to protect critical functions required by Sequential Label and Supply to provide electronic commerce functions. It doesn't say that we are to instrument every device in that network segment."

Miller looked sour. He said, "In my *professional* opinion we need to put an operating sensor on every device in the DMZ. You can't be sure that even a QA server won't get hacked, and then they can get to anything we have running out there."

Kelvin knew that Miller was compensated by the hour and also got a commission for every IDS sensor he installed. He also knew Laverne had been with Sequential for eight years, but had only been working in information security for the past eight months. He pondered his next question.

DISCUSSION QUESTIONS:

1. What factors must be considered to decide correctly on the better of the two conflicting recommendations?
2. How could Kelvin restructure the project team to avoid these kinds of dilemmas

LEARNING OBJECTIVES:

Upon completion of this material you should be able to:

- Define and identify the various types of firewalls.
- Discuss the approaches to firewall implementation.
- Discuss the approaches to dial-up access and protection.
- Identify and describe the two categories of intrusion detection systems.
- Discuss the two strategies behind intrusion detection systems.
- Discuss scanning, analysis tools, and content filters.
- Understand trap and trace technologies.
- Discuss the process of encryption and define key terms.
- Identify and discuss common approaches to cryptography.
- Compare and contrast symmetric and asymmetric encryption.
- Discuss various approaches to biometric access control.

Introduction

Information security is a discipline that relies on the synthesis of people, policy, education, training, awareness, procedures, and technology to improve the protection of an organization's information assets. Technical solutions, properly implemented, can maintain the confidentiality, integrity, and availability of information in each of its three states (storage, transmission, and processing). In this chapter, firewalls, intrusion detection systems, encryption-based systems, and some other widely used technologies are discussed. This chapter is designed to give you a fundamental understanding of how to evaluate technical solutions for the physical design of an information security program. For those students who seek to become recognized experts on the configuration and maintenance of these types of systems, additional educational and training is required.

Physical Design of the SecSDLC

The physical design phase of the SecSDLC is made up of two parts: security technologies and physical security, which are covered by Chapters 8 and 9 respectively. Physical design takes the logical design, expressed by the information security blueprint developed in Chapter 6 and the contingency planning elements designed in Chapter 7 and extends the design to the next level. Figure 8-1 provides a visual representation of how these topics fit into the overall process of the SecSDLC.

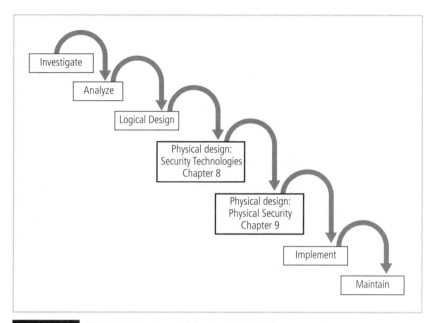

FIGURE 8-1 Physical Design within the SecSDLC

The physical design phase encompasses the selection of technologies and processes that implement controls to manage risk from threats to the information assets of the organization. At the end of the physical design phase you have:

- Selected technologies needed to support the information security blueprint
- Defined a successful solution for a secured environment
- Designed physical security measures that support the technical solution
- Prepared to create project plans in the implementation phase to follow

The material in this chapter is sequenced to effectively introduce you, as students of computer science and information systems, to these topics. If you have not studied these subjects, this material may prove difficult. The challenge is to maintain perspective on each of the technical disciplines while focusing on the overall objective. That objective is to select technology that brings benefits of protection that exceed the costs of the technology. As noted in earlier chapters, few information security units operate with unlimited budgets. This means that information security programs must almost always balance cost with the effectiveness and protection delivered to achieve the needs of the information security blueprint. The discussion of information security technology begins with the most widely used of the technical solutions, firewalls.

Firewalls

In commercial and residential construction, firewalls are concrete or masonry walls that run from the basement through the roof, to prevent fire from jumping from one section of the building to another. In the aircraft and automotive industries, a **firewall** is an insulated metal barrier that keeps the hot and dangerous moving parts of the motor separate from the inflammable interior where the passengers sit. A firewall as part of an information security program is any device that prevents a specific type of information from moving between the outside world, known as the **untrusted network**, (e.g., the Internet) and the inside world, known as the **trusted network**, and vice versa. The firewall may be a separate computer system, a service running on an existing router or server, or a separate network containing a number of supporting devices.

Development of Firewalls

Firewalls have made significant advances since their earliest implementations. The first generations of firewall devices were routers that perform only simple packet filtering operations. More recent generations of firewalls offer increasingly complex capabilities, including the increased security and convenience of creating a DMZ or demilitarized zone (described below). At the present time, there are five generally recognized generations of firewalls, and these generations can be implemented in a wide variety of architectures. The following is a summary of the technical capabilities of each generation.

First Generation

The first generation of firewalls are called **packet filtering firewalls**, because they are simple networking devices that filter packets based on their headers as they travel to and from the organization's networks. In this case the firewall examines every incoming packet header and can selectively filter packets (accept or reject) based on these and other factors:

- Address
- Packet type
- Port request (HTTP or Telnet)

First generation firewalls scan network data packets looking for compliance with or violation of the rules of the firewall's database. A first generation firewall inspects packets at the network layer or Layer 3 of the OSI model.[1] If it finds a packet that matches a restriction, it simply refuses to forward it from one network to another. The restrictions most commonly implemented in packet filtering firewalls are based on a combination of the following:

- IP source and destination address
- Direction (inbound or outbound)
- Transmission Control Protocol (TCP) or User Datagram Protocol (UDP) source and destination port requests

Early firewall models examine one aspect of the packet header: the destination and source address. They enforce **address restrictions**, rules designed to prohibit packets with certain addresses or partial addresses, from passing through the device. They accomplish this through access control lists (ACLs), created and modified by the firewall administrators.

Figure 8-2 shows how a packet filtering router can be deployed as a simple firewall to filter data packets from inbound connections and allow outbound connections unrestricted access to the public network.

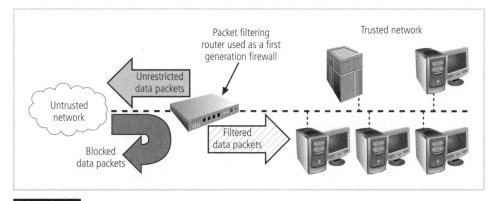

FIGURE 8-2 Packet Filtering Firewall

For example, if administrators configured a simple rule, based on the example shown in Table 8-1, they would be denying any attempt for a connection by an external packet from computers or network devices in the 192.168. address range (192.168.0.0-192.168.255.255[2]) to access any internal service, such as HTTP, Telnet, FTP, or to communicate at all through the firewall. The ability to restrict a specific service represents a more advanced version of the first generation firewall, rather than just the ability to filter based on IP addresses.

TABLE 8-1 Sample Firewall Rule and Format

Source address	Destination address	Service (HTTP, SMTP, FTP, Telnet)	Action (allow or deny)
172.16.x.x	10.10.x.x	Any	Deny
192.168.x.x	10.10.10.25	HTTP	Allow
192.168.0.1	10.10.10.10	FTP	Allow

The ability to restrict a specific service is now considered standard in most modern routers and is invisible to the user. Unfortunately, these systems are unable to detect the modification of packet headers, which occurs in IP spoofing attacks.

Second Generation
The next generation of firewalls is called the **application-level firewall** or **application firewall**. The application firewall is frequently a dedicated computer separate from the filtering router and quite commonly used in conjunction with a filtering router. The application firewall is also known as a **proxy server**, since it runs special software designed to serve as a proxy for a service request. For example, suppose an external user wanted to view a Web page from an organization's Web server. Rather than expose the Web server to direct traffic from the users and to potential attacks as well, the organization can install a proxy

server, configured with the registered domain's URL. This proxy server receives the request for an internal Web page, accesses the Web server itself on behalf of the external client, and then returns the requested page to the user. These servers can store the most recently accessed pages in their internal cache, and are, therefore, also called **cache servers**. The benefits from this type of implementation are significant. With this configuration the proxy server, rather than the Web server, is in the DMZ exposed to the outside world. A **demilitarized zone (DMZ)** is an intermediate area between a trusted network and an untrusted network. Additional filtering routers can be implemented behind the proxy server, restricting the access of internal systems to the proxy server alone, and thereby further protecting internal systems.

One common example of an application-level firewall (or proxy server) is a firewall designed to restrict requests for and responses to requests for Web pages and services. These are still widely used to implement electronic commerce functions, although most users of this technology have upgraded them to take advantage of the DMZ approach as discussed below. The primary disadvantage of application-level firewalls is that they are designed for a specific protocol and cannot easily be reconfigured to protect against attacks on protocols for which they are not designed.

Third Generation
The next generation of firewalls, **stateful inspection firewalls**, keep track of each network connection established between internal and external systems using a **state table**. These state tables track the state and context of each packet in the conversation, by recording which station sent what packet and when. Like first generation firewalls, stateful inspection firewalls perform packet filtering, but they take it a step further. Whereas simple packet filtering firewalls only allow or deny certain packets based on their address, a stateful firewall can restrict incoming packets by denying access to packets that are responses to internal requests. If the stateful firewall receives an incoming packet that it cannot match in its state table, then it defaults to its ACL to determine whether to allow the packet to pass.

The primary disadvantage of this type of firewall is the additional processing requirements of managing and verifying packets against the state table. This can possibly expose the system to a DoS attack. In such an attack, the firewall can be subjected to a large number of external packets, slowing it down as it attempts to compare all of the incoming packets first to the state table and then to the ACL. On the positive side, these firewalls can track connectionless packet traffic, such as UDP and remote procedure calls (RPC) traffic.

Fourth Generation
While static filtering firewalls, such as first and third generation, allow entire sets of one type of packet to enter in response to authorized requests, a **dynamic packet filtering firewall** allows only a particular packet with a particular source, destination, and port address to enter through the firewall. It does this by understanding how the protocol functions, and opening and closing "doors" in the firewall, based on the information contained in the packet header.[3] With this functionality, dynamic packet filters are an intermediate form, between traditional static packet filters and application proxies.

Fifth Generation

The final form of firewall is the **kernel proxy**, a specialized form that works under the Windows NT Executive, which is the kernel of Windows NT. It evaluates packets at multiple layers of the protocol stack, by checking security in the kernel as data is passed up and down the stack. Cisco implements this technology in the security kernel of its Centri Firewall. The Cisco security kernel contains three component technologies:[4] the Interceptor/Packet Analyzer, the Security Verification Engine, and Kernel Proxies. The Interceptor captures packets arriving at the firewall server. Once the Interceptor captures a network packet, it passes it to the Packet Analyzer. The Packet Analyzer reads the header information of the packets, extracts signature data, and passes both the data and the packets to the Security Verification ENgine (SVEN). The SVEN receives this information and determines whether to drop the packet, map it to an existing session, or to create a new session. If a current session exists, the SVEN passes it through a custom-built protocol stack created specifically for that session, which is a customized implementation of the approach widely known as network address translation. The SVEN enforces the security policy as configured into the device in the final piece of the puzzle, the Kernel Proxy, as it inspects each packet.

Firewall Architectures

Each of these firewall generations can be configured in a number of network connection architectures. These approaches are sometimes mutually exclusive and sometimes can be combined. The relatively straightforward approach of packet filtering, screened host, and dual-homed host architectures is discussed, followed by the more advanced screened-subnet (or DMZ) and SOCKS server architectures.

The configuration that works best for a particular organization depends on three factors: the objectives of the network, the organization's ability to develop and implement the architectures, and the budget available for the function. Although literally hundreds of variations exist, there are four common architectural implementations of firewalls. These implementations are packet filtering routers, screened host firewalls, dual-homed firewalls, and screened subnet firewalls. Each of these is examined in more detail below.

Packet filtering Routers

Most organizations with an Internet connection have some form of a router as the interface to the Internet at the perimeter between the organization's internal networks and the external service provider. Many of these routers can be configured to filter packets that the organization does not allow into the network. This is a simple but effective means to lower the organization's risk to external attack. The drawbacks to this type of system include a lack of auditing and strong authentication. The complexity of the access control lists used to filter the packets can grow and degrade network performance. Figure 8-2 (above) is an example of this type of architecture.

Screened Host Firewall Systems

The next type of architecture combines the packet filtering router with a separate, dedicated firewall, such as an application proxy server. This approach allows the router to prescreen packets to minimize the network traffic and load on the internal proxy. The application proxy examines an application layer protocol, such as HTTP, and performs the proxy services. This separate host is often referred to as a **bastion host**, as it represents a single, rich target for external attacks, and should be very thoroughly secured. Even though the bastion host/application proxy actually contains only cached copies of the internal Web documents, it can still present a promising target. Compromise of the bastion host can disclose the configuration of internal networks and possibly provide external sources with internal information. Since the bastion host stands as a sole defender on the network perimeter, it is also commonly referred to as the **sacrificial host**. To its advantage, the proxy requires the external attack to compromise two separate systems, before the attack can access internal data. In this way the bastion host protects the data more fully than the router alone. Figure 8-3 shows a typical configuration of a screened host architectural approach.

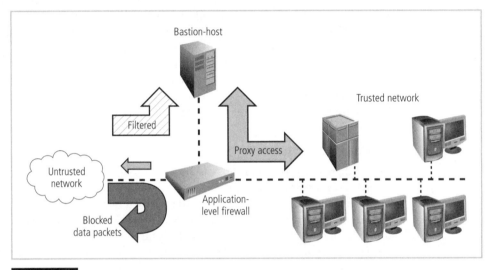

Bastion-host

Trusted network

Filtered

Proxy access

Untrusted network

Application-level firewall

Blocked data packets

FIGURE 8-3 Screened Host Firewall

Dual-homed Host Firewalls

The next step up in firewall architectural complexity is the dual-homed host. With this configuration, the bastion host contains two NICs (network interface cards), rather than the one contained in the bastion host configuration. One NIC is connected to the external network, and one is connected to the internal network, providing an additional layer of protection. With two NICs all traffic *must* physically go through the firewall to move between the internal and external networks. A technology known as network address translation is commonly implemented with this architecture. **Network address translation (NAT)** is a method of mapping real, valid, external IP addresses to special ranges of internal IP addresses, creating yet another barrier to internal intrusion. These internal addresses can consist of three different ranges. Organizations that need Class A addresses can use the 10.x.x.x range, which has over 16.5 million usable addresses. Organizations that need Class B addresses can use the 192.168.x.x range, which has over 65,500 addresses. Finally, organizations with smaller needs, such as those needing only a few Class C addresses, can use the 172.16.0.0 to 172.16.15.0 range, which has 16 Class C addresses or about 4000 usable addresses. Messages sent with internal addresses within these three reserved ranges cannot be routed externally. This means that if a computer with one of these internal-use address ranges is directly connected to the external network, and avoids the NAT server, its traffic cannot be routed on the public network. Taking advantage of this, NAT prevents external attacks from reaching internal machines with addresses in specified ranges. If the NAT server is a multi-homed bastion host, it translates between the true, external IP addresses assigned to the organization by public network naming authorities and the internally assigned, nonroutable IP addresses. NAT translates by dynamically assigning addresses to internal communications and tracking the conversations with sessions to determine which incoming message is a response to which outgoing traffic. Figure 8-4 shows a typical configuration of a dual-homed host firewall that uses NAT and proxy access to protect the internal network.

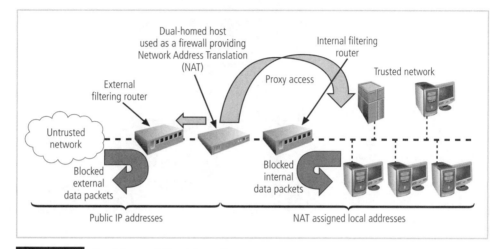

FIGURE 8-4 Dual-homed Host Firewall

Another benefit of a dual-homed host is the ability to translate between the protocols of different data link layers, such as Ethernet, Token Ring, Fiber Distributed Data Interface (FDDI), and asynchronous transfer method (ATM). On the downside, if this dual-homed host is compromised it can disable the connection to the external network and as traffic volume increases, it can become overloaded. Overall, however, this architecture provides strong protection with minimal expense compared to more complex solutions.

Screened Subnet Firewalls (with DMZ)

The final architecture presented here is the screened subnet firewall. The subnet firewall consists of two or more internal bastion hosts, behind a packet filtering router, with each host protecting the trusted network. There are many variants of the screened subnet architecture. The first general model consists of two filtering routers, with one or more dual-homed bastion hosts between them. In the second general model, as illustrated in Figure 8-5, the connections are routed as follows:

- Connections from the outside or untrusted network are routed through an external filtering router.
- Connections from the outside or untrusted network are routed into—and then out of—a routing firewall to the separate network segment known as the DMZ.
- Connections into the trusted internal network are allowed only from the DMZ bastion host servers.

As depicted in Figure 8-5, the screened subnet is an entire network segment that performs two functions: it protects the DMZ systems and information from outside threats;

and it protects the internal networks by limiting how external connections can gain access to internal systems. Although extremely secure, the screened subnet can be expensive to implement and complex to configure and manage. To use the architecture, the value of the information it protects must justify the cost.

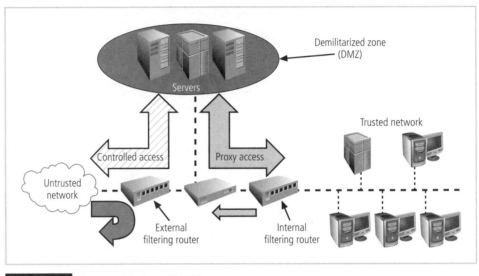

FIGURE 8-5 Screened Subnet (DMZ)

The architecture of a screened subnet firewall provides a DMZ. The DMZ can be a dedicated port on the firewall device linking a single bastion host, or it can be connected to a screened subnet as shown in Figure 8-5. Until recently, servers providing services through an untrusted network were commonly placed in the DMZ. Examples include Web, file transfer protocol (FTP), and certain database servers. More recent strategies using proxy servers have provided much more secure solutions.

SOCKS Servers
Deserving of brief special attention is the SOCKS firewall implementation. SOCKS is the protocol for handling TCP traffic through a proxy server. The SOCKS system is a proprietary circuit-level proxy server that places special SOCKS client-side agents on each workstation. The general approach is to place the filtering requirements on the individual workstation, rather than on a single point of defense (and thus point of failure). This frees the entry router from filtering responsibilities, but then requires each workstation to be managed as a firewall detection and protection device. A SOCKS system can require additional support and management resources to configure and manage possibly hundreds of individual clients, versus a single device or set of devices.

Selecting the Right Firewall
Selecting the optimum firewall for your organization depends on a number of factors. The most important of these is the extent to which the firewall design provides the

desired protection. When evaluating a firewall for your networks, your questions should cover the following topics:[5]

1. "What type of firewall technology offers the right balance between protection and cost for the needs of the organization?
2. "What features are included in the base price? What features are available at extra cost? Are all cost factors known?
3. "How easy is it to set up and configure the firewall? How accessible are the staff technicians who can competently configure the firewall?
4. "Can the candidate firewall adapt to the growing network in the target organization?"

Question two addresses the second most important issue, cost. The cost of a firewall may keep a certain make, model, or type out of reach for a particular security solution. As with all security decisions, certain compromises have to be made to provide a viable solution under the budgetary constraints stipulated by management.

Configuring and Managing Firewalls

Once the firewall architecture and technology has been selected, the initial configuration and ongoing management of the firewall(s) needs to be considered. Chapter 7 noted that each firewall device, whether a filtering router, bastion host, or other firewall implementation, must have its own set of configuration rules that regulate its actions. As indicated in the section on packet filtering firewalls, these rules may be simple statements regulating source and destination addresses, specific protocol or port usage requests, or indicators of whether to allow or deny these types of requests. In actuality, the configuration of firewall policies can be something of a nightmare. Those of you familiar with application programming can appreciate the problems associated with debugging both syntax errors and logic errors. Syntax errors in firewall policies are usually easy to identify, as the systems alert the administrator of incorrectly configured policies. However, logic errors, such as the following, are another story: allowing instead of denying, specifying the wrong port or service type, and using the wrong switch. These and a myriad of other simple mistakes can take a device designed to protect users' communications and turn it into one giant choke point. The choke point can restrict all communications, or the incorrectly configured rule can cause other unexpected results. An example of this problem occurred when novice firewall administrators improperly configured a virus-screening e-mail gateway (think of this as a type of e-mail firewall), resulting in the blocking of all incoming e-mail. Users experienced a great deal of frustration when the e-mail gateway blocked all e-mail, with or without attachments, instead of screening selected e-mail to protect users from malicious code. As is evident, configuring firewall policies is as much an art as a science. Each rule must be carefully crafted, debugged, tested, and even sorted. This process ensures that the actions are performed in the correct sequence, so that the most resource-intensive actions are performed after the most restrictive, to reduce the number of packets that must undergo intense examination. When configuring firewalls, keep one thing in mind: when security rules conflict with the performance of business, security loses. If users can't work because of a security restriction, the security administration is usually told, in no uncertain terms, to remove the safeguard. Organizations are much more willing to live with a potential risk than a certain failure.

Best Practices for Firewalls

This section outlines some of the best-business practices for firewall use:[6]

1. All traffic from the trusted network is allowed out. This allows members of the organization to access the services they need. Filtering and logging of outbound traffic is possible when indicated by specific organizational policy goals.

2. The firewall device is never accessible directly from the public network. Almost all access to the firewall device is denied to internal users as well. Only authorized firewall administrators access the device through secure authentication mechanisms, with preference for a method based on cryptographically strong authentication using two-factor access control techniques, which have been described in earlier chapters.

3. Simple Mail Transport Protocol (SMTP) data is allowed to pass through the firewall, but it should all be routed to a well-configured SMTP gateway to securely filter and route messaging traffic.

4. All Internet Control Message Protocol (ICMP) data should be denied. Known as the ping service, it is a common method for hacker reconnaissance and should be turned off to prevent snooping.

5. Telnet (terminal emulation) access to all internal servers from the public networks should be blocked. At the very least, telnet access to the organization's Domain Name Service (DNS) server should be blocked to prevent illegal zone transfers, and to prevent hackers from taking down the organization's entire network. If internal users need to come into an organization's network from outside the firewall, you should be using a virtual private network (VPN) client, or other secure authentication system.

6. When Web services are offered outside the firewall, HTTP traffic should be denied from reaching your internal networks by using some form of proxy access or DMZ architecture. That way, if any employees are running Web servers for internal use on their desktops, the services are invisible to the outside Internet. If your Web server is behind the firewall, you need to allow HTTP or HTTPS (SHTTP) through for the Internet at large to view it. The best solution is to place the Web servers containing critical data inside the network and use proxy services from a DMZ (screened network segment). It is also advisable to restrict HTTP traffic coming to internal network addresses to responses to requests that originated at internal addresses. This restriction can be accomplished through NAT or firewalls that can support stateful inspection or are directed at the proxy server itself. All other incoming HTTP traffic should be blocked. If the Web servers only contain advertising, they should be placed in the DMZ and rebuilt when they are compromised (not *if*, but *when*).

Dial-up Protection

Before the Internet emerged as a public network option, organizations created private networks and allowed individuals and other organizations to connect to them using dial-up or leased line connections. In the current networking environment firewalls are used as a protection that safeguards the connection between an organization and its Internet (public network) connection. The equivalent level of protection has always been and continues to be needed to protect connections to private networks. While internal network connection via private networks are now less popular because of the high cost of installation, maintenance, and protection, dial-up connections are still quite common. It is a widely held view that unsecured, dial-up access represents a substantial exposure to attack. An attacker who suspects that an organization has dial-up lines can use a device called a **war dialer** to locate the connection points. A war dialer is an automatic phone-dialing program that dials every number in a configured range (e.g., 555-1000 to 555-2000), and checks to see if a person, answering machine, or modem picks up. If a modem answers, the war dialer program makes a note of the number and then moves to the next target number. The attacker then returns at a later time and attempts to hack into the network through the identified modem connection using a variety of techniques. Network connectivity through dial-up connections are usually much simpler and less sophisticated than those deployed with Internet connections. For the most part, simple username and password schemes are the only means of authentication. Some newer technologies have improved this process, including RADIUS systems, CHAP password systems, and even systems that use strong encryption. The dominant of these approaches, RADIUS and TACACS, are discussed below.

RADIUS and TACACS

RADIUS and TACACS are systems that authenticate the credentials of users who are trying to access an organization's network through a dial-up connection. RADIUS stands for **Remote Authentication Dial-in User Service**. Typical dial-up systems place the responsibility for the authentication of users on the system directly connected to the modems. If there are multiple points of entry into the dial-up system, this authentication system is difficult to manage. The RADIUS system centralizes the management of user authentication by placing the responsibility for authenticating each user in the central RADIUS server. When a remote access server (RAS) receives a request for network connection from a dial-up client, it passes the request along with the user's credentials to the RADIUS server. RADIUS then validates the credentials and passes the resulting decision (accept or deny) back to the accepting remote access server (RAS). Figure 8-6 shows the typical configuration of a RAS system.

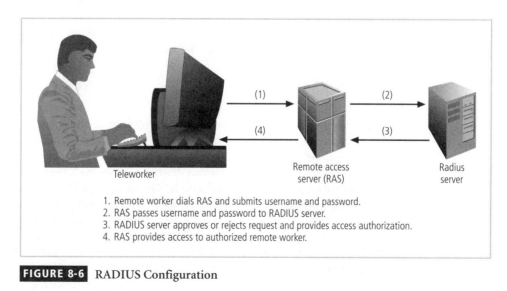

1. Remote worker dials RAS and submits username and password.
2. RAS passes username and password to RADIUS server.
3. RADIUS server approves or rejects request and provides access authorization.
4. RAS provides access to authorized remote worker.

FIGURE 8-6 RADIUS Configuration

Similar in function to the RADIUS system is the **Terminal Access Controller Access Control System (TACACS).** TACACS is another remote access authorization system that is based on a client/server configuration. It contains a centralized database, such as RADIUS, and validates the user's credentials at the TACACS server. There are three versions of TACACS: TACACS, Extended TACACS, and TACACS+. The original version combines authentication and authorization services. The extended version separates the steps needed to provide authentication of the individual or system attempting access from the steps needed to authorize that the authentic individual or systems are able to make this type of connection. The extended version then keeps records that show that the action of granting access has accountability and that the access attempt is linked to a specific individual or system. The plus version uses dynamic passwords and incorporates two-factor authentication.[7]

Intrusion Detection Systems (IDS)

Information security **intrusion detection systems (IDS)** work like a burglar alarm. When the alarm detects a violation of its configuration (as in an opened or broken window), it activates the alarm. This alarm can be an audible and visual (noise and lights), or it can be a silent alarm that sends a message to a monitoring company. With almost all IDS, the administrators can choose the configuration and alarm levels. Many IDS enable administrators to configure the systems to notify themselves through e-mail and numerical or text paging. The systems can also be configured to notify an information security service organization that is external, just as burglar alarms do. As with firewall systems, IDS require complex configurations to provide the level of detection and response desired. IDS operate as either network based, as when the technology is focused on protecting network information assets, or host based, as when the technology is focused on protecting server or host information assets. IDS use one of two detection methods, signature based or statistical anomaly based. In Figure 8-7, two typical approaches to intrusion detection using IDS are being used to monitor both network connection activity and current information states on host servers. Each of these approaches to intrusion detection is examined in additional detail in the following sections.

Host-based IDS

A **host-based IDS** resides on a particular computer or server, known as the host, and monitors activity on that system. Most host-based IDS work on the principle of configuration or change management, in which the systems record the file sizes, locations, and other attributes of the files, and then report when one or more of these attributes changes, when new files are created, and when existing files are deleted. Host-based IDS can also monitor systems logs for predefined events. Host-based IDS examine these files and logs to determine if an attack has occurred, and if the attack was successful, they report this information to the administrator. IDS maintain its own log files. Therefore, when hackers successfully modify a systems log in an attempt to cover their tracks, IDS provide independent verification that the attack occurred. Once properly configured, host IDS are very reliable. The only false positive readings typically presented by host IDS occur when an authorized user changes a monitored file. This action can be quickly reviewed and dismissed as acceptable by an administrator, who can then decide to disregard subsequent changes to the same set of files.

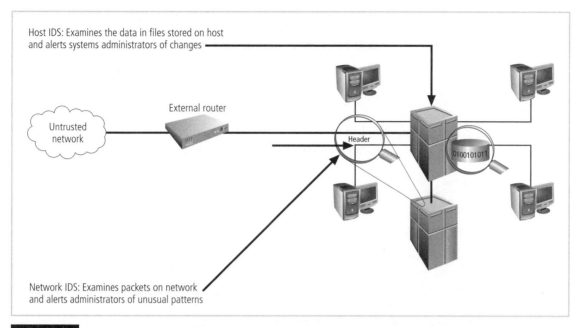

Host IDS: Examines the data in files stored on host and alerts systems administrators of changes

External router

Untrusted network

Header

0100101011

Network IDS: Examines packets on network and alerts administrators of unusual patterns

FIGURE 8-7 Intrusion Detection Systems

Host-based IDS work through the configuration and classification of various categories of systems and data files. In many cases, IDS only provide a few general levels of alert notification. For example, an administrator can configure IDS to report the following types of changes as reportable, security events: changes in a system folder (e.g., C:\Windows or C:\WINNT); and changes within a security-related application (C:\TripWire). Administrators can configure the system to report as a reportable security event any changes within a critical data folder. They can configure changes to an application folder (e.g., C:\Program Files\Office) as a normal, and hence unrecorded, event. Administrators can configure the system to instantly page them if a reportable security event occurs, to e-mail them with a priority code if a reportable security event occurs, or simply to log any activity that generated a normal event. While this seems simplistic, most administrators are only concerned if changes occur in unauthorized and sensitive areas of the host. Applications frequently modify their internal files, such as dictionaries and configuration templates. Users are constantly updating their data files. Unless they are very concisely configured, these actions can generate a large volume of false alarms.

Host-based IDS that are managed can monitor multiple computers simultaneously. They do this by storing a client file on each monitored host and by making that host report back to the master console, which is usually located on the systems administrator's computer. This master console monitors the information provided from the managed clients and notifies the administrator when predetermined attack conditions occur. Figure 8-8 provides a sample screen from Tripwire, a popular host-based IDS (see *www.tripwire.com*).

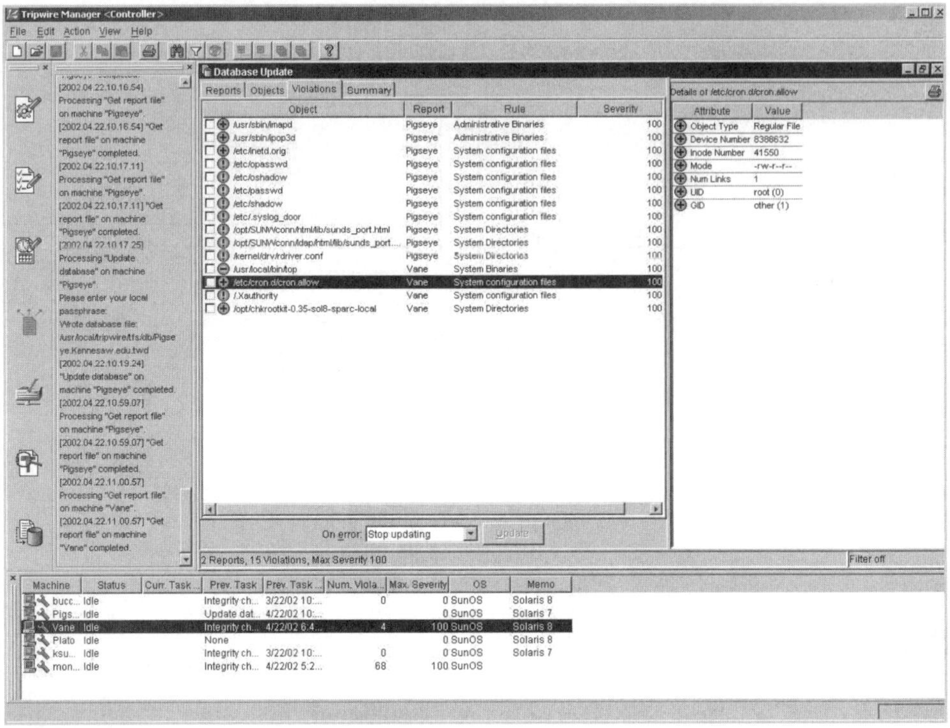

Courtesy of Tripwire®

FIGURE 8-8   Host-based IDS

Network-based IDS

Network-based IDS work differently than their host-based counterpart. While host-based IDS reside on a host (or hosts) and monitor only activities on the host, network-based IDS monitor network traffic. When a predefined condition occurs, network-based IDS respond and notify the appropriate administrator. While host-based IDS look for changes in file attributes (create, modify, delete), the network-based IDS looks for patterns of network traffic, such as large collections of related traffic that can indicate a denial-of-service attack, or a series of related packets that could indicate a port scan in progress. Network IDS, therefore, require a much more complex configuration and maintenance program than do host-based IDS. Network IDS must match known and unknown attack strategies against their knowledge base to determine whether or not an attack has occurred. Network IDS result in many more false positive readings than do host-based IDS, as the systems are attempting to read into the pattern of activity on the network to determine what is normal and what is not. Figure 8-9 shows a sample screen from Demarc Pure Secure (see *www.demarc.com*), displaying events generated by the Snort Network IDS Engine (see *www.snort.org*).

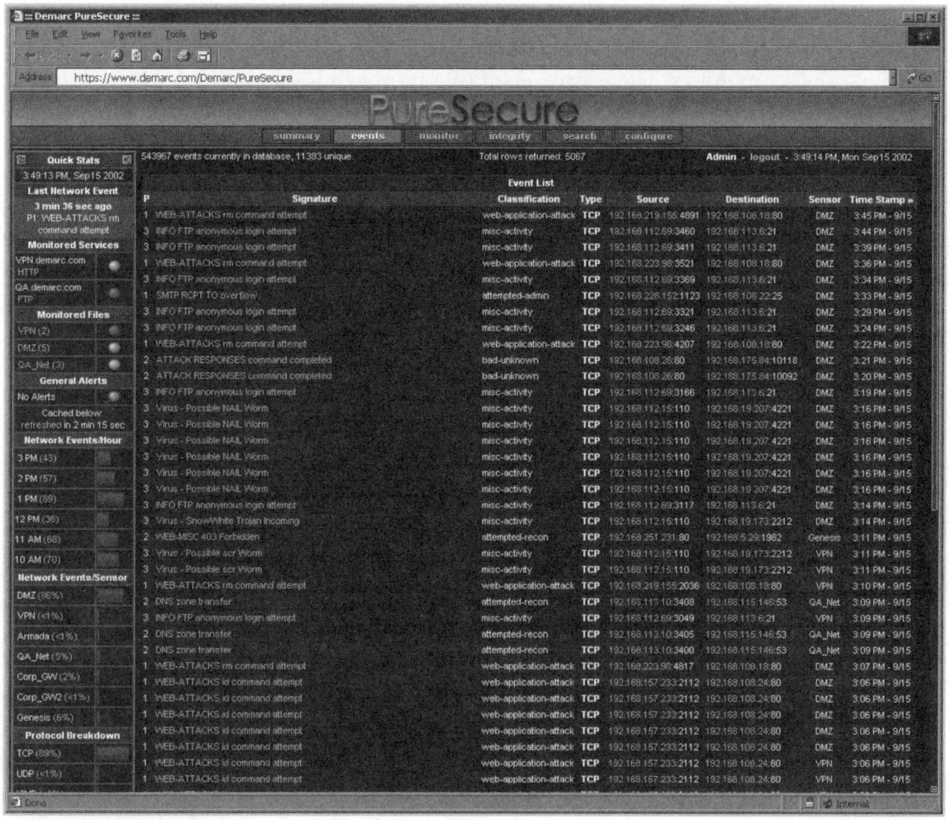

Courtesy Demarc Security, Inc.

FIGURE 8-9 Demarc Pure Secure Total Intrusion Detection System (TIDS)

Signature-based IDS

IDS that use signature-based methods work like antivirus software. In fact, antivirus software can be classified as a form of signature-based IDS. **Signature-based IDS** or **knowledge-based IDS** examine data traffic in search of something that matches signatures, which are preconfigured, predetermined attack patterns. The problem with this approach is that the signatures must be continually updated, as new attack strategies are identified. Failure to stay current allows attacks using new strategies to succeed. Another weakness of this method is the time frame over which attacks occur. If attackers are slow and methodical, they may slip undetected through IDS, as their actions may not match the signature that includes factors based on duration of the events. The only way to resolve this is to collect and analyze data over longer periods of time, which requires substantially larger data storage ability and additional processing capacity.

Statistical Anomaly-based IDS

Another common method used in IDS is the **statistical anomaly-based IDS (stat IDS)** or **behavior-based IDS**. Stat IDS collect data from normal traffic and establish a baseline. Once the baseline is established, IDS periodically samples network activity, based on statistical methods, and compares the samples to the baseline. When the activity is outside the baseline parameters (known as a **clipping level**), IDS notify the administrator. The baseline variables can include a host's memory or CPU usage, network packet types, and packet quantities. The advantage of this approach is that the system can detect new types of attacks, as it looks for abnormal activity of any type. Unfortunately these systems require much more overhead and processing capacity than signature-based versions, as they must constantly attempt to match patterns of activity to the baseline. These systems also may not detect minor changes to system variables and may generate many false positives. If the actions of the users or systems on the network vary widely with periods of low activity and periods of frantic packet exchange, this type of IDS may not be suitable, as the dramatic swing from one level to another almost certainly will generate false alarms. As a result, this type of IDS is less commonly used than the signature-based approach.

Scanning and Analysis Tools

Although some may not perceive them as defensive tools, scanners, sniffers, and other analysis tools are invaluable to security administrators in enabling them to see what the attacker sees. Scanner and analysis tools can find vulnerabilities in systems, holes in security components, and unsecured aspects of the network. Unfortunately, they cannot detect the unpredictable behavior of people. Some of these devices are extremely complex and others not. Some are extremely expensive commercial products. But, many of the best tools are those that the hackers themselves use, and are available free on the Web. Good administrators should have several hacking Web sites bookmarked to enable them to look for discussion of new vulnerabilities, recent conquests, and favorite assault techniques. This can also enable them to discover the best tools for identifying weaknesses in security defenses. There is nothing wrong with a security administrator using the tools used by hackers to examine his defenses and find areas that require additional attention. In the military, there is a long and distinguished history of generals inspecting the troops before battle, walking down the line checking out the equipment and mental preparedness of each soldier. The security administrator, using vulnerability analysis tools such as IDS, can inspect his forces in a similar way. A word of caution, though, should be heeded: many of these tools have distinct signatures, and some Internet service providers (ISPs) scan for these signatures. If the ISP discovers someone using hacker tools, it can pull access privileges. It's best to establish a working relationship with the ISP and notify it of the purpose and extent of the signatures.

Scanning tools are used to collect information needed by an attacker to succeed. One of the preparatory parts of an attack is the collection of information about a potential target, a process known as footprinting. **Footprinting** is the organized research of the Internet addresses owned or controlled by a target organization. The attacker uses public Internet data sources to perform keyword searches to identify the network addresses of the organization. This research is augmented by browsing the organization's Web pages. Web pages usually contain quantities of information about internal systems, individuals developing Web pages, and other tidbits, which can be used for social engineering attacks. The Reveal Source option on most popular Web browsers allows the user to see the source code behind the graphics. A number of clues can provide additional insight into the configuration of an internal network: the locations and directories for Common Gateway Interface (CGI) script bins and the names or possibly addresses of computers and servers.

To assist in the data collection process, another type of scanner can be used. This is an enhanced Web scanner, such as Sam Spade (*www.samspade.org*), which is a utility that, among other things, can scan entire Web sites for valuable information, such as server names and e-mail addresses. A sample screenshot from Sam Spade is shown in Figure 8-10. Sam Spade can also do a host of other probes and scans such as sending multiple ICMP information requests (Pings), attempting to retrieve multiple and cross-zoned DNS queries, and performing network analysis queries (known as traceroutes from the commonly used UNIX command to perform the analysis), all of which are powerful diagnostic and hacking activities. Sam Spade is not considered as hackerware (or hacker-oriented software), but is a useful utility for the network administrator and miscreant alike.

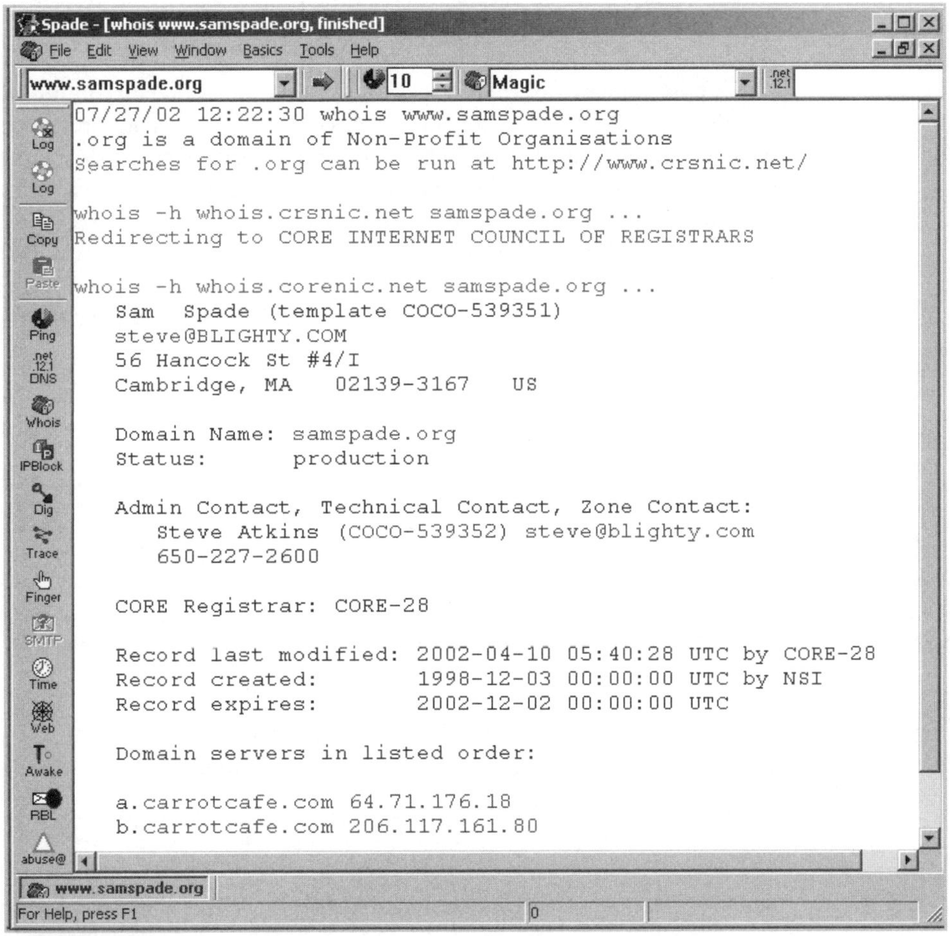

FIGURE 8-10 Sam Spade

The next phase of the preattack data-gathering process is called **fingerprinting**. This is the systematic examination of all of the Internet addresses of the organization (collected during the footprinting phase noted above). Accomplished with tools discussed in the next section, fingerprinting reveals useful information for the anticipated attack.

Port Scanners

Port scanning utilities (or **port scanners**) are tools used to identify (or fingerprint) computers that are active on a network, as well as the ports and services active on those computers, the functions and roles the machines are fulfilling, and other useful information. These tools can scan for specific types of computers, protocols, or resources, or their scans can be generic. It is helpful to understand the environment that exists on and in the network you are using, so that you can use the best tool for the job. The more specific the scanner is, the better it can give you detailed information that will be useful later. However, it is also recommended that you keep a generic, broad-based scanner in your toolbox as well. This helps to locate and identify rogue nodes on the network of which administrators may be unaware.

A **port** is a network channel or connection point in a data communications system. Within the TCP/IP networking protocol, TCP and User Datagram Protocol (UDP) port numbers differentiate between multiple communication channels used to connect to network services being offered on the same network device.[8] Each layer utility of TCP/IP has a unique port number assigned. Some have default ports but can also use other ports. Some of the well-known port numbers are presented in Table 8-2. In all, there are 65,536 port numbers in use (64K). The well-known ports are those from 0 through 1023. The registered ports are those from 1024 through 49151, and the dynamic and private ports are those from 49152 through 65535.

TABLE 8-2   Commonly Used Port Numbers

Port numbers	Description
20 and 21	File Transfer Protocol (FTP)
25	Simple Mail Transfer Protocol (SMTP)
53	Domain Name Services (DNS)
67 and 68	Dynamic Host Configuration Protocol (DHCP)
80	Hypertext Transfer Protocol (HTTP)
110	Post Office Protocol (POP3)
161	Simple Network Management Protocol (SNMP)
194	IRC chat port (used for device sharing)
443	HTTP over SSL
8080	Used for proxy services

Why secure open ports? Simply put, an **open port** can be used to send commands to a computer, gain access to a server, and exert control over a networking device. The general rule of thumb is to remove from service or secure any port not absolutely necessary to conduct business. If a business doesn't host Web services, there may be no need for port 80 to be available on its servers.

Vulnerability Scanners

Vulnerability scanners scan networks for highly detailed information. As a class, they identify exposed usernames and groups, show open network shares, and expose configuration problems and other vulnerabilities in servers. An example of a vulnerability scanner is Nmap (*www.insecure.org/nmap*), a professional freeware utility. Nmap uses IP packets to determine the hosts available on the network, the services (ports) they are offering, the operating system and OS version they are running, the type of packet filters and firewalls in use, and dozens of other characteristics. GFI LANguard Network security scanner (N. S. S.), which is available as freeware for non-commercial use, is another example of a vulnerability scanner. Figures 8-11 and 8-12 show sample LANguard and Nmap result screens.

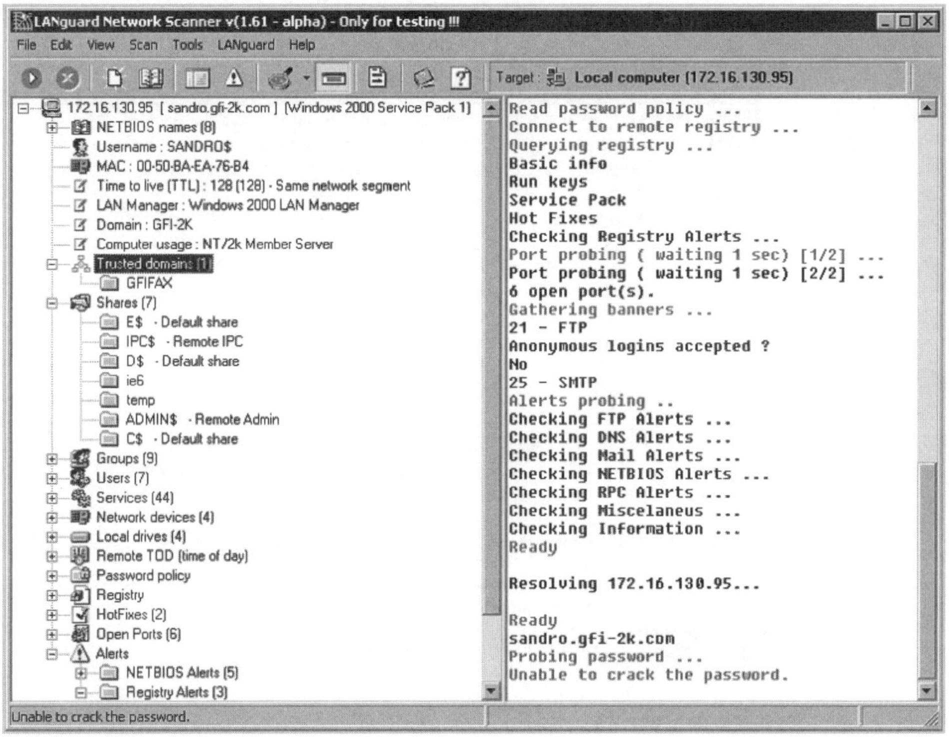

Courtesy of GFI Software Ltd.

FIGURE 8-11 GFI LANguard Network Security Scanner

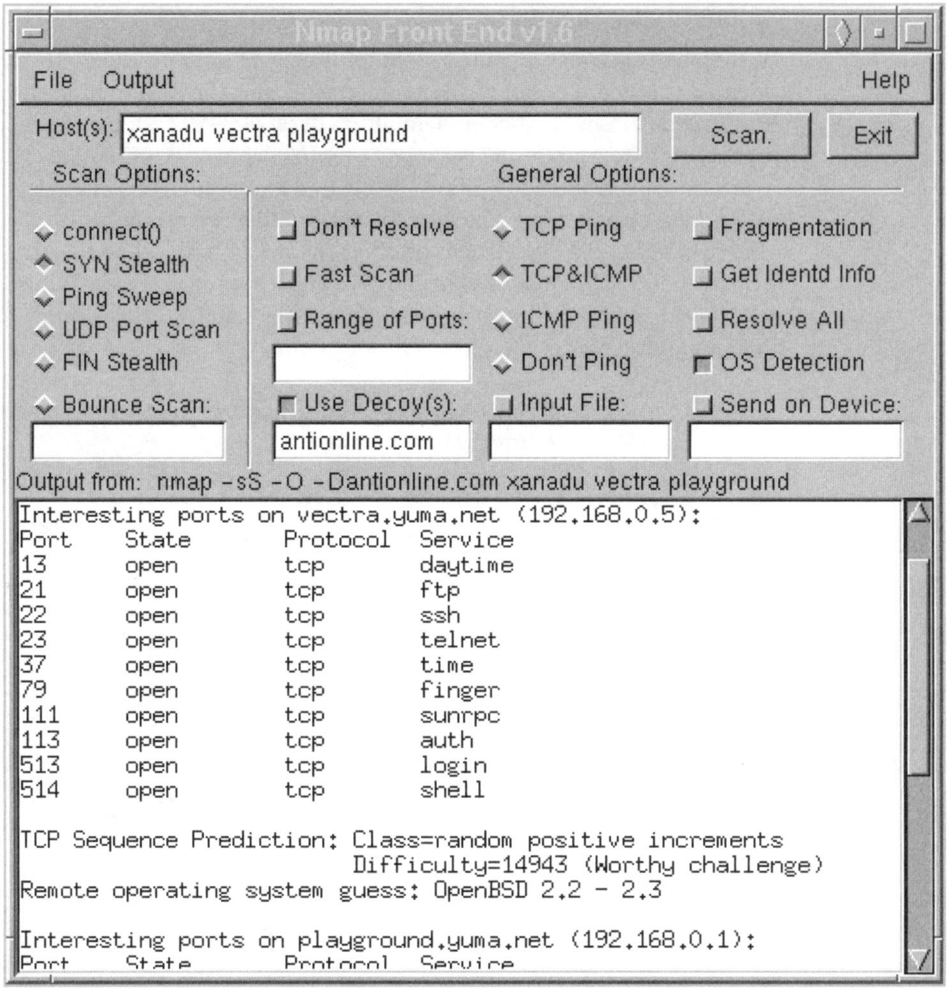

Courtesy of Insecure.org—http://www.insecure.org/nmap

FIGURE 8-12 Nmap Vulnerability Scanner

Packet Sniffers

One last tool worth mentioning here is the packet sniffer. A **packet sniffer** is a network tool that collects copies of packets from the network and analyzes them. It can provide a network administrator with valuable information to diagnose and resolve networking issues. In the wrong hands, a sniffer can be used to eavesdrop on network traffic. There are commercially available and open-source sniffers, such as Sniffer, which is a commercial product, and Snort, which is open-source software mentioned earlier. An excellent free, network protocol analyzer is Ethereal (*www.ethereal.com*). Ethereal allows the administrator to examine data from both live network traffic and captured data. Ethereal has several features, including a language filter and TCP session reconstruction utility. Figure 8-13 shows a sample screen from Ethereal. Typically, to use these types of programs most effectively, you must be internal to a network. Simply tapping into an Internet connection floods you with more data than you can process, and technically constitutes a violation of the wiretapping act. To use a packet sniffer legally, you must be: 1) on a network that the organization owns; 2) under direct authorization of the owners of the network, and 3) have knowledge and consent of the content creators (users). If all three conditions are met, the administrator can selectively collect and analyze packets to identify and diagnose problems on the network. Conditions one and two are self-explanatory, and three is usually a stipulation for using the company network, requiring users' signatures when their usernames and passwords are issued. Incidentally, these are the same requirements for employee monitoring in general, and in fact, packet sniffing can be construed as employee monitoring.

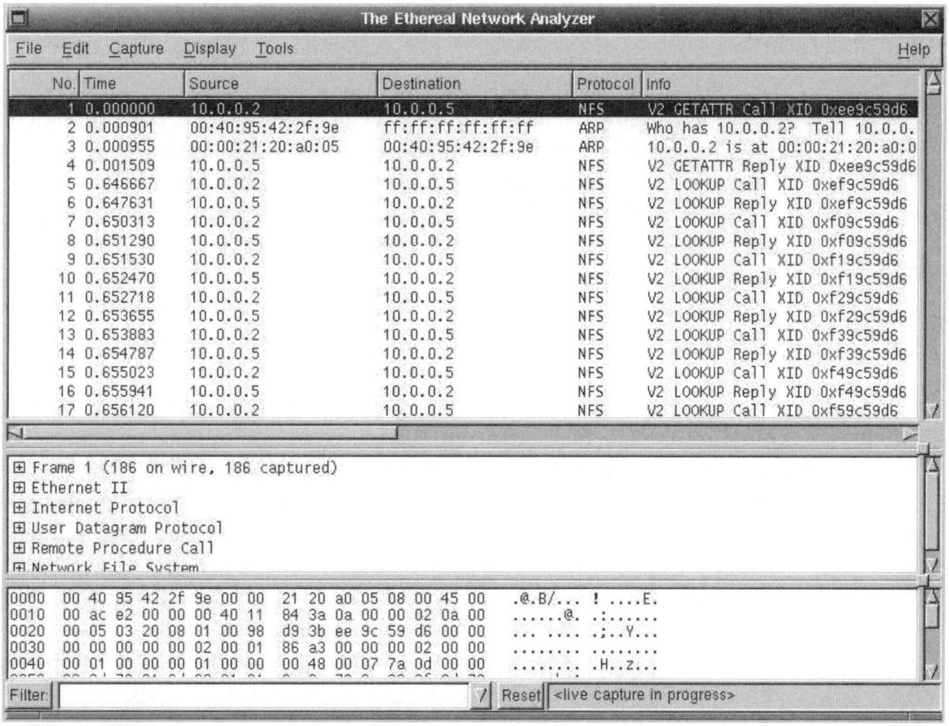

FIGURE 8-13 Ethereal Sample Screen

Content Filters

Another utility that effectively protects the organization's systems from misuse and unintentional denial-of-service is the **content filter**. Although technically not a firewall, a content filter is a software filter that allows administrators to restrict accessible content from within a network. The most common application of a content filter is the restriction of Web sites with nonbusiness related material, such as pornography. Another application is the restriction of spam e-mail from outside sources. Content filters can be small add-on software for the home or office, such as NetNanny, SurfControl, or major corporate applications, such as the Novell Border Manager. The advantage of content filters is the assurance that employees are not distracted by nonbusiness material and cannot waste organizational time and resources. The downside is that these systems require extensive configuration and on-going maintenance to constantly update the list of unacceptable destinations or the source addresses for incoming restricted e-mail. Some newer content filtering applications come with a service of downloadable files that update the restricted database, similar to an antivirus program. These applications work by matching either a list of disapproved or approved Web sites and by matching key content words, such as "nude" and "sex." Content creators have realized this and are working to bypass the restrictions by suppressing these types of trip words, thus creating additional problems for networking and security professionals.

Trap and Trace

Another set of technologies, the trap and trace categories of applications, which were described briefly in Chapter 6, are growing in popularity. The trap function describes software designed to entice individuals who are illegally perusing the internal areas of a network. These individuals either discover directly or find indicators of rich content areas on the network that turn out to be areas set up exclusively to distract potential miscreants. Better known as honey pots, these directories or servers distract the attacker while notifying the administrator.

The newest accompaniment to the trap is the trace. Similar in concept to caller ID, the trace is a process by which the organization attempts to determine the identity of someone discovered in unauthorized areas of the network or systems. If this individual turns out to be someone internal to the organization, the administrators are completely within their purview to track them down and turn them over to internal or external authorities. If it turns out that the individual is outside the security perimeter, then numerous legal issues arise, as described in earlier chapters. One of the most popular professional software suites is ManTrap and ManHunt, by Recourse Technologies (*www.recourse.com*). ManTrap is the honey pot application, presenting a virtual network running from a single server. ManHunt is an intrusion detection system with the capability to initiate a TrackBack function to trace a detected intruder as far as the administrator wishes, usually to an administrative boundary. It is possible, with this technology, to coordinate with an ISP that might have similar technology to hand off a trace to the upstream neighbor.

Cryptography and Encryption-based Solutions

Although not a specific application or security tool, encryption represents a sophisticated approach to security that is implemented in many security systems. In fact, many security-related tools use embedded encryption technologies to protect sensitive information handled by the application. **Encryption** is the process of converting an original message into a form that is unreadable by unauthorized individuals, that is, anyone without the tools to convert the encrypted message back to its original format. The science of encryption, known as **cryptology** encompasses **cryptography**, from the Greek words *kryptos*, meaning hidden, and *graphein*, meaning to write, and **cryptanalysis**, the process of obtaining the original message (or **plaintext**) from an encrypted message (or **ciphertext**), without the knowledge of the algorithms and keys used to perform the encryption. The field of cryptology is so complex it can fill many volumes. As a result, only a general overview of one branch of cryptology is presented in the Appendix on cryptography at the end of this chapter. This portion of Chapter 8 is dedicated to the foundations of encryption, followed by cryptology tools commonly used in information security.

Encryption Definitions

You can better understand the tools and functions popular in encryption security solutions after being introduced to some basic definitions:

- **Algorithm:** The mathematical formula used to convert an unencrypted message into an encrypted message

- **Cipher:** The transformation of the individual components (characters, bytes, or bits) of an unencrypted message into encrypted components

- **Ciphertext** or **cryptogram:** The unintelligible encrypted or encoded message resulting from an encryption

- **Code:** The transformation of the larger components (words or phrases) of an unencrypted message into encrypted components

- **Cryptosystem:** The set of transformations necessary to convert an unencrypted message into an encrypted message

- **Decipher:** To decrypt or convert ciphertext to plaintext

- **Encipher:** To encrypt or convert plaintext to ciphertext

- **Key** or **cryptovariable:** The information used in conjunction with the algorithm to create the ciphertext from the plaintext. The key can be a series of bits used in a mathematical algorithm, or the knowledge of how to manipulate the plaintext

- **Keyspace:** The entire range of values that can possibly be used to construct an individual key

- **Link encryption:** A series of encryptions and decryptions between a number of systems, whereby each node decrypts the message sent to it and then reencrypts it using different keys and sends it to the next neighbor, until it reaches the final destination

- **Plaintext:** The original unencrypted message that is encrypted and results from successful decryption

- **Steganography:** The process of hiding messages; for example, messages can be hidden within the digital encoding of a picture or graphic

- **Work factor:** The amount of effort (usually in hours) required to perform cryptanalysis on an encoded message

The notation used to describe the encryption process differs depending on the source. Two versions are presented here. The first uses the letter M to represent the original message, C to represent the ending ciphertext, and E to represent the encryption process: thus $E(M) = C$.[9] This formula represents the application of encryption to a message to create ciphertext. D represents the decryption or deciphering process, thus $D[E(M)] = M$. In other words, if you decipher an enciphered message, you should get the original message. K is used to represent the key, therefore $E(M, K) = C$, or encrypting the message with the key results in the ciphertext. Similarly $D(C,K) = D[E(M,K),K] = M$.

Another annotation method used later in this text during the discussion of Kerberos uses a slightly different approach. Many of the letters are the same, but C represents the client, and s the server. $K_c[M]$ means the message was encrypted with the private key of the client. (See the discussion in subsequent sections to understand private and public keys.) This annotation is actually more concise, as the E and D are inferred operations, and thus not represented in the notation. However for pedagogical purposes, the first notation set is used in this chapter, except in the discussion of Kerberos.

Now that you know the vocabulary, take a look at a simple form of encryption based on two concepts: the block cipher and the exclusive OR operation. With the block cipher method, the message is divided into blocks, e.g., 8- or 16-bit blocks, and then each block is transformed using the algorithm and key. The exclusive OR operation (XOR) is a function of Boolean algebra whereby two bits are compared, and if the two bits are identical, the result is a binary 0. If the two bits are the same, the result is a binary 1. Table 8-3 provides additional detail on this operation.

TABLE 8-3   Exclusive OR Operations

Bit 1	Bit 2	Exclusive OR result
0	0	0
0	1	1
1	0	1
1	1	0

Now you can combine these two concepts into a simple, but powerful operation. Given the following binary message, a block size of 8 bits is used, and an exclusive OR operation. You use the key = 0 1 0 1 0 1 0 1, and perform the XOR on the message, 8 bits at a time, until the entire message is enciphered. The resulting ciphertext can then be transmitted to the receiver, who must know the algorithm (XOR) and key (01010101) to decipher the message.

Here is an example:

Message:	0011010101000101001101010010101110010101
Message blocks:	00110101 01000101 00110101 00101011 10010101
Key:	01010101 01010101 01010101 01010101 01010101
Ciphertext:	01100000 00010000 01100000 01111110 11000000

If you cannot apply the key to the ciphertext and derive the original message, the cipher was misapplied. You should be able to tell that it would be impossible to decipher the ciphertext without both the algorithm and the key. Instead of using the exclusive OR operation, you could have chosen to use a different operation, such as a transposition or substitution, described in the following paragraph.

Encryption Operations

In encryption the most commonly used algorithms include two functions: substitution and transposition. In a **substitution cipher**, you substitute one value for another. For example, you can substitute the message character with the character three values to the right in the alphabet.

Thus: Plaintext = `ABCDEFGHIJKLMNOPQRSTUVWXYZ` becomes
Ciphertext = `DEFGHIJKLMNOPQRSTUVWXYZABC`, such that `MOM` becomes `PRP`.

This is a simple enough method by itself but very powerful if combined with other operations. Incidentally, this type of substitution is based on a **monoalphabetic substitution**, since it only uses one alphabet. More advanced substitution ciphers use two or more alphabets, and are referred to as **polyalphabetic substitutions**. To continue the previous example, consider the following block of text:

Plaintext =	`ABCDEFGHIJKLMNOPQRSTUVWXYZ`
Substitution cipher =	`DEFGHIJKLMNOPQRSTUVWXYZABC`
Substitution cipher =	`GHIJKLMNOPQRSTUVWXYZABCDEF`
Substitution cipher =	`JKLMNOPQRSTUVWXYZABCDEFGHI`
Substitution cipher =	`MNOPQRSTUVWXYZABCDEFGHIJKL`

In this example, the plaintext is the first line of code, and the next four lines are four sets of substitution ciphers. In this example, you can encode the word `TEXT` as `WKGF`, as you select letters from the second row for the first letter, third row for the second letter and so on. This type of encryption would be substantially more difficult to decipher without the algorithm (rows of ciphers) and key (use of the second row for first letter, third for second, and so on). It is also easy to completely randomize the cipher rows to create more complex operations. Another simple example of the substitution cipher is the daily cryptogram in your local newspaper, or the once famous "Little Orphan Annie" decoder ring. Caesar reportedly used a three-value shift to the right, so that A becomes D, and so on, giving that particular substitution cipher his name—the "Caesar Cipher."

The next type of cipher operation is the transposition. Just like the substitution operation, the transposition cipher is simple to understand but can be complex to decipher if properly used. Unlike the substitution cipher, the **transposition cipher** (or **permutation cipher**) simply rearranges the values within a block to create the ciphertext. This can be done at the bit level or at the byte (character) level. Here is an example.

Plaintext:	`0010010101101011100101010101001001`
Key:	$1\rightarrow4, 2\rightarrow8, 3\rightarrow1, 4\rightarrow5, 5\rightarrow7, 6\rightarrow2, 7\rightarrow6, 8\rightarrow3$

(Read as bit 1 moves to position 4, and so on, with bit position 1 being the far right bit.)

The following shows the plaintext broken into 8-bit blocks (for ease of discussion) and the corresponding ciptertext, based on the application of the key to the plaintext:

Plaintext 8-bit blocks:	`00100101 01101011 10010101 01010100`
Ciphertext:	`00001011 10111010 01001101 01100001`

To make this easier to follow, consider the following example in character transposition:

Plaintext:	`MY_DOG_HAS_FLEAS.` (spaces count as characters and are shown as underscores)
Key:	Same Key as above, but characters transposed, not bits. (Note that spaces are transposed as well.)
Plaintext 8 character blocks:	`MY_DOG_H   AS_FLEAS`
Ciphertext:	`_DYOHM_G AFSLSA_E`

Transposition ciphers and substitution ciphers can be used together in multiple combinations to result in a highly secure encryption process. To make the encryption stronger (more difficult to cryptanalyze) the keys and block sizes can be made much larger (64 bit or 128 bit), resulting is substantially more complex substitutions or transpositions.

Vernam Cipher

Also known as the one-time pad, the Vernam cipher was developed at AT&T and uses a one-use set of characters, the value of which is added to the block of text. The resulting sum is then converted to text. When the two are added, if the values exceed 26, 26 is subtracted from the total (Modulo 26). The corresponding results are then converted back to text as shown in the example below.

Plaintext:	M	Y	D	O	G	H	A	S	F	L	E	A	S
Corresponding values:	13	25	04	15	07	08	01	19	06	12	05	01	19
One-time pad:	F	P	Q	R	N	S	B	I	E	H	T	Z	L
Pad corresponding values:	06	16	17	18	14	19	02	09	05	08	20	26	12
Results: (Plaintext)	13	25	04	15	07	08	01	19	06	12	05	01	19
One time pad:	06	16	17	18	14	19	02	09	05	08	20	26	12
Sum:	19	41	21	33	21	27	03	28	11	20	25	27	31
Subtraction:	15		07		01		02					01	05
Ciphertext:	P	O	U	G	U	A	C	B	K	T	Y	A	E

Book or Running Key Cipher

Another method, made popular by spy movies, is the use of text in a book as the algorithm to decrypt a message. The key consists of knowing which book to use and a list of codes representing the page number, line number, and word number of the plaintext word. For example, from a copy of a particular popular novel, one can send the message: `67,3,1;145,9,4;375,7,4;394,17,3`. Dictionaries and thesauruses make the most popular sources as they guarantee every word needed, although almost any book suffices. If the receiver knows which novel is used, he goes to page 67, line 3 and selects the first word from that line, then goes to page 145, line 9 and uses the fourth word, and so forth. The resulting message `cancel operation, target compromised` can then be deciphered. When using dictionaries, use only the page and word number. An even more sophisticated version can use multiple books, with a new book in a particular sequence for each word or phrase.

OFFLINE

Does Encryption Key Size Really Matter?

Many encryption applications and cryptosystems are described by their key size. Does the size of the encryption key really matter? How does the key size affect the strength of the algorithm? What is the strength of an algorithm? First, the keyspace, as defined earlier in the chapter, is the amount of space from which the key can be drawn. In a simple example, you have an algorithm that uses a 3-bit key. In binary, 3 bits represent values from 000 to 111, which corresponds to 0 to 7 in decimal, a keyspace of 8 keys. That

continued

means you have eight keys to choose from (0 to 7 in binary: 000, 001, 010, 011, 100, 101, 110, 111). Knowing how many keys to choose from, you can program a computer to simply try all the keys and see if you can crack the encrypted message. This presumes a few things: 1) you know the algorithm, 2) you have the encrypted message; and 3) you have time on your hands. It is easy to satisfy the first criteria. The encryption tools that use the Data Encryption Standard (DES) can be purchased over the counter. Many of these tools are based on encryption algorithms that are standards, such as DES, so it is relatively easy to get a cryptosystem based on DES that would allow you to decrypt an encrypted message, if you have the key. The second criterion requires the interception of an encrypted message, which is illegal, but not impossible. As to the third criterion, once set to a task, computers do not require much adult supervision, so you do not have to quit your day job. The result is a brute force attack, in which the computer randomly (or sequentially) selects possible keys of the known size and applies them to the encrypted text, or a piece of the encrypted text. If the result is plaintext, bingo! The strength of the algorithm is how long it takes to guess the key. As indicated in this chapter, it can take quite a long time to exert brute force on the more advanced cryptosystems.

But how big is big? As mentioned earlier, a three-bit system has eight keys to guess. An eight-bit system has 256 keys to guess. Table 8-4 shows how quickly the numbers grow with additional bits.

TABLE 8-4 Bits and Values

Bits	Values
8	256
16	65536
24	16777216
32	4.29E+09
56	7.21E+16
64	1.84E+19
128	3.4E+38
192	6.28E+57
256	1.16E+77

If you use a 32-bit key, puny by modern standards, you still have to guess almost 16.8 million keys to guess them all.

Why do systems such as DES use multiple different operations? Consider the following: if you use the same operation (XOR, substitution, or transposition) multiple times in a row, you gain no additional benefit. For example if you use a substitution cipher, and substitute B for A, and then R for B, and then Q for R, it is essentially the same as substituting Q for A (if A = B, and B = C, then A = C). So no benefit is gained from the additional operations. Similarly if you transpose a character in position 1, then position 4, then position 3,

continued

what's the difference between moving it to 3 to begin with? Since there is no net advantage for sequential operations, each subsequent operation must be different. Therefore, if you substitute, then transpose, then XOR, then substitute again, you have dramatically scrambled, substituted, and recoded the original plaintext with ciphertext that is untraceable without the key.

Now perhaps you have a better appreciation for the strength of the key. In cryptosystems, key size *does* matter.

Symmetric Encryption

The method described in the syntax example that required the same key to both encipher and decipher the message is also known as **private key encryption**, or symmetric encryption. **Symmetric encryption** indicates that the same key, also known as a **secret key**, is used to conduct both the encryption and decryption of the message. Symmetric encryption methods can be extremely efficient, requiring minimal processing to either encrypt or decrypt the message. The problem is that both the sender and the receiver must know the encryption key. If either copy of the key is compromised, an intermediate can decrypt and read the messages. One of the challenges of symmetric key encryption is getting a copy of the key to the receiver, a process that must be conducted out of band (meaning through an alternate channel or band than the one carrying the ciphertext) to avoid interception. Figure 8-14 illustrates the concept of symmetric encryption.

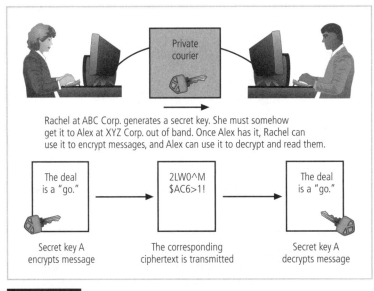

Rachel at ABC Corp. generates a secret key. She must somehow get it to Alex at XYZ Corp. out of band. Once Alex has it, Rachel can use it to encrypt messages, and Alex can use it to decrypt and read them.

| The deal is a "go." | 2LW0^M $AC6>1! | The deal is a "go." |

Secret key A encrypts message — The corresponding ciphertext is transmitted — Secret key A decrypts message

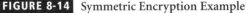

FIGURE 8-14 Symmetric Encryption Example

There are a number of popular symmetric encryption cryptosystems. One of the most familiar is **Data Encryption Standard (DES)**. DES was developed in 1977 by IBM and is based on the Data Encryption Algorithm (DEA), which uses a 64-bit block size and a 56-bit key. The algorithm begins by adding parity bits to the key (resulting in 64 bits) and then applies the key in 16 rounds of XOR, substitution, and transposition operations. With a 56-bit key, the algorithm has 2^{56} possible keys to choose from (over 72 quadrillion).

DES is a federally approved standard for nonclassified data (see Federal Information Processing Standards Publication 46-2). DES was cracked in 1997 when Rivest-Shamir-Aldeman (RSA) put a bounty on the algorithm. The term, RSA, reflects the last names of the three developers of the RSA algorithm, which is discussed later in this chapter. RSA offered a $10,000 reward for the first person or team to crack the algorithm. Fourteen thousand (14,000) users collaborated over the Internet to finally break the encryption. **Triple DES**, or **3DES**, was developed as an improvement to DES and uses up to three keys in succession. It is substantially more secure than DES, not only because it uses up to three keys to DES's one, but because it also performs three different encryption operations as described below:

1. In the first operation, 3DES encrypts the message with key 1, then decrypts it with key 2, and then it encrypts it with key 1 again. Decrypting with a different key is essentially another encryption, but it reverses the application of the traditional encryption operations. Essentially, [E{D[E(M,K1)],K2},K1].
2. In the second operation, it encrypts the message with key 1, then it encrypts it again with key 2, and then it encrypts it a third time with key 1 again, or [E{E[E(M,K1)],K2},K1].
3. In the third operation, 3DES encrypts the message three times with three different keys; [E{E[E(M,K1)],K2},K3]. This is the most secure level of encryption possible with 3DES.

The successor to 3DES is **Advanced Encryption Standard (AES)**. AES is based on the Rijndael Block Cipher, which is a block cipher with a variable block length and a key length of either 128, 192, or 256 bits. In 1998, it took a special computer designed by the Electronic Freedom Frontier (*www.eff.org*) over 56 hours to crack DES. It would take the same computer approximately 4,698,864 quintillion years (4,698,864,000,000,000,000,000) to crack AES.

Asymmetric Encryption

Another category of encryption techniques is **asymmetric encryption**, also known as **public key encryption**. Whereas the symmetric encryption systems are based on a single key to both encrypt and decrypt a message, asymmetric encryption uses two different keys. Either key can be used to encrypt or decrypt the message. If, however, Key A is used to encrypt the message, only Key B can decrypt it, and if Key B is used to encrypt a message, only Key A can decrypt it. Although at first this method seems inefficient or even pointless, its uses can be elegant, as you will see. This technique has its highest value when one key is used as a private key, and the other key as a public key. Why is it called the public key? The public key is stored in a public location, where anyone can use it. Obviously, the private key is called that, because it must be kept private, or else there is no benefit from the encryption. The private key, as its name suggests, is a secret known only to the owner of the key pair. Consider the following example, illustrated in Figure 8-15. Alex at ABC Corporation wants to send an encrypted message to Rachel at XYZ Corporation. Alex goes to a public key registry and obtains Rachel's public key. Remember the foundation of asymmetric encryption is that the same key cannot be used to both encrypt and decrypt the same message. So when Rachel's public key is used to encrypt the message, only Rachel's private key can be used to decrypt it, and that private key is held by Rachel alone. Similarly, if Rachel wants to respond to Alex's message, she goes to the registry where Alex's public key is held, and uses it to encrypt her message, which of course can only be read by Alex's private key.

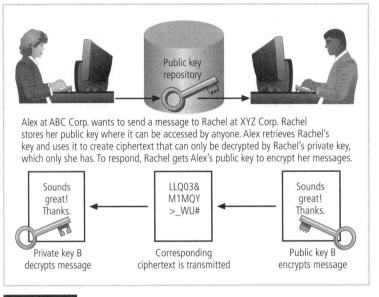

Alex at ABC Corp. wants to send a message to Rachel at XYZ Corp. Rachel stores her public key where it can be accessed by anyone. Alex retrieves Rachel's key and uses it to create ciphertext that can only be decrypted by Rachel's private key, which only she has. To respond, Rachel gets Alex's public key to encrypt her messages.

FIGURE 8-15   Using Public Keys

The problem with asymmetric encryption is that it requires four keys to hold a single conversation between two parties. If four organizations want to frequently exchange communications, they each have to manage their private key and four public keys. It can be confusing to determine which public key is needed to encrypt a particular message. With more organizations in the loop, the problem expands. Also, asymmetric encryption is not as efficient as symmetric encryptions in terms of CPU computations. As a result, the hybrid system described in the section on Public Key Infrastructure (see below) is more commonly used, instead of a pure asymmetric system. For more information on asymmetric encryption, read the Technical Details box entitled, "How Asymmetric Algorithms Work."

Digital Signatures

An interesting thing happens when the asymmetric process is reversed, that is the private key is used to encrypt a short message. The public key can be used to decrypt it, and the fact that the message was sent by the organization that owns the private key cannot be refuted. This is known as **nonrepudiation**, which is the foundation of digital signatures. **Digital Signatures** are encrypted messages that are independently verified as authentic by a central facility (registry).

RSA

One of the most popular public key cryptosystems is RSA. As described earlier, RSA stands for Rivest-Shamir-Aldeman, its developers. RSA is the first public key encryption algorithm developed and published for commercial use. RSA is very popular and is part of both Microsoft and Netscape Web browsers. There are a number of extensions to the RSA algorithm including: RSA Encryption Scheme - Optimal Asymmetric Encryption Padding (RSAES-OAEP); and RSA Signature Scheme with Appendix - Probabilistic Signature Scheme (RSASSA-PSS).

TECHNICAL DETAILS

How Asymmetric Algorithms Work

Asymmetric algorithms are based on one-way functions. A one-way function is simple to compute in one direction, but complex to compute in the opposite. Public-key encryption is based on a hash value, calculated from an input number using a hashing algorithm. The hash value is essentially a summary of the original input values. It is virtually impossible to derive the original value without knowing how the values were used to create the hash value. For example, if you multiply 45 by 235 you get 10,575. Simple enough. Now if you have the number 134,575, can you determine which two numbers were multiplied to determine this number? Now assume that each number is 200 digits long and prime. The resulting multiplicative value would be up to 400 digits long. Try factoring that one out. There is a shortcut, however. In mathematics it is known as a trapdoor. A **trapdoor** is a "secret mechanism that enables you to easily accomplish the reverse function in a one-way function."[10] With a trapdoor, you can use two keys to encrypt or decrypt the ciphertext, but not both. The public key can be the true key, and the private key can be derived from the public key using the trapdoor.

In RSA, the keys are generated as follows:

- "Choose two large prime numbers, p and q of equal length, compute p x q = n, which is the public modulus.
- "Choose a random public key, e, so that e and (p-1)(q-1) are relatively prime.
- "Compute e x d = 1 mod (p – 1)(q – 1), where d is the private key.
- "Thus $d = e^{-1} mod[(p – 1)(q – 1)]$."

"(d, n) is the private key; (e, n) is the public key. P is encrypted to generate ciphertext C as $C = P^e mod \, n$, and is decrypted to recover the plaintext, P as $P = C^d mod \, n$."[11]

PKI

Public Key Infrastructure is the entire set of hardware, software, and cryptosystems necessary to implement public key encryption. PKI systems are based on public key cryptosystems and include digital certificates and certificate authorities (CAs). Common implementations of PKI include: systems to issue digital certificates to users and servers; encryption enrollment; key issuing systems; tools for managing the key issuance; verification and return of certificates; and any other services associated with PKI.

PKI protects information assets in several ways:[12]

- **Authentication:** Digital certificates in a PKI system permit individuals, organizations, and Web servers to validate the identity of each of the parties in an Internet transaction.

- **Integrity:** A digital certificate demonstrates that the content signed by the certificate has not been altered while being moved from server to client.

- **Privacy:** Digital certificates keep information from being intercepted during transmission over the Internet.
- **Authorization:** Digital certificates issued in a PKI environment can replace user IDs and passwords, enhance security, and reduce some of the overhead required for authorization processes and controlling access privileges for specific transactions.
- **Nonrepudiation:** Digital certificates can validate actions, making it less likely that customers or partners can later repudiate a digitally signed transaction, such as an online purchase.

For more information on PKI, see the Offline box entitled, "The Risks of PKI."

What are Digital Certificates and Certificate Authorities?

As alluded to earlier, a **digital certificate** is an electronic document, similar to a digital signature, attached to a file certifying that this file is from the organization it claims to be from and has not been modified from the original format. A **certificate authority** is an agency that manages the issuance of certificates and serves as the electronic notary public to verify their worth and integrity. This is easily seen when downloading and updating software on the Internet (see Figure 8-16). The pop-up window shows that the downloaded files did in fact come from the purported agency, and thus can be trusted.

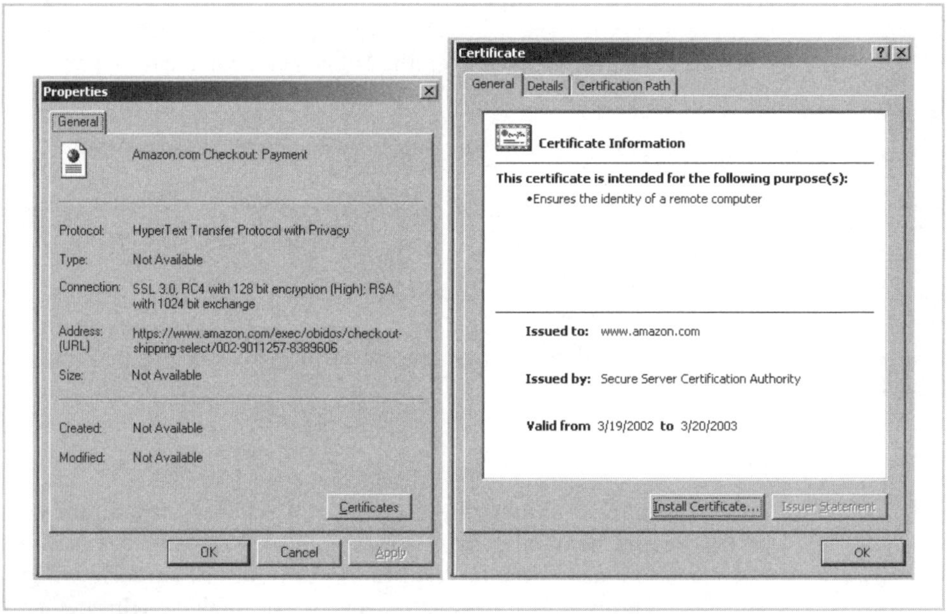

FIGURE 8-16 Digital Certificates

OFFLINE

"Ten Risks of PKI: What You're not Being Told about Public Key Infrastructure" [13]

Adapted from an article by C. Ellison and B. Schneier, *Computer Security Journal*, 2000.

"Risk #1: Who do you trust, and for what?" There's a risk to the imprecise use of the word "trust." A CA is often defined as "trusted." Who gave the CA the authority to grant such authorizations? Who made it trusted?

"Risk #2: Who is using my key?" Depends on how well you protect your own data. If your data is compromised, someone may have your key. Repudiate that.

"Risk #3: How secure is the verifying computer?" Not very, after all it isn't protecting secrets, only public keys.

"Risk #4: Which John Robinson is he?" Will the real John Robinson please stand up? You may know only one John Robinson personally, but how many does the CA know? How can you determine that the certificate you receive is from the same guy you think it is?

"Risk #5: Is the CA an authority?" Depends, it may be an authority on issuing certificates, but not necessarily an authority on what the certificate contains.

"Risk #6: Is the user part of the security design?" Not really, the user cannot be expected to validate a certificate, or to verify the certificate is actually legitimately associated with the e-commerce site on which it is presented.

"Risk #7: Was it one CA or a CA plus a registration authority?" In response to the accusation that CAs are not authorities on the content of a certificate, some CAs have created registration authorities (RAs), run by authorities on the certificate contents. Some haven't.

"Risk #8: How did the CA identify the certificate holder?" Some did by requiring a signature in person, some didn't.

"Risk #9: How secure are the certificate practices?" No more so than systems that run them. As a result they should be used with caution, and concern.

"Risk #10: Why are you using the CA process, anyway?" Maybe because authentication is a royal pain, and you would prefer not to have to deal with it. Maybe it's the latest snake oil. Maybe because there's not much else out there. Or, why not?

Hybrid Systems

In practice, asymmetric key encryption is not widely used except for digital certificates. Asymmetric key encryption is more often used in conjunction with symmetric key encryption creating a hybrid system. The current process is based on the **Diffie-Hellman Key Exchange method**, which is a method for exchanging private keys using public key encryption. Diffie-Hellman avoids the exposure to third parties that is sometimes associated with out-of-band key exchanges. With Diffie-Hellman, asymmetric encryption is used to exchange symmetric keys, so that two organizations can conduct quick, efficient, secure communications based on symmetric encryption. Diffie-Hellman provided the foundation for subsequent developments in public key encryption. The process is illustrated in Figure 8-17 and works this way. Because symmetric encryption is more efficient than asymmetric for sending messages, and asymmetric encryption doesn't require out-of-band key exchange, asymmetric encryption can be used to transmit symmetric keys in a hybrid approach. Alex at ABC wants to communicate with Rachel at Company XYZ, so Alex first creates a session key. A **session key** is a limited-use symmetric key for temporary communications. Alex encrypts a message with the session key, and then gets Rachel's public key. Alex uses Rachel's public key to encrypt both the session key and the message that is already encrypted. Alex transmits the entire package to Rachel, who uses her private key to decrypt the package containing the session key and the encrypted message, and then uses the session key to decrypt the message. Rachel can then continue the electronic conversation using only the more efficient symmetric session key.

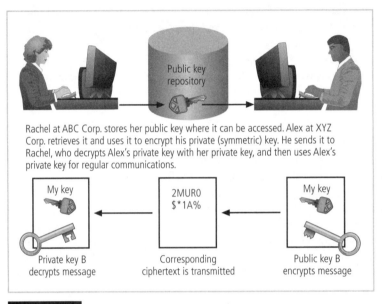

Rachel at ABC Corp. stores her public key where it can be accessed. Alex at XYZ Corp. retrieves it and uses it to encrypt his private (symmetric) key. He sends it to Rachel, who decrypts Alex's private key with her private key, and then uses Alex's private key for regular communications.

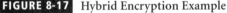

FIGURE 8-17 Hybrid Encryption Example

Securing E-mail

A number of cryptosystems have been adapted in an attempt to inject some degree of security into e-mail, a notoriously unsecured medium. Some of the more popular adaptations included Secure Multipurpose Internet Mail Extensions (S/MIME), Privacy Enhanced Mail (PEM), and Pretty Good Privacy (PGP). Each of these is briefly examined here.

S/MIME builds on the encoding format of Multipurpose Internet Mail Extensions (MIME) by adding encryption and authentication through digital signatures based on public key cryptosystems. Privacy Enhanced Mail (PEM) was proposed by the Internet Engineering Task Force (IETF) as a standard to function with the public key cryptosystems. PEM uses 3DES symmetric key encryption and RSA for key exchanges and digital signatures. Pretty Good Privacy (PGP) was developed by Phil Zimmerman and uses the IDEA Cipher, a 128-bit symmetric key block encryption algorithm with 64-bit blocks for message encoding. IDEA performs 8 rounds on 16-bit subblocks using algebraic calculations. PGP also uses RSA for symmetric key exchange and for digital signatures. PGP is much like the approach to trust represented by the idea that the friend of my friend is my friend. In PGP, if station A has established a trusting relationship with station B, and station B has a trusting relationship with station C, then station A is presumed to have a trusting relationship with station C and can exchange encrypted information.

Securing the Web

Just as PGP, PEM, and S/MIME work to secure e-mail operations, a number of cryptosystems work to secure Web browsers, especially at electronic commerce sites. Among these are Secure Electronic Transactions (SET), Secure Socket Layer (SSL), Secure Hypertext Transfer Protocol (SHTTP), Secure Shell (SSH-2), and IP Security (IPSec). Each of these is discussed in additional detail below.

Secure Electronic Transactions (SET) was developed by MasterCard and VISA in 1997 to provide protection from electronic payment fraud. SET works by using the credit card transfers with DES for encryption and RSA for key exchange, much as other algorithms do. SET provides the security for both Internet-based credit card transactions and the encryption of the swipe systems of credit cards in retail stores. Secure Socket Layer was developed by Netscape in 1994 to provide security in online electronic commerce transactions. It uses a number of algorithms, but mainly relies on RSA for key transfer and IDEA, DES, or 3DES for encrypted symmetric key-based data transfer. Figure 8-16, which was described earlier, shows the certificate and SSL information that is displayed when you are checking out of an e-commerce site. If the Web connection does not automatically display the certificate, you can right click in the window and select properties to view the connection encryption and certificate properties.

Secure Hypertext Transfer Protocol (SHTTP) is an encrypted solution to the unsecured version of HTTP. It is an alternative to the aforementioned protocols and uses a number of different algorithms to provide secure e-commerce transactions as well as encrypted Web pages for secure data transfer over the Web. **Secure Shell (SSH)** provides security over remote access connections using tunneling. (In tunnel mode, the entire IP packet is encrypted and is then placed as the payload in another IP packet.) SSH provides authentication services between a client and server.

IP Security (IPSec) is the cryptographic authentication and encryption product of the IETF's IP Protocol Security Working Group. It is defined in Request for Comments (RFC) 1825, 1826, and 1827. IP Security (IPSec) is used to create Virtual Private Networks (VPNs), described in the following section. IPSec itself is actually an open framework for security development within the TCP/IP family of protocol standards. A Cisco Systems white paper describes how IPSEC combines several different cryptosystems as follows:

- Diffie-Hellman key exchange for deriving key material between peers on a public network
- Public key cryptography for signing the Diffie-Hellman exchanges to guarantee the identity of the two parties
- Bulk encryption algorithms, such as DES, for encrypting the data
- Digital certificates signed by a certificate authority to act as digital ID cards.[14]

IPSec includes: 1) the IP Security Protocol itself, which defines the information to add to an IP packet, as well as how to encrypt packet data; and 2) the Internet Key Exchange, which uses an asymmetric-based key exchange and negotiates the security associations. IPSec works in two modes of operation: transport and tunnel. In **transport mode** only the IP data is encrypted, not the IP headers themselves. This allows intermediate nodes to read the source and destination addresses. As defined earlier, in **tunnel mode** the entire IP packet is encrypted and is then placed as the payload in another IP packet. This requires other systems at the beginning and end of the tunnel to act as proxies to send and receive the encrypted packets. These systems then transmit the decrypted packets to their true destinations.

The implementation of these technologies is commonly used in the process known as **Virtual Private Networks (VPNs)**. A VPN is a network within a network. In the most common implementation, a VPN allows a user to turn the Internet into a private network, free from the prying eyes of unwanted observers. As you know, the Internet is anything but private. However, using the tunneling approach described earlier, an individual or organization can set up tunneling points across the Internet and send encrypted data back and forth, using the IP-packet-within-an-IP-packet method to get the data across safely and securely. VPNs are simple to set up and maintain and usually require only that the tunneling points to be dual-homed, connecting a private network to the Internet or to another outside connection point. There is VPN support built into most Microsoft server software, including NT and 2000, as well as client support for VPN services built into XP. While true private network services connections can cost hundreds of thousands of dollars to lease, configure, and maintain, a VPN can cost next to nothing.

Securing Authentication

One last set of cryptosystems discussed here provide secure third-party authentication. The first is **Kerberos**, named after the three-headed dog of Greek mythology (spelled Cerberus in Latin), which guarded the gates to the underworld. Kerberos uses symmetric key encryption to validate an individual user to various network resources. Kerberos keeps a database containing the private keys of clients and servers, which, in the case of a client, is the client's encrypted password. Network services running on servers in the network register with Kerberos, as do the clients that use those services.[15] The Kerberos system knows these private keys and can authenticate one network node (client or server) to another. For example, Kerberos can authenticate a client to a print service. To understand Kerberos, think of a friend introducing you around at a party. Kerberos also generates temporary session keys, which are private keys given to the two parties in a conversation. The session key is used to encrypt all communications between these two parties. Typically a user logs into the network, is authenticated to the Kerberos systems, and is then authenticated by the Kerberos system to other resources on the network by the Kerberos system itself.

Kerberos consists of three interacting services all using a database library:

1. Authentication server (AS), which is a Kerberos server that authenticates clients and servers.
2. Key Distribution Center (KDC), which generates and issues session keys.
3. Kerberos ticket granting service (TGS), which provides tickets to clients who request services. In Kerberos a **ticket** is an identification card for a particular client that verifies to the server that the client is requesting services and that the client is a valid member of the Kerberos system and therefore authorized to receive services. The ticket consists of the client's name and network address, a ticket validation starting and ending time, and the session key, all encrypted in the private key of the server from which the client is requesting services.

Kerberos works based on the following principles:

- "The KDC knows the secret keys of all clients and servers on the network.
- "The KDC initially exchanges information with the client and server by using these secret keys.

- "Kerberos authenticates a client to a requested service on a server through TGS and by issuing temporary session keys for communications between the client and KDC, the server and KDC, and the client and server.
- "Communications then takes place between the client and server using these temporary session keys."[16]

Figures 8-18 and 8-19 illustrate this process.

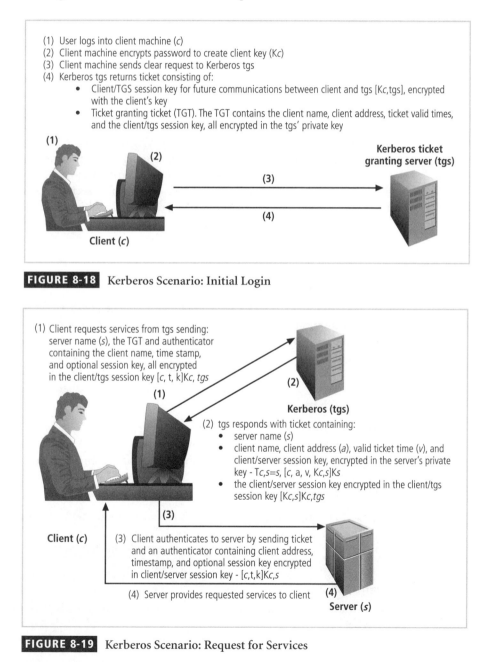

(1) User logs into client machine (*c*)
(2) Client machine encrypts password to create client key (K*c*)
(3) Client machine sends clear request to Kerberos tgs
(4) Kerberos tgs returns ticket consisting of:
  • Client/TGS session key for future communications between client and tgs [K*c*,tgs], encrypted with the client's key
  • Ticket granting ticket (TGT). The TGT contains the client name, client address, ticket valid times, and the client/tgs session key, all encrypted in the tgs' private key

Kerberos ticket granting server (tgs)

Client (*c*)

FIGURE 8-18   Kerberos Scenario: Initial Login

(1) Client requests services from tgs sending: server name (*s*), the TGT and authenticator containing the client name, time stamp, and optional session key, all encrypted in the client/tgs session key [*c*, t, k]K*c*, tgs

Kerberos (tgs)

(2) tgs responds with ticket containing:
  • server name (*s*)
  • client name, client address (*a*), valid ticket time (*v*), and client/server session key, encrypted in the server's private key - T*c*,*s*=*s*, [*c*, a, v, K*c*,*s*]K*s*
  • the client/server session key encrypted in the client/tgs session key [K*c*,*s*]K*c*,tgs

Client (*c*)

(3) Client authenticates to server by sending ticket and an authenticator containing client address, timestamp, and optional session key encrypted in client/server session key - [*c*,t,k]K*c*,*s*

(4) Server provides requested services to client

Server (*s*)

FIGURE 8-19   Kerberos Scenario: Request for Services

Kerberos may be obtained free of charge from MIT at *http://web.mit.edu/is/help/kerberos/*, but if you use it, you should be aware of some fundamental problems. If the Kerberos servers are subjected to denial-of-service attacks, no client can request services. If the Kerberos servers, service providers, or clients' machines are compromised, their private key information may also be compromised.

Sesame

To solve some of the problems associated with Kerberos, a new, European research and development project evolved, which was partly funded by the European Commission. This is the Secure European System for Applications in a Multivendor Environment (SESAME). SESAME is similar in part to Kerberos in that the user is first authenticated to an authentication server to receive a token. The token is then presented to a privilege attribute server (instead of a ticket granting service) as proof of identity to gain a privilege attribute certificate (PAC). The PAC is like the ticket in Kerberos; however, a PAC conforms to European Computer Manufacturers Association (ECMA) and the International Organization for Standardization/International Telecommunications Union (ISO/ITU-T) standards. The differences lie in the security protocols and distribution methods. SESAME uses public key encryption to distribute secret keys. SESAME also builds on the Kerberos model by adding "heterogeneity, sophisticated access control features, scalability of public key systems, better manageability, audit and delegation."[17]

Access Control Devices

This section examines a final set of technologies associated with access control. There are a number of components to the physical design of a successful access control. The most important is the need for strong authentication, which is two-factor authentication. This authentication can consist of the user's personal password or passphrase but requires at least one other factor to represent strong authentication. Frequently a physical device is used for the second factor. If you remember from Chapter 4, when considering access control you address:

- What you know: for example, passwords and passphrase
- What you have: tokens and smart cards
- Who you are: fingerprints, hand topography, hand geometry, retinal, and iris recognition
- What you produce: voice and signature pattern recognition

The technology for what you know is integrated into the networking and security software executed in the systems already described. The last three are implemented in some form of identification technology that seeks to provide the desired level of authentication.

Authentication

Authentication is the validation of a user's identity, in other words, "Are you whom you claim to be?"

What You Know

This area of authentication deals with what the user knows, be it a password, pass phrase, or other unique authentication code, such as a personal identification number or PIN.

A **password** is a private word or combination of characters that only the user should know. One of the biggest debates in security concerns the complexity of passwords. The password should be difficult to guess, which means it cannot be something that is easily associated with the user, such as a spouse's, children's, or pet's name. Nor should it be a series of numbers commonly associated with the user, such as a phone number, social security number, or birth date. In juxtaposition, the password must be something the user can easily remember, which means it should be short or commonly associated with something the user can remember.

A **passphrase** is a series of characters, typically longer than a password, from which a **virtual password** is derived. For example, while a typical password might be 23skedoo, a typical passphrase can be MayTheForceBeWithYouAlways, which can also be represented as MTFBWYA.

What You Have

The second area of authentication addresses something the user carries in their possession—something they have. These include **dumb cards**, such as ID cards or ATM cards with magnetic stripes containing the digital (and often encrypted) user personal identification number (PIN) against which a user input is compared. A better version is the **smart card**, which contains a computer chip that can verify and validate a number of pieces of information above and beyond the PIN. Another device often used is the token, a computer chip in a display that presents a number used to support remote login authentication. Tokens are synchronous or asynchronous. Once **synchronous tokens** are synchronized with a server, each device (server and token) uses the time or a time-based database to generate a number that is entered during the user login phase. **Asynchronous tokens** use a challenge-response system, in which the server challenges the user during login with a numerical sequence. The user places this sequence into the token and receives a response. The user then enters the response into the system to gain access. This system does not require the synchronization of the previous system and therefore does not suffer from mistiming issues.

What You Are

The third area of authentication deals with something represented in the person of the user or something they are. This involves the entire area of biometrics discussed earlier. Biometrics include:

- Fingerprints
- Palm scan
- Hand geometry
- Hand topology
- Keyboard dynamics
- ID cards (face representation)
- Facial recognition
- Retina scan
- Iris scan
- Voice recognition

With all these metrics, only three human characteristics are considered truly unique:

- Fingerprints
- Retina of the eye (blood vessel pattern)
- Iris of the eye (random pattern of features found in the iris including: freckles, pits, striations, vasculature, coronas, and crypts)

Figure 8-20 depicts some of these human recognition characteristics.

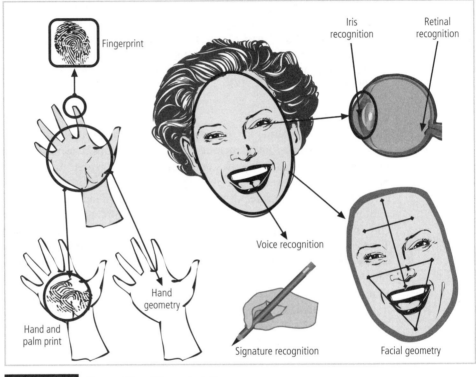

FIGURE 8-20   Recognition Characteristics

Most of the technologies that scan human characteristics convert these images to some form of **minutiae**. Minutiae are unique points of reference that are digitized and stored in an encrypted format. Each subsequent scan is also digitized and then compared with the encoded value to determine if users are whom they claim to be. The problem is that some human characteristics can change over time, due to normal development, injury, or illness.

What You Do

The fourth and final area of authentication addresses something the user performs or something they produce. This includes technology in the areas of signature recognition and voice recognition. Signature recognition has become commonplace. Retail stores use signature recognition, or at least signature capture, for authentication during a purchases. The customer signs his or her signature on a special pad, with a special stylus that captures the signature. The signature is digitized and either simply saved for future reference, or compared to a database for validation. Currently, the technology for signature capturing is much more widely accepted than that for signature comparison, because signatures change over time due to a number of factors, including age, fatigue, and the speed with which the signature is written. Voice recognition works similarly. There are several voice recognition software packages on the market today. These monitor the analog waveforms of a human's speech and attempt to convert them into on-screen text. Voice recognition for authentication is much simpler, as the captured and digitized voice is only compared to a stored version for authentication, rather than for text recognition. Systems that use voice recognition provide the user with a phrase that they are expected to read. This phrase is then compared to a stored version for authentication, for example, "My voice is my password, please verify me. Thank you."

Effectiveness of Biometrics

Biometric technologies are evaluated on three basic criteria: first, the false reject rate, which is the percentage of authorized users that are denied access; second, the false accept rate, which is the percentage of unauthorized users allowed access; finally, the crossover error rate, which is the point at which the number of false rejections equals the false acceptances. Each of these is examined in detail in the following sections.

False Reject Rate

The **false reject rate** is the percentage or value associated with the rate at which authentic users are denied or prevented access to authorized areas, as a result of a failure in the biometric device. This error rate is also known as a Type I error. This error rate, while a nuisance to authorized users, is probably of the least concern to security individuals. Rejection of an authorized individual represents no threat to security, but simply an impedance to authentic use. As a result, it is often overlooked, until the rate increases to a level high enough to irritate users. Most of you have experienced the frustration of having a frequently used credit card or ATM card fail to perform because of problems with the magnetic strip. In biometrics, similar problems can occur through a failure of the system to pick up the various information points it uses to properly authenticate a user.

False Accept Rate

The **false accept rate** is the percentage or value associated with the rate at which fraudulent or nonusers are allowed access to systems or areas as a result of a failure in the biometric device. This error rate is also knows as a Type II error. This type of error is unacceptable to security, as it represents a clear breach of security. Frequently multiple measures of authentication are required to back up a device that may fail and result in the admission of mistakenly accepted individuals.

Crossover Error Rate (CER)

The **crossover error rate** is the point at which the number of false rejections equals the false acceptances, also known as the equal error rate. This is possibly the most common and important overall measure of the accuracy of a biometric system. Most biometric systems can be adjusted to compensate for both false positive and false negative errors. Adjustment to one extreme creates a system that requires perfect matches and results in high false rejects, but almost no false accepts. Adjustment to the other extreme allows low false rejects, but produces high false accepts. The trick is to find the balance with low false accepts, but also low false rejects, to both ensure security and minimize the frustration level of authentic users. The optimal setting is somewhere near the equal error rate or CER. CERs are used to compare various biometrics and may vary by manufacturer. A biometric device that provides a CER of one percent is considered superior to one with a CER of five percent.

Acceptability of Biometrics

A balance must be struck between the acceptability of a system to its users and the effectiveness of the same systems. Many of the biometric systems that are highly reliable and effective are considered somewhat intrusive to users. As a result, to avoid confrontation and possible user boycott or bypass of the biometric controls, some agreement should be reached that allows use of biometrics with acceptable effectiveness rates and low perceptions of intrusiveness. It is interesting to note that the order of effectiveness and order of acceptance is opposite, as shown in Table 8-5.

TABLE 8-5 Orders of Effectiveness and Acceptance [18]

Effectiveness of biometric authentication systems ranking from most secure to least secure	Acceptance of biometric authentication systems ranking from most accepted to least accepted
Retina pattern recognition	Keystroke pattern recognition
Fingerprint recognition	Signature recognition
Handprint recognition	Voice pattern recognition
Voice pattern recognition	Handprint recognition
Keystroke pattern recognition	Fingerprint recognition
Signature recognition	Retina pattern recognition

While the use of one authentication area is necessary for access to the system, the more devices used the better. To obtain **strong authentication**, the systems must use two or more authentication areas.

Chapter Summary

- A firewall as part of an information security program is any device that prevents a specific type of information from moving between the outside world, known as the untrusted network, and the inside world, known as the trusted network, and vice versa.
- Types of firewalls include packet filtering firewalls, application-level firewalls, stateful inspection firewalls, dynamic packet filtering firewalls, and kernel proxies. There are four common architectural

implementations of firewalls: packet filtering routers, screened host firewalls, dual-homed firewalls, and screened subnet firewalls.

- A host-based IDS is a system that resides on a particular computer or server and monitors activity on that system. A network-based IDS monitors network traffic and, when a predefined condition occurs, responds and notifies the appropriate administrator.

- Signature-based IDS, also known as knowledge-based IDS, examine data traffic looking for something that matches signatures, which are preconfigured, predetermined attack patterns. Statistical anomaly-based IDS (also known as behavior-based IDS) collect data from normal traffic and establishes a baseline. When the activity is outside the baseline parameters (clipping level), IDS notify the administrator.

- The science of encryption, known as cryptology, encompasses cryptography, from the Greek words *kryptos*, meaning hidden, and *graphein*, meaning to write, and cryptanalysis, the process of obtaining the original message from an encrypted code without the use of the original algorithms and keys.

- In encryption, the most commonly used algorithms include two functions: substitution and transposition. A substitution cipher substitutes one value for another. The transposition cipher or permutation cipher simply rearranges the values within a block to create the ciphertext.

- Symmetric encryption uses the same key, also known as a secret key, to both encrypt and decrypt a message. Asymmetric encryption (public key encryption) uses two different keys.

- Public Key Infrastructure (PKI) is the entire set of hardware, software, and cryptosystems necessary to implement public key encryption.

- A digital certificate is an electronic document attached to a file certifying that the file is from the organization it claims to be from and has not been modified from the original format.

- A number of cryptosystems have been adapted to make e-mail more secure. Examples include Pretty Good Privacy (PGP), Secure Multipurpose Internet Mail Extensions (S/MIME), and Privacy Enhanced Mail (PEM).

- A number of cryptosystems work to secure Web browsers, including Secure Electronic Transactions (SET), Secure Socket Layer (SSL), Secure Hypertext Transfer Protocol (SHTTP), Secure Shell (SSH-2), and IP Security (IPSec).

- Authentication is the validation of a user's identity or "are you whom you claim to be?" Authentication devices can address one or more of four issues: what you know, what you have, what you are, and what you produce.

- Biometric technologies are evaluated on three basic criteria: the false reject rate, the false accept rate, and the crossover error rate.

- The use of one authentication factor is necessary for access to the system. To obtain strong authentication, the systems must use two or more authentication factors.

Review Questions

1. What role does physical design play in the SecSDLC?
2. What is the typical relationship between the untrusted network, the firewall, and the trusted network?
3. How is an application layer firewall different from a packet filtering firewall? Why is an application layer firewall sometimes called a proxy server?

4. What special function does a cache server perform? Why is this useful for larger organizations?

5. How does a screened host architecture for firewalls differ from a screened subnet firewall architecture? Which offers more security for the information assets that remain on the trusted network?

6. What is the DMZ? Is this really a good name for the function this type of subnet performs?

7. What is RADIUS? What advantage does it have over TACACS?

8. How does network-based IDS differ from host-based IDS?

9. What is network footprinting? What is network fingerprinting? How are they related?

10. Why do many organizations ban port scanning activities on their internal networks? Why would ISPs ban outbound port scanning by their customers?

11. Why is TCP port 80 always critically importance when securing an organization's network?

12. What kind of data and information can be found using a packet sniffer?

13. What is a spam filter in the context of e-mail? Where is it placed in the network to gain the best result for the organization?

14. What are the main components of cryptology?

15. Explain the relationship between plaintext and ciphertext?

16. Define steganography. Why would this be of concern to the information security professional?

17. One tenet of cryptography is that increasing the work factor to break a code increases the security of that code. Why is that true?

18. Explain the key differences between symmetric and asymmetric encryption. Which can the computer process faster? Which lowers the costs associated with key management?

19. How can asymmetric keys help to verify the identity of a buyer in an online transaction?

20. What is a VPN? What are some reasons it is widely popular in many organizations?

21. Are there any biometric recognition characteristics you can think of that were not listed in the text? How could they be used as a biometric authorization device?

22. What is a false reject rate? What is a false accept rate? How are they related to the crossover error rate?

23. What is the most widely accepted biometric authorization technology noted in the text? Why do you think this is the case?

24. What is the most effective biometric authorization technology noted in the text? Why do you think this is the case?

25. The future of biometric authorization is not certain. How do you think biometric technology will be used in the future?

Exercises

1. Create a spreadsheet that takes value input into eight cells and apply a transposition cipher to them. Then create a row that takes the results and apply a substitution cipher (substitute 0 for 5, 1 for 6, 2 for 7, 3 for 8, 4 for 9, and vice versa).

2. Using the Web, identify the technology known as "personal firewalls." Examine the various alternatives available and compare their functionality, cost, features, and type of protection.

3. Using the Web, locate one of the market leaders in the digital certificate market, VeriSign. Determine if VeriSign serves as a registration authority, certificate authority, or both. Download their free guide to PKI and summarize VeriSign's services.

4. Using the Web, go to *http://csrc.nist.gov* and locate FIPS 197. What encryption standard does this address use? Examine the contents of this publication and describe the algorithm discussed. How strong is this algorithm? How does it encrypt plaintext?

5. Using the Web, locate vendors of biometric products. Find one vendor with a product designed to examine each of the characteristics presented in Figure 8-20. What is the CER associated with each product? Which would be more acceptable to users? Which would be preferred by security?

Case Exercises

I. Sticky Fingers

Adapted from "Gummy Fingers' Fool Fingerprint Readers"[19]

By Brett Glass, *Extremetech.com*, May 23, 2002.

Biometrics is almost infallible, because it's almost impossible to fool a fingerprint reader. Or at least that's what manufacturers would have you believe. Unfortunately 'sticky fingers' may have beaten the system. Tsutomu Matsumoto, a Japanese mathematician and scientist, claims to have been able to fool modern fingerprint readers with false fingers made from—of all things—'Gummi' candies. The same materials used to make the popular candy was used to fill a fingertip mold to produce a fingerprint accurate enough to fool some of the industry's best scanners. The gelatin-based phonies are imbedded with fingerprints made from a victim's finger, created from a mold of epoxy-glass and copper circuit boards, and etched with the stamp fingerprint. Matsumoto's findings are significant enough to send biometric makers scrambling to find a means to counter this somewhat simple bypass. What's next? Contact lenses with someone else's iris?

1. What are some of the fundamental problems with the types of biometric readers that can be fooled so easily? What type of error does this represent? Is there a way to counter it?

2. What other biometric devices can be fooled with "forged" body parts? What can manufacturers do to counter these threats?

II. Catching a Thief

Adapted from "Steganography: Hidden data"[20]

By Deborah Radcliff, *Computerworld*, June 20, 2002.

A technology organization thought it had an insider leaking trade secrets. But there was no evidence. Even when e-mail, office machine, and storage materials of the engineer in question were searched, nothing was found. Then, someone noticed that his outgoing e-mail contained graphics. The graphics were turned over to a company specializing in computer forensics, and Bingo! The graphics contained subtly embedded codes that when deciphered contained the organization's most valuable schematics. The process of steganography can involve sound messages and graphics. The concept underlying steganography placed into graphics is rather simple, but the process of implementing it is complex. The culprit simply changes the last bit in each byte of a color pixel's three bytes (a 24-bit code) to reflect the data bits. To the naked eye, it's almost undetectable. To a specially designed computer code, it's simple data hiding. A standard image of 300 x 200 pixels contains over 60,000 pixels. Each pixel can contain three bits of data, resulting in 180Kb of encoded data. Larger more complex graphics can contain more.

Sayan Chakraborty, vice president of engineering at Sigaba Corporation in San Mateo, California, claims the process has been around for a millennium. During the Roman Empire, he explains, secret information was tattooed on a messenger's shaved head. When the hair grew back, the messenger was sent out with the secret message on his scalp and a decoy message in hand.[21] What would they have done if the message was time sensitive?

"'Most people study steganography either as an academic discipline or a curiosity, but I don't know if even terrorist groups would actually use it, says Chakraborty."[22] Neils Provos, a Ph.D. candidate in computer science at the University of Michigan in Ann Arbor, created a detection and cracking tool to examine images as part of his dissertation work. He examined millions of images at a popular auction Web site. What did he find? Nothing.

"Steganography becomes the focus of attention, dies down, and then the public is all over it again, says Provos. But it will never be pervasive, because the amount of data you can actually hide in the images is fairly small. And if someone wanted to steal intellectual property, it'd be easier to copy the data on a disk and carry it out in your pocket."[23]

While steganography isn't prevalent now, that doesn't mean it won't be in the future. If organizations develop tools to examine images and sound bites now, abuse of this type is less likely in the future.

1. What would prompt an individual to use a complex process like steganography when smuggling a diskette would be easier? What can an organization do to protect itself from this type of trade secret theft?

2. What implications does steganography have for national security? Will there be a need for federal agencies to begin screening Web images for possible imbedded messages?

Endnotes

1. Webopedia, "OSI." *Webopedia Online* (25 January 2002) [Cited 1 July 2002]; available from the World Wide Web *http://www.webopedia.com/TERM/O/OSI.html*.

2. Any address ending in .0 is actually a network address and any address ending in .255 is actually a broadcast address. This is simply an example.

3. Avolio and Blask, "Application Gateways and Stateful Inspection: A Brief Note Comparing and Contrasting," *Avolio Consulting Online* (22 January 1998) [Cited 1 July 2002]; available from the World Wide Web *http://www.avolio.com/apgw+spf.html*.

4. Cisco Systems, Inc., "Inside the Cisco Centri Firewall." *Cisco Online* [Cited 1 July 2002]; available from the World Wide Web *http://www.cisco.com/univercd/cc/td/doc/product/ iaabu/centri4/user/scf4ch5.htm#xtocid157876*.

5. Elron Software, Inc., "Choosing the Best Firewall for Your Growing Network." *Elron Online* (22 April 2002) [Cited 1 July 2002]; available from the World Wide Web *http://www.elronsoftware.com/connection/story67a.html*.

6. Laura Taylor, "Guidelines for Configuring your Firewall Rule-Set." *Tech Update Online* (12 April 2001) [Cited 1 July 2002]; available from the World Wide Web *http://techupdate. zdnet.com/techupdate/stories/main/0,14179,2707159,00.html*.

7. Shon Harris, *CISSP Certification: All in One Exam Guide* (Berkeley, CA: Osborne McGraw-Hill, 2001), 163.

8. FOLDOC, "User Datagram Protocol." *FOLDOC Online* (19 June 2002) [Cited 1 July 2002]; available from the World Wide Web *http://wombat.doc.ic.ac.uk/foldoc/ foldoc.cgi?query=port&action=Search*.

9. Ronald L. Krutz and Russell Dean Vines, *The CISSP Prep Guide: Mastering the Ten Domains of Computer Security* (New York: John Wiley and Sons Inc., 2001), 131.

10. Ronald L. Krutz and Russell Dean Vines, *The CISSP Prep Guide: Mastering the Ten Domains of Computer Security* (New York: John Wiley and Sons Inc., 2001), 155.

11. Ronald L. Krutz and Russell Dean Vines, *The CISSP Prep Guide: Mastering the Ten Domains of Computer Security* (New York: John Wiley and Sons Inc., 2001), 156.

12. Verisign. "Understanding PKI." *Verisign Online* [Cited 1 July 2002]; available from the World Wide Web *http://verisign.netscape.com/security/pki/understanding.html.*

13. Carl Ellison and Bruce Schneier, "Ten Risks of PKI: What You're not Being Told about Public Key Infrastructure," *Computer Security Journal* 16, no. 1 (Winter 2000): 1–7.

14. Cisco Systems, Inc., "White Paper: IPSec." *Cisco Online* (21 November 2000) [Cited 1 July 2002]; available from the World Wide Web *http://www.cisco.com/warp/public/cc/so/neso/sqso/eqso/ipsec_wp.htm.*

15. Jennifer G. Steiner, Clifford Neuman and Jeffrey I. Schiller, "An Authentication Service for Open Network Systems," (paper presented for Project Athena 30 March 1988); available from the World Wide Web *ftp://athena-dist.mit.edu/pub/kerberos/doc/usenix.txt.*

16. Ronald L. Krutz and Russell Dean Vines, *The CISSP Prep Guide: Mastering the Ten Domains of Computer Security* (New York: John Wiley and Sons Inc., 2001), 40.

17. Computer Security and Industrial Cryptography, "SESAME," *COSIC Online* [Cited 1 July 2002]; available from the World Wide Web https://www.cosic.esat.kuleuven.ac.be/sesame/html/sesame_what.html.

18. Harold F. Tipton and Micki Krause, *Handbook of Information Security Management* (Boca Raton, LA: CRC Press LLC, 1998), 39–41.

19. Brett Glass,. "'Gummy Fingers' Fool Fingerprint Readers" *Extremetech.Com* (May 23, 2002): 1.

20. Deborah Radcliff, "Steganography: Hidden data" *Computerworld* 36 (24) (Jun 10, 2002): 52.

21. *Ibid.*

22. *Ibid.*

23. *Ibid.*

Appendix: Cryptography

(This appendix is contributed by
Anthony J. Nichols, MSIS,
Kennesaw State University)

A

> Yet it may roundly be asserted that human
> ingenuity cannot concoct a cipher which
> human ingenuity cannot resolve.
>
> **EDGAR ALLAN POE, THE GOLD BUG**

Introduction

This appendix is designed to supplement Chapter 8 with additional detail on the history and content of cryptography, cryptosystems, and cryptanalysis. This appendix describes the foundations of cryptography, methods of encryption, and the operation and function of some of the more popular encryption protocols. Table A-1 is an overview of the history of cryptosystems. It is followed by definitions from the field of cryptography and a technical discussion on encryption algorithms and protocols.

TABLE A-1   History of Cryptography

1900 B.C.	Egyptian scribes used nonstandard hieroglyphs while inscribing clay tablets; this is the first documented use of written cryptography.
1500 B.C.	Mesopotamian cryptography surpassed that of the Egyptian, with a tablet approaching a modern level with an encrypted formula for pottery glazes; the tablet used special symbols that appear to have different meanings.
500 B.C.	Hebrew scribes writing the book of Jeremiah used a reversed alphabet substitution cipher known as the ATBASH.
487 B.C.	The Spartans of Greece developed the Skytale, a system consisting of a strip of papyrus wrapped around a wooden staff. Messages were written down the length of the staff, and the papyrus was unwrapped. To read the message the papyrus had to be wrapped around a shaft of similar diameter.
50 B.C.	Julius Caesar used a simple substitution in governmental communications. To form an encrypted text, Caesar shifted the letter of the alphabet three places. In addition to this monoalphabetic substitution cipher, Caesar strengthened his encryption by substituting Greek letters for Latin letters.
Fourth and fifth centuries	The Kama Sutra of Vatsayana listed cryptography as the 44th and 45th of the 64 arts (yogas) that men and women should practice: 44) The art of understanding writing in cipher, and the writing of words in a peculiar way 45) The art of speaking by changing the forms of the word
725	Abu 'Abd al-Rahman al-Khalil ibn Ahman ibn 'Amr ibn Tammam al Farahidi al-Zadi al Yahmadi wrote a text (now lost) of cryptography; he additionally solved a Greek cryptogram by guessing the plaintext introduction.
855	Abu Wahshiyyaan-Nabati, a scholar, published several cipher alphabets which were used for encrypted writings of magic formulas.
1250	Roger Bacon, an English monk, wrote *Secret Works of Art and the Nullity of Magic* in which he described several simple ciphers.
1392	*The Equatorie of the Planetis*, possibly written by Geoffrey Chaucer, contained a passage in a simple substitution cipher.
1412	Subhalasha, a 14-volume Arabic encyclopedia, contained a section on cryptography, including both substitution and transposition ciphers, and ciphers with multiple substitutions that had never been used before.
1466	Leon Battista Alberti is considered the Father of Western cryptography based on his work with polyalphabetic substitution; he also designed a cipher disk.

TABLE A-1 History of Cryptography (continued)

1518	Johannes Trithemius wrote the first printed book on cryptography invented a steganographic cipher, in which each letter was represented as a word taken from a succession of columns. He also described the polyalphabetic ciphers in the now-standard rectangular substitution form. He is credited with the introduction of the method of changing alphabets with each letter.
1553	Giovan Batista Belaso introduced the idea of the passphrase (password) as a key for encryption; this polyalphabetic cipher is misnamed "Vigenère" today.
1563	Giovanni Battista Porta wrote a classification text on ciphers; he classified ciphers as transposition, substitution, and symbol substitution.
1623	Sir Francis Bacon described a cipher by employing one of the first uses of steganography; his messages were encrypted by slightly changing the typeface of a random text, so that each letter of the cipher was hidden within the text's letters.
1790s	Thomas Jefferson created a 26-letter wheel cipher, which he used for official communications while ambassador to France; the concept of the wheel cipher would be reinvented in 1854, and again in 1913.
1854	Charles Babbage appears to have reinvented Thomas Jefferson's wheel cipher.
1861-5	During the U.S. Civil War, Union forces used a substitution of select words cipher; the Confederacy used a polyalphabetic cipher whose solution had just been published before the start of the Civil War.
1914-17	World War I: The Germans, British, and French used a series of transposition and substitution ciphers in radio communications throughout the war. All sides spent considerable effort to intercept and decode communications, thereby bringing about the birth of the science of cryptanalysis. British cryptographers broke the Zimmerman Telegram, in which the Germans offered Mexico U.S. territory in return for Mexico's support of Germany. This decryption helped to bring the United States into the war.
1917	William Frederick Friedman, the father of U.S. cryptanalysis, and his wife, Elizabeth, were employed as civilian cryptanalysts by the U.S. government. Friedman later founded a school for cryptanalysis in Riverbank, Illinois.
1917	Gilbert S. Vernam, an AT&T employee, invented a polyalphabetic cipher machine using a nonrepeating random key.
1919	Hugo Alexander Koch filed a patent in the Netherlands for a rotor-based cipher machine; in 1927, Koch assigned the patent rights to Arthur Scherbius, the inventor of the Enigma Machine, which was a mechanical substitution cipher.
1927-33	During prohibition, criminal cryptography was born.
1937	The Japanese developed the Purple machine, which was based on principles of the Engima and used telephone-stepping relays to electrically encrypt diplomatic messages; by late 1940, a team headed by William Friedman broke the code generated by this machine and constructed a machine that could automatically decode Purple's ciphers.
1939-42	The fact that the Allies secretly broke the Enigma undoubtedly shortened World War II.

TABLE A-1	History of Cryptography (continued)
1942	Navajo windtalkers entered World War II; in addition to speaking a language that was unknown outside a relatively small group within the United States, the Navajos developed code words for subjects and ideas that did not exist in their native tongue.
1948	Claude Shannon suggested using frequency and statistical analysis in the solution of substitution ciphers.
1970	Dr. Horst Feistel lead an IBM research team in the development of the Lucifer cipher.
1976	A design based upon Lucifer, chosen by the U.S. NSA as the Data Encryption Standard, found worldwide acceptance.
1976	Whitefield Diffie and Martin Hellman introduced the idea of public key cryptography.
1977	Ronald Rivest, Adi Shamir, and Leonard Adleman developed a practical public key cipher for both confidentiality and digital signatures; the RSA family of computer encryption algorithms was born.
1978	The RSA algorithm was published in the Communication of ACM.
1991	Phil Zimmermann released the first version of PGP (Pretty Good Privacy); PGP was released as freeware and became the worldwide standard for public cryptosystems.
2000	Rijndael's cipher was selected as the Advanced Encryption Standard.

Definitions

The Appendix begins with a definition of basic terms. Note that some of these terms have been covered in Chapter 8, but are repeated here for your convenience and for review.

Cryptology is the science that includes all areas of cryptography and cryptanalysis. **Cryptography** is the realm of knowledge that deals with creating methods to assure that messages are secretly sent and received. **Cryptanalysis** encompasses the methodologies to obtain information from encoded messages.

Cryptosystems are manual or computer-based systems used to **encrypt** or transform data for secure transmission and storage. Upon receipt of an encrypted message, cryptosystems are also used to perform **decryption** or decoding operations to reveal the secret message. Cryptosystems are designed to provide confidential transmission of data, authentication of sender identity, transmission integrity, and nonrepudiation services between a sender and a receiver. Steganography and cryptography are both methods that have evolved to allow secret messages to be communicated between a sender and a receiver. The goal of **steganography** is to hide the existence of a secret message. A steganographic message does not use **algorithms** (mathematical calculations) nor does it use **keys** (random and secret values placed within the algorithm to encrypt the information); instead the secret data is hidden. Methods such as invisible inks, microdots, character arrangement and selection, digital signatures, and watermarks allow a sender to hide a secret message, preventing the detection of the message's existence, and thereby hiding the contents of the message. Modern steganographic techniques allow messages to be hidden in computer graphics and sound files or placed on unused space or sectors of a floppy disk or hard drive. The Technical Details box and Figure A-1 provide an example of how steganography can be used.

As noted, cryptography is the art and science of rendering a message unintelligible and meaningless to all except the intended recipients. As with steganography, the goal of cryptography is to protect meaning, but with cryptography the presence of a secret message is not concealed. **Plaintext** or **cleartext** is the original message that is encoded to protect the contents. It may be in a human-readable form, such as a diplomatic memo. The plaintext can also be used as input to a computer program that yields a document, such as a letter, memorandum, report, or spreadsheet. **Ciphertext** is formed when the plaintext data is encrypted and can only be read by individuals possessing both the decrypting algorithm and the **key**. The **cipher** or **cryptographic algorithm** forms the basic unit of the ciphertext; it is a mathematical function that is used for the encrypting and decrypting of the plaintext. The key provides the randomization variable to allow for separate communications sessions to be established for each message using the same cipher algorithm. **Codes** or **code words** consist of distinct words or phrases replacing other words or phrases within the original plaintext syntax prior to encryption.

TECHNICAL DETAILS

Steganography

Adapted from: "How it Works" [1]
By Russell Kay, *ComputerWorld Online,* **June 10, 2002**

Location A in Figure A-1 shows the 24 bits that make up a solitary pixel in a graphical image. Each image consists of a combination of red, green, and blue color bytes, to create 256 different color values per color, resulting in over 16.7 million color combinations.

Location B in Figure A-1 shows the message to be encoded via steganography–the word "Aha!" This word requires four 8-bit bytes (32 bits). To hide this message, a number of pixels in the selected graphical image would be altered. For this to carry data, both the sender and receiver must know which pixels are being used. The bits on the far right of each byte, the least important bits, are used.

Location C in the Figure A-1 shows the modified bits behind the 11 pixels. The result is an undetectable message that uses 32 of the available 264 bits. Because of the coincidence that some bits already contained the desired value, of the 264 bits and 11 pixels used, only 15 bits and eight pixels were modified.

continued

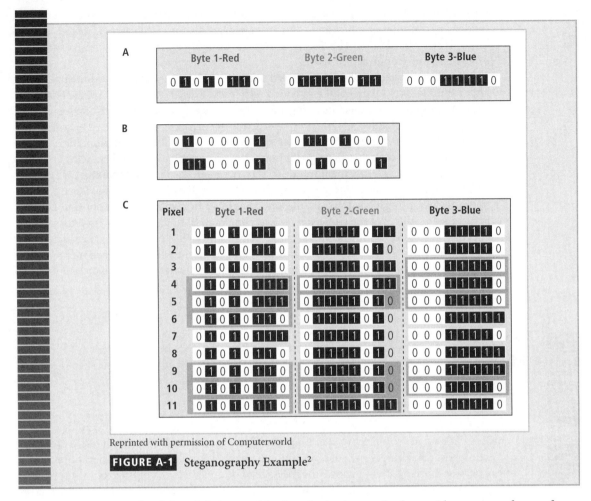

Reprinted with permission of Computerworld

FIGURE A-1 Steganography Example[2]

The **cipher alphabet** used in the substitution methods provides a cross-reference for each letter, number, and symbol used in the encoding algorithm. To increase the effectiveness and security of an enciphered text, homophones and nulls may be employed. **Homophones** are alternate letters or letter combinations that may be used for the same plaintext letter or letter combinations to add complexity without changing meaning. Examples of this are the letters "c" and "k" being freely substituted for each other and letter combination substitutions like "i" for "eye" or "ur" for "you are." **Nulls** have no meaning and are often removed in the cipher text to add to the complexity of decoding when the algorithms and keys are unknown. Additionally, multiple-cipher alphabetic systems **(polyalphabetic)** may be used to increase the security above that of a single alphabetic **(monoalphabetic)** system. The ciphertext is **decoded** or **deciphered** by the person who knows the algorithm and the correct key to reverse the process of encryption.

Hash functions are mathematical algorithms that generate a message summary or **message digest** that allows a **hash algorithm** to confirm that the content of a specific message has not been altered.

Today most cryptographic algorithms can be grouped into two broad categories: symmetric and asymmetric. **Symmetric ciphers** use the same key for both the encryption and decryption of plaintext; in contrast, **asymmetric ciphers** use unlike (but related) keys for each operation.

Types of Ciphers

As noted, encryption methods have historically been divided into two categories: substitution and transposition ciphers. In **substitution**, the letters, numbers, and symbols are replaced by other letters, numbers, or symbols. In each case, however, both the sender and receiver must possess knowledge of the algorithm and identical keys to decrypt the encoded messages. The oldest known substitution cipher is the Caesar cipher, which is attributed to the Roman general Julius Caesar. Any cipher that achieves a ciphertext through a shift of a cryptoalphabet is generically referred to as a **Caesar cipher**.

Today substitution ciphers are classified as either monoalphabetic or polyalphabetic. As the name implies, a monoalphabetic substitution cipher is achieved by mapping the plaintext to one replacement scheme. Monoalphabetic ciphers are highly insecure in practice, as they are relatively easy to break by brute force attacks. Viewed from current perspectives, they are methods for scrambling meaning as opposed to methods for concealing meaning. Here is an example of a substitution encryption:

Plaintext alphabet:

a b c d e f g h i j k l m n o p q r s t u v w x y z

Cipher alphabet:

w d j n t r p v z u m e c y f s l g q x h a b i k o

Plaintext:	Call home
Ciphertext:	jwee vfct

Polyalphabetic Substitution Ciphers

Polyalphabetic substitution ciphers increase the complexity of decipherment by using multiple alphabets for the encryption. In a polyalphabetic encryption, the plaintext is enciphered by using several cryptoalphabets and rules agreed on for switching between the alphabets. One of the most common polyalphabetic substitution ciphers is the Standard Vigenère, which uses an array of 26 by 26 cells, as illustrated in Table A-2.

TABLE A-2 Standard Vigenère Table

A	B	C	D	E	F	G	H	I	J	K	L	M	N	O	P	Q	R	S	T	U	V	W	X	Y	Z
B	C	D	E	F	G	H	I	J	K	L	M	N	O	P	Q	R	S	T	U	V	W	X	Y	Z	A
C	D	E	F	G	H	I	J	K	L	M	N	O	P	Q	R	S	T	U	V	W	X	Y	Z	A	B
D	E	F	G	H	I	J	K	L	M	N	O	P	Q	R	S	T	U	V	W	X	Y	Z	A	B	C
…	…	…	…	…	…	…	…	…	…	…	…	…	…	…	…	…	…	…	…	…	…	…	…	…	…
Z	A	B	C	D	E	F	G	H	I	J	K	L	M	N	O	P	Q	R	S	T	U	V	W	X	Y

Several variants of the Standard Vigenère encryption include: Beaufort, Variant Vigenère, and Vigenère with unordered alphabets. In a Standard Vigenère encryption, the participants agree on a keyword, e.g., "FORTUNE." The letters of the plaintext are written below the repeated keyword:

Keyword: FORTUNEFORT
Plaintext: MEETMEATSIX

The plaintext letters are assigned to the first row, and the keyword letters are assigned to the far left column of the 26 by 26 array. The intersection of the plaintext row and key-word column gives each individual encrypted letter.

Keyword: FORTUNEFORT
Plaintext: MEETMEATSIX
Ciphertext: RSVMGREYGZQ

To decrypt the message, copy the letters of the keyword above the encrypted message. Each letter of the keyword indicates the row of the encrypted letter. After the encrypted letter has been located within the correct keyletter row, the top row in letter position gives the decrypted letter.

Famous polyalphabetic cryptosystems include the Enigma and Purple used by the German and Japanese military, respectively, during World War II.

Transposition Ciphers

In **transposition** cryptosystems, the characters of the plaintext are shifted by following a predefined algorithm and key. Classical transposition or permutation ciphers hide the text message by rearrangement of letter order. The Skytale used by the Spartans is an example. While transposition cryptosystems have increased in complexity, their ease of decryption renders them unreliable for secure communications.

Transposition Example:
Plaintext: Call home
Ciphertext: lacl eohm

Both simple substitution and transposition cryptosystems are vulnerable to attacks that use **frequency analysis**. Effective cryptosystems must use algorithms that mask the patterns of plaintext to prevent key decryption. Modern cryptosystems employ a combination of polyalphabetic substitution and transposition encryption to develop algorithms that produce ciphertext that is more robust and complex and does not yield itself as readily to attacks using frequency analysis.

Hash Functions

Hash functions are mathematical algorithms that generate a message summary or digest (sometimes called a fingerprint) to confirm the identity of a specific message and to confirm that there have not been any changes to the content. While not directly related to the creation of a cipher text, hash functions are used in confirmation of message identity and integrity, both of which are critical functions in e-commerce.

Hash algorithms are publicly known functions that create a message digest by the conversion of variable-length strings into a single fixed-length value. The **message digest** creates a fingerprint of the author's message to compare with the receiver's hash of the same message. If both hashes are equal after transmission, the message has arrived without modification; hash functions are therefore considered one-way operations. Each participant of the communication uses the same hash function to create a message digest from the same message. The security lies in the determination of an equal hash value (message digest) by the recipient. Unlike ciphertext, there is no decryption process involved, only a determination that the message digests are identical. Hashing functions occur without the use of keys. Each participant has a copy of the publicly available hash algorithm to establish and prove message integrity. However, a message authentication code (MAC), which is a key-dependent, one-way hash function, may be attached to the message to allow only specific recipients to access the message digest. The MAC is essentially a one-way hash value that is encrypted with a symmetric key. The recipients must posses the key to access the message digest and to confirm message integrity.

Because hash functions are one-way, they are used in password verification systems to confirm the identity of the user. A hash value is calculated based upon the originally issued password, and this message digest is stored for later comparison. When the user logs on for the next session, the system calculates a hash value based on the user's inputted password. The newly calculated hash value is compared against the stored value to confirm identity.

The NIST (FIPS 180-1) **Secure Hash Standard (SHS)** specifies SHA-1 (Secure Hash Algorithm 1) as a secure algorithm for computing a condensed representation of a message or data file. (NIST stands for the National Institute of Standard and Technology.) SHA-1 produces a 160-bit message digest, which can then be used as an input to a digital signature algorithm. SHA-1 is based on principles modeled after MD4. (The MDx family of hash functions was created by Ronald Rivest.) New hash algorithms (SHA-256, SHA-384, and SHA-512) have been proposed by NIST as standards for 128, 192, and 256 bits, respectively, of security against collision attacks.

SHA-256 is a 256-bit hash designed to provide 128 bits of security against collision attacks. Under SHA-256, similar to SHA-1, the message to be hashed is:

1. Padded so that the result is a multiple of 512 bits
2. Parsed into 512-bit message blocks

Each message block is compressed one at a time in a sequential manner. SHA-256 is essentially a 256-bit block cipher algorithm, creating a key by encrypting the intermediate hash value with the message block functioning as the key. The compression function operates on each 512-bit message block and a 256-bit intermediate message digest. [3]

Cryptographic Algorithms

Today most cryptographic algorithms can be grouped into two broad categories: symmetric and asymmetric. In practice, most popular cryptosystems use a hybrid combination of symmetric and asymmetric algorithms. Symmetric and asymmetric algorithms can be distinguished by the types of keys used for encryption and decryption operations. Symmetric ciphers use a single key for both the encryption and decryption of plaintext, and asymmetric ciphers do not.

The security of encrypted data is not a consequence of keeping the encrypting algorithm secret; algorithms should be published to allow for research to uncover weaknesses. Effective security is maintained through the size (bit length) of the keys as well as by maintaining proper procedures and policies on key distribution.

Symmetric or Private Key Cryptography

Symmetric cryptography, sometimes called private key cryptography, is built on symmetric encryption and uses a single key for both the encryption and decryption of data. Each participant in the secure communication must posses his or her own set of the identical keys. Secure communication can be accomplished over insecure channels with a symmetric cryptosystem. Because the symmetric encoding and decoding algorithm is public, the level of security generated by a symmetric cipher depends on the key length and the system's ability to protect the key. A pseudo-random array is constructed, forming a key table, which initiates the encryption process. The key table consists of an array of pseudorandom numbers generated by the algorithm's pseudorandom number generator (PRNG). The PRNG begins the process by acquiring an input or seed. The seed can be collected from a variety of sources such as a PC's mouse movement, cursor position, date and time to the millisecond, or internally generated electrical signals coming from the thermal noise within a computer system. This process initializes the key and provides the algorithm with key values that are sufficiently long and random to ensure a satisfactory level of encryption. At the sender's end of the process, the encryption algorithm uses the key values taken from the key table to encode the plaintext into a ciphertext and then, at the recipient's end of the process, to decode the ciphertext back into a cleartext message.[4] This process is illustrated in Figure A-2, which shows plaintext that is encrypted to produce a ciphertext and communicated to the recipient where it is decrypted using another copy of the same key.

Symmetric ciphers are widely used because they tend to be faster when enciphering large amounts of data and can be executed efficiently. There are two basic types of symmetric cipher algorithms in use today: block and stream.

Symmetric Block Ciphers. The algorithms of **symmetric block ciphers** encrypt data in blocks of bytes, rather than a single byte at a time. The algorithm breaks the plaintext into independent blocks of 8 – 16 bytes and encrypts each block independently. The plaintext message is padded to complete the block size, so that all blocks are of equal byte size. The decryption algorithm must recognize that padding has occurred to successfully decrypt the ciphertext. Block algorithms tend to be slower than stream ciphers, but they are somewhat more secure.

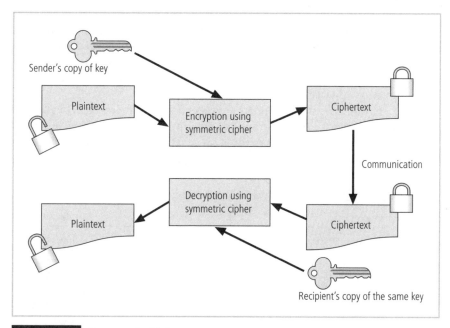

FIGURE A-2 Symmetric Cipher

If the same block of plaintext data appears in two separate places, it is encrypted into the same ciphertext. In **Electronic Code book (ECB)** mode, each plaintext block is encrypted independently. ECB does not eliminate the possibility of identical blocks of plaintext encrypting into identical blocks of ciphertext. **Cipher Block Chaining (CBC)** mode was designed with a feedback loop to eliminate duplicate blocks of ciphertext making the message vulnerable to a possible attack. In CBC mode, each plaintext block is XOR'ed with the previous ciphertext block before further encryption occurs. After a block of plaintext is encrypted, the resulting ciphertext is stored in a feedback buffer. Before the next block of plaintext is encrypted, it is XOR'ed with the content of the feedback buffer. The result is a ciphertext in which any given block of encrypted text depends not only on the plaintext for that block and on the key value used as input, but also on the text content of all the previous plaintext blocks in the original plaintext document. This ensures that all plaintext containing identical blocks is encrypted differently and the resulting ciphers are more secure. The encrypted cipher is again stored and the cycle is repeated. As with standard block algorithms, the last block of plaintext is padded, if required, to make the block size even. This process assures that any patterns in the plaintext are concealed and eliminates the possibility of duplicate blocks of ciphertext. **Cipher feedback mode (CFB)** and **output feedback mode (OFB)** are further refinements to block the cipher encryption process using modified XOR functions with the plaintext.

Symmetric Stream Ciphers. Symmetric stream ciphers **(stream cipher algorithms)** operate on smaller units of plaintext, usually bits. The ciphertext is always the same size as the original plaintext; however, because they use smaller units of the plaintext, ciphertext duplication does not occur. The stream cipher algorithm generates a key stream—a sequence of bits to be used as the keys. Encryption occurs when the plaintext is XOR'ed with the randomly generated keystream. To increase security, the keystream generation can be isolated and independent from the plaintext and ciphertext. Effective stream ciphers are an approximation of the action of one-time pad cryptosystems. A **one-time pad cryptosystem** uses a string of pseudo-randomly generated bits that are combined with the plaintext, generating a theoretically high level of security. The keystream is a practical application of the one-time pad concept.

Symmetric stream ciphers are faster and require less code but are not as generally secure as block ciphers. Symmetric encryptions can be attacked by analyzing the random bit generator, because the random bit generator must be repeatable to allow the recipient to decipher the ciphertext. Table A-3 compares block and stream ciphers.

TABLE A-3   Block and Stream Cipher Comparisons

Characteristic	Block	Stream
Encryption speed	Slower	Faster
Lines of code	Fewer lines	More lines
Encryption keys	Reusable	One time use
Interoperability	Standard algorithms: AES, DES, Triple DES RC2, RC5, IDEA, Blowfish, and Rijndael	Nonstandard algorithm: RC4

Asymmetric Cryptography or Public Key Cryptography

Asymmetric cryptography uses a key pair, consisting of a public key and private (secret) key. The public key encrypts, but cannot decrypt. Asymmetric encryption is popular because one of the keys can be published and widely distributed, thereby allowing anyone to use another's public key to encrypt data; however, only the person with the corresponding private key can decrypt the data. This makes encrypted data secure, as long as the private keys remain secure. Although the keys are related mathematically, it is very difficult to calculate the private key by knowing the public key. RSA (Rivest-Shamir-Adleman) is the most commonly used asymmetric cryptosystem.

The public and private keys for the RSA algorithm are in two parts. The first part, or modulus, is a 512-bit number (64 bytes) that is the product of two 256-bit secret primes, and it is the same for both the public and private key. The second part, the exponent, is a number of variable length. The exponent of the public key is usually the smaller of the two; however, the exponents are related mathematically. In RSA the plaintext (viewed as a binary number) is raised to the power of the public exponent and the result is divided by the modulus. The remainder is the ciphertext. For decryption, the ciphertext is raised to the power of the private exponent and then divided by the modulus; the remainder gives the plaintext values. Asymmetric cryptosystems, such RSA, operate at a slower rate than symmetric systems but provide easier and more manageable key distribution and maintenance. [5] Table A-4 lists some of the various symmetric and asymmetric algorithms.

TABLE A-4	Symmetric and Asymmetric Algorithms	
Symmetric algorithms	**Asymmetric algorithms**
DES, Triple DES	RSA
RC2, RC4, RC5	PGP
IDEA	
Blowfish	
Rijndael, AES	

The flow of the plaintext, keys, and ciphertext is shown in Figure A-3. In the figure, the plaintext is encrypted using the recipient's public key. The resulting ciphertext is transmitted to the receiver, who uses his private key to decrypt the message. If the integrity of the keys has been maintained, the sender can be assured that the message can be read only by the specified receiver.

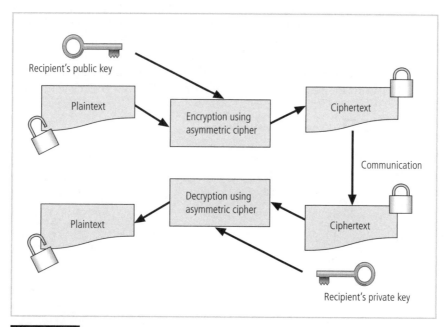

 **FIGURE A-3** Asymmetric Cipher

Hybrid Cryptosystems

To increase the security of communications, a combination of symmetric and asymmetric algorithms is often employed. A symmetric encryption algorithm is used to encrypt the main body of plaintext, and then the symmetric key (private) is encrypted using the stronger but slower public key (asymmetric) process. This encrypted public key can then be securely included within the body of the ciphertext. Decryption allows the retrieval of the asymmetrical key as well as the symmetrically encrypted plaintext message. Hybrid cryptosystems are beneficial because they provide faster encryption for the bulk of the data to be encrypted as well as strong encryption of the enclosed key. This process has the additional benefit of a digital signature that cannot be repudiated.

Popular Cryptographic Algorithms

The pages that follow include a description and some simple examples of the most popular encryption algorithms in use in current cryptographic products.

Data Encryption Standard (DES)

IBM's Lucifer algorithm, which was originally based on a key length of 128-bits, was modified to a key length of 56-bits, renamed **Data Encryption Standard (DES)**, and adopted in 1976 by NIST as a federal standard for encryption of nonclassified information. With the official approval of NIST, DES became widely employed as the encryption standard. However, by 1997 it was realized that a 56-bit key was insufficient to maintain an acceptable level of secure communications. In 1998, using a specially designed computer, the Electronic Frontier Foundation broke DES in less than three days. It has been theoretically determined that a dedicated attack supported by the proper hardware can break a DES key in less than four hours.

DES encrypts and decrypts data in 64-bit blocks, and the parity bits are ignored, producing an effective key length of 56 bits. Decryption uses the same the key as encryption with reversed key scheduling. A 64-bit block of plaintext is encrypted into a 64-bit block of ciphertext, as the DES algorithm executes 16 times. Key scheduling, the initial step, is accomplished by passing the 64-bit key through the Permuted Choice 1 (PC-1) table, as shown in Table A-5.

TABLE A-5 PC-1: Permuted Choice 1[6]

Bit	0	1	2	3	4	5	6
1	57	49	41	33	25	17	9
8	1	58	50	42	34	26	18
15	10	2	59	51	43	35	27
22	19	11	3	60	52	44	36
29	63	55	47	39	31	23	15
36	7	62	54	46	38	30	22
43	14	6	61	53	45	37	29
50	21	13	5	28	20	12	4

To determine the new 56-bit key, locate each byte value in Table A-5 and add the row and column headers together:

EX: Value of byte in original 64-bit key = 13
13 is located in row (50) and column (1)
New key: 1 + 50 = 51

With the new 56-bit key, the next step is to generate sixteen 48-bit subkeys (K), using a fixed subkey rotation table, as shown in Table A-6, and a PC-2 table, as shown in Table A-7. Both are used in each of the 16 rounds of the DES algorithm. Beginning with T1 (round 1), divide the current 56-bit key into two 28-bit blocks Left (L(i)) and Right (R(i)). Rotate L(i) and R(i) by the number of bits specified in the subkey rotation table, using 1 for round 1

(T1) and so on. L(i) joined to R(i) forms **k**, which when permuted by PC-2 forms the new *K*. Continue through subsequent rounds until all 16 subkeys K(1 –16) have been created.[7]

TABLE A-6 Subkey Rotation[8]

Round number	1	2	3	4	5	6	7	8	9	10	11	12	13	14	15	16
Number of bits to rotate	1	1	2	2	2	2	2	2	1	2	2	2	2	2	2	1

TABLE A-7 PC-2: Permuted Choice 2[9]

Bit	0	1	2	3	4	5
1	14	17	11	24	1	5
7	3	28	15	6	21	10
13	23	19	12	4	26	8
19	16	7	27	20	13	2
25	41	52	31	37	47	55
31	30	40	51	45	33	48
37	44	49	39	56	34	53
43	46	42	50	36	29	32

A plaintext block to be enciphered is initially permutated through the initial permutation table (IP). The plaintext byte is located within the IP table, of which column and row headings are summed to give permutation. A complex key-dependent computation is completed, which is converted into a permutation. This permutation is the inverse of the initial permutation (IP-1). The cipher function, F, is a result of the key-dependent computation and the key schedule KS. The generation of the permuted plaintext is similar to the creation of the 56-bit key. The actual encryption or decryption is performed by the main DES algorithm beginning with the input of a 64-bit block of data, which is divided into two 32-bits halves, Left (L) and Right (R). The process is repeated 16 times during standard DES encryption process, as illustrated in Figures A-4 and A-5.

The 64 bits of the input block are subjected to the initial permutation (IP). This permuted block is then used as an input into the key-dependent algorithm forming the pre-output. The pre-output is then permuted as the inverse of the initial permutation.

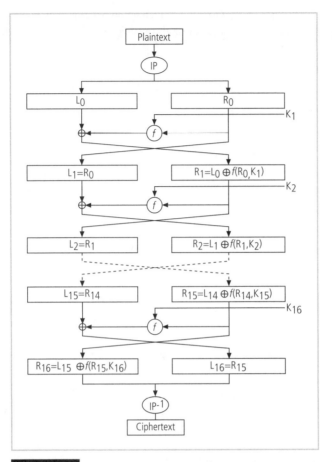

FIGURE A-4 Flow of Enciphering of DES Computation Algorithm[10]

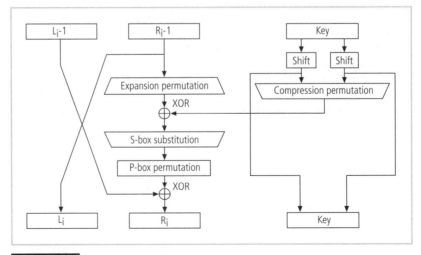

FIGURE A-5 Round 1 of DES[11]

Data Encryption Core Process

The inverse initial permutation (IP-1) is now applied to the pre-output of the DES algorithm completing the encryption process. Figure A-6 show the inverse initial permutation process used in DES. Decrypting the ciphertext uses a similar process modified so that the subkeys are applied in reverse order.

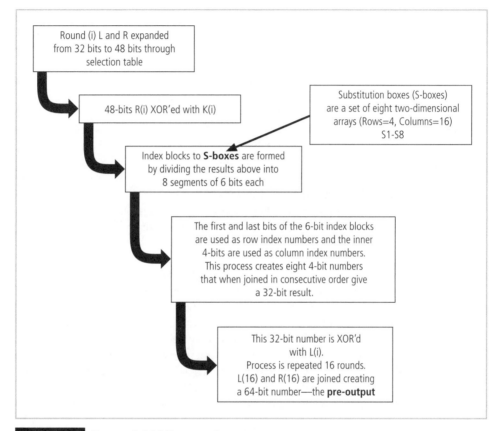

FIGURE A-6 Inverse Initial Permutation

Four modes of operation are available with DES: electronic code book (ECB) and cipher block chaining (CBC) are block processing modes. Cipher feedback (CFB), and output feedback (OFB) are stream-processing modes. Table A-8 compares the various DES options.

TABLE A-8 DES Modes

Mode	Characteristic	Advantage	Disadvantage
Electronic code book	Message broken into independently encrypted blocks	Useful when sending and encrypting a few blocks at a time	Repetitions in plaintext can be reflected in ciphertext

TABLE A-8	DES Modes (continued)		
Cipher block chaining	Message blocks linked during encryption	More secure than ECB	Initiation value must be known by both parties; errors can propagate through encryption
Cipher feedback	Message treated as a stream of bits; result is fed back for the next encryption	Very secure	Errors can propagate through encryption; slower than ECB
Output feedback	Message treated as a stream of bits; results of block cipher are added to message and then fed back for the next encryption	Used when error feedback is problematic	Less secure than CFB; sender and receiver must remain synchronized

Triple Data Encryption Standard (3DES)

Triple DES is an advanced application of the principles of DES and is designed to replace DES. As it has been demonstrated that DES is not strong enough for highly classified communications, 3DES was created to provide a level of security far beyond standard DES. There was a 2DES; however, it was statistically shown that the double DES did not provide significantly stronger security than DES. 3DES takes three 64-bit keys for an overall key length of 192 bits. Triple DES encryption is the same as standard DES; however, it is repeated three times. Triple DES can be employed using two or three keys, and a combination of encryption or decryption to obtain additional security. The most common implementations are to encrypt with two different keys, E[K1],E[K2],E[K1]; three different keys, E[K1],E[K2],E[K3]; and to encrypt and decrypt with either two keys E[K1],D[K2],E[K1] or three keys E[K1],D[K2],E[K3]. 3DES employs 48 rounds in its encryption computation, generating ciphers that are approximately 2^{56} stronger than standard DES while requiring only three times longer to process.

Advanced Encryption Standard (AES)

AES is a Federal Information Processing Standard (FIPS) that specifies a cryptographic algorithm for use within the U.S. government to protect unclassified information. Requirements for AES stipulate that the algorithm is unclassified, publicly disclosed, and available royalty-free worldwide. AES has been developed to replace DES, which has been repeatedly compromised, although 3DES remains an approved algorithm. Historically, cryptographic standards approved by FIPS have been adopted on a voluntary basis by organizations outside government entities. The AES selection process involved cooperation between the U.S. government, private industry, and academia from around the world. MARS, RC6, Rijndael, Serpent, and Twofish were selected as the five finalists for AES consideration from the worldwide submissions. On October 2, 2000, NIST announced the selection of Rijndael as the finalist to propose the AES. AES was approved by the Secretary of Commerce as the official federal governmental standard as of May 26, 2002. Rijndael is now being adopted worldwide as the standard for symmetric key cryptology.

RSA is a public key encryption technique published in 1977 by Ronald **R**ivest, Adi **S**hamir, and Leonard **A**dleman. The patented **RSA algorithm** has become the *de facto* standard for public use encryption applications. The security of the algorithm is based on the computational difficulty of factoring large composite numbers and computing the *eth roots modulo*, a composite number for a specified odd integer *e*. The RSA algorithm has been employed in most of the Internet-driven encryption requirements. Among others, PGP (Pretty Good Privacy, which is explained in more detail below), Netscape Navigator, and Microsoft Explorer are using implementations of RSA as their encryption standard.

With public key encryption using RSA, users can send secure and verifiable messages to each other. The public key is used to encrypt the plaintext, while the private key is used to decrypt the cipher. Only one member of the key pair can encrypt and decrypt the messages. A message encrypted by the public key cannot be decrypted with the public key, thereby assuring that any unauthorized recipient cannot decipher the message, as presented in Figure 8-15.

A message can be digitally signed by the user, as illustrated in Figure 8-16, using his or her private key to encrypt the message. The recipient can then use the sender's public key to decrypt the message, thus assuring that the private key holder has sent the message. This process however, does not protect the secrecy of the message, as anyone in possession of the sender's public key can decipher the message. A sender can send a digitally signed encrypted message with public key cryptography by initially encrypting the message with the recipient's public key and then encrypting it a second time with his or her private key. The recipient then validates the digital signature by decryption with the sender's public key. The encrypted message can then be deciphered with the recipient's private key.

Encryption in RSA is accomplished by raising the message M to a nonnegative integer power e. The product is then divided by the nonnegative modulus n (n should have a bit length of at least 1024 bits), and the remainder is the ciphertext C. This process results in one-way operation when n is a very large number.

$C = M^e \bmod n$

In the decryption process, the ciphertext C is raised to the power d, a nonnegative integer, as follows:

$d = e^{-1} \bmod ((p\text{-}1)(q\text{-}1))$

C is then reduced modulo n. In order for the recipient to calculate the decryption key, the p and q factors must be known. The modulus n, which is a composite number, is determined by multiplying two large nonnegative prime numbers, p and q:

$n = p \times q$

Essentially the RSA algorithm can be divided into three steps:

1. *Key generation*: Prime factors p and q are statistically selected by a technique known as probabilistic primality testing and then multiplied together to form n. The encryption exponent e is selected, and the decryption exponent d is calculated.
2. *Encryption*: M is raised to the power of e, reduced by modulo n, and remainder C is the cipher text.
3. *Decryption*: C is raised to the power of d and reduced by modulo n.

The sender publishes the public key, which consists of modulus n and exponent e. The remaining variables; d, p, and q are kept secret.

A message can then be encrypted by: $\quad$ C= M^e(recipient) mod n(recipient)

Digitally signed by: $\quad$ C'= M'^{d}(sender) mod n(sender)

Verified by: $\quad$ M' = C'^{e}(sender) mod n(sender)

Decrypted by: $\quad$ M = C^d(recipient) mod n(recipient)

Example Problems

As this appendix presents complex information, the following sections contain practice examples to help you better understand the machinations of the various algorithms.

RSA Algorithm Example: [12] Work through the following steps to better understand how the RSA algorithm functions.

1. Choose randomly two large prime numbers: P, Q (usually P, Q > 10^100) → This means 10 to the power 100.
2. Compute:

   N = P × Q

   Z = (P – 1)(Q – 1)
3. Choose a number relatively prime with Z and call it D.

   D < N ; relatively prime means that D and Z have *no* common factors, except 1.
4. Find number E, such that → E × D = 1 mod Z
5. The public key is: (N, E); the private Key is (N, D).
6. Create Cipher (Encrypted Text):

   C= | TEXT |^E (MOD N)

   C → Encrypted text → this is the text that's transmitted

   | TEXT | → Plain Text to be encrypted (its numerical correspondent)
7. Decrypt the message:

   D= Plaintext= C^D (MOD N), C=Cipher text from part 6.

   Note that it is almost impossible to obtain the private key, knowing the public key, and it's almost impossible to factor N into P and Q.

RSA Numerical Example: [13] Work through the following steps to better understand RSA Numericals:

1. Choose P=3, Q=11 (two prime numbers). Note that small numbers have been chosen for the example, so that you can easily work with them. In real life encryption, they are larger than 10^100.
2. N = P × Q = 3 × 11 = 33; Z=(P-1)(Q-1)=2 × 10 =20
3. Choose a number for D that is relatively prime with Z, for example, D=7 → (20 and 7 have no common divisors, except 1).
4. E=? such as E × D = 1 MOD Z (1 MOD Z means that the remainder of E/D division is 1).

   E × D / Z → E × 7 / 20 → **E=3**

   Check E × D / Z → 3 × 7 / 20 → 21/20 → Remainder = **1**
5. So, the public key is (N,E) = (33,3) →This key will be used to encrypt the message. The private key is (N,D) = (33,7) →This key will be used to decrypt the message.

English Alphabet and Corresponding Numbers for Each Letter: [14] In real life applications the ASCII code is used to represent each of the characters. Here, the position of the letter in the alphabet is used instead to simplify the calculations.

A= 01 ; B= 02 ; C= 03 ; D= 04 ; E= 05 ; F= 06 ; G= 07 ; H =08 ; I= 09 ; J 10

K=11 ; L=12 ; M=13 ; N=14 ; O=15 ; P=16 ; Q=17 ; R=18 ; S=19 ; T=20

U =21 ; V =22 ; W= 23 ; X =24 ; Y =25 ; Z =26

Encrypt The Word "Technology": [15] Now you can use the numerical values from the previous examples and the previous calculations to calculate values for the public key (N,E)= (33,3) and the private key (N,D)=(33,7):

TABLE A-9 Encryption

Plain text	Text value	(Text)^E	(Text)^E MOD N = Cipher
T	20	8000	8000 MOD 33 = 14
E	05	125	125 MOD 33 = 26
C	03	27	27 MOD 33 = 27
H	08	512	512 MOD 33 = 17
N	14	2744	2744 MOD 33 = 05
O	15	3375	3375 MOD 33 = 09
L	12	1728	1728 MOD 33 = 12
O	15	3375	3375 MOD 33 = 09
G	07	343	343 MOD 33 = 13
Y	25	15625	15625 MOD 33 = 16

So, the cipher (encrypted message) is: 14262717050912091316 → This is what is transmitted over unreliable lines. Note that there are two digits per letter.

TABLE A-10 Encryption

Cipher	(Cipher)^D	(Cipher)^D MOD N = |Text|	Plain Text
14	105413504	105413504 MOD 33 = 20	T
26	8031810176	8031810176 MOD 33 = 05	E
27	10460353203	10460353203 MOD 33 = 03	C
17	410338673	410338673 MOD 33 = 08	H
05	78125	78125 MOD 33 = 14	N
09	4782969	4782969 MOD 33 = 15	O
12	35831808	35831808 MOD 33 = 12	L
09	4782969	4782969 MOD 33 = 15	O
13	62748517	62748517 MOD 33 = 07	G
16	268435456	268435456 MOD 33 = 25	Y

Note that although very small P and Q numbers were used, as you can see in Table A-10, the numbers required for decrypting the message are relatively large. Now you have a good idea of what kind of numbers are needed when P and Q are large (for example 10^{100} numbers long).

So if P and Q are not big enough for the cipher to be secure, P and Q must be increased. The strength of this encryption algorithm relies on how difficult it is to factor P and Q from N, if N is known. If not, it's even harder to break.

Since the introduction of RSA, several extensions and enhancements have been added including RSAES-OAEP (RSA Encryption Scheme – Optimal Asymmetric Encryption Padding) and RSASSA-PSS (RSA Signature Scheme with Appendix – Probablilistic Signature Scheme). RSAES-OAEP is a public key encryption method combining the RSA algorithm with the OAEP method. **OAEP** is an encoding method that uses a randomly generated seed, message padding, and two mask-generation functions. RSASSA-PSS is a RSA algorithm-signing scheme using one RSA decryption and hashing, while verification occurs using one RSA encryption with hashing, which produces a signature the size of the modulus. [16]

Public Key Infrastructure (PKI)

Public Key Infrastructure is an integrated structure of software, encryption methodologies, protocols, legal agreements, and third-party services that enable users to securely communicate across the insecure Internet. Third-party suppliers integrate public key cryptography, digital certificates, and certification authority into an enterprise-wide solution to provide authenticated and secure communications between participants.

A typical PKI solution protects the transmission and reception of secure information by integrating the following components:

- A **certificate authority (CA)** that issues, manages, authenticates, signs and revokes a digital certificate containing the user's name, public key, and other identifying information.

- A **registration authority (RA)** that operates under the trusted collaboration of the certificate authority and can be delegated day-to-day certification functions, such as verifying registration information about new registrants, generating end-user keys, revoking certificates, and validating that users possess a valid certificate.

- **Certificate directories** are central locations for certificate storage, providing a single access point for administration and distribution.

- **Management protocols** organize and manage the communications between CAs, RAs, and end users. This includes the functions and procedures to register and initialize new users, recover, update and revoke keys, as well as enable the transfer of certificates and status information among the parties involved in a PKI trust.

- **Policies and procedures** assist an organization in the application and management of certificates, formalization of the legal liabilities and limitations, and actual business practice use.

The certification authority (CA) manages the critical function of establishing a trust relationship with an end user to generate and maintain a valid certificate. The CA is used in the organization to manage the issuance, update, and revocation of certificates, which are electronic containers for the key values needed for the use of a cryptosystem. The CA manages the housekeeping details of tracking who has been assigned which key, providing a directory of public key values for use across the organization, assisting users in safeguarding their private keys, and helping the organization manage common workplace events that could threaten the safety of keys in use. If the trust relationship is broken, such as when a private key has been compromised or the key holder no longer has authority to manage the key, the certificate may be revoked. The CA periodically distributes a certificate revocation list (CRL), which contains a signed time-stamped listing of all revoked certificates. The CA's users can then check against the most recent CRL to determine which, if any, certificates have been revoked.

Key pairs provide encryption and nonrepudiation required for secure e-business transactions. The key pair can be generated either by the end user or by the CA (or designated RA). A key pair generated by the end user can provide nonrepudiation; however, encryption and transport to a CA may reduce the level of security. A central system operated by a CA or RA can generate cryptographically strong keys that can be independently trusted and can provide private key backup and recovery as well.

The strength of a cryptosystem relies on both the raw strength of the key complexity and quality of the overall key management security processes. PKI solutions can provide several mechanisms to limit access and possible exposure of the private keys. These mechanisms include password protection, smart cards, hardware tokens, and other hardware-based, key storage devices that are memory capable (like PC cards). PKI users should select the key security mechanisms that can provide an appropriate level of key protection. Managing the security and integrity of private keys used for nonrepudiation or the encryption of data files is a critical activity for all members of the trust network. [17]

Digital Signatures

Digital signatures based on the Digital Signature Standard (DSS) have been approved and endorsed by state, federal, and several international governments to authenticate the author of an electronic document. NIST has approved three algorithms for generating and verifying digital signatures: DSA, RSA, and **ECDSA (Elliptic Curve Digital Signature Algorithm)** when used in conjunction with the Secure Hash Standard, which was described earlier. The DSS approach uses a hash function to create a message digest, which is then input into the digital signature algorithm along with a random number to generate a digital signature. The digital signature function also depends upon the sender's private key and a set of parameters provided by the CA. The encrypted message containing the digital signature is then verified by the recipient by using the sender's public key.

Digital Certificates

Digital certificates are electronic documents issued by a reputable third party that certify the identity of a user and the proof of identification associated with the presentation of a public key. In contrast to digital signatures, which help authenticate the origin of a message, digital certificates authenticate the company that provides the verification of the authenticity of the digital signature, much as the Federal Deposit Insurance Corporation helps assure individual bank customers that the bank is official. Time and date stamps may be included, as a CA validates the identity of a certificate requestor, issues the electronic certificate, and certifies to recipients that the entity presenting the certificate is in fact who it claims to be. Different types of certificates are in use to assure authentication in client-server applications:

- CA certificates identify and establish a trust relationship with a CA to determine what additional certificates can be authenticated.
- Secure/Multipurpose Internet Mail Extension (S/MIME) certificates are used for signed and encrypted e-mail as well as for form signing. These certificates are part of a single sign-on solution. (S/MIME is explained in detail later in this appendix.)
- Object-signing certificates are used to identify signers of object-oriented code and scripts.
- Server SSL certificates for are used to authenticate servers via SSL in order to establish an encrypted SSL session. **SSL** is a Secure Sockets Layer protocol more fully described later in this appendix.
- Client SSL certificates are used to authenticate users, sign forms, and are part of a single sign-on solution via Secure Socket Link (SSL).

TABLE A-11   **X.509 v3 Certificate Structure**[18]

Version
Certificate serial number
Algorithm identifier   ■ Algorithm   ■ Parameters
Issuer name
Validity   ■ Not before/Not after date
Subject name
Subject Public Key Information   ■ Algorithm   ■ Parameters   ■ Key
Issuer unique identifier (optional)
Subject unique identifier (optional)
Extensions   ■ Type   ■ Criticality   ■ Value
Signature

Two popular certificates that are in use today are Pretty Good Privacy (PGP) and the International Telecommunication Union's (ITU-T) X.509 version 3. You should know that X.509 v3 is an ITU-T recommendation that essentially defines a directory service that maintains a database of information about a group of users. The directory is a repository of the public key certificates issued by the CA. An X.509 v3 certificate binds a **distinguished name (DN)**, which is a series of name-value pairs that uniquely identify a certificate entity, to a user's public key. The certificate is signed and placed in the directory by the CA for retrieval and verification by the users' associated public key. X.509 v3 does not specify an encryption algorithm; however, RSA with its hashed digital signature is recommended. Table A-11 outlines the X.509 v3 certificate structure.

Pretty Good Privacy (PGP)

Pretty Good Privacy (PGP) is a hybrid cryptosystem originally designed in 1991 by Phil Zimmermann. PGP combined some of the best available cryptographic algorithms to become the open source *de facto* standard for encryption and authentication of e-mail and file storage applications. Both freeware and low-cost commercial versions are available for a wide variety of platforms. Table A-12 provides the routines for PGP.

TABLE A-12   PGP Routines[19]

Routine	Algorithm	Application
Public key encryption	RSA/SHA or DSS/SHA	Digital signatures
Conventional encryption	3DES, RSA, IDEA or CAST	Message encryption
File management	ZIP	Compression

PGP Suite of Security Solutions

The PGP security solution provides six services: authentication by digital signatures, message encryption, compression, e-mail compatibility, segmentation, and key management.

SHA-1 is used to hash a message into a 160-bit hash code. The hash code is then encrypted with DSS or RSA and appended to the original message. The receiver uses the sender's public key to decrypt and recover the hash code. Using the same encryption algorithm, the receiver then generates a new hash from the same message, which is the comparison of the two identical hash codes that authenticates the sender.

In addition to sending a digitally signed message, the sender may want the entire contents of the message protected from unauthorized view. 3DES, IDEA, or CAST, which are all standard algorithms, may be used to encrypt the message contents with a unique, randomly generated 128-bit session key. The session key is encrypted by RSA, using the recipient's public key, and then appended to the message. The receiver uses his private key with RSA to decrypt and recover the session key. The recovered session key can now be used to decrypt the message. Authentication and message encryption can be used together by first digitally signing the message with a private key, encrypting the message with a unique session key, and then encrypting the session key with the intended recipient's public key.

PGP uses the freeware ZIP algorithm to compress the message, after it has been digitally signed but before it is encrypted. This saves space and generates a more secure encrypted document.

Radix-64 conversion assures e-mail compatibility by maintaining the required 8-bit blocks of ASCII text. The format maps three octets of data into four ASCII characters; a cyclic redundancy check (CRC) is attached to detect transmission errors.

With many Internet facilities imposing restrictions on maximum message size, PGP can automatically subdivide messages into a manageable stream size. The segmentation is completed after all other encryption and conversion functions have been processed. At the recipient end, PGP reassembles the segment's message blocks prior to decompression and decryption.

While PGP does not impose a rigid structure for public key management, several approaches are suggested. PGP can assign a level of trust within the confines of PGP, but it does not manage the trust function. Trust can be addressed and assured by using the public key ring structure. In a public key ring structure, each specific set of public key credentials is associated with a key legitimacy field, a signature trust field, and an owner trust field. These fields contain a trust-flag byte that identifies whether the credential is trusted in each of these three regards. In the event that the trust of a given credential has been broken, as when a key is compromised, the owner can issue a digitally signed key revocation certificate that updates the credential trust bytes when the credential is next verified.

Protocols for Secure Communications

Many current applications used on the Internet and within organizations are not true cryptosystems in and of themselves. Instead they rely on the addition of cryptography-based protocols to provide the needed level of security. It has been said that the Internet and its corresponding protocols were not designed with security in mind, and rather had security added afterwards. This is due, in no small part, to the lack of threats during the Internet's construction and infancy. As the level of threats grew, so did the need for additional security. You could say the growth of the Internet created the need for its own security. The following sections overview some of the key protocols used to add security to existing applications and protocols used in data communications.

S-HTTP and SSL

S-HTTP (Secure Hypertext Transfer Protocol and **SSL** (Secure Sockets Layer) are two protocols designed to enable secure communications across the Internet. S-HTTP and SSL ensure Internet security through different functionalities and can be used independently or together. S-HTTP is the application of SSL over HTTP, which allows the encryption of all information passing between two computers through a protected and secure virtual connection.

Netscape developed the SSL protocol, which uses public key encryption, to secure the channel in Internet communications. Most popular browsers, including Internet Explorer, support the implementation of SSL. In addition to providing data encryption, integrity, and server authentication, SSL when properly configured, can provide client authentication as well.

SSL provides two layers of protocol within the TCP framework. The **SSL Record Protocol** provides basic security and communication services to the top levels of the SSL protocol stack. **Standard HTTP** provides the Internet communication services between client and host. The SSL Record Protocol is responsible for the fragmentation, compression, encryption, and the attachment of a SSL header to the cleartext prior to transmission. Received encrypted messages are decrypted and reassembled for presentation to the higher levels of the protocol.

After a normal HTTP session has been established between a client and a server, and the client has accessed a portion of the Web site that requires secure communications, the server sends a message to the client indicating that a secure connection needs to be established. The client responds back by sending its public key and security parameters. The handshaking phase is completed when the server finds a public key match and responds to the client by authenticating with its digital certificate. The client must then verify that the received certificate is valid and trustworthy. The SSL session is established and maintained for the duration of the secure communication between client and server. As long as the session remains active, any amount of data can be transmitted securely. Either client or server can sever the secure connection at any time during the communication.

Secure-HTTP (S-HTTP) is an extension of the Hypertext Transfer Protocol to provide for the encryption of individual messages between a client and server across the Internet. Unlike SSL, in which a secure channel is established for the duration of the session, S-HTTP is designed to send only individual messages across the Internet; therefore each individual transmission must be preestablished. The client and server must have compatible cryptosystems and agree on the configuration. The S-HTTP client sends the server its public key to generate a session key. The session key is encrypted with the client's public key and returned to the client. The client and server now possess identical session keys, which are used to encrypt messages between the two parties. S-HTTP can provide for confidentiality, authentication, and data integrity through a variety of trust models and cryptographic algorithms. S-HTTP is designed for easy integration with existing HTTP applications and for implementation in conjunction with HTTP. The cleartext message is transmitted transparently, complete with all pertinent HTTP information within the S-HTTP wrapper.

Secure/Multipurpose Internet Mail Extension (S/MIME)

S/MIME is the second generation of enhancement to the Internet e-mail format standard STMP/ RFC 822. Initially, **MIME** was developed to address some of the shortcomings and limitations in the use of SMTP. Problems associated with SMTP/RFC 822 included the inability to transmit executable files or binary object, and the limit to the 7-bit ASCII. The MIME specification included five new message header fields, predefined content types, and conversion transfer encoding in order to resolve many of the issues with SMTP, as illustrated in Table A-13. Conversion encodings such as 7-bit, 8-bit, binary, and Radix-64 are provided to assure reliable delivery across a wide range of systems. A canonical form format is employed in both MIME and S/MIME to relate and standardize content type for use between systems.

TABLE A-13   MIME Message Header Fields[20]

Header fields	Function
MIME-version	States conformity to RFCs 2045 and 2046
Content-ID	Identifies MIME entities
Content-type	Describes data in the body of message
Content-description	Text description of the body object
Content-transfer-encoding	Type of conversion used in message body

Built on improvements to MIME, S/MIME has the additional ability to sign, encrypt, and decrypt messages. S/MIME is functionally similar to PGP and incorporates some of the same algorithms, as illustrated in Table A-14.

TABLE A-14   S/MIME Functions and Algorithms

Function	Algorithm
Hash code for digital signatures	SHA-1
Digital signatures	DSS
Encryption session keys	ElGamal (variant of Diffie-Hellman)
Digital signatures and session keys	RSA
Message encryption	3DES, RC2

Internet Protocol Security (IPSec)

IPSec is an open source protocol to secure communications across any IP-based network such as LANs, WANs, and the Internet. The protocol is designed to protect data integrity, user confidentiality, and authenticity at the IP packet level. IP layer security is obtained by application of an **AH (application header)** or an **ESP (encapsulating security payload)** protocol. A security association which contains the encryption and authentication keys, algorithms, and key lifetimes can implement either the AH or the ESP protocol, but not both. If the security functions of both the AH and ESP are required, multiple security associations must be bundled to provide the correct sequence through which the IP traffic must be processed, delivering the desired security features.

The authentication header protocol is designed to provide data integrity and authentication of IP packets. Although confidentiality protection is not provided by AH, IP packets are protected from replay attacks and address spoofing as well as other types of cyberattacks against open networks. Figure A-7 provides insight into the packet format of the IPSec authentication header protocol. IPSec authentication service can be employed in either a transport mode or in a tunnel mode. In transport mode, under IPv4, the AH is placed after the IP header and before the TCP segment, whereas under IPv6, the AH is placed after the hop-by-hop, routing, and fragmentation headers. In either case, IPv4 or IPv6, authentication secures the entire packet, excluding mutable fields in the new IP header. In tunnel mode, however, the entire inner IP packet is secured by the authentication header protocol.

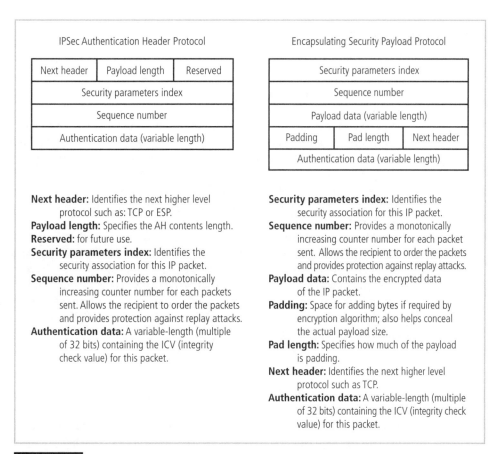

IPSec Authentication Header Protocol

Next header	Payload length	Reserved
Security parameters index		
Sequence number		
Authentication data (variable length)		

Encapsulating Security Payload Protocol

Security parameters index		
Sequence number		
Payload data (variable length)		
Padding	Pad length	Next header
Authentication data (variable length)		

Next header: Identifies the next higher level protocol such as: TCP or ESP.
Payload length: Specifies the AH contents length.
Reserved: for future use.
Security parameters index: Identifies the security association for this IP packet.
Sequence number: Provides a monotonically increasing counter number for each packets sent. Allows the recipient to order the packets and provides protection against replay attacks.
Authentication data: A variable-length (multiple of 32 bits) containing the ICV (integrity check value) for this packet.

Security parameters index: Identifies the security association for this IP packet.
Sequence number: Provides a monotonically increasing counter number for each packet sent. Allows the recipient to order the packets and provides protection against replay attacks.
Payload data: Contains the encrypted data of the IP packet.
Padding: Space for adding bytes if required by encryption algorithm; also helps conceal the actual payload size.
Pad length: Specifies how much of the payload is padding.
Next header: Identifies the next higher level protocol such as TCP.
Authentication data: A variable-length (multiple of 32 bits) containing the ICV (integrity check value) for this packet.

FIGURE A-7 IPSec Headers[21]

The Encapsulating Security Payload Protocol provides confidentiality services for IP packets across insecure networks. ESP can also provide the authentication services of AH. Figure A-7 also provides information on the packet header for ESP. ESP in tunnel mode can be used to establish a virtual private network, assuring encryption and authentication between networks communicating across the Internet. In tunnel mode, the entire IP packet is encrypted with the attached ESP header. A new IP header is attached to the encrypted payload, providing the required routing information. In this manner the packet can be securely routed across the Internet.

An ESP header is inserted into the IP packet prior to the TCP header, with an ESP trailer placed after the IPv4 packet. Additionally, if authentication is desired, an ESP authentication data field is appended after the ESP trailer. The complete transport segment, in addition to the ESP trailer, is encrypted. For an IPv6 transmission, the ESP header is placed after the hop-by-hop and routing headers. Encryption under IPv6 covers the transport segment and the ESP trailer. Authentication in both IPv4 and Ipv6 covers the ciphertext data plus the ESP header. IPSec ESP complaint systems must support the implementation of the DES algorithm utilizing the CBC (cipher block chaining) mode which includes the following: Triple DES, IDEA, RC5, CAST, and Blowfish.

Attacks on Cryptosystems

Historically unauthorized access to secure communications has been attempted by brute force attacks in which the ciphertext is repeatedly searched for clues that can lead to the algorithm's structure. Searching for common text structure, wording, or syntax can assist the attacker in mounting a **ciphertext attack** in a frequency analysis of the encoded text. However, modern algorithms attempt to remove the repetitive and predictable statistical bias from the cipher text. Occasionally, the cryptanalysts may obtain duplicate texts, one in ciphertext and one in plaintext, which enable the attacker to reverse engineer the encryption algorithm in a **known-plaintext attack** scheme. Alternatively an attacker may conduct a **selected-plaintext attack** by sending the potential victim a selected text that he wants encrypted and returned. Reverse engineering may lead to the discovery of the cryptosystem that is being employed.

Most publicly available encryption methods are generally released to the user community for testing of the encryption algorithm's resistance to cracking. Although this serves the purpose of developing a more secure algorithm, the cryptanalysts are informed of which methods of attack have failed, allowing them to devote time to other potential weaknesses in the cryptosystem or routes to obtain the needed keys. Although many of these attacks were discussed in Chapter 2, they are reiterated here in the context of cryptosystems and their impact on these systems.

Man-in-the-Middle Attack

A **man-in-the-middle attack**, as discussed in Chapter 2, is designed to intercept the transmission of a public key or to even insert a known key structure in place of the requested public key. Attackers attempt to place themselves between the sender and receiver, intercepting the request for key exchanges. The attacker sends each participant a valid public key, which is known by the adversary. Encrypted communication appears to occur normally between the participants; however, the attacker receives each encrypted message and decodes it with the key given to the sending party. The decoded message is then encrypted and sent to the originally intended recipient. Establishment of public keys with digital signatures can prevent the traditional man-in-the-middle attack, as the attacker cannot duplicate the signatures.

Correlation Attacks

As the complexities of encryption methods have increased, so too have the tools and methods of cryptanalysts in their attempts at attacking the cryptosystems. **Correlation attacks** attempt to deduce statistical relationships concerning the structure of the key and the output of the cryptosystem. Differential and linear cryptanalysis have been used to mount successful attacks on block cipher encryptions such as DES. Factoring of the public key, if achieved in a reasonable time, allows all messages written with the key to be decrypted.

Dictionary Attacks

Dictionary attacks require the attacker to use the target cryptosystem to encrypt every word in a given dictionary. Much like the selected-text attack, the attacker is attempting to locate a match between the target cipher text and a given enciphered plaintext. Dictionary attacks can be successful when the cipher text consists of relatively few characters, such as usernames and passwords. If an attacker possesses a password file, he or she can run hundreds of thousands of potential passwords against the one-way hashed functions by searching for matching values from both sets of data. After a match is located, the attacker has identified a potential valid password for the system under attack.

Timing Attacks

In **timing attacks**, the attacker eavesdrops during a user's session. Statistical analysis of the user's typing patterns and interkeystroke timings can be used to discern sensitive session information. While timing analysis may not directly result in the decryption of sensitive data, it can be used to eliminate candidate information, narrowing the search criteria. Once attackers have successfully broken an encryption, a **replay attack** may occur when they attempt to resubmit the deciphered authentication to gain entry into a secure source.

Encryption is a very useful tool in protecting the confidentiality of information while in storage and transmission. However, it is just that, another tool in the information security administrator's arsenal of weapons against threats to information security. Frequently, unenlightened individuals describe information security in terms of encryption and firewalls, and possibly virus protection software. Encryption in and of itself is simply hiding the true meaning of information. Over the millennia, mankind has developed dramatically more sophisticated means of hiding information from those who should not see it. No matter how sophisticated encryption and cryptosystems have become, they have retained the same flaw that the first systems contained thousands of years ago. If you know the key, which is the method and secret to encryption, you can determine the message. Key management is a human factor, even in automated key distribution systems. People tend to be the weakest link in cryptosystems, as much as in any other aspect of information security.

Encryption can, however protect information when it is the most vulnerable, when it is outside the organization's systems. Information in transit, through public or leased networks, is outside the organization's control. With loss of control can come loss of security. Encryption provides this last frontier of security for the protection of information, preventing those who sniff, spoof, and otherwise skulk around these public and leased networks from uncovering private information. As such encryption is a vital piece of the security puzzle.

Endnotes

1. Russell Kay, "How It Works" ComputerWorld Online, June 10, 2002, [Cited 31 July, 2002]. Available from the World Wide Web <http://www.computerworld.com/securitytopics/security/story/0,10801,71728,00.html>.

2. *Ibid.*

3. Torbjorn Anderson. "Polyalphabetic Substitution." *Le Canard Volant Non Identifie Online.* 30 January 1999. [Cited 29 July 2002]. Available from the World Wide Web <http://www.cvni.net/radio/nsnl/>.

4. William Stallings, *Cryptography and Network Security, Principles and Practice* (New Jersey: Prentice Hall, 1999).

5. Information Systems Audit and Control Association. "Java Security." [Cited 29 July 2002]. Available from the World Wide Web <http://www.isaca.org.hk/document/cisa_slide/Java%20Security/index.htm>.

6. National Institute of Standards and Technology, *Data Encryption Standards (DES).* FIPS PUB 46-3. (25 October 1999).

7. *Ibid.*

8. *Ibid.*

9. *Ibid.*

10. *Ibid.*

11. *Ibid.*

12. Special thanks to our reviewer for this example: Robert Statica, Associate Director, Cryptography and Telecommunications Laboratory, New Jersey Institute of Technology.

13. *Ibid.*

14. *Ibid.*

15. *Ibid.*

16. Steve Burnett and Stephen Paine, *RSA Security's Official Guide to Cryptography* (New York: Osborne/McGraw-Hill, 2001).

17. Stefan Kelm. "The PKI Page." *Secorvo Security Consulting Online.* [Cited 29 July 2002]. Available from the World Wide Web <http://www.pki-page.org/>.

18. William Stallings, Cryptography and Network Security, Principles and Practice (New Jersey: Prentice Hall, 1999).

19. The International PGP Home Page. *PGPI Online.* [Cited 29 July 2002]. Available from the World Wide Web <http://www.pgpi.org/>

20. William Stallings, Cryptography and Network Security, Principles and Practice (New Jersey: Prentice Hall, 1999).

21. Behrouc A. Forouzan, TCP/IP Protocol Suite (Boston: McGraw Hill, 2003).

Physical Security

If someone really wants to get at the information, it is not difficult if they can gain physical access to the computer or hard drive.

MICROSOFT WHITE PAPER, JULY 1999

AMY WINDAHL WAS BACK EARLY from lunch. She was walking toward the building from the parking lot when she saw one of the accounting clerks go through the building's double glass doors. He walked past the security guard station in the lobby, heading for the elevator. She also saw someone else she didn't recognize following him: a tall, blond man in nondescript business casual clothes. Amy got into the next elevator and pressed the button for her floor.

When the elevator doors opened, Amy saw the same blond man standing in the second floor elevator lobby looking at the company's phone list. She walked over to the doors and cocked her right hip where her badge was clipped toward the sensor for the locks. When she heard the magnetic lock release, Amy pulled the door open and went through. But, as the door began to shut, the stranger grabbed it and came through behind her.

Now, Amy realized she had a tailgater, a person who follows those with badges through checkpoints. Amy had seen the security bulletin just last week emphasizing that tailgaters should be reported. Everyone in the staff meeting had a good laugh about turning each other in the next time two of them came through the door together. Now she understood the seriousness of the bulletin.

Amy did a quick spin and came face-to-face with the blond man. "Excuse me," she said as she headed back into the lobby. The stranger stepped back to let her pass and then continued down the hall. Amy picked up the lobby phone and dialed the number for building security.

"Security," a voice answered.

"Hi, Amy Windahl here. I work at the Help Desk. I just had a stranger tailgate into the second floor offices. Do you guys want to check it out?"

"Yes ma'am. We have someone on the floor already. I'll have him meet you in the lobby in a minute or two," said the security dispatcher.

When the security officer appeared, Amy said, "He went down the hall, toward the programming offices. He's tall, heavy, has green slacks, a tan shirt—oh, and he has blond hair."

The guard said, "Wait here. If he gets past me, call dispatch at 3333. I'll be right back."

Amy sat down in the chair by the phone. Three or four minutes went by when she saw the blond man walking briskly toward the doors. The guard was right behind him. As the stranger opened the door, the guard called out, "Sir. Please stop. I need to speak with you. What's your name?" Before he could answer, the elevator opened, and two more guards came into the lobby.

The stranger responded, "Alan Gaskin."

The guard asked, "What's your business here?"

"Just visiting a friend," said the stranger.

"And who would that be?" the guard asked.

The stranger looked a bit surprised, and then said, "Uh, William Walters, uh, in the Accounting Department, I think."

The guard reached for his wireless handheld terminal and punched a few buttons. Then he said, "Mr. Gaskin, there are no employees with that name working here, in Accounting or any other department. Do you want to try another answer?"

The stranger looked a little confused and took a quick step toward the stairwell. The other two guards had moved up in the meantime and cut him off. As they took him by the upper arms to keep him from escaping, a brown paper bag dropped to the floor, the contents spilling out on the carpet. Amy saw several office badges, a watch, two palm pilots, and several cell phones.

The first guard immediately radioed Dispatch. "Contact the city police and advise them we have a trespasser. We will press charges." The other guards led the man toward the elevators, while the first guard told Amy, "You need to call your supervisor and tell her you will be delayed. We have to take your statement."

DISCUSSION QUESTIONS:

1. What security awareness and training documents and posters were important to this event?
2. Should Amy have done anything differently? What?

LEARNING OBJECTIVES:
Upon completion of this material you should be able to:

- Understand the conceptual need for physical security.
- Identify threats to information security that are unique to physical security.
- Describe the key physical security considerations for selecting a facility site.
- Identify physical security monitoring components.
- Grasp the essential elements of access control within the scope of facilities management.
- Understand the criticality of fire safety programs to all physical security programs.
- Describe the components of fire detection and response.
- Grasp the impact of interruptions in the service of supporting utilities.
- Understand the technical details of uninterruptible power supplies and how they are used to increase availability of information assets.
- Discuss critical physical environment considerations for computing facilities.
- Discuss countermeasures to the physical theft of computing devices.

Introduction

As discussed in Chapter 1, information security encompasses the protection of both data and physical information assets. A wide variety of subjects that focus on the technical aspects of data have been examined: firewalls, intrusion detection systems, and monitoring software. In addition, a number of management topics, such as risk assessments, risk analysis, and risk control have been presented. The focus of this chapter is the second part of information security: physical security.

Physical security addresses the design, implementation, and maintenance of countermeasures that protect the physical resources of an organization. This means the physical protection of the people, hardware, and the supporting system elements and resources associated with the management of information in all its states: transmission, storage, and processing. Most of the technology-based controls discussed to this point can be circumvented if an attacker gains physical access to the devices being controlled. For example, when employees fail to secure the server console, the operating system running on that computer is vulnerable to attack. Some computer systems are constructed in such a way that it is easy to steal the hard drive and the information it contains. As a result, physical security should receive as much attention as logical security in the security development life cycle. This attention assures a solid foundation for the security program.

In earlier chapters, you have encountered a number of threats to information security that can be classified as threats to physical security. For example, in the physical environment a potential act of human error or failure can be represented by an employee accidentally spilling coffee on his or her laptop computer. A compromise to intellectual property can include an employee without an appropriate security clearance copying a classified marketing plan. A deliberate act of espionage or trespass could be exemplified by a competitor sneaking into a facility with a camera. Deliberate acts of sabotage or vandalism can be physical attacks on individuals or property with the intent to sabotage or deface; deliberate acts of theft are perhaps the most common of these threats. Examples include employees stealing computer equipment, credentials, passwords, and laptops. Quality of service deviations from service providers, especially power and water, also represent physical security threats. Technical hardware failures or errors and technological obsolescence both have common examples in physical security. In his book, *Fighting Computer Crime,* Donn B. Parker lists the "Seven Major Sources of Physical Loss" as follows:

1. "Extreme temperature: heat, cold
2. "Gases: war gases, commercial vapors, humid or dry air, suspended particles
3. "Liquids: water, chemicals
4. "Living organisms: viruses, bacteria, people, animals, insects
5. "Projectiles: tangible objects in motion, powered objects
6. "Movement: collapse, shearing, shaking, vibration, liquefaction, flows waves, separation, slide
7. "Energy anomalies: electrical surge or failure, magnetism, static electricity, aging circuitry; radiation: sound, light, radio, microwave, electromagnetic, atomic"[1]

Just as with all other areas of security, physical security requires sound organizational policy for direction. Policy guides the planning of physical security in the development life cycle and serves as a reference to organizational objectives through ongoing maintenance and use. These physical security policies direct users of information assets in the appropriate use of computing resources and information assets, as well as the protection of their own personal safety in day-to-day operations.[2] Physical security is designed and implemented in several layers. Each community of interest in the organization is responsible for components within these layers.

- **General management:** Responsible for the security of the facility in which the organization is housed and the policies and standards for secure operation. This includes exterior security, building access, as well as other controls noted below.
- **IT management and professionals:** Responsible for environmental and access security in technology equipment locations and for the policies and standards of secure equipment operation. This includes access to server rooms, server room temperature and humidity controls, as well as other controls noted below.
- **Information security management and professionals:** Perform risk assessments and implementation reviews for the physical security controls implemented by the other two groups.

Access Controls

There are a number of physical access controls that are uniquely suited to the physical entry and exit of people to and from the organization's facilities. Sometimes the technology of physical security control can overlap logical security control technologies. Some of these overlaps include biometrics, smart cards, or wireless enabled keycards, which are used for controlling access to locked doors, information assets, and information system resources.

Before examining access controls, you need to understand the concept of a secure facility and its design. The organization's general management oversees physical security. Commonly, access controls for a building are operated by a group called **facilities management**. Larger organizations may have an entire staff dedicated to facilities management, while smaller organizations often outsource these responsibilities.

From the point of view of facilities management, a **secure facility** is a physical location that has been engineered with controls designed to minimize the risk of attacks from physical threats. The concept of the secure facility brings to mind military bases, maximum-security prisons, and nuclear power plants. It is not always necessary to sacrifice aesthetics to minimize risk from physical attacks, but some compromises are often part of the process. A secure facility can use the natural terrain, traffic flow, and urban development to its advantage. A secure facility can complement these features with protection mechanisms, such as fences, gates, walls, guards, and alarms.

Controls for Protecting the Secure Facility

There are a number of physical security controls and issues that the organization's communities of interest should consider when implementing physical security inside and outside the facility. Some of the major issues are:

Walls, Fencing, and Gates

One of the oldest and most reliable methods of providing physical security on the premises, these controls deter unauthorized access to the facility.

Guards

Guards and security agencies have the ability to apply human reasoning. Other controls are either static, and therefore unresponsive to actions, or they are programmed to respond with specific actions to specific stimuli. Guards are employed to evaluate each situation as it arises and to make reasoned responses. Most guards have clear, standing operating procedures (SOPs) that help them to act decisively in unfamiliar situations. In the military, guards are provided with general orders (see the Offline on guard duty) and special orders that are unique to their posts.

OFFLINE

Guard Duty

Adapted from "Guard Duty," *www.armystudyguide.com/guard_duty/studyguide.htm*
And from "General Military Knowledge" *http://www.military-net.com/education/mpdgeneral.html*

In the military, guard duty is a serious responsibility. A guard must memorize, understand, and comply with his general orders, and the orders particular to his assignment.
"General Orders:
1) I will guard everything within the limits of my post and quit my post only when properly relieved.
2) I will obey my special orders and perform all of my duties in a military manner.
3) I will report violations of my special orders, emergencies, and anything not covered in my instructions to the commander of the relief."[3]

continued

How do guards comply with the responsibilities of their assignments? They apply the force necessary to accomplish their missions, including deadly force in approved situations. Deadly force is the power to cause death or severe bodily harm. It is applied only to the minimum extent necessary to make an apprehension.

"Deadly force can only be used for:
1. Self-defense in the event of imminent danger of death or serious bodily harm;
2. To prevent the actual theft or destruction of property designated for protection; and
As directed by the Standard Operating Procedures of his individual guard post."[4]

Dogs

If the organization is protecting highly valuable resources, dogs can be a valuable part of physical security if they are integrated into the plan correctly and managed properly. Guard dogs are useful because their keen sense of smell and hearing can detect intrusions that human guards cannot and they can be placed in harm's way, rather than risk the life of a human.

ID Cards and Badges

One area of access control that ties physical security with information access control is the use of identification cards (ID) and name badges. An ID card is typically worn concealed, whereas a name badge is visible. These devices can serve a number of purposes. First, they are simple forms of biometrics (facial recognition) to identify and authenticate an authorized individual with access to the facility. With the addition of a magnetic strip or radio chip that can be read by automated control devices, the ID card can allow authorized individuals access to restricted areas within the facility. However, these devices are not foolproof, and the cards used to communicate with the locks can be easily duplicated, stolen, and modified. Because of this inherent weakness, a name badge or ID should not be the only control for access to restricted areas.

Another inherent weakness of access control technologies is the human-factor known as **tailgating**. This occurs when an authorized individual presents a key and a door is opened, but other individuals, who may or may not be authorized, also enter the unlocked door. As the opening scenario showed, an awareness campaign about tailgating is one way to combat this problem. Other technical means are available to help avoid tailgating, but they are usually expensive or inconvenient or both.

Locks and Keys

There are two types of locks: mechanical and electromechanical. The mechanical lock relies on a key of carefully shaped pieces of metal that turn tumblers to release secured loops of steel, aluminum, or brass (in brass padlocks). Or a dial can cause the proper rotation of slotted discs until the slots on multiple disks are aligned, permitting the retraction of a securing bolt (combination and safe locks). Though simple in concept, some of the technologies that go into the development of these physical security devices are quite complex. Modern enhancements have created the electromechanical lock. These devices can accept a variety of inputs including keys that are magnetic strips on ID cards, radio signals from name badges, personal identification numbers (PINs) typed into a keypad, or some combination of these.

Locks are divided into four categories: manual, programmable, electronic, and biometric. Manual locks, padlocks, and combination locks are commonplace and well understood. If you have the key (or combination) you can gain access to the resources secured behind the lock. These locks are often preset by the manufacturer and therefore unchangeable. Programmable locks tend to be a bit more sophisticated, allowing the owner to reset the access method (key or combination) to upgrade security. Examples of many of these types of locks are presented in Figure 9-1. Mechanical push button locks are popular for securing computer rooms and wiring closets, as they have a resettable code and don't require electricity to operate.

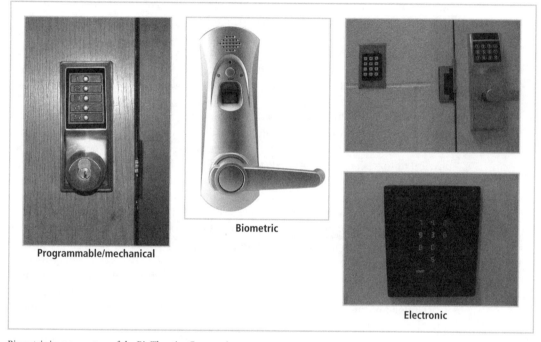

Biometric image courtesy of the BioThentica Corporation

FIGURE 9-1 Locks

Manual locks are installed into doors and cannot be changed, except by highly trained locksmiths. Their use is often limited to controlling access to a single door. Programmable locks can be changed, after they are put in service, allowing for combination or key changes without a locksmith.

Electronic locks can be integrated into alarm systems and other building management systems. The number of ways that sensors and locks can be integrated to combine the various features into locking behaviors is quite numerous. These combinations can include using fire alarms and locks in a combined system to change the degree of authorization needed to access a location if it is in an alarm condition, or the use of a lock to notify guard stations that the lock has been activated. Some common forms of electronic locks include the electric strike locks that are used when you announce yourself and are buzzed into a building. Electronic locks can be deactivated by a switch controlled by an agent, usually a secretary or guard. Electronic push button locks, like their mechanical cousins, have a numerical keypad over the knob, allowing the individual user to enter a personal code and open the door. They usually use battery backups to power the keypad in case of a power failure.

As mentioned in the ID card section, some locks require keys that contain computer chips. These smart cards can carry critical information, provide strong authentication, and offer a number of other features. Keycard readers based on smart cards are commonly used for securing computer rooms, communication closets, and other restricted areas. The card reader can track entry and provide accountability. Individuals can be allowed or denied access depending on their current status, without requiring replacement of the lock. A specialized type of keycard reader is the **proximity reader**, which does not require the insertion of the keycard into the reader. Instead the individual simply places the card within the lock's range to be recognized. With some of these readers, the lock can recognize the card even when it is inside a pocket.

The most sophisticated locks are **biometric locks**. Finger, palm and hand readers, iris and retina scanners, voice, and signature readers fall into this category. The technology that underlies biometric devices was discussed in Chapter 8.

As part of general management's responsibility for the physical environment, the management of keys and locks is a fundamental concern. When they have complete access to the facility, locksmiths should be carefully screened and monitored. As discussed in Chapter 11, when individuals are hired, fired, laid off, or transferred, their access controls, whether physical or logical, must be properly adjusted. Failure to do so can result in instances of employees cleaning out their offices by taking more than their personal effects.

Sometimes locks fail and facilities need alternative procedures for access. The procedure must take into account that locks fail in one of two ways: when the lock of a door fails and the door becomes unlocked, that is a **fail-safe lock**; when the lock of a door fails and the door remains locked, this is a **fail-secure lock**. The most common failure modes for technically sophisticated locks are loss of power and activation through fire control systems. A fail-safe lock usually secures an exit, where it is essential for human safety in the event of a fire.[5] A fail-secure lock is used when human safety is not a factor.

Understanding lock mechanisms is important, because locks can be exploited by an intruder to gain access to the secured location. If an electronic lock is short circuited, it may become fail-safe and allow the intruder to bypass the control and enter the room.

Mantraps

A common enhancement for locks in high security areas is the mantrap. A **mantrap** is a small enclosure that has an entry point and a different exit point. The individual entering the facility, area, or room, enters the mantrap, requests access through some form of electronic or biometric lock and key, and if verified, is allowed to exit the mantrap into the facility. This is called a mantrap, because if the individual is denied entry, the mantrap does not allow exit until a security official overrides the automatic locks of the enclosure. Figure 9-2 provides an example of a typical mantrap layout.

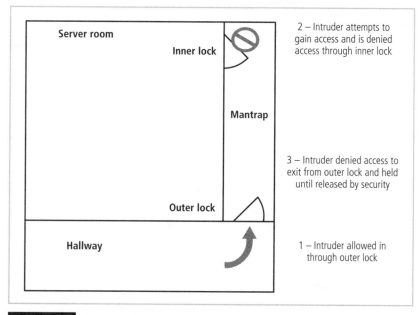

FIGURE 9-2 Mantraps

Electronic Monitoring

To record events within a specific area that guards and dogs might miss, or to record events in areas where other types of physical controls are not practical, monitoring equipment can be used. Many of you are accustomed to video monitoring, with cameras viewing you from odd corners and with the ever present silver globes found in many retail stores. On the other end of these cameras are video cassette recorders (VCRs) and related machinery that captures the video feed. Electronic monitoring includes closed-circuit television systems (CCT), some of which collect constant video feeds while others rotate input from a number of cameras, sampling each area in turn.

These systems have drawbacks: for the most part they are reactive and do not prevent access or prohibited activity. Others are monitored in real time. For video recordings, someone has to review the information collected. Science has not yet developed intelligent systems capable of reliably evaluating this data to determine if unauthorized activities have occurred. Therefore every minute of taped monitoring must be reviewed to determine if an unauthorized action has occurred. For this reason, CCT is most often used as a data collection device for areas that have been broken into, and thus it becomes more a collective device than a detective instrument. In high security areas, however, personnel monitor these systems constantly, looking for improprieties. Banks, casinos, and shopping centers are areas where security personnel constantly look for suspicious activity.

Alarms and Alarm Systems

Closely related to monitoring are the alarm systems that notify the appropriate individual when a predetermined event or activity occurs. This could be a fire, a break-in or intrusion, an environmental disturbance, such as flooding, or an interruption in services, such as a loss of power. The burglar alarm is common in residential and commercial environments. These alarms detect intrusions into unauthorized areas and notify either a local or remote security agency to react. These systems rely on a number of sensors that detect the intrusion: motion detectors, thermal detectors, glass breakage detectors, weight sensors, and contact sensors. Motion detectors detect movement within a confined space and are either active or passive. Some motion sensors emit energy beams, usually in the form of infrared or laser light, ultrasonic sound or sound waves, or some form of electromagnetic radiation. If the reflected beam from the room being measured is disrupted, the alarm is activated. Other types of motion sensors are passive, in that they read energy from the monitored space, usually infrared, and detect rapid changes in the energy in the monitored area. Energy signatures can be blocked or disguised and are therefore fallible. Thermal detectors work by detecting rates of change in the ambient temperature in the room. They are also used in fire detection as described in later sections. The addition of a human with a radiation of 98.6 degrees Fahrenheit into a 65 degrees Fahrenheit room changes the temperature. Contact and weight sensors work when two contacts are connected, for example by a foot stepping on a pressure sensitive pad under a rug, or a window pin and spring sensor detecting when a window is opened. Vibration sensors also fall into this category, except that they detect movement of the sensor rather than movement in the environment.

Computer Rooms and Wiring Closets

Computer rooms and wiring and communications closets are facilities that require special attention to ensure the confidentiality, integrity, and availability of information. For an outline of the physical and environmental controls needed for computer rooms, read the Technical Details entitled "Physical and Environmental Controls for Computer Rooms." Logical access controls are easily defeated, if an attacker gains physical access to the computing equipment. As mentioned previously, rumors have arisen in the past of technology professionals being employed as custodians at the offices of their competition. Custodial staff are often the least scrutinized of employees and nonemployees who have access to offices. Yet custodians are given the greatest degree of unsupervised access. They are often handed the master keys to the entire building and then ignored. Custodians collect paper from every office, dust desks, and move large containers from every area. It is therefore not difficult for this type of worker to gather critical information, computer media, and copy proprietary and classified information. This is not to accuse the custodial staff of espionage but to state that this role can be used by competitors to gain unauthorized information and should be carefully managed not only by the organization's general management but also by IT management.

Interior Walls and Doors

The security of information assets can sometimes be compromised because of the construction of the walls and doors of the facility. The walls in a facility are typically of two types: standard interior and firewall. Building codes require that each floor have a number of **firewalls** to limit the area of damage should a fire break out in an office. Between the firewalls, standard interior walls are erected to compartmentalize the individual offices. Unlike firewalls, they reach only part way to the next floor. This type of construction allows ventilation systems to inexpensively collect return air from all the offices.

For security this means that when there are several offices on the same floor, an individual can climb over the wall from one to the other. The space above the ceiling, below the floor above, is called a **plenum** and is usually 12 to 24 inches high. As a result, all high-security areas, such as computer rooms and wiring closets, must have firewall-grade walls surrounding them. This provides not only physical security from potential intruders but from fires as well.

The doors that allow access into these types of secured rooms should also be evaluated. Standard office-grade doors provide little or no security. For example, one of the authors of this textbook once locked himself out of his office by accidentally breaking the key off in the lock. When the locksmith arrived, he carried a curious contraption. Instead of disassembling the lock or using other locksmith secrets, he carried a long piece of heavy-duty wire, bent into the shape of a bow, with a string tied to each end. He slid one end of this bow through the one-inch gap under the door, levered the contraption on end and yanked the string. The locksmith's wire bow slid over the door handle and looped the string over it. When he yanked the string, the door swung open. This information is not meant to teach you how to access interior offices but to warn you that no office is completely secure. How can you avoid this problem? In most interior offices you can't. Instead, IT security professionals must educate the organization's employees to secure their information and systems within their offices.

In computer rooms and wiring closets, push or crash bars can be installed. These are much more difficult to open than the usual door handles from the outside and still provide the needed levels of safety in the event of an emergency. Such devices meet building codes, but provide much higher levels of security than the standard door pull handle.

TECHNICAL DETAILS

Physical and Environmental Controls For Computer Rooms

Adapted from "Guide for Developing Security Plans for Information Technology Systems"[6] by M. Swanson, NIST Special Publication 800-18, December 1998.

The following list of physical and environmental controls for computer rooms is intended to be representative, not comprehensive.

- Card keys for building and entrances to work area
- Twenty-four-hour guards at all entrances and exits
- Cipher lock on computer room door
- Raised floor in computer room
- Dedicated cooling system
- Humidifier in tape library
- Emergency lighting in computer room
- Four fire extinguishers rated for electrical fires
- One fire extinguisher with a combination of a class B and class C fire control rating (note that fire control ratings are discussed below)
- Smoke, water, and heat detectors
- Emergency power shutoff switch by exit door
- Surge suppressor
- Emergency replacement server
- Zoned dry-pipe sprinkler system
- Uninterruptible power supply for LAN servers
- Power strips and suppressors for peripherals
- Power strips and suppressors for computers
- Controlled access to file server room
- Plastic sheets for water protection
- Closed-circuit television monitors

Fire Safety

The most important principle of physical security is the safety of the people who work in the organization. The most serious threat to that safety is the possibility of fire. Fires account for more property damage, personal injury, and death than any other threat to physical security. As a result, it is imperative that physical security plans examine and implement strong measures to detect and respond to fires and fire hazards.

Fire Detection and Response

Fire suppression systems are devices installed and maintained to detect and respond to a fire, potential fire, or combustion situation. These devices typically work to deny an environment of one of the three requirements for a fire to burn: temperature (ignition source), fuel, and oxygen.

While the temperature of ignition or **flame point** may vary by combustible fuel type, it can be as low as a few hundred degrees. Paper, the most common combustible in the office, has a flame point of 451 degrees Fahrenheit (as in Ray Bradbury's novel). Paper can reach that temperature when it is exposed to a carelessly dropped cigarette butt, malfunctioning electrical equipment, or other accidental or purposeful misadventures.

Water and water mist systems, which are described in detail in subsequent paragraphs, work to reduce the temperature of the flame to extinguish it and to saturate some categories of fuels to prevent ignition. Carbon dioxide systems (CO_2) rob fire of its oxygen. Soda acid systems deny fire its fuel, preventing spreading. Gas-based systems, such as halon and its Environmental Protection Agency-approved replacements, disrupt the fire's chemical reaction but leave enough oxygen for people to survive for a short time. However before a fire can be suppressed, it must be detected.

Fire Detection

Fire detection systems fall into two general categories: manual and automatic. **Manual fire detection systems** include human responses, such as calling the fire department, as well as manually activated alarms, such as sprinklers and gaseous systems. One consideration with manual fire detection systems is the fire alarm itself. Organizations must use care when manually triggered alarms are tied directly to suppression systems, as false alarms are not uncommon. Organizations should also ensure that proper security remains in place, until all employees and visitors have been cleared from the building and their removal has been verified. During the chaos of a fire evacuation, an attacker can easily slip into offices and obtain sensitive information. As part of a complete fire safety program, it is advisable to designate individuals as floor monitors.

There are three basic types of fire detection systems: thermal detection, smoke detection, and flame detection. The **thermal detection systems** contain a sophisticated heat sensor that operates in one of two ways. In the first, known as **fixed temperature**, the sensor detects when the ambient temperature in an area reaches a predetermined level, usually between 135 degrees Fahrenheit and 165 degrees Fahrenheit, or 57 degrees Centigrade to 74 degrees Centigrade. [7] In the second, known as **rate-of-rise**, the sensor detects an unusually rapid increase in the area temperature, within a relatively short period of time. In either case, if the criteria are met, the alarm and suppression systems are activated. Thermal detection systems are inexpensive and easy to maintain. Unfortunately, thermal detectors usually don't catch a problem until it is already in progress, as in a full-blown fire. As a result, thermal detection systems are not permitted in areas where human safety could be at risk. They are also not recommended for areas with high-value items, or items which could be easily damaged by high temperature.

Smoke detection systems are perhaps the most common means of detecting a potentially dangerous fire, and they are required by building codes in most residential dwellings and commercial buildings. Smoke detectors operate in one of three ways. In the first, **photoelectric sensors** project and detect an infrared beam across an area. If the beam is interrupted (presumably by smoke), the alarm or suppression system is activated. In the second, an **ionization sensor** contains a small amount of a harmless radioactive material within a detection chamber. When certain by-products of combustion enter the chamber, they change the level of electrical conductivity with the chamber and activate the detector. These types systems are much more sophisticated than photoelectric sensors and can detect fires much earlier, as the invisible by-products are detected long before enough visible material enters a photoelectric sensor to trigger a reaction. The third category of smoke detectors is the air-aspirating detector. **Air-aspirating detectors** are very sophisticated systems, which are used in high-sensitivity areas. They work by taking in air, filtering it, and moving it through a chamber containing a laser beam. If the laser beam is diverted or refracted by smoke particles, the system is activated. These types of systems are typically much more expensive than the less effective models. However they are much better at early detection and more commonly used in areas where extremely valuable materials are stored.

The third major category of fire detection systems is the **flame detector**. The flame detector is a sensor that detects the infrared or ultraviolet light produced by an open flame. These systems require direct line of sight with the flame and compare the flame "signature" to a database to determine whether or not to activate the alarm and suppression systems. While highly sensitive, flame detection systems are expensive and must be installed where they can scan all areas of the protected area. They are not typically used in areas with human lives at stake; however, they are quite suitable for chemical storage areas where normal chemical emissions might activate smoke detectors.

Fire Suppression

Fire suppression systems can consist of portable, manual, or automatic apparatus. Portable extinguishers are used in a variety of situations where direct application of suppression is preferred, or fixed apparatus is impractical. Portable extinguishers are much more efficient for smaller fires, because they avoid the triggering of an entire building's sprinkler systems and the damage that can cause. Portable extinguishers are rated by the type of fire they can combat as described below.

- **Class A:** Fires that involve ordinary combustible fuels such as wood, paper, textiles, rubber, cloth, and trash. Class A fires are extinguished by agents that interrupt the ability of the fuel to be ignited. Water and multipurpose, dry chemical fire extinguishers are ideal for these types of fires.
- **Class B:** Fires fueled by combustible liquids or gases, such as solvents, gasoline, paint, lacquer, and oil. Class B fires are extinguished by agents that remove oxygen from the fire. Carbon dioxide, multipurpose dry chemical, and halon fire extinguishers are ideal for these types of fires.

■ **Class C:** Fires with energized electrical equipment or appliances. Class C fires are extinguished with agents that must be nonconducting. Carbon dioxide, multipurpose, dry chemical, and halon fire extinguishers are ideal for these types of fires. Never use a water fire extinguisher on a Class C fire.

■ **Class D:** Fires fueled by combustible metals, such as magnesium, lithium, and sodium. Fires of this type require special extinguishing agents and techniques.[8]

The Technical Details box on halon and the EPA provides additional details on the ban on new installations of halon-based systems and the approved replacements.

TECHNICAL DETAILS

Halon Q & A

"Halon Substitutes Under SNAP as of 26 April 2000"[9]
By The Environmental Protection Agency, Online, July 10, 2002.

"When was the production of halons banned?

"Under the Clean Air Act (CAA), the United States banned the production and import of virgin halons 1211, 1301, and 2402 beginning January 1, 1994, in compliance with the Montreal Protocol On Substances That Deplete The Ozone Layer. Recycled halon and inventories produced before January 1, 1994, are now the only sources of supply. EPA's final rule published March 5, 1998, (63 FR 11084), bans the formulation of any blend of two or more of these halons with one exception. An exemption is provided for halon blends formulated using recycled halon solely for the purpose of aviation fire protection, provided that blends produced under this exemption are recycled to meet the relevant purity standards for each individual halon. A fact sheet summarizing this rule is also available from the Stratospheric Ozone Protection Hotline.

"Must I now dismantle my halon fire protection system?

"No. It is legal to continue to use your existing halon system. It is even legal to purchase recycled halon and halon produced before the phase-out to recharge your system.

However, because halons deplete the ozone layer, users are encouraged to consider replacing their system and making their halon stock available for users with more critical needs.

"Are there any federal laws on emissions of halons?

"EPA's final rule published March 5, 1998, (63 FR 11084) prohibits the intentional release of halon 1211, halon 1301, and halon 2402 during the testing, repairing, maintaining, servicing, or disposal of halon-containing equipment or during the use of such equipment for technician training. The rule also requires appropriate training of technicians regarding emissions reduction and proper disposal of halon and halon-containing equipment. The rule became effective April 6, 1998.

"What are the acceptable substitutes for Halon?

"There are a number of acceptable substitutes for Halon 1211 and 1301 (the two most common types of Halon-based systems)." These are presented in Table 9-1.

continued

Table 9-1 Acceptable Substitutes

Acceptable Substitutes for Halon 1211 Streaming Agents Under the Significant New Alternatives Policy (SNAP) Program as of April 26, 2000[10]

Substitute	Trade Name	Comments
HCFC-123	FE-232	Nonresidential uses only
HCFC-124	FE-241	Nonresidential uses only
[HCFC Blend] B	Halotron 1	Nonresidential uses only
[HCFC Blend] C	NAF P-III	Nonresidential uses only
[HCFC Blend] D	Blitz III	Nonresidential uses only
Gelled Halocarbon/ Dry chemical suspension	Envirogel	Allowable in the residential use market
[Surfactant Blend] A	Cold Fire, Flameout	
Water mist systems using potable or natural sea water		
Carbon dioxide		
Dry chemical		
Water		
Foam		

Acceptable Substitutes for Halon 1301 Total Flooding Agents Under the Significant New Alternatives Policy (SNAP) Program as of April 26, 2000

Substitute	Trade Name	Comment
Powdered Aerosol C	PyroGen, Dynameco	For use in unoccupied areas only
Powdered Aerosol A	SFE	For use in unoccupied areas only
Carbon dioxide system		Design must adhere to OSHA 1910.162(b)(5) and NFPA Standard 12
Water		
Water mist systems using potable or natural sea water		
Foam A	Phirex+	This agent is not a clean agent, but is a low-density, short duration foam

Manual and automatic fire response can include installed systems designed to apply suppressive agents. These are usually either sprinkler or gaseous systems. All **sprinkler systems** are designed to apply liquid, usually water, to all areas in which a fire has been detected. In sprinkler systems, the organization can implement wet-pipe, dry-pipe, or pre-action systems. A **wet-pipe** system has pressurized water in all pipes and has some form of valve in each protected area. When the system is activated, the valves are opened allowing water to sprinkle the area. This is best for areas where fire represents a severe risk to people, but where damage to property is not a major concern. The most obvious drawback to this type of system is damage to office equipment and materials through soaking. This type of system is completely inappropriate in computer rooms, wiring closets, and anywhere electrical equipment is used or stored. There is also the risk of accidental or intentional misactivation. Figure 9-3 shows a water sprinkler system that works this way: when the ambient temperature reaches 140 degrees Fahrenheit to 150 degrees Fahrenheit, the plastic pin melts, releasing the stopper to allow water to hit the diffuser that sprays water throughout the area.

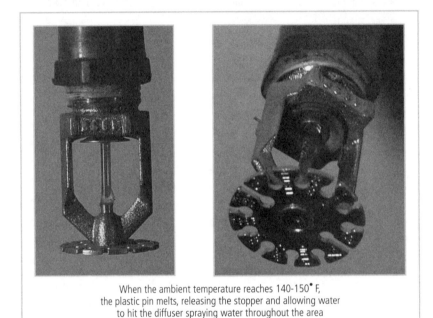

When the ambient temperature reaches 140-150° F, the plastic pin melts, releasing the stopper and allowing water to hit the diffuser spraying water throughout the area

FIGURE 9-3 Water Sprinkler System

A **dry-pipe** system is designed to work in areas where electrical equipment is used. Instead of the system containing water, it contains pressurized air. The pressurized air holds valves closed, keeping the water away from the target areas. When a fire is detected and the sprinkler heads are activated, the pressurized air escapes, water fills the pipes, and exits through the sprinkler heads. This reduces the risk of accidental activation of the system with its resulting damage. It is not, however, the optimal solution for computing environments, as other more sophisticated systems can both suppress the fire and maintain the integrity of computing equipment.

A third type of sprinkler system is the **pre-action system**. Unlike either the wet- or dry-pipe systems, the pre-action system has a two-phase response to a fire. The system is normally maintained with nothing in the delivery pipes. When a fire has been detected, the first phase is initiated, and valves allow water to enter the system. Like the wet-pipe, however, the pre-action system does not deliver water until the individual sprinkler heads are triggered, and then water is sprinkled into the area. A variation of the pre-action system is the **deluge system**, in which the valves are kept open, and as soon as the first phase is activated, valves allow water to be immediately applied to various areas without waiting for the second phase to trigger the individual heads.

Water mist sprinklers are the newest form of sprinkler systems and rely on microfine mists instead of traditional shower-type systems. The water mist systems work like traditional water system in reducing the ambient temperature around the flame, therefore minimizing its ability to sustain the necessary temperature needed to maintain combustion. Unlike traditional water sprinkler systems, the foglike mist stays buoyant (airborne) much longer, as the droplets are much less susceptible to gravity. As a result a much smaller quantity of water is required, extinguishing the fire more quickly and causing less collateral damage. Unlike some of the gaseous systems, water-based systems are low cost, nontoxic, and require minimal retrofit for an existing sprinkler system.

Gaseous Emission Systems

Chemical gas systems can be used in the suppression of fires. These systems are either self-pressurizing or must be pressurized with an additional agent. Until recently there were only two major types of gaseous systems: carbon dioxide and halon. Carbon dioxide robs a fire of its oxygen supply. Unfortunately, any living organisms that also rely on oxygen are similarly robbed of their oxygen supply. As a result, carbon dioxide systems are not commonly used in residential or office environments. The alternative is halon. Halon is one of a few chemicals designated as a **clean agent**, which means that it does not leave any residue when dry, nor does it interfere with the operation of electrical or electronic equipment. As a result it is the preferred solution for computer rooms and communications closets. Unlike carbon dioxide, halon does not rob the fire of its oxygen and produces instead a chemical reaction with the flame to extinguish it. As a result it is much safer than carbon dioxide when people are present and the system is activated. Although it can cause suffocation, it requires a much higher dosage than carbon dioxide and therefore provides additional time for people to exit the area safely. As mentioned in the Offline on halon, the EPA has classified halon as an ozone-depleting substance, and therefore new installations are prohibited in commercial and residential locations. There are a number of alternatives, as presented in the Offline box, although, like the refrigerant freon, they are reported to be less effective than halon. These alternative clean agents include the following:[11]

- FM-200 (very similar to halon 1301) is safe in occupied areas
- Inergen is a high-pressure agent composed of nitrogen, argon, and carbon dioxide
- Carbon dioxide, although riskier than halon, is an acceptable alternative
- FE-13 (trifluromethane) is one of the newest and safest clean agent variations of the most commonly used clean agents (FE-13, Inergen, and FM-200). FE-13 is safe for human exposure until concentrations reach 30 percent and can therefore allow additional time for safe egress. Unlike FM-200, FE-13 also can be installed with high ceiling nozzles and can be used in low-temperature situations.

As part of a physical security plan, every building is required to have clearly marked fire exits and maps posted throughout the facility. It is important to rehearse fire alarm response and ensure that individuals are designated to escort everyone from the building and ensure no one is left behind. It is also important to have fire suppression systems (see Figure 9-4), which are both manual and automatic, inspected and tested regularly.

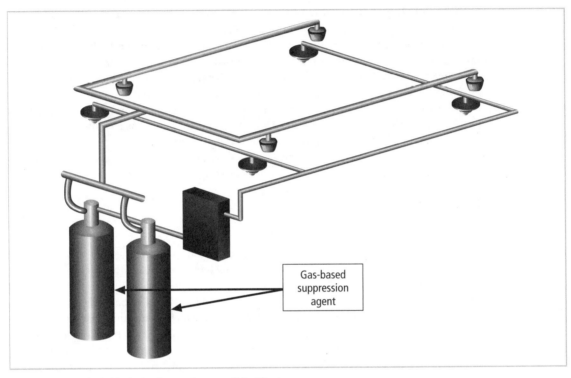

Gas-based
suppression
agent

Image is courtesy of Reliable Fire Equipment Company, Alsip, Illinois

FIGURE 9-4 Fire Suppression System

Failure of Supporting Utilities and Structural Collapse

Supporting utilities, such as heating, ventilation and air conditioning, power, water, and other utilities, have a significant impact on the continued safe operation of a facility. Extreme temperatures and humidity levels, electrical fluctuations and the interruption of water, sewage, and garbage services can create conditions that inject vulnerabilities in systems designed to protect information. Each utility must be properly managed in order to prevent potential damage to information and information systems. Each of these is examined in additional detail below.

Heating, Ventilation, and Air Conditioning

Although traditionally a facilities management responsibility, the operation of the heating, ventilation, and air conditioning (HVAC) system can have dramatic impact on information and information systems operations and protection. Specifically there are four areas within the HVAC system that can cause damage to information-carrying systems: temperature, filtration, humidity, and static electricity.

Temperature

Computer systems are electronic and as such are subject to damage from extreme temperature. Temperatures as high as 100 degrees Fahrenheit can damage computer media, and at 175 degrees Fahrenheit computer hardware can be damaged and destroyed. On the other hand, when the temperature approaches 32 degrees Fahrenheit, media is susceptible to cracking, and components can actually freeze together. Rapid changes in temperature, from hot to cold, or from cold to hot can produce condensation, which can create short circuits or otherwise damage systems and components. The optimal temperature for a computing environment (and people) is between 70 and 74 degrees Fahrenheit.

Humidity and Static

Humidity is the amount of moisture in the air. High humidity levels create condensation problems, and low humidity levels can increase the amount of static electricity in the environment. With condensation comes the short-circuiting of electrical equipment and the potential for mold and rot in paper-based information storage. **Static electricity** is caused by a process called **triboelectrification** that occurs when two materials are rubbed or touched and electrons are exchanged, resulting in one object becoming more positively charged and the other more negatively charged. When a third object with an opposite charge or ground is encountered, electrons flow again, and a spark is produced. One of the leading causes of damage to sensitive circuitry is **electrostatic discharge (ESD)**. Integrated circuits in a computer use between two and five volts of electricity. Voltage levels as low as 200 can cause microchip damage. Static electricity is not even noticeable to humans until levels approach 1,500 volts, and you can't see the little blue spark until it approaches 4,000 volts. A person can generate up to 12,000 volts of static current by walking across a carpet.[12] Table 9-2 shows some static charge voltages and the damage they can cause to systems.

Table 9-2 Static Charge Damage in Computers [13]

Volts	Damage caused
40	Damages sensitive circuits and transistors
1,000	Scrambles monitor display
1,500	Causes disk drive data loss
2,000	Shuts down a system
4,000	Jams printers
17,000	Permanently damages chips

Two types of failures can result from ESD damage to chips. Immediate failures, also known as catastrophic failures, occur right away, are usually totally destructive, and require chip replacement. Latent failures or delayed failures can occur weeks or even months after the damage is done. The damage may not be noticeable, but the chip may suffer intermittent problems. It has been observed, however, that with the overall poor quality of some of the current versions of popular operating systems, this type of damage may be hard to notice. As a result, it is imperative to maintain the optimal level of humidity, which is between 40 and 60 percent, in the computing environment. Humidity levels below this range create static, and levels above create condensation. Humidification or dehumidification systems can assist in the regulation of these conditions.

Ventilation Shafts

One last discussion point within the topic of HVAC is the security of the ventilation system air ductwork. While in residential buildings the ductwork is quite small, in large commercial buildings it can be large enough for an individual to climb though. This is one of Hollywood's favorite methods for villains or heroes to enter buildings. In practice, these ventilation shafts aren't quite as negotiable as Hollywood would have you believe. In fact with moderate security precautions, these shafts can be completely removed from security's concern. In most new buildings the vent feeds to the individual rooms are no larger than 12 by 24 inches. This precludes most adults from access, especially with the sharp screws sticking through the sides where the ducts are anchored to supports. If the vents are much larger, security can install wire mesh grids at various points to compartmentalize the runs. In any case, the ventilation system is one more area within the HVAC that must be evaluated.

Power Management and Conditioning

Of additional concern is the quality of electrical power. As discussed in Chapter 2, not only is electrical quantity (the voltage level and the amperage rating) of concern, but the quality of the power (cleanliness and proper installation) are of importance. Clean power is properly delivered power, without unwanted fluctuations or embedded signaling. It is possible to use the wire and cable built into your homes to send communications signals on purpose or by accident. Some so-called wireless intercom systems, telephone extensions, and home computer networking devices use this effect to communicate over the power lines already in place. The most critical factor for power systems used by information-processing equipment is that the power infrastructure be properly installed and correctly grounded. Interference with the normal pattern of the electrical current is also referred to as **noise** in the current. Computers can use the normal 60 Hertz cycle of the electricity in alternating current to synchronize their clocks. Any noise that interferes with this cycle can result in inaccurate time clocks or, even worse, unreliable internal clocks inside the CPU.

Grounding

Grounding ensures that the returning flow of current is properly discharged to the ground. If this is not properly installed, anyone touching a computer or other electrical device could be used as a ground source, causing damage to equipment and injury or death to the person. Similarly computing and other electrical equipment in areas where water can accumulate must be uniquely grounded, with ground fault circuit interruption (GFCI) equipment. GFCI is capable of quickly identifying and interrupting a ground fault, in which an individual has come into contact with water and represents a better ground than the electrical circuit's current source. Power should also be provided in sufficient amperage to support needed operations. Nothing is more frustrating than plugging in a series of computers, only to have the circuit breaker trip. Consult a qualified electrician when designing or remodeling computer rooms to ensure sufficiently high amperage circuits are available to provide the needed power. Overloading a circuit not only causes problems with the circuit tripping, but can also overload the power load on an electrical cable, creating the risk of fire.

Uninterruptible Power Supplies (UPS)

In case of power outage, a **UPS** is a backup power source for major computer systems. Figure 9-5 shows a number of UPS types. Of those shown, this section describes the following basic configurations: the standby, ferroresonant standby, line-interactive, and the true online (also known as double conversion online). Each of these is examined in detail.[14]

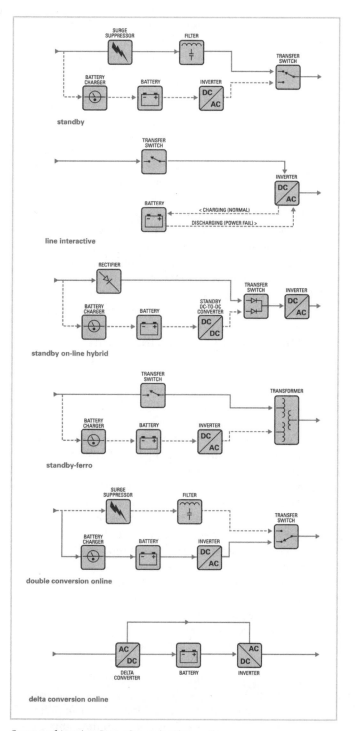

Courtesy of American Power Conversion Corporation

FIGURE 9-5   Types of Uninterruptible Power Supplies

Because UPS is not truly uninterruptible, it is often referred to as a **standby power supply (SPS)**. SPS is an offline battery backup that detects the interruption of power to the power equipment. The primary power source is the electrical service. When the power stops flowing to the equipment, the SPS kicks in to activate a transfer switch, which then provides power from the batteries, through a DC to AC converter, until the power is restored or the computer is shut down. Various types of UPS are listed below. The advantage of SPS is that it is the most cost-effective type of UPS. However, the significant drawbacks, such as run time and switch time (the amount of time it takes to switch from standby to active) may outweigh the cost savings. Switch time may become an issue, as very sensitive computing equipment may not be able to handle the delay in transfer once the power stops, and thus reset and even suffer data loss or damage. These systems also provide no power conditioning, which is a drawback discussed in the coverage of more sophisticated UPS. As a result, SPS is seldom used in critical computing applications and is best suited for home and light office use. UPS capacity is measured by the units volt-ampere (or VA) power output rating. These devices typically run up to 1,000 VA and can be engineered to exceed 10,000 VA. A typical PC might use 200 VA, and a server in a computer room may need 2,000 to 5,000 VA depending on needed running time. The four types of UPS are outlined below:

A **standby or offline UPS** is an offline battery backup that detects the interruption of power to the power equipment. The primary power source is the electrical service. When the power stops flowing to the equipment, the UPS kicks in activating a transfer switch which then provides power from the batteries, through a DC to AC converter, until the power is restored or the computer is shut down.

A **ferroresonant standby UPS** improves upon the standby UPS design. This UPS is still an offline UPS, with the electrical service still providing the primary source of power and the UPS serving as a battery backup. The primary difference is that a ferroresonant transformer replaces the UPS transfer switch. The transformer provides power conditioning and line filtering to the primary power source, reducing the effect of power problems. This transformer also stores energy in its coils providing a buffer to fill in the gap between interruption of service, and activation of the battery backup. This greatly reduces the probability of system reset and data loss. These systems are better suited to settings that require a large capacity of conditioned and reliable power, since they are available in up to 14,000 VA. However, with the improvement in other UPS designs, many manufacturers have abandoned this design in favor of more recent models.

The **line-interactive UPS** has a substantially different design than the previous models. In the line-interactive UPS the internal components of the standby models are replaced with a pair of inverters and converters. The primary power source, like both the SPS and the ferroresonant UPS, remains the power company, with the battery as backup. However the inverters and converters both charge the battery and provide power when needed. Once the power supply ceases, the inverters and converters begin supplying power to the systems. As this device is always connected to the output, instead of relying on a switch, this model has a much faster response time and also incorporates power conditioning and line filtering.

The **true online UPS** works in the opposite fashion to a standby UPS. In an online UPS, the primary power source is the battery, with the power feed from the utility constantly recharging the batteries. This model allows constant feed to the system, while completely eliminating power problems. By controlling these problems, the computing systems are fed a constant, smooth, conditioned power stream. If the power fails, the computer systems are unaffected, as long as the batteries hold out. The online UPS is considered the top of the line and as such is the most expensive. The only major drawback, other than cost, is that the process of constantly converting from an AC feed to DC battery storage and back to an AC feed creates high levels of heat. An improved model resolves this issue by incorporating a device known as a delta-conversion unit, which allows some of the incoming power to be fed directly to the destination computers, thus reducing the amount of energy wasted and heat generated. Should the power fail, the delta unit shuts off, and the batteries automatically compensate for the increased power draw; the systems still do not detect a change in voltage levels.

Selecting the best UPS can be a lesson in electrical engineering, because you must calculate the load the attached systems place on an active UPS. This can be quite challenging. Fortunately, many UPS vendors provide sample scenarios that aid in the selection of the optimal device. Because a high-quality UPS costs several thousand dollars, it is advisable to select the smallest UPS necessary to provide the needed support. To manually calculate the rating needed in a UPS, you begin by examining the computer systems and connected support equipment to be protected. For example, the back panel of a monitor can indicate that it is rated at 110 volts and 2 amps. You can then calculate the wattage you need to run this device by multiplying the two, since volts times amps equals watts. The multiplication shows that the rating of the monitor is 220 VA. The computer draws 3 amps at 110 volts and therefore have a rating of 330 VA. Together the total is 550 VA. You can then select a UPS capable of supporting this voltage level. The UPS provides information on how long it would run at a specific voltage level. Some smaller scale UPSs can run approximately six minutes at 600 VA at full voltage. You should look for a UPS that provides enough time to both ride out the minor power fluctuations and give the user enough time to safely shut down the computer before the UPS completely gives out.

Emergency Shutoff

One important aspect of power management in any environment is the need to be able to stop power immediately should the current represent a risk to human or machine safety. Most computer rooms and wiring closets are equipped with an emergency power shutoff, which is usually a large red button, prominently placed to facilitate access, with an accident-proof cover to prevent unintentional use. These devices are the last line of defense against personal injury and machine damage in the event of flooding or sprinkler activation. The last person out of the computer room hits the switch, preventing the water from short-circuiting the computers and destroying computers that are active. While it is never advisable to allow water to come into contact with a computer, there is a much higher probability of recovery if the systems were not active when wet. Some disaster recovery companies specialize in water damage recovery. At a minimum, hard drives and other sealed devices may be recoverable. The list below defines relevant terms for electrical power influences:

- **Fault**: Momentary interruption in power
- **Blackout**: Prolonged interruption in power
- **Sag**: Momentary drop in power voltage levels
- **Brownout**: Prolonged drop in power voltage levels
- **Spike**: Momentary increase in power voltage levels
- **Surge**: Prolonged increase in power voltage levels

Water Problems

Another critical utility infrastructure element is water service. Lack of water poses problems to systems, including the functionality of fire suppression systems, and the ability of water chillers to provide air-conditioning. On the other hand, a surplus of water, or water pressure, poses a real threat. Flooding, leaks, and the resulting presence of water in areas where it should not be is catastrophic to paper and electronic storage of information. Water damage can result in complete failure of computer systems and the structures that house them. It is therefore important to integrate water detection systems into the alarm systems that regulate overall facilities operations.

Structural Collapse

Unavoidable environmental factors or forces of nature can cause failures of structures that house the organization. Structures are designed and constructed with specific load limits, and overloading these design limits, intentionally or unintentionally, inevitably results in structural failure. Personal injury and potential for loss of life are also high in these conditions. Periodic inspections by qualified civil engineers assist in identifying potentially dangerous structural conditions before the structure fails.

Testing Facility Systems

Just as with any phase of the security process, the physical security of the facility must be constantly documented, evaluated, and tested. Documentation of the facilities configuration, operation, and function is integrated into disaster recovery plans and standing operating procedures. Testing provides information necessary to improve the physical security in the facility and identifies weak points.

Interception of Data

The next major area of physical security is the physical interception of data. There are three methods of data interception: direct observation, interception of data transmission, and electromagnetic interception. With direct observation, an individual must be close enough to the information to breach confidentiality. The physical security mechanisms described in the previous sections restrict the possibility of an individual accessing unauthorized areas and therefore directly observing information. There is, however, a corresponding risk when the information is removed from a protected facility. If an employee is browsing documents over lunch in a restaurant or takes work home, the risk of direct observation rises substantially. If a competitor knows that an organization's employees frequently take classified information home, it can more easily intercept vital information at the employee's home than at the office. Incidences of interception, such as shoulder surfing, can be avoided, if employees are either prohibited from removing sensitive information from the office or required to implement strong security at their homes.

On the other hand, if attackers can access the transmission media, they need not be anywhere near the source of information. In some cases, as with Internet usage, the attacker can use sniffer software, which has been described in previous chapters, to collect information. Other interceptions, such as tapping into a LAN, require some proximity to the organization. It is important for network administrators to periodically conduct a physical inspection of all data ports, to insure no unauthorized taps have occurred. If direct wiretaps are a concern, the organization should consider fiber-optic cable, as the difficulty in splicing into fiber makes it much more resistant to tapping. If wireless LANs are used, the organization should be concerned about eavesdropping on networks, as the individual snooper may be hundreds of feet outside the building, depending on the strength of the wireless access points (WAPs). For this reason alone, all wireless communications should be secured via encryption. Modern hackerware does not require a user to log into a network to eavesdrop on wireless transmissions. Cellular scanners enable snoopers to listen in on cellular conversations, and nosy neighbors use FM radios to eavesdrop on cordless phone conversations. By the way, the Federal wiretapping act does not cover wireless communications, as courts have ruled that users have no "expectation of privacy" with radio-based communications media.

The third area of interception of data is a bit more like a "Star Trek" espisode. For decades scientists have known that electricity moving through cables emits electromagnetic signals (EM). It is possible to eavesdrop on those signals, and therefore to determine the data carried on the cables without actually tapping into them. In 1985, scientists proved that computer monitors also emitted radio waves, and that the screens could be reconstructed from these signals.[15] More recently scientists determined that certain devices with LED displays actually emit information encoded in the light that pulses in these LEDs.[16]

TEMPEST is a technology that involves the monitoring of devices that emit electromagnetic radiation (EMR) in such a manner that the data can be reconstructed. Some believe that the acronym was originally a code word created by the U.S. government in the 1960s, but was later defined as Transient Electromagnetic Pulse Emanation Surveillance Technology or Telecommunications Electronics Material Protected from Emanating Spurious Transmissions. James Atkinson, a TEMPEST engineer certified by the National Security Agency (NSA) says that there is no such thing as TEMPEST monitoring. He claims it's an urban legend stating that most modern computers are shielded to prevent interference, not eavesdropping. Atkinson states that receiving monitor emanations is theoretically possible, but it would be extremely difficult, expensive, and impractical.[17]

Legend or not, a good deal of money is being spent by the government and military protecting computers from TEMPEST monitoring. This involves the following: ensuring that computers are placed as far as possible from outside perimeters (see Chapter 8 for more information), installing special shielding inside the CPU case, and implementing a host of other restrictions, including maintaining distances from plumbing and other infrastructure components that carry radio waves. Standards for these types of protection are available from the NSA at *www.nsa.gov/isso/bao/tep.htm*. Regardless of whether there is a real threat from eavesdropping or emanations, many systems that protect against emanations also protect against threats to physical security.

Mobile and Portable Systems

Although the physical security associated with mobile and portable solutions substantially overlaps other security areas, these solutions are important enough to warrant additional mention. With the increased threat to overall information security for laptops, handhelds, and PDAs, mobile computing requires even more security than the average in-house system. Many of these mobile computing systems not only have corporate information stored within them, many are configured to facilitate the user's access into the organization's secure computing facilities. Forms of access include VPN connections, databases of passwords, locations of files, and storage of information on organizational structure. Many users allow the underlying operating systems to conveniently remember usernames and passwords to simplify the access to information. In addition, many people have multiple accounts, with different usernames and passwords. It is tempting to allow the systems to assist in the access of frequently needed accounts. The downside is obvious: loss of the system means loss of the access control mechanisms.

New technology to support the location of lost or stolen laptops can provide additional security. The first type of new technology is CompuTrace, computer software that is stored on a laptop's hardware, as described in Figure 9-6. Periodically, when the computer is on the Internet, the software reports itself and the electronic serial number of the computer on which it is installed to a central monitoring center. If the laptop is reported stolen, the computer can be traced to its current location and possibly recovered. The software is so versatile that it is undetectable on the system, even if the thief knows the software is installed. It even remains installed if the drive is formatted and the operating system is reinstalled.

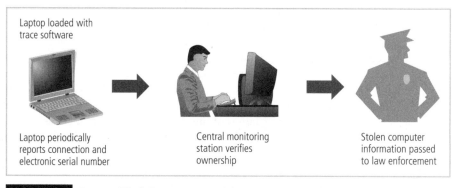

Laptop loaded with trace software

Laptop periodically reports connection and electronic serial number

Central monitoring station verifies ownership

Stolen computer information passed to law enforcement

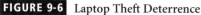

FIGURE 9-6 Laptop Theft Deterrence

Also available for laptops are burglar alarms made up of a PC card that contains a motion detector. If the alarm in the laptop is armed, and the laptop is moved beyond a configured distance, the alarm triggers an audible alarm. The system also shuts down the computer and includes an encryption option to completely render the information unusable.

For maximum security, laptops should be secured at all times. If you are traveling with a laptop, you should have it in your possession at all times. Special care should be exercised when flying, as laptop thefts in airports are common. The list below outlines steps you can take to prevent your laptop from being stolen and comes from the Metropolitan Police of the District of Columbia:

- "Don't leave a laptop in an unlocked vehicle, even if the vehicle is in your driveway or garage, and never leave it in plain sight, even if the vehicle is locked—that's just inviting trouble. If you must leave your laptop in a vehicle, the best place is in a locked trunk. If you don't have a trunk, cover it up and lock the doors.
- "Parking garages are likely areas for thefts from vehicles, as they provide numerous choices and cover for thieves. Again, never leave your laptop in plain sight; cover it or put it in the trunk.
- "Do be aware of the damage extreme temperatures can cause to computers.

- "Carry your laptop in a nondescript carrying case, briefcase, or bag when moving about. Placing it in a case designed for computers is an immediate alert to thieves that you have a laptop.
- "Going to lunch, or taking a break? Don't leave a meeting or conference room without your laptop. Take it with you, or you run the risk that it won't be there when you return.
- "Lock the laptop in your office during off-hours.
- "Don't have your own office? Use a cable lock that wraps around a desk or chair leg. Or put the laptop in a locked closet or cabinet.
- "Don't let unaccompanied strangers wander around in your workplace. Offer assistance and deliver the visitors to their destinations.
- "Apply distinctive paint markings to make your laptop unique and easily identifiable. Liquid white-out is a good substance to apply.
- "Consider purchasing one of the new theft alarm systems specially made for laptops.
- "Be aware that if your computer is stolen, automatic logins can make it easy for a thief to send inappropriate messages with your account.
- "Back up your information on disks today, and store the disks at home or the office."[18]

Remote Computing Security

Remote site computing is rapidly growing in popularity. Remote site computing includes a wide variety of computing sites that are distant from the base organizational facility and includes the entire spectrum of telecommuters (or telecomputers). **Telecommuting** involves computing using telecommunications facilities. These facilities include the Internet, dial-up connections, or leased point-to-point links. Individual employees may need to access home networks on business trips, telecommuters need access from their home systems, and some organizations even have satellite offices that need to be tightly integrated into the overall information technology infrastructure.

Individuals telecommuting from home deserve special attention. As more individuals consider telecommuting, the risk to organizational information through these often unsecured connections is substantial. With overcrowding in large metropolitan cities, more and more employees are considering telecommuting. By avoiding the traffic congestion, sparse parking, and long commutes, these employees can focus on the job without risking commuter accidents. The problem is that few organizations provide their employees with secure connections to their office networks, and even fewer provide secure systems, should the employee's home computer be compromised. To provide a secure extension of the organization's internal networks, all external connections must be secured. To secure the entire network, the organization must dedicate security resources to protecting these home connections. Although the installation of a VPN may go a long way toward protecting the data in transmission, frequently telecommuters store office data on their home systems, in home filing cabinets, and on off-site media. To complete the security process, the computers that telecommuters use to access the network must be more secure than the organization's systems, as they are outside the security perimeter. An attacker breaking into someone's home would probably find a much lower level of security than if the same attacker were to access an office system. Most office systems have some form of native operating system that requires login, in addition to the network connection requiring additional authentication, but the home computer is probably the employee's personal machine, with a much less secure operating systems and preconfigured access. As mentioned earlier, this home machine is most probably set up for the OS to remember key username and password data as well. To solve this problem, telecommuters must refrain from allowing the system to remember their passwords. They must use a modern operating system that requires authentication, such as Windows NT/2000/XP. They must store all loose data in locking filing cabinets and loose media in locking fire safes. They must treat the home office more carefully than they would the on-site office, as the general level of security for the average home is lower than that of a commercial building.

The same goes for the mobile computer and the off-site office worker. Employees using notebooks in hotel rooms should presume that their unencrypted transmissions are being monitored, and that any unsecured notebook computer can be stolen. The off-site worker using leased facilities, does not know who else is physically attached to the network, and therefore who is listening to conversations. VPNs are a must in all off-site to on-site communications, and the advanced authentications systems discussed in Chapter 8 are strongly advised.

Although it is possible to secure remote sites, organizations cannot assume that employees will invest their own funds for security. Many organizations barely tolerate telecommuting for a number of reasons, including the expectation that the employee must be issued two sets of computing equipment, one for the office and one for the home. This extra expense is difficult to justify, especially when the employee is the only one gaining the benefit from telecommuting. In those rare cases in which allowing an employee or consultant to telecommute is the only way to gain extremely valuable skills, the organization is usually willing to do what is necessary to secure its systems. Only when additional research into telecommuting clearly displays a financial bottom-line advantage to telecommuting do organizations begin to invest sufficient resources into the securing of the telecommuters equipment. As a caveat, there are several quality organizations that openly embrace and support telecommuting. These organizations are typically one of three groups. The first is the mature and therefore fiscally sound organization with a sufficient budget to support telecommuting and the need to enhance its standing with employees and to improve its organizational image. In recent years, the availability of telecommuting has become a factor in the ranking contests undertaken by various magazines. Some organizations seek to improve employee work conditions and also gain a higher level in the best-places-to-work ranking by adding telecommuting as an option for employees. The second group is the new high-technology company, with a large number of geographically diverse employees, who telecommute almost exclusively. These companies use technology extensively and are determined to make the adoption of technology and its use the cornerstone of the organization. The third group overlaps with the second and is referred to as the virtual organization. A **virtual organization** is a group of individuals brought together for a specific task, usually from different organizations, divisions, or departments. These individuals form a virtual company, either in leased facilities or through 100 percent telecommuting. When the job is done, the organization is either redirected or dissolved. These organizations rely almost exclusively on remote computing and telecommuting to function. However, these organizations are extremely rare and therefore not well documented or studied.

Special Considerations for Physical Security Threats

Now that the field of physical security has been introduced, there are a number of special considerations for physical security threats that should be examined. The first of these is the decision to develop physical security in-house or to outsource it. As with any aspect of information security, the make or buy decision should not be made lightly. There are a number of qualified and professional agencies that provide consulting and services in the physical security area. The benefit of outsourcing physical security includes gaining the experience and knowledge of these agencies, many of which have been in the field for decades. Outsourcing unfamiliar operations always frees the organization to focus on its primary objectives, rather than being distracted by support operations. The downside includes the high expense of outsourcing physical security, the loss of control over the individual components of the physical security solution, and the level of trust that must be placed in another company. An organization must not only trust the processes used by the contracted company but also its ability to hire and retain trustworthy employees who respect the privacy of the hiring organization, even though they have no allegiance to it. This level of trust is often the most difficult aspect of the decision to outsource, because nonemployees are providing physical security for the organization's information resources, and in doing so are providing a safeguard that the organization administers only marginally. The decision is not easy.

Another area of physical security deals with social engineering. As discussed in previous chapters, social engineering is the use of people skills to obtain information from employees without their knowing it. While most social engineers prefer to use the telephone and computer to make their contacts and solicit information, there are those who brazen accessing the information more directly. In addition to the urban legend of the janitor spy, there are a number of ways an outsider can gain access to the organization's resources. Most organizations do not distribute a list of nonemployees who are authorized to access the facility. As a result, no one gives the wandering repairman, service worker, or city official a second look. It is not difficult to dress like a telephone repairman, construction worker, or building inspector and move freely throughout a building. To go almost anywhere in a building, all one really needs is a clipboard and an attitude. If you look as if you have a mission and you look competent, most people leave you alone. How can organizations combat this type of attack? By requiring that all individuals entering the facility display appropriate visitor's badges and be escorted by a security individual when in restricted areas.

Inventory Management

As with other organizational resources, computing equipment should be inventoried and inspected on a regular basis. The management of a computer inventory is an important part of physical security. How else does corporate security know if an employee has been pilfering computer supplies or has quit and taken organizational equipment home? Similarly, classified information should also be inventoried and managed. In the military, whenever a classified document is reproduced, a stamp is placed on the original before it is copied. This stamp states the document's classification level and prints "___ of ___," so that the person making the copies can mark what the number of the copy is out of the total number of copies. If 25 copies are to be made, the person responsible for copying the document writes 26 in the right blank, makes copies, and then numbers them. Why 26 and not 25? The original is always document number one. Then each classified copy is issued to its receiver, who signs for the document. While this procedure is overkill for most organizations, it ensures that the inventory management of classified documents is secure at all times. The formality of having to sign for a document cements its worth in the mind of the receiver.

Chapter Summary

- Physical security addresses the design, implementation, and maintenance of countermeasures that protect the physical resources of an organization. This means the physical protection of the people, hardware, and the supporting system elements, and resources associated with the management of information in all its states.

- Many threats to information security can also be classified as threats to the physical security. Policy guides the planning of physical security in the development life cycle and serves as a reference to organizational objectives through ongoing maintenance and use.

- In the context of facilities management, a secure facility is a physical location that has been engineered with controls designed to minimize the risk of attacks from physical threats. A secure facility can use the natural terrain, traffic flow, urban development, and can complement them with protection mechanisms, such as fences, gates, walls, guards, and alarms to provide the effective protection of information resources and people.

- A part of general management's responsibility for the physical environment, the management of keys and locks is a fundamental concern.

- A fail-safe lock is usually used on an exit, where it is essential for human safety in the event of a fire. A fail-secure lock is used when human safety is not a factor.

- Monitoring equipment can record events that guards and dogs might miss and can be used in areas where other types of physical controls are not practical.

- Just as with any phase of the security process, the physical security of the facility must be constantly documented, evaluated, and tested.

- Fire suppression systems are devices installed and maintained to detect and respond to a fire, potential fire, or combustion. Fire suppression systems typically block an environment from one of the three requirements for fire: temperature, fuel, or oxygen.

- There are three basic types of fire detection systems: thermal detection, smoke detection, and flame detection.

- There are four conditions controlled by HVAC systems that can cause damage to information-carrying systems: temperature, filtration, humidity, and static electricity.

- Computer systems depend on specific power needs to function; when power levels are too high, too low, or too erratic, computer circuitry can be damaged or destroyed. Power is termed as clean when it is properly delivered, contains no unwanted fluctuations, and has no embedded signaling.

- Water problems and the weakening and subsequent failure of a building's physical structure clearly represent potential threats to the integrity and availability of information assets.

- Data can be intercepted electronically and manually. There are three routes of data interception: direct observation, interception of data transmission, and electromagnetic interception.

- TEMPEST is a technology that involves the monitoring of devices that emit electromagnetic radiation (EMR) in such a manner that the data can be reconstructed.

- With the increased threat to overall information security for laptops, handhelds, and PDAs, organizations should be aware that mobile computing requires even more security than the average in-house system.

- Remote site computing requires a secure extension of the organization's internal networks and special attention to security for any connected home or off-site computing technology.

- Classified information should also be inventoried and managed. If multiple copies of a classified document are made, they should be numbered and tracked.

Review Questions

1. What is physical security? What are the primary threats to physical security? How are they manifested in attacks against the organization?

2. What are the seven major sources of physical loss? How do they map into the primary threats noted above?

3. How do the roles of IT, security, and general management differ with regard to physical security?

4. In what ways is physical security like logical security with regard to policy? How is physical security like logical security with regard to the three communities of interest?

5. How does physical access control differ from logical access control as described in earlier chapters? How is it similar?

6. Describe facilities management. How does facilities management vary with the size of the organization?

7. Define a secure facility. What is the primary objective of designing such a facility? What are some of the secondary objectives you might strive to achieve in designing a secure facility?

8. Why are guards considered the most effective control for situations that require human reasoning? Why are they usually the most expensive controls to deploy? When should dogs be used for physical security?

9. List and describe the four categories of locks. Taken in the order presented in the text, what attribute increases as you move down the list? In which situation is each preferred?

10. What are the two described failure modes for locks? What implications does this have for human safety? In which situation is each preferred?

11. What is a mantrap? When should it be used?

12. What is the primary drawback to electronic monitoring systems? How has this affected their use?

13. What is the most common form of alarm? What does it detect? What types of sensors are commonly used in this type of alarm system?

14. Describe a construction firewall that is used in buildings. List reasons for needing a firewall for physical security controls.

15. What is considered the most serious threat within the realm of physical security? Why is it valid to consider this threat the most serious?

16. What are the three requirements for a fire to start and continue? How do fire suppressions systems use the three requirements to interrupt fires?

17. List and describe the three fire detection technologies covered in the chapter. Which is the most commonly used in the world today?

18. List and describe the four classes of fire described in the text. Does the class of the fire dictate how to control the fire?

19. What is the problem with halon?

20. What does HVAC stand for? Why is this a topic of concern for physical security? What four physical characteristics of the indoor environment are controlled by a properly designed HVAC system? What are the optimal temperature and humidity ranges for computing systems?

21. List and describe the ways in which electrical power quality can be degraded. Why is static electricity a problem for computing systems? Is a UPS required to overcome each specific degradation?

22. List and describe the four primary types of UPS systems. Which is the most effective and the most expensive and why?

23. What two critical factors are impacted when water is not available in a facility? Why are these factors important to the operation of the organization's information assets?

24. List and describe the three fundamental ways that data can be intercepted. Why is data interception considered a part of physical security? How can you protect against each?

25. What can you do to reduce the risk of laptop theft?

Exercises

1. Assume that your organization is planning a lights-out server room in the data center. Describe the fire control system(s) you would include in that room. (A lights-out room functions without human beings through the automation of functions.)

2. Assume you have converted part of a former area of general office space in an existing building into a server room. Describe the factors you would consider for each of the following topics:
   a. Walls and doors
   b. Access control
   c. Fire detection
   d. Fire suppression
   e. Heating, ventilating, and air conditioning
   f. Power quality and distribution

3. Assume you have been asked to review the power needs for a stand-alone computer system. It processes important, but noncritical, data and does not have to be online at all times. It does, however, store valuable data that could be corrupted if power were to suddenly cease. What factors of the various UPS systems should concern you? What would you recommend as the lowest cost solution for this situation?

4. Using a map of your town, identify three areas where you would feel confident locating a secure data facility. What are the strengths and weaknesses of each?

5. Using the Web, search for hacker sites that provide information on breaching physical security. At a minimum, find one site on how to pick mechanical locks, one on social engineering, and one on bypassing biometric devices.

6. Using a floor plan from a building you are familiar with, design an electronic monitoring plan that includes closed-circuit television, burglar alarms with appropriate sensors, fire detectors, and suppression and access controls for key entrances.

7. Select a building at your institution. Identify the existing fire suppression and detection systems components. What fire extinguishing equipment is present and what classes of fires are they rated to combat?

8. Define the required wattage for a UPS for the following systems:
   a. Monitor: 2 amps; CPU: 3 amps; printer: 3 amps
   b. Monitor: 3 amps; CPU: 4 amps; printer: 3 amps
   c. Monitor: 3 amps; CPU: 4 amps; printer: 4 amps

9. Using the Web, find a UPS that provides the wattage necessary to run the systems listed in Exercise 8 for at least 15 minutes during a power outage.

Case Exercises

I. HVAC Security Important Piece of Security Puzzle

Adapted from "More HVAC security guidelines continue to surface"[19]

By Mark P Skaer, *Air Conditioning, Heating & Refrigeration*, May 20, 2002.

As a direct result of the terrorist attacks on the United States, the newly formed Office of Homeland Security has formed a task force to specifically address the physical security that protects buildings from terrorist attacks. This task force, the Interagency Workgroup on Building Air Protection, is composed of representatives of over 30 federal government agencies.

The first task at hand was to formulate a series of policies to guide individuals and organizations tasked with construction, management, and maintenance of facilities on securing facilities from terrorist attack. The first deliverable of this working group was the development of a "Guidance for Protecting Building Environments from Airborne Chemical, Biological, or Radiological Attacks" developed primarily in conjunction with the National Institute of Occupational Safety and Health. This document was specifically designed to address HVAC physical security: filtration, airflow, systems administration, and training of maintenance staff.

An overview of these guidelines includes requirements to:

- Restrict access and secure air intakes and returns
- Secure building HVAC systems
- Develop emergency capabilities
- Use caution in the implementation of security measures that impact the function of the systems

A particular problem with the security of buildings against terrorist chemical and biological attacks is that measures to protect against these attacks can adversely affect the normal operations of HVAC, fire, and other physical plant systems. Therefore there is a need for specific guidelines.

1. Why would HVAC security be important to physical security in light of the anthrax attacks?

2. What can an organization do to protect their HVAC systems and thus minimize this threat?

II. The Physical Security Physical

Adapted from "Had a security physical lately?"[20]

By Curtis E. Dalton, *Business Communications Review*, May, 2002.

Although information security professionals are quick to mention the need for electronic intrusion detection and prevention, the need for physical intrusion detection may not get the same attention. The acts of September 11 have changed the perspectives of many companies.

Just as an organization conducts security evaluations of its electronic access controls, the security team should also conduct evaluations of its physical security profiles. It is common to say that electronic security can do little to stop a well-placed brick.

Some common sense mechanisms include not advertising the company's mission if it involves sensitive data. Other mechanisms include the following: guard entry and exit points correctly; require physical access measures including ID cards and name badges; and make sure implemented controls are adequately enforced, because guards who don't check people entering and exiting a facility are worse than no guards at all. It is also important to audit these controls, to make sure that unusual activities are not occurring.

It is sometimes frustrating to realize that many physical control measures can be fooled or circumvented. Just ask any 18- to 20-year-old, and you find that counterfeit identifications are possible to obtain.

Physical security should also be appropriate to the situation. For example, data center access should be substantially more restricted than front door security. Without proper support, however, physical security mechanisms, like other controls, provide less than desired levels of security. All security measures must be maintained and monitored.

Realistic training is needed for security staff, in the areas of physical as well as electronic security. Simulations of breaches of physical security should be performed, with the results documented, evaluated, and improvements made. Management should be as involved with measures of physical security as they are with measures of electronic security.

The bottom line is that physical security should support the operations and goals of the business, without undue interference. When business and security clash, security loses.

1. What should a physical security physical involve? What areas should be audited?

2. How can physical security interfere with the operations of a business? What special considerations should management evaluate in the implementation of physical security?

Endnotes

1. Donn B. Parker, *Fighting Computer Crime* (New York: John Wiley and Sons Inc., 1998), 250-251.

2. Marianne Swanson, *Guide for Developing Security Plans for Information Technology Systems (December 1998)*, National Institute of Standards and Technology, SP 800-18, 28-30 [Cited 10 July 2002]; available from the World Wide Web *http://csrc.nist.gov/publications/nistpubs/800-18/Planguide.PDF*.

3. Military-net.com, "General Military Knowledge," *Military-net.com Online* [Cited 10 July 2002]; available from the World Wide Web *http://www.military-net.com/education/mpdgeneral.html*.

4. Army Study Guide.com Online [Cited 23 September 2002]; available from the World Wide Web *http://armystudyguide.com/guard_duty/studyguide.htm*.

5. Security Management Consulting, "Types of Locks," *Security Management Consulting Online* [Cited 10 July 2002]; available from the World Wide Web *http://www.secmgmt.com/equipmentspecs/tol.php*.

6. Marianne Swanson, *Guide for Developing Security Plans for Information Technology Systems (December 1998)*, National Institute of Standards and Technology,SP 800-18, 30 [Cited 10 July 2002]; available from the World Wide Web *http://csrc.nist.gov/publications/nistpubs/800-18/Planguide.PDF*.

7. Nick Artim, *An Introduction to Fire Detection, Alarm, and Automatic Fire Sprinklers*, Emergency Management, Technical Leaflet 2, sec. 3, (Middlebury: Fire Safety Network).

8. The University of Texas, "Environmental Health and Safety Operations Guide," *UTSA Online* [Cited 10 July 2002]; available from the World Wide Web *http://www.utsa.edu/compliance/enviro/Section%2007/Sec07-06.html*.

9. Environmental Protection Agency, "Halon Substitutes Under SNAP as of 26 April 2000," *EPA Online* [Cited 10 July 2002]; available from the World Wide Web *http://www.epa.gov/ozone/snap/fire/halo.pdf*.

10. *Ibid.*

11. Firewall.com, Online [Cited 23 September 2002]; available from the World Wide Web *http://www.fireline.com/firesuppressionsystems/firesuppressionsystems.html*

12. "Static Electricity and Computers," *www.webopedia.com/DidYouKnow/2002/March/static.html*

13. Webopedia, "Static Electricity and Computers," *Webopedia Online* (March 2002) [Cited 10 July 2002]; available from the World Wide Web *http://www.webopedia.com/DidYouKnow/Computer_Science/2002/static.html*.

14. Charles M. Kozierok, "Uninterruptible Power Supply Types," *PC Guide Online* (17 April 2001) [Cited 10 July 2002]; available from the World Wide Web *http://www.pcguide.com/ref/power/ext/ups/types.htm*.

15. Wim Van Eck, "Electromagnetic Radiation from Video Display Units: An Eavesdropping Risk?" *Computers & Security* 4 (1985): 269-286.

16. Joe Loughry and David A. Umphress, "Information Leakage from Optical Emanations," *ACM Transactions on Information and System Security* 7, no. 7, accepted March 2002.

17. PC Privacy, "Is Tempest a Threat or Hoax?" *PC Privacy* 8, no. 4 (April 2000).

18. Metropolitan Police of The District of Columbia, "Tips for Preventing Laptop Computer Theft," *Government of The District of Columbia Online* [Cited 10 July 2002]; available from the World Wide Web *http://mpdc.dc.gov/info/consumer/laptop_theft.shtm*.

19. Mark P. Skaer, "More HVAC Security Guidelines Continue to Surface," *Air Conditioning, Heating & Refrigeration News* 216, no.3 (20 May 2002): 31.

20. Curtis E. Dalton, "Had a Security Physical Lately?" *Business Communications Review* 32, no. 5 (May 2002): 44-45.

Implementing Security

> Change is good. You go first!
>
> **DILBERT (BY SCOTT ADAMS)**

KELVIN URICH ARRIVED EARLY FOR the change control meeting. Sitting in the large conference room, he reviewed his notes and then flipped through the handouts one final time. After his meeting with the technical review committee last week, he felt he had hammered out a tight, well-ordered project plan.

This was Kelvin's first technical review meeting. Once this meeting was over, he knew that his salvo of change requests would keep the technical analysts of Sequential Label and Supply busy for months to come. At this moment, he felt everything was under control. His handout was loaded with columns of tasks, subtasks, and action items. He had assigned dates to every action step, and he already had names assigned for the implementation of each task.

Naomi Jackson, the change control supervisor also arrived a few minutes early. She saw Kelvin, gave him a nod, and then began passing out the weekly change reports to seating places around the conference table. Charlie Moody came in and also nodded to Kelvin before taking his usual seat.

Once the room filled, Naomi said "Time to get started." She picked up her copy of the report and announced the first change control item for discussion, Item 742.

One of the members of the Windows support team responded, "As planned." His short statement meant to all of the regular attendees that this item was routine maintenance that was going to happen in the planned maintenance window next Sunday afternoon.

Since no one else said anything, Naomi continued down the list in numeric order. Most items received the response, "As planned" from the sponsoring team member. Once in a while, someone answered "Cancelled" or "Will be rescheduled," but almost all the change items were routine, until they came to Kelvin's group of change requests for information security.

Naomi said, "Items 761 through 767. Kelvin Urich from the security team is here to discuss these items as a group."

Kelvin started by splitting his pile of handouts in two and sending them around the table in both directions. He waited a moment with great anticipation as the stacks were distributed. When everyone had a copy he began, "I'm sure most of you are already aware of the information security upgrades we have been working on for the past few months. We created an overall strategy based on the revised policies that were published last year and a detailed analysis of the threats we face for the systems we have. Since I've been named the project manager, I have created what I think is a very workable plan. First, these seven change requests are all network changes and are all top priority. I have more changes for later, but I thought I'd give everyone a copy as a heads up. That way, each department knows who's next on the list for changes to the security controls. As you can see, there are more changes coming, and I hope we can all work together to make this a success." He looked up at Naomi to indicate he was finished.

"Uh, comments or discussion?" asked Naomi.

Instantly six hands shot into the air. All of them were senior technical analysts. Kelvin realized that none of them were on the technical review committee for networks. And, while others, such as Amy Windahl from the user group and training committee, were busy pulling calendars and PDAs out of briefcases and bags, Davey Martinez from Accounting was busy having a private but heated discussion with Charlie Moody, Kelvin's boss. Charlie did not look pleased.

Above the noise, Kelvin heard someone ask, "Wasn't this supposed to be a preliminary meeting?" This sudden state of chaos during an otherwise orderly meeting made Kelvin realize that his plan was not as simple as he thought.

It was going to be a very long meeting.

DISCUSSION QUESTIONS:

1. Look back at Chapter 6 in which Kelvin was assigned to this project. Did Charlie give him adequate coaching and information about his role in the company?
2. Given the responses at today's meeting, what should Kelvin do next?
3. Had you been in Kelvin's place, what would you have done differently from the time of the assignment in Charlie's office until this meeting?

LEARNING OBJECTIVES:

Upon completion of this material you should be able to:

- Understand how the organization's security blueprint becomes a project plan.
- Understand the numerous organizational considerations that must be addressed by the project plan.
- Grasp the significant role and importance of the project manager in the success of an information security project.
- Understand the need for professional project management for complex projects.
- Take in the technical strategies and models for implementing the project plan.
- Grasp the nontechnical problems that organizations face in times of rapid change.

Introduction

Kelvin got off to a bad start with some of his coworkers. As the assigned project manager, Kelvin failed to consider a number of issues when developing his draft project plan. Implementing an information security project takes time, effort, and a great amount of communication and coordination within an organization. As discussed in Chapter 1, the security systems development life cycle (SecSDLC) is made up of six phases. This chapter and the next discuss two primary stages in the implementation phase and how to successfully execute the information security blueprint. In general the implementation phase is accomplished by changing the configuration and operation of the organization's information systems to make them more secure. It includes changes to:

- Procedures (for example, through policy)
- People (for example, through training)
- Hardware (for example, through firewalls)
- Software (for example, through encryption)
- Data (for example, through classification)

As you recall from earlier chapters, the security systems development life cycle (SecSDLC) is a process for collecting information about the organization's objectives, its technical architecture, and the information security environment. These elements form the information security blueprint, from which the protection of the confidentiality, integrity, and availability of information is built. Whether the information is in storage, being transmitted, or is being processed, it is secured through the application of controls that include policy, education and training, and technology.

During the implementation phase, the organization translates its blueprint for information security into a concrete **project plan**. The project plan delivers instructions to the individuals who are executing the implementation phase. These instructions focus on the security control changes needed to the hardware, software, procedures, data, and people that make up the organization's information systems. The project plan as a whole must describe how to acquire and implement the needed security controls and create a setting in which those controls achieve the desired outcomes.

Before a project plan can be developed, management should already have articulated and coordinated the organization's information security vision and objectives with the communities of interest involved in the execution of the plan. This type of coordination insures that only the controls that add value to the organization's information security program are incorporated into the project plan. If, however, a statement of vision and objectives has not yet been developed for the organization's security program, it is crucial that one be incorporated into the project plan. The vision statement should be concise. It should state the mission of the information security program and its objectives. In other words, the project plan is built upon the vision statement, which serves as a compass for guiding the changes necessary for the implementation phase. The components of the project plan should never conflict with the organization's statement of vision and objectives.

Figure 10-1 shows where the implementation phase occurs in the SecSDLC methodology.

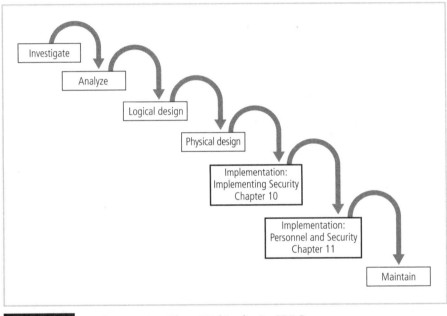

FIGURE 10-1 Implementation Phase Within the SecSDLC

Project Management in the Implementation Phase

Once the organization's vision and objectives are documented and understood, the processes for translating the blueprint into a project plan can be defined. As the scenario of this chapter illustrates, organizational change is not easily accomplished. The following pages discuss the issues a project plan must address, including leadership, managerial, technical, and budgetary considerations, plus organizational resistance to the change.

The major steps in executing the project plan are:

- Planning the project
- Supervising tasks and action steps
- Wrapping up

The project plan can be developed in any number of ways. Each organization has to determine its own project management methodology for IT and information security projects. Whenever possible, information security projects should follow the organizational practices of project management. If your organization does not have clearly defined project management practices, you can apply the general guidelines on project management which are presented in the following pages.

Developing the Project Plan

Planning for the implementation phase involves the creation of a detailed project plan. Creating a project plan to implement the information security blueprint is often assigned to either a project manager or the project champion. This individual can manage the project and delegate parts of it to other decision makers. Often the project manager is an individual from the IT community of interest, because most other employees lack the information security background and the appropriate position within the organization to accomplish the goals of an information security project.

The creation of the project plan itself can be accomplished using a simple planning tool, such as the **work breakdown structure (WBS)** shown below. The WBS can be prepared with a simple desktop PC spreadsheet program or other more complex project management software tools. Using complex project management tools often results in **projectitis**, which is a common pitfall of IT and information security projects. This phenomenon can be recognized when the project manager spends more time documenting project tasks, collecting performance measurements, recording project task information, and updating project completion forecasts than in accomplishing meaningful project work. Recall Kelvin's handout from the opening scenario, which was loaded with dates and details. Clearly, Kelvin fell into the trap of projectitis by developing an elegant, detailed plan before gaining consensus for the changes that it required. As Kelvin did not realize, using simple tools helps the project manager focus on organizing and coordinating with the individuals assigned to the project team.

When using a WBS approach, the project plan is first broken down into several major tasks. Each of these major tasks is placed on the WBS task list. The common attributes for each task are:

- Work to be accomplished (activities and deliverables)
- Individuals (or skills set) assigned to perform the task
- Start and end dates for the task (when known)
- Amount of effort required for completion in hours or work days
- Estimated capital expenses for the task
- Estimated noncapital expenses for the task
- Identification of task interdependencies

Each major task on the WBS is then further divided into either smaller tasks or specific action steps. For the sake of simplification and discussion of the project plan, the sample project plan below divides each task only into action steps. Be aware that in an actual project plan, tasks are often more complex than the example provided below and may require the subdivision of major tasks into subtasks before action steps can be determined and assigned to the individual or skill set. Although there are few hard-and-fast rules about what level of detail is appropriate, there are some indicators that show when a task or subtask becomes an action step: it becomes an action step when it can be completed by one individual or skill set and when it includes a single deliverable as defined below.

Work To Be Accomplished

The first step is to identify the work to be accomplished. This encompasses both activities and deliverables. A **deliverable** is a completed document or program module that can serve either as the beginning point for a later task or becomes an element in the finished project. Ideally, the project planner provides a label for the task followed by a thorough description. The description should be complete enough to avoid ambiguity during the later tracking process, yet, not so detailed as to make the WBS unwieldy. For instance, if the task is to write firewall specifications for the preparation of a request for proposal (RFP), the planner would note that the deliverable is a specification document suitable for distribution to vendors.

Assignees

The project planner should describe the skill set or individual person (often called a **resource**) needed to accomplish the task. Naming individuals should be avoided in the early planning efforts, a rule Kelvin ignored in the opening scenario when he named individuals for every task in the first draft of the project plan. Instead of assigning individuals, the plan should focus on roles or known skill sets as they are used in the organization. For example, if any of the engineers in the networks group can write the specifications for a router, the assigned resource would be "network engineer" on the WBS. As planning progresses, however, the specific tasks and action steps should be assigned to individuals. For example, when only the manager of the networks group can evaluate the responses to the RFP and make an award for a contract, the planner identifies the network manager as the resource.

Start and End Dates

In the early stages of planning, the project planner should focus on determining only completion dates for major milestones within the project. A **milestone** is a specific point in the project plan when a task and its action steps are complete and have a noticeable impact on the progress of the project plan as a whole. For example, the date for sending the final RFP to vendors is considered a milestone, because it signals all RFP preparation work is complete. Early in the planning process, assigning too many dates to too many tasks causes projectitis to increase. This is another mistake Kelvin made in the opening scenario and a significant cause of resistance. By assigning only key or milestone start and end dates early in the process, planners can avoid this pitfall. Later in the planning process additional start and end dates can be added as needed.

Amount of Effort

Planners need to estimate the effort required to complete each task, subtask, or action step. Estimating effort hours for technical work is a complex process. Even when an organization has formal governance, technical review processes, and change control procedures, it is always good practice to ask the individuals who are most familiar with the work or familiar with similar types of work to make the estimates. Then, all individuals assigned to action steps should review the estimated effort hours, understand the tasks, and agree with the estimates. Had Kelvin collaborated with his peers more effectively and adopted a more flexible planning approach, much of the resistance he encountered in the meeting would not have emerged.

Estimated Capital Expenses

Planners need to estimate the expected capital expenses for the completion of this task, subtask, or action item. While each organization budgets and expends capital according to its own established procedures, most differentiate between expenses for durable assets and expenses for other purposes. Be sure to determine the practices in place at the organization where the plan is to be used. For example, a firewall device costing $5,000 may be a capital expense for a given organization, but the same organization might not consider a $5,000 software package as a capital expense.

Estimated Noncapital Expenses

Planners need to estimate the expected noncapital expenses for the completion of the task, subtask, or action item. Some organizations require that this cost include a recovery charge for staff time, while others exclude employee time and only plan contract or consulting time as a noncapital expense. Organizations follow their own established procedures in classifying different kinds of expenses as being capital or noncapital. As mentioned earlier, it is important to determine the practices in place at the organization where the plan is to be used. For example, an information security management program costing $600,000 may be considered a noncapital expense, but a network router that costs $600 may be considered a capital expense.

Task Dependencies

Planners should note wherever possible the dependencies of other tasks or action steps on the task or action step at hand. The tasks or action steps that come before the specific task at hand are called **predecessors**. Tasks or action steps that come after the task at hand are called **successors**. Understand that there is more than one type of dependency, and most courses on project management cover this subject in detail.

An example project plan is provided below to help you better understand the process of creating one. In this example, a small information security project has been assigned to Jane Smith for planning. The project is to design and implement a firewall for a single small office. The hardware is a standard organizational product and will be installed at a location that already has a network connection.

Jane's first step is to list the major tasks:

1. Contact field office and confirm network assumptions.
2. Purchase standard firewall hardware.
3. Configure firewall.
4. Package and ship firewall to field office.
5. Work with local technical resource to install and test.
6. Coordinate vulnerability assessment by penetration test team.
7. Get remote office sign-off and update all network drawings and documentation.

Jane's first draft WBS is shown in Table 10-1.

Table 10-1   Example of WBS, Early Draft

	Task or subtask	Resources	Start and end dates	Estimated effort in hours	Estimated capital expense	Estimated non-capital expense	Dependencies
1	Contact field office and confirm network assumptions	Network architect	S:9/22 E:	2	0	200	
2	Purchase standard firewall hardware	Network architect and purchasing group	S: E:	4	4,500	250	1
3	Configure firewall	Network architect	S: E:	8	0	800	2
4	Package and ship to field office	Student intern	S: E:10/15	2	0	85	3
5	Work with local technical resource to install and test	Network architect	S: E:	6	0	600	4
6	Complete vulnerability assessment by penetration test team	Network architect and penetration test team	S: E:	12	0	1,200	5
7	Get remote office sign-off and update all network drawings and documentation	Network architect	S: E:11/ 30	8	0	800	6

After all individuals involved have reviewed and refined the plan, additional detail is added and more dates are assigned to tasks. Another, more detailed version is shown in Table 10-2. Note the project plan has been further developed and illustrates the breakdown of tasks 2 and 6 into action steps.

Table 10-2   Example of WBS, Later Draft

	Task or SubTask	Resources	Start and End Dates	Estimated Effort in Hours	Estimated Capital Expense	Estimated Non-capital Expense	Dependencies
1	Contact field office and confirm network assumptions	Network architect	S:9/22 E:9/22	2	0	200	
2	Purchase standard firewall hardware						
2.1	Order firewall through purchasing group	Network architect	S:9/23 E:9/23	1		100	1
2.2	Order firewall from manufacturer	Purchasing group	S:9/24 E:9/24	2	4,500	100	2.1
2.3	Firewall delivered	Purchasing group	E:10/3	1		50	2.2
3	Configure firewall	Network architect	S:10/3 E:10/5	8	0	800	2.3
4	Package and ship to field office	Student intern	S:10/6 E:10/15	2	0	85	3
5	Work with local technical resource to install and test	Network architect	S:10/22 E:10/31	6	0	600	4
6	Penetration test						
6.1	Request Penetration test	Network architect	S:11/1 E:11/1	1	0	100	5
6.2	Perform Penetration test	Penetration test team	S:11/2 E:11/12	9	0	900	6.1
6.3	Verify that results of penetration test were passing	Network architect	S:11/13 E:11/15	2	0	200	6.2
7	Get remote office sign-off and update all network drawings and documentation	Network architect	S:11/16 E:11/30	8	0	800	6.2

Project Planning Considerations

As the project plan is developed, adding detail is not always straightforward. The section below discusses important considerations for project planners as they decide what should be included in the work plan, how to break tasks into subtasks and action steps, and how to accomplish the objectives of the project. In the opening scenario, Kelvin did not examine the following considerations and constraints in his draft project plan.

Financial Considerations

No matter what information security needs exist in the organization, the amount of effort that can be expended depends on the funds available. A cost benefit analysis (CBA), prepared earlier in the life cycle, must be verified prior to development of the project plan. The CBA identifies the impact that a specific technology or approach can have on the organization's information assets and what it may cost.

Each organization has its own approach to the creation and management of budgets and expenses. In many cases, the information security budget is a subsection of the overall IT budget. In some organizations information security is a separate budget category that may have parity with the IT budget. Regardless of where in the budget information security items are located, monetary constraints determine what can be accomplished. Both public and private organizations have budgetary constraints, albeit of a different nature.

Public organizations are the most predictable in their budget processes. Based on the results of legislative budget meetings, they usually know in advance the amount of the next fiscal year's budget. The downside is that if during a fiscal year additional funding is needed for operations such as information security, the funds must come from a different spending category. In addition, some public organizations are based on temporary or renewable grants. The expenses must be determined when the grants are written. If new expenses arise, funds must be requested in new grant applications. Grant expenditures are usually audited and cannot be misspent. There is one unique twist to the budgets at many public institutions: all budgeted funds must be spent in one fiscal year. If not, the budget is reduced by that amount the next fiscal year. The result is an "end-of-fiscal-year-spend-a-thon," to spend all the remaining funds before the end of the fiscal year. If you are employed by a public organization, this is often the best time to acquire that remaining piece of technology needed for the information security architecture.

Private (for-profit) organizations on the other hand have different budgetary constraints. The marketplace, not a legislature, drives their constraints. If a for-profit organization does not generate revenue, there can be no funding for any information security expenditure.

When a for-profit organization needs to fund a project to improve security, the funding comes from the company's capital and expense budgets. Each for-profit organization determines its capital budget and the rules for managing capital spending and expenses differently. In any case, budgetary constraints impact the expenditures for information security. For example, a preferred technology or solution may be sacrificed for a less desirable but more affordable solution. The budget ultimately guides the information security implementation.

To justify an amount budgeted for a security project at either a public or for-profit organizations, it may be useful to benchmark expenses of similar organizations. Most for-profit organizations publish the components of their expense reports. Similarly, public organizations must show how funds were spent. The savvy security project manager can find a number of similarly sized organizations with larger expenditures for security and use these as justification for his planned expenditures. While such tactics may not improve this year's budget, they could improve the budget in future years. Attackers can also help to justify the information security budget. If, during the year, attacks have successfully compromised secured information systems, management may be more willing to support the information security budget.

Priority Considerations

In general, the most important information security controls in the project plan should be scheduled first. As explained above, however, with budgetary constraints there are also constraints when assigning priorities. As discussed in Chapters 4 and 5, the implementation of controls is guided by the prioritization of threats and the value of the information assets that are threatened. A control that costs a little more and is a little lower on the prioritization list but addresses many more specific vulnerabilities and threats has higher priority than a less expensive, higher priority component that only addresses one particular vulnerability (such as encryption).

Time and Scheduling Considerations

Time is another constraint that has a broad impact on the development of the project plan. Time can impact a project plan at dozens of points in its development, including the following: time to order and receive a security control due to backlogs of the vendor or manufacturer; time to install and configure the control; time to train the users; and time to realize the return on investment of the control. The one universal rule is that time waits for no one. If a control must be in place before a new electronic commerce product can be implemented, the selection of a particular type or model of technology may be influenced by the speed of acquisition and implementation of the alternatives.

Staffing Considerations

The lack of enough qualified, trained, and available personnel also constrains the project plan. Experienced staff is often needed to implement available technologies and to develop and implement policies and training programs. If no staff members are trained to configure a firewall that is being purchased, someone must be trained, or someone must be hired who is experienced with that particular technology.

Scope Considerations

It is unrealistic for an organization to install all information security components at once. Related to the constraints of time and effort-hours is the project scope. The project plan should not attempt to implement the entire security system at one time. (See the discussion of the bull's-eye approach later in this chapter.) In addition to the constraints of handling so many complex tasks at one time, there are the problems of interrelated conflicts between the installation of information security controls and the daily operations of the organization. In addition, the installation of new information security controls may conflict with existing controls. For example, installing a new packet filtering router and a new application proxy firewall at the same time can cause a conflict between the controls, and as a result, the organization's users are blocked from accessing the Web. Which technology caused the conflict? Was it the router, firewall, or an interaction between the two? As this example shows, it is best to limit the scope of implementation to manageable tasks. This does not mean that the project can allow change to only one component at a time; it does mean that it is prudent to cut back on the number of tasks that are planned to occur at the same time in a single department. Recall that in the opening scenario all of Kelvin's change requests were in the area of networking. If the changes were not deployed exactly as planned, this could have caused extensive disruption to Sequential Label and Supply's ability to function.

Procurement Considerations

All IT and information security planners must consider the acquisition of goods and services. There are a number of constraints on the selection process for equipment and services in most organizations, specifically in the selection of certain service vendors or products from manufacturers and suppliers. These constraints may change the specifics of a particular technology or even eliminate the technology as a viable choice. For example, in a recent budget cycle, the authors' lab administrator was considering selecting an automated risk analysis software package. The leading candidate promised to integrate everything, from soup to nuts, including vulnerability scanning, risk weighting, and control selection. Upon receipt of the RFP, the vendor issued a bid to accomplish the desired requirements for a heart-stopping $75,000, plus a 10 percent annual maintenance fee. For an organization with an annual information security capital budget of $30,000, this completely eliminated that solution from consideration. Procurement and budget constraints are but two of several constraints, which may require reconsideration as the project plan develops.

Organizational Feasibility Considerations

Another consideration is the ability of the organization to adapt to change. Policies require time to develop and new technologies require time to be installed, configured, and tested. In addition, employees need training on both the new policies and new technology components. Employees need to understand how the new information security program impacts their working lives. The goal of the project plan is to avoid new security components from directly impacting the day-to-day operations of the individual employees. This means that changes should be transparent to systems users, unless the new technology causes changes to procedures, such as requiring additional authentication or verification. The organization must develop and conduct training sessions that minimize the impact of the changes, before the new technologies come online. Waiting until the processes are in place, after the users have had to deal with changes without preparation, can create tension and resistance, and possibly undermine security operations altogether. Unless properly trained, users may develop ways to work around difficult or unfamiliar security procedures, bypassing controls and creating additional vulnerabilities. Conversely, users should not be prepared so far in advance that they forget the new training techniques and requirements. The optimal time is usually one to three weeks before the new policies and technologies come online.

Training and Indoctrination Considerations

The size of the organization and the normal conduct of business may preclude a single large training program on new security procedures or technologies. As a result, the organization should conduct a phased-in or pilot approach to implementation (see later section), such as roll-out training for one department at a time. In the case of policies, it may be sufficient to brief all supervisors on new policy and assign the supervisors the task of updating end users in regularly scheduled meetings. Ensure that compliance documents are also distributed, requiring all employees to read, understand, and agree to the new policies.

Change Control and Technology Governance Considerations

In organizations that have IT infrastructures of significant size, the change control and technology governance issues become essential. This topic is discussed in more detail in the "Technical Topics of Implementation" section that follows.

The Need for Project Management

Project management requires a unique set of skills and a thorough understanding of a broad body of specialized knowledge. The cursory overview of project management provided here does not prepare an individual for the role of project manager for a project of any significant size. In the opening scenario, Kelvin's inexperience as a project manger makes this all too clear. It is realistic to assume that most information security projects require a trained project manager, a CISO, or a skilled IT manager, who is versed in project management techniques and can oversee the project. In addition, when selecting advanced or integrated technologies or outsourced services, even experienced project managers are advised to seek expert assistance when engaging in a formal bidding process.

Supervising Implementation

Although it is not an optimal solution, some organizations may choose to designate a champion from the general management community of interest to supervise the implementation of the project plan for security information. In this case, groups of tasks are delegated to individuals or teams from the IT and information security communities of interest. An alternative is to designate a senior IT manager or the CIO of the organization to lead the implementation. In this case, the detailed work is delegated to cross-functional teams. The optimal solution is to designate a suitable person from the information security community of interest, because the inherent focus is on the information security needs of the organization. In the final analysis, it is up to each organization to find the leadership for a successful project implementation that best suits its specific needs and the personalities and politics of the organizational culture.

Executing the Plan

Once a project is underway, it is managed to completion using a process known as a **negative feedback loop** or cybernetic loop, which ensures that progress is measured periodically. The measured results are compared to expected results. When significant deviation occurs, corrective action is taken to bring the task that is deviating from plan back into compliance with the projection, or else the estimate is revised in light of new information. See Figure 10-2 for an overview of this process.

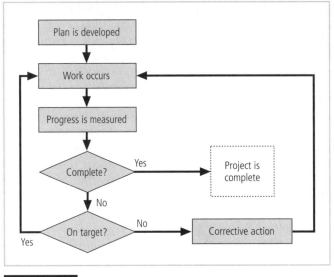

FIGURE 10-2   Negative Feedback Loop

Corrective action is required because of two basic situations: either the estimate was flawed or performance has lagged. When an estimate is flawed, as when a faulty estimate for effort-hours is made, the plan should be corrected and downstream tasks updated to reflect the change. When performance has lagged, for example due to high turnover of skilled employees, correction is accomplished by adding resources, lengthening the schedule, or by reducing the quality or quantity of the deliverable. The decisions are usually expressed in terms of trade-offs. Often a project manager can adjust one of the three following planning parameters for the task being corrected:

- Effort and money allocated
- Elapsed time or scheduling impact
- Quality or quantity of the deliverable

When a task is lagging behind expectations, it is failing in one or more of these parameters. When too much effort and money is being spent, you can either slow down and take longer or lower the deliverable quality or quantity. If the task is taking too long to complete, add more resources in staff time or money or else lower deliverable quality or quantity. If quality is too low, add more resources in staff time or money, or take longer to complete the task. Of course, there are dynamics between these variables, and these simplistic solutions do not serve in all cases, but this simple trade-off model can assist the project manager in analyzing the options available.

Wrap-up

Project wrap-up is usually handled as a procedural task assigned to a mid-level IT or information security manager. These managers collect documentation, finalize status reports, and deliver a final report and a presentation at a wrap-up meeting. The goal of the wrap-up is to resolve any pending issues, critique the overall effort of the project, and draw conclusions about how to improve the process for the future.

Technical Topics of Implementation

Some parts of the implementation process are technical in nature and deal with the application of technology, while others are not and deal instead with the human interface to technical systems. In the following section, the topics of conversion strategies, prioritization among multiple components, outsourcing, and technology governance are discussed.

Conversion Strategies

As the components of the new security system are planned, provisions must be made for the changeover from the previous method of performing a task to the new method. Borrowing from the changeover strategies of information systems, there are four basic approaches to changing from an old method to the new.

- **Direct changeover:** Also known as going "cold turkey," a **direct changeover** involves stopping the old method and beginning the new. This could be as simple as having employees perform one way one week, and the new way the next. Some cases of direct changeover are simple, such as requiring a new password on Monday with stronger authentication; some may be more complex, such as disabling an old firewall and activating the new one. The primary drawback to this approach is that if the new system fails or needs modification, the users may be without services while the system's bugs are worked out. Complete testing of the new system in advance of the direct changeover helps to reduce the probability of these problems.

- **Phased implementation:** A **phased implementation** is the most common approach and involves rolling out a piece of the system across the entire organization. This could mean that the security group implements only a small portion of the new security profile, giving users a chance to get used to it, and resolving small issues as they arise. This is usually the best approach to security rollouts.

- **Pilot implementation:** The **pilot implementation** involves implementing all security improvements in a single office, department, or division, and resolving issues within that group before expanding to the rest of the organization. The pilot implementation works well when an isolated group can serve as the "guinea pig" without dramatically impacting the performance of the organization as a whole. The operation of a research and development group, for example, may not impact the real-time operations of the organization and could assist security in resolving issues that emerge.

- **Parallel operations: Parallel operations** involve running the new methods alongside the old methods. In information systems, this means running two systems concurrently. Although usually a complex operation in IS, in security this can mean running two firewalls concurrently, and allowing the old system(s) to back up the new systems if they fail or are compromised. Drawbacks usually include the need to deal with both systems and maintain both sets of procedures.

The Bull's-eye Model for Information Security Project Planning

A proven method for prioritizing a program of complex change is the bull's-eye method. This model has been used by many organizations and called many different things. The fundamental concept is that issues are addressed from the general to the specific and that the focus is on systematic solutions instead of individual problems. By reviewing the information security blueprint and the current state of the organization's information security efforts in terms of the four layers of this model, project planners can find guidance about where to lobby for expanded information security capabilities. The increased capabilities can include increased budgets or increased expenditures for resources that have been budgeted. As presented here and diagrammed in Figure 10-3, the approach relies on a process of evaluating project plans in a progression through four layers: policy, network, systems, and applications. Each is defined below:

1. **Policies:** The outer layer in the bull's-eye diagram is policies. As noted many times in this textbook and fully detailed in Chapter 6, the foundation of all effective information security programs is sound information security and information technology policy.

2. **Networks:** In the past, most information security efforts have focused on this layer, and until recently information security was often considered synonymous with network security. In the network layer of the bull's-eye model the threats from public networks meet the organization's networking infrastructure. Those organizations new to the Internet find that the primary effort in this layer is the design and implementation of an effective DMZ and the balance of authentication and authorization needed when connecting to public networks.

3. **Systems:** Many organizations find that the problems of configuring and operating information systems in a secure fashion become more difficult as the number and complexity of these systems grow. This layer includes computers used as servers, desktop computers, and systems used for process control and manufacturing systems.

4. **Applications:** The final layer is that of application software systems used by the organization to accomplish its work. This includes packaged applications, such as office automation and e-mail programs as well as high-end enterprise resource planning (ERP) packages than span the organization. Custom application software developed by the organization for its own needs is also included.

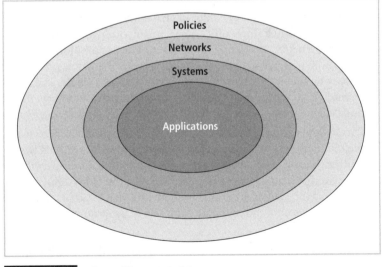

FIGURE 10-3   The Bull's-eye Model

The bull's-eye model can be used to evaluate the sequence of steps taken to integrate parts of the information security blueprint into a project plan. To put it simply, this means that:

- Until sound and useable IT and information security policy is developed, communicated, and enforced, no additional resources should be spent on other controls.
- Until effective network controls are designed and deployed, all resources should be spent to achieve that goal (unless, of course, resources are needed to revisit the policy needs of the organization).
- After policy and network controls are implemented, implementation should focus on the information, process, and manufacturing systems of the organization. Until there is well-informed assurance that all critical systems are being configured and operated in a secure fashion, all resources should be spent on reaching that goal.
- Once there is assurance that policy is in place, networks are secure, and systems are safe, attention should move to the assessment and remediation of the security of the organization's applications. This is a complicated and vast area of concern for many organizations. Most organizations neglect to analyze the impact of information security on existing purchased and self-developed systems. As in all planning efforts, attention should be paid to the most critical applications first.

It is important to remember that implementing the bull's-eye model or any other model must be tempered with judgment and experience.

To Outsource or Not

Not every organization needs to develop an information security department or program of its own. Just as some organizations outsource part of or all of their IT operations, so too can organizations outsource part of or all of their information security programs. The expense and time it takes to develop an effective information security program may be beyond the reach of some organizations, and it is in their best interest to hire competent professional services to be available to their IT Departments.

When an organization has outsourced most or all of its IT services, information security should be part of the contract arrangement with the outsourcer. When an organization retains its own IT Department, it may choose to outsource some of the more specialized information security functions. It is not at all unusual for small- and medium-sized organizations to hire outside consultants for penetration testing and information security program audits. It is also common to find that organizations of all sizes outsource the network monitoring functions both for quality of service and the network break-in period.

The subject of outsourcing for IT, information security, and other common infrastructure and corporate services continues to be a focus for many organizations. Because of the complex nature of these decisions, it is best to hire the finest outsourcing specialists, and then have the best attorneys possible to negotiate and verify the legal and technical intricacies of the outsourcing contract.

Technology Governance and Change Control

Other factors that determine the success of an organization's IT and information security are **technology governance** and **change control** processes. Technology governance is a complex process that an organization uses to manage the impacts and costs caused by technology implementation, innovation, and obsolescence. This matter deals with how frequently technical systems are updated, and how technical updates are approved and funded. Technology governance also facilitates the communication about technical advances and issues across the organization.

Medium or large organizations deal with the impact of technical change on the operation of the organization through a change control process. By managing the process of change the organization can:

- Improve communication about change across the organization
- Enhance coordination between groups within the organization as change is scheduled and completed
- Reduce unintended consequences by having a process to resolve potential conflict and disruption that uncoordinated change can introduce
- Improve quality of service as potential failures are eliminated and groups work together
- Assure management that all groups are complying with the organization's policies regarding technology governance, procurement, accounting, and information security

Effective change control is an essential part of the IT operation in all but the smallest organizations. The information security group can also use the change control process to insure that essential process steps that assure confidentiality, integrity, and availability are followed as systems are upgraded across the organization.

Nontechnical Aspects of Implementation

Other aspects of the implementation process are not technical in nature and deal with the human interface to technical systems. In the section that follows, the topics of creating a culture of change management as well as considerations for organizations facing change are discussed.

The Culture of Change Management

In any major project, the prospect of change, the familiar shifting to the unfamiliar, can cause employees to unconsciously or consciously resist. Whether the changes are perceived as good as in the case of information security implementations, or perceived as bad, such as a downsizing or massive restructuring, employees prefer the old way of doing things. Even when employees embrace changes, the stress of making changes and adjusting to the new procedures can increase the probability of mistakes or create vulnerabilities in systems. By understanding and applying some of the basic tenets of change management, the resistance to change can be lowered, and you can even build resilience for changes, making ongoing change more palatable to the entire organization.

The basic foundations of change management require that those making the changes understand that there is a fundamental organizational culture that represents the mood and philosophy for the general conduct of business. Disruptions to this culture that are caused by change must be properly addressed to minimize their effects. One of the oldest models of change is the Lewin change model, which consists of:[1]

- Unfreezing
- Moving
- Refreezing

Unfreezing is when you thaw out hard and fast habits and established procedures. Moving is the transition between the old way and the new. Refreezing is the integration of the new methods into the organizational culture, by creating an atmosphere in which the changes are accepted as the preferred way of accomplishing the requisite tasks.

Unfreezing

The process of unfreezing can be categorized as three subprocesses, each of which must be effective for employees to feel ready and motivated to change:

1. **Disconfirmation:** To assist employees you must instill the feeling that unless they change to the new standards, they will fail to achieve their goals (survival anxiety), or to perform their duties to their own satisfaction (survival guilt). This is a necessary part of getting the employees to break with their old habits.
2. **Induction of Guilt or Survival Anxiety:** To reinforce these feelings, the employee must feel that the reasons behind their survival guilt are valid. The validity of these feelings can be thwarted by the anxiety that comes from the feeling that you must change because you are imperfect or flawed (learning anxiety). Learning anxiety can promote fear and lead to a loss of self-esteem or effectiveness. The change process can accommodate this risk by creating some degree of psychological safety as planning for change occurs.
3. **Creation of Psychological Safety or Overcoming Learning Anxiety:** "The key to effective change management, then, becomes the ability to balance the amount of threat produced by disconfirming data with enough psychological safety to allow the change target to accept the information, feel the survival anxiety, and become motivated to change."[2]

Moving

Like unfreezing, the process of moving is composed of three subprocesses that are necessary for change to be realized.

1. **Cognitive redefinition:** Moving is the process of enabling the employees to realize that there is no shame in accepting the new learning. "Cognitive restructuring," also known as frame breaking or reframing, occurs when new information allows the individual to identify the new way of doing things as acceptable.
2. **Imitation and positive or defensive identification with a role model:** The easiest way to get the employees to accept new procedures is to use role models. Role models are frequently used in social circles and include big brothers and mentors. An organization can designate as a role model an employee who is respected by others, who adopts the new methods, and demonstrates that the new methods do not threaten status or well-being. If no positive role models exist, then you have to create the environment for "scanning."
3. **Scanning (insight or trial and error learning):** Scanning is the process whereby the employees learn by scanning their environment, talking to coworkers, and generally learning new methods on their own. The problem with scanning is that it is easy for the employee to scan poor reinforcement or negative reinforcement for the proposed changes. "Change agents" such as trained employees or consultants can support scanning, if they meet with the employees in training sessions and demonstrate the positive results of the change process. Once the new learning has occurred, the employee goes through a period of trial and error. At this time, if the new learning is not reinforced, it results in a new scanning process.

Refreezing

For change to become permanent, it must be refrozen through personal and relational refreezing. Personal refreezing occurs when each individual employee comes to an understanding that the new way of doing things is the best way, and that no other way will suffice. Relational refreezing occurs when a group comes to a similar decision. Both can be accomplished if the group is trained in new methods, and through the training comes to an understanding of the procedures involved in the new methods. Then each individual applies the new training in his respective work environment, reinforcing the group learning, and solidifying the personal refreezing.

Considerations for Organizational Change

Steps can be taken to make an organization more amenable to change. These steps reduce resistance to change at the beginning of the planning process and modify the organization to be more flexible as changes occur during project implementation.

Reducing Resistance to Change from the Start

The level of resistance to change impacts the ease with which an organization works through the process described above. The more ingrained the previous methods and behaviors, the more difficult the change. It's best to start in the early phases of the SecSDLC to improve the interaction between the affected members of the organization and the project planners. The interaction between these groups is improved through a three-step process: communicate, educate, and involve.

Communications is the first step and the most crucial. You communicate with the employees, notifying them that a new security process is being considered, and that their feedback is necessary to make it work. You constantly update the employees on the progress of the SecSDLC and provide information on the expected completion dates. This ongoing series of updates prevents the process from being a surprise at the last minute, and allows the individuals to accept the change when it finally arrives.

Simultaneously, the updates should educate the employees on exactly how the proposed changes will affect them both personally and within the organization. While detailed information may not be available in earlier stages, as the SecSDLC progresses, more detail is provided. Education also involves teaching employees to use the new systems once they are in place. This means a high-quality training program delivered at the appropriate times, as discussed earlier.

Finally, involvement means getting key representatives from user groups to serve as members of the SecSDLC development process. In systems development this is referred to as **joint application development** or **JAD**. This means that some users are part of the development team and report to their coworkers on the progress of the project, and report to the project team the concerns of their coworkers. This representative approach serves the team well in early planning stages, when unforeseen problems with acceptance of the project are addressed.

Developing a Culture that Supports Change

An ideal organization fosters resilience to change. This resilience means the organization has come to expect that change is a necessary part of the culture, and that to embrace change is more productive than fighting it. To develop such a culture the organization must successfully accomplish many projects that require change. A resilient culture can be either cultivated or undermined by management's approach. Strong management support for change, with a clear executive-level champion, enables the organization to recognize the necessity and strategic importance of the change. Weak management support, with delegated responsibility and no champion, sentences the project to certain failure. In this case, employees sense the low priority that has been given to the project and do not communicate with representatives of the development team, because the effort seems useless.

Chapter Summary

- The implementation phase of the security systems development life cycle is accomplished by making changes to the configuration and operation of the organization's information systems in order to make them more secure. It includes changes to procedures, people, hardware, software, and data.

- During the implementation phase, the organization translates its blueprint for information security into a concrete project plan which instructs individuals on the execution of the implementation phase.

- Before developing a project plan, management should articulate and coordinate the organization's information security vision and objectives with the involved communities of interest.

- The major steps in executing the project plan are planning the project, supervising tasks and action steps within the project plan, and wrapping up the project plan.

- Each organization determines its own project management methodology for IT and information security projects. Whenever possible, information security projects should follow organizational practices for project management.

- Planning for the implementation phase involves the creation of a detailed project plan.

- The project plan itself can be created by using a simple planning tool, such as the work breakdown structure (WBS) prepared with a simple desktop PC spreadsheet program or with more complex project management software tools. The common attributes of WBS tasks are: work to be accomplished (activities and deliverables); individuals (or skills set) assigned to perform the task; start and end dates for the task (when known); amount of effort required for completion in hours or days; estimated capital expenses for the task; estimated noncapital expenses for the task; and identification of task interdependencies.

- Constraints and considerations should be addressed when developing the project plan, including financial, procurement, priority, time and scheduling, staffing, scope, organizational feasibility, training and indoctrination, change control, and technology governance.

- Instead of designating a professional project manager to lead a security information project, some organizations designate a champion from the general management community of interest. This individual supervises the implementation instead of a senior IT manager or the CIO of the organization.

- Once a project is underway, it is managed to completion using a process known as a negative feedback loop or cybernetic loop.

- As the components of the new security system are planned, provisions must be made for the changeover from the previous method of performing a task (or not performing the task in some cases) to the new method(s).

- The bull's-eye model is a proven method for prioritizing a program of complex change is. Using this method, you address issues from the general to the specific and focus on systematic solutions instead of individual problems.

- When the expense and time it takes to develop an effective information security program is beyond the reach of an organization, it is best to outsource to competent professional services.

- Technology governance is a complex process that an organization uses to manage the impacts and costs caused by technology implementation, innovation, and obsolescence.

- The change control process is a method which medium and large organizations use to deal with the impact of technical change on the operation of the organization.

- As with any project, there are certain aspects of change that must be addressed. In any major project, the prospect of change and moving from the familiar to the unfamiliar can cause employees to consciously or unconsciously resist the changes.

Review Questions

1. What categories of controls can be applied to secure information?
2. What is a project plan? List what a project plan can accomplish.
3. What is the primary objective of the implementation phase of a project plan for information security?
4. What is the value of a statement of vision and objectives? Why is it needed before a project plan is developed?
5. What five categories of constraints to project plan implementation are noted in the chapter? Explain each of them.
6. List and describe the three major steps in executing the project plan.
7. What is a work breakdown structure (WBS)? Is it the only way to organize a project plan?
8. What is projectitis? How is it cured or its impact reduced? *p 506 Keep is simple*
9. List and define the common attributes of the tasks of a WBS. *P 395*
10. How does a planner know when a task has been subdivided to an adequate degree and can be classified as an action step?
11. What is a deliverable? Name two uses for deliverables.
12. What is a resource? What are the two types?
13. Why is it a good practice to delay naming specific individuals as resources early in the planning process?
14. What is a milestone and why is it significant to project planning?
15. Why is it good practice to assign start and end dates sparingly in the early stages of project planning?
16. Who is the best judge of effort estimates for project tasks and action steps? Why?
17. Are there concrete rules about what is a capital expense and what is not? What is a general guideline?
18. Within project management, what is a dependency? What is a predecessor? What is a successor?
19. List and describe the consideration and constraint categories of project planning discussed in the chapter. In your opinion, which is the most significant and why?
20. What is a negative feedback loop? How is it used to keep a project in control?
21. What are the three planning parameters for each task? Describe them.

22. When a task is not meeting the plan, what two circumstances are likely to be involved?

23. List and describe the four basic approaches to conversion to a new system as described in the chapter. Which is the best approach?

24. Describe the bull's-eye model for information security project planning. List and describe the four layers of the bull's-eye.

25. What is technology governance? What is change control? How are they related?

Exercises

1. Create a first draft of a WBS from the scenario below. Make assumptions as needed based on the section about project planning considerations and constraints in the chapter. In your WBS, describe the skill sets required for the tasks you have planned .

   Scenario

   Sequential Label and Supply is having a problem with employees surfing the Web to access material the company has deemed inappropriate for use in a professional environment. The technology exists to insert a filtering device in the company Internet connection that blocks certain Web locations and certain Web content. The vendor has provided you with some initial information about the filter. The hardware is an appliance that costs $18,000 and requires a total of 150 effort-hours to install and configure. Technical support on the appliance costs 18 percent of the purchase price and includes a training allowance for the year. A software component is needed for administering the appliance that runs on the administrator's desktop computer and it costs $550. A monthly subscription provides the list of sites to be blocked and costs $250 per month. The administrator must spend an estimated four hours per week for ongoing administrative functions.

   Items you should consider:

   - Your plan requires two sections, one for deployment and another for ongoing operation after implementation.
   - The vendor offers a contracting service for installation at $140 per hour.
   - Your change control process requires a 17-day lead time for change requests.
   - The manufacturer has a 14-day order time and a 7-day delivery time for this device.

2. If you have access to a commercial project management software package (Microsoft Project for example), use it to complete a project plan based on the data shown in Table 10-2. Prepare a simple WBS report (or Gantt chart) showing your work.

3. Write a job description for Kelvin Urich, the project manager described in the opening scenario of this chapter. Be sure to identify key characteristics of the ideal candidate as well as work experience and educational background. Also, justify why your job description is suitable for potential candidates of this position.

4. Search the World Wide Web for job descriptions of project managers. You can use any number of Web sites including *www.careerjournal.com/* or *www.dice.com/* to find at least ten IT-related job descriptions. What common elements do you find among the job descriptions? What is the most unusual characteristic among the job descriptions?

Case Exercises

I. Change is Good

Adapted from "Overcoming Insecurity"[3]

By Deborah Radcliff, *Computerworld*, July 17, 2000.

In most organizations security is broken. Organizations react instead of act. Firewalls work contrary to the designs of network managers, clogging traffic, and slowing throughput. Some administrators have almost given up trying to plug all of the holes in the organization's security perimeter. Products are incompatible, not integrated, and in some cases cause more vulnerabilities than they solve. The sheer despair of it all often sours the top management. They see security as a necessary evil that counters productivity.

The challenge is to create a symbiotic relationship between business and security, with all the right buzzwords: scalable, flexible, robust, proactive, and interoperable. So how can security sell this approach? The answer is to change the organization's culture, so that it sees security as beneficial.

As part of an effective change control policy, security should be required to sign off on all projects. Unfortunately this is a difficult problem, as developers focus on systems and software development first and foremost and tend to view security as a delay to development and productivity.

This situation requires security to have a champion, an executive to support the processes. However, such managers must ensure that security goes hand-in-hand with business. Investors won't be tolerant of delays in production that occur while the company tries to resolve security issues. They would rather get the product out, and work the bugs out in the field.

"This is why it's important to change the mind-set of the security group from one that bogs down business to one that enables business. Too many security groups are focused on auditing problems versus proactive enablement of business. The security group needs to change from being the group that says `no' at the end of a project to the group that gets involved in the beginning of a project by building secure hooks into the infrastructure. That means developing review processes and tweaking the infrastructure to keep pace with business development cycles, from concept through change management and beyond."[4]

As IT, security, and business sectors learn to work together, there is an inevitable coming together of operations and activities. Good business operations should be secure, and good security should mean good business and IT should be in support of it all. By setting security as a top priority, the chief information security officer should exert his influence as the individual responsible for the infrastructure.

To get employees to accept this change, security administrators need to rethink their approaches to security, by giving up traditional defenses and focusing on risk management. It requires adaptability and flexibility to adapt security to each unique situation, while keeping in mind restrictions and resource availability.

Only when security proves itself to the executive staff, by balancing business needs against protection requirements, does security receive the corporate respect it needs. And the key is change.

1. How can security sign-off increase acceptance of security in the organization? Aren't these ideas counterproductive?

2. Is the integration and reconciliation of security, IT, and business sectors possible? Realistic? How can this be accomplished through managing change and company culture?

II. Spinning a Secure Web

Adapted from "Web Projects Bring New Scope"[5]

By Yogi Schulz, *Computing Canada*, January 4, 2002.

Traditional project management goes out the window with Web-based development projects. Or does it? When an organization puts a new application on the Web, it dramatically increases its user group, thereby creating a number of difficulties. With literally millions of users to stress an application to the maximum, how can an organization develop an application with no substantial flaws?

Some key rules for a Web project include:

- Focus on high performance. While slow interfaces and so-so performance may be tolerated on internal applications, Web users won't hesitate to surf elsewhere.

- Make the Web experience memorable. Users demand more visual stimulation from the Web than from traditional content.

- "Implement impenetrable security…With the world awash in hackers and script kiddies bent on infiltrating your server complex solely for the bragging rights, more robust security measures are required. Now, your Web application must be deployed behind a firewall and support encryption for sensitive data transmission…Security features add scope to software development and effort to testing that Web project managers must accommodate in their plans."[6]

- Strive for high up-time. Web applications must be 24/7. If the site's not up, neither are sales.

- Design for a wide audience. Web customers use a variety of applications. Although the traditional development market only uses the interface application created by the designers, now systems compatibility can make or break the project.

- Make your applications "integrate-able."

- Be quick to deliver. While traditional applications required quick delivery, Web applications require even shorter delivery times. Balance that requirement with security.

Experienced client/server project managers can deliver successful Web applications if they accept and plan to address the new characteristics that make Web applications so powerful."[7]

1. Apart from the obvious swarm of friendly and unfriendly site users, why does the development of Web applications require more concern for security than traditional applications? How does the management of the security of a Web project differ from that of traditional security applications?

2. How can Web project managers balance the need for quick delivery with the need for ultra-high security? How can a project management sell security in this light?

Endnotes

1. Edgar H. Schein, "Kurt Lewin's Change Theory in the Field and in the Classroom: Notes Toward a Model of Managed Learning," Working paper, MIT Sloan School of Management. [Cited 20 July 2002]. Available from the World Wide Web *http://www/ sol-ne.org/res/wp/10006.html#one.*

2. *Ibid.*

3. Deborah Radcliff, "Overcoming Insecurity," *ComputerWorld* 34, no. 29 (Jul 17, 2000) 44–45.

4. *Ibid.*

5. Yogi Schulz, "Web Projects Bring New Scope," *Computing Canada* 28, no. 1 (Jan 4, 2002) 23.

6. *Ibid.*

7. *Ibid.*

Security and Personnel

> I think we need to be paranoid optimists.
>
> **ROBERT J. EATON**

WHILE SHE DRANK HER COFFEE, Iris opened the e-mail program on her computer screen. Mixed in among the newsletters and unsolicited offers for travel deals and mortgage loans was a message from Charlie Moody. As she opened the message, Iris worried about what a note from the Senior Manager of IT could mean. The e-mail read:

From: Charles Moody [c_moody@slsco.com]
To: Iris Majwabu [i_majwabu@slsco.com]
Subject: You need to see me
Iris,

   I wanted to tell you that the managers in IT and the whole information security team appreciate your diligence and attitude in the Magruder affair. We completed all of the personnel actions on this matter yesterday, and it is now behind us.

   You might like to know that the best guess from the Corporate Security Department is that you helped us catch this in the early stages, and so no company assets were compromised.

   Please set up an appointment with me in the next few days to discuss a few things.
/CM

   "Uh-oh," she thought. As she opened her calendar program to set up the appointment, Iris couldn't imagine what Charlie, who was her boss's boss, could want. Iris was a database administrator, and she hoped he wasn't going to give her more work.

A week later, Iris entered Charlie Moody's office. He was sitting behind his desk and stood as she entered.

"Come in," Charlie said. "Have a seat."

After Iris made herself comfortable in one of the many chairs in the office, Charlie came around his desk and sat down at his worktable next to her. She took a deep breath, eyeing the folder in his hand, which looked like her personnel file.

"I'm sure you're wondering why I asked you here," said Charlie smiling. "Because you did so well in the Magruder affair, I am offering you a transfer to Kelvin Urich's information security group. You were right to bring that issue to your manager's attention and avoid confronting Magruder directly. You made the right choice, you acted quickly, showed a positive attitude throughout the whole situation, and I think you have demonstrated an information security mindset. You are someone I want on Urich's team."

"I'm not sure what to say," she began. "I've been a DBA for three years here. I really don't know much about information security other than what I learned from the company training and awareness sessions."

"That's not a problem," Charlie said. "You can learn. So how about it, are you interested in the job?"

Iris said, "It sounds interesting, but I hadn't thought of a career change just now. I am willing to think about it, but have a few questions...."

DISCUSSION QUESTIONS:

1. What questions should Iris ask Charlie about the new job, about Kelvin's team, and about the future of the company?
2. Do you think Iris has the right stuff for a job in information security? Why? Why not?
3. Do you think Charlie is making the right choice in transferring Iris to his information security group or would he be better served by other options? Think of at least three of those options. What are the advantages and disadvantages of each?

LEARNING OBJECTIVES:

Upon completion of this material you should be able to:

- Understand where and how the information security function is positioned within organizations.
- Understand the issues and concerns about staffing the information security function.
- Know about the credentials that professionals in the information security field can acquire.
- Recognize how an organization's employment policies and practices can support the information security effort.
- Understand the special security precautions necessary for nonemployees.
- Recognize the need for the separation of duties.
- Understand the special requirements needed for the privacy of personnel data.

Introduction

Iris is correct in asking questions before taking the position offered by Charlie. Just as each potential employee and potential employer look for the best fit, each organization should examine the options possible for staffing the information security function. When implementing information security in an organization, there are many human resource issues that must be addressed. First, the entire organization must decide how to position and name the security function within the organization. Second, the information security community of interest must plan for the proper staffing (or adjustments to the staffing plan) for the information security function. Third, the IT community of interest must understand the impact of information security across every role in the IT function and adjust job descriptions and documented practices accordingly. Finally, the general management community of interest must work with the information security professionals to integrate solid information security concepts into the personnel management practices of the organization.

Understanding the impact of change to the personnel management practices of the organization is an important factor in the success of the implementation phase of the security system development life cycle (SecSDLC). During the analysis phases, a behavioral feasibility study should have been conducted that addressed the impact of the changes necessary for implementation. This feasibility study should have included an investigation of the levels of employee acceptance of—and resistance to—change. In the case of information security systems, experience has shown that employees often feel threatened when an organization is creating or enhancing an overall information security program. Employees can perceive such a program as a manifestation of the Big Brother syndrome, which means questions such as the following emerge:

- Is management monitoring my work or my e-mail?
- Will security go through my hard drive looking for evidence to fire me?
- How can I do my job, when I now have to deal with the added delays of the security technology?
- Are we a target of cyberterrorism?

As indicated in Chapter 10, quelling the doubts and reassuring the employees are fundamental parts of the implementation process. It is important to gather feedback and respond to it quickly.

The Security Function Within an Organization's Structure

This chapter, like earlier chapters, briefly covers the placement of the information security function within the organization. For a full discussion of the issues and impact of the placement of the information security function, refer to related textbooks on the management of information security. In addition, a useful and complete discussion of the subject can also be found in the work of Charles Cresson Wood. His book, *Information Security Roles and Responsibilities Made Easy,* offers a chapter entitled "Reporting Relationships," which clearly articulates the following placement options for the information security function.[1] The security function can be placed within the:

- IT function, as a peer of other functions such as networks, applications development, and the help desk

- Physical security function, as a peer of physical security or protective services
- Administrative services function, as a peer of human resources or purchasing
- Insurance and risk management function
- Legal department

The challenge for the entire organization is to design a reporting structure for the information security function that balances the competing needs of each of the communities of interest. In many organizations, the way in which the security unit is placed in the reporting structure can indicate that no one wants to manage it, and that it has been moved from place to place within the organization without regard to the issues that impact its effectiveness. Organizations can find a rational compromise by placing the information security function where it can best balance the needs of enforcement of organizational policy (often called compliance) with the education, training, awareness, and customer service needed to make information security part of the organizational culture.

Wherever it is placed, building the information security team is both an art and a science. As shown in the next section, the information security function should be staffed based on both the science of measuring technical, educational, and work experience and the art of the assessing skills needed for success.

Staffing the Security Function

Selecting information security personnel is based on a number of criteria. Some of these factors are within the control of the organization and others some are not. Consider the fundamental concept of supply and demand. When the demand for any commodity increases too quickly, specifically a critical technical skill needed for many information security roles, supply initially fails to meet the demand. Many potential professionals seek to enter the security market by gaining the skills, experience, and credentials to qualify as a new supply. Until the new supply reaches the demand level, organizations must pay the higher costs associated with the current limited supply. In order to enter the new high-demand market, people change jobs, go to school, or are trained. Once the supply reaches a level at or above demand, the organizations hiring these skills become selective, and the cost they are willing to pay drops. This process continues to swing, like a clock pendulum, because the real economy, unlike an econometric model, is seldom in a state of equilibrium. At the present time (2002), the information security industry is in a period of high demand, with few qualified and experienced individuals available for organizations seeking their services.

Qualifications and Requirements

There are a number of factors that influence an organization's hiring decisions. Because of the recent emergence of information security as a separate discipline, however, there is a lack of understanding of the qualifications needed when hiring competent security personnel. Currently in many organizations, the staff of information security teams lack established roles and responsibilities. For the information security discipline to move forward, these factors must be addressed:

■ The general management community of interest should learn more about the necessary position requirements and qualifications for both information security positions and those IT positions that impact information security.

■ Upper management should also learn more about the budgetary needs of the information security function and the positions within it. That way management can make sound fiscal decisions for both the information security function and the IT functions that carry out many of the information security initiatives.

■ The IT community of interest as well as the general management community need to learn more about the level of influence and prestige the information security function should be given in order to be effective. This is especially true for the chief information security officer.

The following sections address the job requirements for information security professionals, methods for entering the field, descriptions of positions, professional certifications, and finally, recommendations to those who are seeking to enter the field or who are already working in the field.

In most cases, organizations look for a technically qualified information security generalist, with a solid understanding of how an organization operates. In many other career fields, the more specialized professionals become, the more marketable they are. However, in the information security discipline, overspecialization is often a risk. It is important to balance technical skills with general information security knowledge.

When hiring information security professionals, organizations frequently look for individuals who understand:

■ How an organization operates at all levels

■ That information security is usually a management problem and is seldom an exclusively technical problem

■ How to work with people and collaborate with end-users, and have strong communications and writing skills

■ The role of policy in guiding security efforts, and the role of education and training in making the user part of the solution, rather than part of the problem

■ The threats facing an organization and how these threats can become attacks

■ How to protect the organization from information security attacks

■ How business solutions (including technology-based solutions) can be applied to solve specific information security problems

■ Most mainstream IT technologies (not necessarily as experts, but as generalists)

■ The terminology of IT and information security; this is the basis for subsequent knowledge and skill needed for the specific positions

Entry into the Security Profession

Many information security professionals enter the field through one of two career paths: first, ex-law enforcement and military personnel move from their high-stress environments into the more business-oriented world of information security; and second, technical professionals find themselves working on security applications and processes more often than on traditional information systems tasks. Networking experts, programmers, database administrators, and systems administrators are individuals who may find themselves in this circumstance. College graduates and upper division students are now selecting and tailoring their degree programs to prepare for work in the field of security. Figure 11-1 illustrates these career paths.

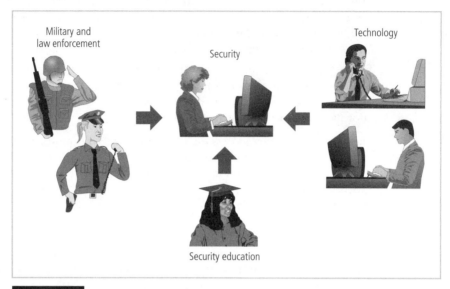

Military and law enforcement

Security

Technology

Security education

FIGURE 11-1   Career Paths to Information Security Positions

The current perception in the field itself is that a security professional must first be a proven professional in another field of IT. IT professionals who move into information security, however, tend to focus on the technology to the exclusion of general information security issues. Organizations can foster greater professionalism in the information security discipline through clearly defined expectations and position descriptions.

Information Security Positions

The use of standard job descriptions can increase the degree of professionalism in the information security field as well as improve the consistency of roles and responsibilities between organizations. Organizations that are revising the roles and responsibilities of information security staff can consult Charles Cresson Wood's book *Information Security Roles and Responsibilities Made Easy*, which offers a set of model job descriptions for information security positions. The book also identifies the responsibilities and duties of IT staff whose work touches on information security.[2] Figure 11-2 shows a common reporting structure for information security positions.

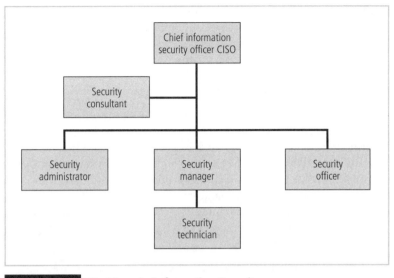

FIGURE 11-2 Positions in Information Security

Another study of information security positions by Schwartz, Erwin, Weafer, and Briney found that positions can be classified into one of three areas: those that *define*, those that *build*, and those that *administer*.

"Definers provide the policies, guidelines and standards…They're the people who do the consulting and the risk assessment, who develop the product and technical architectures. These are senior people with a lot of broad knowledge, but often not a lot of depth…[Builders are] the real techies, who create and install security solutions…[Administrators] operate and administrate the security tools, [and] the security monitoring function and…continuously improve the processes, performing all the day-to-day…work…We often try to use the same people for all of these roles. We use builders all the time… If you break your infosec professionals into these three groups, you can recruit them more efficiently, with the policy people being the more senior people, the builders being more technical and the operating people being those you can train to do a specific task."[3]

Examples of specific job titles that follow this model are discussed in the following sections.

Chief Information Security Officer

This position is typically considered the top information security officer in the organization. As indicated in earlier chapters, the CISO is usually not an executive level position and frequently reports to the chief information officer. Though CISOs are business managers first and technologists second, they must also be conversant in all areas of security, including the technical, planning, and policy areas. The CISO performs the following functions:

- Manages the overall information security program for the organization
- Drafts or approves information security policies
- Works with the CIO on strategic plans, develops tactical plans, and works with security managers on operational plans

- Develops information security budgets based on available funding
- Sets priorities for the purchase and implementation of information security projects and technology
- Makes decisions or recommendations on the recruiting, hiring, and firing of security staff
- Acts as the spokesperson for the security team

Qualifications and Position Requirements. The most common qualification that is expected of a candidate for this type of position is the Certified Information Systems Security Professional (CISSP), which is described later in this chapter. A graduate degree in one of the following areas is also probably required: criminal justice, business, technology, or other related fields. To qualify for this level position, the candidate must demonstrate experience as a security manager (see the following inset text), and presents experience with planning, policy, and budgets. As mentioned earlier, some organizations prefer to hire individuals with law enforcement experience. The following example job description is typical:

"Director of Security, *Responsibilities:* Reporting to the senior vice president of administration, the director of corporate security will be responsible for all issues related to the security and protection of the company's employees, executives, facilities, proprietary data and information. Accountable for the planning and design of the company's security programs and procedures, this individual will facilitate protection from and resolution of theft, threats, and other situations that may endanger the well being of the organization. Working through a small staff, the Director will be responsible for executive protection, travel advisories, employee background checks and a myriad of other activities throughout the corporation on a case-by-case basis. The Director will serve as the company's chief liaison with law enforcement agencies and, most importantly, will serve as a security consultant to all of the company's autonomously run divisions. Travel requirements will be extensive.

"*Qualifications:* The ideal candidate will have a successful background with a federal law enforcement agency, or other applicable experience, that will afford this individual an established network of contacts throughout the country. Additional private industry experience with a sizeable corporation—or as a consultant to same—is preferable. A proactive attitude with regard to security and protection is a must. The successful candidate must be capable of strategically assessing our client's security needs and have a track record in areas such as crisis management, investigation, facility security and executive protection. Finally, the candidate should have a basic understanding of the access and use of electronic information services as they apply to security issues. We seek candidates who are flexible enough to deal with varied business cultures and who possess the superior interpersonal skills to perform well in a consulting role where recommendations and advice are sought and valued, but perhaps not always acted upon. A college degree is required."[4]

Security Manager

Security managers are accountable for the day-to-day operation of the information security program. They accomplish objectives as identified by the CISO and resolve issues identified by technicians. Management of technology requires an understanding of the technology administered, but not necessarily proficiency in its configuration, operation, and fault resolution. Within the information security community, there may be team leaders or project managers who are responsible for certain management-like functions, such as scheduling, setting relative priorities, or administering any number of procedural tasks, but are not necessarily held accountable for making a particular technology function.

Qualifications and Position Requirements. It is not uncommon for a candidate for this position to have a CISSP. Traditionally, managers earn the CISSP while technical professionals earn the Global Information Assurance Certification (GIAC); however, a number of new certifications are discussed later in the chapter. Security managers must have the ability to draft middle- and lower-level policies as well as standards and guidelines. They must have experience in traditional business matters: budgeting, project management, hiring, and firing. They must also be able to manage technicians, both in the assignment of tasks and the monitoring of activities. Experience with business continuity planning is usually a plus. The following example is typical of a security manager job description. However, there are several different types of security managers, as security managers are much more specialized than CISOs. Reading the job description is the best way to determine exactly what the employer is looking for.

"*Position*: IT Security Compliance Manager. *Job description*: A job has arisen for an IT Security Compliance Manager reporting to the IT Security Manager. In this role you will manage the development of the client's IT Security standards and operate a compliance program to ensure conformance at all stages of the systems lifecycle. This is a key, hands-on role with the job holder taking an active part in the delivery of the compliance program. The role will also involve the day-to-day management of IT Security staff and their career development. The principal accountabilities for this role are as follows:

- "Develop and manage an IT security compliance program
- "Develop the client's security standards in line with industry standards and emerging threats and technologies
- "Identify IT-related business risk in new software and game developments and ensure the effective risk management solutions are identified and complied with
- "Manage and conduct IT security compliance reviews in conjunction with Operational and IT Audit staff
- "Conduct investigations into security breaches or vulnerabilities

"*Candidate profile*: The ideal candidate should have five years experience of managing the implementation of technical security controls and related operational procedures and must have sound business risk management skills. You must have a flexible approach to working and must be able and willing to work unsociable hours to meet the demands of the role."[5]

The preceding example illustrates the confusion that currently exists in the information security field regarding job titles and reporting relationships among information security professions. Until commonality of job titles and expected roles and responsibilities emerges, information security professionals should carefully research roles and responsibilities for each position without relying on the implications of the job's title.

Security Technician

Security technicians are the technically qualified individuals tasked to configure firewalls, deploy IDSs, implement security software, diagnose and troubleshoot problems, and coordinate with systems and network administrators to ensure security technology is properly implemented. A security technician is the ideal entry-level position; however, some technical skills are usually required, which is the dilemma of many seeking to enter a new field. It is difficult to get a job without experience, and experience comes with a job. Just as in the networking arena, security technicians tend to be specialized, focusing on one major security technology group (firewalls, IDS, servers, routers, or software) and further specializing in one particular software or hardware package such as Checkpoint firewalls, Nokia firewalls, or Tripwire IDS. These areas are sufficiently complex to warrant a high level of specialization. If individuals hired for one of these positions, however, want to move up in the corporate hierarchy, they must expand their technical knowledge horizontally, gaining an understanding of the general, organizational issues of information security, as well as all technical areas.

Qualifications and Position Requirements. The technical qualifications and position requirements for a security technician are varied. Organizations prefer the expert, certified, proficient technician. Regardless of the area, the particular job description covers some level of experience with a particular hardware and software package. Sometimes familiarity with a technology secures an applicant an interview; however, experience in using the technology is usually required. The following job announcement for a security technician is typical.

"Firewall Engineering Consultant

Job Description: Working for an exciting customer-focused security group within one of the largest managed network providers in Europe. You will have the opportunity to expand your experience and gain all the technical and professional support to achieve within the group. Must have experience to third line technical support of firewall technologies. Checkpoint certified. Experienced in Nokia systems.

"*Package*: Possible company car, discretionary bonus, private health care, on-call pay and overtime pay."[6]

Because overtime and on-call pay are listed, this is probably an hourly rather than a salaried position, which is common for security technicians. The move to a salaried position is typically a move from technician to manager.

Internal Security Consultant

There is a special category of information security professional that warrants examination. The information security consultant is typically an expert in some aspect of information security (disaster recovery, business continuity planning, security architecture, policy development, or strategic planning). The consultant is usually brought in when the organization makes the decision to outsource one or more aspects of its security program. While it is usually preferable to involve a formal security services company, it is not unusual to find a qualified individual consultant. Even when a security services company is employed, typically only one or two consultants are assigned to the task. The security consultant must be highly proficient in the managerial aspects of security and have access to staff that can perform the technical implementations, perhaps through a service agreement. It is widely known that most consultants are idea generators and not implementers. They are frequently called in to solve a problem. The consultants come in, examine the existing systems or structures, design a solution to the problem, and then refer the organization to a service company for follow-through. Not all consultants work in this way, but it is important to clarify the consultants' approach before hiring them.

Information security consultants usually enter the field after working as experts in the discipline. A good security consultant often has experience as a security manager or CISO. Some consultants are recruited by service companies, and as a result, the job description is based on the needs and services of that particular company. The following job description is for an Information Security Consultant:

> "*Job Description*: To join a team delivering high value consultancy to internal and external clients. Security consultants are expected to provide external consultancy to companies in various aspects of security including BS7799, policy design and enforcement, systems architecture and auditing. Internal corporate work will include vulnerability scans, penetration tests and risk assessments, etc. Desirable qualifications are CISSP, CLAS. Sound practical knowledge of Network Security Architecture including monitoring solutions such as IDS, Access Control and Authentication."[7]

Note the emphasis on external consultancy and on security policy and auditing.

Credentials of Information Security Professionals

As discussed earlier, many organizations seek recognizable certifications to indicate the level of proficiency associated with the various security positions. Most existing certifications are relatively new and not fully understood by hiring organizations. The certifying bodies work hard to educate the general public on the value and qualifications of their certificate recipients. Employers are trying to understand the match between certifications and the position requirements, and the candidates are trying to gain meaningful employment based on their newly received certifications. This section presents information on current and planned certifications that are widely recognized in the market. The description of each certification contains the qualifications of recipients, the knowledge tested, and the means of testing. Chapter 3 briefly touched on some of this material in the discussion of professional associations and their codes of ethics.

Certified Information Systems Security Professional (CISSP) and Systems Security Certified Practitioner (SSCP)

Considered the most prestigious certification for security managers and CISOs, the CISSP is one of two certifications offered by the International Information Systems Security Certification Consortium (ISC)[2] (see *www.isc2.org*). The SSCP is the other CISSP Certification was designed to recognize mastery of an international standard for information security and understanding of a common body of knowledge (CBK). In order to sit for the CISSP exam, the candidate must possess at least three years of direct full-time security professional work in one or more of ten domains. The CISSP exam itself consists of 250 multiple-choice questions and must be completed within six hours. The exam covers ten domains of information security knowledge:

- Access control systems and methodology
- Applications and systems development
- Business continuity planning
- Cryptography
- Law, investigation, and ethics

- Operations security
- Physical security
- Security architecture and models
- Security management practices
- Telecommunications, network, and Internet security

As of August 2002, the CISSP certification requires both successful completion of the examination and an endorsement by a qualified third party, typically another CISSP, the candidate's employer, or a licensed, certified, or commissioned professional. Ostensibly, this is to guarantee that the individual meets the qualifications and requirements of the overall process. The breadth and depth covered in each of the ten domains makes it one of the most challenging certifications on the market. Once a candidate receives the CISSP, he or she must earn a specific number of continuing education credits every three years to retain the certification.

With the difficulty in mastering all ten domains, many security professionals seek other, less rigorous, certifications. (ISC)² developed and presented the SSCP certification, which is oriented toward the security administrator. Like the CISSP, the SSCP certification is more applicable to the security manager than the technician, because most questions focus on the operational nature of information security. The SSCP focuses "on practices, roles and responsibilities as defined by experts from major IS industries."[8] However, the information security technician seeking advancement can benefit from this certification.

The SSCP exam consists of 125 multiple-choice questions, and must be completed within three hours. Instead of the ten domains of the CISSP, the SSCP covers seven domains:

- Access controls
- Administration
- Audit and monitoring
- Risk, response, and recovery
- Cryptography
- Data communications
- Malicious code and malware

The SSCP is considered by many to be the little brother of the CISSP. It is a valid certification and is certainly easier to obtain than the CISSP. The seven domains are not a subset of the CISSP domains, but contain slightly more technical content. Just as with the CISSP, a SSCP recipient must earn continuing education credits to retain the certification, or else retake the exam.

Global Information Assurance Certification (GIAC)

The System Administration, Networking and Security Organization, better known as SANS (*www.sans.org*), developed a series of technical security certifications in 1999, known as the GIAC (*www.giac.org*). At the time, there were no technical certifications. Anyone who wished to work in the technical security field could only obtain networking or computing certifications, such as the MCSE (Microsoft Certified Systems Engineer) or CNE (Certified Novell Engineer).

The GIAC family of certifications can be pursued independently or combined to earn the comprehensive certification, GIAC Security Engineer (GSE). Like the SSCP, the

GIAC Information Security Officer (GISO) is an overview certification that combines basic technical knowledge with understanding of threats, risks, and best practices. Unlike other certifications, the GIAC certifications require the applicant to first complete a written practical assignment. This assignment is intended to require the applicant to demonstrate his or her abilities and skills by putting them into practice. These assignments are submitted to the SANS Information Security Reading Room for review by security practitioners, potential certificate applicants, and others with an interest in information security. Only when the practical assignment is complete is the candidate allowed to take the online exam.

SANS defines its steps to obtain GIAC certification as follows:

- "Complete a practical/research paper and one or two exams (depending on your certification track).
- "Your practical must receive a passing grade before you will be authorized to take the exams.
- "Complete the online exams for that particular subject via the GIAC Web site. Most exams are 75 questions (multiple choice), and must be completed within two hours. A few of the exams are 90 questions and must be completed within three hours.
- "If you submit an acceptable practical and pass your exams, you will be GIAC certified."[9]

The various individual GIAC Certifications include:

- GIAC Security Essentials Certification (GSEC)
- GIAC Certified Firewall Analyst (GCFW)
- GIAC Certified Intrusion Analyst (GCIA)
- GIAC Certified Incident Handler (GCIH)
- GIAC Certified Windows Security Administrator (GCWN)
- GIAC Certified UNIX Security Administrator (GCUX)
- GIAC Information Security Officer - Basic (GISO - Basic)
- GIAC Systems and Network Auditor (GSNA)
- GIAC Certified Forensic Analyst (GCFA)
- GIAC Security Leadership Certificate (GSLC)

To obtain the GIAC Certified Engineer, which is considered the pinnacle of GIAC certifications, candidates must earn *all* of the above certifications and receive honors recognition in at least one, before they are even allowed to sit for the final certification. GIAC is designed not only to test knowledge of a field, but also to require application of that knowledge through the practicum. While there are a growing number of entry-level certifications, GIAC currently offers the only advanced technical certifications.

Security Certified Professional

One of the newest certifications in the information security discipline is the Security Certified Professional certification (*www.securitycertified.net*). The SCP certification provides two tracks: the SCNP (Security Certified Network Professional) and the SCNA (Security Certified Network Architect). Both are designed for the security technician and have dominant technical components; however, the latter also emphasizes authentication principles. Even though they both have a networking focus, it is a concentration on network security, rather than on true networking (for example, MSCE and CNE). The SCNP track focuses on firewalls and intrusion detection and requires two exams:[10]

- Network Security Fundamentals (NSF)
- Network Defense and Countermeasures (NDC)

The SCNA program focuses more on authentication, including biometrics and PKI. The two exams in the SCNA certification are:

- PKI and Biometrics Concepts and Planning (PBC)
- PKI and Biometrics Implementation (PBI)

Although not as detailed as the GIAC certifications, these programs provide a useful migration into new areas of security, while developing a vendor-neutral core of practitioner knowledge evaluations.

TruSecure ICSA Certified Security Associate (T.I.C.S.A.) and TruSecure ICSA Certified Security Expert (T.I.C.S.E.)

The ICSA certifications are among the first service vendor certifications. TruSecure Corporation is a well-known service vendor and is promoting the ICSA security practitioner tracks. This is a vendor-neutral approach that focuses on providing "certifications that are skills- and knowledge-based, technology specific, and pragmatic." As with other certifications, a candidate must demonstrate appropriate experience and training before being allowed to sit for the examinations. The promoters of the certification describe it as follows: "Complementary to CISSP, in as much as it is designed for the IT practitioner responsible for ensuring security principles are applied in the context of their daily job scope; and it represents a stepping stone toward higher-level security management."[11] In fact, the managing director of (ISC)[2] has endorsed this as a more technical certification than the SSCP. The T.I.C.S.A. certification is highly technical and is targeted towards network and systems administrators. According to Trusecure, to attain the T.I.C.S.A., a candidate must have two years experience in an area of information security in one of the TruSecure areas of risk (see the following bulleted list), have at least 48 hours of training or coursework in security, complete the written exam, and subscribe to the TruSecure ICSA Security Practitioner Code of Ethics.

Because the examination is based largely on the TruSecure methodology, it cannot be considered vendor neutral. The examination is also based on the following TruSecure six categories of risk:

- "Electronic
    - External and internal
    - Hacking and sniffing
    - Spoofing
- "Malicious code
    - Viruses and worms
    - Java and ActiveX
    - Trojans
- "Physical
    - Theft and terminal hijack
- "Human Social engineering
    - Privacy

- "Downtime
  - DoS attacks
  - Bugs
  - Power
  - Civil unrest
  - Natural disasters"[12]

The exam consists of approximately 70 multiple-choice questions which must be completed within 90 minutes.

Another recent security certification at TruSecure is their expert certification, the T.I.C.S.E., which is still in planning. This certification is designed to be a follow-up to the T.I.C.S.A. and to require an advanced level of knowledge, approaching that of the security manager. The T.I.C.S.E candidate must demonstrate proficiency in the areas of:

- Firewall implementation, including multi- and single-firewall installations, packet filtering, and proxy-servers
- Security policy formulation and implementation
- Risk analysis
- Attack method identification and solutions
- Bastion hosts and system hardening techniques
- Proxy-server filtering properties
- Packet filter definition and filtering criteria
- Basic packet filter rule set design
- VPN deployment
- OS security expertise
- Applied cryptography (PGP, S/MIME, and VPNs)
- Key management issues and solutions
- Incident response planning
- Biometrics
- Network and computer forensics

The candidate also completes both a written and a practical exam. The exam formats and durations have not yet been published.

Security+

CompTIA (*www.comptia.com*) is the company that introduced the first vendor-neutral professional IT certifications, the A+ series. CompTIA is in the process of defining the body of knowledge necessary for their next certification. The Security+ certification will probably be similar to the Network+ certification and to many others in its focus on key skills necessary to perform security, without being tied to a particular software or hardware vendor package. In actuality, several of the other certifications in security are rather vendor-neutral, focusing on the subject areas and bodies of knowledge necessary to manage security, rather than the configuring of security technology. At the time of this publication, the Security+ certification was still in the planning stage and the subject areas to be tested were still unknown.

Certified Information Systems Auditor (CISA)

The CISA certification, while not specifically a security certification, contains many information security components. The Information Systems Audit and Control Association & Foundation promotes the certification for auditing, networking, and security professionals. Many of the CISA certifications have requirements that are common to all security certifications, including:

- Successful completion of the CISA examination
- Experience as an information systems auditor, with a minimum of five years' professional experience in information systems auditing, control, or security
- Agreement to the Code of Professional Ethics
- Agreement to the Information Systems Auditing Standards
- Continuing education policy requires maintenance fees and a minimum of 20 contact hours of continuing education annually. In addition, a minimum of 120 contact hours is required during a fixed three-year period.

The exam covers the following areas of information systems auditing:

- The IS audit process (10 percent)
- Management, planning, and organization of IS (11 percent)
- Technical infrastructure and operational practices (13 percent)
- Protection of information assets (25 percent)
- Disaster recovery and business continuity (10 percent)
- Business application system development, acquisition, implementation, and maintenance (16 percent)
- Business process evaluation and risk management (15 percent)

The exam is only offered once a year, so advanced planning is a must.

Certified Information Systems Forensics Investigator

There is a new certification under development by the Information Security Forensics Association (*infoforensics.org*). This group is developing an examination for a certified information systems forensics investigator, which evaluates the tasks and responsibilities of a security administrator or security manager in dealing with incident response, working with law enforcement, and auditing incidences. Although the certification exam has not been developed yet, the common body of knowledge has been tentatively defined to include information on:

- Countermeasures
- Auditing
- Incident response teams
- Law enforcement and investigation
- Traceback

Related Certifications

There are a number of related certifications, with security components or strong vendor ties, including those developed by the following:

- "Brainbench
- "Check Point Software Technologies Ltd.
- "Cisco Systems
- "Entrust
- "Information Systems Audit and Control Association
- "International Webmasters Association
- "Learning Tree International
- "Novell Corporation
- "Microsoft Corporate
- "Sun Corporation
- "Pine Mountain Group
- "Prosoft Training
- "RSA Security Inc.
- "Symantec
- "Tivoli Systems"[13]

The details of these certificates are too varied to cover here. For additional information on these and other certifications, check the Web.

Cost of Being Certified

Certifications cost money, and the better certifications can be quite expensive. Some certification exams can run as much as $450 for one examination, and the entire track can cost several thousand dollars. Additionally, the cost for formal training to prepare the candidate for the certification can be significant. Although you should not attempt to earn a certification with only the certification preparation course as preparation, these courses can help candidates round out their knowledge and fill in gaps. As mentioned earlier, some of the exams, such as the CISSP, are very broad and others very technical. Even an experienced professional would find it difficult to sit for one of these exams without some preparation. Many candidates teach themselves through trade press books. Others prefer the structure of formal training, because it includes practicing the technical components on equipment the candidate may not be able to access. At any rate, certifications are designed to recognize experts in their respective fields, and the cost of certification inhibits those who take exams just to see if they can pass. Most examinations admit only those with two and three years of expertise in the skills being tested. Before attempting a certification exam, do your homework. Look into the exam criteria, its purpose, and requirements in order to ensure that the time and energy spent pursuing the certification are well spent. Figure 11-3 shows several approaches to preparing for security certification.

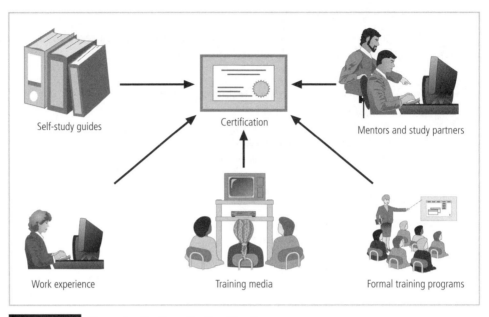

Self-study guides

Certification

Mentors and study partners

Work experience

Training media

Formal training programs

FIGURE 11-3 Preparing for Security Certification

Advice for Information Security Professionals

As a future information security professional, you can benefit from the following suggestions on entering the information security job market.

- Always remember: Business first, technology last. Technology is a tool for solving business problems. Information security professionals are sometimes guilty of looking for ways to apply the newest technology to problems that do not require technology-based solutions. When evaluating a problem, look at the source of the problem first, see what factors impact the problem, and see if you can design a solution that is independent of technology; then, count on technology to go the last mile. Technology can provide elegant solutions for some problems, but for others it only adds to the difficulties.

- Your job is to protect the organization's information and information systems resources. Never lose sight of the goal: protection.

- Be heard and not seen. Information security should be transparent to the users. With minor exceptions, the actions taken to protect the information should not interfere with the users' actions. Information security supports the work of end users, not the other way around. The only communications that should be conducted between users and security should be the periodic awareness messages, training announcements, newsletters, and e-mails.

- Know more than you say, and be more skillful than you let on. Don't try to impress users, managers, and other nontechnical people with your level of knowledge and experience. One day you just might stumble across the Jedi master who puts you in your place.

- Speak *to* users, not *at* them. While you are talking to users, use their language, not yours. Users aren't impressed with techno-babble and jargon. They may not comprehend the TLAs (three letter acronyms), technical components, software, and hardware necessary to protect their systems, but they do know how to short-circuit your next budget request or pick out the flaws in your business report.

■ Your education is never complete. As sensitive as you are to the idea that information technology is ever evolving, you must be equally sensitive to the idea that security education is never complete. Just when you think you have mastered the latest skills, you will encounter changes in threats, protection technology, your business environment, or the regulatory environment. As a security professional, you must expect to continue the learning process. This is best accomplished through periodic seminars, training programs, and formal education. Even if the organization (or your pocketbook) cannot afford the more extensive and expensive training programs and conferences, you can keep abreast of the market by reading trade literature (magazines), textbooks, and news articles on security. You can also subscribe to the many mailing lists for security professionals. Several are listed in the Offline entitled "What's In a Name?" Join at least one professional security association, such as the Information Systems Security Association (*www.issa.org*). Whatever approach you take, keep on top of the reading, never stop learning, and make yourself the best security professional possible. It can only enhance your worth to the organization and your career.

OFFLINE

What's in a Name?

Here are some of the titles listed in job search databases, which were reviewed to prepare this section. The databases searched are presented at the end of the Offline. See if you can guess the position level based on the title.

■ Senior security analyst
■ SAP security analyst
■ Security supervisor
■ Direct loss prevention manager
■ Security officer (not a guard job)
■ Loss prevention consultant
■ Site supervisor—security
■ Safeguards and security specialist

http://justsecurityjobs.com
http://securityjobs.net
http://www.itsecurityjobs.com
http://www.ssr-personnel.com/NewPage/vacs.htm

Employment Policies and Practices

The general management community of interest should integrate solid information security concepts into the organization's employment policies and practices. The section that follows examines important concepts associated with recruiting, hiring, firing, and managing human resources in the organization. If the organization can include security as a documented part of every employee's job description, information security will be taken more seriously. Discussion begins with the hiring issues related to information security that management faces.

Hiring and Termination Issues

From an information security perspective, the hiring of employees is a responsibility laden with potential security pitfalls. The CISO and information security manager should establish a dialogue with the Human Resources Department to provide an information security viewpoint for hiring personnel. Figure 11-4 highlights some of the hiring issues.

Background checks

Certifications

Policies

Covenants and agreements

Contracts

FIGURE 11-4 Hiring Issues

Job Descriptions

Inserting information security perspectives into the hiring process begins with reviewing and updating all job descriptions. To prevent people from applying for positions based solely on access to sensitive information, the organization should avoid revealing access privileges to prospective employees when advertising positions.

Interviews

The next point of contact with a potential employee is the job interview. Some interviews are conducted with members of the Human Resources staff, and others include members of the department for which the new position is being offered. An opening within the Security Information Department opens up a unique opportunity for the security manager to educate HR on the various certifications, the specific experience each requires, and the qualifications of a good candidate. For all other areas of the organization, information security should advise HR to limit information which is provided to the candidate on the responsibilities and access rights the new hire would have, for many of the same reasons mentioned during the discussion of job descriptions. For those organizations that include on-site visits as part of initial or follow-up interviews, it is important to exercise caution when showing a candidate around the facility. Avoid tours through secure and restricted sites. Candidates who are shown around can retain enough information about the operations or information security functions to represent a potential threat.

Background Checks

A background check should be conducted before the organization extends an offer to a candidate. A background check is an investigation into the candidate's past, specifically looking for criminal behavior that could indicate potential for future misconduct. There are a number of regulations that govern what the organization can investigate, and how much of the information can influence the hiring decision. The security manager and HR manager should discuss these matters with the competent counsel to determine what local and state regulations impact the hiring process.

Background checks differ in the level of detail and depth with which the candidate is examined. In the military, background checks determine the individual's level of security classification, a requirement for many positions. In the business world, a background check can determine the level of trust the business places in the individual. Individuals considered for security positions should expect some level of background check. Those considering careers in law enforcement or high-security positions may even be required to submit to polygraph tests. The following list contains a number of types of background checks with the type of information each looks into:

- Identity checks: Personal identity and social security number validation
- Education and credential checks: Institutions, degrees and certifications earned, and certification status
- Previous employment verification: Where candidates worked, why they left, what they did, and for how long
- References checks: Validity of references and integrity of reference sources
- Worker's compensation history: Claims from worker's compensation
- Motor vehicle records: Driving records, suspensions, and DUIs
- Drug history: Drug screening and drug usage, past and present
- Credit history: Credit problems, financial problems, and bankruptcy
- Civil court history: Involvement as the plaintiff or defendant in civil suits
- Criminal court history: Criminal background, arrests, convictions, and time served

As mentioned, there are federal regulations regarding the use of personal information in employment practices, include the Fair Credit Reporting Act (FCRA), which governs the activities of consumer credit reporting agencies, and the uses of the information procured from these agencies.[14] These reports contain information on a job candidate's credit history, employment history, and other personal data.

Among other things, the FCRA prohibits employers from obtaining these reports unless the candidate is informed in writing that such a report will be requested as part of the employment process. FCRA also allows the candidate to request information on the nature and type of reporting used in making the employment decision and subsequently enables the candidate to learn the content of these reports. The FCRA also restricts the periods of time these reports can address. Unless the candidate earns more than $75,000 per year, the information can only contain seven years' worth of adverse information. If the candidate earns $75,000 or more per year, there is no time limitation. Note that "any person who knowingly and willfully obtains information on a consumer from a consumer reporting agency under false pretenses shall be fined under title 18, United States Code, imprisoned for not more than two years, or both."[15]

Employment Contracts

Once a candidate has accepted the job offer, the employment contract becomes an important security instrument. Many of the policies discussed in Chapter 6 require an employee to agree in writing, specifically through fair and responsible use policies, to monitoring and non-disclosure agreements. If an existing employee refuses to sign these contracts, the security personnel are placed in a difficult situation. They not may be able either to force the employee to sign, or to deny the employee access to the systems necessary to perform his duties. New employees, however, are in a different situation. These policies may be classified as "employment contingent upon agreement," whereby the employee is not offered the position unless he agrees to the binding organizational policies. Although this may seem harsh, it is a necessary component of the security process. After the candidates have signed the security agreements, the remainder of the employment contracts may be executed.

New Hire Orientation

As new employees are introduced into the organization's culture and workflow, they should receive as part of their new employee orientation an extensive information security briefing. All major policies should be explained, as well as procedures for performing necessary security operations and other requirements for information security within the new position. The levels of authorized access are outlined, and training is provided on the secure use of information systems. By the time employees are ready to report to their positions, they should be thoroughly briefed on the necessary security component of their particular jobs, as well as the rights and responsibilities of all personnel in the organization.

On-the-Job Security Training

As part of the new hire's ongoing job orientation, and as part of every employee's security responsibilities, the organization should conduct the periodic security awareness and training described in Chapter 6. Keeping security at the forefront of employees' minds and minimizing employee mistakes is an important part of the information security mission. Formal external and informal internal seminars also increase the level of security awareness for all employees, especially security employees.

Performance Evaluation

To heighten information security awareness and change workplace behavior, organizations should incorporate information security components into employee performance evaluations. Employees pay close attention to job performance evaluations, and if the evaluations include information security tasks, employees are more motivated to perform these tasks at a satisfactory level.

Termination

Leaving the organization may or may not be a decision made by the employee. Organizations may downsize, be bought out, taken over, shut down, run out of business, or simply may be forced to lay off, fire, or relocate their work force. In any event, when an employee leaves an organization, there are a number of security-related issues. Key among these is the continuity of protection of all information to which the employee had access. When an employee prepares to leave an organization, the following tasks must be performed:

- Access to the organization's systems must be disabled
- Removable media must be returned

- Hard drives must be secured
- File cabinet locks must be changed
- Office door lock must be changed
- Keycard access must be revoked
- Personal effects must be removed from the organization's premises

After the employee has delivered keys, keycards, and other business property, he or she should be escorted from the premises.

In addition to the tasks listed above, many organizations use an **exit interview** to remind the employee of contractual obligations, such as nondisclosure agreements and to obtain feedback on the employee's tenure in the organization. At this time, the employee should be reminded that that should he or she fail to comply with contractual obligations, civil or criminal action may result.

Of course, most employees are allowed to clean out their own offices, collect their personal belongings, and simply asked to return their keys. From a security standpoint, however, regardless of the level of trust in the employee or the level of cordiality in the office environment, security cannot risk the exposure of organizational information. The simplest and best method to handle the outprocessing of an employee is to select one of the scenarios that follows, based on the employee's reasons for leaving.

Hostile departures (nonvoluntary) include termination, downsizing, lay off, or quitting. Before the employee knows he is leaving, security terminates all logical and keycard access. As soon as the employee reports for work, he is escorted into his supervisor's office for the bad news. Upon receiving the termination notice, he is escorted to his office, cubicle, or personal area and allowed to collect personal effects. No organizational property is allowed to be taken from the premises, including diskettes, pens, papers, and books. Regardless of the claim the employee has on organizational property, he is not allowed to take it from the premises. To protest these procedures, employees can submit, in writing, a list of the property they want to retain and state their reasons. After their personal property has been gathered, the employees are asked to surrender all keys, keycards, other organizational identification and access devices, PDAs, pagers, cell phones, and all remaining company property. They are then escorted out of the building.

Friendly departures (voluntary) include retirement, promotion, or relocation. In this case, the employee may have tendered notice well in advance of the actual departure date. This actually makes it much more difficult for security to maintain positive control over the employee's access and information usage. Employee accounts are usually allowed to continue with a new expiration date. Employees come and go at will and usually collect their own belongings and leave under their own cognizance. They are asked to drop off all organizational property "on their way out the door."

In either circumstance (involuntary or voluntary), the offices and information used by the employee must be inventoried, files must be stored or destroyed, and all property must be returned to organizational stores. It is possible in either situation that the employees foresee departure well in advance and begin collecting organizational information and, for whatever reason, taking home files, reports, data from databases, and anything that could be valuable in their future employment. This may be impossible to prevent. Only by scrutinizing systems logs after the employee has departed and sorting out authorized actions from systems misuse or information theft can the organization determine if there has been a breach of policy or a loss of information. In the event that information is illegally copied or stolen, the action should be declared an incident and the appropriate policy followed. Figure 11-5 overviews some termination activities.

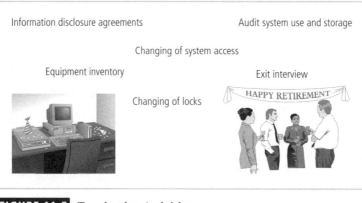

Information disclosure agreements   Audit system use and storage

Changing of system access

Equipment inventory   Exit interview

Changing of locks   HAPPY RETIREMENT

FIGURE 11-5 Termination Activities

Security Considerations for Nonemployees

A number of individuals who are not subject to rigorous screening, contractual obligations, and eventual secured termination often have access to sensitive organizational
information. Relationships with individuals in this category should be carefully managed
to prevent a possible information leak or theft as outlined in the sections that follow.

Temporary Employees

Temporary employees are hired by the organization to serve in a temporary position or
to supplement the existing workforce. These employees may not actually work for the
organization they are performing their duties for, but may instead be the paid employees
of a "temp agency" or organization that provides specifically qualified individuals at the
paid request of another company. Temps typically perform secretarial or administrative
support, and may be exposed to a wide range of information. As they are not employed
by the host organization, they are often not subject to the contractual obligations or general policies of other employees. If these individuals breach a policy or cause a problem,
the strongest action the host organization can take is to terminate the relationships with
the individuals and request that they be censured. The employing agency is under no
contractual obligation to do so, but may seek to appease a powerful or lucrative client.

From a security standpoint, access to information for these individuals should be
limited to that necessary to perform their duties. The organization can attempt to have
temporary employees sign nondisclosure agreements and fair use policies, but the temp
agency may refuse, forcing the host organization to either dismiss the temp worker or
allow him or her to work without the agreement. This can create a situation that is awk-
ward and potentially dangerous. Temporary workers may have access to information that
does not directly relate to their responsibilities. The only way to combat this threat is to
ensure that the temp's supervisor restricts the information to which he or she has access
and makes sure all employees follow good security practices, especially the clean desk

policies and the security of classified data. Temps can provide great benefits to the host organization, but should not be employed at the cost of sacrificing information security.

Contract Employees

Contract employees are typically hired to perform specific services for the organization. The host company often makes a contract with a parent organization rather than with an individual for a particular task. Typical contract employees include groundskeepers, maintenance service people, electrical contractors, mechanical service contractors, and other service repair people. Although some individuals may require access to virtually all areas of the organization to do their jobs, they seldom need access to information or information resources, unless, for example, the organization has leased computing equipment or has contracted with a disaster recovery service. Contract employees may need access to various facilities; however, this does not mean they should be allowed to wander freely in and out of buildings. In a secure facility, all contract employees are escorted from room to room, as well as into and out of the facility. When these employees report for maintenance or repair services, the first step is to verify that these services are actually scheduled or called for. As indicated in earlier chapters, it is not unheard of for an attacker to dress up as a telephone repairman, maintenance technician, or janitor to gain physical access to a building, and therefore, direct supervision is a necessity. There is also the need for certain restrictions or requirements to be negotiated into the contract agreements when they are activated. The following regulations should be negotiated well in advance: the facility requires 24 to 48 hours notice of a maintenance visit; the facility requires all on-site personnel to undergo background checks; and advanced notice is required for cancellation or rescheduling of a maintenance visit.

Consultants

Sometimes on site contracted employees are self-employed or employees of an organization hired for a specific, one-time purpose. These people are typically referred to as **consultants** and have their own security requirements and contractual obligations. Consultants should be handled the same as contract employees, with special requirements for information or facility access requirements integrated into the contract before these individual are allowed outside the conference room. Security and technology consultants especially must be pre-screened, escorted, and subjected to nondisclosure agreements to protect the organization from possible intentional or accidental breaches of confidentiality. Many consultants like to brag about the complexity of a particular job or an outstanding service provided to another client. If the organization does not want the consultant to mention its client relationship, or to disclose the least detail about its particular system configuration, the organization must write these restrictions into the contractual agreement. Although these professionals typically request the permission to present their work to other companies as part of their resumes, the organization is not obligated to grant this permission and can explicitly deny it in writing. Just because you pay a security consultant doesn't make the protection of your information his or her number one priority.

Business Partners

On occasion, businesses find themselves in strategic alliances with other organizations, desiring to exchange information, integrate systems, or simply to discuss operations for mutual advantage. In these situations, there must be a prior business agreement that specifies the level of exposure both organizations are willing to endure. Sometimes one division of a business enters a strategic partnership with an organization that directly competes with one of its own divisions. If the strategic partnership evolves into an integration of the systems of both companies, competing groups may be provided with information that neither parent organization expected. As a result, there must be a meticulous, deliberate process of determining what information is to be exchanged, in what format, and to whom. Nondisclosure agreements must be in place. And as discussed in Chapter 2, the level of security of both systems must be examined before any physical integration takes place, as system connection means that the vulnerability of one system is the vulnerability of all.

Separation of Duties and Collusion

Separation of duties is a cornerstone in the protection of information assets and in preventing financial loss. **Separation of duties** is a control used to reduce the chance of an individual violating information security and breaching the confidentiality, integrity, or availability of the information. The completion of a significant task that involves sensitive information should require two people. If one person has the authorization to access a particular set of information, there may be nothing to prevent this individual from copying it and removing it from the premises. This is especially important when the information is financial. Consider for example, that in a bank two people are required to issue a cashier's check. The first is authorized to prepare the check, acquire the numbered financial document, and ready the check for signature. The process then requires a second person, usually a supervisor, to sign the check. Only then can the check be issued. If only one person has the authority to perform both functions, that person can write a number of checks to fellow conspirators, sign them, and steal large sums from the bank. The same level of control can be applied to critical data. One programmer updates the system, and a supervisor or coworker accesses the file location in which the updates are stored. Or, one employee can be authorized to run backups to the system, and another to install and remove the physical media. This check and balance method requires two or more people to conspire to commit an incident, which is known as **collusion**. The odds that two people are willing and able to misuse or abuse the system are much lower than one. Related to the concept of separation of duties is that of **two-man control**, the requirement that two individuals review and approve each other's work before the task is categorized as finished. This is distinct from separation of duties, in which the two work in sequence. In two-man control, each person completely finishes the necessary work, and then submits it to the coworker. Each coworker examines the work performed, double checking the actions performed, and making sure no errors or inconsistencies exist. Figure 11-6 illustrates these operations.

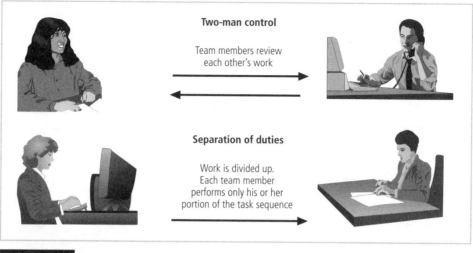

Two-man control

Team members review
each other's work

Separation of duties

Work is divided up.
Each team member
performs only his or her
portion of the task sequence

FIGURE 11-6 Preventing Collusion

Another control used to prevent personnel from misusing information assets is job rotation. **Job rotation** or **task rotation** is the requirement that every employee be able to perform the work of another employee. If it is infeasible that one employee learn the entire job of another, then ensuring that all critical tasks have multiple individuals capable of performing the tasks can greatly increase the chance that one employee could detect misuse of the system or abuse of the information of another. This way no one employee is performing actions that cannot be physically audited by another employee. In general, this method makes good business sense. One threat to information is the inability of the organization to perform the tasks of one employee, in the event that the employee is unable or unwilling to perform his duties. If everyone knows at least part of the job of another person (a human RAID system), the organization can survive the loss of any one employee.

This leads to the concept of mandatory vacations. Why require them? A mandatory vacation, of at least one week, provides the organization with the ability to audit the work of an individual. Individuals who are stealing from the organization or otherwise misusing information or systems are reluctant to take vacations, for fear that their actions are detected. Therefore, all employees should be required to take at least one one-week vacation, so that their jobs can be audited. This does not imply that employees are untrustworthy, but ensures that employees who want to abuse the system know that there is a strong probability of being caught.

One last topic to be covered has been mentioned before, but warrants repeating. Employees should be provided access to the minimal amount of information for the minimal amount of time necessary for them to perform their duties. This is referred to as the principle of **least privilege**. Similar to the concept of need-to-know, least privilege ensures that no unnecessary access to data occurs, and that only those individuals who must access the data do so. There is no need for everyone in the organization to have access to all information. The whole purpose of information security is to allow those people with a need to use information to do so without concern for the loss of confidentiality, integrity, and availability. Everyone who can access data probably will, resulting in numerous potential losses.

Privacy and the Security of Personnel Data

Another personnel and security topic is the security of personnel and personal data. Organizations are required by law to protect employee information that is sensitive or personal. This includes employee addresses, phone numbers, social security numbers, medical conditions, and even names and addresses of family and relatives. This responsibility also extends to customers, patients, and business relationships, as discussed in Chapter 3. While personnel data is in principle no different than other data that security protects, there is a great deal more regulation covering its protection. As a result, security should ensure that this data receives at least the same level of protection as the other important data in the organization.

Chapter Summary

- The placement of the information security function within the organization is a key decision facing the entire organization. The most popular options are within the IT function or within the physical security function. Organizations searching for a rational compromise should place the information security function where it can balance the needs of enforcement of organizational policy with customer service.

- Selecting information security personnel is based on a number of criteria. Some of these factors are within the control of the organization and others are not. At the time of writing this textbook (2002), the information security industry is in a period of high demand, with few qualified individuals available.

- In most cases, organizations look for a technically qualified information security generalist, with a solid understanding of how an organization operates and with the following attributes:
  - Agreement that information security is usually a management problem not an exclusively technical problem
  - Good people skills, communications skills, and writing skills, and a tolerance for users
  - An understanding of the role of policy in guiding security efforts
  - An understanding of the role of education and training in making the user part of the solution
  - An understanding of the threats facing an organization and how these threats can become attacks, as well as how to protect the organization from information security attacks
  - A working knowledge of many of the most common technologies, and a general familiarity with most mainstream IT technologies

- Many information security professionals enter the field through one of two career paths: from being former law enforcement or military personnel or from being technical information systems professionals.

- During the hiring process, using standard job descriptions can increase the degree of professionalism of those hired and also improve the consistency of roles and responsibilities between organizations that have positions in the information security discipline. Studies of information security positions have found that they can be classified into one of three areas: those that define, those that build, and those that administer. Among the most common job titles are:
  - Chief information security officer
  - Security manager
  - Security technician
  - Security consultant
- Many organizations seek individuals with recognizable certifications to indicate the level of proficiency associated with the various security positions. Among the most visible are:
  - Certified Information Systems Security Professional (CISSP) and Systems Security Certified Practitioner (SSCP)
  - Global Information Assurance Certification (GIAC) family of certifications
  - Security Certified Professional (SCP)
  - TruSecure ICSA Certified Security Associate (T.I.C.S.A.) and TruSecure ICSA Certified Security Expert (T.I.C.S.E.)
  - Security+
  - Certified Information Systems Auditor (CISA)
  - Certified Information Systems Forensics Investigator
- The general management community of interest should integrate solid concepts on information security into the organization's employment policies and practices. Areas of integration should include:
  - Hiring: Job descriptions, interviews, and background checks
  - Employment contracts
  - New hire orientation
  - On-the-job security training
  - Performance evaluation
  - Termination
- Organizations may need the special services of nonemployees, and the resulting relationships should be carefully managed to prevent information leaks or theft. The categories of nonemployees are:
  - Temporary employees
  - Contract employees
  - Consultants
  - Business partners
- Separation of duties is a control used to reduce the chance of any one individual violating information security and breaching the confidentiality, integrity, or availability of the information. Any major task that involves sensitive information should require two people to complete.
- A final topic within the area of personnel and security is the privacy and security of personnel and personal data. These information assets have government-mandated requirements for special security considerations and must be covered in the organization's information security program.

Review Questions

1. Which department should decide where the information security function should be located in the organizational structure? Why?

2. List and describe the options available for the location of the information security functions within the organization.

3. Based on your response to the previous question, discuss the advantages and disadvantages for each option.

4. If a thorough review of job descriptions for information security tasks is undertaken, which job descriptions are reviewed? Which IT jobs, not directly associated with information security, should be reviewed?

5. What is a behavioral feasibility study? When should it be completed? What is its purpose and why is it needed?

6. List and describe the criteria for selecting information security personnel.

7. What are some of the factors that influence an organization's hiring decisions?

8. What attributes do organizations seek in a candidate when hiring information security professionals? Prioritize the list and justify your ranking.

9. What are the critical considerations when dismissing an employee? Do these change based on whether the departure is "friendly" or "hostile"?

10. How do the security considerations for temporary or contract employees differ from those of the regular full-time employee?

11. What two career paths are often used by experienced professionals when moving into the information security discipline? Are there other pathways and if so describe them?

12. Why is it important to use standard job descriptions for hiring information security professionals?

13. What functions does the CISO perform, and what are the key qualifications and requirements for the position?

14. What functions does the security manager perform, and what are the key qualifications and requirements for the position?

15. What functions does the security technician perform, and what are the key qualifications and requirements for the position?

16. What functions does the internal security consultant perform, and what are the key qualifications and requirements for the position?

17. What is the rationale for acquiring professional credentials?

18. List and describe the certification credentials available to the information security professional.

19. Who should pay for the expenses of certification? Why?

20. What is the most significant advice for future information security professionals offered in this chapter? Do you agree or disagree? Why?

21. List and describe the standard personnel practices that are part of the information security function. What happens to these practices when they are integrated with information security concepts?

22. Why shouldn't you show an employee candidate secure areas during interviews?

23. List and describe the typical associations that information security organizations have with nonemployees. What are the special security considerations for workers involved in these associations and why are they significant?

24. What is separation of duties? How can it be used to improve an organization's information security practices?

25. What is collusion? How does the separation of duties impact collusion?

Exercises

1. Reread the opening scenario about Iris and Charlie. In light of the material in the chapter, create a position in Kelvin Urich's group and create a job description for it.

2. Reread the opening scenario about Iris and Charlie. Based on the material in the chapter, develop a list of questions Iris should ask to make an informed decision about the job offer.

3. Using the Web, find at least five job postings for a security administrator. What qualifications do the listings have in common?

4. Go to the (ISC)² Web site (*www.isc2.org*). Research the knowledge tested for both the CISSP and the SSCP. What areas must you study that are *not* covered in this text?

5. Using the Web, search for three different employee hiring and termination policies. Review each and look carefully for inconsistencies. Do they each have sections addressing security of information requirements? What clauses should a termination policy contain to prevent disclosure of an organization's information? Create your own variant of either a hiring or termination policy.

Case Exercises

I. The Truth, the Whole Truth ...

Adapted from Stephanie Armour, "Security checks worry workers; Padded resumes could be exposed," *USA TODAY*, June 19, 2002.[16]

When employees apply for jobs, they want to represent themselves in the best possible light and hope to be the best qualified for the position. In fact, they may want the position so badly, that they pad their resumes just a little. Who's going to know, right?

Wrong. With the increased emphasis on information security and screening for terrorists, Security and Human Resources Departments are carefully reviewing all applicants' qualifications. The result is that seemingly innocent "exaggerations" are seen as falsified applications. Potential job candidates become rejected applicants. "More than 40 percent of applicants misrepresented their education or employment history, according to a survey by computing service firm, Automatic Data Processing."[17]

The problem is growing. With a downturn in the economy, more people are out of work. Jobs are becoming harder to find, and therefore job hunters are more desperate and likely to fib on their applications.

"Headlines are a stark reminder that such misrepresentations can kill careers. Sandra Baldwin quit as U.S. Olympic Committee chairman after it came to light that she listed a Ph.D. she hadn't earned. And last month, Washington, D.C., Fire Chief, Ronnie Few, resigned because he had claimed a college degree he didn't have."[18]

While some companies are willing to overlook some embellishment, most prefer total honesty, especially in their security personnel.

1. If organizations don't check with each other during the hiring process, how can Security or Human Resources Departments detect these "little white lies?" What's so serious about a little enhancement?

2. What should organizations do if they detect applicants who are falsifying applications and claiming certifications they don't have or degrees they don't possess?

II. Money Where Your Mouth Is

Adapted from Sean Dugan, "Certifiably secured" InfoWorld, July 9, 2001.[19]

"After 20 years in the U.S. Navy, Steve Akridge had the technical skills for a civilian career in information security. Yet, he still had to prove he could address bottom-line problems and direct security outside the military. Knowing this, Akridge wanted information security certification. According to [the] Gartner Group ... by 2004 InfoSec certification will be required for 60 percent of CISOs and staff positions and for 40 percent of day-to-day technical positions. 'With CISSP, I was exposed to new concepts—commercial concepts,' Akridge says. 'A CISSP proves my worth with senior executives.'"[20] Akridge recently completed a tour of duty as the CISO for the Georgia Technology Authority in Atlanta and has since moved onto private security consulting. Certification was critical to his post-service success.

Finding qualified technology administrators and technicians is tough. Finding qualified security technologists and managers is a nightmare. Until recently it was almost impossible to determine the skill and knowledge levels of security personnel. With the increase in security certifications, it is becoming easier to distinguish defined skill sets. That doesn't make them any more common. Just as with any market-driven certification, security certifications weren't prevalent ten years ago, because they weren't in demand. It's a circular problem. People didn't get security certifications, because organizations didn't recognize the need for certified security professionals. Agencies didn't offer them, because people didn't demand them. Organizations didn't expect them, because they weren't "popular." Now that they are available, the best security personnel have credentials to back up their knowledge and skills.

"The breadth of skills and management breadth required for strong information security puts unusual demands on organizations and professionals. 'I'm a very strong advocate of hiring people that have more than one focus.' says Micki Krause, CISSP and director of information security at PacifiCare Health Systems, in Santa Ana, Calif."[21]

Even though it's the most popular, the CISSP isn't the only certification offered. It is commonly understood that the CISSP is the managerial security certification of choice, and the GIAC is the technical and specialized security certification of choice. Some industry experts feel that there is a greater need in the short term for technical specialists, and a more long-term need for managers. In either case, the political issues associated with navigating the corporate budgets, planning requirements, and organizational culture, still make security management certification a big-demand item.

But certification is the beginning of a learning journey, not the destination of a career. While technology changes rapidly, security moves like a hurricane. Keeping up with changes is a full time job in itself. It will be a challenge for the certification exams to keep pace. One additional challenge to the certifications and the security profession is the inevitable arrival of "paper certifications." Paper certification is the consequence of viewing certification as more valuable than the knowledge and expertise the certification is expected to represent. This issue has already been discussed in connection with networking. Individuals use "certification boot-camps" and self-study "idiot" guides to earn unwarranted certifications. Organizations should use care when hiring certified security administrators to ensure they choose individuals who have the ability to backup their credentials.

1. What is the benefit of the generalized, managerial approach of the CISSP? When and where is it preferred over the more technical GIAC certification? Why is a managerial certification needed in security, when so few other career fields have managerial certifications?

2. What can the certification agency do to reduce the presence or impact of paper certifications? What can industry do to help?

Endnotes

1. Charles Cresson Wood, *Information Security Roles and Responsibilities Made Easy* (Houston, Tex.: PentaSafe Corporation, 2002), 95.

2. *Ibid.* 55-94.

3. Eddie Schwartz, Dan Erwin, Vincent Weafer, and Andy Briney, "Roundtable: Infosec Staffing Help Wanted!" *Information Security Magazine Online* (April 2001) [Cited 22 July 2002]; available from the World Wide Web *http://www.infosecuritymag.com/ articles/april01/features_roundtable.shtml.*

4. Security Jobs Network, Inc, "Sample Job Descriptions: Director of Security," *Security Jobs Network, Inc. Online* [Cited 21 July 2002]; available from the World Wide Web *http:// securityjobs.net/documents/Director%20of%20Security%20Position,%20Cox. html.*

5. IT Security Jobs, "IT Vacancies," *SSR Personnel Online* (22 July 2002) [Cited 22 July 2002]; available from the World Wide Web *http://www.ssr-personnel.com/vacancies/ IT.HTM#t1525l.*

6. IT Security Jobs, "623873 – Firewall Engineering Consultant," *SSR Personnel Online* (16 July 2002) [Cited 22 July 2002]; available from the World Wide Web *http://www.itsecurityjobs.com/ vacancies.htm.*

7. *Ibid.*

8. International Information Systems Security Certification Consortium, Inc, *"About SSCP Certification,"* ISC² Online [Cited 22 July 2002]; available from the World Wide Web *http://www.isc2.org/cgi/content.cgi?category=20.*

9. Global Information Assurance Certification, "GIAC: Steps to Certification General Instructions," *SANS Institute Online* [Cited 22 July 2002]; available from the World Wide Web *http://www.giac.org/steps.php#instructions.*

10. Security Certified Programs, "Certifications," *Ascendant Learning, LLC Online* [Cited 22 July 2002]; available from the World Wide Web *http://www.securitycertified.net/ certifications.htm.*

11. Trusecure, "TICSA Certification," *Trusecure Online* [Cited 22 July 2002]; available from the World Wide Web *http://www.truesecure.com/solutions/certifications/ticsa/.*

12. *Ibid.*

13. GoCertify, "Security Certifications," *Anventure Online* [Cited 21 July 2002]; available from the World Wide Web *http://gocertify.com/security.*

14. Background Check International, LLC, "BCI," *BCI Online* [Cited 22 July 2002]; available from the World Wide Web *http://www.bcint.com/legal.html.*

15. Federal Trade Commission, *Fair Credit Reporting Act,* 2002, 15 U.S.C., S. 1681 et seq.

16. Stephanie Armour, "Security checks worry workers; Padded resumes could be exposed," *USA TODAY*. (Jun 19, 2002): B01.

17. *Ibid.*

18. *Ibid.*

19. Sean Dugan. "Certifiably secured" InfoWorld. July 9, 2001. Volume 23 Issue 28 26-27

20. *Ibid.*

21. *Ibid.*

Information Security Maintenance

> The only thing we can predict with certainty is change.
>
> **JAYNE SPAIN, DEPARTMENT OF CHILDREN AND FAMILY LEARNING, STATE OF MINNESOTA**

CHARLIE MOODY LEANED BACK IN his chair. It was Monday morning after the biggest conversion weekend for the implementation of the information security project. Charlie had just completed his review of the results of the implementation steps. Everything was working as expected. The initial penetration tests run on Sunday afternoon were clean. Charlie was eager for everything to return to normal, that is, to the way things had been before the attack on Sequential's network had triggered the changes of the past few months.

Kelvin Urich tapped on the open door of Charlie's office. "Hey Charlie," he said. "Have you seen the e-mail I just sent? There's an urgent vulnerability report on Bugtraq about the version of UNIX we use. The vendor just released a critical patch to be applied right away. Should I get the system programming team started on an acceptance test for the patch?"

"Oh yes. Get them to pull a download from the vendor's FTP site as soon as they can," said Charlie. "Then get them to patch the test lab servers. If that looks okay, have them patch the development servers for the HQ development team. Oh, and get these into change control ASAP, and add the production server change request for the overnight change window tonight."

"Okay," Kelvin said. He turned to leave and then turned back. "Also, the consultant from the implementation team got the news about the new vulnerability. When he reviewed the CERT report, he said he figured out a way for the IDS to detect anyone trying to run the exploit and taking advantage of the vulnerability. He wanted permission to spend the day working on the IDS signature and testing it in our lab. I approved his request."

Charlie responded, "Good. I agree. Keep me posted on that."

Kelvin left Charlie's office as Charlie pulled up the CERT home page on his PC. He was reading about the new vulnerability when there was another knock on the doorjamb. It was Iris Majwabu.

When Charlie looked up, Iris said, "Hi Charlie. Got a second?"

"Sure, Iris. How have you been? Settling in with Kelvin's team, okay?"

She smiled. "Oh sure. They are a good group. They have me studying the documentation trail from the time before the security program was implemented. I came to see you about the reassessment of the information asset inventory and the threat-vulnerability update."

Charlie looked a little confused for a second, and then his memory kicked in and he grimaced just a little. "Oh, yes. I had put the quarterly asset and threat review out of my mind while we were busy with the implementation of the blueprint. I suppose it's time to start planning for the regular reviews, isn't it?"

Iris handed him a folder and said, "Here's the first draft of the plan for the review project. Kelvin has already seen it and suggested I review it with you. Let me know when you would like to go over it."

DISCUSSION QUESTIONS:

1. Is the consultant's idea about the IDS on the right track? Or, is he trying to pad his invoice?
2. What should Charlie look for when he reviews Iris' project plan?

LEARNING OBJECTIVES:

Upon completion of this material you should be able to:

- Understand the need for the ongoing maintenance of the information security program.
- Become familiar with recommended security management models.
- Understand a model for a full maintenance program.
- Understand key factors for monitoring the external and internal environment.
- Learn how planning and risk assessment tie into information security maintenance.
- Understand how vulnerability assessment and remediation tie into information security maintenance.
- Learn how to build readiness and review procedures into information security maintenance.

Introduction

Upon the successful implementation and testing of a new and improved security profile, an organization might feel more confident of the level of protection it is providing for its information assets. It shouldn't. By the time the organization has completed implementing the changes mandated by an upgraded security program, a good deal of time has passed. In that time, everything that is dynamic in the organization's environment has changed. What is dynamic? Virtually everything. The threats that were originally assessed in the early stages of the SecSDLC have probably changed, and new priorities have emerged. New variants and types of threats emerge, such as viruses, worms, denial-of-service attacks, and a host of other variables outside and inside the organization.

A comprehensive list is beyond the scope of this text, but some of the factors that are likely to shift in the information security environment are:

- New assets are acquired.
- New vulnerabilities associated with the new or existing assets emerge.
- Business priorities shift.
- New partnerships are formed.
- Old partnerships dissolve.
- Organizational divestiture and acquisition occur.
- Employees who are trained, educated, and made aware of the new policies, procedures, and technologies leave.
- New personnel are hired, thus possibly creating new vulnerabilities.

As the preceding list shows, by the time a cycle of the SecSDLC is completed, the environment changes so much that you must assure management that the information security program has accommodated that change. If the program is not adjusting adequately to change, it may be necessary to begin the cycle again. That decision depends on how much change has occurred and how well the organization and its program for information security maintenance can accommodate change. If an organization deals successfully with change and has created procedures and systems that can flex with the environment, the security program can probably continue to adapt successfully. The information security team continues to adapt to the changes as they occur using an information security maintenance model as a guide. How the maintenance component of the SecSDLC fits into the overall methodology is shown in Figure 12-1.

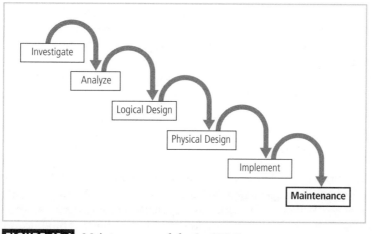

FIGURE 12-1 Maintenance and the SecSDLC

The CISO determines whether the information security group can adapt adequately and maintain the information security profile of the organization or whether the macroscopic process of the SecSDLC must start anew to redevelop a fundamentally new information security profile. It is less expensive and more effective when an information security program is designed and implemented to deal with change. It is more expensive to reengineer the information security profile again and again. Note that even when an information security program is adapting and growing, those processes of maintenance and change mirror the overall process of the SecSDLC, differing only in scope. As deficiencies are found and vulnerabilities pinpointed, projects to maintain, extend, or enhance the program follow the SecSDLC steps. Therefore, for maintenance, the steps include investigation, analysis, design, and implementation.

Before explaining the recommended maintenance model and the components of the model, some background on the management and operation of the information security program is in order. The section that follows outlines an approach to the management and operation of an information security program that aims to keep an organization and its information assets safe.

Managing for Change

Once an organization has improved the security posture of the organization, the security group must turn its attention to the maintenance of security readiness. To do so, the information security community of interest, led by the CISO, must constantly monitor the three components of the **security triple** (threats, assets, and vulnerabilities). As the organization continues to function, the team constantly monitors its systems and the environments in which the systems operate. The team also reviews security publications, notification lists, and e-mails to stay on top of the latest general and specific threats to its information security. As each threat evolves or new vulnerabilities in systems emerge, the information security team must determine if a shift in the prioritization of the organization's security posture is required. If so, the team must reevaluate the entire matrix of threat priorities and the corresponding interlocking system of controls. If no change in the security posture is required, monitoring continues. Similarly, as the organization acquires new assets, the team reevaluates the asset prioritization list and adapts it to shifts in the equations for information asset value. Only by creating an aggressive external and internal monitoring program can the information security team hope to stay abreast of changes in the environment.

Security Management Models

To assist the information security community to manage and operate the ongoing security program, a management model must be adopted. In general, management models are frameworks that structure the tasks of managing a particular set of activities or business functions. An example discussed in the next section is a modified variant of the ISO network management model.

The ISO Network Management Model

The ISO network management model is a five-layer approach that provides structure to the administration and management of networks and systems. The core ISO model addresses management and operation thorough five topics:

- Fault management
- Configuration and name management
- Accounting management
- Performance management
- Security management

While in its original form, the ISO model is not directly applicable to the management of an information security program, a modification of the model supports the various administrative tasks in most information security programs. The five areas of the ISO model are transformed into the five areas of security management as follows:

- Fault management
- Configuration and change management
- Accounting and auditing management
- Performance management
- Security program management

Each of the five key areas is examined in detail in the sections that follow.

Fault Management

In the ISO model, fault management is the process of identifying, tracking, diagnosing, and resolving faults in the system. Information security involves systems based both on people and technology; fault management also applies to people and technology. Fault management of information security involves identifying faults in the applied information security profile and then addressing them through remediation. Remediation includes vulnerability assessment, technical fault detection and correction, and general user security support. **Vulnerability assessment** involves the physical and logical assessment of the vulnerabilities present in both information security and related nonsecurity systems. This is most often accomplished with penetration testing. **Penetration testing** involves security personnel simulating or performing specific and controlled attacks to compromise or disrupt their own systems by exploiting documented vulnerabilities. Penetration testing from outside the organization is commonly performed on network connections, as security personnel attempt to exploit vulnerabilities in the system from the attacker's viewpoint. The information security personnel, who are often consultants or outsourced contractors, are commonly referred to as **whitehat hackers**, **ethical hackers**, **tiger teams**, or **red teams**. What they are called is less important than what they do. Information security administrators who have not looked at their systems through the eyes of an attacker are failing to maintain readiness. The best procedures and tools to use in penetration testing and other vulnerability assessments are the procedures and tools of the hacker community. The list that follows outlines some of the more common tools. Fortunately, many intrusion detection systems detect the signatures of these tools and can alert information security management of their use. The tools listed here in alphabetical order provide valuable services to network and system administrators. The easy availability and functionality of these tools means that they are also used by hackers even though they were certainly not created for hacking. As a security professional, you should incorporate these tools into your own toolbox of software to examine your systems and test your security.

- **Ethereal:** (*www.ethereal.com*) Ethereal is a freeware network protocol analyzer for UNIX and Windows. Ethereal allows the user to capture data over a network or from a data disk. The user can then review the data, data summaries, and details. Ethereal includes a filter and allows the user to recreate a TCP session data stream.

- **Nessus:** (*www.nessus.org*) Nessus is a freeware, remote security scanner. Nessus provides the user with the ability to perform vulnerability analysis on a given system. It allows the user to identify which services are running on which ports, and which will attempt to exploit the vulnerability.

- **NMAP:** (*www.nmap.org*) NMAP (network mapper) is an open-source tool to provide network exploration and vulnerability testing. NMAP uses raw IP packets to determine what hosts are available on the network, what services they offer, what operating system and version are installed, and what packet filters and firewalls are in use.

- **Sam Spade:** (*www.samspade.org*) Sam Spade is a virtual toolbox providing utilities normally available only to UNIX/Linux users. The utilities include the following:
  - **Ping:** Pings a host to see and time the responses
  - **Nslookup:** Resolves an IP address from a hostname and vice versa
  - **Whois:** Queries a whois server for a domain name's owner (you can specify the server or Sam Spade queries the nearest server)
  - **IP block whois:** Is a whois for a range of IP addresses
  - **Dig:** Asks a DNS server for all available information about a host
  - **Traceroute:** Prints the hops between you and a destination
  - **Finger:** Provides information about users on a specific system if available
  - **SMTP VRFY:** Queries a mail server to verify an e-mail address as an original, a forwarding address, or false
  - **Web browser:** Views naked HTML, without activated file downloads or Java scripts
  - **Keep-alive:** Keeps a dialup link active by communicating with an ISP's Web server
  - **DNS zone transfer:** Queries a DNS server for information about a domain and identifies the authoritative server
  - **SMTP relay check:** Identifies whether or not a mail server is secure
  - **Usenet cancel check:** Identifies cancelled messages in Usenet groups
  - **Web site download:** Copies an entire web site to disk
  - **Website search:** Queries an entire web site for a specified search pattern
  - **E-mail header analysis:** Examines the header of an e-mail to identify if the address has been spoofed
  - **Blacklist lookups:** Looks for an address on blacklists
  - **Abuse.net query:** Identifies the abuse reporting address for a given domain
  - **Time:** Retrieves the time maintained by a specific host

- **Snort:** (*www.snort.org*). Snort is an open-source network intrusion detection system that can examine real-time traffic on IP networks. Snort performs protocol analysis, content searching and matching, and can detect attacks and probes, such as buffer overflows, stealth port scans, CGI attacks, server message block (SMB) probes, and OS fingerprinting attempts. Snort also has real-time alert messaging and can be used as a straight packet sniffer, a packet logger, or as a complete network IDS.

Another aspect of fault management is the monitoring and resolution of user complaints. After all, as discussed in earlier chapters, the first clue that an attack is underway often comes from reports of observant users. In many organizations, help desks handle these reports as well as other systems problems. If a help desk does not exist, one may be needed, or provisions for reporting suspicious systems problems may have to be established. The Offline on help desks discusses the function and organization of the help desk. Help desk personnel must be trained to recognize a security problem as distinct from other system problems. As the help desk personnel screen problems, they track the activities for resolving the complaint in a help desk information system, such as the fictional ISIS system in the Chapter 1 scenario. The tracking process is commonly referred to as a **trouble ticket**. The ticket is opened when the user calls, and is closed when technical support or help desk personnel resolve the issue. One key advantage to formal help desk software is the ability to create and develop a knowledge base of common problems and solutions. This knowledge base can be searched when a user problem comes up, speeding up the process of resolving the complaint when it replicates a problem that has already been resolved. This knowledge base can also generate statistics on the frequency of problems by type, by user, or by application, and can detect trends and patterns in the data. User problems can be created or influenced by a security program. Modifications to firewalls, implementations of IDS rules, or new systems policies in the network may directly impact how users interact with the systems. A significant number of help desk trouble tickets are related to user access issues including passwords and other authentication, authorization, and accountability issues. Proper user training and ongoing awareness campaigns can reduce these problems; however, they are never completely eliminated.

As mentioned earlier, the tracking of trouble tickets includes tracking problem resolution. This may require that a technical support technician visit the user's office to examine equipment or observe the user's procedures. Or it may require that the technical support technician interact with other departments or workgroups. It is not uncommon for the help desk team to include a security technician. In any case, the technician working to resolve the trouble ticket must document not only the diagnosis, but also the resolution, as both are invaluable components of the knowledge base and are useful for resolving similar trouble tickets. Once the problem has been resolved and the results documented, the ticket is closed.

OFFLINE

The Help Desk

With a relatively small investment in an IT help desk, an organization can improve the quality of the IT support and information security functions. A small help desk with only a few call agents can provide good—perhaps excellent—service for an organization of several hundred users. If managed properly and funded adequately, large organizations can provide high-quality services using one or more help desks.

A help desk functions differently in various organizations but commonly provides:

- A single point of contact for service requests from users
- Initial screening of requests, answering the most common questions, solving the most common problems, and dispatching other types of calls to other units

continued

- Data entry of all calls into a tracking system
- Dispatch of service providers to respond to calls
- Reporting and analysis of call volumes, patterns, and process improvement

Other services that may be integrated into the help desk often include:

- Deskside support for common IT support functions such as Windows, end-user computing tools and common applications
- New-user management
- User removal processes
- Password management
- Smart card management
- Knowledge management for service requests and optimum resolutions
- Server configuration
- Network monitoring
- Server capacity monitoring
- Virus activity monitoring and virus pattern management

While each organization has its own approach to creating and evolving a help desk solution, many evolve through discernable phases and alter the mix of services they offer over time.[1] The smooth operation of a help desk, when integrated with the IT and information security functions, can greatly increase the quality of both the IT and information security services.

Configuration and Change Management

The information security management model continues with **configuration management** and **change management**. Configuration management is the administration of the configuration of the components of the security program. Change management is the administration of changes in the strategy, operation, or components of the information security program. Both configuration and change management administration involve nontechnical as well as technical changes.

Nontechnical changes impact procedures and people. Technical changes impact the technology implemented to support security efforts in the hardware, software, and data components. The IT managers and professionals of the organization are responsible for the information-processing systems of the organization. The information security community, however, should ensure that the technical systems of information security are managed independently from traditional IT equipment, except when there is overlap, such as with a filtering router. In cases of overlap, joint management is necessary. The ultimate goal is to ensure that all security technology is properly managed with perspective focusing on information security.

Nontechnical Change Management. When implementing changes to the information security program, the organization must probably implement a number of new policies and procedures. The documents that result from these efforts should be changed when they are insufficient, outdated, or inaccurate. As a result, the document manager should maintain a master copy of each document, record and archive revisions made, and keep copies of the revisions, along with editorial comments on what was added, removed, or modified. This library of documents can become unwieldy. As a result, the organization may wish to implement online archives to maintain the documents and revisions. It is important to be able to track changes to these documents, and to determine why and by whom they were created or modified. The record should include insight into the environment that caused the change. Without this type of record keeping, members of the organization may be following older versions of critical policy or procedure documents, while management is expecting performance according to a newer version.

As mentioned in earlier chapters, policy revisions are not considered implemented and enforceable until they have been disseminated, read, understood, and agreed to. As revisions are made, the updated versions must be disseminated to the involved personnel, and agreement must be documented. The management of the agreement documentation constitutes an administrative challenge, as many security policies and procedures contain sensitive information that the organization may not wish to disclose. The most effective way to manage changes to documents is to include the revision version number in the header, along with the file name, and revision date, and to physically distribute the documents to all parties affected. As the new documents are distributed, all older versions should be collected and destroyed, to prevent the end users from throwing them out carelessly or continuing to use them. To support the distribution and control of the documents, each copy should be labeled as discussed in previous chapters, as "Copy ____ of ____." As employees receive new copies and old versions are collected, the employees should sign for the new revision. Employees should also be given a conformation form with a due date requiring them to read and agree to the policies by a specified date.

The organization of these documents is easier if each employee or end user is issued a special binder for storing the most current version of all plans, policies, and procedures. This binder can be uniquely colored, labeled, and stored to prevent binder camouflage, which is the loss of a binder on a shelf of similar binders. One must be careful not to overdo the unique coloring and labeling of binders, as overuse can cause as much confusion as the use of the bland, white, unlabeled alternative. The storage of these binders should reflect the level of sensitivity of the documents that they contain.

Modern, Web-based software is available to make the creation, modification, dissemination, and agreement documentation processes more manageable. One example product, as noted in Chapter 6, is PentaSafe Policy Center (*www.pentasafe.com/products/vpc/*). It is coupled with policy writing aids from Charles Cresson Wood and allows organizations to require its users to be tested on policy knowledge. This product can also record agreement to policy and document that users have read and understood the policy or procedure.

Technical Configuration and Change Management. Just as documents have version numbers, revision dates, and requirements to monitor and administer change, so do technical components. There are several terms associated with the management of configuration and change in the technical components of systems (software, hardware, and firmware). Each of these is presented here:

- **Configuration item:** A hardware or software item that is to be modified and revised throughout its life cycle.
- **Version:** The recorded state of a particular revision of a software or hardware configuration item. These are often noted in a specific format as the version number in

the form M.N.b. In this notation, "m" is the major release number and "N.b" can be various minor releases and build numbers within that major release.

- Major release: A significant revision of the version from its previous state.
- Minor release (update or patch): A minor revision of the version from its previous state.
- Build: A snapshot of a particular version of software assembled (or linked) from its various component modules.
- **Build list:** A list of the versions of components that make up a build is called a build list.
- **Configuration:** A configuration is a collection of components that make up a configuration item.
- **Revision date:** The date associated with a particular version or build.
- **Software library:** A collection of configuration items that is usually controlled and that developers use to construct revisions and to issue new configuration items.

To make these definitions more palatable, consider the following hypothetical example: XYZ Security Solutions Corporation develops a new software application: Panacea—the Ultimate Security Solution. Panacea is the configuration item. Panacea's configuration consists of three major software components: See-all, Know-all, and Cure-all. Panacea is Version 1.0, and it is built from its three components. The build list is See-all 1.0, Know-all 1.0, and Cure-all 1.0, as this is the first major release of the overall application, as well as its components. The revision date is the date associated with the first build. The programmers pulled information from their software library to create Panacea. If the programmers discover a minor flaw in a subroutine while the application is being used in the field, they can issue the minor release, Panacea 1.1. If they need to make a major revision to the software for changing market needs or substantial problems with the subcomponents, they can issue a major release, Panacea 2.0.

In any case, both product developers and users perform configuration management. The developers focus on managing the build list and keeping up with the development of major and minor releases, while the users monitor the implementation of versions and track the latest releases and where the versions are implemented.

There are four procedures associated with configuration management.[2]

1. **Configuration identification:** The identification and documentation of the various components, implementation, and states of configuration items
2. **Configuration control:** The administration of changes to the configuration items and the issuance of versions
3. **Configuration status accounting:** The tracking and recording of the implementation of changes to configuration items
4. **Configuration audit:** Auditing and controlling the overall configuration management program

Of these four, configuration control is usually only performed by an entity that actually develops its own versions of configuration items. The other three should be performed by any organization that uses technology to solve problems. The physical management of configuration and changes should be implemented so that it does not interfere with the use of the technology. One individual in the security team should be appointed as the configuration manager or change manager to maintain the appropriate data elements in the organization's cataloging mechanism, including the specific version, revision date, and build associated with each piece of hardware and software implemented. In the maintenance model described later in this chapter much of this data is used in the risks, threats, and attacks database to make tracking vulnerabilities more meaningful. In some cases it may be better to have someone outside the implementation process document the process, as he or she is not distracted by the installation, configuration, and troubleshooting of the new installation. In the case of minor revisions, it may be simpler to have a procedure in plan, in which the final actions are documenting the machines on which the revision was installed, the date and time of the installation, and the installer. While the documentation procedures required for these processes may seem onerous, they are necessary to quickly and accurately determine exactly which systems are impacted when a new vulnerability arises. When stored in a comprehensive database along with risk, threat and attack information, configuration information provides a mechanism that quickly responds to new and rapidly changing threats and attacks.

Accounting and Auditing Management

The next category in the ISO security management model involves chargeback accounting and systems monitoring. **Chargeback accounting** enables organizations to internally charge their departments for system use. In other words, when Department A uses 30 seconds of CPU time on a mainframe, it is charged for that amount of use. While chargebacks for CPU cycle time are seldom used today, certain kinds of resource usage are commonly tracked, such as resources on a computing system (like a server or a desktop computer), or charges are made on a human effort-hour basis. These chargebacks allocate the recovery of IT costs from non-IT units. A useful byproduct of this process is measuring when organizational growth is approaching a level that requires additional resources. Accounting management involves the monitoring of the use of a particular component of a system. In networking, it may be simple to determine which users are using which resources. In security, however, it may be easy to track which resources are being used but difficult to determine who is using them. At this point, accounting management begins to overlap with performance management, which is addressed in the next section. With accounting management you begin to determine optimal points of systems use as indicators for upgrade and improvement.

In this context, **auditing** is the process of reviewing the use of a system, not to check performance, but to determine if misuse or malfeasance has occurred. Most computer-based systems used in security can create logs of their activity. These logs are a vital part of the detective functions associated with identifying what happened, when it happened, and how it happened. The management of systems logs in large organizations is a complex process and can be considered an art in itself. Unless the security (or systems) administrators are vigilant in the review of these logs, they can pile up quickly, as systems constantly write the activity that occurs. Fortunately, automated tools can consolidate various systems logs, perform comparative analysis, and detect common occurrences or behavior that is of interest. This can include anomalous network activity (such port scanning), malware signatures, hacking attempts, and illicit use of controlled network resources or computer systems. Considered part of some IDS approaches, these log analyzers can detect activities in real time. The IDS engines (both host and network based) also create logs. These logs are invaluable document summaries of events and should be archived and stored for future review as needed. It is not unheard of for systems intruders to attempt to cover their tracks by erasing entries in logs. As a result, wise administrators configure their systems to create duplicate copies of the logs, preferably to sources that cannot be easily modified, like write once, read many (WORM) technologies, such as CD-R and DVD-R.

Many vendors offer log consolidation and analysis features. One multiple-vendor approach is offered by the PentaSafe Corporation in their VigilEnt Intrusion Manager product (*http://www.pentasafe.com/products/vim/*). This software product, like offerings from other vendors, allows the analysis of its own IDS components. PentaSafe is similar to other leading software companies in the field of information security management in providing for the integration of log files from other vendor's products, such as firewall vendors and network equipment vendors.

Performance Management

Because many information security technical controls are implemented on common IT processors, they are affected by the same factors as most computer-based technologies. It is therefore important to monitor the performance of security systems and their underlying IT infrastructure to determine if they are working effectively. This type of monitoring is especially important for systems, such as Internet usage monitors that look for inappropriate use of Internet resources and operate as pass-by devices. When they are not sized correctly or kept tuned for proper performance, the actions they are intended to block are not stopped.

Some common system and network metrics used in performance management are also applicable in security, especially when the components being managed are associated with the ebb and flow of network traffic. The following list offers a few rules of thumb for use when exploring the issues of system and network performance.[3]

- When the memory usage associated with a particular CPU-based system averages 50-60 percent or more over prolonged periods, it may be time to consider adding more memory.

- When the CPU usage associated with a particular CPU-based system averages 50-60 percent or more over prolonged periods, it's time to consider an upgrade for the CPU.

- When the network traffic on a particular link averages 50-60 percent or more for prolonged periods, it's time to consider an upgrade to the link, either by increasing the bandwidth available or by segmenting the traffic.

- When the amount of data stored on a particular hard drive averages 50-60 percent or more of available capacity for a prolonged period, it's time to consider an upgrade for the hard drive, either by replacing the hard drive with a larger drive or by adding additional drives.

To evaluate the performance of a security system, the administrators must establish performance baselines within the system. Previous chapters covered establishing procedural baselines across industries and organizations. In this context, a **performance baseline** is an expected level of performance against which all subsequent levels of performance are compared. In other words, network traffic levels are deemed to be high when traffic reaches or surpasses the level of the performance baseline. The planning of capacity upgrades should begin before users complain about the slow loading Web pages. Organizations must establish baselines for a number of different criteria and for various periods of time: days of the week, weeks of the year, months of the year, times of day (AM and PM), among others. To accomplish this effectively, the organization must monitor all possible variables, collecting and archiving performance baseline data and then analyzing it. After the performance baseline matrix is established, continued monitoring and data collection allows the administrators to compare current performance against the performance baseline to determine if an abnormal level of activity is occurring. Performance baselines are established for network traffic and also for firewall performance and IDS performance. In fact, many other security-related technologies rely on some form of performance baseline to interpret various levels of computer activity. Many systems establish their own baselines, such as behavior-based (statistical anomaly) IDS. These systems compare activity against their baselines to determine if an attack or intrusion is occurring.

Security Program Management

Once an information security program is functional, it must be operated and managed. The ISO five-area framework that is currently being discussed is designed to support the structuring of a management model; however, it focuses on ensuring that various areas are addressed, rather than guiding the actual conduct of management. In order to assist in the actual management of information security programs, a formal management standard can provide some insight into the processes and procedures needed. The British Standard BS 7799 mentioned in previous chapters contains two such standards, which are designed to assist in this effort. The first part of this standard is the BS7799/ISO17799 Code of Practice for Information Security Management. An overview of these standards was presented in an earlier chapter.

The second part is the BS 7799 (Part 2), which specifies requirements for establishing, implementing, and documenting an information security management system (ISMS). Part 2 of the BS 7799 document introduces a process model with a set of steps called Plan-Do-Check-Act. These steps are part of a management system approach to developing, implementing, and improving the effectiveness of an organization's information security management with regard to the management of risk. The Plan-Do-Check-Act process is as follows:[4]

- **Plan:** Perform a risk analysis of the vulnerabilities faced by the organization.
- **Do:** Apply internal controls to manage risk.
- **Check:** Undertake periodic and frequent review to verify effectiveness.
- **Act:** Develop incident response plans as necessary.

As these standards are not truly open standards (you have to pay to get them), dissemination is restricted. However, a popular standard such as the BS series can fill in any gaps in the management of information security that an organization's CISO might discover.

While there are other management approaches, this modified version of the ISO model provides the needed overview for the overall management of the security program, even when it does not offer all of the required detail. Within that management framework, the maintenance of the security program requires specific management efforts, as discussed in the next section.

The Maintenance Model

While a management model such as the ISO model discussed in the previous section deals with methods to manage and operate systems, a maintenance model is intended to complement the chosen management model and focus organizational effort on maintenance. A recommended approach for dealing with change caused by information security maintenance is presented in Figure 12-2. This figure diagrams a full maintenance program and forms a framework for the discussion of maintenance that follows.

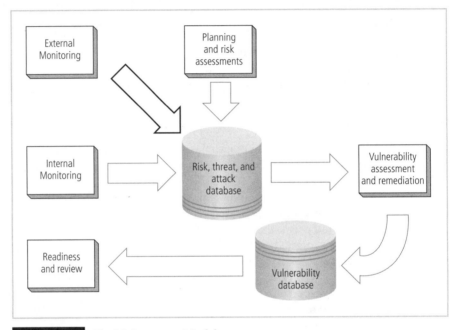

FIGURE 12-2   The Maintenance Model

The recommended maintenance model is made up of five subject areas or domains. They are:

- External monitoring
- Internal monitoring
- Planning and risk assessment
- Vulnerability assessment and remediation
- Readiness and review

In the sections that follow, each of these domains is explored and their interaction discussed.

Monitoring the External Environment

During the Cold War of the twentieth century, the western alliance, led by the United States and Britain, confronted the Soviet Union and its allies. A key component of the western alliance's defense was early warning of attack. The image of the ever vigilant team of radar operators scanning the sky for incoming attacks using a global network of sensors translates into the current world of information security. While the stakes are no longer at the level of nuclear Armageddon, they are still high for many modern, information-dependent organizations.

The objective of the **external monitoring domain** within the maintenance model shown in Figure 12-2 is to provide the early awareness of new and emerging threats, threat agents, vulnerabilities, and attacks that is needed to mount an effective and timely defense. Figure 12-3 shows the primary components of the external monitoring process.

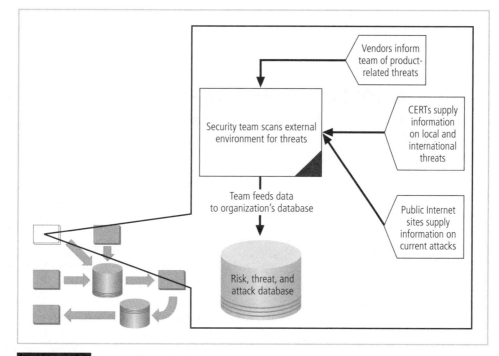

FIGURE 12-3 External monitoring

External monitoring entails collecting intelligence from data sources, and then giving that intelligence context and meaning for use by decision makers within the organization.

Data Sources

Acquiring data about threats, threat agents, vulnerabilities, and attacks is not difficult. There are many sources (see the list in Table 12-1 that follows) and few costs associated with gathering the raw intelligence. What is challenging and can be expensive is turning this flood of good and timely data into information that decision makers can use. Some organizations outsource this component of the maintenance model. Companies such as TruSecure can provide a complete tailored supply of processed intelligence to the organizations that can afford the subscription fees. Other providers supply varying levels of analysis and timeliness for those who partner with them.

As shown in Figure 12-3, external intelligence can come from three classes of sources:

- **Vendors:** When specific products are used as part of the information security program, the software provider often provides direct support or indirect tools to allow the user communities to support each other. This support often includes intelligence on emerging threats.

- **CERT organizations:** Computer emergency response teams exist in varying forms around the world. Often, the CERT Coordination Center (*www.cert.org*) is viewed as definitive, but it is not the only CERT in existence. Many states have CERT agencies, and many countries have CERT organizations to deal with specific national issues and threats.

- **Public network sources:** Many publicly accessible information sources, both mailing lists and Web sites, are open to all. Table 12-1 lists some of these information security intelligence sources.

TABLE 12.1   External Intelligence Sources

Source Name	Type	Comments
Bugtraq	Mailing list	Bugtraq is a moderated mailing list for detailed, full-disclosure discussions and announcements of computer security vulnerabilities. Topical coverage includes identifying vulnerabilities, documenting how they are exploited, and reports on how to remediate them. Individuals can register for all Bugtraq mailing lists at *online.securityfocus.com/cgi-bin/sfonline/subscribe.pl*.
Bugtraq focus-ids	Mailing list	This mailing list contains information about intrusion detection systems vulnerabilities, and discusses both how to exploit them and how to use them in defending networks.
Bugtraq focus-ms	Mailing list	This mailing list takes up where Bugtraq leaves off. It discusses the inner workings and underlying software weaknesses of Microsoft software products. It includes detailed discussions of the various security mechanisms available to help assess, secure, and remediate Microsoft software products.
Bugtraq forensics	Mailing list	This mailing list is a discussion of technical and process methodologies for the application of computer forensics. The discussion is centered around technical methodology, audit trail analysis (technical), general postmortem analysis (technical), products and tools for use in this field (technical), process methodology evidence-handling (technical), search and seizure (nontechnical policy discussion), evidence handling policies (nontechnical policy discussion).

| TABLE 12.1 | External Intelligence Sources (continued) |||

Source Name	Type	Comments
Bugtraq incidents	Mailing list	This is a lightly moderated mailing list to facilitate the quick exchange of security incident information. Topics include: information about root kits and backdoors, new Trojan horses, viruses and worms, sources of attacks, and telltale signs of intrusions.
Bugtraq pen-test	Mailing list	The penetration-testing mailing list is designed to allow people to converse about professional penetration testing. The list is not OS specific and has discussions on many varieties of networks and devices.
Bugtraq vuln-dev	Mailing list	This mailing list allows reports of potential or undeveloped vulnerabilities. This is a full-disclosure list and can include exploit code.
Bugtraq focus-virus	Mailing list	This mailing list discusses the inner working and underlying issues of the various products, tools, and techniques available to help secure systems from virus threats.
CERT	Web site	The CERT Coordination Center (CERT/CC) is a center of Internet security expertise and is located at the Software Engineering Institute, a federally funded research and development center operated by Carnegie Mellon University. This Web site is usually considered definitive when emerging threats become demonstrated vulnerabilities. *www.cert.org*
CERT Advisory Mailing List	Mailing list	The CERT sends e-mail copies of each advisory and summary to the mailing list. Individuals can register for the advisory list at *http://www.cert.org/contact_cert/certmaillist.html*
ISS	Web site	Commercial site with a focus on their commercial IDS and other security products. *www.iss.net*
Insecure Mailing List Archive	Web site	List of information security related lists. *http://lists.insecure.org/*
NESSUS-DEVEL	Mailing list	This is a noncommercial Web site dedicated to the Nessus vulnerability test product. It can contain information about emerging threats and how to test for them. *www.nessus.org*
Nmap-hackers	Mailing list	This list is intended to facilitate the development of nmap, a free network exploration tool. Read the file at *http://lists.insecure.org/about/ nmap-hackers.txt* to learn how to subscribe.

TABLE 12.1 External Intelligence Sources (continued)		
Source Name	**Type**	**Comments**
Packet Storm	Web site	Commercial site with a focus on current security tool resources. *packetstorm.decepticons.org*
Security Focus Online	Web site	Commercial site with general coverage and commentary on information security. *online.securityfocus.com*
snort-sigs	Mailing list	This mailing list includes announcements and discussion of Snort open source IDS and its rules and signatures. It can be useful for detecting emerging threats. Individuals can register for this mailing list at *lists.sourceforge.net/lists/listinfo/snort-sigs*

Regardless of how the organization collects external monitoring data, the CISO evaluates the actions and personnel needed to act on the information. The responsibility for establishing a viable external monitoring program extends to:

- Creating documented and repeatable procedures
- Providing proper training to primary and backup staff assigned to perform the monitoring tasks
- Equipping assigned staff with proper access and tools to perform the monitoring function
- Designing criteria and cultivating expertise among the monitoring analysts, so that they can perform analytic steps to cull meaningful summaries and actionable alerts from the vast flow of raw intelligence
- Developing suitable communications methods for moving weighted external intelligence to designated internal decision makers in all three communities (IT, information security, and general management)
- Integrating the incident response plan (IRP) with the results of the external monitoring process for appropriate, timely responses

Monitoring, Escalation, and Incident Response

The basic function of the external monitoring process is to monitor activity, report results, and escalate warnings. The optimum approach for escalation is to rely on a thorough integration into the planning and process steps of the IRP (discussed in Chapter 6). The monitoring process has three primary deliverables:

- Specific warning bulletins issued when developing threats and specific attacks pose a measurable risk to the organization. The bulletins should assign a meaningful risk-level to the threat to help decision makers in the organization formulate the appropriate response.
- Periodic summaries of external information. The summaries present either statistical results (for example, the number of new or revised CERT advisories per month) or itemized lists of significant new vulnerabilities.

■ Detailed intelligence on the highest risk warnings. This information prepares the way for the detection and remediation of vulnerabilities in the later steps of vulnerability assessment. This intelligence can include current signature status for IDS engines and documented knowledge of external approaches already underway to provide remediation of the vulnerability.

Data Collection and Management

Over time, the external monitoring processes should capture knowledge about the external environment in a format that can be referenced both across the organization as threats emerge and for historical use. This can be accomplished using e-mail, Web pages, databases, or even paper-and-pencil recording methods, so long as the essential facts are communicated, stored, and can be used to make queries when needed. In the final analysis, external monitoring collects raw intelligence, filters it for relevance to the organization, assigns it a relative risk impact, and communicates these findings to the decision makers in time to make a difference.

Monitoring the Internal Environment

It is just as important to monitor the internal computing environment as it is the external environment. The primary goal of the **internal monitoring domain** is to maintain an informed awareness of the state of all of the organization's networks, information systems, and information security defenses, as shown in Figure 12-4. This awareness must be communicated and documented, especially for components that face the external network. This is accomplished by:

■ Building and maintaining an inventory of network devices and channels, IT infrastructure and applications, and information security infrastructure elements

■ Active participation in, or leadership of, the IT governance process within the organization to integrate the inevitable changes found in all network, IT, and information security programs

■ Real-time monitoring of IT activity using intrusion detection systems (IDS) to detect and initiate responses to specific actions or trends of events that introduce risk to the organization's information assets

■ Periodic monitoring of the internal state of the organization's networks and systems. This recursive review of the network and system devices that are online at any given moment and any changes to the services offered on the network is needed to maintain awareness of new and emerging threats. This can be accomplished through automated difference detection methods that identify variances introduced to the network or system hardware and software.

The value of internal monitoring is high when the resulting knowledge of the network and systems configuration is fed into the vulnerability assessment and remediation domain (discussed in the section that follows). However, this knowledge becomes invaluable when incident response processes are invoked and disaster recovery processes are engaged. Figure 12-4 shows the component processes of the internal monitoring domain, which are discussed in the sections that follow.

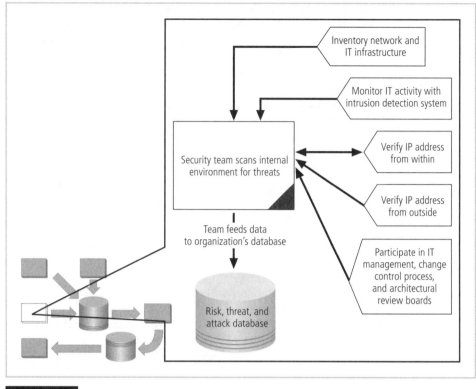

FIGURE 12-4 Internal monitoring

Network Characterization and Inventory

Each organization should have a carefully planned and fully populated inventory for all network devices, communication channels, and computing devices. This inventory should certainly include servers, and it is advisable to include desktop applications and partner interconnections. These **partner interconnections** are network devices, communications channels, and applications that may not be owned by the organization, but are essential to the continued operation of the partnership. The process of collecting this information can be called **characterization**, which is the systematic collection of the characteristics of the network and computer devices present in the environment.

Once the characteristics have been identified, they must be carefully organized and stored using a mechanism, manual or automated, that allows timely retrieval and rapid integration of disparate facts. For all but the smallest network environments, this demands a relational database. The attributes to be stored have been discussed in earlier chapters (in the discussion on information asset identification), but the characteristics should be highly accurate, timely, and flexible. The technology underpinning the stored data should be stand-alone and portable. When this data is called into action to support incident responses and disaster responses, server or network access may be reduced as a result of an incident or disaster.

The Role of IT Governance

The topic of IT governance has been discussed in earlier chapters as well. The primary value of active engagement in an organization-wide IT governance process is the increased awareness of the impact of change. The process of becoming aware of change is documented in the list that follows. This awareness must be translated into a description of the risk that is caused by the change. Such a description is developed in the planning and risk assessment domain of operational risk assessment, which is discussed in the sections that follow.

Awareness of change that flows from IT governance comes from two primary parts of the IT governance process:

- **Architecture review boards:** Many organizations have a group designated to plan, review, and approve managed technology. This group also coordinates the acquisition and adoption of new technologies. The group can be called many things from **technical architecture team** to **network review board**. Whatever the name, the group directs the orderly introduction of change in information technology across the organization. After alerting the information security team of changes to come, this group has a second valuable effect: by being present on the governance committee, the group's information security participant(s) can educate the IT community about the information security impact of the change. The participants can also educate the IT community on correct processes, so that the information security risk becomes part of the decision to adopt and deploy new information technology.

- **IT change control process:** Most organizations of appreciable size have implemented one or more mechanisms to control change in the network, IT infrastructure, and IT applications. The change control forum serves the multiple purposes of:
  - Making the information security group aware of planned changes in IT systems
  - Making the IT community aware of changes planned in the information security infrastructure
  - Allowing the information security participant(s) to educate the change control community about information security risk and how risk is managed in the organization

Making Intrusion Detection Systems Work

Earlier chapters, especially Chapter 8, discussed the technology of intrusion detection systems. To be effective, IDS must be integrated into the maintenance process. An endless flow of alert messages makes little difference to the effectiveness of the information security program. After all, the IDS is reporting events that have already occurred. The most important value of the raw intelligence provided by the IDS is to prevent risk in the future.

Whether the organization has outsourced IDS monitoring, staffs IDS monitoring 24/7, staffs IDS monitoring during business hours, or merely ignores the real-time alerts from IDS, the log files from the IDS engines can be mined to add information to the internal monitoring knowledge base. Traffic analysis is often critically important, because it identifies the most frequently used devices. Analyzing attack signatures for unsuccessful system attacks can identify weaknesses in various security efforts. One example is the need to mask device signatures. The default configuration setting of most network devices notifies every connection that asks what kind of device it is. Many organizations require that all devices be reconfigured to conceal their device signatures. If the analysis of unsuccessful attacks reveals that lesser-known UNIX attacks are being launched, this might inform the organization that the server under attack is responding to requests for OS type with its device signature. Of course, break-in reports can identify the compromised systems that need to be recovered and then remediated.

Detecting Differences

One approach that achieves good results is to perform combinations of manual and automated difference analyses to identify changes to the internal environment. Table 12-2 shows how several kinds of difference analyses can be used.

TABLE 12-2 Types of Difference Analysis

Suggested frequency	Manual or automated	Looking for	Result
Quarterly	Manual	Firewall rules	Verify that new rules follow all risk assessment and procedural approvals; identify illicit rules; ensure removal of expired rules; and detect tampering
Quarterly	Manual	Edge router rules	Verify that new rules follow all risk assessment and procedural approvals; identify illicit rules; ensure removal of expired rules; and detect tampering
Quarterly	Manual	Internet footprint	Verify that public Internet presence (addresses registered to the organization) are accurate and complete
Monthly	Automated	Fingerprint all IP addresses from the inside	Verify that only known and approved servers (and other devices offering critical services) can be reached from the internal network
Weekly	Automated	Fingerprint services on critical servers on the internal network	Verify that only known and approved services are offered from critical servers in the internal network
Daily	Automated	Fingerprint all IP addresses from the outside	Verify only known and approved servers (and other devices) can be reached from the public network
Hourly	Automated	Fingerprint services on critical servers exposed to the Internet	E-mail notification if new services become available on critical servers exposed to the Internet

Be sure to note that Table 12-2 comprises suggestions of possible difference analyses. Each organization should identify what differences it wants to measure and criteria for action. The value of difference analysis depends on the quality of the baseline, which is the initial snapshot portion of the difference comparison. It also depends on the degree to which the notification of discovered differences can induce action.

Planning and Risk Assessment

The primary objective of the **planning and risk assessment domain** is to keep a weather eye on the entire information security program. This is done in part by identifying and planning ongoing information security activities that further reduce risk. Also, the risk assessment group identifies and documents risks introduced by both IT projects and information security projects. Further, it identifies and documents risks that may be latent in the present environment. The primary outcomes from this domain are:

- Establishing a formal information security program review process that complements and supports both the IT planning process and strategic planning processes
- Instituting formal project identification, selection, planning and management processes for information security follow-on activities that augment the current information security program
- Coordinating with IT project teams to introduce risk assessment and review for all IT projects, so that risks introduced by the launching of IT projects are identified, documented, and factored into decisions about the projects
- Integrating a mindset of risk assessment across the organization to encourage the performance of risk assessment activities when any technology system is implemented or modified

Figure 12-5 illustrates the relationships between the components of this maintenance domain. Note that there are two pivotal processes: planning for the information security program, and operational risk assessments. A discussion of both of these topics plus their relationship to both IT and information security projects follows.

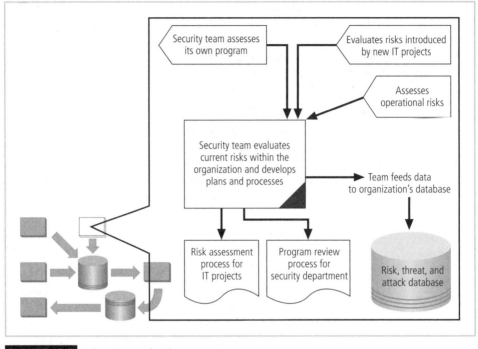

FIGURE 12-5   Planning and risk assessments

Information Security Program Planning and Review

Periodic review of an ongoing information security program coupled with planning for enhancements and extensions is a recommended practice for each organization. The strategic planning process should examine the future IT needs of the organization and the impact those needs have on information security.

A recommended approach takes advantage of the fact that most organizations have annual capital budget planning cycles. In this approach, the IT organization has an annual project planning process that closely follows the other organizational units' annual operational planning process. The IT organization develops an annual idea list for project planning. This list of projects is then sized and risks are preliminarily assessed for each project. These assessments become part of the project-planning document. When capital and expense budgets are made final, the projects to be funded are chosen using the planning information already prepared. This allows executives to make informed decisions about which projects to fund. The organization then follows up with quarterly reviews of progress, which include an updated project risk assessment. As each project nears completion, an operational risk assessment group reviews the impact of the project on the risk profile of the organization. The sponsors of the project, and perhaps other organization executives, then determine if the risk level is acceptable, if the project requires additional risk remediation, or if the project must be aborted.

Information Security Improvement through Ongoing Projects

The previous section discussed projects that organizations might fund to maintain, extend, or enhance the information security program. As noted in the introduction of this chapter, the projects follow the SecSDLC model for development and implementation if the organization does not have a SDLC methodology that would supercede its use. After the program is in place, monumental information security projects should be broken into smaller, incremental projects for several reasons:

- Smaller projects tend to have more manageable impacts to the networks and users.
- Larger projects tend to complicate the change control process in the implementation phase.
- Shorter planning, development, and implementation schedules reduce uncertainty for IT planners and financial sponsors.
- Most large projects can easily be assembled from smaller projects, giving more opportunities to change direction and gain flexibility as events occur and circumstances change.

Security Risk Assessments

A key component in the engine that drives change in the information security program is a relatively straightforward process called an **information security operational risk assessment** (RA for short). The RA is a method to identify and document the risk that a project, process, or action introduces to the organization and, perhaps, offer suggestions for controls that can reduce that risk. The information security group often finds itself in the business of coordinating the preparation of many different types of RA documents including:

- **Network connectivity RA:** Used to respond to network change requests and network architectural design proposals. May be part of or support a business partner RA.
- **Dialed modem RA:** Used when a dial-up connection is requested for a system.
- **Business partner RA:** Used when a proposal for connectivity with business partners is being evaluated.
- **Application RA:** Used at various stages in the life cycle of a business application. Content depends on the project's position in the life cycle when the RA is prepared. Usually, multiple RA documents are prepared at different stages. The definitive version is prepared as the application is readied for conversion to production.
- **Vulnerability RA:** As vulnerabilities emerge or change over time, an RA format can assist in communicating the background, details, and proposed remediation.
- **Privacy RA:** Used to document applications or systems that contain protected personal information that needs to be evaluated for compliance with privacy policies of the organization and relevant laws.
- **Acquisition or divesture RA:** Used when planning for reorganization as units of the organization are acquired, divested or moved.
- **Other RA:** Used when a statement about risk is needed for any project, proposal, or fault which is not contained in the preceding list.

The RA process identifies risks and proposes controls. Most RA documents are structured to include the sections shown in Table 12-3. Most training programs on information security include training sessions for the preparation of RA documents.

TABLE 12-3 Risk Assessment Documentation Components

Component	Description	When and how used
Introduction	Standard opening description to explain the RA to readers who are unfamiliar with the format. The exact text varies for each RA template. Here is an example: "The primary purpose of the security risk-assessment is to identify computer and network security risks to information assets that may be introduced to the organization by the issue described in this risk assessment document. This security risk assessment is also used to help identify security controls planned or proposed. Further, the sections below may identify risks that are not adequately controlled by the planned controls."	Found in all RA document templates
Scope	A statement of the boundaries of the RA. Here is an example: "To define the security and control requirements associated with project X running application Y with access via Internet and the migration of that application into the organization's environment."	Found in all RA document templates
Disclaimer	Include language to identify at what point in the project life cycle the report was developed. This positioning indicates how comprehensive the report is. This statement is sometimes removed in the final RA. Here is an example: "The issues documented in this report should not be considered all inclusive. A number of strategic and tactical decisions will be made during the development and implementation stages of the project, and therefore the security control deliverables may change based on actual implementation. Any changes should be reassessed to insure that proper controls will still be enacted."	Found in all draft RA document templates. Some issues may remain in the disclaimer in some final RA templates.

TABLE 12-3   Risk Assessment Documentation Components (continued)

Component	Description	When and how used
Information security resources	Name the information security team members who collected information, analyzed risk, and documented the findings.	Found in all RA document templates
Other resources	Name the other organization members who provided information, assisted in analyzing risk, and documented the findings.	Found in all RA document templates
Background	Document the proposed project, including network changes, application changes, and other issues or faults.	Found in all RA document templates
Planned controls	Document all controls that are planned in the proposed project, including network changes, application changes, and other issues or faults.	Found in all RA document templates
IRP and DRP planning elements	Document the incident response and disaster planning elements that have been or will be prepared for this proposed project, including network changes, application changes, and other issues or faults.	Recommended in all RA document templates
Opinion of risk	Summary statement of the risk to the organization introduced by the proposed project, network change, application, or other issue or fault. Here is an example: "This application as it currently exists, is considered high risk. IMPORTANT NOTE: Because of the high risk of the current implementation and the potential for high impact to the organization if system or data is compromised in any way, this notification needs to be escalated to the director or manager who would be held responsible for the added expense or loss of revenue from such a compromise. In addition, an acknowledgement and sign off on the understanding of the nature of the risk and the urgency of correcting it must be returned to the CISO of the organization."	Found in all RA document templates

TABLE 12-3	Risk Assessment Documentation Components (continued)	
Component	**Description**	**When and how used**
Recommendations	When required, state what needs to be done to bring the risk from the proposed project, including network changes, application changes, and other issues or faults.	Found in all RA document templates
	Here is an example: "A project team should be formed to assist the operating unit and technical support team to create a comprehensive plan to address the security issues within application X. Specific areas of concern are: authentication and authorization. The continuing corrections of configuration errors found in the platform security validation process must continue. All user accounts need to be reviewed and scrubbed to determine whether the user or service account required access. All user accounts need to be reviewed and assigned the appropriate privileges. Integrity: The Web server function of application X needs to be separated from the application and database server."	

TABLE 12-3   Risk Assessment Documentation Components (continued)

Component	Description	When and how used

Information security controls recommendations summary	The controls that are planned or needed should be summarized using the architectural elements as an organizing method. The following columns of information are recommended to be documented in tabular form:
	
	■ **Security architecture elements and what they provide:**
	  ■ Authentication: The user is verified as authentic.
	  ■ Authorization: The user is allowed to use the facility or service.
	  ■ Confidentiality: Secrecy of content from unintended recipients.
	  ■ Integrity: Data storage must be secure, accurate and precise.
	  ■ Accountability: Actions and data usage can be attributed to specific individuals.
	  ■ Availability and reliability: Systems work when needed.
	  ■ Privacy: System complies with organizational privacy policy.
	■ **Security requirement: Statement on what each element must provide. Suggested texts are:**
	  ■ Authentication: Must conform to organization authentication policies.
	  ■ Authorization: Must conform to inbound and outbound use policies.
	  ■ Confidentiality: Must protect data from interception and misuse in transit using hard encryption.
	  ■ Integrity: Data must be stored in ways that insure completeness and freedom from corruption.
	  ■ Accountability: Actions and data used in business must be tracked and monitored as required.
	  ■ Availability and reliability: Solutions must be available that measure up to current organizational levels of expectation.
	  ■ Privacy: Data processed, stored, and transmitted must be protected to ensure sufficient confidentiality to meet legal privacy requirements.
	■ **Security controls planned or in place: identify controls for each architectural element.**
	■ **Planned completion date when the control will be fully operational.**
	■ **Who is responsible: Which group or individuals are accountable for implementing the control?**
	■ **Status: What is the status of the control implementation?**
		Recommended in all RA document templates

A risk assessment's identification of the systemic or latent vulnerabilities that introduce risk to the organization can provide the opportunity to create a proposal for an information security project. When used as part of a complete risk management maintenance process, the RA can support the information security program as a powerful and flexible tool to identify and document risk and help remediate it as well.

Vulnerability Assessment and Remediation

The primary goal of the **vulnerability assessment and remediation domain** is the identification of specific, documented vulnerabilities and their timely remediation. This is accomplished by:

- Using vulnerability assessment procedures which are documented to safely collect intelligence about network (internal and public facing), platforms (servers, desktops, and process control), dial-in modems, and wireless network systems
- Documenting background information and providing tested remediation procedures for the reported vulnerabilities
- Tracking, communicating, reporting and escalating to management the itemized facts about the discovered vulnerabilities and the success or failure of the organization to remediate them

Figure 12-6 illustrates the process flow of the vulnerability and remediation domain. Using the inventory of environment characteristics stored in the risk, threat, and attack database, the vulnerability assessment processes identify and document vulnerabilities. These vulnerabilities are stored, tracked, and reported using the vulnerability database until they are remediated.

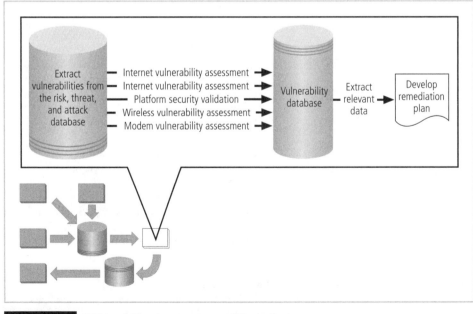

FIGURE 12-6   Vulnerability Assessment and Remediation

Introducing Vulnerability Assessment

The process of identifying and documenting specific and provable flaws in the organization's information asset environment is called **vulnerability assessment**. While the exact procedures can vary, the following five vulnerability assessment processes can serve many organizations as they attempt to balance the intrusiveness of vulnerability assessment with the need for a stable and effective production environment. Some organizations pursue a strategy of monthly vulnerability assessment using all five processes. Others perform an Internet assessment weekly and choose from the other four processes on a rotating monthly or quarterly basis. These choices depend on the quantity and quality of the resources dedicated to vulnerability assessments.

Internet Vulnerability Assessment

The **Internet vulnerability assessment** process is designed to find and document the vulnerabilities that may be present in the public-facing network of the organization. Because attackers from this direction take advantage of any loophole or flaw, this assessment is usually performed against all public-facing addresses, using every possible penetration testing approach. The steps in the process are:

- **Planning, scheduling, and notification of the penetration testing:** Large organizations often take an entire month to perform the data collection phase using nights and weekends and avoiding change control blackout windows. These are periods when changes are not allowed on the organization's systems or networks. This degree of scanning results in vast quantities of test results and many hours of analysis effort (as explained in the section that follows). A rule of thumb is that every hour of scanning results in two to three hours of analysis. Therefore, planning should accommodate spreading out the scanning times, so that analysis is being performed on fresh scanning results over the course of the assessment period. The various technical support communities are given the detailed plan, so that they know when each device is scheduled for testing and what tests are used. This makes disruptions caused by invasive penetration testing easier to diagnose and recover from.

- **Target selection:** Working from the network characterization database elements that are stored in the risk, threat, and attack database, the penetration targets are selected. As previously noted most organizations select every device that faces the public.

- **Test selection:** Using the external monitoring intelligence generated previously, the test engine (such as Nessus) is configured for the tests to be performed. The selection of the test library to be employed usually evolves over time to match the evolution of the threat environment. After the ground rules are established, there is little debate about the risk level of the tests used. After all, if a device is placed in a public-facing role, it must be able to take everything the Internet can send its way, including the most aggressive penetration test scripts.

- **Scanning:** The penetration test engine is unleashed at the scheduled time using the planned target list and test selection. The results of the entire test run are logged to text log files for analysis. This should be a monitored process, so that if an invasive penetration test causes a disruption to a targeted system, the outage can be reported immediately for recovery. Also note that the log files generated, along with all of the data generated in the rest of this maintenance domain, must be treated as highly confidential.

- **Analysis:** A knowledgeable and experienced vulnerability analyst screens the test results for the **candidate vulnerabilities** logged during scanning. During this step, the analyst:

  - Classifies the risk level of the candidate vulnerability as needing attention or as an acceptable risk

  - Validates the existence of the vulnerability when it is deemed to be a significant risk, that is, the risk is higher than the risk appetite of the organization. This validation establishes the reality of the risk using manual testing, human judgment, and a large dose of discretion. The goal of this step is to tread lightly and cause as little disruption and damage as possible while removing false positive candidates from further investigation. These proven cases of real vulnerabilities can now be considered **vulnerability instances**.

  - Document the results of the verification by saving a **trophy** (usually a screenshot) that can be used to convince skeptical system administrators that the vulnerability is real.

- **Record keeping:** Record the details of the documented vulnerability in the vulnerability database, identifying the logical and physical characteristics and assigning a response risk level to the vulnerability to differentiate the truly urgent from the merely critical. When coupled with the criticality level from the characteristics in the risk, threat, and attack database, these records can help the system administrators discern which items to remediate first.

As the list of documented vulnerabilities is identified for the Internet information assets, these confirmed items are moved to the remediation stage.

Intranet Vulnerability Assessment

The **intranet vulnerability assessment** process is designed to find and document selected vulnerabilities that are likely to be present on the internal network of the organization. Attackers from this direction are often internal members of the organization, affiliates of business partners, or automated attack vectors (such as viruses and worms). This assessment is usually performed against selected critical internal devices with a known, high value by using selective penetration testing. The steps in the process are almost identical to the steps in the Internet vulnerability assessment, except as noted.

- **Planning, scheduling, and notification of the penetration testing:** Most organizations are amazed at how many devices exist inside even a moderately sized network. Bigger networks contain staggering numbers of networked devices. In order to plan a meaningful assessment process, the planner should be aware that any meaningful degree of scanning will result in vast quantities of test results and many hours of analysis effort (see the description that follows). The same rule of thumb noted previously for Internet vulnerability assessment applies: for every hour of scanning, two to three hours of analysis result. So plan accordingly. Just as in Internet scanning, the various technical support communities should be notified, and these are probably different individuals than those notified for Internet scanning. Like the Internet support teams, the intranet support teams use this information to make any disruptions caused by invasive penetration testing easier to diagnose and recover from. Often, for cases in which Internet system administrators prefer the penetration testing be performed at low-demand periods (such as nights and weekends for commercial operations), intranet administrators prefer penetration testing (both scanning and analysis) be performed during working hours. The best process takes the system administrator's planning needs into account when the schedule is built.

- **Target selection:** Also like the Internet vulnerability assessment process, the intranet scan starts with the network characterization database elements stored in the risk, threat, and attack database. Intranet testing has so many target possibilities that a more selective approach is indicated. At first, the penetration test scanning and analysis should focus on testing only the highest value, most critical systems. As the configuration of these systems is improved, and fewer candidate vulnerabilities are found in the scanning step, the target list can be expanded. The list of targeted intranet systems should eventually reach equilibrium so that it targets as many systems as can be scanned and analyzed with the resources dedicated to the process.

- **Test selection:** The testing for intranet vulnerability assessment usually uses different criteria than Internet scanning. The selection of the tests to be performed usually evolves over time to match the evolution of the threat environment. Most organizations focus their intranet scanning efforts on a few, very critical vulnerabilities at first, and then expand the test pool to include more test scripts. The degree to which an organization is willing to accept risk while scanning and analyzing also affects the election of test scripts. If the organization is unwilling to risk disruptions to critical internal systems, test scripts that pose such risks should be avoided and alternate means to confirm safety from those vulnerabilities pursued.

- **Scanning:** Intranet scanning is the same process as used for Internet scanning. Just as in Internet scanning, the process should be monitored, so that if an invasive penetration test causes disruption, it can be reported for repair.

- **Analysis:** Given the differences in targets and tested vulnerabilities, the intranet scan analysis is identical to the Internet analysis. It follows the same three steps: classify, validate, and document.

- **Record keeping:** Once again, this process step is identical to the one followed in Internet vulnerability analysis. Use the commonality of the processes to your advantage by leveraging the database, the reports, and the procedures used for record keeping, reporting, and follow-up.

In this way, leveraging the common processes and observing the differences of the intranet vulnerability assessment steps, a list of documented internal vulnerabilities is identified and the organization is prepared for the remediation stage.

Platform Security Validation

The **platform security validation (PSV)** process is designed to find and document the vulnerabilities that may be present because of misconfigured systems in use within the organization. These misconfigured systems fail to comply with company policy or standards as adopted by the IT governance groups and communicated in the information security and awareness program. Fortunately, automated measurement systems are available to help with the intensive process of validating the compliance of platform configuration with policy. Two products known to provide this function are Symantec Enterprise Security Manger and PentaSafe VigilEnt Security Manager. Other products are also available that can perform this function, but the approach and terminology presented here were developed while using the PentaSafe product.

- **Product selection:** Typically an organization implements a PSV solution in the information security program deployment. That solution serves for ongoing PSV compliance as well. If a product has not yet been selected, a separate information security project is required to select and deploy a PSV solution.

- **Policy configuration:** As organizational policy and standards evolve, the policy templates of the PSV tool must change to match. After all, the goal is for the tool to measure how well the systems comply with policy.

- **Deployment:** All systems that are mission critical should be enrolled in PSV measurement. If the organization can afford the licensing and support costs and can dedicate sufficient resources to the PSV program, all devices should be enrolled. Attackers often come into a network using the weakest link, which may not be a critical system itself, but could be connected to critical systems.

- **Measurement:** Using the PSV tools, measure the compliance of each enrolled system against the policy templates. Deficiencies should be reported as vulnerabilities.

- **Exclusion handling:** Some provision should be made for the exclusion of specific policy or standard exceptions. For instance, one metric is to determine the user accounts that never expire. Some organizations have adopted practices that assume the risk for having service accounts that do not expire or that have change intervals that are longer than standard user accounts. If the proper organizational decision makers have made an informed decision to assume that risk, the automated PSV tool should be able to exclude the assumed risk factor from the compliance report.

- **Reporting:** Using the standard reporting components in the PSV tool, most organizations can inform the system administrators of deficiencies that need remediation.

- **Remediation:** Systems out of compliance need to be updated with configurations that comply with policy. When the PSV process shows an outstanding configuration fault that has not been promptly remedied, it should flow to the vulnerability database to assure remediation.

The ability of PSV software products to integrate with a custom vulnerability database is not part of the standard product, but most products on the market have the ability to provide data extracts that can be imported to the organization's vulnerability database for integrated use in the remediation phase. If this degree of integration is not needed or cannot be justified, the stand-alone reporting capabilities of the products can generate sufficient reports for the remediation functions of this maintenance domain.

Wireless Vulnerability Assessment

The **wireless vulnerability assessment** process is designed to find and document the vulnerabilities that may be present in the wireless local area networks of the organization. Because attackers from this direction are likely to take advantage of any loophole or flaw, this assessment is usually performed against all publicly accessible areas using every possible wireless penetration testing approach. The steps in the process are:

- **Planning, scheduling, and notification of the wireless penetration testing:** This is a noninvasive scanning process, and can be done almost anytime without notifying system administrators. When notification is provided, periodic unannounced scans should be part of the process, because administrators have been known to turn off wireless access points on scheduled test days to avoid detection and the resulting remediation effort. Times and days should be rotated over time to detect wireless devices that are used for intermittent projects.

- **Target selection:** All areas of the organization's premises should be scanned with a portable wireless network scanner, with special attention to the following: all areas that are publicly accessible; all areas in range of commonly available products (such as 802.11b); and areas where visitors might linger without attracting attention. Because the radio emissions of wireless network equipment can act in surprising ways, all locations should be tested periodically.

- **Test selection:** Wireless scanning tools should look for all wireless signals that do not meet the organization minimum level of encryption strength.

- **Scanning:** The walking scan should survey the entire target area and identify all wireless local area network (WLAN) access points that are not cryptographically secure.

- **Analysis:** A knowledgeable and experienced vulnerability analyst screens the test results for the WLANs that have been logged as previously described. During this step, the analyst performs these steps:

  - Removes false positive candidates from further consideration as vulnerabilities while causing as little disruption or damage as possible

  - Documents the results of the verification by saving a trophy. This serves a double purpose. It can convince skeptical system administrators that the vulnerability is real. It also documents the wireless access point which is a transient device that may be off the air at a later time.

- **Record keeping:** Good reporting makes the effort to communicate and follow-up much easier. Just as in earlier vulnerability assessment phases, effective reporting maximizes results.

At this stage in the process, the wireless vulnerabilities are documented and ready for remediation.

Modem Vulnerability Assessment

The **modem vulnerability assessment** process is designed to find and document any vulnerability that is present on dial-up modems connected to the organization's networks. Because attackers from this direction take advantage of any loophole or flaw, this assessment is usually performed against all telephone numbers owned by the organization, using every possible penetration testing approach. One of the elements of this process, using scripted dialing attacks against a pool of phone numbers, is often called **war dialing**. The steps in the process are:

- **Planning, scheduling, and notification of the dial-up modem testing:** Most organizations find that they need to continuously run the dial-up modem-testing appliance (dedicated system and software) such as PhoneSweep. Because this is a 24/7 operation, planning of schedules and notification is not required.

- **Target selection:** All telephone numbers controlled by the organization should be in the test pool, unless the configuration of the premises phone equipment can assure that the number cannot be dialed from the worldwide telephone system.

- **Test selection:** The entire set of tests in the testing product should be used, including dial-in modems, callback modems, and facsimile testing.

- **Scanning:** This is a 24/7 process. The raw vulnerability reports should be prepared daily or weekly for the analysis steps that follow.

- **Analysis:** A knowledgeable and experienced modem vulnerability analyst screens the test results to eliminate false positives and document the vulnerabilities using the process steps common to the Internet, intranet, and wireless vulnerability assessments already noted. The end result is a list of documented modem vulnerabilities ready for remediation.

Now that each group of vulnerability assessments has been performed, a discussion of the record keeping process is in order.

Documenting Vulnerabilities

The vulnerability database, like the risk, threat, and attack database, both stores and tracks information. It should provide details about the vulnerability being reported as well as a link to the information assets characterized in the risk, threat, and attack database. While this can be done through manual data storage, the low cost and ease of use of relational databases makes them a more realistic choice.

The data stored in the vulnerability database should include:

- A unique vulnerability ID number for reporting and tracking remediation actions
- Linkage to the risk, threat, and attack database based on the physical information asset underlying the vulnerability. The IP address is a good choice for this linkage.
- Vulnerability details usually based on the test script used for the scanning step of the process. If using the Nessus scanner, each test script has an assigned code (NASL or Nessus attack scripting language) that can identify the vulnerability effectively.
- Dates and times of notification and remediation activities
- Current status of the vulnerability instance, such as found, reported, or repaired
- Comments are always useful to add to the vulnerability instance.
- Other fields can be added as needed to mange the reporting and tracking processes in the remediation phase.

The vulnerability database is an essential part of effective remediation to avoid losing track of specific vulnerability instances as they are reported and remediated.

Remediating Vulnerabilities

The final process in the vulnerability assessment and remediation domain is the remediation phase. The objective of remediation is to repair the flaw causing a vulnerability instance or remove the risk from the vulnerability. As a last resort, informed decision makers with the proper authority can accept the risk.

When approaching the remediation process, it is important to recognize that building relationships with those who control the information assets is the key to success. Success depends on the organization adopting a team approach to remediation, in place of cross-organizational push and pull.

Acceptance of Risk. In some instances, risk must simply be acknowledged as part of an organization's business process. The information security professional must assure the general management community that the decisions made to assume risk for the organization are made by properly informed decision makers. Further, these decision makers must have the proper level of authority within the organization to assume the risk. Many situations where risk is assumed violate this intent:

- Decisions are made at the wrong level of the organization. For example, system administrators should not decide to skip using passwords on a critical application server because it causes them more work.

- Decisions are made by uninformed decision makers. For example, if a project manger convinces an application sponsor that database-level security is not needed in an application and that all users need unlimited access to all data, the sponsor may not realize all of the implications of that decision.

In the final analysis, the information security group must make sure the right people make risk assumption decisions with complete knowledge of the impact of the decision balanced against the cost of the possible security controls.

Threat Removal. In some circumstances, threats can be removed without repairing the vulnerability. For example, if an application can only run on an older desktop system that cannot support passwords, the system can be removed from the network and stored in a locked room or equipment rack. The vulnerability can no longer be exploited, and the risk has been removed. Other vulnerabilities may be amenable to other controls that allow an inexpensive repair and still successfully remove the risk from the situation.

Vulnerability Repair. The optimum solution in most cases is to repair the vulnerability. Applying patch software or implementing a workaround to the vulnerability often accomplishes this. In the cases of some recent vulnerabilities in Web services on Windows operating systems, when Web services are not needed on the server, simply disabling the service removes the vulnerability. In other cases simple remedies are possible. For instance, if an account is flagged as a vulnerability because it has a password that has not been changed for longer than the specified interval, changing the password removes the vulnerability. Of course, the most common remedy is the application of a software patch to make the system function in the expected fashion and to remove the vulnerability.

Readiness and Review

The primary goal of the **readiness and review** domain is to keep the information security program functioning as designed and to keep it continuously improving over time. This is accomplished by:

- **Policy review:** Sound policy needs to be reviewed and refreshed from time to time to provide a current foundation for the information security program.
- **Readiness review:** Major planning components should be reviewed on a periodic basis to ensure they are current, accurate, and appropriate.
- **Rehearsals:** When possible, major plan elements should be rehearsed.

The relationships among the sectors are shown in Figure 12-7. As the diagram indicates, policy review is the primary initiator of the readiness and review domain. As policy is revised or current policy is confirmed, the various planning elements are reviewed for compliance, the information security program is reviewed, and rehearsals are held to make sure all participants are capable of responding as needed.

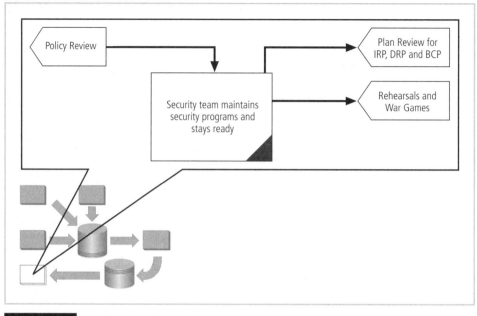

FIGURE 12-7 Readiness and review

Policy Review and Planning Review

Policy needs to be reviewed periodically. The topic of policy management and policy review was covered in Chapter 6. The planning and review process for IRP, DRP, and BCP was covered in Chapter 7.

Program Review

As policy needs shift, a thorough and independent review of the entire information security program should be undertaken. While an exact timetable for review is not proposed here, many organizations find that the CISO should conduct a formal review annually. Earlier in this chapter, the role of the CISO in the maintenance process was discussed. The CISO uses the results of maintenance activities and the review of the information security program to determine if the *status quo* is adequate to the threats at hand,

If the current information security program is not up to the challenges, the CISO must determine if incremental improvements are possible, or if it is time to launch a new initiative to restructure the information security function within the organization.

Rehearsals and War Games

Where possible, major planning elements should be rehearsed. Rehearsal adds value by exercising the procedures, identifying shortcomings, and providing the opportunity to improve the plan before it is needed. In addition, rehearsals make people more effective when an actual event occurs.

Rehearsals that closely match reality are called **war games**. A war game or simulation uses a subset of plans that are in place to create a realistic test environment. This adds to the value of the rehearsal and can enhance training.

When CISOs can't sleep, what is keeping them awake? CISOs find themselves counting sheep because of the maintenance issues covered in this chapter. A solid maintenance program can complement every information security program, and over time can even strengthen a weak program.

REMEMBER HOW AMY'S DAY STARTED at the beginning of this book, and imagine how it could have been. It started out like any other day for Amy at the Sequential Label and Supply Company. She liked her technical support job at the help desk. Taking calls and helping the office workers with PC problems was not glamorous, but it was challenging and paid pretty well.

The phone rang. That was not a big deal for Amy; after all, that was her job. She answered the phone about 35 times an hour, eight to ten hours a day, 20 days a month. This call began like so many others, with a worried user hoping Amy could help him out of a jam. The call display on her screen gave her all the facts: the user's name, his phone number, the department, the location of his office on the company campus, and a list of all the support request calls he'd made in the past.

"Hi, Bob," she said. "Did you get that document-formatting problem squared away after our last call?"

"Sure did, Amy. Hope we can figure out what's going on today."

"I'll try, Bob. Tell me about it."

"Well, I need help setting a page break in this new spreadsheet template I'm working on," Bob said.

Amy smiled to herself. She knew spreadsheets well, so she could probably close this call on first contact. That would help her call statistics, which was one of the ways her job performance was measured.

Roughly four minutes before Amy's phone had rung, a specially programmed computer out at the edge of the SLS network had made a programmed decision. This computer was known to the world as postoffice.seqlbl.com, but was called the e-mail gateway by the networking, messaging, and information security teams at SLS. The decision it had made, just like many thousands of other decisions in a typical day, was to block the transmission of a file that had been attached to an e-mail addressed toBob.Hulme@seqlbl.com. The gateway had determined that Bob didn't need an executable program attached to an e-mail from somewhere on the Internet that contained a forged reply-to address from Davey Martinez at SLS.

The attachment didn't go through.

The e-mail came to Bob Hulme, who had seen that another unsolicited commercial e-mail with an unwanted executable had been blocked. He had deleted the nuisance message without a second thought.

Amy looked up to see Charles Moody walking calmly down the hall. Charlie, as he liked to be called, was the senior manager of the server administration team and also the company's chief information security officer. Kelvin Urich and Iris Majwabu were trailing him as he walked from his office to the door of the conference room. Amy thought, "It must be time for the weekly security status meeting."

She was the user representative on the company information security oversight committee. She was due at that meeting, and would join them for coffee and bagels as soon as she finished her call with Bob.

Chapter Summary

- Change is a reality for most organizations, and procedures are required to deal with change in the operation and maintenance of the information security program.
- The CISO decides whether the information security program can adapt to change as it is implemented or whether the macroscopic process of the SecSDLC must start anew to redevelop a fundamentally new information security profile.
- The recommended maintenance model is made up of five subject areas or domains. They are:
  - External monitoring
  - Internal monitoring
  - Planning and risk assessment
  - Vulnerability assessment and remediation
  - Readiness and review
- To stay current, the information security community of interest, led by the CISO, must constantly monitor the three components of the security triple (threats, assets, and vulnerabilities).
- To assist the information security community to manage and operate the ongoing security program, a management model must be adopted. Management models are frameworks that are structured along the tasks of managing a particular set of activities or business functions.
- In this chapter, a modified version of the ISO management model, the security management model, contains the following elements:
  - Fault management
  - Configuration and change management
  - Accounting and auditing management
  - Performance management
  - Security program management
- The maintenance model is made up of five areas, or process domains:
  - External monitoring
  - Internal monitoring
  - Planning and risk assessment
  - Vulnerability assessment and remediation
  - Readiness and review
- The objective of the external monitoring domain within the maintenance model is to provide the early awareness of new and emerging threats, threat agents, vulnerabilities, and attacks in order to mount an effective and timely defense.
- The objectives of the internal monitoring domain are to maintain an informed awareness of the state of all the organization's networks, information systems, and information security defenses. The security team documents and communicates the awareness, particularly concerning components that face the external network.
- The primary objective of the planning and risk assessment domain is to keep a weather eye on the entire information security program.
- The primary goal of the vulnerability assessment and remediation domain is the identification of specific, documented vulnerabilities and their timely remediation.
- The primary objectives of the readiness and review domain are to keep the information security program functioning as designed and to keep it improving over time.

Review Questions

1. List and define the factors that are likely to shift the information security environment.
2. Who decides if the information security program can adapt to change adequately?
3. List and briefly describe the five domains of the maintenance model.
4. What is the security triple? Why is it important? *P 454*
5. In general, what is a management model? What does it accomplish?
6. What changes were noted in this chapter when moving from the standard ISO model to the modified ISO model?
7. What is fault management? What are its steps? *455*
8. What is vulnerability assessment?
9. What is penetration testing? *455*
10. What is the difference between configuration management and change management?
11. What are four procedures associated with configuration management?
12. What is a performance baseline?
13. Describe the Plan-Do-Check-Act process. What does it accomplish? *463*
14. What are the objectives of the external monitoring domain of the maintenance model?
15. List and describe four vulnerability intelligence sources. Of those that you listed, which seems the most effective? Why?
16. What does CERT stand for? Is there more than one CERT? *P 466*
17. Explain how external monitoring is related to incident response.
18. What are the primary objectives of the internal monitoring domain?
19. What is network characterization? When is it done?
20. Which of the different analysis methods listed in the chapter would add the most value to organizations? Why?
21. What is the objective of the planning and risk assessment domain of the maintenance model? Why is this important?
22. What is the primary goal of the vulnerability assessment and remediation domain of the maintenance model? Is this important to an organization with an Internet presence? Why?
23. List and describe the five vulnerability assessment processes described in the text. Can you think of others not described?
24. What is a candidate vulnerability? When does it become a vulnerability instance?
25. What is a trophy as described in the text?
26. What are the primary objectives of the readiness and review maintenance domain?

Exercises

1. Using a browser on the World Wide Web, find the forum of incident response teams. In your own words, what is their mission?
2. Using a browser on the World Wide Web, locate two or more sites that discuss the ISO management model. What other components of network management, outlined by this model, can be adapted to the security management model?

3. The text lists five tools that can be used by security administrators, network administrators, and hackers alike. Using a browser on the World Wide Web, find three to five other tools that fit this same description. Who do the sites promoting these tools claim to support?

4. Using the list of tools from Exercise 3, and a browser on the World Wide Web, find a site that claims to be dedicated to supporting hackers. Do you find any references to the same tools on the hacker sites?

5. Using the risk assessment documentation components presented in the chapter, draft a tentative risk assessment of one area of your university (a lab, department, or office). Outline the critical faults found and discuss these with your class.

Case Exercises

I. A Slap on the Wrist

Adapted from "Corporate America is Lazy, Say Hackers"[5]
By Dan Verton, *Computerworld*, July 22, 2002.

In July 2002, a group of hackers defaced the Web site of a U.S. newspaper by uploading fake news stories. Big news? Not in today's headlines. What the hackers did was to highlight the importance of security management for all organizations with Web sites.

When security breaches occur, people often point fingers at technology departments, when they should really be focusing on administration. Administration? Not firewalls, intrusion detection systems, and proxy servers? Nope, administration. Alert administrators can rebuff attacks by paying careful attention to the uploading of patches, testing of changes, and closing of unneeded ports. This takes administrative rather than technological expertise.

"We found in our auditing that 90 percent of all attacks stem from poor configuration and administrators that do not consistently update the software they use," said EPiC, the leader of a whitehat hacker group known as Hack3r.com. A hacker who goes by the nickname Hackah Jak agreed. "I can in minutes code a scanner to scan the Internet for two-year-old known vulnerabilities," he said. "I've hit a lot of workstations this way and then worked my way through the network to the server."[6]

Hackers openly admit that most of their successful exploits are caused by the failure of administrators to keep up with updates, patches, and even well known vulnerabilities. When you add incorrect permissions, misconfigured servers and software to the list of misadministered software, it's a miracle everyone isn't taken down. So many servers, so little time, so few hackers.

"However, the real problem isn't laziness; it's trust," said Genocide, the leader of the Genocide2600 hacker group. "Most administrators and managers simply trust that their systems are secure," he said. "That is their first and biggest mistake."[7]

In defense of administrators, it has been estimated that they can spend up to 20 percent of their workweek doing nothing but updating and patching existing servers. When can they find time to deploy new systems?

The moral of the story is: close the barn door, before all your livestock is gone.

1. If vulnerabilities are so well known, why don't administrators know about them? Where can they go to find out?

2. What can administrators do to resolve the problem of not having enough time and energy to constantly update systems? Considering the flood of new exploits discovered daily by tools such as Bugtraq, can the administrators ever catch up? Should they try? What priorities should they set?

II. Security Ambulance Chasers: Beware!

Adapted from "Help Wanted: Security Management"[8]
By John Zipperer, *Internet World*, July 2002.

In the wake of the dot com gold rush and the inevitable market crash, it seems that the next get-rich-quick scheme is to set up your own information security company. Just hang up a shingle and promise to "harden servers, conduct penetration testing, and evaluate information security" and you're sure to make a quick buck.

The problem is multifold: 1) Security vendors don't offer the entire spectrum of products; 2) security consultants often advise and don't "do"; and 3) companies really don't know what they need, so they don't know what to ask for or expect.

The need for security is great. It is so great that even if a security consultant can't do everything, the customer is better off than before. "Some security now is better than perfect security never."[9] One of the most critical needs is in the area of security management.

"It's a mess, " agrees Stephen Crutchley, chief security officer of 4FrontSecurity, a new information security infrastructure provider and services firm. "It's a very fragmented market; there are so many security [vendors] out there, " says Christopher Parker, 4Front's CEO. "The problem with security is that it's always a retrofit. People say, 'You're the nearest guy to the door, so you're going to look after it now.'"[10]

In the beginning of a gold rush, consultants offer what is easiest to learn and deliver: technical solutions. New vendors offer the firewalls, IDS, cryptographic systems and the like. Only more recently have the real needs—security management programs, policy development, risk assessments, and security reporting—been added to the product offerings.

"We're absolutely seeing management being crucial in any type of protection," says Steve Quane, product group manager for antivirus maker Trend Micro. He says customers are demanding greater management, and the most demanding aspect of management has been reporting.

To compound the problem, not only do customers have different components from different developers (software, hardware and networking), because of lack of standards and compatible protocols, different security vendors offer products that don't work together. It's a lot like having a box of jigsaw puzzle pieces, with a handful from a number of different puzzles.

Only recently have vendors begun offering—and companies demanding—integrated solutions that address all of their needs, beginning with managerial concerns, and working their way down to the technical issues.

1. Why are technical components of security offered first? After all, isn't it easier to learn to write policy than it is to learn to configure a firewall?

2. Why is the market so slow to offer integrated "soup-to-nuts" solutions? How has the "education" of companies resulted in an eventual demand for these solutions?

Endnotes

1. Jeanne Cuff, "Grow Up: How Mature Is Your Help Desk?" *Compass America, Inc.* [Cited August 15, 2002]; available from the World Wide Web *http://www.compassamerica.com/white_papers/GrowUpWP.pdf.*

2. R. L Krutz, and R.D.Vines, *The CISSP Prep Guide.* (New York: Wiley 2001), p. 253.

3. Varun Singh, "Intelligent Networking", *Network Computing*, [Cited September 10, 2001]; available from the World Wide Web *http://www.nc-india.com/coverstories/stories/31284.html.*

4. Gamma. "BS7799: How it works" [Cited August 15, 2002]; available from the World Wide Web *http://www.gammassl.co.uk/bs7799/works.html.*

5. Dan Verton, "Corporate America is Lazy, say Hackers," *Computerworld*, 36, no. 30 (July 22, 2002): 7.

6. *Ibid.*

7. *Ibid.*

8. John Zipperer, "Help Wanted: Security Management," *Internet World*, 8, no. 7 (July 2002): 14.

9. *Ibid.*

10. *Ibid.*

Glossary

3DES   Synonymous with Triple DES. An enhancement to the Data Encryption Standard (DES). An algorithm that uses up to three keys to perform three different encryption operations.

A

access   The ability to use, manipulate, modify, or affect an object.

access control   A security measure such as a badge reader that admits or prohibits users from entering sensitive areas.

access control list   A list of people or other entities permitted to access a computer resource.

accurate   Computer data that is free of errors and has a value the user expects.

acquired value   The value an asset has gained over time within an organization.

address restrictions   Rules designed to prohibit data packets with certain addresses or partial addresses from passing through devices.

Advanced Encryption Standard (AES)   A Federal Information Processing Standard (FIPS) that specifies a cryptographic algorithm for use within the U.S. government to protect unclassified information.

after-action review   A detailed examination of the events that occur from the first detection of a security breach to the final recovery.

aggregate information   Information created by combining pieces of data that are not considered private in themselves, but raise privacy concerns when taken together.

air-aspirating detectors   Sophisticated systems that are used in high-sensitivity areas. They filter air by moving it through a chamber containing a detector.

alert message   A scripted description of a security breach that points the recipient to a specific section of a response plan for immediate action.

alert roster   A document containing contact information on the individuals to be notified in the event of a security breach.

algorithm   A set of steps or mathematical calculations used in solving a problem.

annualized loss expectancy (ALE)   The element of a formula for calculating the overall loss an organization could incur from the specified threat over the course of an entire year. ALE=SLE X ARO (annualized loss expectancy equals single loss expectancy times annualized rate of occurrence)

annualized rate of occurrence (ARO)   The element of a formula for calculating the overall loss an organization could incur from a potential risk that represents the anticipated rate of occurrence of a loss from the specified threat. ALE=SLE X ARO (annualized loss expectancy equals single loss expectancy times annualized rate of occurrence).

application header (AH)   A feature of the IPSec protocol that can enhance protection from address spoofing and other modes of attack on open networks.

application-level firewall   Synonymous with application firewall. A device, typically a computer, that provides a defense between a network inside the firewall and a network outside the firewall (the Internet) that could pose a threat to the inside network. All traffic to and from the network must pass through the firewall, so that unauthorized traffic can be blocked.

asset   The organizational resource that is being protected. An asset can be logical, such as a Web site or information owned or controlled by the organization; or an asset can be physical, such as a computer system, or other tangible object.

asset valuation   The process of assigning financial value or worth to each information asset.

Association of Computing Machinery   An organization that focuses on the ethics of security professionals.

asymmetric cipher   A category of cryptographic algorithm that uses unlike but related keys for the encryption and decryption of plaintext.

asymmetric encryption   Synonymous with public key encryption. A method of communicating on a network using two different but related keys, one to encrypt and the other to decrypt messages.

asynchronous token   A device that uses a challenge-response method, in which a server challenges a user during login with a numerical sequence. The user places the sequence into a token, which generates a response that is entered to gain access.

attack   An act that is an intentional or unintentional attempt to compromise the information and/or the systems that support it.

attack profile   A detailed description of the activities that occur during an attack.

attack scenario end case   The summary that describes the attack, and the most likely outcome from the attack and associated costs from that outcome when assessing the impact to information assets from a specific attack profile.

authenticity   A quality or state of information characterized by being genuine or original rather than reproduced or fabricated.

availability   A quality or state of information characterized by being accessible and correctly formatted for use without interference or obstruction.

availability disruption   A situation in which a product or service is not delivered to the organization as expected.

avoidance   The risk control strategy that attempts to prevent the exploitation of the vulnerability.

B

back door   Synonymous with trap door. An electronic hole in software that is left open by accident or intention. Can be installed by a virus or worm.

back hack   Hacking into a hacker's system to find out as much as possible about the hacker.

baseline   A value or profile of a performance metric against which changes in the performance metric can be usefully compared.

bastion host   A dedicated server that receives screened network traffic. Usually prepared with extra attention to detail and hardened for use in an unsecured or limited security zone. Sometimes referred to as a sacrificial host.

behavior-based intrusion detection system (IDS)   Synonymous with statistical anomaly-based IDS. A device that collects data from normal traffic to establish a baseline. The IDS compares periodic data samples with the baseline to highlight irregularities.

behavioral feasibility   Synonymous with operational feasibility. The examination of user acceptance of proposed security measures.

benchmarking   The process of seeking out and studying the practices used in organizations that produce desired results in your organization.

benefit   The value that an organization recognizes by using controls to prevent losses associated with a specific vulnerability.

best business practices   Synonymous with best practices and recommended practices. Procedures that provide a superior level of security for an organization's information.

best security practices   Security efforts that seek to provide a superior level of performance in the protection of information.

biometric lock   An access control device that uses a biometric detection device as a release mechanism.

blackout   A lengthy loss of power.

boot virus   A program that infects the key operating system files located in a computer's boot sector.

bottom-up approach   A method of establishing security policies that begins as a grassroots effort in which systems administrators attempt to improve the security of their systems.

brownout   A prolonged drop in voltage.

brute force attack   The application of computing and network resources to try every possible combination of options of a password.

buffer overflow   An application error that occurs when more data is sent to a buffer than it can handle.

business continuity plan (BCP)   A plan for the continuation of business activities if a catastrophic event occurs, such as the unrecoverable loss of an entire database, building, or operations center.

business impact analysis   The first phase in the development of the continuity planning process. It extends the risk assessment process to determine the priority for risks in the area of information security.

business recovery site   Synonymous with hot site. A remote location with systems identical or similar to a home site for use after a disaster.

C

cache server The server used by proxy servers to temporarily store frequently accessed pages.

Caesar cipher Any cipher that develops ciphertext through a shift of a cryptoalphabet.

candidate vulnerability A possible vulnerability detected by an automated tool. Will be screened by an analyst to ascertain if it is an actual vulnerability.

capability table Synonymous with capabilities table. A list that specifies data items or physical devices (for example printers) that users are authorized to access.

CERT Coordination Center Center of Internet security expertise located at the Software Engineering Institute. A federally funded research and development center operated by Carnegie Mellon University.

certificate authority An agency that manages the issuance of digital certificates and serves as the electronic notary public to verify their worth and integrity.

champion An executive who manages a security project.

change control A process to assure an organization that changes to systems are managed and all parties that need to be informed are aware of the planned changes.

change management The administration of changes in strategy, operations, or components of the information security program.

characterization The systematic collection of the characteristics of the network and computer devices present in an environment.

chargeback accounting A method for organizations to internally charge their departments for system use.

C.I.A. triangle The industry standard for computer security since the development of the mainframe. It is based on three characteristics that describe the utility of information: confidentiality, integrity, and availability.

cipher Synonymous with cryptographic algorithm. A mathematical function that is used to encrypt and decrypt an original message (plaintext).

cipher alphabet Used in the substitution method of encryption, a cross-reference for each letter, number, and symbol that is used in an encoding algorithm.

cipher block chaining (CBC) A mode of encryption in which a feedback loop eliminates duplicate blocks of ciphertext from making the message vulnerable to attacks.

cipher feedback mode (CFB) A refinement to the symmetric block cipher that blocks the cipher encryption process by using modified XOR functions with the plaintext.

ciphertext A message that is formed when plaintext data is encrypted.

ciphertext attack A method of cryptanalysis that uses frequency analysis of the ciphertext to make use of expected word frequency and/or common text structures from the underlying plaintext.

civil law A wide variety of laws that are recorded in volumes of legal code available for review by the average citizen.

clean agent A fire suppression system active ingredient that leaves no residue after application, nor does it interfere with the operation of electrical or electronic equipment.

clean desk policy Rules that require each employee to secure all information in its appropriate storage container at the end of each day.

cleartext Synonymous with plaintext. The unencrypted message that will be encrypted into ciphertext for transmission over an unsecured channel.

clipping level As detected by an intrusion detection system, a level of network activity that is higher than an established baseline and therefore suspect.

code Synonymous with code words. The distinct words or phrases that replace other words or phrases within the original plaintext syntax before encryption.

cold site An alternate site that can be used by an organization if a disaster occurs at the home site. Contains rudimentary services and facilities.

collusion The act of conspiring together to commit a security breach.

Communications Act of 1934 An act that regulates interstate and foreign telecommunications.

Communications Decency Act (CDA) of 1996 An act that attempted to define indecency and was immediately ensnarled in legal debate.

community of interest A group of individuals united by shared interests or values within an organization.

competitive advantage The leverage gained by an organization that supplies superior products or services. Establishing a competitive business model, method, or technique allows an organization to provide a product or service that is superior to others in the marketplace.

competitive disadvantage The leverage lost by an organization that supplies products or services perceived to be inferior to other organizations.

competitive intelligence Information gained legally that gives an organization an advantage over its competition.

computer forensics   The process of collecting, analyzing, and preserving computer-related evidence related to a breach of security.

Computer Fraud and Abuse Act (CFA) of 1986
The cornerstone of many computer-related federal laws and enforcement efforts. Defines and formalizes laws to counter threats from computer-related acts and offenses.

Computer Professionals for Social Responsibility (CPSR)   A public organization for technologists concerned with the impact of computer technology on society.

computer security   A term that in the early days of computers specified the need to secure the physical location of hardware from outside threats. This term later came to stand for all actions taken to preserve computer systems from losses. It has evolved into the current concept of information security as the scope of protecting information in the organization has expanded.

Computer Security Act of 1987   An act that requires all federal computer systems that contain classified information to contain surety plans, and requires periodic security training for all individuals who operate, design, or manage such systems.

Computer Security Division of the National Institute of Standards and Technology   An organization that raises the awareness of issues on information security, especially on new and emerging technologies.

Computer Security Institute (CSI)   An organization that focuses on information protection, especially policy development, risk analysis, and security awareness.

confidentiality   The quality or state of information that prevents disclosure or exposure to unauthorized individuals or systems.

configuration management   The administration of the configuration of the components of a system.

consultant   A self-employed individual who is hired for a specific, one-time purpose.

content filter   A software device that allows administrators to work within a network to restrict accessibility to information.

contingency planning (CP)   The program developed to prepare for, react to, and recover from events that threaten the security of the information assets of an organization.

contract employee   An individual who is hired to perform specific services for the organization.

control   Synonymous with safeguard and countermeasure. A security mechanism, policy, or procedure that can counter system attack, reduce risks, and resolve vulnerabilities.

correlation attack   An attempt to deduce the statistical relationships of the structure of the key and the output of the cryptosystem.

cost avoidance   The money saved by using a control to avoid the financial impact of an incident.

cost benefit analysis   Synonymous with economic feasibility study. The comparison of the cost of protecting an asset with the worth of the asset or the costs of the compromise of an asset.

countermeasure   Synonymous with safeguard and control. A security mechanism, policy, or procedure that can counter system attack, reduce risks, and resolve vulnerabilities.

crack   To attempt to reverse calculate a password.

cracker   An individual who removes an application's software protection that is designed to prevent unauthorized duplication, or a criminal hacker.

criminal law   Laws that address violations harmful to society and that are actively enforced through prosecution by the state.

crisis management   The actions taken during and after a disaster.

crossover error rate   Evaluation criteria for biometric technologies, the crossover rate is the point at which the number of false rejections (denial of access to authorized users) equals the number of the false acceptances (granting of access to unauthorized users).

cryptanalysis   The methodologies used to obtain information from encoded messages when the cryptographic algorithm and/or keys are unknown.

cryptographic algorithm   Synonymous with cipher. A mathematical function that is used to encrypt and decrypt an original message (plaintext).

cryptography   From the Greek work *kryptos*, meaning hidden, and *graphein*, meaning to write. The enciphering and deciphering of coded messages.

cryptology   The science of encryption. A field of study that encompasses cryptography and cryptanalysis.

cryptosystem   The manual or computer-based systems that are used to code or transform data for secure transmission and storage.

cultural mores   Fixed moral attitudes or customs of a particular group.

cyberactivism   The use of computer-related technologies to advance a political agenda.

cyberactivist Synonymous with hacktivist. An individual who uses technology as a tool for civil disobedience.

cyberterrorist The act of hacking to conduct terrorist activities through network or Internet pathways.

D

data classification scheme A method of categorizing the levels of confidentiality of an organization's data.

data custodians Individuals who are responsible for the storage, maintenance, and protection of information.

Data Encryption Standard (DES) An algorithm that is federally approved for encryption. The algorithm is based on the Data Encryption Algorithm (DEA), which uses a 64-bit block size and a 56-bit key.

data owners Individuals who determine the level of classification associated with data.

data user Synonymous with end user. An individual who uses computer applications for his daily work.

Database Right A United Kingdom version of the Directive 95/46/EC.

database shadowing A process that duplicates data in real-time using databases at a remote site or to multiple servers.

de facto **standards** Informal norms. Early Internet connections were based on *de facto* standards.

de jure **standards** Formally recognized norms. As the Internet developed, *de jure* standards were established for its connections.

deciphered Synonymous with decoded. The act of using an algorithm and the correct key to reverse the process of encryption.

decoded Synonymous with deciphered. The act of using an algorithm and the correct key to reverse the process of encryption.

decryption The decoding of data to reveal a secret message.

defense in depth The multiple levels of security controls and safeguards that an intruder faces.

deliverable A completed document or program module that can serve either as the beginning point for a later task or become an element in the finished project.

Delphi technique Named for the oracle at Delphi, a process in which a group rates or ranks asset values or threats to assets.

deluge system A sprinkler system that contains valves that are kept open, so that when the first phase of sprinkler heads are activated, the water is immediately applied to various areas without waiting for a second phase to trigger the individual sprinkler heads.

demilitarized zone (DMZ) An intermediate area between a trusted network and an untrusted network.

denial-of-service (DoS) An attack in which the abuser sends a large number of connection or information requests to overwhelm and cripple a target.

detective control A measure that warns organizations of violations of security principles, organizational policies, or of attempts to exploit vulnerabilities.

dictionary attack A form of brute force attack on passwords that uses a list of commonly used passwords instead of random combinations.

differential backup The storage of all files that have been changed or added since the last full backup.

Diffie-Hellman key exchange method A method for exchanging private keys using public key encryption.

digital certificate An electronic document attached to a file that certifies the file is from the organization it claims to be from and has not been modified from the original format.

Digital Millennium Copyright Act (DMCA) An American version of an international effort to reduce the impact of copyright, trademark, and privacy infringement, especially through the removal of technological copyright protection measures.

digital signature An encrypted message that is independently verified as authentic by a central facility (registry).

direct attack An attack on a computer system that is initiated from the computer of an abuser.

direct changeover A modification to work practices that involves stopping the old method and beginning the new.

Directive 95/46/EC A European Union act that regulated the processing of personal data and the transmittal of such data to protect individual rights.

disaster recovery plan (DRP) A program to limit losses during a disaster and resume business afterwards.

discretionary access control A type of data access control in which data users are allowed to grant access to their peers.

disk striping For backup purposes, the creation of one large logical volume across several hard disk drives and the storage of data in segments, called strips, across all the disk drives in an array.

distinguished name   Used with digital certificates, a series of name-value pairs that uniquely identify a certificate entity to a user's public key.

distributed denial-of-service (DDoS)   An attack in which a coordinated stream of connection requests is launched against a target from many locations at the same time.

dry-pipe   A sprinkler system that is designed to work in areas where electrical equipment is used by spraying pressurized air rather than water.

due care   The actions that demonstrate that an organization makes sure that every employee knows what is acceptable or not acceptable behavior, and knows the consequences of illegal or unethical actions.

due diligence   The actions that demonstrate that an organization has made a valid effort to protect others.

dumb cards   ID cards or ATM cards with magnetic stripes containing the digital (and often encrypted) user personal identification number (PIN) against which a user input is compared.

dumpster diving   The retrieval of information from refuse that could prove embarrassing to the company or could compromise the security of information.

duplexing   For backup purposes, the use of twin drives, each with its own drive controller.

dynamic packet filtering firewall   A firewall that allows only a particular packet with a particular source, destination, and port address to enter through the firewall.

E

e-mail spoofing   The process of sending an e-mail with a modified field. The modified field is often the address of the originator.

Economic Espionage Act (EEA) of 1996   An act designed to prevent abuse of information gained by an individual working in one company and employed by another.

economic feasibility study   Synonymous with cost benefit analysis. The comparison of the cost of protecting an asset with the worth of the asset or the costs if the asset is compromised.

electronic code book (ECB)   A mode of encryption in which each plaintext block is encrypted independently.

Electronic Communications Privacy Act of 1986   Synonymous with the Federal Wiretapping Act. A collection of statutes that regulate the interception of wire, electronic, and oral communication. These statutes work in conjunction with the Fourth Amendment of the U.S. Constitution, which provides protections from unlawful search and seizure.

electronic vaulting   The transfer of large batches of data to an off-site facility.

electrostatic discharge   A spark produced from a buildup of static electricity.

encapsulating security payload (ESP)   A component of the IPSec protocol that provides confidentiality to the data packets being transmitted.

encryption   The process of converting an original message into a form that is unreadable by unauthorized individuals.

end user   Synonymous with data user. An individual who uses computer applications for his daily work.

enticement   The process of attracting attention to a system by placing tantalizing bits of information in key locations.

entrapment   The act of luring an individual into committing a crime to get a conviction.

ethical hacker   Synonymous with tiger team, white-hat hacker, and red team. Consultants or outsourced contractors who are hired to perform controlled attacks to compromise or disrupt systems by using documented vulnerabilities.

ethics   Behaviors that are socially acceptable.

European Council Cyber-Crime Convention   An organization designed to create an international task force to oversee a range of security functions associated with Internet activities and to standardize technology laws across international borders.

evidence   The proof of an action or intent.

exit interview   A discussion at the end of employment that reminds an employee of contractual obligations, such as nondisclosure agreements and obtains feedback on the employee's tenure in the organization.

expert hacker   A master of several programming languages, networking protocols, and operating systems, who also exhibits a mastery of the technical environment of the targeted system.

exploit   A technique used to compromise a system.

exposure   A single instance of a system being open to damage.

external monitoring domain   The sector of a maintenance model that provides early awareness of new and emerging threats.

F

facilities management The operation of an organization's physical security commonly including access controls for a building.

fail-safe lock A lock that ensures ability to exit. When the lock of a door fails, the door becomes unlocked.

fail-secure lock A lock that ensures entrance is prohibited. When the lock of a door fails the door remains locked.

false accept rate The percentage or value associated with the rate at which fraudulent users or nonusers are allowed access to systems or areas as a result of a failure in the biometric device.

false reject rate The percentage or value associated with the rate at which authentic users are denied or prevented access to authorized areas as a result of a failure in the biometric device.

fault The complete loss of power for a moment.

ferroresonant standby uninterruptible power supplies (UPS) A device that replaces a UPS transfer switch. The transformer provides power conditioning and line filtering to the primary power source, reducing the effect of power outages.

field change order (FCO) An authorization issued by an organization for the repair, modification, or update of a piece of equipment.

file hashing Method for ensuring information validity. Involves a file being read by a special algorithm that uses the value of the bits in the file to compute a single large number called a hash value.

Financial Services Modernization Act Synonymous with the Gramm-Leach-Bliley Act of 1999. This act contains provisions on facilitating affiliation among banks, securities firms, and insurance companies. The act has significant impact on the privacy of personal information used by these industries.

fingerprinting A data-gathering process that discovers the assets that can be accessed from a network. Usually performed in advance of a planned attack. This is the systematic examination of the entire set of Internet addresses of the organization.

firewall Synonymous with application firewall and application-level firewall. A computer that provides a defense between a network inside the firewall and a network outside the firewall (the Internet) that could pose a threat to the inside network. All traffic to and from the network must pass through the firewall, so that unauthorized data can be blocked.

firewall subnet Multiple firewalls that create a buffer between networks inside and outside an organization.

fixed temperature A fire detection system that contains a sensor that detects when the ambient temperature in an area reaches a predetermined level.

flame detector A sensor that detects the infrared or ultraviolet light produced by an open flame.

flame point The temperature of ignition.

footprinting The identification of the Internet addresses that are owned or controlled by an organization.

framework The outline from which a detailed security blueprint evolves.

Freedom of Information Act (FOIA) of 1966 An act that provides every person the right to request access to federal agency records or information that are not matters of national security.

frequency analysis A method of cryptanalysis that uses patterns of words or usage to assist in breaking a code.

G

gateway router A device that is designed primarily to connect the organization's systems to the outside world.

general security policy An executive-level document that outlines the organization's approach and attitude towards information security.

grounding A process that ensures that the returning flow of current is properly discharged to the ground.

H

hacker A person who uses and creates computer software for enjoyment or to gain access to information illegally.

hacking Writing computer programs for enjoyment or gaining access to a computer illegally.

hacktivist Synonymous with cyberactivist. An individual who uses technology as a tool for civil disobedience.

hash algorithm A security utility that mathematically combines every character in a message to create a fixed-length number (usually 128 bits in length) that is a condensation, or fingerprint, of the original message.

hash function A mathematical algorithm that generates a message summary or message digest that allows a hash algorithm to confirm that the content of a specific message has not been altered.

hash value Synonymous with message digest. A single large number created when a file is read by a special algorithm that uses the value of the bits in the file to compute the number. The hash value ensures information validity.

Health Insurance Portability and Accountability Act of 1996 (HIPPA) Synonymous with the Kennedy-Kassebaum Act. This act protects the confidentiality and security of health care data by establishing and enforcing standards for the storage and transmission of sensitive personal information.

hierarchical roster A list of names of people who are called in the case of an emergency. Each person in turn calls the next person.

homophone Used in the substitution method of encryption, the alternate letters or letter combinations that may be used for the same plaintext letter or letter combinations to add complexity without changing meaning.

honeynet A network or system subnet that is configured to misdirect hackers by resembling networks or system subsystems that are rich with information.

honeypots Computer servers configured to misdirect hackers by resembling production systems that contain substantial information.

host-based intrusion detection systems (IDSs) Devices that are installed on a computer system to monitor the status of files stored on that system and protect them from security breaches.

hot site Synonymous with business recovery site. A remote location with systems identical or similar to a home site for use after a disaster.

human firewall The concept that automated systems by themselves are not able to provide the most effective defense against electronic attackers and that human judgment is an essential part of any planned defense of information assets.

humidity The amount of moisture in the air.

I

inadvertent act A deed for which malicious intent is absent or cannot be proven.

incident An attack on an organization's information assets.

incident classification The process of determining whether an actual security breach occurred.

incident damage assessment The determination of the scope of a breach of the confidentiality, integrity, and availability of information immediately following an incident.

incident reactions Actions outlined in an incident response plan for security information that guide an organization in attempting to stop an incident, mitigate the impact of an incident, and provide information for recovery.

incident response Activities taken to plan for, detect, and correct the impact of an incident on information assets.

incident response plan A program to establish procedures an organization's staff would follow if it were attacked.

incremental backup The archives of files that have been modified on a particular day.

indirect attack An attack on a computer system that is initiated from a system or resource that itself has been attacked.

industrial espionage Information gained illegally that gives an organization an advantage over its competition.

information classification A process of assigning an information security category to various information assets so that efforts in defending them are applied based on valid organizational priorities.

information security The protection of information and the systems and hardware that use, store, and transmit that information.

information security operational risk assessment A method to identify and document the risk that a project, process, or action introduces to the organization.

information security program Synonymous with security profile and security posture. The implementation of an organization's security policies, procedures, and programs.

information system (IS) The entire set of software, hardware, data, people, and procedures necessary to use information as a resource in the organization.

Information Systems Audit and Control Association (ISACA) A professional association focused on auditing, control, and security.

Information Systems Audit and Control Association's Certified Information Systems Auditor (CISA) An organization that focuses on auditing information security, business process analysis, and information security planning.

Information Systems Security Association (ISSA) A nonprofit society of information security professionals.

information warfare An offensive organized and lawful operation conducted by a sovereign state that involve the use of information technology.

integrity   The quality or state of being whole, complete, and uncorrupted.

International Information Systems Security Certification Consortium (ISC)² . Systems Security Certified Professional (SCCP)   An international consortium dedicated to improving the quality of security professionals.

International Standard Organization (ISO) model   An approach that provides a five-layer structure to the administration and management of networks and systems.

Internet Engineering Task Force (IETF)   A group of professionals in the fields of computing, networking, and telecommunications who develop the Internet's technical foundations.

Internet vulnerability assessment   The process of finding and documenting the vulnerabilities that may be present in the public-facing network of an organization.

intranet vulnerability assessment   The process of finding and documenting vulnerabilities that are likely to be present on the internal network of an organization.

intrinsic value   The essential worth of an asset.

intrusion detection systems (IDSs)   Devices that inspect data communication flows to identify patterns that may indicate that hacking is underway.

ionization sensor   A smoke detection device that contains a small amount of a harmless radioactive material within a detection chamber. When certain by-products of combustion enter the chamber, they change the level of electrical conductivity with the chamber and activate the detector.

issue-specific security policy   A program that addresses specific areas of technology and contains a statement on the organization's position on each specific issue.

J

job rotation   Synonymous with task rotation. A security check that requires that every employee is trained to perform the work of another employee.

joint application development (JAD)   A process in which users are part of the systems development team and report to their coworkers on the progress of the project, and also report to the project team the concerns of their coworkers.

jurisdiction   A court's right to hear a case because a wrong was committed in its territory or involving its citizenry.

K

Kerberos   A cryptosystem that uses symmetric key encryption to validate an individual user to various network resources.

kernel proxy   The fifth and final form of a firewall.

key   A random and secret value that is placed within an algorithm to code information.

knowledge-based intrusion detection system (IDS)   Synonymous with signature-based IDS. A device that examines data traffic for signature matches with predefined, preconfigured attack patterns.

known-plaintext attack   A method of attacking a cryptosystem that relies on knowledge of some or all of the plaintext that was used to generate a ciphertext.

L

lattice-based access control   A matrix of authorizations that control access to data.

laws   Rules adopted for determining expected behavior in modern society and drawn from ethics.

least privilege   A security measure by which employees are provided access to a minimal amount of information for a minimal amount of time necessary for them to perform their duties.

liability   The legal obligation of an entity that includes responsibility for a wrongful act and the legal obligation to make restitution.

likelihood   The overall rating of the probability that a specific vulnerability within an organization will be successfully attacked.

long arm jurisdiction   A law that reaches across the country or around the world to pull an accused individual into its court systems.

M

macro virus   A virus that is contained in a downloaded file attachment such as word processing documents, spread sheets, and database applications.

mail bomb   Synonymous with denial-of-service attack. An attack in which the abuser sends a large number of connection or information requests to overwhelm and cripple a target.

malicious code   Synonymous with malware. Software designed to damage, destroy, or deny service to the target system.

malware   Synonymous with malicious code. Software designed to damage, destroy, or deny service to the target system.

man-in-the-middle   Synonymous with TCP hijacking. An attack in which the abuser records data packets from the network, modifies them, and inserts them back into the network.

management controls   Security processes that are designed by strategic planners and implemented by the security administration of an organization.

mandatory access controls   The regulations that control access to information resources.

mantrap   A small physical enclosure that is used in secure facilities that has an entry point and a different exit point.

manual fire detection systems   Manually activated alarms, such as sprinklers and gaseous systems.

message digest   Synonymous with hash value. A single large number created when a file is read by a special algorithm that uses the value of the bits in the file to compute the number. The hash value ensures information validity.

methodology   A formal approach to solving a problem based on a structured sequence of procedures.

milestone   A specific point in the project plan when a task and its action steps are complete and have a noticeable impact on the progress of the project plan as a whole.

minutiae   Used in biometrics, unique points of reference that are digitized and stored in an encrypted format for comparison with scanned human characteristics.

mirroring   For backup purposes, the use of twin drives in a computer system with both drives managed by a drive controller.

mission   A written statement of an organization's purpose.

mist sprinkler   A sprinkler system that distributes microfine mists instead of traditional shower-type sprays.

mitigation   A control approach that attempts to reduce the impact caused by the exploitation of vulnerability through planning and preparation.

modem vulnerability assessment   The process of finding and documenting any vulnerability that is present on dial-up modems connected to an organization's networks.

monoalphabetic   In encryption, characterized by using a single alphabet.

monoalphabetic substitution   In encryption, the substitution of one value for another using a single alphabet.

Multipurpose Internet Mail Extension (MIME)   A specification developed to increase the security of e-mail that includes five message header fields, predefined content types, and conversion transfer encoding.

mutual agreement   A contract between two or more organizations that specifies how each assists the other in the event of a disaster.

N

National InfraGard Program   A cooperative effort between the FBI's Cleveland Field Office and local technology professionals to protect critical national information.

National Infrastructure Protection Act of 1996   An act that modified several sections of the Computer Fraud and Abuse Act and increased penalties for selected crimes.

National Infrastructure Protection Center (NIPC)   An organization that serves as the U.S. government's center for threat assessment, warning, investigation, and response to threats or attacks against critical U.S. infrastructures.

National Security Agency (NSA)   The organization responsible for signal intelligence and information system security.

need-to-know   A category within a data classification structure that grants access to individuals based on the fact that they require the information to perform their jobs.

negative feedback loop   Synonymous with cybernetic loop. A process to manage a project that insures that progress is measured periodically and that measured results are compared to expected results.

network address translation (NAT)   A method of mapping real, valid, external IP addresses to special ranges of internal IP addresses, creating a barrier to internal intrusion.

network-based intrusion detection systems (IDSs)   Devices that are installed on networks to monitor patterns of network traffic to detect unusual and therefore threatening activity.

network review board   Synonymous with technical architecture team. A group that directs the orderly introduction of change in information technology across the organization.

null Used in encryption, a null has no meaning and is often removed in the cipher text to add to the complexity of decoding when the algorithm and keys are unknown.

O

object A passive entity in an information system that receives or contains information.

object of attack The object or entity being attacked.

offline UPS Synonymous with standby uninterruptible power supplies (UPS). An offline battery backup that detects the interruption of power to equipment.

one-time pad cryptosystem A process that uses a string of pseudo-randomly generated bits that are combined with the plaintext to generate a theoretically high level of security.

open port A network channel or device used to send commands to a computer, gain access to a server, and exert control over a networking device.

operational controls Measures that deal with the operational functionality of security in an organization.

operational feasibility Synonymous with behavioral feasibility. The examination of user acceptance of proposed security measures.

optimal asymmetric encryption padding (OAEP) An encoding method that uses a randomly generated seed, message padding, and two mask-generation functions.

organizational feasibility A comparison of how proposed information security alternatives contribute to the efficiency, effectiveness, and overall operation of an organization.

output feedback mode (OFB) A refinement to symmetric block ciphers that blocks the cipher encryption process by using modified XOR functions with the plaintext.

P

packet filtering firewall Networking devices that filter data packets based on their headers as they travel in and out of an organization's network.

packet sniffer A network tool that collects copies of packets from the network and analyzes them.

parallel operations A method of modifying work practices that involves using the new methods alongside the old methods.

partner interconnections The network devices, communication channels, and applications that may not be owned by the organization, but are essential to the continued operation of a partnership.

passphrase A series of characters, typically longer than a password, from which a virtual password is derived.

password A private word or combination of characters that only the user knows.

password attack An attempt to repeatedly guess passwords to commonly used accounts.

penetration testing A simulation performed by security personnel to compromise or disrupt their own systems by exploiting documented vulnerabilities.

performance baseline An expected level of system performance against which all subsequent levels of performance are compared.

performance gap The difference between the measure of an organization's success and that of others.

permutation cipher Synonymous with transposition cipher. The rearranging of values within a block to create coded information.

phased implementation An approach to implementing new security systems that involves rolling out a piece of a new system across the entire organization.

photoelectric sensors A type of smoke detector that projects and detects an infrared beam across an area. If the beam is interrupted (presumably by smoke), the alarm or suppression system is activated.

phreaker A person who hacks the public telephone network to make free calls and disrupt services.

physical security An aspect of information security that addresses the design, implementation, and maintenance of countermeasures that protect the physical resources of an organization.

pilot implementation The changing of work practices that involves implementing all security improvements in a single office, department, or division, and resolving issues within that group before expanding to the rest of the organization.

plaintext Synonymous with cleartext. The unencrypted message that will be encrypted into ciphertext for transmission over an unsecured channel.

planning and risk assessment domain The domain of the security maintenance model concerned with keeping a "weather eye" on the entire information security program by identifying and planning organization information security activities that further reduce risk.

platform security validation (PSV)   A process designed to find and document the vulnerabilities that may be present because of misconfigured systems that are in use within an organization.

plenum   In an office building the space above the ceiling, below the floor above.

policy   A body of expectations that describe acceptable and unacceptable behaviors of employees in the workplace.

policy administrator   The champion and manager of an information security policy.

polyalphabetic   In encryption, characterized by using multiple alphabets.

polyalphabetic substitutions   In encryption, the substitution of one value for another, using two or more alphabets.

polymorphic threat   A threat that changes its apparent shape over time, to become a new threat not detectable by techniques looking for a preconfigured signature.

port   A network channel or connection point in a data communications system.

port scanners   The tools used to identify (or fingerprint) computers that are active on a network.

possession   The quality or state of having ownership or control of some object or item.

pre-action system   A sprinkler system that has a two-phase response to a fire.

predecessors   In a project plan, the tasks or action steps that come before the specific task at hand.

pretty good privacy (PGP)   A hybrid cryptosystem that combines some of the best available cryptographic algorithms. PGP is the open source *de facto* standard for encryption and authentication of e-mail and file storage applications.

preventive control   The implementation of an organizational policy or a security principle, such as authentication or confidentiality to protect a vulnerability.

privacy   The state of being free from unauthorized observation.

private key encryption   Synonymous with symmetric encryption. Private key encryption is a method of communicating on a network using a single key to both encrypt and decrypt a message.

private law   Laws that regulate the relationship between the individual and the organization, and that encompass family law, commercial law, and labor law.

program   An activity performed within the organization to improve security.

program security policy   A document that outlines the process of implementing security in an organization.

project plan   A program that delivers instructions to individuals for carrying out the implementation stage of the security systems development life cycle.

project team   For information security, a group of individuals with experience in the requirements of both technical and nontechnical fields.

projectitis   The phenomenon of becoming so engrossed in project administration that the project itself suffers.

proximity reader   A type of access control device that does not require keycard insertion.

proxy server   Synonymous with proxy firewall. A server that is configured to look like a Web server and performs actions on behalf of that server to protect it from hacking.

public key encryption   Synonymous with asymmetric encryption. A method of communicating on a network using two different keys, one to encrypt and the other to decrypt a message.

public key infrastructure certificate authority   A software application that provides cryptographic key management services.

public law   A law that regulates the structure and administration of government agencies and their relationships with citizens, employees, and other governments.

Q

quantitative assessment   The evaluation of an organization's assets, estimated values, and formulas.

R

rate-of-rise   A fire detection system in which a sensor detects an unusually rapid increase in the area temperature, within a relatively short period of time.

readiness and review domain   The domain of the security maintenance model concerned with keeping the information security program functioning as designed and keeping it continuously improving over time.

recommended practices   Synonymous with best practices and best business practices. Procedures that provide a superior level of security for an organization's information.

red team Synonymous with ethical hacker, tiger team, and white-hat hacker. Consultants or outsourced contractors who are hired to perform controlled attacks to compromise or disrupt systems by using documented vulnerabilities.

redundancy The implementation of multiple types of technology that prevent the failure of one system from compromising the security of information.

Remote Authentication Dial-in User Service (RADIUS) a system that authenticates the credentials of users who are trying to access an organization's network through a dial-up connection.

remote journaling The transfer of live transactions to an off-site facility.

replay attack An attack in which an abuser has successfully broken an encryption and attempts to resubmit the deciphered authentication to gain entry to a secure source.

residual risk The risk that remains to an information asset after an existing control has been applied.

resource An individual or skill set whose function is detailed in a project plan.

restitution The compensation for a misdeed.

risk The probability that something can happen.

risk appetite The quantity and nature of risk that organizations are willing to accept.

risk assessment The analysis of a danger to assign a risk rating or score to an information asset.

risk assessment specialist An individual who understands financial risk assessment techniques, the value of organizational assets, and security methods.

risk identification The formal process of examining and documenting the security of an organization's information technology.

risk management The process of identifying vulnerabilities in an organization's information system and taking steps to assure its confidentiality, integrity, and availability.

role-based control A type of access control in which individuals are allowed to use data based on their positions in an organization.

RSA algorithm The *de facto* standard for public use encryption applications. The security of the algorithm is based on the computational difficulty of factoring large composite numbers and computing the *eth roots modulo*, a composite number for a specified odd integer *e*.

S

sacrificial host Synonymous with bastion host. A dedicated firewall that enables a router to prescreen data packets to minimize the network traffic and load on a proxy server.

safeguard Synonymous with control and countermeasure. A security mechanism, policy, or procedure that can counter system attacks, reduce risks, and resolve vulnerabilities.

sag A momentary incidence of low voltage.

salami theft Aggregation of information used with criminal intent.

script kiddies Hackers of limited skill who use expertly written software to exploit a system, but do not fully understand or appreciate the systems they hack.

secret key In symmetric encryption, the single key shared by both parties. In asymmetric encryption, the private key retained by the owner for use in decrypting messages encrypted with owner's public key.

secure facility A physical location that has been engineered with controls designed to minimize the risk of attacks from physical threats.

Secure Hash Standard (SHS) An encryption norm that specifies SHA-1 (Secure Hash Algorithm 1) as a secure algorithm for computing a condensed representation of a message or data file.

Secure Hypertext Transfer Protocol (S-HTTP) A protocol designed to enable secure communications across the Internet. S-HTTP is the application of SSL over HTTP, which allows the encryption of all information passing between two computers through a protected and secure virtual connection.

Secure Multipurpose Internet Mail Extensions (S/MIME) A specification developed to increase the security of e-mail that adds encryption and user authentication.

Secure Sockets Layer (SSL) A protocol for transmitting private information securely over the Internet.

Secure Sockets Layer (SSL) Record Protocol A protocol that provides basic security and communication services to the top levels of the SSL protocol stack.

security To be protected from adversaries—from those who would do harm, intentionally or otherwise.

Security and Freedom Through Encryption Act of 1999 An attempt by Congress to provide guidance on the use of encryption. Provided measures for public protection from government intervention.

security blueprint A plan for the implementation of new security measures in an organization.

security clearance A level of authorization to classified material that an individual is granted after a formal evaluation process.

security domain An area within a computer system in which users can safely communicate.

security education, training, and awareness (SETA) program An education program designed to reduce the number of security breaches that occur through the lack of employee security awareness.

security model A collection of security rules that represents the implementation of a security policy.

security perimeter The edge between the outer limit of an organization's security and the beginning of the outside world.

security policy Synonymous with security program policy (SPP), a general security polity, IT security policy, and information security policy. A set of rules developed to protect an organization's assets.

security policy developer An individual who understands the organizational culture, existing policies, and requirements for developing and implementing security policies.

security posture Synonymous with security profile and information security program. The implementation of an organization's security policies, procedures, and programs.

security professional A specialist in the technical and nontechnical aspects of security information.

security profile Synonymous with security posture and information security program. The implementation of an organization's security policies, procedures, and programs.

security systems development life cycle (SecSDLC) A methodology for the design and implementation of security for information systems.

security triple The key aspects of an organization's security system: threats, assets, and vulnerabilities.

selected-plaintext attack A crypto system attack in which the attackers send a target a section of plaintext they want encrypted and returned in order to reveal information about the target's encryption systems.

separation of duties A control used to reduce the chance of an individual violating information security and breaching the confidentiality, integrity, or availability of the information.

sequential roster A list of people who are called by a single person in the case of an emergency.

service bureau A service agency that provides a service for a fee.

service level agreement The contract of a Web host provider covering responsibility for Internet services as well as for hardware and software used to operate the Web site.

session key A limited-use symmetric key for encrypting electronic communication.

shoulder surfing The act of observing information without authorization by looking over a shoulder or spotting information from a distance.

signature-based intrusion detection system (IDS) Synonymous with knowledge-based IDS. A device that examines data traffic for signature matches with predefined, preconfigured attack patterns.

single loss expectancy (SLE) The calculation of the cost incurred in a single instance when a specific asset within an organization is attacked.

smart card A device that contains a computer chip that can verify and validate a number of pieces of information about an individual above and beyond a PIN.

smoke detectors Systems that detect a potentially dangerous fire and are required by building codes in most residential dwellings and commercial buildings.

sniffer A program or device that can monitor data traveling over a network.

social engineering The process of using social skills to convince people to reveal access credentials or other valuable information to the attacker.

software piracy The unlawful use or duplication of software-based intellectual property.

spike A momentary increase in voltage.

spoofing A technique used to gain unauthorized access to computers, whereby the intruder sends messages to a computer with an IP address indicating that the message is coming from a trusted host.

sprinkler system Devices that are designed to apply liquid, usually water, to all areas in which a fire has been detected.

standards Detailed statements of actions that comply with policy.

standby UPS Synonymous with offline uninterruptible power supplies (UPS). An offline battery backup that detects the interruption of power to equipment.

stateful inspection firewall   Devices that track network connections that are established between internal and external systems.

static electricity   The spark that occurs when two materials are rubbed or touched and electrons are exchanged, resulting in one object becoming more positively charged and the other more negatively charged.

statistical anomaly-based intrusion detection system (IDS)   Synonymous with behavior-based IDS. A device that collects data from normal traffic to establish a baseline. The IDS compares periodic data samples with the baseline to highlight irregularities.

steganography   A method of hiding the existence of a secret message.

strategic planning   The process of moving an organization towards its vision by accomplishing its mission.

stream cipher algorithm   Synonymous with symmetric stream cipher. An algorithm that operates on small units of plaintext, usually bits.

strong authentication   In access control, security systems that use two or more authentication mechanisms.

subject   An *active* entity that interacts with an information system and causes information to move through the system for a specific purpose. Examples include individuals, technical components, and computer processes.

subject of attack   A computer or other system that is used as an active tool to conduct an attack.

substitution   The replacement of letters, numbers, and symbols by other letters, numbers, and symbols for encryption.

substitution cipher   In encryption, the substitution of one value for another.

successors   In a project plan, the tasks or action steps that come after the task at hand.

sunset clause   Prevents a temporary policy from becoming a permanent mistake by specifying a discontinuation date.

surge   A prolonged increase in voltage.

symmetric block cipher   A type of cipher in which algorithms encrypt data in blocks of bytes rather than a single byte at a time.

symmetric cipher   A category of cryptographic algorithms that uses the same key for both the encryption and decryption of plaintext.

symmetric encryption   Synonymous with private key encryption. Symmetric encryption is a method of communicating on a network using a single key to both encrypt and decrypt a message.

symmetric stream cipher   Synonymous with stream cipher algorithm. An algorithm that operates on small units of plaintext, usually bits.

synchronous tokens   Authentication devices that are synchronized with a server, so that each device (server and token) uses the time or a time-based database to generate a number that is entered during the user login phase.

System Administration, Networking, and Security Institute (SANS)   A professional organization dedicated to the protection of information and systems.

System Administration, Networking, and Security Institute (SANS) Global Information Assurance Certification   A collection of 12 individual certifications that can be tied into six tracks, or culminate in the capstone GIAC Security Engineer certification.

system administrator   An individual responsible for administering information systems.

systems development life cycle (SDLC)   A methodology for the design and implementation of an information system.

systems-specific policy   A program that addresses the particular use of certain systems. This could include firewall configuration policies, systems access policies, and other technical configuration areas.

T

tailgating   A security breach that occurs when an authorized individual gains admission to a secure area by presenting a badge or key and is directly followed into the area by an unauthorized individual.

task rotation   Synonymous with job rotation. A security check that requires that every employee is trained to perform the work of another employee.

task-based control   A type of data access control in which individuals are allowed to use data, based on their job responsibilities.

TCP hijacking   Synonymous with man-in-the-middle. An attack in which the abuser records data packets from the network, modifies them, and inserts them back into the network.

team leader   For information security, a project manager who understands project management, personnel management, and technical requirements.

technical architecture team   Synonymous with network review board. A group that directs the orderly introduction of change in information technology across the organization.

technical controls   Measures that address the tactical and technical issues related to designing and implementing security in an organization, as well as issues related to examining and selecting the technologies appropriate to protecting information.

technology   The technical implementation of the policy defined by the organization.

technology governance   A complex process that an organization uses to manage the impacts and costs caused by technology implementation, innovation, and obsolescence.

Telecommunications Deregulation and Competition Act of 1996   An act that attempted to modernize the archaic terminology of the 1934 act.

telecommuting   The act of working at a site that is distant from the base organizational facility.

TEMPEST   A technology that involves the monitoring of devices that emit electromagnetic radiation (EMR) in such a manner that the data can be reconstructed.

Terminal Access Controller Access Control System (TACACS)   A remote access system that validates a user's credentials.

The Federal Privacy Act of 1974   An act that regulates the government in the protection of individual privacy. Created to insure that government agencies protect the privacy of individual and business information and to hold those agencies responsible if any portion of this information is released without permission.

theft   The act of stealing.

thermal detection system   A fire detection system that contains a sophisticated heat sensor.

threat   An object, person, or other entity that represents a danger to an asset.

threat agent   A specific instance or component that represents a danger to an organization's assets. Threats can be accidental or purposeful, for example lightning strikes or hackers.

threat assessment   The examination of a danger to assess its potential to impact an organization.

ticket   In a client/server environment, an identification card for a particular client that verifies to a server that the client is requesting services and that the client is a valid member of a system and therefore authorized to receive services.

tiger team   Synonymous with ethical hacker, white-hat hacker, and red team. Consultants or outsourced contractors who are hired to perform controlled attacks to compromise or disrupt systems by using documented vulnerabilities.

time-share   A site that is leased by an organization in conjunction with a business partner for use if a disaster occurs at the home site.

timing attack   An attack in which an abuser explores the contents of a Web browser's cache. These attacks allow a Web designer to create a malicious form of cookie to store on the client's system.

top-down approach   A methodology of establishing security policies that is initiated by upper management.

tort law   Laws that allow individuals to seek recourse against others in the event of personal, physical, or financial injury.

transference   The control approach used by an organization to shift the risks from one asset to another.

transport mode   One of the two modes of operation of the IP Security Protocol. In transport mode, only the IP data is encrypted, not the IP headers.

transposition cipher   Synonymous with permutation cipher. The rearranging of values within a block to create coded information.

trap and trace   A combination of resources that detect an intrusion and trace it back to its source.

trap door   Synonymous with back door. An electronic hole in software that is left open by accident or intention. Can be installed by a virus or worm.

trespass   The act of entering a premises or system without authorization.

triboelectrification   A process that causes static electricity and occurs when two materials are rubbed together causing electrons to be exchanged and one object to become more positively charged and the other more negatively charged. When a third object with an opposite charge or ground is encountered, electrons flow again and a spark is produced.

triple DES   Synonymous with 3DES. An enhancement to the Data Encryption Standard (DES). An algorithm that uses up to three keys to perform three different encryption operations.

Trojan horses   Software programs that hide their true nature (usually destructive), and reveal their designed behavior only when activated.

trophy A piece of evidence (usually a screenshot) that can be used to convince skeptical system administrators that the vulnerability is real.

trouble ticket A process for tracking problems reported to an information technology help desk.

trusted network A network such as an intranet that is inside an organization's firewall and is therefore protected from security breaches.

tunnel mode One of the two modes of operation of the IP Security Protocol. In tunnel mode, the entire IP packet is encrypted and placed as payload into another IP packet.

two-man control A security check that requires that two individuals review and approve each other's work before a task is categorized as finished.

U

U.S. Secret Service A department within the Department of the Treasury. Provides protective services for key members of the U.S. government and detects and arrests any person committing a United States federal offense relating to computer fraud.

U.S.A. Patriot Act of 2001 This act modified a wide range of existing laws to provide law enforcement agencies with a broader latitude of actions to combat terrorism-related activities.

uninterruptible Power Supplies (UPS) A backup power source for major computer systems.

United Nations Charter The mission statement of the U.N., which includes provisions for information security during information warfare.

unskilled hacker An individual who depends on the expertise of others to abuse systems.

untrusted network A network outside an organization's firewall, such as the Internet.

user involvement The inclusion of users in the organizational process of developing security systems.

utility The quality or state of having value for an end purpose. Information has utility if it serves a purpose.

V

virtual organization A group of individuals brought together through electronic communication for a specific task, usually from different organizations, divisions, or departments.

virtual password A password calculated or extracted from a passphrase that meets system storage requirements.

virtual private networks (VPNs) A network within a network that typically allows a user to use the Internet as a private network.

virus Software that attaches itself to another program and can cause damage when the host program is activated.

virus hoaxes E-mails sent warning of the latest and most dangerous viruses that are fictitious.

vision A written statement of the organization's goals.

vulnerability Weakness or fault in a system or protection mechanism that exposes information to attack or damage.

vulnerability assessment The process of identifying and documenting specific and provable flaws in the organization's information asset environment.

vulnerability assessment and remediation domain The identification of specific, documented vulnerabilities and their timely remediation.

vulnerability instance The existence of a vulnerability that is deemed a significant risk.

vulnerability scanner A device that scans servers to identify exposed usernames, shows open network shares, and exposes configuration problems and other vulnerabilities.

W

war dialer An automatic phone-dialing program that dials every number in a configured range (e.g., 555-1000 to 555-2000), and checks to see if a person, answering machine, or modem picks up.

war dialing An attack that uses scripted dialing against a pool of phone numbers.

war game A simulation of an attack on an organization's information assets.

warm site An alternate site that can be used by an organization if a disaster occurs at the home site. Frequently includes computing equipment and peripherals with servers but not client workstations.

waterfall model A methodology of the system development life cycle in which each phase of the process begins with the information gained in the previous phase.

well-known vulnerabilities   System weaknesses that have been examined, documented, and published.

wet-pipe   A type of sprinkler system that contains pressurized water in pipes and has a valve in each protected area.

white-hat hacker   Synonymous with ethical hacker, tiger team, red team. Consultants or outsourced contractors who are hired to perform controlled attacks to compromise or disrupt systems by using documented vulnerabilities.

wireless vulnerability assessment   The process designed to find and document the vulnerabilities that may be present in wireless local area network.

work breakdown structure (WBS)   A planning approach that breaks a project plan into specific action steps.

worm   A virus that replicate itself on other machines.

Z

zombies   Machines that have been compromised and directed towards a target. They are executed remotely (usually by a transmitted command) by the attacker.

Index

A

acceptance, risk management, 161–162

access, defined, 27

access control list (ACL), 144. *See also* access controls

  ACL policies, 200–202

access controls. *See also* controls; physical security

  authentication, 312–315

  defined, 143

  discretionary controls, 144

  in general, 143, 312, 358–359

    alarms, 363–364

    computer rooms and closets, 364

    dogs, 360

    electronic monitoring, 363

    facilities management, 359

    guards, 359–360

    ID cards, 360

    interior walls and doors, 364–365

    locks and keys, 360–362

    mantrap, 362–363

    secure facility, 359

    walls, fencing, gates, 359

  nondiscretionary controls

    role-base controls, 144

    task-based controls, 144

  tailgating, 360

  types

    lattice-based access control, 143

    mandatory access controls, 143

accessibility. *See also* availability

  compared to availability, 10–11

  vs. security, 18–19

accident, 98, 224

account, as incident, 247, 248, 251

accountability, 213

  risk control, 166

accounting management

  ISO model, 461–462

    chargeback accounting, 461

accuracy, 11. *See also* integrity

ACL. *See* access control list

ACM. *See* Association of Computing Machinery

acts of god. *See also* physical security; threat

  forces of nature, 61–63

    dust, 63

    earthquake, 62

    electro-static discharge, 63

    fire, 61–62

    flood, 62

    hurricane, 62

    landslide, 62

    lightning, 62

    tornado, 62

    tsunami, 62–63

  in general, 61

Adams, Scott, 391

administration. *See also* management; security professionals

  responsible individual, 204–205

  systems administrators, 31

Advanced Encryption Standard (AES), 303. *See also* encryption

  discussed, 340–344

Advanced Research Project Agency (ARPA/ARPANET), 5, 6, 7

AES. *See* Advanced Encryption Standard

alarms, 363–364. *See also* access controls

alert message, 249

alert roster, 249, 259

algorithm, defined, 297, 326

Amazon.com, 55, 170

analysis phase, SDLC, 22

Anderson, James, 3, 179

applications, safe operation assurance, 42

architecture. *See* security architecture

ARPANET. *See* Advanced Research Project Agency

Arthur Andersen, 193–194

assessment. *See also* risk assessment; vulnerability assessment

  qualitative assessment, 181

asset. *See also* asset identification and valuation

  acquired value, 167

  defined, 27, 121

  information asset

    classification, 127

    prioritizing assets, 129–130

    valuation, 127–129, 141–142, 167–168

  intrinsic value, 167

asset identification and valuation

  cost benefit analysis, 167–171

  in general, 123–124